POVERTY AND HISTORY

THE AGE OF THE SENTIMENTAL MERCENARY

Clive Hart

authorHOUSE®

AuthorHouse™ UK Ltd.
500 Avebury Boulevard
Central Milton Keynes, MK9 2BE
www.authorhouse.co.uk
Phone: 08001974150

First published by AuthorHouse   5/12/2011.

ISBN: 978-1-4567-7394-6 (sc)

Where are the prophets,

Where are the visionaries,

Where are the poets,

To breach the dawn of the sentimental mercenary?

Marillion. Fugazi.

This book is written in memory of my great-great-great-great-grandfather, Richard Cruttenden, farmer, labourer and pauper, in that order, who died a dependent of All Saints' Parish, Hastings, in 1854.

Also of his son, George, agricultural labourer, who, with his wife Mary and two young children, was removed from the parish of Bodiam to Brede in 1822, and who died in Rye Union Workhouse in 1874.[1]

1 I am indebted to my aunt, Molly Ward, for this information. I should also like to thank Sue Ray for inspiring me to write this book, and for the eviction photograph on the front cover.

Contents

Introduction   1

The Village   6

Strollers   19

Cataclysm   31

The Price of Vulnerability   50

The Elephant on the Sofa Part One   85

The Elephant on the Sofa Part Two   128

The Thing   184

The Sentimental Mercenary   326

Nadir?   358

Introduction
Poverty in the Age of Improvement

An oldish man, who had been telling me one evening how they used to live in his boyhood, looked pensively across the valley when he had done, and so stood for a minute or two, as if trying to recover his impressions of that lost time. At last, with appearance of an effort to speak patiently, "Ah," he said, "they tells me times are better now, but I can't see it"; and it was plain enough that he thought our present times the worse. <u>George Sturt. Change in the Village. 1912.</u>

This book is not for the faint-hearted. It is about our ancestors, our own flesh and blood, and not all that long ago. It concerns an era of our history when conditions of life for a huge proportion of the people of this country underwent a drastic long-term deterioration. It begins at a time of relative well-being and fulfilment; and follows the declining fortunes of ordinary people, through dispossession, displacement, proletarianisation, deprivation, disease and death. Whilst this much, it is to be hoped, is established as historical fact, it is not the story that we would wish to hear, or which we are accustomed to hearing. On the face of it, it represents a huge challenge to our notions of progress and improvement, of the superiority of modernity over the past. But if the past, and by inference the world we live in, is to be properly understood, it is a story which needs to be told; and a phenomenon which needs to be explained.

There is a common perception, at least in the wealthy nations of the modern world, that the sum of human suffering in the present day is much less than it used to be. But why is that so? Most people, perhaps, would be tempted to account for it, at least in part, by the passing of time. We are now living in the twenty-first century, they might say, with a certain sense of pride and superiority; we are no longer living in the dark ages; *we have progressed*. If asked to be a little more concrete, they would no doubt invoke the many advantages which we in the modern world possess, which were not available to our ancestors – perhaps to the capitalist system, to the welfare state, to education, to technical innovation, etc. etc. They would say that the widespread poverty and misery which existed in the past has, at last, been overcome by all these means. But that is an explanation in reverse, which does not begin to explain why poverty existed in the first place. You cannot explain a historical phenomenon by the lack of something which happened subsequently. To do so leads to the unquestioning assumption that poverty and misery were inevitably and inseparably connected with the past; merely part of the landscape of our history; and prevents us from asking the questions which lead to an understanding of why such suffering existed.

People were poor, as someone once expressed it to me, because "they hadn't got round to doing anything about poverty yet". A cursory analysis of the assumptions inherent in that statement would fill a chapter!

The idea of progress is as universally held as it is strange. We all of us like to be thought progressive, modern, liberal, eager to embrace technical innovation, unafraid of change, liberated from tradition. No one wishes to be thought retrograde, backward-looking, reactionary or Luddite.

And this makes us very reluctant to accept or understand a long period of deteriorating conditions in the relatively recent past.

People these days have a very limited conception of the past. It is as if we have just turned a corner, and are now unable to see where we have come from. The past has become unfashionable. History is invaded, on one side, by nationalism, which teaches us to think in terms of our historic national glories, and the important part which this country played in the progress of the world; and, on another, by political correctness, which exaggerates the importance of certain subjects way beyond what is scientifically justifiable, and ignores many others. On all sides, history is perverted to substantiate certain pre-conceived orthodoxies. We change history to suit our ideas; rather than base our ideas upon historical fact. If we wish for a scientific understanding of the past, the only truly valid questions, those which alone we are entitled to ask, are; What happened? Why? All the others are loaded.

Popular ideas about the past can more or less be condensed into three strands. One sees the past in terms of great and colourful figures and events, kings and queens, battles and revolutions; wars and dates which need to be memorised. Another is the nostalgic strand; the idea of quaintness is important here; where the past is seen as a simpler, slower, more relaxed world, free from many of the stresses and strains of modern living. But to temper this, the third strand is brought to mind – that of the rose-tinted spectacles through which we must not be tempted to look. Living in the past involved much toil and distress; times were hard; people were poor; life, as is commonly quoted, was "nasty, brutish and short." Very few see the past as a place populated by their ancestors; people genetically connected to themselves; evolved to an equal extent; as intelligent and as human; facing the challenges of their situation as we face ours; lacking modern sophistication, maybe, but, as conditioned by their experiences, possessed of multitudes of knowledge and abilities which we, alas, will never be privy to. If times were hard for them; if they were distressed and poor and miserable, (which they may or may not have been), why was that so?

The whole problem is made the more intractable because the period of history in question was a time of rapid economic change. It was the age of the so-called industrial and agricultural revolutions, which, received wisdom maintains, were the beginnings of the modern age, and the foundations of our present prosperity.

The fortunes and misfortunes of ordinary people can easily be obscured by the dazzling glories of banking, scientific discovery, agricultural change, industrialisation, and the rise of our nation to global pre-eminence. All too easily, history can come to be written in terms of a progression towards the state of affairs observable, or even imagined, in the present day; which, itself, is often treated almost as the highest possible point of perfection. Assume, for argument's sake, that we are currently living in a modern, industrial democracy, in which society is possessed of unheard-of wealth, and where even the poorest have a standard of living well above subsistence, thanks to intervention by government in the form of the welfare state. The past will then be seen as a process culminating in a society with those characteristics; and every stage along the route to that culmination will assume great importance and emphasis, whilst trends and events of an opposite tendency will be skimmed lightly over, or omitted altogether. A lengthy period of intensifying mass immiseration does not tune in very well with this progressive process; less well if it is found to coincide with the events that are supposed to be the foundation of the improvement; less well still if it is found to be caused by them.

A well-known historian of modern times, writing a study of the period from 1763 to 1867, went so far as to entitle his work 'The Age of Improvement'. As part of his authority for doing this, he pointed out, quite rightly, that improvement was a popular theme of the time. It was to be found in the works of Defoe and Johnson; it was thought, in the 1780s, that the "discoveries and improvements" of the time seemed to diffuse "a glory over this country unattainable by conquest or dominion."

The agricultural and mechanical innovations were said to be "unparalleled in the chronicles of the world". In 1836, G. R. Porter prefaced his statistical survey entitled 'The Progress of the Nation' with the comment that "this country and….the present generation….have made the greatest advances in civilisation that can be found recorded in the annals of mankind."[1]

History is thus viewed as a process of amelioration, at times, as in this period, rapid, and at other times, more or less stagnant. And this unavoidably involves the assumption that, in the past, people were in a worse condition, less happy and less enlightened, than in the present; and that the farther back in history one goes, the more miserable was their state.

Most writers of the time seemed to agree that the state of primitive peoples was one of the most abject indolence, wretchedness, deprivation and ferocity. Even William Godwin, one of the least intellectually encumbered of writers, put forward his theories of the perfectibility of man on the basis of the vast improvements made on the savage state, especially in language. He points out that both radical and establishment thinkers agree in viewing "man first as a miserable savage….They call to mind with horror the fierce and unrelenting passions of savages and barbarians." But how did they know? Contemporary views of what are called primitive peoples, the sources from which they were derived, and their tenuous relationship with reality, form a subject wide enough, and important enough, to merit a book all on their own. Nevertheless, Godwin saw them as "destitute of all the advantages and refinements of a civilised state", personal security being "the great nourisher of leisure, disinterestedness, science and wisdom." They were "scarcely above the brutes".[2]

Are the brutes, then, miserable, in their natural state? A tour of any modern livestock farm will reveal far more cases of sickness and poor condition amongst the domesticated animals of the fields and buildings, than amongst the inhabitants of the hedgerows, the woods and the skies. Sheep in the wild, for example, would suffer very rarely from many of the afflictions that are the bane of the modern shepherd. Foot rot, intestinal worms, fly strike and lambing difficulties would all more or less disappear, either as a result of a healthier, more natural way of life, or else selectively bred out of existence. In fact, unlike the members of our modern human society, it is very rare to see a wild animal diseased, overweight, or wasting away from hunger. If we are to put forward theories about progress and improvement, it is the state of nature which must be our starting-point.

In The Age of Improvement, Asa Briggs makes the surprising statement that "contemporaries were divided about the merits of improvement, but they were at one in admitting that it existed." This is partly nonsensical, and partly wrong. Indeed, on the one hand we have the historian H. T. Buckle, for whom the rate of progress justified the belief that the human race in the future would be transported "to a state of happiness and virtue, which a fond imagination loves to ascribe to the primitive condition of man." "Innocence and simplicity", associated with "the traditions of the theologian and the dreams of the poet", would be recovered in a new age of bliss.[3]

But, on the other hand, a great many contemporaries thought that the changes of the 18th and 19th centuries represented a worsening of the conditions of life for most people, not an improvement. They saw the political system as having degenerated from a state of relative purity, to one of abject corruption, and saw the solution as a move back into the past. The radical, William Cobbett, was one such, who saw himself as a conservative, and the establishment as innovators. Cobbett savagely satirised the whole concept of improvement; and quoted with heavy irony the mantra of Britain as "the envy of surrounding nations and admiration of the world."

---

1 Asa Briggs. The Age of Improvement. Introduction.
2 W. Godwin An Enquiry into Political Justice. P. 30. See also The Enquirer.. Not everyone subscribed to Godwin's consensus on the savage state. See, for example, R. Price. Observations on Reversionary Payments. P. 279. Or Dr. John Gregory. Comparative View.
3 Asa Briggs. The Age of Improvement. P. 3.

"In this now miserable country, where….thousands are caused to wallow in luxury, to be surfeited with food and drink, while the millions are continually on the point of famishing….there must be a complete and radical change; or England must become a country of the basest slavery that ever disgraced the earth."[4]

It is curious, but instructive, to reflect, that Buckle and Cobbett were both writing of much the same time.

Cobbett was the foremost, but he was far from alone. In defiance of Briggs's supposed consensus in favour of improvement, many writers expressed similar views. Thomas Paine summed up the whole argument very acutely.

"Customary language has classed the condition of man under the two descriptions of civilised and uncivilised life. To the one, it has ascribed felicity and affluence; to the other, hardship and want. But however our imaginations may be impressed by painting and comparison, it is nevertheless true, that a great portion of mankind in what are called civilised countries, are in a state of poverty and wretchedness, far below the condition of an Indian. I speak not of one country, but of all. It is so in England, it is so all over Europe. Let us inquire into the cause."[5]

Let us, indeed, do that very thing!

Poverty can take a variety of forms, and be defined in various ways. It can be defined merely as the absence of wealth. Relative poverty can affect those who have plenty to eat and drink, and have no difficulty in procuring clothing and shelter; but who feel themselves in a disadvantaged position with regard to the more opulent sections of society. These people do not form the subject of this book; we are not dealing here with those who feel disgruntled because they have only one television and only one car. On the other hand, certain forms of poverty are inevitable. Even among wild animals, the aged, the sick, the injured, and the orphaned, will unavoidably fall by the wayside; among human populations, the same will apply, unless the victims are cared for by other members of the species. This type of poverty is also, in the main, not the subject of this book. What you never see among the fauna of the landscape, unless subjected to sudden natural catastrophe of some description, is vast numbers of a species all wasting away together, from hunger and deprivation, as was the case with the human population in England in the earlier part of the 19th century. Man himself was at one time one of the fauna of the landscape. Whenever, in so-called civilised countries, his condition falls below that of the beasts of the woods and the fowls of the air; whenever, that is, he is wasting from hunger or perishing from cold, one is entitled to ask why that should be. How does it happen, that men live worse as members of a civilised society, than they did as the fauna of nature? By examining a period when this was the case, this book asks precisely that question, and attempts to discuss possible explanations.

History, it is said, is written by the victors. This, of course, is not history; it is propaganda; and according to this propaganda, whatever actually happens will, of course, be good. In this alternative reality, all really is for the best. Inevitably, progress will be inevitable. Ideas of progress and advancement become of the essence to the conceptual framework of many people; and are utilised and reinforced by advertisers and propagandists who try to persuade us to purchase or accept things which a more reasoning or objective mode of thought might, perhaps, counsel us against. When we encounter an idea, or a trend, inconsistent with this framework, we tend either to block it out; or else hammer it into shape by inventing explanations for it which may be more or less absurd or detached from reality.

---

4   William Cobbett. Rural Rides. Penguin Ed. Pp. 295 and 316.

5   Thomas Paine. The Rights of Man II. In The Complete Writings of Thomas Paine. Ed. S. Foner. P. 212.

In today's global economy, the proportion of people who do not have enough to eat and drink; who have inadequate clothing and shelter; is not vastly different from the proportion of paupers in Cobbett's England. The idea that many, many millions of people living in this modern, civilised and technological global economy of ours, are actually living to a standard below that of the deer that live in the woods and the fox that steals the chickens from the garden, is not one which we find easy to accept. So we object that people living in the poorer parts of the modern world have yet to go through the process of social and economic change that we have gone through; that they are developing or underdeveloped; in short, that they have not *progressed*......

So the massive immiseration of the population which took place in England during the 18th and 19th centuries will inevitably constitute a huge challenge to our assumptions and preconceptions. For sure, contemporary writers were not lacking who chose to account for the increasing wretchedness of the people as an inevitable part of the "progressive improvement of society"; but this is a paradox far more real than merely apparent. To make an objective analysis of why people starve and freeze, when they are actually perfectly capable of supporting themselves, it is necessary to cast aside our assumptions and preconceptions. Only then can we ask that all-important question – Why was this so? – without flinching from uncomfortable answers. The almost contemporaneous lifespans of Malthus and Cobbett were a time when deepening misery engendered a lively debate on the causes of poverty; which often raises questions about the motives and psychological propensities of those who took part. But, in essence, the period is in an example, which, it is hoped, may provide the key to, and ask the questions necessary for, an understanding of many other periods of our past. Above all, it is a parable of our times....

The Village
Rural society before the age of the stereotype

"A time there was, ere England's griefs began,
When every rood of ground maintained its man;
For him light labour spread her wholesome store,
Just gave what life required, but gave no more.
His best companions, innocence and health;
And his best riches, ignorance of wealth." Oliver Goldsmith. The Deserted Village

This story begins in the village of Wigston Magna in Leicestershire, four miles south of Leicester. Of this village, the historian W. G. Hoskins wrote a brilliant and remarkable, and perhaps undervalued history, which was published in 1957. Here is how he describes the village, by way of introduction.

"It was, before the ancient plan was destroyed by the modern builder, a completely nucleated village, profoundly characteristic of the Midlands. Its farmhouses, cottages and shops gathered together along the village streets; the little crofts lay behind the farm-houses or to one side of them, and the farmyards opened directly off the street. The village stood in the centre of the parish with nearly three thousand acres of open fields all around it, the spire of the parish church visible from almost every corner of its territory."

Hoskins called his book a study of a peasant culture.

"The broad pattern of Wigston's social and economic history between the ninth century and the eighteenth is abundantly clear; it is a village with a large and persistent class of free peasant landowners without any resident lord of the manor at any time; and it is a village which maintained unimpaired its traditional open-field husbandry when so many other villages….in the Midlands….were being enclosed and depopulated for sheep and cattle pastures.

"It is a study of a rural society based upon an open-field economy, and though it cannot be called typical in all its aspects, for every community is a unique organism in some way, with its own peculiar flavour and individuality, it may perhaps be regarded as a portrait of the kind of society which existed over a considerable part of central England for the best part of a thousand years."

The farmers of Wigston made up a traditional rural society. No rural society can be called typical of all. Shades of difference, no doubt, can be traced between Wigston Magna and the surrounding villages of the open-field Midland belt. Greater differences existed between the open-field villages of the Midlands, and, for example, the long enclosed villages of Devon and Cornwall, or the woodland parishes of Kent and Sussex; greater contrasts still with, say, the Highlanders of Scotland. But the connection with the land runs as a common thread through all these various types of rural community, and was what shaped them. The exigencies of nature, of soil and climate, the need to provide for themselves, food and clothing and shelter, were what determined their patterns of living and working, their institutions, their customs. The connection with the land was the common factor binding together all traditional rural societies, and distinguishing them from our modern societies;

with a sharpness which renders the differences between the Midland peasant and the Scottish Highlander mere shades of subtlety.

It is a massive and almost unbridgeable gulf that separates the traditional rural society exemplified by the farmers of Wigston Magna from us in our modern world. In our society, the problem of subsistence is merely a question of money – the earning of it, and the spending of it. Money comes from employment, which is highly unlikely to be connected with the land; food and clothes come from shops; houses are bought with money borrowed from the bank or building society. So much is taken for granted. Luxuries and holidays and fashions are what occupy the concerns of moderns. And the means of earning money, and the ways of spending it – all are provided by the capitalist system. The idea that food, and clothing, and accommodation, all have to be provided by the local environment, and forged from it by the sweat of the brow, is all totally foreign. The forms of society produced by this need are probably outside the experience of most in our own day. I think I am not insulting too many of my readers, if I assert that the wealthy people of the modern world have neither the hardiness, nor the skills, nor the knowledge, to provide for themselves the necessaries of life.

This gulf of understanding began to open up at the time of the extinguishing of the rural communities. George Sturt observed one such community in its death-throes. In his book on the valley of the Bourne in Surrey, written in 1912, he shows himself a perceptive and sympathetic observer and magical narrator of the process. He describes the polarisation of village society between the traditional peasant class, now the employed, and the middle class newcomers, the employers.[1]

"From a position in which the world's distinctions of class and caste were hardly noticed – a position which was, so to speak, an island of refuge, where self-respect could be preserved in preserving the old rough peasant ways, the valley folk have been forced into such relations with the outside world that they are no longer a separate set, unclassified, but a grade has been assigned to them in the classification of society at large, and it is well nigh the lowest grade of all....they have become degraded, humiliated."

On the other hand, "the employing class as a whole has moved on, leaving the labourers where they were, until now a great gulf divides them. Merely in relative wealth, if that were all, the difference has widened enormously.

"The employers have discarded much of their provincialism – in beliefs and tastes they are a new people – the countrified speech, common to village and town fifty years ago, has become a subject of derision – like distinct races, one dominant, the other subject."

This new separation sent the country folk back into their shells.

"A sort of reserve in the village temper, a want of gaiety, a subdued air – this is probably the shadow cast upon the people from the upraised middle class.

"The people appear enigmatic. They keep their own counsel....no sign escapes them when members of the employing class are by."[2]

This is how the Morning Chronicle described the agricultural labourer in 1849.[3]

"When you accost him....he is timid and shrinking, his whole manner showing that he feels himself at a distance from you greater than should separate any two classes of men. He is often doubtful when you address him, and suspicious when you question him; he is seemingly oppressed with the interview, and obviously relieved when it is over."

This acquired secretiveness contributed to widen the gulf that was already opening up for other reasons. A lack of informed judgment characterised the writings of many of the authors on rural

1 George Sturt. Pseud. Bourne.. Change in the Village. P. 111-2
2 George Sturt pseud. Bourne. Change in the Village p. 112
3 The Morning Chronicle of 1ˢᵗ December 1849 quoted by K. D. M. Snell. The Annals of the Labouring Poor. P. 6

society of the nineteenth century, and has translated itself into many modern histories; which tend to assess the situation of the labouring poor by criteria which they themselves would hardly have recognised.[4]

But if comprehension was lacking, hostility was not. Here is George Sturt again.

"While the labouring people, on their side, betray little or no class feeling of hostility towards employers, the converse is not true, but jealousy, suspicion, some fear – the elements of bitter class war, in fact, frequently mark the attitude of middle-class people towards the labouring class."

And following hostility, contempt was not far behind.

"One hears them spoken of as an alien and objectionable race, worth nothing but to be made to work….In truth, I have heard it expressed dozens of times, in dozens of ways….that the English labouring classes are a lower order of beings, who must be treated accordingly."[5]

In our own day, we, of course, live at a much greater distance still from the traditional rural society. Our only opportunities to observe it today exist in far distant parts of the globe, at almost as great a separation in space as is the English peasantry in time. There is not now so much a lack of comprehension of these societies, as a total lack of awareness that they ever existed. The contempt, however, remains.

We live in a world where the dominant political creed roundly condemns many forms of prejudice and stereotyping, some real, some imagined. And yet, in some quarters, there runs rampant a quite socially acceptable anti-rural prejudice. One has only to think of the outrageous anti-farmer campaigns conducted through the media at the time of the governments of Margaret Thatcher and John Major; or the many attempts over the years to blacken the characters of the generality of farmers with such issues as farm subsidies, salmonella and BSE. Tony Blair, in his "forces of conservatism" speech, clearly had in mind the rural population as foremost among the advocates of reaction, and attempted to stereotype them as 'toffs' whose only interest was in hunting and killing foxes. Among sections of modern society, there is a widespread perception of farmers as uncultured individuals who think only of milking the state and chasing after wildlife. A recent newspaper article will serve to illustrate this prejudice. At the outset, the author admits that she detests the country.

"There is seldom anything good in the country", she asserts. "Much of nature, until moulded by the artifice of man, is not a very pretty sight – it consists of a great deal of weeds, mud, and cowpats."

The connection drawn between rusticity and ignorance, already popular among writers and intellectuals in the eighteenth century, is alive and well and living in Belgravia.[6] In the article, Karl Marx is quoted as saying that the town had liberated men from "the idiocy of rural life".

"The country makes fools out of its inhabitants. Why else would we refer to the village idiot as opposed to the city one?...[7]

"In some parts of Devon and Cornwall, employers from London find it hard to get efficient workers as many of the locals are backward, lazy and occasionally unconventional in appearance."[8]

It gets worse.

---

4   K. D. M. Snell. The Annals of the Labouring Poor. Introduction.
5   George Sturt. Pseud. Bourne. Change in the Village. Pp. 107-109
6   See, for example Thomas Alcock. Observations on the Defects of the Poor Laws. P. 41. Or Patricia James. Population Malthus. P. 26.
7   Because we are city people.
8   This particular village idiot is greatly indebted for this godsend to Petronella Wyatt. The article was published in the Daily Mail on 25th July 2008.

"The country fosters more than idiocy. It can foster the sinister and the evil....The young men who were to make up Hitler's youth movement and then his soldiers lit campfires in dark forests and communed with nature. Hitler himself was entranced by Wagnerian landscapes.

"Goering, who obsessively conserved his vast forest estate just north of Berlin, would have been a hero of Al Gore and the Green Movement.

"Robert Mugabe has waxed lyrical over the sun setting on the tundra, while Saddam Hussein was wont to croon over greenery."

If the author had used such types of argument to describe immigrants or homosexuals, we all know what would have happened. But the fact that such irrational and prejudiced anti-rural views can be published in a popular national daily newspaper shows that they are both socially acceptable and widespread.

The very word 'peasant' was already acquiring negative connotations in the eighteenth century. But, in essence, peasant is a neutral, objective term for a small farmer; more particularly for one who has some sort of proprietary interest in the soil which he cultivates. A yeoman is more or less the same thing. But whereas a yeoman has connotations of sturdiness and reliability, the use of the term peasant casts aspersions of backwardness, ignorance and uncouthness; almost to the extent that it is better not to use it.

Many agricultural theorists and historians have subscribed to this disparaging view of the peasant and his culture. A dominant strand of thought contends that traditional peasant farms and open fields obstructed 'progress'. One historian writes that "peasant ownership had often meant stagnation, poverty, ignorance"; another that "small farms generally lacked the acreage and capital to undertake convertible husbandry or improve the quality of their stock or grasslands, and they tended to be ignorant and opposed to change." Traditional peasant society, so the argument runs, needs to be cleared away in order for development to take place, leading in turn to a modern society - the end-product of all progress. In the process, labour is 'freed' from farming, to take up employment in modern manufacturing.[9]

Whether the former small farmer living as a parish pauper in a dilapidated hovel; or the Manchester slum-dweller as he recalled his or his father's cottage in the country; would have considered themselves 'freed' from farming; are questions to which it should not be hard to imagine an answer.

Clearly anyone displaying the above kinds of anti-rural mindset will regard the displacement and starvation of the world's rural communities, if not as a positive good, at least with a degree of equanimity. The will to understand why people have to live in misery, and starve or freeze to death, depends upon a giant leap of comprehension, empathy and objectivity.

What can we say, then, about this alien culture, this lost and unknown civilisation, made up and exemplified for us by the farmers of Wigston Magna in Leicestershire?[10] At the beginning of the seventeenth century, it was a community of about 140 households. Most of the population "consisted of the middling farmers, the true peasantry, and the freehold cottagers, men with ten to thirty acres of land, some with none at all but a cottage, a cow or two, and certain rights upon the common". In most villages such as this, the connection with the land probably ran right throughout the village, as hardly anyone, if anyone at all, did not engage in some way in growing crops or raising livestock

---

9   Most of this paragraph is based on R. C. Allen. Enclosure and the Yeoman. Ch. 1 on Agrarian Fundamentalism.

10 Most of this section is based on W. G. Hoskins. The Midland Peasant. Ch. 7.

on his own account.[11] There was no manufacturing in the village; only the traditional local crafts, many of the practitioners of which would have been smallholders as well. Of the roughly 3000 acres surrounding the village, by far the greater part belonged to those small farmers. Most of this was divided into three huge open fields, called Mucklow, Thythorn Hill, and Goldhill. One field each year would be left fallow; the other two divided into strips. Each farmer would be allotted a greater or smaller number of strips in the open fields, and crops, mainly of grain and pulses, would be grown in them. The villagers' livestock would be grazed on the fallow, on the stubbles following the crops, and on various enclosed areas of grass and meadow. Supplementing this, and essential to the whole system, was the common. This was a large area of open, uncultivated ground, dedicated mostly to the grazing of livestock. This underpinned the agriculture of the village, by providing alternative grazing for the farmers' livestock from the time the grass started to grow in the spring, until mowing time; allowing the production of that most essential commodity – hay.[12] It was also an integral part of the cottage economy of those who owned little or no land – perhaps no more than a large garden. It provided longer-term grazing for their sheep and cows, pigs and poultry of all kinds. There on the common could be found timber for building, and turf, furze, or firewood for cooking and warmth.

It was a system of farming, indeed a way of life, stretching back through many centuries, its origins almost lost in the mists of time; not completely unchanging, it is true, but evolving only gradually; stable. Hoskins imagines a farmer of 1525 visiting the village a century later.

"….he would have felt at home, back in a timeless world in which all the fields had their familiar names; in which many of the families that he had known still carried on the remembered trades or cultivated the ancestral acres as of old; and in which all the familiar boundaries and landmarks were still to be found where he had always known them, the same mills, wells, springs, lanes and hedges." And a good chance existed that he would even have met his own descendants; for Wigston was a stable community; 44 per cent of its families in 1670 had lived there for over a century; and 20 per cent for double that time. Ancient and unchanging the life of the village may have been; but not timeless; for now it is all gone, and this book, in part at least, is about its destruction.

Farming in the open-field village was a largely cooperative venture, originating, probably, in the needs of ancient settlers, and in particular in the practice of communal ploughing, where a number of farmers would yoke their several oxen to one plough.[13] By the seventeenth century, this practice had largely died out, but survived in the form of the town plough kept in Wigston church, for the use of those who could not afford their own. Nevertheless, cooperation survived both in spirit and in practice. The village community was not just a social unit; nor just an agricultural one; it was also a unit of self-government. The system of farming required communal action, discussion, agreed rules and organisation, and all this was reflected in the parish constitution. Meetings of farmers and smallholders would be called to decide on the uses to which the common fields could best be put, or for deciding disputes. They would also appoint the village officials. Wigston was governed through the churchwardens, the petty constables, and the overseers of the poor. There were also two other, more purely agricultural types of official – the field-reeve and the evener. The duties of all these officials bring sharply into focus the communal nature of this society. We find, for example, the churchwardens making payments to those who "had greate losse by fire". How many people in the modern world would be prepared to share the misfortunes of their neighbours in this way? The duties of the field-reeves were numerous, and were mainly connected with the arable operations. For example, "they mended the gates leading into the fields, paid someone to guard the peas….and let out the 'town balks' for pasture. They kept the 'toun plow' in the church….cleared out the ditches

11 G. Slater. The English Peasantry and the Enclosure of Common Fields. P. 130.
12 Society of Farmers. A Political Enquiry into the Consequences of Enclosing Waste Lands. P. 41.
13 G. Slater. The English Peasantry and the Enclosure of Common Fields. P. 87.

in the fields, and scoured 'Newgate pool' where the village women did their washing." The eveners' duties were more closely connected with organising the grazing of the livestock. They employed the herdsman, acquired and deployed the town bull, and made sure that those among the smaller owners who had no grazing of their own could rent some cheaply from the wealthier farmers.

The traditional rural society was most strikingly distinguished from the modern world by its localism and its self-sufficiency. Let Hoskins tell his own story.

"Wigston produced all its own food, clothing, light, power and building materials, and nearly all its own heat, out of the most commonplace natural resources; for the parish was not specially endowed by Nature in any single respect beyond the fact that its clays, with constant hard labour, were capable of producing good crops. For its buildings – houses, barns, and boundary walls – it had its own clay, used in the preparation of the long-lasting mud walls. The boulders in the clay, of every size from pebbles upwards, provided the necessary footings for all these mud walls, and the mortar that bound them came from Wigston's own lime-pit. Wheat-straw or selected reeds from some special corner of the parish provided the material for thatching houses and copings for mud walls. The parish had its own sand-pits and gravel-pits....and in the last quarter of the seventeenth century good brick-earth was found right in the village.

"The willows that fringed the streams of the parish provided wattles for sheep-hurdles and other temporary fences, besides the framework for 'wattle-and-daub' farmhouses, a more substantial construction than mud alone. The furze of the common pastures, though there was not much of it, was burnt in bakehouses, brewhouses, and kitchen fires, as were the 'shreddings' or loppings off the hedgerows also.

"As for its crops, the parish grew enough flax and hemp to meet its own needs for linen sheets, napkins, towels and clothing; it produced enough wool from its own sheep to keep the five or six village tailors well supplied. Its barley, grown over several hundred acres every year, supplied food and drink; and its wheat, rye oats, peas and beans provided food for all men and beasts. Every cottage and farmhouse had its own poultry (chiefly geese, but ducks and hens were numerous), and most kept pigs and bees. All had herb-gardens and many had small orchards; so the village had meat, bacon, eggs, cheese, butter, milk, honey, apples, and herbs of all kinds. The parish generated its own power; for the wind did not blow to waste, but was harnessed to two or three windmills; and the waters of the little river Sence were not allowed to flow unused across the parish boundary. Since the middle of the twelfth century they had turned the water-wheel at Crow Mill, and from time out of mind they had yielded a few precious fish, the only fishing water in the whole parish.

"Wigston was not exceptional in practising this high economy of natural resources, nor was it by any means exceptionally endowed. It was, indeed, less fortunate than a great number of other parishes, for it lacked building stone, coal, a sufficiency of large timber for building purposes, iron for farm implements and gear, and the inevitable salt; and most of these things had to be brought in from elsewhere, though usually not from far."

This was a society and economy based on thrift – on wasting nothing; on making use of every resource, no matter how trivial, to us, it may appear.

"....these trifles, down to the pebbles under the clay or the bee-hives in the garden and the feathers on the goose's breast, were the very foundation of that old peasant economy which thought all the time in terms of goods and services and not of money."

For sure, money was in use in the village; indeed, its use was increasing; but it did not play the predominant part that it does today. George Sturt, in his study of the Surrey peasantry, makes the observation in more detail.

"Under the old regime, although probably a small regular expenditure of money had been usual, yet in the main the peasant's expenditure was not regular, but intermittent. Getting so much food and firing by his own labour, he might go for weeks without needing more than a few shillings to make up occasional deficiencies….A man's chief savings were in the shape of commodities ready for use or growing into use. They were, too, a genuine capital inasmuch as they supported him while he replaced and increased them. The flitches of bacon, the little stores of flour and home-made wine, the stack of firing, the small rick of fern or grass, were his savings-bank, which, while he drew from it daily, he replenished betimes as he planted his garden, and brought home heath and turf from the common, and minded his pigs and his cow, and put by odd shillings for occasional need. At a pinch, he could even do without the money, paying for what he wanted with a sack of potatoes, or a day's work with his donkey-cart."[14]

It was a world where one good turn deserved another.

What, then, of the people themselves, who inhabited this alien social landscape? Hoskins's account is based on the written records of several centuries ago. From these, we can tell that the village was a stable and cohesive community. The village families were constantly marrying into other families, and outsiders were rarely brought in by marriage. The village was almost like a tribe, the community spirit being based not just on social and agricultural needs, but on a large degree of kinship. These farmers were hard-headed businessmen, who participated in a constantly active market in land. Parcels of ground were forever changing hands, from sizeable areas right down to plots of an acre or so. And they were quite prepared to go to law to defend their own interests, and quite capable of acting in concert when they did so. In 1606, for example, Sir William Faunt brought a lawsuit against the villagers over a couple of mills. Twenty-eight small owners appeared as defendants, quite possibly successfully. The village spirit was active, dynamic, and formidable.

But to penetrate a little further beneath the surface of the traditional villager, we will need an eye-witness account; and so will revert again to George Sturt's work on the valley folk of Surrey, written in 1912.

Regarding that surface;-

"The men had a very rough exterior, so rough that I have known them to inspire timidity in the respectable who met them on the road, and especially at night, when, truth to tell, those of them who were out were not always too sober….I admit that their aspect was unpromising enough at first sight. A stranger might have been forgiven for thinking them coarse, ignorant, stupid, beery, unclean…. Many of the men were physically powerful….Through all their demeanour they displayed a hardness which in some cases went far below the surface, and approached real brutality."[15]

No peaceful rural idyll this; it was a commonplace in political writings of the eighteenth and nineteenth centuries that the small farmers of the English countryside made the hardiest and bravest soldiers.[16] During the troubled times of the eighteenth century, when disputes broke out between villagers and the soldiery stationed nearby, the resulting skirmishes nearly always ended with the country folk as victors.[17] Peasant life at times could be violent enough, and murders were not unknown.

And yet, "after you got to know them….you knew that there was rarely any harm in them…. Seeing them casually in their heavy and uncleanly clothes, no one would have dreamed of the great

14   George Sturt, pseudo. Bourne. Change in the village. P. 91
15   George Sturt. Pseud. Bourne. Change in the Village. Pp. 20-1.
16   See, for example, Joseph Massie. 1758. P. 63 on yeoman soldiers.
17   J. Bohstedt. Riots and Community Politics in England and Wales 1790-1810. P.172

qualities in them – the kindliness and courage and humour, the readiness to help, the self-control, the patience. It was all there, but they took no pains to look the part; they did not show off."

All the knowledge, the abilities, the characteristics even, of the peasant, came from the localism and self-sufficiency of his life, and his connection with the rural environment.

"All the things of the countryside had an intimate bearing upon his own fate; he was not there to admire them, but to live by them – or, say, to wrest his living from them by familiar knowledge of their properties. From long experience – experience longer than his own, and traditional amongst his people – he knew the soil of the fields and its variations almost foot by foot; he understood the springs and streams; hedgerow and ditch explained themselves to him; the coppices and woods, the water-meadows and the windy heaths, the local chalk and clay and stone, all had a place in his regard – reminded him of the crafts of his people, spoke to him of the economies of his own cottage life; so that the turfs or the faggots or the timber he handled when at home called his fancy while he was handling them, to the landscape they came from." In this landscape, "he did not merely reside; he was part of it, and it was part of him. He fitted into it as one of its native denizens, like the hedgehogs and the thrushes."[18]

To forge a living out of this landscape required not only a detailed and intimate knowledge of it, but also the most bewildering array of skills, talents and abilities.

"Amongst themselves they would number a few special craftsmen – a smith, a carpenter or wheelwright, a shoemaker, a pair of sawyers, and so on; yet the trades of these specialists were only ancillary to the general handiness of the people, who with their own hands raised and harvested their crops, made their clothes, did much of the building of their homes, attended to their cattle, thatched their ricks, cut their firing, made their bread and wine or cider, pruned their fruit-trees and vines, looked after their bees, all for themselves. And some at least, and perhaps most of these economies were open to the poorest labourer."[19]

If anyone should think that these are unskilled tasks, fit only for mindless drudges, let him see how long it takes to master them, indeed any one of them; and what satisfaction is gained in case of success. Is it not a little incongruous, in these days of dumbing down; when advertisers see ease and simplicity as major selling points for their products; when the greatest challenge which many people face in a day is knowing which button to press; that we should profess contempt for these masters of the primary life skills?

Along with the knowledge and abilities necessary for survival in the countryside, and connected with them, a certain attitude of mind underpinned the lives of all the villagers, and it was this which first drew George Sturt's attention to the existence of a peasant culture. This attitude betrayed itself in crisis situations, where quick thinking and prompt action were needed.

"If a horse falls in the street, ten chances to one it is some obscure labouring fellow who gets him up again. Whether there is danger or no, in emergencies which demand readiness and disregard of comfort, the common unskilled labourer is always to the fore....[20]

"The courage, the carelessness of discomfort, the swiftness to see what should be done, and to do it, are not inspired by any tradition of chivalry, any consciously elaborated cult. It is habitual with these men to be ready, and those fine actions which win our admiration are but chance disclosures in public of a self-reliance constantly practised by the people amongst themselves – by the women quite as much as by the men – under stress of necessity.

"....if you follow the clue on, it leads very quickly to the scene where self-reliance is so to speak at home, where it seems the natural product of the people's circumstances – the scene, namely, of their

18   George Bourne pseud. Sturt. Change in the Village. P 80
19   Ibid. P. 78.
20   Ibid P. 15

daily work. For there, not only in the employment by which the men earn their wages, but in the household and garden work of the women as well as the men, there is nothing to support them but their own readiness, their own personal force....a sort of intrepidity grows customary with them."

And this intrepidity was the product of the centuries. "The necessity which compels the people to be their own servants would not make them so adaptable as they are, were there not, at the back of them, a time-honoured tradition teaching them how to go on."[21]

Everything was "appraised by an ancient standard of the countryside....the men and women, and the very children....are living by an outlook in which the values are different from those of easy-going people, and in which, especially, hardships have never been met by peevishness, but have been beaten by good humour."[22]

The "ancient standard of the countryside" showed itself also in other ways. Sturt observed a great "independence of convention" among the village people. Social relations consisted of "a sort of bonhomie, of good temper and good sense. With this for a guide, the people had no need for the etiquette called 'good manners', but were at liberty to behave as they liked, and talk as they liked, within the bounds of neighbourliness and civility....In few other grades of society could men and women dare to be so outspoken together, so much at ease, as these villagers still often are. Their talk grows Chaucerian at times. Merrily or seriously, as the case may be, subjects are spoken of which are never alluded to between men and women who respect our ordinary conventions."[23]

(This was written in 1912)

"The average country labourer can talk with less restraint because he has really less to conceal than many men who would look down upon him. He may use coarse words, but his thoughts are wont to be cleanly, so that there is no suspicion of foulness behind his conversation, rank though it sound.

"The main fact is that the two sexes, each engaged daily upon essential duties, stand on a surprising equality the one to the other....And the absence of convention extends to a neglect – nay to a dislike – of ordinary graceful courtesies between them. So far as I have seen, they observe no ceremonial. The men are considerate to spare women the more exhausting or arduous kinds of work; but they will let a woman open the door for herself, and will be careless when they are together who stands or who sits, or which of them walks on the inside of the path, or goes first into a gateway. And the women look for nothing different. They expect to be treated as equals....

"Illegitimacy has been very common in the village. But once a man and a woman are married, they settle down into a sober pair of comrades, and instead of the looseness which might be looked for there is on the whole a remarkable fidelity between the married couples....the unions usually last long, the man and wife growing more affectionate, more tender, more trustful, as they advance in years....I have no distinct memory of having heard during twenty years of any certain case of intrigue or conjugal misbehaviour amongst the cottage folk. The people seem to leave that sort of thing to the employing classes. It scandalises them to hear of it. They despise it."

All this probably amounts to a very superficial sketch of the characteristics of what clearly was a very complex phenomenon – the traditional village community. All of us, I guess, have ancestors who lived in this way, but it is clear how very far removed we in the modern world are. The differences are many and fundamental. The changes brought about by education and the capitalist system are too obvious to need pointing out. But we should also bear in mind the intelligence and the talents necessary for the life of rural self-sufficiency which we have now lost; the independence of outlook has likewise disappeared, as we now all expect the state and our employers to look after us, and large companies to supply all our needs. Perhaps the most important change is psychological; the

---

21 Ibid. Pp. 17-19.
22 Ibid. P. 75.
23 Ibid. Pp 25-27.

cooperative spirit of the small village community being far more congenial to the human psyche than the vast competitive society in which we live now. As the developing human craves identity and community, in the city there is often little or nothing to fulfil his needs; and thus many adolescents are driven to courses which may be destructive or self-destructive; less likely with the peasant, as a member of his tribe, his little group of folk, who "in their successive generations, were the denizens of their little patch of England – its human fauna."[24]

✳

During the early part of the seventeenth century, the community of farmers at Wigston Magna wore an air of considerable well-being. True, the population had been increasing quite rapidly, which led to some degree of overcrowding; as more houses had to be crammed into the same built-up area; the farmland being far too valuable to be encroached upon. This populousness thus led to unhealthfulness; in 1609, for example an epidemic killed around forty villagers. But in most other respects, things were looking rosy at Wigston.[25]

The sharp rise in prices of the sixteenth century, we will call depreciation; in common with the writers of the eighteenth and nineteenth centuries. It was caused largely by the influx of precious metals from the mines of South America, reducing the value of the currency by making it more plentiful. The term inflation is a modern propaganda ploy, which shifts the onus of responsibility from the providers of currency, where it belongs, on to the providers of goods and services. In any case, this depreciation of the sixteenth century, as we shall call it, benefited anyone who had surplus goods to sell; and this included most of the farmers of Wigston Magna. Those who had no surplus to sell, but nevertheless produced some or most of the necessaries of life for themselves, were, at worst, shielded from the unfavourable effects of this depreciation. There would have been hardly anyone in the village who did not fit in to one or other of the above categories.

There was virtually no poverty in the Tudor village – not, at least, in the sense in which we will come across it later. There were no poor 'as a class'. There were, as there always are, people who were incapable of producing their own subsistence through old age, infancy, sickness or injury, but if these people could not be looked after by their own families, then voluntary charity sufficed. Money would be left in wills to "the poore man's boxe" in the church. In general, farming families could afford to look after their own old folks. The retired farmer, or else his widow, would be given a parlour in the farmhouse, and a small area of land in which to 'potter'.[26]

The material standard of living at Wigston Magna seems to have more than doubled in less than a century, and the most obvious manifestation of this growing prosperity was in housing. Up until the 1560s, villagers lived in houses of one or two rooms only. From then on, improvements proliferated. By 1640, many of the village houses had been completely rebuilt; most of the rest improved or enlarged. Kitchens started to make their appearance as a third room in the house. From the 1570s, upstairs rooms were being created by boarding over the ends of the house. Glazed windows started to become common from 1583. And 1599 saw the first house to have a complete upper storey created by the boarding over of the main hall. By the end of this period, the houses of the village had grown much larger; and in general contained more fireplaces; they were much more comfortable and had come to provide a greater degree of privacy. And these developments can be mirrored from all over England. A survey of the houses on the Wilton estate in Wiltshire taken in 1631-2 shows that out of the 355 houses, the traditional peasant one-roomed house made up only four per cent of the total.

---

24 Ibid. P. 81.
25 G. W. Hoskins. The Midland Peasant. Ch. vii
26 W. G. Hoskins. The Midland Peasant. P. 189.

15

Building and rebuilding in the countryside throughout most of England is ample evidence of rural prosperity.

"One has only to look at the villages of almost any county in England….to see how many of them were rebuilt in the years between 1580 and 1640, and how well they were built, with what profound assurance and serenity of mind."[27]

Increasing domestic comfort is also demonstrated by the contents of these houses, as detailed in the inventories made on the deaths of the peasant farmers. A great variety of furniture and domestic goods were listed, along with increasing amounts of tools, implements, grain, hay and livestock. All in all, the estate left by an average farmer rose from between two and four pounds in the early sixteenth century, to between ten and twenty pounds a century later. Allowing for the depreciation of the currency, this still represented a doubling of the standard of living.

Even those described as labourers, on occasion, left wills, inventories, and estates, which suggest a considerable degree of well-being. Some of these survive from the Leicestershire villages surrounding Wigston. A labourer from Skeffington, who died in 1670, left property to the value of £10-7-0. His cottage had little furniture; but he left "two old cows and a yearling calf", barley, peas, and hay. Another, from the same village and dying in the same year, left three sheep, three cows, a yearling heifer, peas hay, barley, and malt, valued at £22-19-4. Rather more startling was Robert Arden of Sutton Cheney, who left a bedstead, a feather bed, napkins, sheets, tablecloths, ten yards of "new flaxen cloth", pewter, brassware, two cows and a yearling, four sheep, three lambs, two growing pigs and a hog, hay, corn and peas.[28] Whilst it is clearly unlikely that all the members of the lowest stratum of society were as well-off as this, these inventories are an indication of what could be achieved by the cottage economy combined with hard work. Many of the cottagers of Wigston owned their own homes, with, perhaps, a single strip in each field pertaining, together with grazing rights on the common. Some cottagers had no land, but still possessed common rights. Collectively, those cottagers who owned no land, possessed, in 1670, somewhere in the region of 35 cows and 220 sheep, around an eighth of the village total, according to the records of the village constables. It was incumbent upon the wealthier farmers to rent grazing to such landless cottagers, at a reasonable rate, when necessary. The cottager could avail himself of the services of the communal herdsman or shepherd; put his cow to the town bull; and use the town plough for free. Cottages had gardens, where pigs, poultry and bees could be kept, and fruit and vegetables grown. All this could be supplemented with labouring for other farmers for money, or even combined with a small craft. In the sixteenth and seventeenth centuries, even the poor could live comfortably.

In this society, it is misleading to think of rigid classes of rich and poor. Everyone in the village belonged to the same class, the social system being continually fluid, and allowing a relatively high degree of mobility. Village society had gradations and hierarchy like any other, and a young farmer might start at the bottom of the ladder, and end up a substantial farmer later in life. But he was still a farmer.

Essential to this mobility was the institution of farm service. Farm servants were young, unmarried farm workers who lived as part of the household of the farmer; and indeed were accounted part of the family. The institution flourished mainly in open-field villages, in areas where small to medium farms predominated; and where a constant demand for reliable labour existed throughout the year.

Servants tended to be the children of small farmers, cottagers and labourers; they would enter service around the age of thirteen of fourteen, relieving the parents of the burden of maintenance.

---

27 Ibid. P.194.
28 Ibid. P. 200.

They would remain in service, though not necessarily on the same farm, until they married, and set up households of their own.[29]

A farm servant lived a good life. While living as a member of the farmer's household, he enjoyed the same standard of living as his employer. Food and lodging would be provided, and this gave the servant the opportunity to save for future needs. The reviewer of the agriculture of Staffordshire estimated that servants could save up to two-thirds of their wages. In case of lack of work from bad weather, or whatever cause, wages still had to be paid; similarly if the servant fell sick or got injured; and this was enforceable at law. Wages could be paid by the provision of grazing; a few sheep kept with those of the master could form the nucleus of a future flock, or be easily sold for cash. The period of service provided the opportunity to learn about many aspects of agriculture; and some servants would move from farm to farm in order to learn about the different systems prevalent in different places and situations.

A pamphlet published in 1785 gives a striking account of how the institution of service interacted with common rights to promote social mobility within the village. It enumerates the advantages accruing to cottagers, craftsmen and small shopkeepers from the ability to graze their livestock on the open common; and especially to agricultural labourers.[30]

"The children of these cottagers brought up under an industrious father and mother, are sent to yearly service amongst farmers etc. and if in the course of a few years service, the young man can scrape up £20 or £30 and finds a young woman that he likes, possessed with nearly an equal sum, they strike a bargain and agree to marry as soon as they can find a cottage near the common, they then stock their cottage with cows, calves, sheep, hogs, poultry etc. as much as their little fortunes will admit of. He then hires himself as a labourer to a neighbouring farmer, and the wife stays at home to look after the livestock. I could mention many cottagers in my neighbourhood under this predicament, who keep two or three milch cows, two or three calves a-rearing, forty or fifty sheep, two or three hogs, and poultry consisting of chickens, ducks, geese, and turkies, to the amount in number of fifty to a hundred in a year, according as they may have had success."

The couple might occupy a cottage with an orchard or garden attached, with perhaps a piece of meadow ground for winter feed, which would cost them, in rent, perhaps £5-11-0.

"By this means, I have known instances of the wife's management of the livestock, together with the earnings of herself and her children in hay time, and harvest etc., produce nearly as much in the course of the year, as her husband by all his labour during the same time....The greatest part of the livestock, viz. of cows, sheep, hogs, poultry, etc., seen upon the commons in general, in my neighbourhood, which are very numerous and extensive, are the property of cottagers...."

And thus, asserts our pamphleteer, whoever he may have been, common-rights became an incentive to industry and an encouragement to young men and women to intermarry; providing a means of supporting children with credit and comfort, rendering them very valuable members of society.

But there was no reason why that should be the limit of their success. In 1795, the peasant occupiers of the Isle of Axholme successfully resisted an attempt to divide and enclose their common fields. This was an unusual achievement, the wisdom of which was amply demonstrated later. In his masterful study of enclosure, published in 1909, Gilbert Slater showed how the flexible system of allocating strips in the open fields on the Isle of Axholme produced social mobility in a peasant society, albeit at a later date.[31]

---

29 A. Kussmaul. Servants in Husbandry in early Modern England. Passim.
30 A Society of Farmers. A Political Enquiry into the Consequences of Enclosing Waste Lands. P. 43.
31 G. Slater. The English Peasantry and the Enclosure of Common Fields. Pp. 57-60.

"How the upward ladder is used was well explained by a Mr. John Standring, himself a holder of ten acres, before the Select Committee of the House of Commons on Small Holdings in 1889….

"When the labourer who has been living in marries and takes a cottage, he also takes up a holding in the fields. He begins with one 'land', then takes a second, a third, and so on….

"The eighty holders occupying from half an acre to two acres would all be men in regular employment, as a rule, agricultural labourers….the more enterprising of these labourers do not rest content with so small a holding, and these pass into the next class, those who hold up to ten acres. 'Many such' says Mr. Standring, 'keep a horse and a cow and a few pigs. And on some of the stronger land two or three of these will yoke their horses together and work their own land, and also land belonging to other men similarly situated who do not keep horses. As a rule they have done very well – I scarcely know a failure.'

"The most successful of these again recruit the ranks of the larger farmers. 'I do not believe there is one in ten in my parish, and in the adjoining parish, among those who are renting from 50 to 100 acres, but what, in my time, has been an agricultural labourer or an agricultural servant before he was married; and each of them, to my knowledge, has commenced with two or three acres, and in some cases not more than an acre….one man who is now occupying 200 acres was a labourer in his early days.'

"These bigger farmers sometimes move elsewhere, and take larger farms, or bring up their sons in other occupations than farming, so that the farm of 150 to 200 acres becomes again available for division into small holdings. Thus, in spite of the continual growth of the holding occupied by individual men at different stages of their career, the average size of holdings does not show any tendency to increase."

It is difficult to believe that this is not just one variant of a system of some antiquity and possibly wide geographical distribution. One would guess that a similar system provided the rationale behind that very active land market in Wigston Magna. Slater adds the following comment;-

"The Isle of Axholme has been singularly successful in preserving the spirit of the common field system – social equality, mutual helpfulness, and an industrial aim directed rather towards the maximum gross product of food than towards the maximum gross profit."

On the moderately flourishing and comfortable situation of rural England, before the changes occurred which are the subject of this book – the progress of which we in the modern world are so proud – let the last words be spoken by W. G. Hoskins and by George Sturt.

"No social system is perfect, but if it offers the possibility of well-being to the majority of men able and willing to work it can be called good; and the peasant system did that. It made it possible for men to get on in a modest but satisfying way, to enjoy well-being, to acquire a standing and some measure of respect in their own community by reason of the quality of their work."[32]

"The 'peasant' tradition in its vigour amounted to nothing less than a form of civilisation – the home-made civilisation of the rural English. To the exigent problems of life it furnished solutions of its own – different solutions, certainly, from those which modern civilisation gives, but yet serviceable enough. People could find in it not only a method of getting a living, but also an encouragement and a help to live well. Besides employment there was an intense interest for them in the country customs. There was scope for modest ambition too….It seems singular to think of now; but the very labourer might hope for some satisfaction in life, nor trouble about 'raising' himself into some other class, so long as he could live on peasant lines."[33]

---

32 W. G. Hoskins. The Midland Peasant. P. 200.
33 George Sturt. Pseud. Bourne. Change in the Village. P. 77.

Strollers

From Hull and Halifax and Hell,
Good Lord deliver me. <u>The Dalesman's Litany</u>

Change was afoot. In 1670, an assessment was made for the hearth tax in Wigston Magna, and it survives.[1] It shows some worrying trends – worrying, that is, for the well-being of the rural community. Of the 161 households in the village, 47 were exempted from paying the tax because of poverty. If it is assumed that as many as one half of these were poor on account of age, sickness or infirmity, that still leaves around one sixth of the village as a permanent class of able-bodied poor – a class which, as we have seen, was almost completely non-existent a century earlier. This poverty seems to have been closely associated with immigration into the village from surrounding areas. Bishop Wake's survey of his diocese, made in 1705, reveals a total of 200 families living in Wigston, an increase of 40 families since 1670, or 25 per cent; and the unfamiliar surnames appearing in the parish register at this time indicate that most had probably come in from outside.[2]

When Celia Fiennes rode through Leicestershire in 1700, she observed it "a very rich country – Red land, good corn of all sorts and grass, both fields and inclosures. You see a great way upon their hills the bottoms full of Enclosures, woods, and different sorts of manureing and herbage".[3] Around the beginning of the seventeenth century, a movement began for dividing and enclosing the open communal field and commons of the Midlands, and Leicestershire was at the centre of it. "Above one hundred towns inclosed in Leicestershire", wrote John Moore already in the 1650s.[4] The movement probably intensified at the time of the commonwealth, and continued thereafter. Enclosure at this time generally, though perhaps not invariably, entailed the conversion of large areas of corn-growing land into pasture; and the consolidation of small farms into large ones. Large grazing farms did not require much labour, and ambitious landlords did not want people on their estates who would consume the produce, and eat into the profits through the poor-rate. Thus, the little rural communities were deprived of their farms and their cottages and their livelihoods, and dispersed through the country. In this way arose the close parish, in the hands of one or two landowners, and worked by a small number of wealthy, capitalist tenant farmers. Of the one hundred towns mentioned by John Moore, "how few amongst them all are not unpeopled and uncorned?"

Examples abound all over the Midlands, and elsewhere, but especially in Leicestershire. In the 1780s, Rev John Howlett received the following intelligence from a correspondent in the county.[5]

"As to enclosures, I can mention two villages in the county within two miles of each other, Wishow and Foston, which formerly contained 34 or 35 dwellings; but by enclosure Foston is reduced

---

1 W. G. Hoskins. The Midland Peasant. P. 195.
2 W. G. Hoskins. The Population of an English Village. Transactions of the Leicestershire Archaeological Society. 1952. P. 27.
3 G. Slater. The English Peasantry and the Enclosure of Common Fields. P. 200.
4 Ibid. P. 201.
5 Rev J. Howlett. Enquiry into the Influence which Enclosures have had upon the Population of the Kingdom. P. 12.

to three habitations; the parsonage-house accommodates one family, and the two other buildings are occupied by shepherds, who manage the stock for their distant renters, as the whole lordship belongs to one person. And as to Wishow, the 34 mansions have vanished in a very few years, and no dwelling remains but the late Sir Charles Halford's hall-house, who owned the lordship; and theses are called improvements; for double and treble rents ensue, and double or treble the old value of land and house rents, and so of provisions."

In neighbouring Nottinghamshire, the historian Dr. Robert Thoroton, writing in 1677, provides a list of villages depopulated by enclosure. At Langer and Barnston, "Earl Howe hath made a park of the Closes….nigh his House, which is well stocked with deer, much better than the towns are with people, where so considerable part of the Fields are inclosed; the too common fate of good land in this county." Cotham "is now decayed, the houses pulled down and most of it enclosed being the inheritance of the Duke of Newcastle." And Hawton was "a Lordship very much depopulated since the war and a great part of it enclosed since then too, which never fails to produce that effect." [6]

The consequences of the pursuit of such a policy by landlords were illustrated by, among many others, John Cowper, in a pamphlet published in 1732.[7] Once a village is enclosed, he says, hedging and ditching may employ several hands, but for less than a year. After that, three or four old men in a parish were sufficient to keep everything in repair; apart, that is, from those who tended the livestock; and "who among the country people live lazier Lives than the Grazier and the Dairyman?"[8]

"In most Open-field parishes there are, I believe, taking them at a medium….six Hundred and forty Persons, Men, Women and Children. These make up a Country-Town or Village, and besides their employment in Husbandry, carry on large Branches of the Woollen and Linnen Manufactories, and are in general the consumers of their own produce….And shall so many honest useful Subjects, so many industrious pains-taking Families be driven from their Settlements, and sent to beg their Bread among Strangers, merely to humour the insatiable Avarice, the Pride or the Luxury of a few, whose Fortunes are already too large for their souls?"[9]

On commons, Cowper had this to say;

"For when a Common, that has been the main Support of perhaps forty or fifty poor Families, and some of them large ones too, is thus taken from them, they will certainly be thereby render'd incapable of maintaining themselves as usual in that Parish: This will put them under a Necessity of forsaking their old Habitations, (which in their mean circumstances must be a great Loss and Hardship) and wandring about till they can find some other Place, where they may enjoy their former Priviledges, without which they cannot subsist."[10]

But a parish did not have to be enclosed in order to be depopulated. Its population might be considerably reduced merely by the practice of engrossing small farms into large ones. That it was common policy among landlords of the early eighteenth century to raise rents by means of amalgamating farms and eliminating the small owners and occupiers is demonstrated by a treatise on estate stewardship written by land surveyor Edward Laurence in 1727.

"A Steward, as much as in him lieth, and without Oppression, should endeavour to lay all the small Farms, let to poor indigent People, to the great ones. But this must be done with discretion, as it may be with Reason and Justice, as the Heads of Families happen to fall, without continuing the Farms to the poor Remains….

6   J. D. Chambers. Nottinghamshire in the Eighteenth Century. P. 189.

7   John Cowper. An Essay Proving that Inclosing Commons and Common-field-lands is contrary to the Interest of the Nation. P. 5.

8   Ibid. P. 15.

9   Ibid. Pp. 3-4.

10   Ibid. P. 2.

"A Steward should not forget to make the best Enquiry into the disposition of any of the Freeholders within or near any of his Lord's Manors, to sell their lands, that he may use his best Endeavours to purchase them at as reasonable a price as may be for his Lord's Advantage and Convenience.... (He should be) zealous, for his Lord's sake, in purchasing all the Freeholders out as soon as possible, especially in such Manors where Improvements are to be made by inclosing Commons and Common-Fields."[11]

That Laurence's advice was widely put into practice has been well demonstrated by Gordon Mingay.[12] On the Duke of Kingston's open-field estates in Nottinghamshire, the larger farms were growing both in number and acreage throughout the eighteenth century; at the expense of the smaller farms. At Colgrave, for example, between 1691 and 1740, the number of farmers of over one hundred acres rose from one to seven, whilst the number occupying between twenty-one and one hundred acres halved. Much the same was happening in the long-enclosed parishes of Staffordshire belonging to the Bagots. Between 1724 and 1764 there was a big rise of 44 per cent in the number of farms over one hundred acres and a forty per cent rise in their acreage. In Sussex, farm size was growing steadily both in the long-enclosed village of Laughton, belonging to the Pelhams, as well as in nearby open-field areas.

Such a process could be almost as deleterious in its effects on the rural community as enclosure itself. In Nottinghamshire, Dr. Thoroton noted the parish of Elton, where "engrossing of farms was the depopulation first complained of....there being not so much above half so many farms as in old time altogether."[13] And engrossing could affect areas which had long since ceased to farm on the open-field system, perhaps never had done so; in Devon, for example, as William Chapple tells us, in his Risdon's Survey of Devon, of 1785.

"The pernicious practice of uniting small farms, which heretofore had their due share of tillage, and converting them into large feeding farms, I am sorry to observe, begins to gain too much footing in parts of this, as well as other counties; witness the many Cottage-houses let down within the last 30 years, and the refusal of some landlords to renew the leases for lives even in their smaller farms as well as others....Such grazing engrossers of land, being enabled to manage their farms with a few servants (especially when prohibited from tillage) have little or no occasion to hire labourers; and hence these are cruelly deprived not only of the opportunities of getting bread-corn at any rate at home, but also of that employment which might enable them to procure it elsewhere; and moreover obliged to quit their ruinous cottages, which are no longer thought worth repairing."[14]

The depopulation of a village was, in fact, illegal, as Arthur Young pointed out in 1786.

"(We) could (not) understand, nor was it fully explained to us, how, in any case, the proprietors could drive the poor away. To act in that manner would be pursued in many parts of the kingdom if the law permitted, but the laws of settlement effectually prevent it. Those for the maintenance of the poor render the others necessary."[15]

The poor laws made it incumbent upon every parish in the country to maintain its own poor, and the law of settlement directed that poor people wandering away from home should be returned to their parish of settlement. Like a true propagandist, Young argued that because depopulation was illegal, it did not happen. But we know, and he knew, that it did; indeed, that it was a common practice. The law was transgressed on a massive scale, and the whole issue passed lightly over by contemporaries and historians alike. It is interesting to speculate whether any enterprising overseer

---

11   Edward Laurence. The Duty of a Steward to his Lord. Pp. 35-7.
12   G. Mingay. The Size of Farms in the Eighteenth Century. Economic History Review. 1962..
13   J. D. Chambers. Nottinghamshire in the Eighteenth Century. P. 189.
14   William Chapple. Risdon's Survey of Devon. Pp. 42-43.
15   Arthur Young. 10 Days Tour to Mr. Bakewell's. Annals of Agriculture. 1786.

ever attempted to repatriate wanderers from these 'close' parishes, and what the probable outcome of such temerity may have been.

Of the actual physical process of depopulation, we seem to possess few details. The Commission on Depopulation of 1517 gave an account of the enclosure of the village of Stretton super Street, in Warwickshire, in 1498, by Henry Smith, who caused "messuages and cottages to be demolished and laid waste", and converted the land to pasture. Eighty persons who were occupied in the cultivation, "and who dwelled in the said messuages and cottages were compelled to depart, tearfully and against their will. Since then they have remained idle and thus they lead a miserable existence, and indeed they die wretched".[16]

But once the poor laws were in operation, how were these countrymen induced to leave, tearfully against their will? We know that, in Ireland, evictions and clearances could be attended with much violence, and even deaths.[17] But how were clearances effected in England? In some cases, landlords sought to do this gradually; cottages might be demolished as they fell vacant, and any land or grazing rights pertaining to them attached to the bigger holdings; in other cases it was done by eviction.[18] At least one writer mentions the use of the cart and the whip for driving away the villagers.[19]

"….The engrossing and monopolizing of land….must necessarily send the inhabitants at least out of the villages. Lesser farmers, labourers, etc. are thereby deprived of their employments, and if they are not immediately forced out of their houses, they are left to starve in them. But they must leave them soon; want of food, and indeed want of comfortable shelter (in such miserable ruinous cottages as those in the inclosures become, in a little time) oblige them to flee. Their landlords in general are glad to get rid of them, that they may not become burdensome, and to save the expences of repairing their old houses."[20]

Edward Laurence drops a clear hint as to how villagers might be moved on. Once the head of a small farming family had died, he suggests, "the poor Remains….may as well betake themselves to other Employments; or if unable, had better be provided for otherwise; And this will be a means of keeping a multitude of poor out of the Parish, who generally care not to come where they must live by hard labour." In other words, a spot of harsh treatment might serve to drive out the riff-raff![21]

The connection between poverty on the one hand, and movement, migration and wandering on the other, is common to nearly all writers on these subjects at the time, no matter on which side of the controversy they stood – surely an indication that the able-bodied poor were, to a large extent, the victims of displacement from the farms and commons of their native villages. Cowper was told by an eminent surveyor that a third of all the land in England had been enclosed within eighty years. And this, according to his estimate, had set adrift twenty thousand farmers, and the same number of cottagers.[22]

As if to illustrate the point, Thomas Alcock, in a pamphlet published in 1752, persistently refers to poor people as 'strollers'. "It is their misfortune", he reluctantly concedes, "that they are in some measure obliged to wander and stroll about to pick and steal, urged on as they are with hunger and want, and not knowing otherwise how to get a piece of bread".[23]

---

16 R. C. Allen. Enclosure and the Yeoman. P. 37.
17 See, for example, Alexander Somerville. The Whistler at the Plough. Pp. 500-5 and 539.
18 Christopher Clay in Agrarian History of England and Wales. Vol. 5. Part 2. P. 237.
19 Roger North. A Discourse of the Poor.
20 Stephen Addington. An Inquiry into the Reasons for and against Inclosing Open-fields. Pp. 42-3.
21 Edward Laurence. The Duties of a Steward to his Lord. 1727. P. 35.
22 J. Cowper. An Essay Proving That Inclosing Commons and Common-field-Lands is contrary to the Interest of the Nation. 1732. P. 5.
23 Thomas Alcock. Observations on the Defects of the Poor Law. 1752. P. 69.

According to Joseph Massie, writing in 1758, the practice of strolling originated around the time of Charles II, when the decay of manufacturing led to a great increase of the poor, and a country-wide distress. By his own day there had arisen a great inequality of employment between one district and another, "so that Multitudes of common working People cannot be Employed in their native Places, nor constantly in any one place, but must travel from County to County in order to find Employment".[24]

When the members of a rural community were dispossessed, uprooted and dispersed, their first thought would have been to find somewhere where they could find employment and subsistence; "where they may enjoy their former priviledge", as John Cowper put it. And this, of course, meant an open-field village, as yet unenclosed, and possessing a common. Such a place was Wigston Magna. But the dispersal of the inhabitants of a number of rural communities could wreak havoc with the economies of neighbouring villages. F. M. Eden visited Deddington in Oxfordshire in 1797, where he noted the high poor rates in this parish, of over 6s in the pound; a circumstance he ascribed to "the common-field of which the land principally consists; whereas the neighbouring parishes have been inclosed many years, and many small farms in them have been consolidated; so that many small farmers, with little capitals, have been obliged, either to turn labourers, or to procure small farms in Deddington, or other parishes that possess common-field. Besides this, the neighbouring parishes are, many of them, possessed by a few individuals, who are cautious in permitting new comers to obtain a settlement".[25]

Open villages would soon become overstocked with hungry labourers; unemployment and underemployment became endemic in the English countryside, as this farmer from Nottinghamshire later noted. He writes of the pain of seeing "….the honest labourer asking from door to door 'for leave to toil' that he may thereby get his daily bread, but asking in vain….This is no imaginary case, but an undeniable fact, the constant occurrence of which under our own eyes, has induced me to allude to it. Can we wonder at men, born with the feelings of Englishmen, turning droopingly away, inwardly feeling that no man careth for them, and that our very cattle are regarded more than they?" He writes of their broken spirit, and dejected mien.[26]

A grazing common, remaining open, would also act as a magnet to the dispossessed of adjoining areas. At Hothfield, in Kent, Eden noted that "half the labouring poor are certificated persons from other parishes. The common, which affords them the means of keeping a cow or poultry, is supposed to draw many poor into the parish."[27] And thus the common, like the labour market, would become overstocked. The parish of Chailey, in Sussex, contained around 1000 acres of common grazing, scattered around the parish; but situated upon it were a large number of pauper tenements, and half-tenements; and the poor-rates in the village were as high as 9s in the pound.[28] Should we connect this to the close proximity of the estate of Lord Sheffield, a well-known 'improving' landlord, and not noted for his sympathy to the poor? At Sutton Coldfield in Warwickshire, an inspired method of managing the common attracted many to attempt to settle there. "Hence an influx of inhabitants more than adequate to the increased employment; the want of which the rights of common cannot compensate." Poor rates there, too, were very high.[29]

So the displaced and wandering populations of close parishes caused much pressure and disruption for those that remained open; like Wigston Magna. "But if these inclosures become general", asked

---

24 J. Massie. Considerations Relating to the Poor. 1758. P. 61.
25 F. M. Eden. The State of the Poor. 1797. P. 501.
26 J. D. Chambers. Nottinghamshire in the Eighteenth Century. P. 184.
27 F. M. Eden. The State of the Poor. 1797. P. 288.
28 Arthur Young in Annals of Agriculture 1785-6. P. 221.
29 J. Howlett. Enclosures a Cause of Improved Agriculture and Plenty. P. 80. Quoting Eden.

John Cowper prophetically in 1732, "whither must they go? Or how will they get their bread?"[30] The answer was supplied by John Wedge, reporting to the Board of Agriculture on Warwickshire in 1793.

"About 40 years ago the southern and eastern parts of this county consisted mostly of open fields. There are still about 50,000 acres of open field land, which in a few years will probably be all inclosed….These lands being now grazed want much fewer hands to manage them than they did in the former open state. Upon all enclosures of open fields the farms have generally been made much larger; from these causes the hardy yeomanry have been driven for employment to Birmingham, Coventry and other manufacturing towns."[31]

One might hazard a guess that those who made it to Birmingham were the lucky ones.[32] Indeed, some displaced farmers did very well for themselves, if they possessed the requisite degrees of luck, ruthlessness, drive and entrepreneurship. Many of the best-known figures of the so-called industrial revolution originated in the English countryside – Peel, Strutt, Wedgwood and Darby, for example. Radcliffe and Fielden had both been dispossessed by acts of enclosure, and started in business from scratch and without capital.[33] For the majority of strollers, however, a multitude of mischances awaited. Here again is the perceptive Joseph Massie in 1758.

"Persons when out of their own Parishes, as some Hundred Thousands of working People probably are at all Times; most of whom get together a small Stock of Money before they leave their native Places, and being then in Health and Strength; they may reasonably hope to support themselves by honest Industry; but Sickness, Want of Employment, or other Misfortunes, bring great Numbers of these People to Poverty, when they are far from Home."[34]

The hazards of strolling were legion. While huge numbers of people could not find work, begging was illegal as a form of roguery. In the seventeenth century, the law laid it down that "valiant rogues", as these able-bodied wanderers were denominated, should be "stockt, stript, and whipt", and then sent to their several parishes of habitation. Even simple loitering could incur this penalty.[35]

"The Law makes only a Cobweb Partition between Stealing and Begging – distressed People may well be expected not to make a thicker."[36]

Thus they might easily be driven to thieving or prostitution, and the gallows might present itself as an alternative to starvation.

"Who will be to answer for What these distressed Persons DO or SUFFER, the great SEARCHER of all HEARTS only can tell."[37]

"….as to a poor Man or Woman being hunted out of one Parish, and DYING for WANT, in the next, why, it is a sad Thing, to be sure, but the Overseers comfort themselves with not knowing of the Distress."[38]

It is a curious fact that at the end of the eighteenth century, and in the nineteenth, we hear very rarely of people dying of starvation. We know that they did. William Cobbett talks of labourers dying

---

30 J. Cowper. An Essay Proving that Inclosing Commons and Common-field-Lands is contrary to the Interest of the Nation. P. 5.
31 G. Slater. The English Peasantry and the Enclosure of Common Fields. P. 101.
32 Rev. J. Howlett. The Insufficiency of the Causes to which the Increase of our Poor, and of the Poor's Rates, have been commonly ascribed.
33 J. L. and B. Hammond. The Town Labourer. P. 8.
34 J. Massie. Considerations Relating to the Poor. P. 54.
35 J. D. Chambers. Nottinghamshire in the Eighteenth Century. P. 248.
36 J. Massie. Considerations Relating to the Poor. P. 55.
37 Ibid. Pp. 54-55.
38 Ibid. P. 59.

in the fields with sorrel in their bellies; and the rioters of 1816 and 1830 frequently claimed that a quick death by the bullet was far preferable to a slow one by starvation. But in general contemporaries did not mention this distasteful fact. No such delicacy seems to have affected the writers of the 1750s; when conditions had not yet plumbed the depths experienced in the nineteenth century.

"....the Reluctance, or ill Success, with which such unfortunate People do practise begging, is frequently manifested by a poor and emaciated Man or Woman being found drowned or starved to Death...."[39]

Thus Joseph Massie.

Henry Fielding, novelist, writer, and magistrate in London, also noted mortality from starvation.[40]

"While a Million yearly is raised among the (rich), many of the (poor) are starved; many more languish in Want and Misery."

Death by starvation, he claimed, a little unconvincingly, was little known about, because it was little seen.

"They starve, and freeze, and rot among themselves; but they beg and steal and rob among their betters."

Nevertheless, huge numbers of the displaced peasantry did, in fact, make it to the manufacturing centres. Already by 1612 complaints came from Nottingham of a "confluence of poor persons from forraine parts." Some years later, the magistrates of the county wrote to the Privy Council that "where houses are pulled downe the People are forced to seeke new habitations. In other tounes....(which) are (thereby) pestred so as they are hardly able to live by one another....And Causes Rogues and Vagabonds to increase." The authorities in Nottingham were being continually forced into measures to keep out migrants and their families, such as prohibitions on building cottages and converting barns into dwellings.[41]

It almost seemed as if the whole of the Midlands was on the move. Concentrations of displaced country folk seeking employment stimulated the founding and expansion of industries, whilst in turn the presence of manufacturing attracted people to settle. Domestic industries were established in many of the more northerly areas in the Midlands, both in the towns and in the large open industrial villages; and in these migrants congregated. In this way, framework-knitting proliferated in Leicestershire, Nottinghamshire and Derbyshire, producing stockings and gloves. Weaving was carried on in northern Oxfordshire; boots and shoes were produced in Northamptonshire; and blankets at Witney.[42]

Generally, in much of the southern Midlands, there was little manufacturing carried on, and so London became the destination of the wanderers. Incredibly, the population of London almost trebled during the seventeenth century, most of which increase must have come from the countryside. Indeed, the Midlands supplied almost a third of the apprentices to London companies between 1570 and 1640.

But it was not just the Midlands. Country people flooded into the woollen towns of Yorkshire; into the metal-working towns of Sheffield and Birmingham; and in Lancashire farmers and cottagers turned themselves by the thousand into handloom-weavers. In Devon, where population movements were caused not by enclosure, but by the absorption of small farms into large ones, and the conversion of arable to pasture, the poorer parts of Exeter were clearly receiving immigrants. St. Sidwells parish,

---

39   Ibid. P. 50.
40   H. Fielding. A Proposal for Making an Effectual Provision for the Poor. P. 10.
41   J. D. Chambers. Nottinghamshire in the Eighteenth Century. P. 190.
42   R. C. Allen. Enclosure and the Yeoman. Pp. 243-5.

situated outside the east gate of the old city, was the poorest parish, the most densely settled, and the fastest growing, with a population which by 1670 had probably doubled in a century.[43]

It was not all bad news. It seldom is. Birmingham had a reputation as a city of good conditions and wages, where labourers could work in a multitude of small workshops, and for small masters. Trade was generally steady; and if one branch of it fell on hard times, it was normally possible, at least in the eighteenth century, to find employment in another branch. From around 1700, migrants into Nottingham found that the obstacles to settlement had been removed; landlords accommodating inmates had merely to register their name with the parish officers.[44] The city's framework-knitting industry was expanding, and labourers were in demand. Through most of the early part of the eighteenth century, employment was easy to find and well paid; trade was regular; and the prices of provisions low.[45]

But the numbers of people driven from their homes and farms and commons by the changes in the countryside were actually far greater than could be comfortably accommodated in the rapidly growing towns, or employed in the new manufacturing. Just as the remaining open villages and commons had their economies disrupted by the influx of strollers; so the towns became physically overstocked with people, and their industries with labour. This, no doubt, was greatly to the advantage of masters and entrepreneurs.

Growing numbers of immigrants flocking into towns meant constantly deteriorating physical conditions. The city of Nottingham was circumscribed by private land which prevented its expansion, so that the inflowing crowds attracted by the rapidly growing stocking manufacture had to be accommodated on a finite amount of space; and this led to complaints about the division of houses, and landlords taking in inmates and lodgers, "to the great danger of ills and contagions, and for depauperisation of the parishioners by overcrowding."[46]

In 1791, a letter was published in the Annals of Agriculture, written by J. H. Campbell Esq., on the dangers accompanying life in Preston, Lancashire.[47]

"Sudden and great call and temptation for hands from the country, of this county and others, and many distant parts; crowded, of course, in their lodgings; tempted by extra gain to long continued application at sedentary work, in air contaminated both by the exhalation and breathing of many people together, and also the effluvia of the material used, in confined spaces, and though getting good wages at what they think easy work, yet (provisions being dear....) perhaps living but poorly in diet, these people are frequently visited, especially in autumn and beginning of winter, with low and nervous fevers, in short, putrid and gaol distempers, that often cuts off men, leaving families behind....such diseases do make havoc among them at times."

Through overcrowding and exploitation, towns were becoming places of ugliness and servility. Those unfortunate enough to be forced into factory labour found themselves under a harsh system of discipline and control, with extortionate fines imposed for trivial offences. Working hours were long, and masters often exerted pressure for longer. Many workers would not see daylight from one end of the working day to the other, and in Manchester spinning factories the temperature would normally be between 80 and 84 degrees. Both the working conditions, and the accommodation in "the dirty, confined parts of the larger towns, in which the poor are most frequently situated", must

43 W. G. Hoskins. Industry, Trade and People in Exeter 1688-1800. P. 120.
44 J. D. Chambers. Nottinghamshire in the Eighteenth Century. P. 271
45 Ibid. P. 292.
46 Ibid. P. 267.
47 Annals of Agriculture. Vol. 15. P. 564. See also Stephen Addington. An Inquiry into the Reasons for and against Inclosing Open Fields. Pp. 47-8.

have presented a stark contrast indeed to those "who are driven thither from the pure air, and more active employment of the country".[48]

This crowding of people into the manufacturing centres affected wages and employment opportunities, as well as living conditions, as the labour markets became oversupplied. The flood of aspiring hand-loom weavers into Lancashire early on brought about a great decrease in wages, which continued as a long-term trend.[49] By the middle of the eighteenth century, the weavers of Nottingham were already beginning to experience distress and poor living conditions, even though trade was still growing and labour in demand, probably through continued migration into the city of country people desperate for work. The journeymen weavers were described as "Poor Men, many of whom (though not Old) are scarce able to get bread".[50]

In London, according to Joseph Massie in 1758, the situation was even worse; it was not just that wages were low; it was even difficult to find work at all. "Thousands of common People are Unemployed, for the many Register Offices for Servants, etc. in this Metropolis, do prove the Want of much WORK, as well as a Desire to find it".[51]

The consequences that this situation might entail for strollers in London were graphically described by magistrate Henry Fielding in 1751.

"Most of the Rogues who infest the Public Roads and Streets, indeed almost all the thieves in general, are Vagabonds in the true Sense of the Word, being Wanderers from their lawful Place of Abode....These Vagabonds do indeed get their livelihood by Thieving, and not as petty Beggars or petty Chapmen; and have their Lodging not in Alehouses, etc. but in private Houses, where many of them resort together, and unite in Gangs, paying each 2d per Night for their Beds."[52]

The following information came from the High Constable of Holborn, a Mr. Welch.

"That in the Parish of St. Giles's there are great Numbers of Houses apart for the Reception of idle Persons and Vagabonds, who have their lodgings there for Twopence a Night; That in the above parish, and in St. George, Bloomsbury, one Woman occupies seven of these Houses, all properly accommodated with miserable beds from the Cellar to the Garret, for such Twopenny Lodgers; That in these Beds, several of which are in the same room, Men and Women, often Strangers to each other, lie promiscuously, the Price of a double Bed being no more than Threepence, as an Encouragement to them to lie together; That as these places are adapted to Whoredom, so are they no less provided for Drunkenness, Gin being sold in them all at a Penny a Quartern; so that the smallest Sum of Money serves for Intoxication; That in the Execution of Search Warrants, Mr. Welch rarely finds less than Twenty of these Houses open for all Comers at the latest Hours; That in one of these Houses, and that not a large one, he hath numbered 58 Persons of both Sexes.

"If one considers the Destruction of all Decency and Morality; the Swearing, Whoredom, and Drunkenness, which is eternally carrying on in these Houses, on the one hand, and the excessive Poverty and Misery of most of the Inhabitants on the other, it seems doubtful whether they are more the Objects of Detestation or Compassion; for such is the Poverty of these Wretches....I have been credibly informed, that a single Loaf hath supplied a whole family with their Provisions for a Week....If any of these miserable Creatures fall sick (and it is almost a Miracle, that Stench, Vermin and Want should ever suffer them to be well) they are turned out in the Streets by their merciless Host or Hostess, where, unless some Parish Officer of extraordinary Charity relieves them, they are sure miserably to perish, with the Addition of Hunger and Cold to their Disease."

---

48 J. L. and B. Hammond. The Town Labourer. Pp. 18-22. Stephen Addington. Op. cit. P. 48.
49 J. L. and B. Hammond. The Town Labourer. P. 13.
50 J. D. Chambers. Nottinghamshire in the Eighteenth Century. Pp. 292-3.
51 J. Massie. Considerations relating to the Poor. P. 54.
52 H. Fielding. An Enquiry into the Causes of the late Increase of Robbers etc. P. 91.

The great precariousness of the existence of huge numbers of people living in cities, towns, and centres of manufactures, resulted, according to Joseph Massie, from the "Removing Multitudes of People from our Natural and Fixed Basis, Land, to the Artificial and Fluctuating Basis, Trade".[53] Notoriously, poor rates were high in such places; not just because the attraction of them to wanderers would overstock the labour market; but also because trade declines and depressions could quickly throw thousands on to their respective parishes. And these could be caused in numberless ways. Changes in fashion were well-known for plunging industries into depression, or else destroying them altogether. Coventry, for example, was dangerously dependent upon the manufacture of ribbons, according to Eden.

"Both the manufacture and the Poor's Rates in this city are very fluctuating. The markets are often overstocked with ribbon, the staple manufacture of this city; and the manufacturers, in consequence of the stagnation of trade, are often thrown on the parish for support; sometimes there is a great demand for this article, at which time the parochial burthens are considerably lessened."[54] The city of Exeter provides a sad instance of the multiplicity of misfortunes that could befall manufacturing populations through no fault of their own. The proportion of Exeter folk dependent on the serge manufacture increased rapidly from 1660, until by 1700 it was said to be four out of five. By the 1720s, however, Devon serges were being replaced in foreign markets by stuffs manufactured in Norfolk. In part, this was the result of changes in fashion; but, more importantly, wage rates around Norwich were considerably below those of Exeter. This led the masters of Exeter to attempt to reduce costs. The large quantities of cheap Irish wool which fed the industry had always been combed and spun in Devon; but it was cheaper to perform these operations in Ireland, and so finished yarn was imported instead. This caused massive distress among Devon combers and spinners, and various serious disturbances at Tiverton had to be put down by military force. But the loss of the markets continued, and the weavers suffered progressive wage reductions through the eighteenth century. By 1743, "the lamentable condition of the woollen trade" was being complained of, with bankruptcies among the masters, worsening unemployment, the truck system being used to reduce labour costs still further, and the prisons and workhouses full.[55] Deteriorating conditions led to high mortality rates, which brought the average family size in the city down to a mere 4.4 persons.[56] And the decline or destruction of an industry could set strollers out on the road all over again.

Meanwhile, back in Leicestershire, the framework-knitting of stockings was establishing itself at the major centres of Hinckley and Leicester. That all was not well with this industry either is demonstrated by Eden's comment in 1797 that great numbers of hands had been taken off by the war, whose families were now being supported by the parish rates.[57] This probably also happened in earlier wars. Nevertheless, in Leicester, the records show that between a quarter and a half of the city's freemen and apprentices were migrants.[58] The displaced persons of the enclosed parishes flocked to Hinckley and Leicester. But they also went to Wigston Magna.

Wigston remained an open village, with communal fields and an open grazing common. Migrants came to it in the hope of finding employment in agriculture; perhaps some pasturage for a cow or poultry; maybe even a small farm. But its economy was increasingly being subjected to pressure and disruption, both from within and without.

---

53 J. Massie. Considerations relating to the Poor. P. 69

54 F. M. Eden. The State of the Poor. P. 740.

55 W. G. Hoskins. Industry, Trade and People in Exeter 1688-1800.

56 Ibid. P. 129.

57 F. M. Eden. The State of the Poor. P. 228.

58 R. C. Allen. Enclosure and the Yeoman. P. 253.

Inside the village, there was occurring a concentration of land into the hands of a few large occupiers. The Pochin and Davenport families, for example, had six yardlands each, and could no longer be considered part of the peasant economy. Many other farms consisted of between two and four yardlands. A peasant family could support itself on from half to one yardland, but for many the possibility of acquiring such a farm had now vanished. This meant that by the time of the poor-rate assessment of 1765, the cohesive village community, the members of which graduated up and down within it, had been replaced by a polarised class system of rich and poor, with an unbridgeable gulf dividing them. The peasant community now subsisted itself on not much more than a quarter of the land of the village, the rest being in large farms of over a hundred acres.[59] Indeed, in England as a whole, it has been estimated that in 1688 the peasantry still occupied two thirds of the land; but by 1800 that proportion had dropped to ten per cent.[60] In Wigston, by 1765, twelve men owned three fifths of the village, less than half of them from local stock. Only sixty families occupied land, a mere thirty per cent of the inhabitants. There were more farmers at the time of the Domesday Survey, with less than half the population. Many families which had been part of the rural community in earlier times were now landless. Some had gone. Some, no doubt, were impoverished.[61]

But in spite of the deteriorating conditions of life in Wigston, the dispossessed and the desperate were still being driven there from surrounding parishes. The resulting pool of cheap labour stimulated the establishment of a framework-knitting industry in the village, which was becoming industrialised by 1700.[62] This, in its turn, continued to attract migrants. The rise in the number of inhabitants came to a halt during the first half of the eighteenth century, and resumed its steady rise from around 1760, when a wave of parliamentary enclosure in Leicestershire was setting people adrift on the roads once again.[63] By 1765, a quarter of the families of Wigston were too impoverished to be assessed for the poor-rate. At the bottom of the social scale existed a large permanent class of landless, able-bodied poor, dependent partly on agricultural labour, partly on the framework-knitting industry, and partly on the parish rate. Already at the end of the seventeenth century, small houses of from one to three rooms were forming an increasing proportion of the housing stock – fifty-three per cent, up from thirty-seven per cent early in the century. The influx of poor people meant that many small cottages had to be built, with just two rooms on the ground floor, with or without one upstairs.[64] Hovels could be quickly and cheaply erected out of mud, and by 1765 the village was congested with dwellings of this sort, occupying every spot that could be found, in the lanes or open spaces. Following overcrowding came disease. Mortality was high throughout the 1760s, when we may strongly suspect typhus as the main culprit. In the 1770s, it got worse; in the 1780s, worse still; and in 1789 the vicar recorded in the parish register twenty deaths from the smallpox.[65]

The agricultural changes of the seventeenth and eighteenth centuries caused a huge amount of economic disruption and dislocation. That sounds a very dry, cold, objective statement, but behind it

59 W. G. Hoskins. The Midland Peasant. Pp. 214-7.
60 R. C. Allen. Enclosure and the Yeoman. P. 85.
61 W. G. Hoskins. The Midland Peasant. P. 247 and 217.
62 Ibid. P. 212.
63 W. G. Hoskins. The Population of an English Village. Transactions of the Leicestershire Archaeological Society. 1957.
64 W. G. Hoskins. The Midland Peasant. Pp. 300-1.
65 W. G. Hoskins. The Population of an English Village. Transactions of the Leicestershire Archaeological Society. 1957.

lay the intense suffering and misery of millions of people. The motivation behind the changes was little more than the acquisitiveness of the landowning class, though that too makes the situation sound a great deal less complex than it actually was, as we shall see. However, that the subsistence of millions should be converted to rent and added to the wealth of those who were wealthy already, does not seem to be a particularly praiseworthy achievement. Yet by many modern historians it has been applauded, and the assertions of the propagandists supporting the changes, ranging from plausible, to wayward, to dishonest, to absurd, have been accepted less critically and questioningly than they ought to have been. That is because the resulting society is perceived as bearing an incipient resemblance to that in which we live today. In short, the changes are seen as progressive; and the progressive aspects of them come to be emphasised, whilst the negative aspects, if acknowledged at all, are so in a low-key, justificatory sort of way.

But the fact was that many parts of the country, as a result of those changes, were in an appalling state of chaos and confusion. Despite the assertions of the propagandists, the lifestyle of a stroller was not, in general, to be envied.

Cataclysm

Enclosure, when suddenly effected, as by a private act, is rightly termed the extinction of a village community. Gilbert Slater. The English Peasantry and Enclosure. 1909.

In the last quarter of the seventeenth century, Wigston Magna had been a magnet for refugees from all the surrounding villages, whose commons and open fields had been divided, enclosed, the farms amalgamated and turned over to pasture. This could be done in parishes where a few large owners could get together and buy out the smallholders, who might have objected to the process. Wigston had escaped such a fate, because in Wigston there were ninety-nine owners, maybe more, the overwhelming majority of whom would strongly have opposed enclosure. However, in the middle of the eighteenth century, a procedure became common, which could overcome this obstacle – enclosure by act of Parliament. To obtain such an act required the consent of the owners of around seventy-five to eighty per cent of the parish by value, according to the land tax or poor rate assessment; so long as these included the lord of the manor and the tithe-owner. The previous trend towards concentration and polarisation of landownership in Wigston meant that the consent of only twenty of the ninety-nine owners would have been enough to instigate the procedure; and many of these would have had no connection with the rural community who lived and worked there; but had plenty of financial interest in accomplishing the enclosure. Four of the promoters of the act were absentee owners, who received between them over a quarter of the parish at enclosure.[1]

At least sixty of the peasant community appear to have been against the enclosure, but they managed to make no representations against the bill presented in Parliament. Stephen Addington, writing against enclosure a few years later, described the situation as follows.

"Many small proprietors of land are hereby greatly injured, and most of the labourers in every parish that is inclosed are deprived of the means of support. There are some in almost all such open parishes, who have houses and little parcels of land in the field, with a right of common for a cow, and three or four sheep, by the assistance of which, with the profits of a little trade, or their daily labour, they procure a very comfortable living. This land furnishes them with wheat and barley for bread, and, in many places, with beans or peas to feed a hog or two for meat; with the straw they thatch their cottage, and with their cow, which gives a breakfast and supper of milk, nine or ten months in the year, for their families. These almost universally disapprove of inclosing; and their number is considerable in many open villages; much greater, than perhaps the constituents of our legislature are generally aware of. Indeed, they cannot well know it, when these unhappy sufferers are not able to make an opposition. If the expences were less, P---t might know much more of the sense of the people on inclosing, than they do at present….many proprietors in parishes that have been inclosed, disapprove of it. Some refuse to sign the petitions, and others heartily repent of signing them after they have been prevailed upon to do it, when they see its unhappy consequences. But the ill success that opposition to inclosing bills has generally met with, discourages the attempt, and the connections of others oblige them to forbear. There are few but would submit to inconvenience and injury, rather

---

1 W. G. Hoskins. The Midland Peasant. Pp. 247-250.

than appear against their superiors, especially those who are in their neighbourhoods; and many are aggrieved, who do not openly complain."[2]

Even Henry Homer, a firm advocate of enclosure, wrote, in the very year of the Wigston award, of the trickery used to frustrate the wishes of the inhabitants.

"One branch proper to be brought under better regulation is the method of transacting the bills, which is often very exceptionable. The whole plan of them is for the most part settled between the solicitors and two or three principal proprietors, without even letting the rest into the secret, till they are called upon to sign the petition. They are in many instances, not so much as indulged with a sight of the bill, or the privilege of hearing it read, till it is tendered to them to be signed, and for that purpose they are taken separately. This leaves them exposed to be practised upon by Agents....Many times the business is hurried on and concluded without a single meeting of the parties concerned to consult about their common interest tho' perhaps the whole property of many is at stake."[3]

The whole process of enclosure in general was ruthlessly skewed against the agricultural community. The rather shocking details are recounted by the Hammonds in The Village Labourer.[4] But the upshot was as stated in Arthur Young's report prepared for the Board of Agriculture in 1813; by a Mr. Elmhurst who had been an enclosure commissioner for fully twenty-eight years.

"Little (owners) would have no weight by opposition, they must submit, was it ever so disadvantageous to them, as it very often happens...."[5]

Parliamentary enclosure was a device for the coercion of the majority of a village community. John Billingsley, writing for the Board on Somerset in 1795, and no doubt propagating the views of the enclosing landlords, noted that enclosures often necessitated an act, "whereby a minority, sanctioned only by ignorance, prejudice, or selfishness, is precluded from defeating the ends of private advantage and public utility." Of course, "the minority" was so only in terms of the value of the lands they held; numerically they were the overwhelming majority.[6]

Here is an example of "ignorance, prejudice, and selfishness", in a petition sent up to the House of Commons by the villagers of Raunds in Northamptonshire; on the subject of an enclosure act relating to their parish, which nevertheless passed in 1797.

"The petitioners beg leave to represent to the House that, under Pretence of improving Lands in the said Parish, the Cottagers and other Persons entitled to Right of Common on the Lands intended to be inclosed, will be deprived of an inestimable Privilege, which they now enjoy, of turning a certain Number of their Cows Calves and Sheep, on and over the said Lands; a Privilege that enables them not only to maintain themselves and their Families in the Depth of Winter, when they cannot, even for their Money, obtain from the Occupiers of other Lands the smallest Portion of Milk or whey for such necessary Purpose, but, in addition to this, they can now supply the Grazier with young or lean Stock at a reasonable Price....And they further conceive, that a more ruinous Effect of this Inclosure will be the almost total Depopulation of their Town, now filled with bold and hardy Husbandmen.... and driving them, from necessity and Want of Employ, in vast Crowds, into manufacturing Towns, where the very nature of their Employment, over the Loom or the Forge, soon may waste their Strength, and consequently debilitate their Posterity....These are some of the injuries....which the Petitioners conceive will follow from this, as they have already done from many Inclosures, but which

---

2 Rev. Stephen Addington. An Inquiry into the Reasons for and against Inclosing Open Fields. 1772. Pp. 33-34.
3 Henry Homer. An Essay on the Nature and Method Etc. 1766. P. 103.
4 J. L. and B. Hammond. The Village Labourer. Ch. 3.
5 G. E. Mingay. Arthur Young and his Times. P. 117.
6 John Billingsley. General View of the Agriculture of Somerset. 1795. P. 49.

they did not think they were entitled to lay before the House....until it unhappily came to their lot to be exposed to them through the Bill now pending."[7]

It will be observed that the petitioners of Raunds based their case on the historical experience of "many Inclosures in other Parishes". In a similar, though much later, instance of "ignorance, prejudice, and selfishness", the petitioners of Foulmere in Cambridgeshire cited the instance of their neighbours in Thriplow, where "the poor inhabitants having similar rights were utterly and most unjustly deprived of their rights and privileges without any compensation whatever"....were "in great difficulty to provide the means of maintenance for their respective families by labour and adequate wages and should the Bill pass without protection Clauses will become utterly destitute and....must become paupers and inmates of a workhouse".[8]

Many enclosure bills were opposed by petitions making points similar to these, most of which were studiously ignored. Nevertheless, the fears which the petitioners voiced for their futures and their livelihoods turned out to be well-founded in the majority of cases.

When the enclosure commissioners arrived in the villages, they had to start the business of assessing claims in order to award allotments. Claims normally had to be presented by a certain date, and in the correct form. The act for the enclosure of Croydon specified claims "in Writing under their Hand, or the Hands of their Agents, distinguishing in such Claims the Tenure of the Estates in respect whereof such Claims are made, and stating such Particulars as shall be necessary to describe such Claims with precision".[9]

If the bureaucratic processes were not correctly carried through, the commissioners could reject the claim; as happened in the enclosure of Knaresborough Forest, according to a petition presented in 1774, because of "mistakes made in the description of such tenements....notwithstanding the said errors were merely from inadvertency, and in no way altered the merits of the petitioners' claims". In the enclosure of Sedgmoor in Somerset, indeed, 2265 claims were discarded out of a total of 4063![10]

But what business did peasant farmers have with bureaucratic processes? Some commoners would have settled in the parish, often as refugees from neighbouring enclosures, building themselves cottages on the waste. Other families would have possessed common rights, of grazing livestock and collecting fuel and building materials, for centuries; the origins of those rights being lost in the mists of time. Customary usage from time immemorial was sometimes admitted as a genuine claim, but more often not. Many claims from small farmers must have been presented wrongly, late, or not at all; and many thousands of the members of the agricultural communities would have lost their rights and their land, possibly their homes, certainly their security and independence, even before the enclosure awards were made.

In Wigston Magna, the award was made on the 17th November 1766. The most striking feature of the remodelled parish was the huge estate presented to the rector in lieu of the great tithes. It could have been worse. In many parishes it was usual to take around one sixteenth of the land to compensate the lord of the manor for the loss of his manorial rights, or some of them. This was a generous compensation, especially considering the increased rentals which followed enclosure; but there being no lord of the manor in Wigston Magna, this at least was one burden which the villagers there were free of. The rector, however, was another matter.[11]

---

7   J. L. and B. Hammond. The Village Labourer. Pp. 15-16.

8   K. D. M. Snell. Annals of the Labouring Poor. P. 179.

9   J. L. and B. Hammond. The Village Labourer. P. 39.

10   Ibid. Pp. 39-40.

11   W. G. Hoskins. The Midland Peasant. Ch. 9.

The tithe was a tenth part of the produce of the village, which traditionally the farmers were compelled to donate for the support of the church. In open-field parishes, when enclosed by act, the tithes were generally replaced; sometimes by cash payments or corn rents; more often by land. The church was in a strong position; it was influential, businesslike, and aggressive in pushing forward its claims. No enclosure could go ahead without the support of the tithe-holder, who usually appointed a commissioner to look after his interests. And the bishops in the House of Lords would block any act which did not meet with their approval.[12]

For these reasons, the rectors and incumbents in the enclosed parishes gained far more than a tenth of the land as their allotments. In Warwickshire, for example, 17.4 per cent of all the land enclosed was set aside for the support of the tithe-holders. Various arguments were put forward to justify this theft, but none made much sense; nor vindicated the huge increases of income enjoyed by the tithe-holders. For example, the annual receipts of James Hodgson, rector of Hillington in Norfolk, rocketed from £200 to £500.[13] Furthermore, since the Reformation, around a third of the great tithes had fallen into the hands of laymen, and benefited the church not at all. This was a situation which, as Cobbett later said, no one of any persuasion seriously considered justifiable....

The rector of Wigston Magna was the Duke of St. Albans. His Grace, together with the vicar, in lieu of the great and small tithes, took between them over 475 acres of the village land; around 16.5 per cent of the total. All the other allotments, therefore, had to be reduced by this proportion.[14] The larger landowners and farmers would acquiesce in this because, as Arthur Young put it, "tythe is such a horrible oppression that men will give enormous compensation to be rid of it"; and because, in boom conditions, they were sanguine about making large profits anyway.[15] But upon the smaller holdings, a reduction in area of one sixth would have an obvious effect on viability.

Nor was this all. Many of the enclosure acts directed that the lord of the manor and the tithe-owner were to have their awards as compact areas, conveniently situated. At the enclosure of Haute Huntre, investigated by the Hammonds, for example, it was laid down that Lord Fitzwilliam was to have his allotment near his gardens.[16] The smaller owners, thus, would perforce be fitted in where possible; and the awkward siting of a farm could have a disastrous effect on its viability. As Mr. Elmhurst, the enclosure commissioner encountered by Arthur Young in Lincolnshire, pointed out;

"A little man may as well have nothing allotted to him as to have it so far off or so inconvenient for him that it is not worth having; as it would prevent him going to his daily labour; and wherefore he must sell his property to his rich and opulent neighbour."[17]

Nor, yet, was even this all. Most enclosure acts laid it down that the tithe-owner was to bear no share of the costs of enclosure; and this indulgence was sometimes extended to the lord of the manor as well.[18] Moreover, in Wigston Magna, the act stated that the lands awarded to the Duke of St. Albans and the vicar were "to be mounded and fenced round by ditches and quickset hedges guarded or fenced with good posts and double rails"; whilst the Duke's lands, in addition, were to be divided internally into fields with hedges and fences of the same high quality; and all this to be done at the expence of the proprietors of the village.[19]

---

12 E. J. Evans. The Contentious Tithe. Pp. 97-8 and 101-2.
13 Ibid. Pp. 98-102.
14 W. G. Hoskins. The Midland Peasant. Ch. 9.
15 E. J. Evans. The Contentious Tithe. P. 98.
16 J. L. and B. Hammond. The Village Labourer. P. 77.
17 G. E. Mingay. Arthur Young and his Times. P. 117.
18 E. J. Evans. The Contentious Tithe. P. 101.
19 W. G. Hoskins. The Midland Peasant. P. 251.

It is abundantly clear, then, that the amount of generosity shown to the tithe-owner, and in some places the lord of the manor also, was a critical factor in determining the future prospects and well-being of the agricultural community. Or lack of them.

If tithes and manorial rights were grossly overvalued by the enclosure commissioners, rights of commonage were routinely undervalued; as even Arthur Young, the arch advocate of enclosures, commented in 1800.

"In the minute I took of these and many other enclosures many instances will be seen in which the small value of common rights is noted from the low rent paid for them; this....is (not) even an argument proving the position for which it is brought, as letting to the inhabitants of other parishes is precluded, and when the home poor are unable to get the stock the price at which a right lets can be no criterion of its value."[20]

In other words, the supposed rental of a common right, on which compensation was based, was much less than its competitive, economic market value; and whilst enhanced post-enclosure rents were ignored when compensating tithe-owners, we might strongly suspect that they were brought into the calculation of the value of commoners' allotments.

The consequence was as related to Arthur Young by a gentleman of St. Neots, the enclosure of which had taken place sixteen years previously.

"(He) complained as I rode thither with him, that notwithstanding the productiveness of the soil was certainly greater, yet that the poor were ill-treated by having half a rood given them in lieu of a cow-keep."[21]

It took around two or three acres to maintain a cow; half a rood was a garden, and a garden was of little use without a cow to manure it. The valuation that really mattered was that a common-right was sufficient to feed a cow; the supposed compensation was not. Cows were the greatest grievance, but not the only one. Commons provided also for sheep, geese, donkeys and pigs. They were a source of fuel for heating and cooking, in the form of wood, turves, furze etc. Wood could be cut also for building, fencing, and tools. Rights might extend to fishing, hunting wildfowl, or cutting hay. All this was lost and replaced with a garden.[22]

But in general even the garden was only given in cases where a common right existed by virtue of the possession of land in the open field, or ownership of a cottage with rights attached. "In some cases," the General Report on Enclosures of 1808 tells us, "many cows had been kept without a legal right, and nothing given for the practice....In others they kept cows by right of hiring their cottages,....and the land going of course to the proprietor, was added to the farms, and the poor sold their cows; this is a very common case. The causes were in this manner various, but the result the same."[23]

A further burden on the smaller owners was the expence involved in enclosure. The enclosure of Wigston Magna cost the villagers a total of £2817 10s 9d. This included the fees of lawyers employed in getting the act through Parliament; of the enclosure commissioners; of surveying the land and awarding allotments; of fencing round the estates of the vicar and the Duke of St. Albans, and dividing the latter into fields; and various other expences. These costs worked out on average at 23s 4d per acre, but were normally allocated according to an allotment's value rather than its acreage.[24] A typical village farmer might be obliged to find from £25 to £35 within ten days of the award to cover those costs. In the case of failure or inability to pay, the enclosure commissioners had the legal

20 G. E. Mingay. Arthur Young and his Times. P. 137.
21 G. E. Mingay. Arthur Young and his Times. P. 101.
22 K. D. M. Snell. Annals of the Labouring Poor. P. 180.
23 Board of Agriculture. The General Report on Enclosures. 1808. Pp. 12-13.
24 W. G. Hoskins. The Midland Peasant. Pp. 259-260.

power to distrain on the offender's goods, or else to appropriate his rents or profits until the required sum had been recovered.[25]

But the outlay did not stop there. Each individual farmer was obliged to fence his new holding, as well around the perimeter, as internally, dividing the farm into fields, and this had to be done in a fairly short space of time. Fencing was an expensive operation. At an enclosure in Lincolnshire, studied in detail, a small farmer who contributed £4 18s 2d to the expences of enclosure, faced a bill of £10 8s 0d for fencing. And roughly such a proportion probably held good also in Wigston Magna.[26]

This was the enforced price to the village community of something which most of them did not want; the price, in fact, of their degradation and impoverishment.

Of course, in many cases, it was both overwhelming and crippling. Even where reductions in acreage had not diminished holdings to below the level of viability, inability to meet the expence would often enforce the sale of the farm. The gentleman of St. Neots, who had complained to Arthur Young about a mere half rood being given in lieu of a common-right, noted the consequence.

"The enclosure of which land costing more than they could afford, they sold the lots at £5, the money was drunk out at the alehouse, and the men, spoiled by the habit, come with their families to the parish."[27]

Mr. Forster was an enclosure commissioner interviewed by Arthur Young at Norwich. Rather surprisingly for a commissioner, he commented;-

"Numbers in the practice of feeding commons cannot prove their right and many, indeed most who have allotments, have not more than one acre, which being insufficient for the man's cow, both cow and land are usually sold to the opulent farmers; that the right sold before the enclosure would produce much less than the allotment after it, but the money is dissipated, doing them no good when they cannot vest it in stock."[28]

Mr. Ewen was a colleague of Mr. Forster's. He "observes that in most of the enclosures he has known the poor man's allotment and cow are sold five times in six before the award is signed."

If the common right was worth in money terms less than the allotment, and yet was nevertheless generally sold before the award and not after, we are surely entitled to suspect some form of pressure or trickery.

In Wigston Magna, the after-effects of the cataclysm were slow to show themselves. It is not until the 1790s that significant changes become visible. A drop in the number of owner-occupiers tells us that some of the smaller farmers had been forced to give up their occupation, and were either letting their fields out to richer men, or had sold up. By the 1830s, and not until then, the traditional community had been all but swept away; with just a few of the familiar names still to be found among the ranks of the smaller farmers; while most had been reduced to just a cottage, or else had been ruined completely. The reason for this delayed extinction was the mortgage. In the face of overwhelming demands for cash, the peasant owner borrowed money on the security of his holding, in order to survive a little longer. This subject of mortgages is glaringly under-researched. Suffice it, for now, to say that the traditional agricultural community of Wigston Magna in Leicestershire was already doomed in 1766; the mortgage delayed its ultimate demise, but made that demise all the more inevitable.[29]

---

25 Ibid. P. 251.
26 Ibid. P. 260 n.
27 G. E. Mingay. Arthur Young and his Times. P. 101.
28 Ibid. P. 137.
29 W. G. Hoskins. The Midland Peasant. Pp. 264-5.

So what sort of physical and social environment was presented by the newly-enclosed village? The concentration of landownership into ever fewer hands, which had already been going on for many years, was reflected in the enclosure award. Eight proprietors were awarded fully one half of the parish, whilst the remaining ninety had to manage with the rest. The trend was accentuated as more and more small owners disappear from view.[30]

The practice of continually enlarging and engrossing farms caused much comment. Here is Rev. David Davies, writing in1794, about his own parish of Barkham in Berkshire.

"The landowner, to render his income adequate to the increased expence of living, unites several small farms into one, raises the rent to the utmost, and avoids the expence of repairs. The rich farmer also engrosses as many farms as he is able to stock; lives in more credit and comfort than he could otherwise do; and out of the profits of several farms, makes an ample provision for one family."[31]

These opulent farmers and landowners were no longer part of peasant society. In Wigston, fully 842 acres now belonged to absentee owners. Although six of the biggest fifteen awards went to traditional village families, these were now wealthy men who had made good, and bore, perhaps, little resemblance to the members of the agricultural community that their ancestors had been. Many of the other awards went to wealthy traders and outsiders.[32] A substantial farmer in the traditional village would have considered himself as of the same class as the labourer with, perhaps, a cottage, an acre and a common right; a more elevated member, it is true; a village elder, perhaps.

"View the farmer before the land was inclosed; and you will find him entertaining his friends with a part of a hog of his own feeding, and a draught of the ale brewed from his own malt presented in a brown jug, or a glass, if it would bear it, which was the utmost of his extravagance; in those happy days you might view the farmer in a coat of the growth of his flock, and spun by his industrious wife and daughters, and his stockings produced from the same quarter of his industry, and his wife and daughters clad from their own hands of industry, and the growth of their own flock their best attire."[33]

But these new rich farmers were of an entirely different hue, and would have considered themselves as different from, and inherently superior to, the mass of the villagers. Here is Country Farmer again.

"On the other hand, the farmers are reduced to one-fourth of their number, and they very opulent, generally having enough to support themselves and families without any kind of business; but to raise fortunes for their families, take one of those large inclosed farms at more than double the rent it used to go at….they….support that luxury which the present age has fallen into, and to which they are no small contributors, as they think themselves upon a footing with the 'squire, and actually have as much formality in receiving and returning visits. Their entertainments are as expensive as they are elegant; for it is no uncommon thing for one of these new-created farmers to spend ten or twelve pounds at one entertainment; and to wash down delicate food, must have the most expensive wines, and those the best of their kind; and to set off the entertainment in the greatest splendour, an elegant side-board of plate is provided of the newest fashion. As to dress no one that is not personally acquainted with the opulent farmer's daughter can distinguish her from the daughter of a Duke by her dress, both wishing to imitate something, but they know not what."[34]

---

30 Ibid. P. 252.
31 Rev. David Davies. The Case of the Labourers in Husbandry. 1794. P. 55.
32 W. G. Hoskins. The Midland Peasant. P. 255.
33 Cursory Remarks on Inclosures by a Country Farmer. 1786. Pp. 21-2.
34 Ibid. Pp. 20-21.

Village society, it might be said, had become polarised; or, more accurately, a higher social echelon had been superimposed upon it, partly from within the village, mainly from without. And the agricultural community had to make way for it. And the most glaring and fundamental manifestation of that making way was that the typical villager became landless; disconnected from the countryside which was his life, his environment and his subsistence.

Nathaniel Kent, writing in 1775, becomes heated upon the subject. "Upon an estate of one thousand pounds a year," he opines, there should be around sixteen farms of mixed sizes. "But instead of this, the generality of large estates do not support a third part of these families….a great many families, which would get a decent livelihood upon the farms of 30l. 40l. and 50l. a year, come to the parish….when they are deprived of this method of supporting themselves….Through the destruction of small farms we see a vast number of families reduced to poverty and misery."[35] Even where small farms did survive, their rental value, through their scarcity and the fierce competition for them, was raised to such a pitch that no small farmer could make a living –"industry itself cannot get a livelihood upon them".[36]

Even the gardens and plots of land pertaining to the cottages were disappearing, as Rev. David Davies tells us.

"But few cottages, comparatively, have now any land about them. Formerly many of the lower sort of people occupied tenements of their own, with parcels of land about them, or they rented such of others. On these they raised for themselves a considerable part of their subsistence, without being obliged, as now, to buy all they want at shops. And this kept numbers from coming to the parish…. These small parcels of ground have been swallowed up in the contiguous farms and inclosures".

Many villagers, when they lost their land, lost their homes also.

"The cottages themselves have been pulled down; the families which used to occupy them are crowded together in decayed farmhouses, with hardly ground enough about them for a cabbage garden….This destruction has been greatly promoted by the system of engrossing farms. For the engrossing farmer, occupying sometimes six farms, converts all the farm-houses, except that in which his own family resides, into dwellings for the poor."[37]

He takes most of the garden for his own use, and divides whatever remains.

The whole process is more fully described by the Earl of Winchilsea, in his letter to Sir John Sinclair, written in 1796. He ascribes the cause to "the dislike farmers have to seeing the labourers rent any land….they rather wish to have the labourers more dependent upon them, for which reasons they are always desirous of hiring the house and land occupied by a labourer, under pretence, that by that means the landlord will be secure of his rent, and that they will keep the house in repair….It is in this manner that the labourers have been dispossessed of their cow-pastures in various parts of the midland counties. The moment the farmer obtains his wish, he takes every particle of land to himself, and relets the house to the labourer, who by this means is rendered miserable, the poor rates increased, the value of the estate to the landlord diminished, and the house suffered to go to decay…."[38]

Overwhelmingly, the most frequently heard complaint arising from this new condition of village landlessness, was the inability of the labouring families to keep cows. Thus the Earl of Winchilsea;-

"Whoever travels through the midland counties, and will take the trouble of enquiring, will generally receive the answer, that formerly there were a great many cottagers who kept cows, but that the land is now thrown to the farmers; and if he enquires still further, he will find that in those parishes the poor's rates have increased in an amazing degree…."

---

35   Nathaniel Kent. Hints to Gentlemen of Landed Property. Pp. 217 and 192.
36   Ibid. P. 219.
37   Rev. David Davies. The Case of the Labourers in Husbandry. Pp. 55-56 and 35.
38   Communications to the Board of Agriculture. Vol. IV. P. 358.

The massive scale of this devastation, or debovinisation, is summed up by Kent.

"Since little farms have been swallowed up in greater, there are thousands of parishes which do not support so many cows as they did by fifty or sixty in a parish...."[39]

Such complaints abound in the General Report on Enclosures of 1808, a document whose tone in general is highly favourable to the enclosure movement. We hear them again and again, about loss of livestock in general, but of cows in particular. From Lanchester, county Durham, for example, it was reported that many cottagers had been "deprived of the convenience of keeping a cow without any recompense in any other respect"; from Donnington in Lincolnshire, that 140 cows belonging to the villagers had been lost.

The disappearance of the house-cow from the villages led directly to a decline in the nutritional status of the cottagers, and more particularly of their children. This was true not only of the cow-keepers themselves, but also of their neighbours, to whom they were accustomed to sell their surplus produce. Large farmers, if they produced milk at all, were normally unwilling to go to the trouble of retailing their produce in small quantities. Consequently, from Souldrop in Bedfordshire, we hear "the condition of the labouring poor much worse now than before the enclosure, owing to the impossibility of procuring any milk for their young families". At Tingewick, in Buckinghamshire, milk could be bought before the enclosure at 1d per quart, but since could not be bought at any price.[40]

In some places, the loss of the villagers' cows seems to have been closely associated with the loss, also, of their homes. From Kirkburn, in Yorkshire, comes this.

"The labourer who previous to the enclosure had his cow-gate, and from thence derived considerable nourishment to his small family, was deprived of this and by his inability to enclose, therefore was under the necessity of selling his tenement to his richer neighbour, and deprived his family of a comfortable refuge."

The desperate and depressing plight into which many thousands of cottagers' families up and down the country were now being abruptly plunged was well summarised by the poor of Alconbury, in Huntingdonshire, in 1791, at a meeting with Arthur Young, at the curate's house.

"Their own account to me, at Mr. Nicholson's, was, that several who kept cows before, were, upon the enclosure, forced to part with them, and have kept none since. The cottage allotments going to the landlords, were thrown together, and the inhabitants left without cows or land. Those who had allotments given in lieu of their rights, not being able to enclose them, were forced to sell, and became as the rest in this respect. Before the enclosure, milk could readily be bought; poor people could lay out a halfpenny, or a penny, every day; but nothing of the sort to be got since; some not a halfpenny in a month, and others not in three."

The overwhelming importance of cows to the economy of the agricultural community is something which might not be readily grasped by a modern readership; whose connection with the bovine species is likely, in most cases, to be remote. But if a salaried employee of modern times were to lose half of his livelihood, and perhaps his home as well, and were forced to work all available hours for the other half, he would still not be in danger of starvation; nevertheless, he might begin to appreciate the enormity of the catastrophe.

"And what a produce is that of a cow!", wrote William Cobbett in 1821. "I suppose only an average of five quarts of milk a day. If made into butter, it will be equal every week to two days of the man's wages; besides the value of the skim milk, and that can hardly be of less value than another day's wages. What a thing, then, is this cow, if she earn half as much as the man! I am greatly under-rating

---

39   Nathaniel Kent. Hints to Gentlemen of Landed Property, P. 226.
40   Board of Agriculture. General Report on Enclosures. Appendix IV.

her produce."[41] Cobbett forgot to mention the annual calf, and the seemingly never-ending supply of manure for the garden.

Small farming families who managed to retain some degree of connection with the land fared much better, and remained in a much more comfortable condition, than the majority of the poor. Arthur Young noted, in various parts of the country, a number of areas where families had built cottages for themselves on commons. He found a hundred such cottages at Chatteris in Cambridgeshire; and thirty such families settled on forty acres with their livestock, at Blofield in Norfolk. The cottagers at Weston Colville, in Cambridgeshire, had plots of land, from large gardens to areas of two or three acres. They had cows and grew corn. Similarly, at Aldershot, they kept cows and pigs. The usual consequence of this was that such families had removed themselves from dependence on parish relief, or virtually so. Young comments;-

"Nothing can be clearer than the vast importance which all these poor people, scattered as they are through many counties, and affected by circumstances so extremely various, attach to the object of possessing land, though no more than to set a cottage upon....

"But the effect which is here proved to attend the possession of a cow, is very extraordinary; they all agree uniformly on this point, and assert that they would rather have a cow than any parish relief here noted, valuing it even so highly as 5s or 6s per week...."[42]

A few enlightened landlords regularised and institutionalised this system, by renting, directly to the labourers, cottages with enough land about them to maintain livestock. Foremost among them was the Earl of Winchilsea, on his estates in Rutland. In 1796, the good earl wrote to the president of the Board of Agriculture on the benefits of this system.

"By means of these advantages, the labourers and their families live better, and are consequently more fit to endure labour; and it makes them more contented, and gives them a sort of independence, which makes them set a higher value on their character....When a labourer has obtained a cow, and land sufficient to maintain her, the first thing he has thought of has been how he could save money enough to buy another....There are from 70 to 80 labourers upon my estate in Rutland, who keep from 1 to 4 cows each...."[43]

None of these cottagers ever required parish relief; and in some cases even, when a labourer died, his son could afford to maintain the widow.

The earl's neighbour, Mr. Barker of Lyndon, wrote that in his parish most of the poor kept cows, to such great advantage "that we can hardly say there are any industrious persons who are really poor, as they are in some places where they have not that advantage".[44]

Where it was not practical for the labourers to keep cows, they would reap much benefit from cottage gardens, provided they were large enough. "There should be as much as will produce all the garden-stuff the family consumes, and enough for a pig, with the addition of a little meal....I have had experience in several places, particularly in two parishes near Newport Pagnell, Bucks, where there never had been any gardens annexed to the labourers' houses, and where, upon being allotted to them, they all, without a single exception, cultivated their gardens extremely well, and profess receiving the greatest benefit from them".[45]

A few landlords followed the earl's example, like Lords Carrington and Scarborough; for some reason nearly all in Rutland and Lincolnshire. In this district, according to the General Report on

41   William Cobbett. Cottage Economy. P. 95.
42   G. E. Mingay. Arthur Young and his Times. Pp. 127 and 132.
43   Communications to the Board of Agriculture. 1796. P. 1.
44   Ibid. P. 3.
45   Ibid. P. 7.

Enclosures of 1808, there were 48 parishes, where 753 cottagers kept between them 1195 cows. "Not one of them receives anything from the parish! Nor did, even in the late scarcities."[46]

"The effect of the poor possessing property in cattle, and occupying land to feed them, has been so powerful a spur to industry and sobriety as to have taken them entirely from the parish; insomuch that wherever the plan has been carried into execution, the poor-rates are as low as they can be, and exist chiefly for objects with which the poor have little concern."[47]

In times of scarcity and high prices, when poor-rates in most places rocketed, "the poor thus favoured" received "no more from the parish than in common times, that is to say, nothing!"

To emphasise the point, a case is noted from Mayfield in Sussex, where a family receiving poor relief even in times of plenty, "ceased to be chargeable in scarcity, from a cow being given by the parish".[48]

In a sense, however, none of this was of great importance. The allotment system flourished only on a few estates and in a few areas. Most landowners, farmers, and writers on the subject, were opposed to it. In spite of continued agitation in its favour over a period of many years, in the whole of Nottinghamshire, in 1888, it was said that the number of labourers who possessed grazing for a cow, was twenty-eight.[49] "To acquire land to build a cottage on," ruefully reflected Arthur Young in 1801, "is a hopeless aim in 99 parishes out of 100." The historical significance of the system lies not in its widespread adoption, but in what it teaches us about the great improvement in living standards which the possession of land and cows brought to labouring families. But, after all, it merely brought them part way back to where they were before the agricultural changes of the seventeenth and eighteenth centuries. The lessons of history were already available to Arthur Young, had they but accorded with the point of view which he was wishing to propagate.

The greater historical significance lies in the corollary; when labouring families were deprived of their land and cows, the result was either out-migration, employment in some branch of trade or industry, or dependence upon labouring by the day, at the behest of some rich farmer, with its almost inevitable consequence of destitution and dependent poverty.

Out-migration, as we have seen, was a major feature of enclosures earlier in the eighteenth century and before; indeed, some later sources still speak of migration to industrial towns, such as the Board of Agriculture's reviewer of Warwickshire, or the petitioners of Raunds. But the parishes which were enclosed later, and by act of Parliament, tended to be those with a large number of owners, where it was more difficult for a few major proprietors to drive out the population. In earlier days, peasant farmers could afford to help their children migrate, by paying the premium for apprenticeships, or by setting them up in a trade. Those days were gone.[50] Besides, the industrial towns were becoming crammed with labour. Conditions were worsening, and the laws of settlement were being enforced more rigorously. From around 1750, therefore, the population displaced by agricultural change tended to stay put. In Wigston Magna, an industrial village, the framework-knitting soaked up much of this displaced labour, and the same was true of much of Leicestershire and the surrounding counties. In the more southerly counties of the Midlands, there was virtually no industry. Here the displaced population had little choice but to remain in the villages, and become part of a continuing nightmare of surplus labour, unemployment, partial employment, and pauperisation.[51]

---

46 Board of Agriculture. General Report on Enclosures. P. 164.
47 Ibid. P. 15.
48 Ibid. P. 165.
49 J. D. Chambers. Nottinghamshire in the Eighteenth Century. P. 185.
50 R. C. Allen. Enclosure and the Yeoman. P. 243.
51 Ibid. P. 237.

The agricultural community, being now, as David Davies put it, "reduced to mere hirelings", was, of a sudden, plunged into a money-based economy, instead of the commodity-based one that they had been used to, and had thrived in.[52] Here is George Sturt, on the "radical alteration of the domestic economy of the cottagers" of his valley, which resulted from their being shut out of their common, albeit at a much later date.

"By the peasant system….people derived the necessaries of life from the materials and soil of their own countryside. Now, so long as they had the common, the inhabitants of the valley were in a large degree able to conform to this system, the common being, as it were, a supplement to the cottage gardens, and furnishing means of extending the scope of the little home industries….

"When the enclosure began to be a fact, when the cottager was left with nothing to depend upon save his garden alone, as a peasant he was a broken man – a peasant shut out from his countryside and cut off from his resources. True, he might still grow vegetables, and keep a pig or two; but there was little else that he could do in the old way. It was out of the question to obtain most of his supplies by his own handiwork; they had to be procured, ready-made, from some other source. That source, I need hardly say, was a shop.

"Under the old regime, although probably a small regular expenditure of money had been usual, yet in the main the peasant's expenditure was not regular, but intermittent. Getting so much food and firing by his own labour, he might go for weeks without needing more than a few shillings to make up occasional deficiencies. His purse was subject to no such constant drain as that for which the modern labourer has to provide. In short, the regular expences were small, the occasional ones not crushing. But today, when the people can no longer produce for themselves, the proportion has changed. It has swung round so completely that nearly all the expences have become regular, while those of the other sort have well-nigh disappeared. Every week money has to be found.

"So the once self-supporting cottager turned into a spender of money….; and of course, needing to spend money, he needed first to get it.

"To a greater or lesser extent, most of them were already wage-earners, though not regularly. If a few had been wont to furnish themselves with money in true peasant fashion – that is to say, by selling their goods, their butter, or milk, or pig-meat, instead of their labour – still the majority had wanted for their own use whatever they could produce in this way, and had been obliged to sell their labour itself, when they required money. Wage-earning, therefore, was no new thing in the village, only the need to earn became more insistent, when so many more things than before had to be bought with the wages….Every hour's work acquired a market value. The sense of taking part in time-honoured duties of the countryside disappeared before the idea – so very important now – of getting shillings with which to go to a shop….

"Unemployment, hitherto not much more than a regrettable inconvenience, became a calamity."[53]

But just at that same time, the pattern of employment in the newly-enclosed village had radically altered. Wigston Magna was typical of open-field villages enclosed before the 1790s, in that a large proportion of the arable land was converted to pasture. Very soon after enclosure the larger farmers of Wigston began to call themselves graziers; and by the time of the agricultural survey of 1801, seven of the parishes surrounding Wigston were described as being overwhelmingly under grass. By 1832, two-thirds of the parish of Wigston were said to be pasture; 1400 acres of tillage had been converted to grassland since enclosure. Pasture land gives rise to much less employment than arable, and in

52   Rev. David Davies. The Case of the Labourers in Husbandry. P. 56.
53   George Sturt. Pseud. Bourne. Change in the Village. Pp. 87-90.

1832 it appears that only forty labourers could work the land of the entire parish, between a quarter and a third of what had been necessary before the enclosure.[54]

The whole system of the large farm and the new agriculture was inimical to employment. The economies of scale, which made the large farm viable, centred predominantly around labour.[55] If the new farmer was an owner-occupier, he came loaded with the costs of enclosure, which impaired his ability to pay wages. If not, he was likely to be a tenant-at-will, reluctant to lay out money on the labour necessary for improving his farm; he was burdened with a high rent, which his tenancy allowed to be increased almost at will, and which in most cases could not be recovered out of greater production.[56] The necessary cost-saving could be effected by keeping wages down as far as possible; or by laying off workers when not needed, and allowing them to be maintained at parish expence. Labour costs could be reduced by employing specialists such as shepherds or hedgers, instead of the multi-skilled labourer of the traditional village; and gangs from outside the village for operations such as carting hay or corn.[57]

The scale of the catastrophe is demonstrated by R. C. Allen, who estimates that between 1676 and 1831, in the south Midlands, over 17,800 farm jobs were lost, whilst the aspiring agricultural workforce increased by over 32,000.[58]

The traditional small village farm was worked by the whole family, with perhaps a live-in servant or two, who counted as family. The new large farm employed only men, and those mainly day-labourers. Whilst employment opportunities for men diminished by twenty-four per cent, those for women declined by twenty-nine per cent, and for children by thirty-six per cent.[59]

The loss of the earnings of the women was a catastrophic blow to the well-being of labouring families. Up until the middle of the eighteenth century, women were extensively involved in the operations of the farm.[60] Almost half were employed full-time, and many more took part in seasonal tasks such as haymaking and harvest; as well as looking after the livestock on the family smallholding.[61] Spinning was a widespread cottage industry in which both women and children could contribute to the family income. David Davies presents the account of a family in which the mother and her daughters work at spinning at home, and thereby provide a decent standard of life for the family, as well as a small cash surplus. Without the spinning the family budget would have been in deficit each year, to the tune of between three and five pounds.[62]

From around 1760, the opportunities for women to earn gradually disappeared. The land and the cows were lost. Their labour was not required on the large farms of the new agriculture, except perhaps at peak times. And domestic industry became less widespread. In particular, the demand for spinning dried up abruptly with the coming of the factory system. Thus, real wage rates, not just for spinning, but for lace-knitting, straw-plaiting, and all types of female employment experienced a drastic, long-term decline.[63]

---

54 W. G. Hoskins. The Midland Peasant. Pp. 261-3.
55 R. C. Allen. Enclosure and the Yeoman. P. 214.
56 K. D. M. Snell. Annals of the Labouring Poor. Pp. 186-92.
57 R. C. Allen. Enclosure and the Yeoman. Pp. 218-220.
58 R. C. Allen. Enclosure and the Yeoman. P. 250.
59 Ibid. P. 235.
60 K. D. M. Snell. Annals of the Labouring Poor. P. 52.
61 R. C. Allen. Enclosure and the Yeoman. P. 251.
62 Rev. David Davies. The Case of the Labourers in Husbandry. P. 86.
63 R. C. Allen. Enclosure and the Yeoman. Pp. 252 and 255. K. D. M. Snell. Annals of the Labouring Poor. P. 57.

David Davies places a heavy emphasis on this important subject, the provision of steady employment for women and girls being, for him, one of the most pressing of necessities.

"At present, the earnings of the wives and children of day-labourers are, in general, very small. Except at hay-making and harvest, their earnings are insignificant. The greater part of their time is unprofitably spent....so that almost the whole burden of providing for their families rests upon the man."[64]

A letter in the Reports of the Society for Bettering the Condition of the Poor notes the problem of women, "a burthen upon the father of the family, and in many cases upon the parish. The wife is no longer able to contribute her share towards the weekly expences. In a kind of despondency she sits down, unable to contribute anything towards the general fund of the family, and conscious of rendering no other service to her husband except that of the mere care of his family."[65]

The large farms of the new agriculture also economised on farm servants, living in the farmhouse. In the traditional village of common land, open fields and farms of mixed sizes, farm service was the first rung on the social ladder of the village. Service gave young people the opportunity to save their wages for a few years, and these savings formed the basis of their independence in later years; when many servants would become small farmers themselves, or cottagers, or commoners. But farm service, it has been said, was "an alien element in the economy of the large farm".[66] Although large farms employed much less labour per acre, as individual units they may have employed more in total, and there were limits to how many could be accommodated in the farmhouse; even had they been welcome. The new breed of opulent farmer, with his lavish entertainments, his fine wines and his splendid sideboard of plate, no longer wished to live with those who ploughed the fields or milked the cows. Still less did his daughter, in her finery indistinguishable from the daughter of a duke. Besides, the whole system was becoming expensive, as food prices rose consistently during the second half of the eighteenth century. Farm service was characteristic of a society where labour was in short supply. It bound the servant to work for the farmer all year, in return for guaranteed wages and maintenance. Enclosing and engrossing created a labour surplus, and a subsistence crisis which forced young people into dependent day-labour. When the labourers were not needed, they could be laid off and consigned to the mercies of the parish overseer, rather than maintained in idleness at the farmer's expence.

In consequence, the practice of hiring live-in servants began to disappear from the 1780s, to a position of near extinction in the nineteenth century, especially in those areas of the country, like the south and the east, where the culture of the large farm prevailed the most.[67]

In the absence of opportunities to become servants, the young men of the village had little choice but to become day-labourers, with all the insecurities which that involved. Wage-earning could be suspended because of bad weather, sickness or injury, slack seasons, or the whim or necessitousness of the employer. Under-employment was chronic in many areas. The man might begin married life, earlier than under the old system, without any savings under his belt, and consequently very susceptible to pauperisation.

For women, the results were worse still. With diminishing employment both in agriculture and in cottage industry, the decline of farm service presented them with a serious problem of subsistence. Marriage often became the only option, as a matter of survival, and was entered into increasingly urgently as the changes in agriculture progressed. The female age at marriage dropped considerably;

---

64 Rev. David Davies. The Case of the Labourers in Husbandry. Pp. 83 and 56.
65 K. D. M. Snell. Annals of the Labouring Poor. P. 57.
66 A. Kussmaul. Servants in Husbandry in Early Modern England. P. 121.
67 Ibid. Ch. 7.

pregnancy before marriage became common, as young women, perhaps, attempted to catch themselves a husband; and illegitimacy rates rose; in part as some of these attempts went awry.[68]

Arthur Young tells us that "young men and women in the country fix their eye on London as the last stage of their hope….The number of young women that fly there is incredible." In London, it might be possible to find work in domestic service, but there were normally thousands of aspiring servants out of employ; and prostitution was the last resort. It was rapidly on the increase. In mid-century, it was estimated that 3,000 prostitutes were working the streets of London. Magistrate Sir John Fielding commented;-

"As beauty is not the particular lot of the rich more often than the poor, many of the girls have great advantages of person; and whoever will look amongst them will frequently see the sweetest features disguised by filth and dirt.

"These are the girls that the bawds clean and clothe for their wicked purposes. And this is done to such a degree that on a search night when the constables have taken up near forty prostitutes, it has appeared on their examination that the major part of them have been of this kind, under the age of eighteen, many not more than twelve, and those, though so young, half eat up with the foul distemper."

Most were dead by the age of twenty-four.[69]

Complaints about the lack of employment in the enclosed villages find their way into the General Report on Enclosures of 1808. From Waddesdon, in Buckinghamshire, we hear that "poverty has been very sensibly increased; the husbandmen come to the parish, for want of employment; the land laid to grass." From Bradwell, in the same county, was reported, "fewer hands employed; rates increased"; and from Castlethorp, "less work for the people".[70] In general, however, the foremost cause of pauperisation was not seen as the lack of employment. Wage-earning in the traditional village had never been more than partial, and only the most visionary of propagandists viewed day-labour as an honest, respectable and secure way of gaining a livelihood. It was the loss of the villagers' lands, and the loss of their cows, which is seen as leading directly to pauperisation; the insecurity of day-labour being such as to make dependent poverty an unavoidable consequence. From Ackworth, in Yorkshire;-

"The parish belonged to near 100 owners, nearly the whole of whom have *come to the parish* since the enclosure, or changed the quantity of their lands."

And from Letcomb, in Berkshire;-

"The poor seem the greatest sufferers; they can no longer keep a cow, which before many of them did, and they are now therefore maintained by the parish."[71]

This point, made forcibly here by Rev. David Davies, about his parish of Barkham in Berkshire, could be illustrated time and time again from contemporary sources.

"The depriving the peasantry of all landed property has beggared multitudes….Thousands of families, which formerly gained an independent livelihood on those separate farms, have been gradually reduced to the class of day-labourers. But day-labourers are sometimes in want of work, and are sometimes unable to work; and in either case their sole resort is the parish. It is a fact, that thousands of parishes have not now half the number of farmers which they had formerly. And in proportion as the number of farmers has decreased, the number of poor families has increased.

---

68   K. D. M. Snell. Annals of the Labouring Poor. P.53.

69   John H. Hutchins. Jonas Hanway. P. 120

70   Board of Agriculture. General Report on Enclosures. 1808. Appendix IV.

71   Ibid.

"Thus an amazing number of people have been reduced from a comfortable state of partial independence to the precarious condition of hirelings, who, when out of work, must immediately come to their parish".[72]

The consequence was seen in the rapid increase of the rates collected for the poor throughout the country; and in the acceleration of that increase. In Wigston Magna, the amount collected during the early 1750s was below £100; by 1776 it had risen to £377; by 1783-5, to £433; and in 1802, it was £1776.[73] At Kibworth Beauchamp, also in Leicestershire, F. M. Eden found the rates "to have been not one third of their present figure before the enclosures, and the people attribute the rise to the enclosures, for they say before the fields were enclosed they were solely applied to the production of corn; that the poor had plenty of employment in weeding, reaping, threshing etc. and would also collect a great deal of corn by gleaning, but that the fields being now in pasturage, the farmers have little occasion for labourers, and the poor being thereby thrown out of employment must of course be supported by the parish."[74]

The correlation between enclosure and rising poor expenditure is brought sharply into focus at East Socon in Bedfordshire. The enclosure award there was made in 1800, when there was said to be an "enormous increase" of families on poor relief. Between 1706 and 1785, expenditure was rarely over £400. Between 1785 and 1795, it averaged £800; and from 1800 to 1819, £1835.[75] Arthur Young mentions a number of parishes where rate assessments had shot up after enclosure; at Lidlington, the assessment rose from 1s in the pound rental value to 4s 6d; at Abington, where rates had not been necessary, an assessment of 2s 6d was imposed; and at March, where it was misleadingly claimed that enclosure had greatly benefited the poor, the assessment doubled. Young points out that where rates in enclosed parishes rose to the same extent as in unenclosed, that represented a much greater sum collected; as the assessment was made per pound rental value, and in enclosed parishes rents had more than doubled. What he omitted to mention, was that even in many unenclosed parishes, the rise was caused, at least in part, by the enclosure of surrounding villages, and the resulting influx of the dispossessed.[76]

Pauperisation, then, was very often the consequence of enclosure for the bulk of the traditional rural society; and enrichment for the upper strata of the new village. This growing dichotomy is well portrayed by Rev. David Davies.

"For since the destruction of small farms, and of cottages having land about them, has so greatly contributed to bring the lower peasantry into the starving condition in which we now see them....This practice has been reducing the generality of small farmers into day-labourers, and the great body of day-labourers into beggars, and has been multiplying and impoverishing even beggars themselves.... it has perhaps elevated the body of farmers above their proper level, enabling many of them not only to tyrannise over their inferiors, but even to vie with their landlords in dissipation and expence."[77]

The new farmer, of large acreages, in the village of the new agriculture, had, perhaps, a heavy burden of enclosure and fencing costs to bear; or else a vastly increased rent to pay. He had a social position to support; a luxurious lifestyle; and possibly demanding and materialistic womenfolk. The

72 Rev. David Davies. The Case of the Labourers in Husbandry. Pp. 55-56.
73 W. G. Hoskins. The Midland Peasant. P. 269.
74 F. M .Eden. The State of the Poor. P. 269.
75 K. D. M. Snell. Annals of the Labouring Poor. P. 206.
76 G. E. Mingay. Arthur Young and his Times. P. 138.
77 Rev. David Davies. The Case of the Labourers in Husbandry. P. 103

much-vaunted increase of produce which was supposed to result from the new methods proved, in most cases, illusory. So many farmers now saw a firm hold over labour as the key to maintaining their position. The clowns should be kept landless, dependent, in surplus, and poor, so as to make them industrious. A pamphlet written by a practical farmer, and published in 1785, complained on this head.

"I know many farmers who….will not employ any cottager who is possessed of any kind of beast, although he may have a just right and conveniency to keep them….(They forbid) cottagers to keep any living creature besides themselves and children, under the pretence, that if they keep any beasts or poultry, they will steal from the farmer's barn for their support; they also say, keep the cottagers poor and you will keep them industrious, etc. – but the real fact, I believe, is that the farmers may have the whole right of common to themselves." The "flinty-hearted farmer" had arrived in the village. Hannah More and her sisters came across many of them in the course of their good works in Somerset. Their writings abound with references to "these rich savages", who "oppress and trample on" their employees and their families. At Cheddar, they found "a dozen wealthy farmers, hard, brutal and ignorant". Hannah More wrote in 1789 of the chief despot of the village, "who is very rich and very brutal". He was even an outsider to the villagers; "I ventured to the den of this monster, in a country as savage as himself, near Bridgewater". His brother was described as "profligate, abusive, depraved, this proud man, this haughty sinner, this gentleman of Cheddar". At Congresbury, wrote Martha More, "we found the poor divided into two classes – the very poor, and what is called gentleman farmers, wealthy, unfeeling and hard". At Nailsea, the farmers were "savages, or heads as they call themselves".[78]

Agricultural change and polarisation brought about social estrangement and class conflict. It appears that there is little evidence of this bitterness of feeling before about 1780, but examples abound subsequently. The following letter demonstrates not only the resentment of the villagers, boiling over into violence; but also the farmers' determination at all costs to prevent the poor from keeping any livestock of their own. It was written in 1816, by the men of Ashill, whose parish had been enclosed in 1786.

"This is to inform you that you have by this time brought us under the heaviest yoke we ever knowed; it is too hard for us to bear….You do as you like, you rob the poor of their common right, plough the grass up that God sent to grow, that a poor man may feed a cow, Pig Horse nor Ass; lay muck and stones on the road to prevent the grass growing….There is 5 or 6 of you have gotten all the whole of the land in this parish in your own hands and you would wish to be rich and starve all the other part of the poor of the parish….Gentlemen, these few lines are to inform you that God Almighty have brought our blood to a proper circulation, that we have been in a very bad state a long time, and now without an alteration of the aforesaid, we meant to circulate your blood with the leave of God…. There was 2 cows and an ass feeding on the road last Saturday, and there was 2 farmers went to the keepers and said they would pound them if they did not drive them away, and one of them….went home, got a plough and horses, and ploughed up the grass on the road….So we shall drive the whole before us….and set fire to all the houses and stacks as we go along; we shall begin in the Night…. we wish to prepare yourselves for action….you have had a good long time….No; we will fight for it and if you win the day so be it"[79]

Note the resignation in that "so be it"; the desperation; the turn of phrase of men who have nothing left to lose.

78   William Roberts. Memoirs of the Life and Correspondence of Hannah More. Vol. II. P.207. Martha More. Mendip Annals. Pp. 49, 78, 34, and73.
79   K. D. M. Snell. Annals of the Labouring Poor. Pp. 68, 102 and 176.

Here is another example of bitterness and ill-feeling; this time a protest at the impending enclosure of a parish.

"Whe right these lines to you who are the Combin'd of the Parish of Cheshunt in the Defence of our Parrish rights which you unlawfully are about to disinherit us of….Resolution is maid by the aforesaid Combin'd that if you intend of inclosing our Communal Commond fields Lammas Meads Marshes etc. Whe resolve before….that bloudy and unlawful act it is finished to have your hearts bloud if you proceede in the aforesaid bloudy act Whe like horse leaches will cry give, give until whe have spilt the bloud of every one that wishes to rob the Inosent unborn. It shall not be in your power to say I am safe from the hands of my Enemy for whe like birds of pray will prively lie in wait to spil the bloud of the aforesaid Charicters whose names and places of abode are as putrefied sores in our Nostrils – Whe declair that thou shall not say I am safe when thou goest to thy bed for beware that thou liftest not thine eyes up in the moist mist of flames."[80]

Being a day-labourer was not vastly different from being a slave, and in some material aspects it was worse. The village community was not just degraded by agricultural change; it was divided, its spirit destroyed by the necessity of a larger number of labourers competing for inadequate employment. As George Sturt observed of the people of his valley in Surrey.

"Competition amongst the labourers seeking to be employed has become the accepted condition of getting a living in the village, and it is to a great extent a new condition. Previously there was little room for anything of the kind. The old thrift lent itself to cooperation rather….Both kindliness and economy would counsel the people to be mutually helpful….Those who had donkey-carts would willingly bring home turfs for those who had none, in return for help with their own turf-cutting. The bread-ovens, I know, were at the disposal of others besides the owners. At pig-killing, at thatching, at cleaning out wells….the people would put themselves at one another's service. They still do so in cases where there is no question of earning money for a living….

"But no spirit of cooperation may now prompt one wage-earner to ask, or another to proffer, assistance in working for wages. As well might one shopkeeper propose to wait on another's customers for him….

"In spite of all the latent good-will, therefore, and in spite of the fact that the cottagers are all on the same social level, intimacies do not thrive amongst them. If there was, formerly any parochial sentiment in the village, any sense of community of interest, it has all been broken up by the exigencies of competitive wage-earning, and each family stands by itself, aloof from all the others. The interests clash. Men who might be helpful friends in other circumstances are in the position of rival tradesmen competing for the patronage of customers."[81]

The rural community, to all intents and purposes, was dead. Formerly, its members had been farmers and cottagers; independent or semi-independent; forging their livelihood from the landscape of their village and its environs; multi-skilled craftsmen, able to perform all the necessary tasks. These people had been responsible for their own well-being, taking decisions on a day-to day basis, on which the welfare of their families depended; and having an input into the agricultural system of the whole village, through the manorial court; appointing the village officials, and taking part in communal decision-making.[82] In their work, they had been motivated by working their own land, and looking after their own livestock; and by the advancement within the village system that was possible under the cooperative regime. The inhabitants of the new village were not recognisable as such. The small farmers and multi-skilled craftsmen had been transformed into part-time day-labourers and part-time paupers. As labourers, they were merely ploughmen, who needed a much narrower range of skills than

80 E. P. Thompson. The Making of the English Working Class. P. 240.
81 George Bourne Pseud. Sturt. Change in the Village, Pp. 96-8.
82 R. C. Allen. Enclosure and the Yeoman. Pp. 289-90.

they actually possessed. Specialisation on the large farm had reduced the amount of abilities that were needed, and workers were now only semi-skilled; and viewed by employers and outsiders as entirely unskilled; and paid as such. The opportunities for acquiring rural skills had vanished, as employment for children was now no longer common, and few farmers required live-in servants. Women, too, had become redundant on the farm for most of the year, and were now merely housewives. The communal institutions of the village were swept away at enclosure; and decision-making and mental exertion no longer played any part in the lives of the villagers. They were dependent; at the mercy of forces outside of their control and no longer in charge of their own destiny. The levels of literacy among country people almost certainly declined sharply; as it did in my own family in Sussex, who could sign their names as farmers in the eighteenth century, but could not as paupers in the nineteenth.[83] As a labour force, they had become indifferent and undermotivated; complaints abounded among farmers that the clowns did not get through as much work as formerly. Why should they? Their reasons for doing so had been taken away. And from this miserable situation there was no escape. The system of social mobility of the traditional village, consisting of service, common, and strips in the open fields, existed no longer. So what had happened to the traditional rural society? Impoverishment fails adequately to describe it; degradation alone will not do; downward social mobility does not encompass all that was involved. Perhaps the closest parallel that we can draw is that of one people conquered by another. No actual military campaign had taken place, but, where people dared to protest, they were increasingly confronted by military force, and memory of past retribution, or the threat of future, was, in general, sufficient to counsel submission. So the agricultural communities had been defeated, dispossessed, and virtually enslaved.

"In their intercourse with the outer world", observed George Sturt, "they have become, as it were, degraded, humiliated, and when they go out of the valley, to earn wages, it is to take the position of an inferior and almost servile race....One hears them spoken of as an alien and objectionable race, worth nothing but to be made to work.....Inferiority has come into their lives; it is expected of them to treat almost everybody else as a superior person."[84]

"Nothing can be a surer mark of slavery than to have but two sorts of people, petty princes and starving beggars."[85]

---

83 I am indebted to my aunt, Mrs. Molly Ward, for this information.
84 George Sturt pseud. Bourne. Change in the Village. Pp. 106-11.
85 William Chapple. Risdon's Survey of Devon. 1785. P. 45.

The Price of Vulnerability

These poor people, in assigning the cause of their misery, agreed in ascribing it to the high price of the necessaries of life. "Everything (said they) is so dear that we can hardly live." <u>Rev. David Davies.</u> <u>The Case of the Labourers in Husbandry.</u>

When we were in Wigston Magna, in happier days, we noted how well the village community fared during the rapid price rises of the sixteenth and early seventeenth centuries; or at least all that section of it which had surplus produce to sell. Even the poorer sections of village society, those who had no surplus, were largely insulated from the adverse effects of rising prices, through producing most or all of their own subsistence. From around 1765, prices stated to climb once more. The movement was relentless, and more or less rapid, and lasted into the next century. In striking contrast to the earlier period of rising prices, the eighteenth century depreciation caused massive distress among the labouring classes, and their families, in countryside and town. Clearly, in the meantime, a radical alteration had taken place in the situation of the bulk of the English people. As Richard Price noted in 1792;-

"The price of corn….has for some time been complained of by the poor as oppressively high, though far from being so high as it generally was at the end of the last century….In the year 1697, wheat was at 3ls a quarter, and other grain proportionably dear. But there was no clamour, and the exportation went on….At present….(even) when wheat is below this price….there is an alarm, the poor are starving, and the exportation is prohibited….This is a striking fact which implies that the lower part of the nation are now more distressed than ever."[1]

Price, perhaps, exaggerated slightly; even by the 1690s there must have been many people who were dependent upon purchasing their subsistence. But the general thrust of the point he is making must surely be correct. And why was this so?

"The high price of bread was not, at the time I have mentioned, of essential consequence to the lower people, because they could live more upon other food which was then cheap; and because also being more generally occupiers of land, they were less under a necessity of purchasing bread. Whereas now, being forced by greater difficulties, and the high price of all other food, to live principally or solely on bread, if that is not cheap, they are rendered incapable of maintaining themselves."[2]

Price illustrates for us how he thinks this situation has come about.

"Let a tract of ground be supposed in the hands of a multitude of little proprietors and tenants, who maintain themselves and families by the produce of the ground they occupy, by sheep kept on a common, by poultry, hogs etc.; and who, therefore, have little occasion to purchase any of the means of subsistence. If this land gets into the hands of a few great farmers, the consequence must be that the little farmers will be converted into a body of men who earn their living by working for others, and who will be under a necessity of going to market for all they want….Parishes….will be more loaded, because the number of poor will be greater. And towns and manufactures will increase, because more will be driven to them in quest of places and employments. – This is the way in which

---

1 Richard Price. Observations on Reversionary Payments. 1792. Vol. II. P. 274n. and P. 284-5.
2 Ibid. P. 285.

the engrossing of farms naturally operates; And this is the way in which, for many years, it has been actually operating in this kingdom."[3]

Relentless agricultural change had catapulted a majority of the labouring classes on to a precarious dependence on wage-labour and the market. Retail shops, "which scarce a village, consisting of a dozen houses, is without", were now the primary source of subsistence.[4] And when the market failed to deliver, or failed to deliver at a manageable price, the inevitable consequence was distress and pauperisation.

The debate over the standard of living during the eighteenth century is perhaps one of the most striking examples of modern values and assumptions being inappropriately imposed on to a historical situation. Most, though not all, historians have conducted this debate almost entirely on the basis of real wages; that is, the relative movements of wages and prices, and the changing amounts of produce which those movements enabled the employed labourer to purchase. In doing so, they are subscribing, consciously or unconsciously, to the unsubstantiated Malthusian fiction that every society, ultimately and inevitably, must resolve itself into a class of proprietors and a class of labourers; and dismissing from the equation all those societies, past and present, which do not conform to this assumed pattern. This assumption, in fact, underlies all modern political philosophy, both economically and conceptually, of whatever wing. The existence of a proletariat is as essential to capitalist elites as it is to socialist ones; and though governments through the years have paid lip-service to the importance of the private enterprise of individuals and small businesses, in practice obstacles have been continually placed in their way over a period of many years, with the result that their numbers have been constantly decreasing, and do so still and at a rapid rate.

Contemporaries, however, saw things differently. Quality of life was assessed by criteria far more complex and more wide-ranging than merely the relative movements of wages and prices. In particular, those who had been reduced, for their quality of life, to dependence on the unsympathetic and unpredictable vagaries of price movements, saw that fact in itself as the major cause of their distress.

In The Annals of the Labouring Poor, the historian K. D. M. Snell presents fascinating evidence of the concerns of displaced members of rural society, in the form of letters written to relatives back in southern England from the new settlements of America. In the letters, wages, prices, and opportunities for purchasing provisions, are seen to be matters of fairly minor importance. Often, they are not mentioned at all, and if they are, it is usually near the end of the letter, as a subsidiary concern. Fewer than one in ten correspondents, apparently, mention wages. On the other hand, issues of self-sufficiency, of the opportunities for providing ones own subsistence, independently of the vagaries of the market, assume much greater significance. And much the same points, according to Snell, could equally be demonstrated from diaries and autobiographies written by members of the labouring classes.[5]

Unsurprisingly, therefore, opportunities to acquire land and livestock loom large amongst the topics of the emigrants' letters. Here is an example.

"There is no difficulty of a man's getting land here….many will let a man have land with a few acres improvement and a house on it without any deposit….I thank God my wife and I never found ourselves so comfortable in England as we do here….we have a good comfortable house to live in and a good cow for our use, and a plenty of firing."

Independence and self-sufficiency remained important to the members of agricultural communities, even after they had been displaced and driven to the colonies.

3 Ibid. Pp. 283-4.
4 Roger Wells. Wretched Faces. Pp.20-1.
5 K. D. M. Snell. Annals of the Labouring Poor. P. 10.

51

"I am going to work on my own farm of 50 acres, which I bought at £55, and I have five years to pay it in. I have bought me a cow and five pigs….if I had stayed at Corsley I never should have had nothing…."

And again;-

"Here you can raise everything of your own that you want to make use of in your family."

In America, game could form a welcome addition to the household fare, unlike in England, where poaching, as it had become, carried ever more severe penalties.

"I can take my gun and go a shooting, as well as any of the farmer's sons; and we can go a fishing when we please, and when we are hunting we don't have no need to be afraid of the gamekeeper. I tell you my dear brothers that if you were here you would be better off than you are now."

All the opportunities provided by the open-field village were looked for in America; the ready availability of paid employment for both men and women; living-in arrangements for employees replicating the institution of service in England, which gave such a good solid start in life to many members of the rural communities; and the good social relationship between masters and men resulting from it, seen as contributing so much to the well-being of the labourers.

"We were very happy and comfortable, and I have plenty of employment for this winter season. I am chiefly threshing for which I get the 10th bushel of all kinds of grain and our board; it is the custom of the country to be boarded and lodged, let you work at what you will; and tradesmen the same; and Master and Mistress and all the family sit all at table, and if there is not room at the table for the whole family to sit down, their children sit by till workmen are served; there is no distinction between the workman and his master, they would as soon shake hands with a workman as they would with a gentleman."[6]

Notwithstanding all this, however, the fact is inescapable that in England, things were no longer like this. The agricultural community was become the proletariat; unavoidably dependent on wage-labour for their subsistence, and needing to purchase this retail at markets and, increasingly, in shops. In this situation, real wage levels, the ever-changing relationship between the price of labour and the price of provisions, became the controlling factor in their now much reduced quality of life.

In the early eighteenth century, wages were low, but prices were lower. Let us go to Nottinghamshire. Here, wages hardly rose between 1710 and 1770. But up until around 1765, prices remained on a par with them. There were very few years of scarcity and high prices during this period, and in Nottingham in 1742 a quartern loaf could be bought for as little as 3d. It has been estimated that at that time a man could feed himself on 4d per day. This would buy him two to three pounds of bread and half a pound of meat or cheese; all of which could be washed down with plentiful amounts of small beer, a gallon then costing a mere 1½d. On this basis, a labourer might spend between £5 and £6 per year on food. Allowing perhaps £1 or £2 for clothes, £1 for rent, and something for his firing and the tools of his trade, he might spend around £9 in a year. If he earned an average wage, say 8d per day, and worked for 300 days in a year, he would be left, at the end of it, with a surplus of £1. In those days, the women and children took a much greater part in agricultural work than they later did; domestic industry, especially spinning, could make a significant contribution to the family budget; and a high proportion of labouring families had gardens, occupied land, and kept livestock. The wife and children had opportunities for earning their own maintenance, rather than being merely dependent on the earnings of the man.[7]

Here follows a list of prices compiled by Charles Deering for his History of Nottingham of 1751. John Throsby, another historian of Nottingham, also produced a list of prices for the 1790s, and where a comparison can be made, his figures follow.

6   K. D. M. Snell. Annals of the Labouring Poor. Pp. 12-3.
7   J. D. Chambers. Nottinghamshire in the Eighteenth Century. Pp. 284-7.

| | Deering[8] | Throsby[9] |
	1750	1790s
Bread corn per bushel.	3s6d-4s0d	7s0d
Malt per bushel.	3s0d-3s6d	
Meat (not bacon) per stone	3s0d 4s8d	
Butter per pound	4d-6d	8½d
Cheese per pound	3d	
Eggs 10-16	4d	8d
Salt-fish per pound	2½d-	3d
Beans and peas per peck	4d-6d	
Carrots, turnips or parsnips per bunch	1d	
Cabbages etc.	In proportion	
Potatoes per peck	6d-8d	5d
Small beer per gallon	1½d	

Perhaps the most significant point about Deering's list is that these are all articles which he denominates "immediate necessaries", and which he distinguishes from another list of "less necessaries"; the implication being that the above foodstuffs were considered as essential for everyone, and were in common use throughout the social hierarchy. With prices at this level, the Nottinghamshire labourer could maintain himself and his family without difficulty, and many did so by working just four days per week, and sometimes less. This brought many complaints from writers and employers. In Nottingham, in 1686, it was noted of the stockingers that "they have been observed seldom to work on Mondays and Tuesdays, but to spend their time at the alehouse....The weavers 'tis common in them to be drunk on Monday, have their headache on Tuesday and their tools out of order on Wednesday". [10] This is clearly propaganda, and we need not take it too seriously in a general sort of way. Labouring was not seen as a full-time occupation in those days; many families would have had their own concerns to attend to, and were not necessarily idle when not employed. Nevertheless, it does illustrate the comparative ease of the labourer, and the lack of pressure involved in gaining a subsistence. Many nostalgic comments were made about this period.

"The labourers who had some partial remembrance of that era, have been many times heard to speak with great complacency of those good old times, 'ere the style was altered, and the pudding lost its place.'"[11]

According to George Dyer, writing in 1793, the plentiful conditions of the early part of the century began to come to an end with the scanty harvest of 1756, which was "attended with very serious consequences."[12]

"There are never wanting persons to turn the calamity of mankind to their own advantage – The price of grain sunk afterwards; but it did not sink to the level it was at prior to 1756, and there has been a gradual increase in the price of provisions." At Mark Lane, the principal London corn market, the price of wheat rocketed to 72s per quarter, and the city of Nottingham saw riots led by the wives of the miners of Wollaton.[13]

---

8   Charles Deering. History of Nottingham. 1751. P.70
9   John Throsby. History of Nottingham, 1795.
10 J. D. Chambers. Nottinghamshire in the Eighteenth Century. P. 277
11 Thomas Batchelor. General View of the County of Bedfordshire. P. 63.
12 George Dyer. Complaints of the Poor People of England. P. 99.
13 J. D. Chambers. Nottinghamshire in the Eighteenth Century. P. 284.

However, it is the bad harvest of 1766 which is usually seen as the beginning of the period of rapidly rising prices. According to petitions sent up to Parliament in that year, the price of veal went up from 2½d – 3½d per pound to 5d-5½d ; of beef from 1s 10d per stone to 2s 4d; of mutton from 2s 2d to 3s; and of pork from 2s to 3s. In Nottinghamshire, the price of bread almost doubled; butter stood at 6d per pound and cheese at 4d. Serious disturbances resulted in Nottingham, in which rioters forcibly prevented the shipment of cheese to London along the Trent; and which ended with the mayor of Nottingham calling on the government for military aid. The historian of Nottinghamshire called this "the beginning of a profound change that rapidly reduced the agricultural labourer to a position of great misery".[14]

The sharp and sustained rise in the cost of living in the second half of the eighteenth century, and the deterioration in living conditions which it brought about, was a major talking-point at the time, and one could fill several chapters with the figures and the resulting comment. However, by way of example, let us visit the west country.

The historian of Wigston Magna, W. G. Hoskins, also wrote a history of Exeter. Like Chambers in Nottinghamshire, Hoskins noted the lack of subsistence pressure on the labouring classes in the early eighteenth century. This was a period of regular employment; for although the city's woollen industry was in decline, those workers who were displaced from it could easily find other sources of employment; wages tended to be steady, or even slightly on the rise. A typical working family in Exeter in the middle of the eighteenth century might earn between them, man, woman and children, 10s in a week. Of this, 3s might be spent on bread; 4s 6d on other foodstuffs; 1s 6d on fuel and light; and 1s on rent. This easy-going situation began to change in the late 1750s, as food prices started to rise; and the trend became marked from the poor harvest year of 1766.[15]

The crucial price was that of wheat. Throughout most of the early part of the eighteenth century the price of a half-peck of wheaten bread stood at around 6d or 7d. Approaching the year of dearth of 1766, it was at 6d in 1762; 7d in 1763 and 1764; and 8d in 1765. The average between 1768 and 1770 was 7¾d. The price of wheat per bushel rose from 3s 7d in 1759 to 6s 1½d in 1766. Other prices followed. Perhaps the most dramatic rise was in meat, the wholesale price of which rose from 16s 9d per hundredweight in the early 1760s, to 22s 4d at the end of the decade. Twelve pounds of butter rose from 5s 0½d to 5s 10d; and cheese from 16s 10d to 20s 4d. And so on.[16]

The year of food shortage of 1766 saw corn riots in Devon as it did in Nottingham. At Exeter there were disturbances in the spring, followed by violence in many towns in the east of the county in August. In September, a mob forcibly unloaded a cargo of corn at Topsham, and sold it to the poor at what seemed a reasonable price. Later in the month, a load of cheese and bacon was intercepted on its way to a nearby market, and a quantity of cheese was taken and distributed from a local warehouse.[17]

The immediate crisis subsided in the years after 1766, but the price rises, or depreciation in the value of money, continued relentlessly. In spite of a few cheap years, like 1769, 1778, and 1779, the price of a half-peck of bread in Exeter rose from 7d in the early 1760s, to 9d in the early 1790s, a rise of thirty per cent; and in a year of poor harvest it might rocket to 1s or 1s 1d. The rise in the price of meat in the same period was double that of wheat; of butter 50 per cent; of cheese 34 per cent; of milk 43 per cent; of peas 57 per cent; and of coal 11 per cent. Altogether, the increase in the price of foodstuffs probably averaged between 40 and 50 per cent; the cost of rent, fuel and candles also rose, but by lesser amounts.[18]

14 Ibid. P. 288.
15 W. G. Hoskins. Industry, Trade and People in Exeter. 1688-1800. Pp. 135-6.
16 Ibid. Pp. 136-138.
17 Ibid. P. 138.
18 Ibid. P. 141. E. Gilboy. Wages in Eighteenth century England. P. 122.

In the face of this continuous rise in the cost of living, what happened to the incomes of labouring families in Devon during the same period? In the latter part of the seventeenth century, the Devon day-labourer could earn 5d per day, with food and drink worth another 5d. His wife could earn food and drink to the value of 3d, with 1d over. In those days, in Devon, wage levels were officially determined by local magistrates, and by the time of the beginning of the surviving series of assessments, in 1700, the daily winter wage with diet included was still 5d, but was 11d when paid all in money. This was raised to 12d in 1732, a rate which prevailed right through to 1778. The summer wage remained stable throughout the entire period, at 6d with food and drink, and 12d without. The wage for mowing hay was assessed at 8d per day with food and drink, and 1s 4d without, a rate which, again, held good through all the years from 1700 to 1778.[19]

When Robert Fraser reviewed the county of Devon for the Board of Agriculture in 1794, he found wages to be 1s per day, with two pints of cider. "In harvest the same, with as much cyder as they chuse to drink."[20] Two years later, William Marshall visited Devon, and reported that the daily wage there was 1s per day with two pints of cider in winter and spring; at haymaking, the wage was the same, only with more cider; and at harvest, the same, but with full board.[21]

It is clear, then, that throughout the eighteenth century, the income of the Devon farm labourer increased scarcely at all; indeed, it appears that the rewards for haymaking actually decreased. And a large part of this period was a time when the cost of living rose rapidly and continuously.

Building labourers in Devon fared a little better, with wages around 1s 2d per day in the early part of the century, and around 1s 4d later on. The pay of journeymen craftsmen in Exeter fluctuated between 1s 8d and 2s per day; but outside Exeter between 1s 4d and 1s 8d.[22]

So the general tendency of wages in eighteenth century Devon was to remain relatively stable. Whilst some classes of workers did better than others, it is clear that no sector of the workforce received a sufficient increase of wages to compensate for the rise in the price of food, estimated at between 40 and 50 per cent. Among the woollen workers of Exeter, and the labourers on the farms of Devon, wages scarcely changed. And in Exeter at least, as the century progressed, employment became harder to come by, as the woollen industry declined, and alternative trades became overstocked with labour. Unemployment added a further complication to an already difficult situation.[23] The income of a labouring family in Exeter in 1688 might total around 9s or 10s per week. By the end of the eighteenth century, it was still the same.

Here are William Chapple's observations on this crisis, published in his Risdon's Survey of Devon in 1785.

"The great Decrease of the Value of Money within the Time here mentioned, seems to require a proportional Advancement of Labourers' Wages; to which there can be no Doubt of their having a just Claim, if it be considered, that Any Diminution of the *Value* of Money....whatever....may be the cause, - is sufficiently evident from its Effects; having within 20, or 25 years at most, rais'd the Price of Provisions and Rents of Estates, and consequently the *pecuniary* Produce of that Labour for which the *Wages* we are here speaking of become payable, by at least *One Third*; of which Addition, the labourer ought in Justice to have his proportional Share, to enable him to obtain common Necessaries at the present advanc'd Prices, and prevent his Family from being too early burdensome on the Parish. – This, and this only, can put our present Labourers on the same footing with their Forefathers."[24]

19 W. G. Hoskins. The Farm Labourer in Devonshire Studies. P. 425.
20 Robert Fraser. General View of the County of Devon. P. 43.
21 William Marshall. Rural Economy of the West of England. Vol. I. P. 321.
22 E. Gilboy. Wages in Eighteenth Century England. P. 106 and 111.
23 W. G. Hoskins. Industry, Trade and People in Exeter. 1688-1800. Pp. 141 and 131.
24 William Chapple. Risdon's Survey of Devon. P. 52 n.

The effects of this crisis were serious and pervasive. The population of Devon was experiencing a steady decline in its standard of living, and the most obvious aspect of this was in diet. The level of nutrition of the average Devonshire family must have undergone a serious lowering. As prices rose, the cheaper barley bread began to take the place of wheaten, and a greater use was made of potatoes. Meat, butter and cheese all disappeared from the diet, partially or completely. This can be illustrated from the menu in the workhouse at Exeter. In 1701, inmates were fed on a diet of bread, cheese, beer, beef, butter, broth, pease pudding, oatmeal, milk porridge, puddings with or without fruit, garden vegetables, etc. As prices rose later in the century, butter was no longer used, peas replaced meat, and bread was made half of barley and half of wheat.[25] Labouring families outside the workhouse would probably have fared not so well as this. When William Marshall visited Devon in 1796, he observed that the food of the people consisted of barley bread, skim-milk cheese and potatoes.[26] Robert Fraser, in 1794, related how in Devonshire bread was made partly out of potatoes. "This is done by simply mashing the potatoes after they have been boiled, and mixing them with the flour or leaven."[27]

Another grave consequence of the Devon labourer's deteriorating position was his increasing dependence on the parish rate. William Marshall observed;-

"The wages of the District, seeing the great rise in the price of living, appears to me too low.... All ranks of people, FARM LABOURERS ONLY EXCEPTED, have had an increase of income, with the increase of the prices of the necessaries of life; or, which is the same thing, with the decrease in the value or price of money. This may, in a great measure, account for the increase of the poor's rates in country parishes...."[28]

In Exeter, during the time of low prices before 1766, applicants for parish relief received on average only 9d per week, and their numbers remained steady. In the poor harvest year of 1766, £1300 was spent on poor relief. By 1776, the figure was £3200, and it stayed at roughly that level until 1785. In 1796, £5000 was levied by the poor rate. In 1803, £7653 was expended. By this time, the numbers receiving relief had dramatically risen, as had the average sum doled out; there were 250 people living in the workhouse, and 200 receiving out-relief.[29] It was, in most cases, a sad misfortune, and an increasingly frequent one, to "be consigned to the care and humanity of the jailor of a workhouse", as William Chapple put it.[30]

When Risdon wrote his original Survey of Devon in 1650, he tells us that labourers were then "allow'd Holidays and Times of Leisure for manly Exercises, such as shooting, wrestling, hurling the Ball, etc. in which the Activity of these West-country men exceeded all others in the Realm". William Chapple brought out his heavily edited version in 1785. In the interval, he tells us, "their Case has been much alter'd; for now the high Price of Provisions in proportion to their Wages, and the Duties charg'd on Soap, Candles, Salt, and other Necessaries of Life, will permit them to keep but few *Holidays*; unless compell'd thereto by the want of Employment, and to turn them into *fasting* Days by their want of Bread; - - which must be the unavoidable Consequence of that Neglect and even Prohibition of Tillage....The Effects of this...., even within the last 30 or 40 Years, have been very perceptible; and most of those Country Villages, Wherein Chearfulness and a kind of rustic Gaiety, might be observ'd among the poor Labourers within our Remembrance, have at present a very different Appearance, and exhibit all the Marks of Poverty and Distress: Instead of that Sprightliness and Alacrity with which they heretofore perform'd their daily Task, and earned a competent Supply

25 W. G. Hoskins. Industry, Trade and People in Exeter 1688-1800. P. 143.
26 William Marshall. Rural Economy of the West of England. Vol. I. P. 27.
27 Robert Fraser. General View of the County of Devon. P. 70.
28 William Marshall. Rural Economy of the West of England. Vol .I. P. 107.
29 W. G. Hoskins. Industry, Trade and People in Exeter 1688-1800. P. 145.
30 William Chapple. Risdon's Survey of Devon. P. 43.

of homely Food for themselves and Families, we now perceive a kind of heavy Gloom on every Face; and instead of having now-and-then (as they formerly had) in a Summer Evening, before Harvest-time came on, an Hour's Recreation after finishing the Work of the Day, - - - they must now endeavour to supply, if possible, the Deficiency of their scanty Wages (being scarce sufficient to purchase two-thirds of the Provision it would have bought 25 Years since), by assisting their craving Families in some Employment at home, or otherwise send them supperless to bed."[31]

✳

The condition of the labouring families of Devon can be used as a benchmark to assess the circumstances of people in other counties. Vancouver speaks of the "general air of wretchedness and misery so often met with in the villages and detached groups of houses"; Chapple of the villagers exhibiting "all the marks of poverty and distress....a kind of heavy gloom on every face". But sad and worsening as the plight of the good people of Devon undoubtedly was, there is good reason to suppose that they were far from being the least prosperous people in England; indeed, that the generality of the inhabitants of vast swathes of southern and south-eastern England, East Anglia and the Midlands, were, in fact, much worse off still. The two great disadvantages suffered by the Devonshire labourers were the lowness of wages in the face of continually rising prices, and the badness of housing.

The Devon wage was reported as inadequate by Vancouver, and even by Marshall. But there were plenty of places where it was no better. Wages in Dorset were only 6s a week, but with enough corn to feed a family at 5s per bushel.[32] In neighbouring Somerset, Hannah More reported wages of 1s per day, a rate which left their "wants and distresses uncommonly great."[33] In Berkshire, they were a little better off, but not much. Since the middle of the century, the advance of wages was "in some places from five to six shillings, in others from six to seven shillings a week; and in some few places, a little more than this".[34] There were some areas of higher wages. In 1794, Nathaniel Kent reported from Norfolk that wages there had until recently remained at 14d a day in summer and 1s in winter; this had then increased to 18d in summer and 14d in winter.[35] But higher wages did not necessarily mean better living conditions. For example, in Sussex, Arthur Young junior computed the average wage in 1793 at 1s 5d in winter and 1s 9d in summer. But at Glynde in that year half a peck of bread cost 1s, whereas in Devon it was 9d.[36] Thomas Davies in 1794 complained of the high price of labour in Wiltshire – "seldom less than 7s per week and frequently 8s" – this constituting "a heavy tax on the farmers"! Yet in the same report he mentions that this increased wage "is now barely sufficient for their subsistence, and a few days illness brings them to the parish".[37] Wages could vary considerably and unaccountably even within fairly small areas. In a Group of six Bedfordshire villages mentioned by Thomas Batchelor, the weekly price of day-labour in 1790 varied in winter from 6s to 8s, and in summer from 9s to 10s.[38] This inexplicable variation was also noted by George Dyer.

"Labourers ought to receive more wages than they commonly do,...and our farmers and manufacturers can, in general, afford to give more....In the course of a year, wages have been raised in some places through which I lately passed two-pence a day, without any inconvenience to the farmers;

31 William Chapple. Risdon's Survey of Devon. Pp. 51-2.
32 John Claridge. General View of the County of Dorset. P. 22.
33 William Roberts. Memoirs of the Life and Correspondence of Hannah More. Vol. II. P. 304.
34 David Davies. The Case of the Labourers in Husbandry. P. 66.
35 Nathaniel Kent. General View of the county of Norfolk. P. 152.
36 Rev. Arthur Young. General View of the County of Sussex. P. 89.
37 Thomas Davies. General View of the County of Wiltshire. Pp. 140 and 154.
38 Thomas Batchelor. General View of the County of Bedfordshire. P. 53.

yet in the very next villages, perhaps, labour keeps at the paltry shilling. Now I have not heard, that there is anything in the circumstances of the farms, in the latter case, to prevent this trifling advance. Indeed, if I am not wrongly informed….in some places wages are even as low as ten-pence."[39]

Shudder as one might to contemplate a labourer struggling to raise a family in the 1790s on 10d a day, many had to manage with less. Most of those working in the new manufactures received a wage below subsistence level, and this included cotton-weavers and framework-knitters. With the ending of apprenticeship regulations, employers could take advantage of hungry countrymen flooding into industry, and the widespread use of child labour on machines that required neither strength nor skill, to force wages down to starvation level. Workers were then left to depend for maintenance partly on the parish, and partly on the earnings of their children.[40] William Hallam, framework-knitter of Nottingham, earned 7s in a week; the rent of his frame, together with other deductions made by his employer, totalled 2s 6d. He and his family had to exist for a week on 4s 6d. 4s 6d was also the standard daily rate for agricultural labour in the Gloucestershire village of Newent.[41]

In point of housing, most observers agreed that Devonians were, on the whole, severely disadvantaged. This was already the case in mid-century, when Mrs. Powys made the following remarks in her diary on Devon cob cottages.

"We were surprised in our travels thro' Devonshire to see their cottages of an appearance really meaner than in any county is usual; and indeed, as by fatal experience, they have found residences terribly unsafe; for on July 2nd, at Offington, near Exeter, more than twenty were demolished; the poor people were in their beds. And one old woman in hers drowned by the rain being prodigious heavy; it came pouring in such torrents from the hills behind, and hurl'd down so great a quantity of stones of such amazing size, that soon broke down the walls built only of a composition of clay and straw called cob. The houses were instantly overflow'd and tumbling to pieces; all were in the utmost consternation, as one may easily imagine, from the ruinous state their habitations are still in. But to quit a subject so dismal…."[42]

Charles Vancouver, reporting on Devon to the Board of Agriculture in 1808, went into considerable detail on the subject, emphasising not just the poor condition of the cottages, but also their increasingly short supply. Quoting from the census of 1801, Vancouver tells us that at that time, in north Devon, there were 7,183 houses, containing 7,845 families. This meant that 642 houses were double-tenanted; but at the same time 401 houses were recorded as uninhabited, - "the greater part of which may fairly be supposed in a state of dilapidation, or utter ruin; or from other causes, equally dependent on the proprietors, without any inhabitants at all".[43]

By 1808, the picture was the same over most of the county. In eastern Devon, the cottages were "in a state of alarming decrease". In some central parishes, "twelve or fifteen families are found absent not having houses to receive them. Farmers having many vacant tenements on their lands, refuse letting them to the poor….; many peasant families are thus expelled from the parishes to which they belong…." In the more easterly of these parishes, the poor were "so indifferently provided with

39   George Dyer. The Complaints of the Poor People of England. 1793 ed. P. 102.

40   J. L. and B. Hammond. The Town Labourer. P. 95. Rev. John Howlett. The Insufficiency of the Causes to which the increase of our Poor, and of the Poor's Rates have been commonly ascribed. P. 64.

41   J. D. Chambers. Nottinghamshire in the Eighteenth Century. Pp. 283-4. David Davies. The Case of the Labourers in Husbandry. P. 160.

42   Diary of Mrs. Philip Lybbe Powys. P. 69. Quoted in G. E. Fussell and C. Goodman. The Housing of the Rural Population. Economic History. Vol. II. P. 76.

43   Charles Vancouver. General View of the county of Devon. P. 403.

habitations, it is deplorable to see the number of cottages that are daily going to ruin, and have fallen down within a few years."[44]

Many of those cottages remaining were becoming dilapidated and unsuitable for living in.

"The general want of cottages through this district, can no where be more clearly shown than in the example of Chilworthy, where three mud walls and a hedge-bank form the habitation of many of the peasantry."[45]

There were exceptions. William Marshall noted the "superior habitations" in the west of Devon, where stone and slate could be obtained easily and cheaply. "Even the cottages are comfortable and sometimes neat." The situation was better on the estates of paternalistic landlords, like Lord Clifford, who "builds very neat cottages for his workmen", or Lord Rolle, who encouraged rural folk to settle on the edges of commons. More usually, Devon cottages were built of mud, known as cob. Even cob cottages were "capable of being rendered clean and comfortable….if afterwards rough-cast and whitewashed." But in general this was not the case.[46]

"The universal prevalence of cob, or mud walls, will serve in a great measure to account for the untenantable state of many buildings, and for the general air of wretchedness and misery so often met with in the villages and detached groups of houses throughout the district. This may be ascribed to the negligence of those who have the care of the estates, and the indifference but too frequently shown by the proprietors, in preserving a sufficient number of cottages on their estates for the accommodation of labourers."[47]

Devon may have been notorious for the badness of its housing, but conditions in many parts of the country were scarcely better. In Suffolk, Arthur Young found the cottages "in general bad habitations; deficient in all contrivance for warmth, and for convenience; the door very generally opening immediately from the external air into the keeping-room, and sometimes directly to the fire-side; the state of reparation bad, and the deficiency of garden too general."[48] Young connected the deficiency of housing with the lowness of agricultural wages; labourers being too poor to pay a rent which would justify the investment required in building cottages. In Devon also, the practice of leaving cottages empty was attributed to the inability of the labourer to pay rent in hard times. Clearly, where cottagers still owned their own homes, their inability to maintain them would have worsened as conditions deteriorated; instance the labourer of Seend in Wiltshire encountered by Eden in 1797, who "cannot afford to repair his ruinous cottage".[49]

The deficiency and dilapidation of cottage housing was associated by many writers with the enclosing and engrossing of farms. 'Improving' landlords would often demolish cottages in order to reduce the number of poor living in a parish, or simply stop repairing them to save the expence. Stephen Addington commented that in almost all enclosed villages, older residents could remember "upwards of an hundred houses and families" in their open-field state, where now there were only eight or ten. The ruins of former dwelling-houses, barns and stables were there for all to see; and villagers were driven away by the state of "such miserable ruinous cottages as those in the enclosures become in a little time."[50]

---

44 Ibid. Pp. 93-4 and 98.

45 Ibid. P. 94.

46 Ibid. P. 92. William Marshall. Rural Economy of the West of England. Vol. 1. P. 27.

47 C. Vancouver. General View of the County of Devon. P. 403.

48 Arthur Young. General View of the County of Suffolk P. 11.

49 C. Vancouver. General View of the County of Devon. P. 93. F. M. Eden. The State of the Poor Vol. III P. 344.

50 Stephen Addington. An Inquiry into the Reasons for and against Inclosing Open-Fields. P. 42.

In Berkshire, David Davies saw the same process at work. Noting the decrease in the number of houses, he tells us;

"A great many *farm-houses* in the hands of engrossing farmers, each of which was formerly occupied by *one* farming family only, are now divided into *two, three,* or even *four* separate dwellings for labouring families. The like happens where cottages are suffered to fall into decay, and no new ones built….The cottages themselves have been pulled down; the families which used to occupy them crowded together in decayed farmhouses, with hardly ground about them for a cabbage garden."[51]

The increasing incidence of multiple tenements in East Anglia became a subject of correspondence to Arthur Young's Annals of Agriculture. The vicar of Icklingham in Suffolk, a Mr. Gwilt, wrote that in his village in 1700 there were 68 houses; at the time of writing there were only 56. But that was no indication of a falling population, as there were now twelve double tenements and one treble. Twenty-five years ago there were none; the village now averaged six to a house. In Ketteringham, it was worse. Out of only twenty houses, five were double tenements and one treble; and there were 8.3 inhabitants to a cottage. At Hamstead, in Essex, where cottages were also disappearing, though families contained on average six persons, the houses held eight; twelve being divided into two, and three into three, out of a total of 52.[52]

As in Devon, there were brighter spots dotted around the country. Some of the great landlords were well-known for providing comfortable dwellings for the workers on their estates, and these included the Duke of Bedford and the Earl of Winchelsea. Of Suffolk, Arthur Young commented that "some very respectable individuals have distinguished themselves most laudably by building neat and comfortable cottages for the poor; but such instances are not general."[53] Eye- witness accounts of the generality of cottages could be quoted at great length, but let us content ourselves with the observations of John Wood, who was an architect at Bath. In preparing 'A Series of Plans for Cottages' in 1792, he felt compelled "to feel as the cottager himself; to enquire after the conveniences he wanted, and into the inconveniences he laboured under."

"The necessity there was of improving the dwellings of the poor labourer became continually more and more apparent….The greatest part of the cottages that fell within my observation, I found to be shattered, dirty, inconvenient, miserable hovels, scarcely affording a shelter for beasts of the forest; much less were they proper habitations for the human species; nay it is impossible to describe the condition of the poor villager, of which I was too often the melancholy spectator."[54]

Wood lists the complaints of the inhabitants of the better sort of these cottages. Many were built in "low dreary spots", perhaps against banks as in Devon, with floors below ground level. They were therefore constantly damp. They were also "cold and cheerless", on account of the lack of a porch, and the poor siting of the doors, windows and chimneys. The external walls were so extremely thin that they let the water through. "I have seen the inside of these walls covered with ice from the roof to the foundation". They were cramped and inconvenient. The lowness and closeness of the rooms, and their facing mainly north or west, made them unhealthy places to live. The dormer windows were often badly fitted and out of repair, allowing yet more water to enter, and leading to the decay of the cottage, starting with the roof.

Of the complaints of the inhabitants of the worse sort of these cottages, Wood makes no mention….

The demolition of cottages; the keeping of them deliberately in short supply; the neglect of the landlord's duty of keeping them in repair; the use of derelict farmhouses; and the crowding of more

51   David Davies. The Case of the Labourers in Husbandry. Pp. 53-56.
52   Annals of Agriculture. Vol. IV. P. 51. Vol. VIII. P. 350. Vol. II. Pp. 332-5.
53   Arthur Young. General View of the County of Suffolk. 1797. P. 11.
54   John Wood. A Series of Plans for Cottages. Pp. 1-3.

than one family into hovels and divided tenements; these were all characteristic, one might say important and salient features, of the new, improved, progressive agriculture. Yet in text-book praises of the agricultural revolution, they find no mention.

Poor wages and housing, then, were the twin evils laboured under by the people of Devon. But despite the well-attested wretchedness and misery prevailing both in town and village, Devonshire families still enjoyed many advantages which the inhabitants of many other parts of England no longer did. In Devon, the family farm was still the norm, and the social gap that had come to separate farmers from their labourers in most of the rest of England had still not opened very wide. The harsh, opulent, 'flinty-hearted', capitalist farmer was late arriving in Devon.

In neighbouring counties, he was already well established. At Cheddar, in Somerset, Hannah More found "twelve wealthy farmers, hard, brutal and ignorant", lording it over 2,000 half-starved villagers.[55] And in nearby Dorset, the reviewer for the Board of Agriculture in 1793 made the following observation.

"The increase of large farms, evidently tends to place the great farmer at too great a distance from the labourer, whom he considers a mere vassal, and though he employs him, and pays, what he calls a customary price; still it is out of the power of the labourer, either by strength or indefatigable industry, scarcely to supply his family with the common necessaries of life; and the moment his activity ceases, he becomes a pauper...."[56]

The relationship between the farmer and the labourer had a material effect on the well-being or otherwise of the lower strata of society, which was an advantage to Devonians, but a further cause of misery to the inhabitants of many other parts. Here is Robert Fraser, on the South Hams district, where the respectable class of yeomanry was said to be more numerous than in any other part of England.

They "live in great comfort, and exercise without parade, that old English hospitality which the refinements of modern manners have banished from many other parts of the kingdom. I observed with much pleasure, the attention they paid to their various dependants around them, and their kindness to the poor. Nothing can evince this more strongly than the agreements they have entered into, in most parts of this district, to supply the labourers and neighbouring poor with grain, at certain fixed moderate prices, an example well worthy of more general imitation."[57]

Despite the lowness of the wages, farmers in Devon looked after their workers far better than in most other parts of England. The practice of providing labourers' families with bread corn at below market price was remarked upon also by Marshall and Vancouver, who considered that it in part compensated for the fall in real wages. By 1808, wheat was supplied at 6s per bushel, and barley at 3s, a family of four or five needing a bushel of wheat per month, or two of barley.[58] This practice was widespread in Devon, and possibly other parts of the West Country,[59] but was dying out elsewhere; a point which was not lost on Nathaniel Kent.

"A farmer is even unwilling to sell the labourer who works for him a bushel of wheat, which he might get ground for 3d or 4d a bushel. For want of these advantages, he is driven to the meal-man or baker, who in the ordinary course of their profit, get at least 10 per cent of them, upon this principal

55   William Roberts. Memoirs of the Life and Correspondence of Hannah More. Vol. II. P. 300.
56   J. Claridge. General View of the County of Dorset. P. 24.
57   R. Fraser. General View of the County of Devon, P. 17.
58   W. Marshall. Rural Economy of the West of England. Vol. I. P. 107. C. Vancouver. General View of the County of Devon. Pp. 361-2.
59   See, e.g. J. Claridge. General View of the County of Dorset. P. 22.

article of their consumption; which they might save, if their employers would supply them with corn, at the common market price."[60]

Many Devon farmers would also provide labourers' families with a small amount of manured land, at a reasonable rent, for growing potatoes.

"This proves a most valuable resource, as the labourer is thereby enabled to keep a small pig, which is generally in good order for slaying about the end of winter, and when cured furnishes a rare but comfortable indulgence."[61]

Thus, the diet of the Devonians, though monotonous, and becoming more so, still contained far more variety than in any other part of England below the northernmost counties. Wheat bread, barley bread, skim-milk cheese, and potatoes were said to be the staples. But Vancouver records districts where, as late as 1808, this diet was still varied with wheat-broth seasoned with meat and pot-herbs; pies made with bacon and potatoes; "pea and other broths, seasoned with pickled pork, bacon, or the fat of mutton, with a profusion of leeks and onions". And he notes the "variety of wholesome food enjoyed by those who inhabit maritime districts", where an ample supply of "fish contributes to sustain the mass of the inhabitants with firmness and vigour to an advanced period of life". Eden also observes, of the increasingly wretched inhabitants of Clyst St. George, that before 1793 their staple diet had consisted of wheaten bread, cheese, and meat about twice a week.[62]

The collapse in dietary standards in other parts of England, the north excepted, had gone much further, and manifested itself largely in the disappearance of variety from the diet. The staple food became, in most cases, almost the only food, and that tended increasingly to be wheaten bread. David Davies observed the process taking place in his parish of Barkham in Berkshire.

"If the working people of other countries are content with bread made of rye, barley, or oats, have they not milk, cheese, butter, fruits, or fish to eat with that coarser bread? And was not this the case of our own people formerly, when those grains were the common productions of our land....? Flesh-meat, butter and cheese, were then at such moderate prices, compared with the present prices, that poor people could afford to use them in common. And with a competent quantity of these articles, a coarser kind of bread might very well satisfy the common people of any country.

"Time, which changes everything, has gradually changed the circumstances of this kingdom.... The prices of meat, butter and cheese, are so much increased....that working people can now scarcely afford to use them in the smallest quantities. So that they depend almost entirely upon the bread they eat for strength to perform their daily labour. That bread should therefore be of a good kind."[63]

The drastic decline in levels of nutrition that took place during the second half of the eighteenth century is perhaps the most glaring and significant manifestation of the diminishing status and worsening conditions of life of the bulk of ordinary folk in England. In Nottingham, in 1751, Charles Deering produced his list of foods which he considered as "immediate necessaries"; in use by all. These included bread, malt, meat, butter, cheese, eggs, salt-fish, pulses, vegetables and beer.[64] At that time, according to the modern historian of Nottinghamshire, a man could feed himself for 4d per day, which would stand him in two to three pounds of bread, half a pound of meat or cheese, and plenty of small beer. Relating to the same period, Hoskins produced a theoretical budget which he considered roughly typical of an average labouring family in Exeter, with an income of around 10s

---

60 N. Kent. Hints to Gentlemen of Landed Property. P. 238. See also D. Davies. The Case of the Labourers in Husbandry. Pp. 33-4.

61 C. Vancouver. General View of the County of Devon. P. 361.

62 C. Vancouver. General View of the County of Devon. Pp. 410-414. W. Marshall. Rural Economy of the West of England. Vol. I. P. 27. F. M. Eden. The State of the Poor. Vol.II. P. 173?

63 David Davies. The Case of the Labourers in Husbandry. Pp. 31-2.

64 Charles Deering. History of Nottingham. P. 70.

per week. This family might have spent 3s per week on bread. With bread fluctuating at between 6d and 7d per half-peck loaf at the time, that represented a weekly consumption of between five and six loaves; a level which remains remarkably constant as the years go by. 4s 6d would be spent on foods other than bread.[65]

Joseph Massie, writing in 1758, made "an estimate of the annual income and expence of a common manufacturer's or working man's family." This was not an actual budget, as "families which are of the same class, have not all like income, nor do they proportion their Expences alike, but some lay out more money in one Thing, and some in another, as Occasion and Inclination direct, so that matters of this sort must be stated in a general manner." Nevertheless, his estimate is not vastly different from Hoskins' theoretical budget. He allows a weekly consumption of 5.5 half-peck loaves, at a cost each of 5¼d, making a weekly expenditure around 2s 5d. Expenditure on other foods totalled 4s – a shilling each on cheese, milk and butter, meat, and beer or cider.[66]

Arthur Young wrote his Farmer's Letters in 1767, the year following the time of scarcity and high prices, from which many historians date the decline in living standards. In it, he published a budget which he claimed was the average of four families of five persons each; and already things were beginning to change. Young allows around 5.75 half-peck loaves per week to each family, but by now the price of such a loaf had shot up to 1s, and weekly expenditure on bread to 5s 8¼d. Thus was now left only 3s 3d to be spent on other foods, which was divided between 1s 9d spent on cheese, at 13 ounces per family per day, and 1s 1d on beer.[67]

In 1775, Nathaniel Kent published his Hints to Gentlemen of Landed Property, in which his assessment of the diets of labouring families shows a further deterioration. He allows a working man one and a half pounds of bread a day, whilst his wife and children would eat, on average, half that amount each. This comes to 42 pounds of bread per week, or 5.25 half-peck loaves; which, at 1½d. per pound, makes a total weekly expenditure on bread of 5s 3d. If total familial income was 8s 6d, as posited by Kent, this left only 3s 3d for all other expences. Kent comments;-

"While the present high price of provisions continues, it is impossible that such a family can eat any thing except bread, which is a very cruel case upon a poor man, whose whole life is devoted to hard labour."[68]

As if to confirm what Kent wrote, a practical farmer, who was also a writer of pamphlets, noted down ten years later that "a man of sixty who has worked on my farm twelve years observed to me that he wondered where all the beef and mutton went to, for he was very certain that not half of the butcher's meat in poor labouring men's families in the country was now consumed as formerly, it being now so dear he was not able to buy it."[69]

Notwithstanding this testimony, it is possible that Kent exaggerated slightly, for when David Davies published his budgets of labouring families, compiled at the end of the 1780s, cheese, butter and meat were all still in use, albeit in the most minute quantities. Davies was the clergyman at Barkham in Berkshire. He collected a number of family budgets from his parishioners, which he considered typical of labouring families. In addition, he sent out to many parts of the country for gentlemen and clergymen to do the same. The number of replies was not great, but those he received he printed. In general, the budgets from the south and Midlands show a remarkable continuity of bread-eating. By working the figures in the budgets, it is possible to arrive at a rough estimate of

---

65 W. G. Hoskins. Industry, Trade and People in Exeter. 1688-1800.
66 Joseph Massie. Considerations Relating to the Poor. 1758. P. 104.
67 Arthur Young. Farmer's Letters. 1771 edition. Pp. 195-202.
68 Nathaniel Kent. Hints to Gentlemen of Landed Property. P. 237.
69 A Society of Farmers. A Political Enquiry into the Consequences of Enclosing Waste Lands. 1785. P. 71.

the amount of bread eaten, on average, in the villages mentioned; and it differs very little from the estimates of Hoskins and Massie for earlier in the century. At Barkham and Pangbourne in Berkshire; at Affpiddle, Bishop's Caundle and Stinsford in Dorset; at Crawley, Longparish, Monk-Sherborne and Basing in Hampshire; and at Holwell in Somerset; bread consumption works out at between five and six half-peck loaves per family per week. Where bread consumption was higher, it was generally associated with unusually large families; like the three budgets from Brington in Northamptonshire, where three families contained a total of twenty-seven persons, and got through about eight half-peck loaves per family per week. Where bread consumption was less, it was either through extraordinary poverty, as at Newent in Gloucestershire, where families managed on less than four half-peck loaves; or through greater affluence. Better-off families were known to give greater priority to foods such as meat, dairy produce and beer.[70] Such families are represented in Davies's budgets by the villagers of Sidlesham in Surrey and Tuntington in Sussex; where families also averaged only around four half-peck loaves.[71]

If the amount of bread consumed had not changed significantly, the cost of that bread undoubtedly had. As against the 3s allowed by Hoskins for Exeter, or the 2s 5d allowed by Massie, the average weekly sums spent on bread in the places listed above varied from 5s 2d at Longparish, to 6s 2d at Bishop's Caundle. At Stinsford in Dorset, expenditure averaged only 4s, as farmers supplied their labourers with wheat at 6s per bushel.

Clearly this left very little to be spent on foods other than bread. At mid-century, Hoskins allowed 4s 6d, and Massie 4s, for alternative foods. But in the villages mentioned above, expenditure ranged from 1s 9d at Affpiddle, to 3s 8d at Bishop' Caundle. The average of the averages was about 2s 6½d. At the much higher prices pertaining in 1790, this bought very little. The meat consumed was mostly bacon, and ranged from half a pound per family per week at Affpiddle, to 1.8lb at Bishop's Caundle. These quantities, needless to say, are nugatory, derisory even. The families of Stinsford, who could buy cheap corn from their employers, managed 2.8lb; whereas the more prosperous families of Sidlesham and Tuntington consumed about 3.25-3.5lb. At Newent in Gloucestershire, where the harshness of the times was felt more keenly than elsewhere, 3.5oz of bacon had to last a family for an entire week.

Cheese was the other main luxury of the poor. In the crisis year of 1766-7, Arthur Young allowed an expenditure of only 1s 9d on this article, but even that bought a labouring family a weekly ration of over 5½lb of cheese. The family budgets collected by Davies around 1790 give a weekly allowance from virtually none in Davies's own parish of Barkham, to a full pound at Crawley in Hampshire. At Holwell, they consumed 2lb per week, whilst, somewhat exceptionally, the families of Bishop's Caundle luxuriated with an average of 3.6lb. The families of Stinsford, favoured with cheap corn by the farmers, and having their rent and fuel paid for to compensate for the lowness of their wages, could afford 4lb.

Typically, the labouring families represented by the budgets used about half a pound of butter in a week, and the same in sugar. At Bishop's Caundle, they had none of these. At Affpiddle, families were peculiarly favoured with milk and cream.

The budgets collected by Arthur Young junior for six families at Glynde in Sussex in 1793 show remarkably similar results to the above, with perhaps a little less spent on bread, and a little more on other foods, notably meat.[72]

The greater variety of diet in Devon, including, as it did, potatoes, pies, broths and fish, presupposes a means of cooking. None of the writers on Devon mention a shortage of firing as a problem for

70   R. Wells. Wretched Faces. P. 19.

71   David Davies. The Case of the Labourers in Husbandry. The budgets are to be found on Pp. 131-187.

72   Rev. Arthur Young. General View of the County of Sussex.

Devonian families. Around mountainous areas, fuel could be collected from the moors, in the form of peat or turf; in more enclosed areas, wood could be used from copse or hedgerow.[73] The cost and availability of fuel was a material factor in the well-being of labouring families, and the situation varied drastically from place to place. William Cobbett mentioned the superior condition of the inhabitants of the Weald of Sussex and Kent, or of the Forest of Dean, on account of the availability of firewood. At Waterbeech, in Cambridgeshire, Arthur Young observed the villagers "uncommonly well-of"', because they had the freedom to dig turf from Joist Fen.[74] David Davies's parishioners at Barkham were similarly blessed, "because a man can in a week cut turf enough on the common to serve the year".[75] Elsewhere, however, the story could be very different. At enclosure, collecting fuel from the accustomed places and in the accustomed ways abruptly became a criminal offence. And in places it was prosecuted and punished as such. Thomas Davis, reporting on Wiltshire to the Board of Agriculture in 1794, complained of the scarcity of fuel, especially on the downs.

"Coals are already advanced very considerably....Wood is the natural, and should be the depending, fuel of a great part of Wiltshire.

"How necessary, therefore, is it for those who have woods, to preserve them, and for those who have not, to plant some?"[76]

In Exeter, coal shot up from a market price of 11s per quarter in 1760, to a subsidised price of between 12s 6d and 13s during the 1780s; at which price level a cooked meal became a rarity.[77] Firing now had a value even in the countryside, and Davies records some fairly astronomical sums paid for it; 30s for a year's fuel was by no means unusual. F. M. Eden notes the very high price of fuel in Oxfordshire, and remarks that the difficulty of procuring firing was a major contributory factor in the monotony of diet and total dependence on bread for subsistence.[78]

Drink was another article in which Devonians were favoured. In Devon, the custom persisted of providing drink as a perquisite of agricultural labour. It was usually cider, but could sometimes be ale, or the light malt beverage mentioned by Vancouver. Fraser tells us that in 1794 labourers were given a quart of cider as part of their daily wages, or, in harvest-time, "as much cyder as they chuse to drink."[79] Chambers's fourpenny menu in Nottingham in mid-century included copious amounts of small beer, a gallon of which could be had for 1½d. Massie allows an expenditure of 1s per week on beer in 1758, and Young 1s 6d in 1767. But over the next twenty years the use of beer virtually died out in labouring families. There is none to be found in the younger Young's budgets from Sussex in 1793,[80] and almost none in Davies's long series of accounts. Only in the relatively affluent parishes of Sidlesham and Tuntington was it noted that families still brewed their own beer. In Barkham itself, "malt is so dear, that they seldom brew any small beer, except against a lying-in or a christening."

"Time was when *small beer* was reckoned one of the necessaries of life, even in poor families; and it seems to have been designed by Providence for the common drink of the people of this country,

73 C. Vancouver. General View of the County of Devon. P. 365. W. Marshall. Rural Economy of the West of England. Vol. 1. P. 27.

74 W. A. Armstrong in Agrarian History of England and Wales. Vol. VI. P. 749.

75 D. Davies. The Case of the Labourers in Husbandry. P. 137.

76 Thomas Davis. General View of the County of Wiltshire. P. 154.

77 W. G. Hoskins. Industry, Trade and People in Exeter 1688-1800. P. 133.

78 F. M. Eden. The State of the Poor. Vol. II. P. 587.

79 C. Vancouver. General View of the County of Devon. P. 404. R. Fraser. General View of the County of Devon. P. 43.

80 J. D. Chambers. Nottinghamshire in the Eighteenth Century. P. 286. Joseph Massie. Considerations Relating to the Poor. P. 105. Arthur Young. Farmers' Letters. 1771 ed. P. 202. Rev. Arthur Young. General View of the County of Sussex.

being deemed a preservative against some of its worst diseases. Were the poor able to afford themselves this wholesome beverage, it would well enough compensate for the scarcity of milk. But on account of the dearness of *malt*, which is, most unfortunately for them, a principal subject of taxation, small beer has been these many years far beyond their ability to use in common.

"Under these hard circumstances, the dearness of malt, and the difficulty of procuring milk, the only thing remaining for them to moisten their bread with was *tea*." The use of tea enabled the propagandists to level at the poor accusations of extravagance; but, retorted Davies, the tea of the poor was not a luxury.

"Spring water, just coloured with a few leaves of the lowest-priced tea, and sweetened with the brownest sugar, is the luxury for which you reproach them. To this, they have recourse from mere necessity; and were they now to be deprived of this, they would immediately be reduced to bread and water. Tea-drinking is....the consequence of the distresses of the poor."[81]

Typically, a labouring family might use one to one and a half ounces of tea per week. But in spite of its miniscule quantity, it could drive a man to the alehouse.

"The same men, who a few years ago could purchase a little malt, and share their wholesome beverage with their families, are tempted to stint their families even of bread, to get their mug of ale at the public house; for the price of malt being so high, the labourer is prevented from having his accustomed barrel at home."[82]

We have travelled a long way from Wigston Magna, where, in happier days, the villagers produced, for themselves, grains of all types, peas and beans, meat, bacon, eggs, cheese, butter, milk, honey, apples and herbs.[83] By the 1790s, much progress had been made towards the all-bread diet. Contemporary propagandists affected to see this as a reckless extravagance; some modern historians as an improvement. Witness those who express surprise that food rioters should concern themselves with the prices of meat and butter, which, supposedly, were not essential foods. What business did the labouring poor have with meat and butter? It is possible that the quality of the bread eaten by the poor improved in these years, as wheaten bread gradually made inroads against bread made of the inferior grains. But it is by no means certain. The bread which the poor bought at the baker's was not the same as they had previously baked for themselves, from corn grown in the vicinity, and ground at the local mill. Much of the top quality wheat from the larger farms went to London, leaving local bread to be made out of inferior grades, or even imported. Abuses could occur, especially in years of shortage. At Honiton in 1766, there were complaints about "the Bakers confounding one sort of Bread with the others for in reality there is no such thing as White Bread made here; what passes for that is only Wheaten, and what is sold for wheaten being in fact Household, and what is denominated Household being a base mixture of fermented Bran ground down and bolted, to which is added the worst kind of meal...."[84]

Whatever the quality of the bread, all the other articles of nutriment had disappeared from the diet by the 1790s, or appeared in it in such minute amounts as to be insignificant. Bread did not replace meat and cheese; the amount of bread consumed around 1790 had not greatly changed since mid-century. Meat and cheese were simply gone without, or nearly so, and "many poor men with families literally live for several months by bread alone."[85]

---

81 David Davies. The Case of the Labourers in Husbandry. Pp. 19 and 38-9.
82 George Dyer. The Complaints of the Poor People of England. P. 100.
83 W. G. Hoskins. The Midland Peasant. P. 191.
84 R. Wells. Wretched Faces. P. 19. W. G. Hoskins. Industry, Trade and People in Exeter 1688-1800. P. 139.
85 G. Dyer. The Complaints of the Poor People of England. 2nd ed. P. 98.

Man is by nature an omnivorous animal, dependent for health, strength, and a full range of nutrients, upon a varied diet. A man reduced to living on one single article alone is in a far worse condition than in a state of nature. Michael Combrune, writing in 1768, commented on the practice of using the price of wheat as the sole indicator of the well-being of the labouring poor.

"To argue on wheat alone, must be supposing this to be sufficient for their support; but bread, and water added to it, is the sustenance allotted to criminals; as yet, it has not been judged to be sufficient food for slaves."[86]

George Dyer developed the point.

"Many poor labourers must content themselves with prisoners' fare, bread and water; and while in prisons may be seen good wheaten bread, barley, oat bread, or potatoes, is frequently the portion of the poor cottager; and even then in too scanty a portion to satisfy the calls of nature."[87]

Because of the relentlessly rising cost of living, and the increasing number of years of dearth, labouring families were being forced to find cheaper substitutes even for wheaten bread; a retreat to barley bread happened sporadically during bad years. But where wages were so low, and the diet so scanty that endemic starvation seems the only possible consequence, we must suspect – potatoes. Used as a supplement, as they were in the north of England or in Devon, potatoes could be a useful defence against famine. But when they formed a substitute even for bread, they represent yet another lowering of the standard of living. Potatoes were more common than we know, because they were grown in cottage gardens and often make little impact on the budgets; but wherever more than ordinary hardship coincided with the availability of garden ground, there potatoes were used. In Wiltshire, where the labourers' wages were "now barely sufficient for their subsistence", and the price of provisions high, potatoes were "very much cultivated in all parts", which was "exceedingly fortunate for the labouring poor, of whose sustenance they now make a very considerable part". [88] Similarly, on the Isle of Wight, potatoes were well cultivated by the small farmers and labouring poor. These lived, "in a great measure, on potatoes, a wholesome and nourishing food, and plentiful with them, as every labourer's family has a plantation annexed to his dwelling, stocked with this useful root. Indeed, without these assistances, they would be scarcely able to exist, as the rate of wages is but low in the island, provisions dear, and the rent of cottages extravagant."[89]

However, it was the womenfolk of Cornwall who took the art of dietary substitution to an altogether new level. With food prices high, the price of tin on the floor, and unemployment rife, the wives of the tin-miners found an ingredient for their broth that could be collected free of charge and without risk of prosecution – snails! Even William Pitt's government, so far as I am aware, never thought of that.[90]

The frequency with which the costs of the diet of poor labouring families falls just a little short of total familial income suggests a degree of careful planning remarkable in a near impossible situation. Nevertheless, food was not the only expence, and other sums had to be found. Rent, normally, had to be paid. The villagers of Stinsford in Dorset had their rent allowed in consideration of the lowness of their wages, but they were the lucky ones. In 1758, Joseph Massie allowed £1 per year for rent; in 1767, Arthur Young allowed £1 10s. In the later 1780s, rents were still at that level in desperately

86   Michael Combrune. An Enquiry into the Prices of Wheat, Malt etc. P. 119.
87   G. Dyer. The Complaints of the Poor People of England. 2nd ed. P. 99.
88   Thomas Davis. General View of the County of Wiltshire. Pp. 153-4.
89   Rev. Mr. Warner. General View of the Isle of Wight. Pp. 64-5.
90   A. K. Hamilton-Jenkins. The Cornish Miner. P. 156.

poor Newent in Gloucestershire; but in the other southern villages covered by Davies's budgets, it could vary between £1 5s and £2 5s. Rents at Hamsey, near Lewes, in Sussex, were said to be £3 3s. It needs hardly to be added that a deterioration in the state of the cottages had taken place in that time; and that rents were inflated partly by the artificial scarcity of cottages.[91]

Other annual costs which are generally added to Davies's budgets are lying-in, sickness, clothes and fuel. The addition of these expences in most cases put the budgets in deficit. Often, these expences are added arbitrarily; in many cases, also, the deficits are clearly unsustainable. For example, the compiler of the budgets for Pangbourne in Berkshire adds the sum of £6 19s to three of his family accounts, and £8 12s to the fourth. This resulted in annual shortfalls ranging from £5 9s 9d to £13 1s 5d. Clearly, this did not happen, or not, at least, for any length of time.[92]

The arrangements made by labouring families for supplying themselves with firing varied almost infinitely. At Stinsford, in Dorset, the poor were allowed fuel, as also rent, in consideration of the lowness of wages. At poverty-stricken Newent in Gloucestershire, "Mr. A. Foley has an annual fall of coppice, and gives the poor all the browse gratis". Nor was anything allowed at Holwell, in Somerset, where "fuel is procured by gathering cow-dung, and breaking their neighbours' hedges". Many, indeed, were the complaints of writers about labouring families who "depend for this article totally on pilfering, breaking hedges and cutting trees." In some places, fuel could still be collected or cut in the vicinity, as was the case at Barkham and Affpiddle, where fuel therefore cost a week's missed earnings, and maybe the carriage home. Elsewhere, fuel had to be bought, and the price for a year's supply could be anything from the 15s paid by the inhabitants of Pangbourne for a load of beech; to the remarkable £3 18s splashed out by a family of Sherbourne, Dorset, who appear to have stinted themselves of food in order to keep warm, and still ended up in surplus.[93]

But there is another expedient which must have been frequently resorted to, which finds little mention in the written sources – going without. In 1792, Hannah More wrote in a letter from Somerset;-

"One widow, to whom we allow a little pension, burnt her only table for firing; another one of her three chairs....No words could describe the sensations of this poor village at seeing a wagon-load of coals we sent enter the place! I feel indignation to think that so small a sum can create such feelings...."[94]

Similar considerations apply to clothing. In 1758, Joseph Massie estimated an allowance of £7 10s for "cloaths, cloth, shoes." Nine years later, Arthur Young allowed £2 10s. In his Barkham budgets of 1787 David Davies still allowed £2 10s arbitrarily to all his families, and was followed in this by several of those from around the country who compiled budgets for him; even at Newent, where wages were 4s 6d per week. In some villages, they spent more than this. In Crawley, Hampshire,, labouring families spent up to £4 2s, and the two families at Holwell in Somerset appear to have stinted themselves for food in order to be able to afford, for clothes, £5 9s 9d and £4 16s 5d respectively. The figures for Sherbourne are a little more realistic, ranging from 10s to £1 10s. But in general the size of the stated deficits makes it unlikely that the sums mentioned for clothing were actually spent on clothing. Many eye-witness accounts of the state of the poor confirm this. Hannah More constantly refers to "those starving and half-naked multitudes" in her Somerset villages; and as Rev.

---

91 David Davies. The Case of the Labourers in Husbandry. Budgets. J. Massie. Considerations relating to the Poor. P. 105. Arthur Young. Farmers Letters I. P. 195. Rev. Arthur Young. General View of the County of Sussex.

92 David Davies. The Case of the Labourers in Husbandry. P. 138.

93 Ibid. Pp. 161 and 179. Arthur Young. A Farmer's Tour through the East of England. Vol.IV. P. 309.

94 William Roberts. Memoirs of the Life and Correspondence of Hannah More. Pp. 315-6. See also E. A. Goodwyn. Selections from Norwich Newspapers. P. 100.

John Howlett described his neighbours in Dunmow in Essex, the father and mother were covered with rags, and their children without shoes or stockings.[95]

David Davies himself remarks;-

"I found our poor families very meanly clothed....And this is visibly the case of the poor in general....In fact it is but little that in the present state of things the belly can spare for the back. Even such persons as may have been provident enough, when single, to supply themselves with a small stock of clothes, are, after marriage, from inability to buy more, soon reduced to ragged garments. And then the women spend as much time in tacking their tatters together, as would serve for manufacturing new clothing...."[96]

As with fuel, clothing could be got in a number of ways. At Brington, in Northamptonshire, clothing was generally bought second-hand, and many garments were distributed amongst the womenfolk by Countess Spencer. From Affpiddle, it was reported that "clothes they get as they can, and the children go nearly naked." Going without was practised in this article also, as one family in Affpiddle appears to have sacrificed the needs of the back to those of the belly almost completely. It was an expedient resorted to habitually in Ireland, where conditions were even worse. In England, by 1790, freezing to death was a very real danger to the poor.

Despite all the shifts and expedients dreamed up by the ingenuity of labouring families, the evidence of the budgets shows that most were permanently insolvent. And these deficits would entail further serious consequences for poor families. Davies concludes, of some of his families, that "the whole amount of the annual outgoings....for rent, fuel, clothing, lying-in, and casualties, must either come out of the poor-rate, or these families must necessarily run in debt, steal, or starve."[97] Indeed, all of these things occurred.

Rising levels of lawlessness were remarked upon by writers throughout the eighteenth century. In Nottingham, for example, during the early part of the century, riots were rare, and crime sporadic, confined to a few instances of highway robbery, burglary and theft. The latter part of the century, with poorly paid workers facing constantly rising prices, saw crime, vice and drunkenness becoming more and more an everyday part of city life; and vigilante groups were formed among the more opulent citizens to combat this menace.[98]

Endemic indebtedness put poor families at the mercy of their creditors. Many artisans and miners were constantly in debt to their employers; and debts could be used as a lever to enforce, for example, systems of truck payment, even after they became illegal. In the countryside, families were often in debt to the small shopkeepers, who thus possessed an undue control over the market. In the village shops of Dorset, "the price is often increased more than 50 per cent before it reaches the consumer, who has it not in his power to complain, because he is seldom able to pay in ready money for the article he wants."[99] A correspondent to the Gentleman's Magazine in 1756 complained that in the Vale of Evesham, bakers made a practice of getting the poor into their debt, and then using the leverage which this gave them to sell bread that was sub-standard and underweight. The bakers and farmers would combine to force up the price, and as a result "all the poor in the neighbourhood have been brought into a starving condition."[100] It was the same in Hertfordshire, "deemed the first corn county

---

95 J. Massie. Considerations relating to the Poor. P. 105. Arthur Young. Farmer's Letters. Vol. I. P. 199. William Roberts. Memoirs of the Life and Correspondence of Hannah More. P. 217. Rev. J. Howlett. Examination of Mr. Pitt's Speech. 1796. P. 48.

96 David Davies. The Case of the Labourers in Husbandry. P. 28.

97 David Davies. The Case of the Labourers in Husbandry. P. 22.

98 J. D. Chambers. Nottinghamshire in the Eighteenth Century. Pp. 50, 69, and 71.

99 J. Claridge. General View of the County of Dorset. P. 25.

100 Gentleman's Magazine. Vol. 25. P. 55.

of the kingdom", where "Yorkshire bacon, generally of the worst sort, is retailed to the poor from little chandler's shops at an advanced price; bread is retailed to them in the same way."[101]

In Ireland, habitual peasant indebtedness was routinely used to deprive the labourers of their livestock and their property;[102] and there is reason to suppose that the same thing occurred at times in England. The compiler of Davies's Newent budgets, the Rev. J. Foley, complained of the "harpy clams of pettifogging attorneys, who are perpetually harassing them in county courts, and plundering them with impunity." Eden found an instance of this at Monmouth, where a labourer, renting a cottage from the corporation and not able to pay his rent, was distrained upon, and lost all his working tools and some of his furniture.[103] Probably, this went on far more than we know.

But perhaps the most pervasive effect of the insolvency of labouring families was to bring them into dependence on the parish rate, and thus under the influence of those entrusted with its administration. Here, again, the denizens of Devon were at an advantage. The poor-rates of Devon advanced only moderately when they were soaring elsewhere. About 2s in the pound was the figure over much of the county; and this was attributed to the longer survival in Devon of domestic industry, as a result of which "the working class in the vicinity of towns meet with constant employment, and at an advance of wages beyond that formerly stated."[104]

"The wool which the county produces being manufactured in private families; by men, women and children, who by this employment, are kept at their own houses, are enured to habits of industry, are enabled to support themselves at all seasons, and are always at hand to assist in the works of husbandry...."[105]

By 1808, the lack of women's work in some areas of Devon was complained of as much as anywhere else. But fifteen years previously, a good spinner could still earn 3s 6d per week.

The parish of Modbury, in Devon, might serve as an example of the situation in many other parts of the country. Here, a manufacture had established itself, attracted crowds looking for work, and then closed down and abandoned them to the overseers. In Modbury, rates were fully 5s in the pound.[106]

In England as a whole, any remnants of domestic industry were one of the factors keeping rates low. At Dunstable, where straw was being worked into hats and baskets, only eighteen families were receiving relief out of a population of a thousand families, and that as late as 1797.[107] But there were vast areas of England that were not so fortunate. The iron industry had disappeared from the Wealden woodlands of Sussex and Kent, as also from the Forest of Dean. In Wiltshire, Thomas Davis attributed the wretchedness of the country people, "above all", to "the failure of the spinning work for the women and children"; and this, in turn, resulted from the "system newly adopted, in the cloathing manufactories, of spinning the wool in the towns, by machines, which used to be done by the women and children in the villages."[108] In Norfolk, the woollen industry was being superseded by that of Yorkshire, with predictable results for the dependence of the poor on the parish rates; and throughout most of the southern Midlands, there was simply no industry at all.

---

101 R. Wells. Wretched Faces. P. 21.

102 A. Somerville. The Whistler at the Plough. See, for example, pp437-9.

103 F. M. Eden. The State of the Poor. Vol. II. P. 439.

104 W. Marshall. The Rural Economy of the West of England. Vol. I. Pp. 50 and 290. C. Vancouver. General View of the County of Devon. P. 414.

105 W. Marshall. The Rural Economy of the West of England. Vol. I. P. 50.

106 Ibid. Pp. 50 and 290.

107 F. M. Eden. The State of the Poor. Vol. II. P. 2.

108 T. Davis. General View of the County of Wiltshire. P. 154.

A glance through F. M. Eden's State of the Poor will reveal, in a general sort of way, high dependency rates in areas where manufacturing had disappeared; where it had never existed; or where the poor were reliant upon it completely. Large farms, high rents, lack of common land, and a high proportion of pasture land, also raised rates; and over much of the country, these factors were becoming more and more prevalent.

The effect of all these causes was a rapid increase of poor expenditure over most of the country from around mid-century. In earlier days, as we saw in Wigston Magna, poor relief was confined to the elderly, the sick, the injured, and the orphaned. A list of the recipients of relief drawn up by the vestry of Linton in Cambridgeshire in 1693 includes no able-bodied at all; they were all old, lame, sick, widowed, or parents with more children than they could cope with; and one idiot. It was a similar story at Bottisham as late as 1728. But as time went on, there were a growing number of payments to able-bodied persons who were clearly either unemployed or under-employed.[109] Account books from around the country show a trend of increasing payments to able-bodied men out of work. In Essex, the trend began in mid-century, and intensified during the 1770s. By the 1780s, 84 per cent of the recipients of relief were said to be adults perfectly capable of working.[110] When Rev. David Davies was writing, poor relief was already being used, not just as unemployment benefit, but as a supplement to wages which were insufficient to support life. Thus, ever-increasing numbers were being brought within the ambit of the poor laws. At Barkham, in Berkshire, out of a population of 200, forty were in receipt of relief.[111]

For the poor, the experience of the poor laws could be infinitely various. In some areas, predominantly, one suspects, where society was still organised along traditional lines, the poor law could be benevolent. In such areas, there was no huge gulf of wealth to divide officials from the poor in their charge; they would have been personally acquainted and would have considered themselves as of the same class. Here, relief could be generous and cover a wide variety of needs. Payments for rent and fuel were usual; there were grants for clothing, boots and shoes, bedding, furniture, working tools, livestock, grain and funeral expences.[112]

On the other hand, in areas where the farmers of the new agriculture were seen as the greatest oppressors of the poor, they were also, often, the overseers. Such seems to have been the case at Barkham.

"It is manifest....that the poor-rate is now in part a *substitute for wages*. And a miserable substitute it is....The distribution of it being left very much to the discretion of the overseers of the poor, who in saving the parish money save their own; and who in distributing it, do not always regard strict justice, many modest and deserving families, that cannot live entirely without relief, receive not sufficient relief from it.

"The receiving that from the parish in the precarious way of alms, which they ought to receive in wages as the reasonable recompense of labour, is a great discouragement to the industrious poor, tends to sink their minds in despondency, and drive them into desperate courses.

"How wretchedly the poor actually live with this aid."[113]

In many places, poorhouses and workhouses were in use. Here, too, standards could be highly various. Diet could be generous, as in the Exeter workhouse already mentioned; or the one in St. Botulph's, Cambridge, where there was a menu of meat, cheese, bread, oatmeal, roots and greens.

109 E. Hampson. The Treatment of Poverty in Cambridgeshire. Pp. 178-9.

110 W. A. Armstrong in Agrarian History of England and Wales. Vol. VI. Pp. 771-2.

111 David Davies. The Case of the Labourers in Husbandry. Pp. 25-7.

112 K. D. M. Snell. Annals of the Labouring Poor. P. 105. E. Hampson. The Treatment of Poverty in Cambridgeshire. P. 184.

113 David Davies. The Case of the Labourers in Husbandry. Pp. 25-7.

Where workhouses were in use for the impotent poor, this was often the case, especially after the passing of Gilbert's Act in 1782. For the increasing numbers of able-bodied paupers, workhouses, by the act of Parliament of 1723, could be established on the principle of deterrence. Such a workhouse was the one built at Bottisham in 1780, "the poor being numerous and at this time very chargeable". Payment of families' rents was ended, and applicants for relief invited to enter the house. The objective was to make conditions so harsh as to discourage the poor from requesting relief at all. This harshness might consist more in a restriction of freedom than of diet. Such was the case with the new workhouse in Cambridgeshire, which did not allow any pauper out of the house.[114] The big houses of industry established by act of Parliament in East Anglia were described by observers as 'pauper palaces', but the poor saw them as prisons; as evidenced by this open letter in a Norwich newspaper to the M. P.s for Norfolk.

"We do implore you....to stop as you easily can, that imprisonment of our persons, that separation from our children, that destruction of our race, that loss to the kingdom, and that curse from the Almighty that must attend the establishing a poor house on the specious fallacy of providing for our comfort by the breaking of our hearts."[115]

But the truly awful workhouses were those contracted out to private individuals, a practice allowed by the act of 1723 on the principle of deterrence.[116] The amount allowed per head after the taking of profits was often below subsistence level, as the Quaker poet John Scott observed in 1776.

"The weekly pittance of two shillings per head is frequently the condition of maintenance for adults and children, able and impotent together; a price considering the present rate of provisions plainly demonstrating, that unsatisfied hunger to all, and oppressive labour to many, must be the consequence....Emaciated forms, with looks of unavailing sorrow or surly discontent, people like unhappy spectres the melancholy gloom within, and watched with earnest solicitude the motions of their implacable master."

The results could be more disastrous still, when paupers were entrusted to contractors at a distance. John Scott mentioned a parish which sent paupers "near twenty miles"; and dispatched them at night "in order to elude the public observation and censure". Most were never seen again. Contractors such as these were operating over various parts of the country, and were sending out advertisements to many towns and parishes, including Royston in Cambridgeshire. It was a solution to the problem of poverty which had more adherents than the written sources might lead us to suspect.[117]

The great likelihood of pauperisation also brought the poor within the scope of the law of settlement. This law provided that any wanderer seeking work outside his native parish could be forcibly returned there whenever he or she was adjudged likely to become chargeable to the parish. This led to multitudes of cruelties and abuses. Single men did not normally become parish paupers, but as soon as they married, or, worse still, when the wife became pregnant, the overseers were often arranging for their removal. Thus, Thomas Hampson worked as a single journeyman wheelwright in Rutland. On his marriage, however, he was threatened with removal. He migrated to Royston and found work, but was nevertheless returned to Lee, the parish of his apprenticeship, where he was likely to be unemployed. Single pregnant women were also dogged by the overseers, as illegitimate children were entitled to relief in the parish of their birth; some of these women were removed actually in childbirth; deaths could result.[118] Old men were roused from their deathbeds and put in the parish cart, in order to avoid the expences of the funeral. The stories go on and on....

114 E. Hampson. The Treatment of poverty in Cambridgeshire. Pp. 81 and 107.
115 E. A. Goodwyn Ed. Selections from Norwich Newspapers. P. 136.
116 E. Hampson. The Treatment of Poverty in Cambridgeshire. P. 95.
117 J. Scott. Observations on the Present State of the Parochial and Vagrant Poor. Pp. 43 and 110n.
118 E. Hampson. The Treatment of Poverty in Cambridgeshire. P. 138.

For the poor man, the influence of the poor law on his standard of life could often be benign; more often, it was not. In either case, conditions were worsening. With prices spiralling ahead of wages, and underemployment and unemployment becoming more and more a common occurrence for the poor, the poor law was under pressure. The trend is clear from around 1780, and intensifies from the famine of 1795. As poor rates soared, overseers were expected to make savings; many types of relief were curtailed, and expedients adopted for reducing expenditure. A standard of life that depended on the poor law was a declining standard of life.

John Howlett, vicar of Dunmow in Essex, attempted to demonstrate this statistically. The total amount collected nationally for the poor in 1753, he reasoned, was £1 million. By 1776, this had risen to £1.5 million. In the same time, the collective expences of the poor rose by £5 million. The increase of wages in that time provided them with £3 million. Of the remaining £2 million, £500,000 were covered by the rise in the rates. "The want of the rest", he asserts, "gradually sunk the Poor deeper and deeper in the gulphs of poverty and wretchedness." Similarly, in the twelve years from 1776, until the time of writing, the necessary annual expences of the poor had shot up by a further £700,000. Wages had risen very little, if at all; in some manufactures, "by the iniquitous, oppressive practices of those who have the direction of them, they are at this moment considerably lower." And yet the amount distributed in poor relief had only risen by £250,000. "The rest is squeezed out of the flesh, and blood, and bones of the Poor."[119]

Howlett later wrote that the purpose of the poor law was only to prevent death by starvation, and to provide assistance during sickness. This, he said, was "generous, humane and benevolent". The poor will ask;-

"How will the poor law maintain us? Not in idleness, ease and plenty; but, as it now maintains many of my neighbours, in rags, in cold, and hunger; and, if not contented with that, it will deprive us of liberty...."[120]

But the heaviest brunt of the operation of the poor law was actually borne by the children. Being in receipt of poor relief rendered parents liable to having their children taken away, a practice highly recommended by a number of writers. A magistrate from Surrey thought that "a watchful attention to infancy and youth" was necessary in order to instil "early habits of virtuous industry, which could scarcely fail of having a sensible and happy effect on the morals of the rising generation." To this end, given that poor children were likely to learn evil ways "from their necessitous, negligent and perhaps wicked parents", infants should "be totally removed from them at a very tender age; certainly not later than ten."

"The children of all persons chargeable to a parish, or themselves chargeable, are compellable to be bound apprentice, to learn husbandry, housewifery, or such trades or manufactures as they are most fit for....Parents who are particularly attentive to bring up their children in habits of virtue and industry; such may be trusted with them longer, but they can scarcely be taken too soon from the idle and dissolute. The law permits children to be taken from their parents after seven years of age; but in practice, from nine to ten will probably be the common age of binding; after ten, it should be a reproach to a parish to have any of their poor infants unapprenticed."[121]

It was the use of the workhouse which enabled magistrates to decide how many children should be left with their parents, and how many taken away. Thus, children came to form an ever-increasing proportion of the inhabitants of workhouses. In 1774, Royston workhouse contained 14 children

---

119 J. Howlett. The Insufficiency of the Causes to which the Increase of the Poor Rates has been at-tributed. Pp. 63-8.
120 J. Howlett. An Examination of Mr. Pitt's Speech. Pp. 6-7.
121 W. Godschall. A General Plan of Parochial and Provincial Police. P. 6-7 and 21-2.

out of 26 inmates; there were 21 children in there the next year. By 1790, at Bottisham, also in Cambridgeshire, nine out of ten inmates were boys.[122]

Conditions could be bleak, or worse than bleak. The investigations of Jonas Hanway in London uncovered workhouses from which not a single child survived over periods of many years. Death rates of 90 per cent were usual. Of the younger children, Hanway wrote;-

"A great many poor infants and exposed bastard children are inhumanely suffered to die by the barbarity of nurses, especially parish nurses, who are a sort of people void of commiseration or religion, hired by the churchwardens to take off a burthen from the parish at the cheapest and easiest rates they can; and these know the manner of doing it effectually, as by the burial books may evidently appear."[123]

John Scott mentions two "female wretches", by the names of Metyard and Brownrigg, who "in the years 1762 and 1767 starved and tortured to death innocent children committed to their care as apprentices by the parish."

At times, the workhouse seems to have been an accepted and organised method of disposing of infants, whose maintenance costs the overseers were not prepared to allow to their parents. It was, indeed, a fine line between deliberate murder, and the exposure of people to the conditions of a workhouse; the results of which might be viewed "with secret complacence", accelerating with impunity "the removal of a burthen, to which the shoulder of avarice had ever submitted with evident reluctance."[124]

Children who survived to the age of seven were compulsorily apprenticed out. A fortunate placing with a good master was no doubt the saving, or even making, of many children. But good masters willing to take pauper apprentices were not so easy to find; and the consequence could be not only ill-treatment, but a pointless servitude in an unskilled trade, perhaps right up until the age of 24.

Some workhouses sent children away in batches, as apprentices to large mills or factories. The workhouse of Exeter placed advertisements in newspapers to the effect that batches of children were available for manufacturing apprenticeships; and a group of 40 or 50 boys and girls was sent to Twerton Mill near Bath, the property of Messrs. Bamford and Co. Another batch of 30, with an average age of nine, also ended up in Twerton. In a few cases, parents unsurprisingly objected to this process, and attempted to keep their children at home. This was countered by the withdrawal of parish relief, which in at least one case brought about the acquiescence of the parent. Exeter workhouse took an active interest in the subsequent welfare of its pauper apprentices, and sent inspectors to those factories within reasonable travelling distance.[125] But many children travelled much further. Apprentices from Devon and East Anglia were sought after by the new factories of the Midlands and the north, as these children would already have experience of cloth manufacture. From London, too, many pauper children were sent northwards.

Robert Blincoe was deserted by his parents in infancy, and was brought up in the workhouse at St. Pancras. There, he was "well fed, decently clad, and comfortably lodged, and not at all overdone as regards work." But in 1799, he was one of 80 children apprenticed to Lowdham Mill in Nottingham. In the mill, hours were long - from fourteen to sixteen a day; discipline was liberally enforced with horse-whips; and diet consisted of milk porridge, rye bread, potatoes and salt. However, treatment here was relatively humane – only one apprentice was injured permanently. When the mill closed down, most of the apprentices moved to Litton Mill, near Tideswell in Derbyshire. Here, callousness was exchanged for sadism. Mr. Ellice Needham employed 160 boys. The diet was so bad that the

122   E. Hampson. The Treatment of Poverty in Cambridgeshire. Pp. 88 and 115.
123   John H. Hutchins. Jonas Hanway. Pp.48-51 and 57.
124   J. Scott. Observations on the Present State of the Parochial and Vagrant Poor. Pp. 43 and 38.
125   W. G. Hoskins. Industry, Trade and People in Exeter 1688-1800. P. 156.

boys stole food from the pigs. Epidemics raged in the prentice house, and boys were driven till they dropped. So many died, that Needham was obliged to make use of several cemeteries[126].

The factory system was based on child labour; largely on bonded child labour. Water-powered mills were located by streams, and young workers brought in from the urban workhouses in vast numbers. These were put to work on machines that required neither strength nor skill, and were almost certainly developed with the express intention of exploiting the reserve of child pauper labour. Both boys and girls could be put to work as early as age five or six. Their hours would begin at five or six o'clock in the morning, and work would go on until about seven or eight at night. The temperatures inside the mills ranged from 75 to 85 degrees F. Discipline was brutal. Not surprisingly, the cotton mills were notorious for epidemics, like the putrid fever that raged at Radcliffe in 1784. These were hushed up as far as possible. But the situation was so serious as to bring forth complaints from magistrates in 1784 and 1796.

The elder Sir Robert Peel was himself a mill-owner. Understandably, he rarely visited his workforce, but, when he did, "was struck with the uniform appearance of bad health, and in many cases, stunted growth of the children; the hours of work were regulated by the interest of the overseer, whose remuneration depending on the quantity of work done, he was often induced to make the poor children work excessive hours."

Factory children in England worked longer hours than the adult slaves on the sugar plantations of the West Indies.[127]

This situation was brought about directly by the transformation of the rural communities into a proletariat; the taking away of their economic independence; their resulting impoverishment; their dependence on parish relief; and their insolvency. Labour was not "freed from farming"; the idea, put forward by Karl Marx that factories liberated people from the "idiocy of rural life" is, itself, idiotic; or worse than idiotic. People were driven into the factories by a combination of coercion and the fear of starvation. In the early years of the factory system, parents would refuse to allow their children into the mills; but as adult wages declined, it became a matter of survival. Vital parish relief could be made conditional upon children being sent to work, and some millowners would only employ adults if they brought their children. The country over, parents relying on the poor rates had limited scope for resistance when the overseer came to take their children.

When Hannah More and her sister visited the mining villages of Shipham and Rowberrow in Somerset, with a view to instituting their good works, they found the people "savage and depraved.... They began by suspecting we should make our fortune by selling their children as slaves."[128] This suspicion, it seems likely, was not so much the result of savageness and depravity, as of bitter experience.

Reviewing the social history of these years, one of the aspects which most forcibly intrudes itself upon the attention is the almost infinite variety of experience undergone by people in different districts and at different times. A great divergence of experience can be traced even within relatively small geographical areas or historical timescales. Nevertheless, the conclusion seems inescapable that for overwhelming numbers of ordinary folk conditions had been deteriorating for many years, and by 1790 represented a state of serious deprivation. We might find wages higher in one area than another; varying levels of employment; agriculture and poor relief conducted more or less paternalistically;

126 J. B. Firth. Highways and Byways in Nottinghamshire. Pp.168-171.
127 J. L. and B. Hammond. The Town Labourer. Pp. 144-60.
128 Martha More. Mendip Annals. P. 27.

cottages appalling or comfortable; a greater or lesser availability of fuel; cow-pastures or none; potato gardens or none; etc. etc. But this great variety of experience, though it has been used thus by some historians, does not conceal the trend, which is clear.

"For a long time now their condition has been going from bad to worse continually. Small indeed is the portion of worldly comforts now left them."[129]

Contemporary eye-witness accounts of the state of the poor confirm what we would otherwise expect.

The deterioration in the physical condition of the poor was noted by many writers. Thomas Davis was a land steward in Wiltshire. He reported to the Board of Agriculture in 1794.

"The farmers complain and with reason, that the labourers do less work than formerly; when, in fact, the labourers are not able to work as they did, at a time when they lived better."

The impeded development of poor children was frequently adverted to. At Holwell, in Somerset, it was said that the children were "of the diminutive kind." And even so renowned an authority as Malthus so far departed from orthodoxy as to observe;-

"The sons and daughters of peasants will not be found such rosy cherubs in real life, as they are described to be in romances. It cannot fail to be remarked by those who live much in the country, that the sons of labourers are very apt to be stunted in their growth, and are a long while coming at maturity. Boys that you would guess to be 14 or 15 are, upon enquiry, frequently found to be 18 or 19."

This physical deterioration extended to their health. It might be expected that the forcing of a large proportion of the population into urban and industrial occupations would have a damaging effect on health, and so it was. J. H. Campbell, quoted earlier, wrote from Preston of those who "work in air contaminated both by the exhalation and breathing of many people together, and also the effluvia of the material used, in confined places; and….perhaps living but poorly in diet, these people are frequently visited, especially in autumn and beginning of winter, with low and nervous fevers, in short, putrid and gaol distempers, that often cuts off men, leaving families behind."[130] Mining was taking a greater toll on the health of its workforce, ironically because of technological progress. Earlier writers all commend the rude health of the Cornish tin-miner – until, that is, the advent of the steam engine, which enabled much deeper seams to be exploited. From then on, those who went below ground were observed to become pale and stunted; to lose their appetite; and many to die from a sort of slow starvation. On average, they did not live beyond 40, and Cornish mining communities came to contain many widows, but no widowers.[131] In the coal mines, the introduction of the Davy lamp had a similar effect, by enabling operations to take place deeper underground. This involved more danger, more accidents, working at higher temperatures, and resulting painful ailments. Coal-miners were already old at 40, and not able to work past 50.[132]

In the larger towns and cities the country over, disease was rife and mortality high. In Exeter, in 1800, the average family size was kept down to 4.4 because of an excessive death rate; and in Plymouth and the smaller woollen towns of the south-west, the situation was even worse.[133]

But even in the countryside, disease and epidemics were becoming more and more commonplace. Writing about Devon in 1808, Vancouver noted the healthfulness and longevity of the peasant class, which he attributed to "the regularity and exercise necessarily connected with rural life."[134] But in

---

129 D. Davies. The Case of the Labourers in Husbandry. P. 40.
130 Arthur Young ed.. Annals of Agriculture. 1791. P. 564.
131 A. K. Hamilton-Jenkins. The Cornish Miner. Pp. 251 and 259-62.
132 J. L. and B. Hammond. The Town Labourer. Pp. 25 and 35.
133 W. G. Hoskins. Industry, Trade and People in Exeter 1688-1800. P. 129.
134 C. Vancouver. General View of the Count of Devon. Pp. 404-16.

this respect also Devon was a better county to live in than many others. In neighbouring Somerset, Hannah and Martha More encountered a very different situation. In a mining parish, in the winter of 1791, 18 people died from putrid fever. At Congresbury, Martha reported that "sickness and death had considerably reduced the size of the school for the present." Smallpox was implicated, and it was also smallpox that was spreading through the population of Nailsea in March 1794.[135] Hannah herself wrote in 1792 about the village of Shipham.

"Our village of Shipham has suffered dreadfully from a raging fever – we lost seven in two days, several of them our poor children. Figure to yourself such a visitation in a place where a single cup of broth cannot be obtained; for there is none to give if it would save a life."[136]

That this situation might not have been exceptional is demonstrated by the records of Wigston Magna, where outbreaks of typhus and smallpox, and a run of unhealthful years between 1760 and 1799 produced a far higher death rate than normal. From around 200 families, there were 74 burials in 1766, 64 in 1767, 45 in 1768, and 60 in 1769.[137]

The writers on cottages all put down the unhealthfulness of villagers to the badness of their housing. Nathaniel Kent condemned the poor accommodation which "led to illness, especially agues; which more frequently visit cottage children than any others, and early shake their constitution."[138]

Even when not disease-ridden, the poor by 1790 were in a terrible state. David Davies speaks of "the starving condition in which we now see them." Hannah More was shocked at discovering "a very large village containing incredible multitudes of poor….among more want, misery and ignorance than any I had supposed to exist." And she and her sister often refer to "these starving and half-naked multitudes" in their Somerset villages.[139] The vicar of Dunmow in Essex, the Rev. John Howlett, wrote in a similar vein about his parishioners and neighbours.

"It is evident that for the past 40 or 50 years, some particularly favoured spots excepted, their condition has been growing worse and worse, and is, at length, become truly deplorable. Those pale famished countenances, those tattered garments, and those naked shivering limbs, we so frequently behold, are striking testimonies of these melancholy truths."[140]

And so they were; and such was the miserable and deteriorating state of our ancestors, just a few generations back, even before the onset of the famines….

Near the end of the 18th century there occurred in England two periods of something we are quite accustomed to today – eccentric weather. The first began in the summer of 1794, when there was a long drought and extreme heat. Constant sunshine ripened the crops quickly, and led to an early harvest. Quality was good, but yield was down on a normal year by about 10 or 15 per cent. Yields of oats and barley were also down.[141]

---

135 Martha More. Mendip Annals. Pp. 80, 102, 105, and 246.

136 William Roberts. Memoirs of the Life and Correspondence of Hannah More. P.315.

137 W. G. Hoskins. The Population of an English Village in Transactions of the Leicestershire Archaeological Society. 1957. P. 30.

138 N. Kent. Hints to Gentlemen of Landed Property. P. 207.

139 David Davies. The Case of the Labourers in Husbandry. P. 103. William Roberts. Memoirs of the Life and Correspondence of Hannah More. Pp. 178, 189 and 217. Martha More. Mendip Annals P. 65.

140 J. Howlett. An Examination of Mr. Pitt's Speech. P. 2.

141 Most of this section, except where otherwise stated, is closely based on R. Wells. Wretched Faces. Pp. 1-74.

The winter which followed is said to have been the third hardest of the century, with temperatures mostly below freezing from December until March, and heavy snowfalls. Periodically, in some areas temperatures rose for a while, melted the snow, and caused flooding. The wheat, which is mainly sown in the autumn, was in some places completely destroyed, in others only partly. Much had to be ploughed in and resown. The spring of 1795 was every farmer's nightmare – cold and dry, with frosts persisting right up until June, which impeded the development of whatever crops had survived, and led to a yield of about three-quarters of what was normally expected.

Conditions in 1796, 1797 and 1798 were normal, and supplies of corn were reasonable. But in 1799 there occurred another sterile spring, cold and dry, in which nothing grew. There were frosts in June and early July; then there occurred a change, from cold and dry to cold and wet. By the middle of August, there were floods, the like of which some had never seen before. Whenever the rain relented, there were attempts to get in crops, in some places unripe and standing in water, in others wind-damaged and flattened. Unsurprisingly, threshers had great difficulty getting the grains out from the ears.

Thus, the sowing season for the 1800 crop was wiped out; in Somerset, "farmers complained that they could not sow wheat" as the land was "so full of water." In many areas, wheat could not be grown this year, or else was sown as late as December, producing a thin and deficient crop. This then had to cope with a drought during the summer of 1800, which was enough to ruin the crops of turnips, hops and potatoes. But just as the good harvesting weather was leading to anticipations of a reasonable crop, the heavens opened, and storms ensued so violent that some were still recalled many years later. Damage caused by the deluge compounded all the ills already being suffered by the crops, and resulted in a yield shortfall of about 20 per cent.

The consequence was as may be expected – food prices rocketed. In Exeter, from 1794 into 1795, half a peck of bread averaged 1s 3d. By the spring of 1796 it was 1s 6d. Although prices fell between the two famines, they did not go back down to their previous levels; price pressure was cumulative. The half-peck loaf averaged 11d between 1796 and 1798. With the poor harvest of 1799, it shot up to 1s 7d; the following year it sold at 2s 7½d, which would have been out of the reach of a large proportion of ordinary families. Other prices rose in sympathy. There was a big shortfall in the amount of milk, cheese, butter, and meat, especially bacon, for sale in the markets. In Exeter, meat reached 10d per pound, and butter 1s 8d. The potato crop was seriously damaged by the drought of 1800, and in Exeter potatoes were selling for 2s per peck, and those of the poorest quality.[142] There were even brief periods when stocks of wheat were exhausted completely, during the summer of 1795, for example; when it was said at Stourbridge that bread could not be bought at any price. In September and October 1800 supplies were near exhaustion in Birmingham, Northampton, and many other towns of the Midlands and north.

The effect of all this, on a population already chronically under-nourished, and poorly clothed and housed, can only be imagined. The second famine was much worse than the first. In a respected series of real wage calculations, ranging from 1541 to 1871, the year from 1799 to 1800 was the seventh hardest year, and from 1800 to 1801 the fourth hardest. As a two year famine, it is said to be the worst subsistence crisis since the mid-16th century. But given the massive proletarianisation that had taken place over those centuries; the removal of the workforce from the means of production; and what we know about the vastly increased dependence on wage-labour and retail markets for subsistence, it seems probable that to find a worse time one would have to look forwards into the 19th century, rather than back into the 16th. It is undoubtedly true that two consecutive years of famine bite more than twice as hard as one, because of the lack of stocks of grain held over to fall back upon. And our ancestors living at the end of the 18th century had two such periods to struggle through, with

142 W. G. Hoskins. Industry, Trade and People in Exeter 1688-1800. Pp. 146-8.

only three average years to separate them. Nevertheless, it seems justifiable to view the pronounced susceptibility of the population to famine manifested at the end of the 18th century as something new – yet another aspect of that vulnerability which is the subject of this chapter. We have already noted Dr. Price, writing in 1792, of the much greater impact which scarcity and high prices had in his day, than previously.

"In the year 1697, wheat was at 31s a quarter, and other grain proportionably dear. At present.... (even) when wheat is below that price....there is an alarm, the poor are starving....The high price of bread was not, at the time I have mentioned, of essential consequence to the lower people, because they could live more upon other food, which was then cheap, and because also being more generally occupiers of land, they were less under a necessity of purchasing bread. Whereas now, being forced by greater difficulties, and the high price of all other food, to live solely or principally on bread, if that is not cheap, they are rendered incapable of maintaining themselves."[143]

Susceptibility to famine was a characteristic of the dependent wage-labourer.

It is true that Price was writing before the nightmares of 1794-1801; but it is also demonstrable that those country folk who retained some connection with the land could see themselves safely and independently through the successive crises. The General Report on Enclosures commented favourably on the Earl of Winchilsea's project for enabling cottagers to keep cows.

"Where the system was established, there poor-rates did not rise on account of the scarcities; the poor thus favoured receiving no more from the parish than in common times, that is to say, nothing!"

Many of the poor thus favoured lived in Lincolnshire and Rutland. There, the Report mentions a group of 48 parishes, where 753 cottagers kept between them 1195 cows.

"Not one of them receives anything from the parish! Nor did, even in the late scarcities."

No doubt examples can be found from around the country. At Mayfield, in Sussex, a family who had been dependent on poor relief during normal times, from being given a cow by the parish, managed to stand on their own feet throughout the famines.[144] At Chatteris, in Cambridgeshire, in 1800, Arthur Young found 100 small cottages built upon the common, none of the occupiers of which received poor relief. Similarly, at Aldershot, cottagers settled on the common with two acres each, and pigs and cows, not only remained independent, but actually contributed to the rates.[145]

However, unfortunately for them, most of the poor were not thus favoured. And for them the consequences of the famines were dire. Without any noticeable rise in wages to offset the spiralling costs of living, labourers' incomes became, progressively, insufficient to purchase subsistence; and then insufficient to purchase even the cereal element of their diets. There obviously resulted a necessity of reducing still further their standards of nutrition, and of resorting to what are euphemistically termed substitutes. F. M. Eden noticed this process at Clyst St. George in Devon in 1797.

"No labourer can at present maintain himself, his wife and children on his earnings. All have relief from the parish, or corn at a reduced rate. Before the war, bread and cheese was their food, and meat twice a week. Now barley bread and no meat. They make great use of potatoes."[146]

In Lincolnshire, where bacon still formed around a quarter of the diet of the people, it was first reduced, then gone without completely. In Hampshire, workers were said to spend the whole of their earnings and allowance on bread alone. Around St. Austell in Cornwall, "People live entirely on Barley, it is the Expence of their Whole Wages to get it alone."

143 R. Price. Observations on Reversionary Payments. 1792 ed. Vol. II. Pp. 274n. and 284-5.
144 Board of Agriculture. General Report on Enclosures. Pp. 15 and 164-5.
145 G. E. Mingay. Arthur Young and his Times. P. 127.
146 F. M. Eden. The State of the Poor. Vol. II. P. 173.

Further sacrifices had to be made. Very often the first step was to substitute barley for wheat. It was not only the manufacturers of Glamorgan who were "reduced to the necessity of making bread of barley", as similar reports came from around the country. This might have worked during the famine of 1794 to 1796, as barley was relatively plentiful. But throughout the second famine it was as scarce and as damaged as wheat, and the price of it rose even faster.

At this time, a clergyman from Catterick reported that;-

"The poor lived upon barley bread as long as there was any, and some few upon oat bread; Peas are much used, and also dry'd Herrings with potatoes or even turnips as a substitute for meat."

But during the second famine, even potatoes and turnips were in short supply and of poor quality as a result of the drought of 1800. In Somerset, at East Brent, labourers resorted to boiled horse beans and salt, whilst at Over Stowey a donation of pease for boiling brought together large crowds of hungry poor.

Stinging nettles, which were already being eaten with salt and pepper in Staffordshire in 1795, became a common foodstuff in 1800. In Oldham market, they fetched 2d per pound.

Making ends meet must, for many, have been a low priority when it became a question of staying alive. In any case, it was impossible. There was no expedient that did not result in insolvency. Craftsmen in Yorkshire, during the first famine, could afford to live on oats, but not on wheat. But farmworkers on the same diet were already incurring a deficit of 1s weekly. By the time of the second famine, even the craftsmen were in deficiency to the tune of £6 9s 3d annually. Elsewhere, the story was the same. On a Wheat diet, during the first famine, the average weekly deficiency in Sussex was around 1s 9d, and in Norfolk around 1s 6d. By 1800, Norfolk families, having substituted barley for wheat, were running up an annual deficit over £6. In Yorkshire, the poorest diet led to a weekly deficiency around 3s 6d, and in Sussex around 2s 9d. In 1801, the situation deteriorated still further, and weekly deficiencies shot up to 4s 6d in Yorkshire, 4s 3d in Norfolk, and 5s 6d in Sussex. Compared to the levels of wages at the time, these were astronomical sums.

Amounts distributed in the form of poor relief soared of course, but were still far from adequate; as is shown by the common practice of families pawning, for money with which to survive, their household goods, their furniture, their bed linen, their clothes, or anything they could get their hands on. During the second famine, in Staffordshire, "many dragged on a miserable existence by pawning everything about them….even to the very Bed they lay upon, to satisfy their hunger". At Oldham, "a Deal of families have sold their household Goods to exist." Of the manufacturers of Derbyshire it was reported in September 1800 that "their children were as naked as well themselves, and that they had neither money nor credit to purchase them clothing against the winter". In the towns and industrial villages, "thousands dressed in shreds during the day went home to forlorn beds, without linen, and covered only with rags." Of the riotous crowds on the streets of London in September 1800, more than half were said to be "poor women, without cloaks or bonnets, some with scarcely clothes to cover them."

The extreme seriousness of the situation is demonstrated by the fact that families on larger incomes and higher up the social scale were also in severe distress. Even highly paid workers, like the skilled metal workers of the north of England, though remaining on a diet that would have been the envy of many, could only maintain their living standards by becoming increasingly indebted to wealthy employers. Many others fared not so well. In 1800, even the clerks of the Home Office complained of being "deprived of the means of support which our situation formerly allowed us." In 1797, at Bradford in Wiltshire, Eden came across a vestry clerk whose income was nearly 20s per week. Nearly the whole of this was spent on food, over three quarters of it on bread. Even he found it very difficult to afford clothes for his family. "It is therefore not to be wondered at," remarks Eden, "that a labourer, who with 8s or 9s a week endeavours to maintain a large family upon bread, should be often half-starved and half-naked."[147] Many, even among the middle classes, were in worse straits still. During the second famine, at Plympton in Devon, half of the recipients of poor relief were self-employed craftsmen, and included a blacksmith, a tailor, a carpenter, a thatcher and three shoemakers. Many middle class folk in the north of England were to be found in the queues at soup kitchens. And at Exeter, in March 1801, "the middle ranks of townspeople are considered proper objects" for food aid.

It was reported in Holborn in London that "not only the lower, but even the Middle Classes of Society, who have hitherto lived in Respectability, feel severely the complicated evil and can scarcely bare the Pressure of the Times."

Many even of the middle classes, the country over, were being forced to subsist on barley alone.

With so many families, so considerable a way up the social scale, being compelled to expend their entire budgets on food alone, there was simply nothing left to spend on services and manufactured goods; and the distress thus spread to tradesmen of all sorts, and even master manufacturers. The collapse of the home market, even at a time of buoyant foreign demand, proved disastrous; and the depths of a recession coincided with the highest point of the food price spiral. Demand for labour of all sorts plummeted. In 1795, in the Midland hosiery trade, there began an attempt to regain demand from the impoverished middle classes, by producing cheap hose known as cut-ups; and the increasing popularity of these over the years began a drastic and long-term decline in the fortunes of the framework-knitters. During the later stages of the second famine, the manufacturing towns and industrial villages of England were among the grimmest places to be.

The alarming physical state of the poor became of great concern to writers and observers. Begging, that bugbear of writers throughout the 18th century, reached heights never before known. The inhabitants of Birmingham witnessed an influx of beggars; whilst Earl Fitzwilliam reported from Northamptonshire in September 1800 that;-

"Never was there such a number of industrious persons begging and seeking work in every district. I find it so in this county. I found it so in a still greater degree when I was lately in Yorkshire."

Scavenging became a way of life. At Wolverhampton, children rummaged for potato peelings on the dunghill; and at Manchester they competed with the dogs for the offal thrown from the kitchens of the rich.

Most striking was the decline in the physical condition of the people.

"It is with very great concern that I state the poor are in a very weakly condition", commented a diarist at Oldham in 1800. The word starvation was on everybody's lips. The same Oldham diarist wrote of "the poor in a most shocking situation – a great deal are starving for bread." In Leicester, centre of the framework-knitting industry, innumerable requests for poor relief were received from "emaciated poor half-starved objects of pity." Of the poor in her Buckinghamshire village, a Mrs. Freemantle wrote;-

"Some are truly starving and look the picture of death."

The children, of course, were of particular concern. A magistrate from Birmingham reported that "many Thousands, especially children, are all but starved." At Poole, in Dorset, the question was put;-

"Can you behold your Littell one hanging on there weeping mother's Necks Lamenting and Mourning for bread".

Even the Cabinet in London were aware of the situation, having been informed by the President of the Board of Trade;-

---

147 F. M. Eden. The State of the Poor. Vol. II. P. 784. But Eden attributes the poverty to the extravagance of eating bread!!!

"The people are nearly starving for want of food, and in the approaching winter are likely to starve also for want of raiment."

Fears of dying by starvation were voiced frequently. Manufacturers in Warwickshire were said to be "dying by inches"; the poor of Devon were likewise said to deserve "a more honourable death than to be starved alive." But it was, and is, a commonplace, both among contemporary writers, and among modern historians, that actual deaths from starvation were relatively rare. That it happened cannot be questioned. Contemporaries asserted that, in general, it could not happen, because the poor laws prevented it. And it is undoubtedly true that the few victims of starvation that we can identify for certain were mostly wanderers away from their parish of settlement. Thus, we know of a stranger in Oldham who "died in a stable….supposed…. in Consequence of the want of Bread"; and of a vagrant who, according to a coroner's jury, dropped dead from starvation in a street in Birmingham; and of a woman who died at Barning in Kent, not settled there, and prevented from returning to her own parish by peculiar circumstances. But the line pursued by the modern historian of the famines is that though mortality rates shot up, most of the deaths occurred from famine-related disease rather than from famine itself. The number of deaths occurring in 1795 was six per cent up on previous years. It was also up in 1800; but rocketed in the three years following. Delayed mortality caused by hunger-induced disease seems to be a feature of famines in general.

A series of epidemical years began from the time of the second famine, which was particularly remarked upon in the industrial centres. The Oldham diarist recorded;-

"Fever is verey prevalent all over the County….it Ended the miseries of many a poor creature." Many of the poor creatures were his neighbours; he knew them; recorded their names; and ascribed their deaths to debilitation arising from long undernourishment.

A local newspaper reported on the fever raging in Sheffield.

"The Poor are perishing in almost every manufacturing town in the kingdom, by a fatal and infectious fever."

In Manchester, doctors attributed the outbreaks to malnutrition, poor housing and over-crowding.

"Fevers are found to prevail most wherever families have been crowded together in small rooms, and especially where there is not a sufficiency of beds and bed covering." Impoverished immigrants were most at risk, "thrust into damp and dismal cellars"; so too, unsurprisingly, were child labourers in the factories, weakened by poor diet and inappropriate hours of work.

Much of the sickness was probably typhus. It was to be found in London. It was to be found in all the industrial centres of the Midlands and north. It was to be found also in the country, notably in the west of England. People died from it in Somerset; but generally survived it, apparently, in Devon.

But death by actual starvation must also have been far more common than we know, affecting not just the occasional unfortunate wanderer. Such deaths were reported. Doctors feared for the lives of many starving inhabitants of the industrial villages of Staffordshire, and confirmed that one "whole family was absolutely perishing from want." In London, in November 1800, it was claimed that 140 people had starved to death in a year. In Yorkshire, a cleric included in his acreage return that starvation had condemned "several to an untimely sepulchre." In Boston, "no less than 18 Died from hunger" in the autumn of 1800.

The grim reaper works in many ways, and it seems unreasonable to dismiss the significance of these reports. Rather, they are likely to be the rare manifestations of something that was happening on a much greater scale than we know. It is hardly to be expected that the cause of deaths by actual starvation should be conscientiously recorded by those, or by the friends of those, whose legal obligation it was to prevent that very thing; or who had a care for the tranquillity of the parishes in which they lived, whose inhabitants were likely to be highly alarmed by such reports.

"An article in the London general bill of mortality...'starved' is an expression which must strike with horror every ear, to which custom has not rendered it familiar."

John Scott, Quaker and poet, in a pamphlet published in 1773, dealt with this very subject.

"The proportion of ten or twenty individuals, who possibly may perish in a year for want of necessaries, to the multitudes perishing for other and inevitable causes, are too inconsiderable to call for censure on the conduct of a whole community. These few individuals, nevertheless, are every one too many; and from the known defects of our parochial registers of mortality, there is reason to suspect that more really die of famine than those who are found dead in the streets; yet such only, it is presumed, are ranked under the article in question; this article also is confined to one city of an extensive and populous nation.

"These records are computed, not from the report of the attending physician or apothecary, but from that of two ignorant females commonly called Searchers. To judge from these accounts, it might be supposed convulsions were the principal endemic of England....The pulmonic consumption is represented as the next most powerful destroyer, though, under that article, may probably be placed a very great number of deaths occasioned by disorders essentially different, and probably many produced by filthiness and hunger."[148]

The implementation of the poor laws, Scott points out, did not always and necessarily prevent death by actual starvation.

"There are, indeed, advocates for avarice, who....will assert with confidence, that, 'if any suffer want, the fault is their own; since all have settlements, and might, (if they would) be provided for'."

But all did not have settlements; and among them the Irish, the Scots, and immigrants of all kinds. Even if resident in his or her own parish, a distressed person must apply for relief to a parish officer, who, "perhaps from natural obduracy, perhaps from inattention, or private pique, refuses to relieve....To summon the overseer before the justice, is to commit an insult, for which pardon must never be expected; the word of a wealthy farmer, or tradesman, is of greater validity, than the oath of a friendless mendicant; who is represented as neither needing or meriting assistance, and therefore dismissed to nakedness and hunger, with an abusive joke or aggravating reprimand. Thus, starving at home, or wandering forth to punishable beggary, becomes the dreadful alternative."[149]

In the last resort, we will probably never know the full extent of the sufferings undergone by our ancestors during these years, barely more than two centuries ago. Observers and writers on the poor were often very cagey about committing the extremities of their distress to the printed page.

"The miseries of the poor I am unable to describe." This from Oldham in 1800.[150]

"It is impossible to describe the condition of the poor cottagers, of which I was too often the melancholy spectator." This from Somerset already in 1792.[151]

Thomas Davis, reviewing Wiltshire for the Board of Agriculture in 1794, thought it unnecessary to go into detail on the subject.

"It is a melancholy fact, that....the labourers of many parts of this county....may be truly said to be at this time in a wretched situation....There is no necessity of heightening this melancholy picture, every landholder of the county knows it too well; and the resident magistrates have it daily in their view."[152]

References such as these could be multiplied.

---

148 J. Scott. Observations on the Present State of the Parochial and Vagrant Poor. Pp. 5-8 and n.
149 Ibid. Pp. 9-13 and 17-8.
150 R. Wells. Wretched Faces. P. 66.
151 John Wood. A Series of Plans for Cottages. P. 2.
152 Thomas Davis. General View of the County of Wiltshire. P. 155.

But at least Davis mentioned the subject. Many of the Board's reviewers devote scarcely more than a few lines to the state of the poor, those who worked the land, telling us little other than the rate of wages and the price of provisions; whilst devoting lengthy chapters to each of the species of agricultural livestock.

Quite apart from the reluctance of writers to describe what was distasteful and unpleasant to be brought to mind, the realistic discussion of the poor became something of a taboo during the 1790s, as we shall see, and it became increasingly difficult to collect information; as all the researchers found.

The family budgets published by David Davies represent a very tiny yield on the large number of requests for information sent out.

"Returns sent out to every county – very few filled out."[153]

The committee on high prices that sat in 1800 under the chairmanship of Dudley Ryder sent out requests to 1845 parishes for information about the wheat crop. From all these parishes, at the height of the second famine, only 31 clergy thought fit to return information about the poor.[154]

In 1800, Arthur Young initiated a study of the effects of over 140 parliamentary enclosures. The aspects enquired into included the production of human food, population, the poor rate, and the situation and comforts of the poor.

"In great numbers", comments Young, "the last article was not to be ascertained; in some, from the enclosure having taken place long ago; in others, from the want of knowledge in my informants; and for other reasons." The "other reasons", of course, are the most interesting.[155]

It was a similar story when F. M. Eden visited the city of Durham in 1797, where the poor were chiefly engaged in the woollen trade; he found prices very high, and wages so low as to bear no proportion to them. "There was so general a reluctance in this city to communicate any information respecting the Poor….the Poor here appear to be very numerous and very necessitous."[156] What privations and miseries were being undergone by the good people of Durham, so severe that the authorities there were unwilling to discuss them, must be left to us, only to surmise and imagine.

But if contemporaries were understandably touchy on this subject, so, too, are many of the historians of our own day. The era of the so-called agricultural and industrial revolutions is portrayed as the beginning of a new age, in which the endemic poverty and suffering, assumed to be inseparable from the past, are supposed to have been overcome by the capitalist system, by technological advance, or by government intervention, whichever happens to be the view. And this leads on to the golden age of prosperity for all in which we are now living. That, starting from a position of relative well-being, a long-term and drastic decline in the conditions of life should take place, affecting the bulk of the people of this country, and leading to extreme distress, and even deaths by actual starvation, does not sit very happily with this scenario. It is an uncomfortable truth.

We will leave the fate of the ordinary man here, and return to him later.

Suffice it, for now, to say that his condition continued to worsen for many years to come, as successive periods of boom and bust, periods of rising prices alternating with times of spiralling unemployment, ratcheted up his distresses and his despair to ever greater heights. For that is what happened in the Age of Improvement.

---

153 David Davies. The Case of the Labourers in Husbandry. P. 7.
154 Board of Agriculture. General Report on Enclosures. P. 13.
155 G. E. Mingay. Arthur Young and his Times. P. 135.
156 F. M. Eden. The State of the Poor. Vol. II. P. 155.

The Elephant on the Sofa
Part One

The causes of poverty and the emergence of an establishment viewpoint

Few evils so universal, but some individuals are benefited thereby, who carefully hide the true causes of the calamity to continue their profits....such undoubtedly will use every pretence, every art, to preserve to themselves the source of their opulence; every means will be taken to divert the attention of the publick from the cause; the records of past ages will be ransacked and misrepresented, the reason will be laid sometimes on one, then on another, often on complicated circumstances. Michael Combrune. An Enquiry into the Prices of Wheat, Malt, etc. 1768.

The great deterioration in the conditions of life in England during these years might be said to be the salient feature of the age. Yet in the literature of the period, at least up until the subject became a political issue in the 1790s, the subject was very little discussed, *per se*. Very few writers set out with the objective of analysing the circumstances of the poor, or of producing rational explanations for their suffering, based on the social and economic circumstances in which they found themselves. Joseph Massie, John Scott and David Davies are all glaring exceptions to this rule, and have all been quoted from already.

Nevertheless, the causes of poverty came to play a prominent part in discussions of related subjects, which occupied the concerns of the chattering classes rather more. One of these was the rapid and accelerating rise of the parish rates collected for the relief of the poor. Another was the continuing agricultural change of the 17th and 18th centuries. And the third, from around the 1750s, was the rising cost of living.

Respecting the relief and employment of the poor, a report was drawn up by the Board of Trade in 1697. Its author was no less eminent an authority than Mr. John Locke. He began by stating the problem.

"The multiplying of the Poor, and the increase of the tax for their maintenance, is so general an observation and complaint, that it cannot be doubted of....it has been a growing burden these many years."

According to Locke, the reason for this multiplying of the poor was not to be found in their conditions of life.

"If the cause of this evil be looked into, we humbly conceive it will be found to have proceeded neither from scarcity of provisions, nor from want of employment for the Poor, since the goodness of God has blessed these times with plenty, no less than the former, and a long peace gave us as plentiful a trade as ever."

Locke was already on shaky ground. The 1690s were a time of considerable hardship, distress and scarcity; England was at war from 1690; and prices peaked in the very year in which Locke was writing; wheat then being 60s per quarter, according to Richard Price. That very fact was probably the occasion of the enquiry. But if Locke mentioned scarcity and unemployment as possible causes of distress, only to reject them, he was completely silent about the possible role of agricultural change. On the practices of engrossing and enclosing of farms, and of depopulating villages, setting adrift multitudes of wanderers, none of the writers on poor laws make any mention; and it remains, conspicuously, as the elephant on the sofa throughout the literature.

On such shaky foundations, then, Locke built his argument.

"The growth of the Poor must therefore have some other cause; and it can be nothing else but the relaxation of discipline and corruption of manners; Virtue and Industry being as constant companions on the one side, as Vice and Idleness are on the other."

Most able-bodied paupers, according to Locke, were merely idlers and work-shy; "begging drones, who live unnecessarily upon other people's labour."

"Upon a very moderate computation, it may be concluded, that above one half of those who receive relief from the parishes, are able to get their livelihood."

Locke condemns "those who have numerous families of children, whom they cannot, or pretend they cannot, support by their labour; or those who pretend they cannot get work, and so live only by begging, or worse."

"For a great number of children giving a poor man a title to an allowance from the parish, this allowance is given once a week, or once a month, to the father in money, which he not seldom spends on himself at the alehouse, whilst his children (for whose sake he had it) are left to suffer, or perish under the want of necessaries, unless the charity of neighbours relieve them."

To Locke, the problem was merely one of suppression; of a stricter enforcement of the law.

"The first step, therefore, towards setting the Poor on work, we humbly conceive, ought to be a restraint of their debauchery, by a strict execution of the laws provided against it; more particularly, by the suppressing superfluous brandy-shops, and unnecessary alehouses."

Much greater severity was needed "for the more effectual restraining of idle vagabonds", and children under fourteen years of age should be "soundly whipt" if found begging outside of their parish.

"These idle vagabonds being thus suppressed, there will not (we suppose) in many country parishes be many men who will have the pretence that they want work."[1]

Problem solved!

Actually clearly not; for in 1704 Sir Humphrey Mackworth introduced into Parliament his bill for the better relief and setting to work of the poor. It passed the Commons; but in the hope of getting it defeated in the Lords, and probably at the instigation of government, Daniel Defoe produced his pamphlet, entitled 'Giving Alms no Charity'. In it, he asserted as a "fundamental maxim" that;-

"There is in England more Labour than Hands to perform it, and consequently a want of People, not of Employment. No Man in England, of sound Limbs and Senses, can be Poor merely for want of work."

Based on this premise, Defoe paints begging as a desirable way of life, chosen by many in preference to working for a living.

"I am oblig'd to call begging an Employment, since 'tis plain, if there is more Work than Hands to perform it, no Man that has his *Limbs* and his *Senses* need to beg.

"Nay the Begging as now practis'd, is a scandal upon our Charity, and perhaps the foundation of all our present Grievance – How can it be possible that any Man or Woman, who being sound in Body and Mind, may as 'tis apparent they may, have Wages for their Work, should be so base, so

---

1 John Locke. A Report of the Board of Trade to the Lords Justices. In An Account of the Origin, Proceedings, and Intentions of the Society for the Promotion of Industry in the Southern District of the Parts of Lindsey in the County of Lincolnshire. 1789. Pp. 101-108 and 113. Note that Locke's views were still being propagated almost a century later!

meanly spirited, as to beg an Alms for God-sake – Truly the scandal lies on our Charity; and people have such a Notion in *England* of being pittiful and charitable, that they encourage Vagrants, and by a mistaken Zeal, do more harm than good.

"The reason so many pretend to want Work is, that they can live so well with the pretence of wanting Work, they would be mad to leave it and Work in earnest."

What was necessary then, according to Defoe, was not to find work for the poor, but to compel them to find it for themselves. Workhouses and charities actually served to attract the poor away from work, and so to increase their number.

"'Tis a Regulation of the Poor that is wanted in England, not a setting them to Work."

Defoe proceeds to set out his objections to the clauses in Mackworth's bill for setting the poor to work.

"The Manufactures that these Gentlemen Employ the Poor upon, are all such as are before exercised in *England* – They are all such as are manag'd to a full Extent, and the present Accidents of War and Forreign Interruption of Trade consider'd rather beyond the vent of them than under it."

Conspicuously, this is in blatant contradiction to Defoe's original premise that there was more work in England than hands to perform it, and completely undermines his original argument.

But whether you set the poor to work, or force them to find work for themselves, either way, the end-result will be the same – work. If you will overstock the manufactures by doing the one, so will you by the other.

Defoe then enumerates a remote and complicated concatenation of catastrophes which would supposedly result from Mackworth's bill. One of them was that every parish would manufacture all the things it needed, and thus would be eliminated the middleman's ability to interpose himself in the trade; another was that all industry would be forcibly removed to London, leaving the provinces bereft![2]

Defoe's article, one might euphemistically say, was seriously flawed. But it convinced the House of Lords, who duly threw out Mackworth's bill; or rather, perhaps, it provided a justificatory rationale for doing something for which they had reasons of their own. It is perhaps easy to see why a House of Lords containing so many improving landlords, and many others maybe contemplating enclosures and depopulations, would swallow with avidity a series of arguments which absolved them from responsibility for the crowds of itinerant misery which were clearly on the increase in many parts of the country. But how such nonsensical and contradictory assertions came to be treated with seriousness and respect by the historians of our own day is an altogether more difficult question; but no less interesting.

Basing his arguments on his original premise that, in England, there was more work to do than hands to do it, Defoe goes on to produce his own explanation for the rapid growth of the parish rates. It was caused, partly, by a lack of good domestic management among the poor.

"Where an *English* labouring Man with his 9s per week lives wretchedly and poor, a *Dutch-man* with that Wages will live very tolerably well, keep the Wolf from the Door, and have everything handsome about him. In short, he will be Rich with the same Gain as makes the *Englishman* poor, he'll thrive when the other goes in Rags, and he'll live when the other starves, or goes a begging."

It was caused, partly, by their gluttony and extravagance.

"*English* Labouring People eat and drink, but especially the latter three times as much in value as any sort of Forreigners of the same Dimensions in the World....The profuse Extravagant Humour of our poor People in eating and drinking, keeps them low, causes their Children to be left naked and starving, to the care of the Parishes, whenever either Sickness or Disaster befalls the Parent."

And it was caused, partly, by their laziness and drunkenness.

---

2 Daniel Defoe. Giving Alms no Charity. Pp. 9-15.

"There is a general Taint of Slothfulness upon our Poor, there's nothing more frequent, than for an *English-man* to Work till he has got his pocket full of Money, and then go and be idle, *or perhaps drunk,* till 'tis all gone, and perhaps himself in Debt; and ask him in his Cups what he intends, he'll tell you honestly, he'll drink as long as it lasts, and then go to work for more.

"This is the Ruine of our poor, the *Wife mourns,* the Children *starves,* the Husband *has Work before him,* but lies at the Alehouse, or otherwise *idles away* his time, and won't Work.

"'Tis the Men that *won't work,* not the Men that *can get no work,* which make the numbers of our Poor.

"I make no Difficulty to promise on a short Summons, to produce above a Thousand Families in *England,* within my particular knowledge, who go in Rags, and their Children wanting Bread, whose Fathers can earn their 15 to 25s *per Week,* (!) but will not work, who may have Work enough, but are too idle to seek after it, and hardly vouchsafe to earn anything more than bare Subsistence, and Spending Money for themselves."[3]

Through the eminence of, and respect paid to, these two thinkers and writers – Locke and Defoe – the stereotyping and abuse of the poor became socially acceptable, respectable even; and in later years were to become, after a fashion, *de rigueur.* Such doctrines came to constitute an orthodoxy among the ruling classes, which formed the basis of the legislation of the period which concerned the poor.

The Statute of 1722, Knatchbull's Act, sought to reduce the poor rates, not by reducing poverty, but by deterring the poor from applying for relief. Its object was simply to save money; and it is probably not too far-fetched to connect it with the South Sea Bubble, which burst the previous year, leaving many landowners severely financially embarrassed. Like Locke and Defoe, it assumed that pauperism was either voluntary – a desirable lifestyle taken up by preference – or else merely the result of the vices of the poor; and it sought to remedy this by applying a workhouse test, which supposedly would distinguish the drones from the worthy objects of relief. It was an enabling act, which authorised parishes, either alone or in combination, to set up workhouses in which paupers were to be lodged; and to pay contractors to look after the poor for profit. The conditions inside workhouses on this system have already been noted, and it is easy to see why the system acted successfully as a deterrent to potential applicants. Those who applied for relief would be "offered the house", and if any refused to live there they would be "put out of the book in which the names of the persons who ought to receive relief are registered, and shall not be entitled to ask or receive relief from the overseers."[4]

This statute, as John Scott put it, was "a dreadful engine of oppression",[5] but it achieved its objective – a considerable reduction in poor rates – and over 100 such workhouses were already established by 1725.

Similar assumptions underlay the Vagrant Act of 1744. By this, the itinerant poor were divided into three classes; the disorderly, in which were included "all persons who, not having wherewith to maintain themselves, live idle without employment and refuse to work for the usual wages, and beggars going from door to door or placing themselves in streets, highways and passages"; rogues and vagabonds, which comprised those who deserted their families, gatherers of alms, either under false pretences or casually, many sorts of travelling salesmen and entertainers, and all persons wandering about and begging; and, finally, incorrigible rogues – those who failed to mend their ways after correction. Nowhere in this act was a category for those dispossessed by the enclosing or consolidation of farms, by depopulations, or set adrift by the failure of manufactures; for those, in other words, starving through no fault of their own. Like the elephant on the sofa, the idea was not countenanced, and poverty had become merely a punishable offence. Rogues were to be whipped, or consigned to

3   Ibid. Pp. 26-27.
4   Sir G. Nicholls. History of the English Poor Law. Vol. II. Pp. 12-17.
5   John Scott. Observations on the Present State of the Parochial and Vagrant Poor. P. 36.

hard labour for up to six months, or two years in the case of the incorrigible variety. Magistrates were given extensive powers to search for, arrest, whip and convict wanderers, and to punish them according to their several degrees of culpability.[6] Poverty had become reprehensible; nothing more than the manifestation of the depravity of the poor.

Much later in the century, the subject of this depravity was taken up by John Howlett, vicar of Dunmow in Essex.

"The increased wickedness and profligacy of the Poor, and that this is a primary cause of the increase of parish expences, was a popular and current complaint more than a hundred years ago, and has probably been continued through every successive generation."

Howlett quotes from Defoe's Giving Alms no Charity, and comments;-

"Here is such a description of idleness and beggary, debauchery and drunkenness, villainy, vice and wickedness, as one would think nothing could well exceed; yet we have been repeatedly assured that they have all been perpetually increasing ever since, and that even very lately 'licentiousness has made rapid progress, and a deluge of iniquity broken in upon us'."[7]

Whenever food prices were high, noted Howlett, so too were the poor rates; and high poor rates invariably brought forth numerous complaints about the increasing depravity of the poor, which was supposed to be the cause. The absurdity of it all he brought out in the following passage.

"It was between the years 1670 and 1690, that Lord Chief Justice Hales, Sir Joseph Child, Mr. Thomas Firmin, etc. lamented the growing burden of our Poor, and ascribed it partly to their increased profligacy, partly to the want of proper employment, partly to the deficiency of our laws; in short, to every cause but the true one....namely, the excessive price of bread-corn, which for almost twenty years together, was upward of six shillings a bushel....In the course of the next eight or ten years the House of Commons turned their attention to this subject, and Mr. Locke, Mr. Cary and others, employed their researches to account for that load, which in the general apprehension, was sinking us into ruin, and, absurd like their predecessors, they again imputed it to the vice and wickedness of the lower orders of our people. The price of wheat mean time, was upwards of seven shillings a bushel.

"The three or four years immediately following, the price of corn was moderate, and we hear few, if any, complaints on this head.

"In 1704, corn again rose to almost six shillings a bushel, and out steps Mr. Daniel Defoe, and addresses the Knights, Citizens and Burgesses in Parliament assembled, and displays much brilliancy of genius (sic) ....upon the idleness and vices of the Poor....

"In the year 1735 wheat was between five and six shillings a bushel; and Mr. Hay, M. P. published 'Remarks on the Laws relating to the Poor', with his Scheme for their better Relief and Employment.

"In 1752 and 1753 wheat was again between five and six shillings a bushel; and Mr. Alcock makes 'Observations on the Defect of our Poor Laws, and on the Causes and Consequences of the great Encrease and Burden of the Poor'....Lord Hilsborough and Sir Richard Lloyd repeat these complaints, and bring forward their respective Plans of Reformation; and Mr. H. Fielding likewise offers his Project of effectual Provision for the Poor, for amending their Morals, and for rendering them useful Members of Society.

"In 1756, 1757, and 1758, wheat was almost seven shillings a bushel; the cries of the Poor were importunate, and publications, complaints, and schemes, again were numerous. Four years after this, in immediate succession, corn was cheap, and all was still and silent; the lower classes of people, it seems, were not quite so wicked and profligate...."

---

6   Sir G. Nicholls. The History of the English Poor Law. Vol. II. Pp. 34-40.

7   J. Howlett. The Insufficiency of the Causes to which the Increase of the Poor Rates has been attributed. Pp. 23-5.

And so on.[8]

The rationale of those who advocated poor law reform and endless different workhouse schemes as a solution for poverty can be broadly classified under two categories. There were those who accepted that pauperism might have social and economic causes, but thought the cure for it too difficult to be implemented; and that improved poor law schemes were necessary as a matter of humanity. And there were the others, who insisted that poverty was merely the result of the vices of the poor; of their idleness, drunkenness, extravagance and debauchery, and that the solution lay in suppression and punishment. In the first category, we may include Mr. Hay, the M. P. mentioned by Howlett, who published his work on the subject in 1735. Hay at least makes mention of "those who had depopulated their parishes, and were grown easy in their poor rates." He labels the Law of Settlement a "sort of Imprisonment", which the poor suffer "not for any Fault, but for a Misfortune in being poor." The overseers of the poor, in order to save money on the rates, do not relieve poor people as they should, so that people turn to begging and thieving, not because they constitute a desirable way of life as Defoe maintained, but out of necessity.

"Many poor Persons who are willing to work, want Employment in their own Parishes. This forces them to seek it in other Places; where, being unknown, they are not employed; so that at last they are compelled to beg, or fall into courses they would otherwise abhor."

Very little care was taken of the poor in England, Hay complained, and he devised his scheme to remedy that. It was not acted upon.[9]

The London magistrate, Henry Fielding, was another who accepted the reality of poverty; but who absolved the rich from guilt on the doubtful grounds that they simply did not know about it....

"The Sufferings of the Poor are indeed less observed than their Misdeeds; not from any Want of Compassion, but because they are less known; and this is the true Reason why we so often hear them mentioned with Abhorrence, and so seldom with Pity. But if we were to make a Progress through the outskirts of this Town, and look into the Habitations of the Poor, we should there behold such Pictures of human Misery as must move the Compassion of every Heart that deserves the Name of human. What indeed must be his Composition who could see whole Families in Want of every Necessary of Life, oppressed with Hunger, Cold, Nakedness, and Filth, and with Diseases the certain Consequence of all these?

"That such Wretchedness as this is so little lamented, arises therefore from its being so little known;....Some Members of Parliament actually made this Progress in Company with Mr. Welch, and owned the Truth exceeded their imagination."

In any case, concluded Fielding, nothing could be done to put an end to the problem.

"So national and atrocious a Grievance....would not have subsisted so long, had it been capable of being redressed....If, after all these Endeavours, the Evil should not be removed or abated; on the contrary, if it should be even increased, surely no Man can be blamed who shall conclude it to be irremediable; and shall compare it to some inveterate Defect in our animal Constitution, to which, however grievous, an honest Physician will advise us to submit, there being no Cure for it in the Art of Physic."[10]

The idea that poverty was natural, and therefore impossible to remove, had a long, long way to run from here.

A third author who recognised the existence of social and economic causes of poverty, which it was not practical to remove, and which therefore gave rise to the need for parish relief as a matter of

---

8 Ibid. Pp. 70-72.
9 W. Hay. Remarks on the Laws Relating to the Poor. Pp. 10-15.
10 H. Fielding. A Proposal for Making an Effectual Provision for the Poor. Pp. 10-11.

humanity, was, perhaps, Howlett himself. In earlier days, Howlett had been a strenuous advocate of the enclosure of farms, and had displayed an intolerant attitude towards the poor. By 1788, his attitude had softened, and Howlett was overtaken by a surge of compassion. It was not that he changed his previous views; indeed, he included a eulogy on that well-known improving landlord, the Duke of Grafton, with whom Howlett clearly had, or hoped for, some connection. The pamphlet which he published in that year was entitled "The Insufficiency of the Causes to which the Increase of our Poor, and of the Poor's Rates, have been commonly ascribed"; and in it, ironically, Howlett put forward an almost totally monofactorial explanation of the poverty of his day, which entirely exonerated the encloser of land, the consolidator of farms, and the depopulator of villages. Howlett's contention was that the increase of poverty and pauperism had only one major cause – "that the price of labour has not advanced as much as the price of provisions". He dismissed as absurd all those writers who invoked the wickedness of the poor. Most of the poor, he maintained, were well-intentioned.

"No young fellow, but would resolve to work his flesh from his bones, rather than sink into the horrid situation (of pauperism). Examples abound of industrious labourers who, in spite of every increasing difficulty, yet by care, economy and incessant exertion, still support themselves and their families, not only above absolute want and misery, but in some degree of comfort and happiness. However it may excite the smile, or provoke the sneer of the unfeeling insolence of wealth, I am persuaded three fourths of our young labourers set out in life with these generous ideas, and for many a year act up to them. At length, their family becoming numerous, they find their scanty earnings inadequate to their increasing necessities; they struggle hard, but all in vain – overwhelmed in hopeless poverty; farewell all future industry, care, economy or neatness, henceforward nothing but increasing sloth, rags and wretchedness."

So "there really is a greater degree of moral depravity, and a greater frequency of vice, of certain particular kinds especially, among our present Poor, than there were formerly. But this....has not been the *cause*, but the *consequence* of their poverty."

The failure of wages to keep pace with the cost of living was merely part of the progressive enrichment of society as a whole.

"So great has been the increase of our people, such the abridgment and facilitation of the work itself, partly from greater dexterity of the workmen, in consequence of the division and simplification of their labours, still more from the invention of machines, and various ingenious contrivances, mean that the price of the workmanship has been little advanced; there being generally hands in abundance to perform it and the master having, as it were, the choice of whom he shall employ."

Poverty, therefore, was "the natural and necessary consequence of the various changes, in other respects, that have take place in this kingdom, and which have been the sources of our greatest prosperity." To extinguish poverty was "to remove what human wisdom never can remove or prevent; and which can only, from time to time, be somewhat alleviated by the more plentiful assistance of those who are able to afford it, either by voluntary donations, or forced contribution."

Howlett's was a humanitarian explanation of poverty, which avoided burdening the rich with blame.

Society had acquired great wealth, in the face of "lowness of wages and the increasing poverty and wretchedness of the labouring classes....And shall we grudge to allow of this abundance two million pounds a year towards the support of those from the labour of whose hands and the sweat of whose brows we have derived the whole? Shall we grind their faces, and squeeze them to death, and then have the cruel absurdity of ascribing their fate to their increasing vice and profligacy?"[11]

---

11   J. Howlett. The Insufficiency of the Causes to which the Increase of our Poor, and of the Poor's Rates, have been commonly ascribed. Pp. 1, 13?, 27, and 73-75.

Many, however, did have precisely that cruel absurdity, and particularly all those writers who followed Locke and Defoe in viewing the laws relating to the poor as necessary instruments of suppression and punishment.

One such was Thomas Alcock, who published his "Observations" in 1752. Alcock started from the same premise as Defoe.

"England is so fruitful a Place, produces all the Necessaries, and most of the Conveniences of Life in plenty, has Tillage and Manufactures in Abundance, and consequently can find sufficient Employ for all her Poor...."

"Few, I believe, if it was not somehow their own Fault, have perished for want of Sustenance."

Although Alcock pays lip service to the existence of "the bashful Poor, the really distressed" who "keep aloof and almost starve in Silence", it is nevertheless clear that he considers poverty in general to be caused by "Idleness, Sloath, Luxury, Drunkenness, Gluttony or Whoredom." For Alcock, most applicants for relief were actually feigning distress. "Some may have private sums. Others deserve chastisement as having brought themselves into Distress by their Vices and Wickedness."

And "as Want is the natural Consequence....so it is the natural Punishment; and neither the laws of God nor man ever design'd that such a Person should be thrown a Burthen upon others." [12]

Accordingly, Alcock recommended the complete abolition of the poor law.

Alcock presents us with a catalogue of the articles of extravagant expence by which the poor had brought themselves into their distressed condition. First, there was smoking and chewing tobacco.

"The Expence to many poor labouring People only on this Article is very considerable. I believe some lay out almost as much in Tobacco, as in Bread, and declare, they can as ill go without the first as the last."

Then there was snuff-taking.

"'Tis now become general among the lowest Class....especially amongst the Females", who are "more or less addicted to this Habit."

Then tea-drinking.

"Several poor Persons, who receive Charity, have their Tea once, if not twice, a Day....For the Expence of the whole Apparatus of Tea, Sugar, Cream, Bread and Butter etc. must be near treble to that of Milk or Broth, or any other wholesome Breakfast....There is also a considerable Loss of Time attends this silly Habit, in preparing and supping their Tea; a Circumstance of no small Moment to those who are to live by their labour."

And trivial imported luxuries.

"The wearing of Ribbands, Ruffles and Silks, and other slight foreign Things, that come dear, and do but little Service."

And also excessive spirit-drinking.

"The Havock and Destruction which Dram-drinking makes among the common People, amongst whom it chiefly prevails....Consider the Miseries and Calamities which it brings, by that means, upon the Nation in general....This monstrous abuse of Spirituous Liquors has most pernicious Effects; it consumes the Gains and Subsistence of the People, and reduces them to Poverty and Want; destroys their Health and Strength, and makes them both unwilling and unable to Work." Etc. Etc.

"Drunkenness is, and has been for some Time, at an amazing Height in this Nation, especially among the common People."

"These then are the new Articles of Expence, unknown to this Nation in former Times. A law to relieve People brought to Want by these Extravagances is unreasonable and impolitic, and in Time must prove fatal to the Nation."

---

12 T. Alcock. Observations on the Defects of the Poor Laws. Pp. 22, 28 and8-10.

Alcock goes on to enlarge at some length upon the criminal tendencies of those people who applied for parish relief.[13]

The respected Dr. Richard Burn, writing his History of the Poor Laws in 1764, followed pretty much in Alcock's footsteps. With such an abundance of employment, he thought, no one in England needed to beg.

"Beggary is now become an art or a mystery, to which many children are brought up from their cradles…."

"No sufficient provision hath been made, to prevent the nusance of *common begging*. It signifies nothing, to provide for the maintenance and employment of those, who can maintain themselves without labour, and without being subject to controul."

Burn's solution was simple.

"Give them nothing. If none were to give none would beg. And the whole mystery and craft would be at an end in a fortnight.…Let all who relieve a common beggar be subject to a penalty."[14]

By this masterstroke of invention and ingenuity, the whole problem of pauperism was solved yet again.

According to John Scott, "amidst the variety of advice which has tended to deprive the suffering vagrant of his most liberal benefactors.…that of the judicious Dr. Burn, and the pious Mr. Hervey has probably (from the celebrity of their names) had the most powerful and extensive influence."

And as John Scott observes, the pious Mr. Hervey does indeed surpass even the judicious Dr, Burn.

"Money or victuals bestowed, on these worthless wretches, is not real beneficence, but the earnest-penny of sloth; it hires them to be good for nothing, and pays them for being public nuisances. Let us then unanimously join to shake off these dead weights from our wheels, and dislodge these swarms of vermin from our state; let us be deaf to their most importunate clamours, and assure ourselves, that by this determined inflexibility, we do God, we do our community, we do them, the most substantial service."[15]

Writing in 1787, William Godschall, a magistrate from Surrey, articulated yet another line of reasoning which became important in discussions of poverty – that of the innate wickedness of the poor. The lower orders of society were possessed by "a diffused depravity", which gave rise, at worst, to the many robberies which had recently been committed, or, at best, to a "general aversion to honest employment of any kind", which manifested itself in idleness and beggary. It was the duty of the rich to restrain such evil; and it was their indolence, thoughtlessness and laxity in performing this duty that the distressed state of the nation was to be attributed.

"*Prevention* should be the great object,…it is the duty of every government to protect their subjects, not only from others, but themselves." The need was "to reform the manners of the people." Idleness must be overcome "by confinement and compelled labour, with humane usage."

"Idleness.…in all well-governed countries is punished as a crime – by some laws esteemed a capital offence.

"If men had not opportunity to be idle, they would not have leisure to be wicked."[16]

All of the above explanations of the causes of poverty and pauperism have this in common – that they were formulated in defiance of reality. The massive changes which took place in the countryside throughout these years, for example, were simply not entered into the equation. They were, without

13 Ibid. Pp. 46-50 and 74.
14 Dr. R. Burn. History of the Poor Laws. Pp. 175, 203 and 207.
15 John Scott. Observations on the Present State of the Parochial and Vagrant Poor. Pp. 26-8.
16 W. Godschall. A General Plan of Parochial and Provincial Police. Pp. 3, 5, 9, and 15. Heaven help the good people of Surrey!

doubt, a salient feature of the age, in a still predominantly agricultural economy. The body of literature dealing with these changes, and the detrimental effects they had on the lives of ordinary people, was extensive and well-informed. It is inconceivable that the writers on the poor laws were unaware of these changes.

It was left to Joseph Massie to bring the discussion back into the realms of the real world.

"It may well be concluded, that *Depravity of Manners is the* CAUSE; but when the Matter comes to be traced….it will more plainly appear, that Depravity is the EFFECT of our POOR'S-LAWS….The Depravity of poor People proceeds from the depraved Treatment of them….HARD-HEARTEDNESS….*produces* ILL TREATMENT of *distressed persons*….The Reluctance, or ill Success, with which such unfortunate People do practise begging, is frequently manifested by a poor and emaciated man or woman being found *drowned*, or *starved to Death*; so that though *Choice, Idleness,* or *Drunkenness* may be reasons why a Number of People are BEGGARS, yet *this Drowning*, and *perishing for Want*, are sad Proofs that the general Cause is NECESSITY."[17]

For Massie, the causes of poverty lay in the many social and economic changes that had taken place over the previous 150 years.

"The modern State of *England*….differs as much from the State there of in the reign of Queen *Elizabeth*, as the *Sea* in a STORM doth from the *Sea in a* CALM."[18]

Massie goes on to detail a complex combination of circumstances which had brought the people of England into their distressed state. Foremost among these circumstances was agricultural change.

"The Inclosure of COMMON FIELDS, or the WHOLE *of any* COMMON that contributes towards the Maintenance of poor labouring Families, is *Ruinous in* POLICY and *Cruel in* NATURE…. The Consequences of LETTING *Five Hundred* ACRES *of* LAND to ONE *Farmer, instead of keeping it in* TEN *Farms*….The LOSS *of* CERTAIN MEANS to *Continue* and *Maintain* NINE FAMILIES in *Existence* and *Substantiality*….NINE FAMILIES *will be thereby brought upon their* PARISHES, or *be obliged to Transport themselves* to *another* COUNTRY."

Actually, it could be ten if the one rich farmer was brought in from outside.

"For such People know well enough, that *their* LOT *will be to* WORK *for* TEN PENCE, etc. *a Day*; whereas if they are rendered incapable of Labour, they have neither LAND NOR HOUSE TO COMFORT THEM; but must go to a *Parish Workhouse*, and have their *Wives* and *Children* subjected to hard Treatment, if not driven to Vagabondry."[19]

The usual motivation behind such changes as these was the increase of rent that could be achieved by them – many writers speak of rents being doubled or trebled. The desire of the rich to be richer still at the expence of the rural communities is railed against by many of the writers who opposed enclosing and consolidation. Here is John Moore, already in 1656.

"These cruell Ones care not how many they ruine so they may be rich, nor how many they make Beggars so they may be Gentlemen; Let them answer me this one Question, viz; How so *many thousand Families* can subsist when their *Livelyhood* is taken away, with their *Trade of Tillage*? and how shall so many *thousands* of Children be disposed of from slavery, Vagrancy or thieving."[20]

John Cowper took up the theme in 1732.

"Some improvements bring profit to one man and ruin 100 families….And shall so many honest useful Subjects, so many industrious pain-taking Families be driven from their Settlements, and sent

17 J. Massie. Considerations relating to the Poor. Pp. 57, 59 and 50.
18 Ibid. P. 61.
19 Ibid. Pp. 63 and 70-73.
20 J. Moore. A Scripture-Word against Inclosure. P. 8.

to beg their Bread among Strangers, meerly to humour insatiate Avarice, the Pride of the Luxury of a few, whose Fortunes are already too large for their Souls?"[21]

Joseph Massie wrote of "Improvements that are not for, but against the General Good of the Nation, such as may bring present profit to one Man, and at the same Time ruin a hundred Families!"

"The Motive to, and Consequence of such Inclosure, is, that some Avaritious Man may buy out all those valuable Families, from the little Inheritances to which they owe their Existence."[22]

Stephen Addington pursued the same theme in 1772.

"Indeed, lords of manors, the clergy, or other impropriators of tythes, and one or two more of the principal proprietors in a parish, are generally the chief gainers...."

And he complains of "petitions to parliament for little else than to obtain leave of the legislature to take a cow a piece from twenty persons who had only two, and to give ten more to one or two wealthy neighbours who had twenty or thirty before....Yet an ingenious writer on the subject tells us, 'Inclosing is a public good....' Can he think this, or any other measure is for the public good, that impoverishes twenty to enrich one?

"But every thing must be sacrificed to the pleasing prospect of raising an estate of five or six hundred a year, to a thousand; and when the landed interest in one parish hear what great things their neighbours boast of doing for themselves by inclosing, they are easily persuaded to make the experiment."[23]

The complaint, of course, was that the enclosing of commons and common fields resulted in a much smaller number of owners and farmers; that the turning over of huge acreages of arable to pasture, which was the usual consequence, at least before the 1790s, eliminated the need for labour; and that the rural community was disconnected from the land. Some parishes would thus become depopulated; others, as a result, overburdened with poor rates. In areas where enclosure was little practised, or had happened centuries before, the same effects could occur through the consolidation of holdings and the increase of pasture land.

"For the pernicious Practice of uniting small Farms, which heretofore had their due Share of Tillage, and converting them into large feeding Farms, I am sorry to observe, begins to gain too much footing in some Parts of *this*, as well as other Counties; Witness the many Cottage-Homes let down within the last 30 Years...."[24]

So wrote William Chapple in 1785.

In all cases, the consequences for the agricultural community could be proletarianisation, vagrancy and pauperisation.

All this was commonplace to the literature opposing agricultural change. And in most cases there was a strong undercurrent that the rich were enriching themselves still further at the expence of the rural communities.

"I may possibly be censured by very respectable Persons, for publishing such an Opinion, but I cannot help thinking it would be wicked in me to conceal the Growth of such a National Evil....for DISEASES must be discovered before REMEDIES can be applied."[25]

Joseph Massie's fear was no doubt realised in conversation, but not, so far as I am aware, in print. In fact, by all those writers who professed to be writing on the increase of the poor and the poor rates, the issues he raised were studiously ignored. No one said Good Morning to the elephant!

21 J. Cowper. An Essay Proving, That Inclosing *Commons*, and Common-field-Lands Is contrary to the INTEREST of the NATION. Pp. 3 and 13.
22 J. Massie. Considerations relating to the Poor. Pp. 14 and 63.
23 S. Addington. An Inquiry into the Reasons for and against Inclosing Open Fields. Pp. 9-11.
24 W. Chapple. Risdon's Survey of Devon. P. 42n.
25 J. Massie. Considerations relating to the Poor. Pp.74-5.

There was, however, an extremely voluminous literature defending the new agriculture on a number of scores; principally, perhaps, from the charge that it impoverished the rural classes. Joseph Lee, a minister of the gospel, produced an early one, concerning the enclosure of Catthorpe in Leicestershire, in which he had a personal interest. According to Lee, there were good enclosures and bad enclosures; and those who wrote against enclosures meant only depopulating enclosures.

"That which is justly condemned is such a joyning house to house and field to field, which is joyned with oppression and injury to others; till there be no place which is not their own, and none left to their poor neighbour; nothing contenteth, but that they alone possess the earth.

"Those evils which do too usually accompany Inclosure of Commons, are not the faults of Inclosure, but of some Inclosers only."

Depopulation, according to Lee, would only occur in parishes in the ownership of one man, or of a very few. Catthorpe was not like that – its 580 acres were in the hands of eight freeholders and five of six "ancient Cottages who are also Freeholders."[26] In Catthorpe, tillage was to be kept up, as it was in many enclosed parishes in the area, which had either been ploughed up within the previous thirty years, or were about to be.[27]

Theoretically, Lee was right. There was no necessary and inherent reason why enclosed land should be monopolised into few hands and turned over to pasture; nor why the rural population should be driven out or pauperised. At Sapcote, in Leicestershire, the landowner turned down all offers of advanced rents from opulent would-be farmers, and continued the enclosed farms to the same previous tenants, and at the same rents as before. Tillage was maintained, and an area of pasture laid out for the use of the poor at a reasonable rent; none of whom came to the parish through the succeeding hard times.[28]

However, where the object of enclosure was a big increase in rent, the impoverishment of the rural community was an almost inevitable consequence. John Moore answered Lee, in a pamphlet of the same year.

"The man speaks of what may be, and not what usually is. He hath fancyes, notions, and dreams of Innocent Inclosure, both from Depopulation and Decay of Tillage. Surely they may make men as soon believe there is no sun in the firmament as that usually depopulation and decay of Tillage will not follow inclosure in our Inland counties. We see it with our eyes; It is so. *De facto*, it is so. They say they doe not intend depopulation and decay of Tillage....Yet I must answer, it is finis operis.[29]

What the eventual outcome was of the Catthorpe enclosure, one can only surmise. But at least Joseph Lee should be given credit for honest intentions. His fancyes, notions and dreams were minor affairs compared with those who came after him. Despite John Moore's fulminations against the levity and untruths of those who defended enclosures, the literature supporting the new agriculture came to exhibit an increasing air of unreality, absurdity, and intellectual trickery.

Charles Fortrey, writing in 1669, denied absolutely that enclosures caused depopulation.

"As to depopulations by inclosures, granting it increaseth plenty, as cannot well be denied, how increase and plenty can depopulate, cannot well be conceived...."

But the only plenty which interested Fortrey was that of money; and that rent and profit are signs of increased production are merely assumed. In fact, the conversion of tillage to pasture normally

---

26 This was still a very few owners compared with, say, Wigston Magna, and one fears the worst for the farmers and cottagers of Catthorpe.

27 Joseph Lee. A Vindication of a Regulated Inclosure. Pp. 32, 13. Title Page. And P. 5.

28 W. G. Hoskins. The Midland Peasant. P. 268.

29 John Moore. A Scripture-Word against Inclosure. Advertisement and p. 9.

involved a decrease of production; though an increase of rent to the landlord, and of profit to the engrossing farmer.

Opposition to enclosure assumes "that inclosure would convert the land to pasture; one hundred acres of which, will scarce maintain a shepherd and his dog, which now maintains many families, employed in tillage; and by experience it is found, that many towns, which when their lands were in tillage had many families, now they are inclosed, have not so many inhabitants in them."

Fortrey admits the fact. But this is not depopulation.

Surely none will "imagine that the people which lived in those towns they call depopulated, were all destroyed, because they lived no longer there; when indeed they were only removed to other places, where they might better benefit themselves, and profit the publick.

"As many or more families may be maintained and employed, in the manufacture of the wooll that may arise out of one hundred acres of pasture, than can be employed in a far greater quantity of arable;[30] who perhaps do not always finde it most convenient for them to live, just on the place where the wooll growth; by which means cities and great towns are peopled, nothing to the prejudice of the kingdom....

"Enclosure really causeth no depopulation, but at most a removal of people thence; where without benefit to the publick, or profit to themselves, they laboured and toiled, to a more convenient habitation, where they might with less pains greatly advantage both....In....manufactures....the Subjects are employed in honest and industrious callings, maintained and preserved from want, and the mischiefs of idleness."

The trouble was that the removal of the people from the land was real, but their alternative employment in manufacturing was, to a large extent, illusory. As Fortrey was well aware.

"It doth not appear that people are wanting, but rather that we have already too many, if we consider the number of poor people that are found in every place; and it might be prudence, first, to employ these, before we endeavour to multiply more.

"It is true considering our present condition, how trade is decayed, and the little encouragement people have to industry we have already more people than are well employed...."[31]

Despite their inherent absurdity, Fortrey's views achieved the status of an orthodoxy; reinforced at the end of the century by the assertions of the two intellectual heavyweights, Locke and Defoe, that there was far more work to do in England than people to do it; and the implied conclusion from that, that rural folk displaced by agricultural change were merely wandering and begging from a desire to live well without working.

Fortrey's themes were developed by the Reverend John Laurence in 1727. Laurence, like Fortrey, measures the productiveness of land in terms of rent; which he uses to posit an increase of food. And he denies absolutely that enclosures can hurt the poor.

"If one should urge, that the Product will be Grass, but no Corn for the Poor; the contrary is notorious in all inclosed Counties; For we see ploughed Land in Inclosures almost every where. But if Pasture should be thereby increased, will not the Wool and Skins, produced by an Acre of Pasture, make greater Employment for the Poor, than the Tillage of such an Acre can do? I think the Answer is plain, they will. And yet there will be an Overplus of Corn for the Poor too."

This miracle is proclaimed on the same page as the Ten-fold increase of Rent sometimes achieved by enclosure, and the Lancashire farm that was ploughed every year, with just an application of marl every twelve years!

Laurence introduces into this article an element which was to appear more regularly in future literature on this subject – the stereotyping and abuse of the rural classes.

---

30 Try doing the mathematics involved in this claim!
31 Charles Fortrey. England's Interest and Improvement. Pp. 17-21 and p. 12.

"*Wastes* and *Open Fields* draw to them the Poor and Necessitous, only for the Advantage of Pilfering and Stealing; who, when an *Inclosure* is once resolved on, will be employ'd for many Years in planting and preserving the Hedges; and afterwards will be set to work, both in the Tillage and the Pasture, wherein they may get an honest Livelihood.

"Inclosure is the greatest Encouragement to *good Husbandry*, and a Remedy for *Beggary*, the Poor being employed by the continual Labour that is bestowed thereon."[32]

Nonsense, replied John Cowper, a few years later. The large amount of employment provided by hedging and ditching was "contrary to constant Experience."

"Raising *Hedges*, and Sinking *Ditches* may indeed employ several Hands for a Year, or hardly so long, but when that is once over, the Work is at an End; for three or four old Men in a *Parish*, are sufficient to keep them in Repair, and the rest must remove to *Open-field Parishes* if they hope for farther Employment....

"But as to the *Poor's* being employed in the inclosed Pasture Fields, no Man living ever saw such a Thing; and therefore it is not *Pasture*, but *Arable*, that must keep them from begging and starving too."[33]

The cynicism and disingenuousness of the literature of the new agriculture is well demonstrated, also in 1727, by land agent Edward Laurence. A good steward, he suggests, will persuade neighbouring freeholders to sign a provisional agreement for enclosing their land. He provides a sample agreement.

"Whereas it is found, by long Experience, that Common or open Fields, where-ever they are suffer'd or continued, are great Hindrances to a publick Good, and the honest Improvement which every one might make of his own, by diligence and a seasonable charge; And whereas the common Objections hitherto rais'd against Inclosures are founded on mistakes, as if Inclosures contributed either to hurt or ruine the Poor; whilst it is plain that (when an Inclosure is once resolv'd on) the Poor will be imploy'd for many years in planting and preserving the Hedges, and afterwards will be set to work both in the Tillage and Pasture, wherein they may get an honest livelihood. And whereas all or most the Inconveniences and Misfortunes which usually attend the *open Wastes* and common Fields have been fatally experienced at _____, to the great discouragement of Industry and good Husbandry in the Freeholders, viz, That the Poor take their Advantage to pilfer and steal and trespass; That the Corn is subject to be spoil'd by Cattle, that stray out of the Commons and Highways adjacent."

This blatant piece of propaganda is completely undermined, just two pages earlier, by Laurence's advice to his intending steward on how to clear an estate of its inhabitants, gradually, without creating too much odium. The families of deceased farmers were to "betake themselves to other Employments". And Laurence clearly implies that the poor are to be driven out, by a severe enforcement of the poor law; possibly by just such methods as were legalised by the act of just five years before.[34]

For certain, the propagators did not always believe their own propaganda.

The traditional rural communities came in for considerable amounts of odium and abuse at the hands of the pro-enclosure writers. Open-field farmers were portrayed as poor, backward and ignorant.

"The Goths and Vandals of open fields touch the civilisation of enclosures."[35]

"I am sensible that not one farmer in five thousand reads at all, but the country abounds in gentlemen farmers, whose ideas are more enlarged, and whose practice is less founded in prejudice.

32   Rev. J. Laurence. A New System of Agriculture. Pp. 32-33.

33   J. Cowper. An Essay Proving That Inclosing *Commons*, and *Common-field- Lands*, Is Contrary to the INTEREST of the NATION. Pp. 4-5 and 16.

34   Edward Laurence. The Duty of a Steward to his Lord. Pp. 37 and 35.

35   Arthur Young. General View of the County of Oxfordshire. Pp. 35-6.

"They who suppose any improvement owing to common farmers are somewhat mistaken. All the well known capital strokes of husbandry are traced accurately to gentlemen."[36]

This was as arrogant as it was factually incorrect.

Open field farmers, it was said, lived no better than their labourers, and worked harder. In addition, they could not afford to farm properly.

"He must be a novice, indeed, in rural oeconomy, who does not know that the small farmers keep no sheep; seldom any cows, and yet fewer hogs."[37]

What they needed was clearing away.

"The open-field school must die off before new ideas can become generally rooted."[38]

Commoners fared worse still. Here is John Arbuthnot writing in 1773.

"The benefit which they are supposed to reap from commons, in their present state, I know to be merely nominal; nay, indeed, what is worse, I know that in many instances, it is an essential injury to them, by being made a plea for idleness; for, some few excepted, if you offer them work, they will tell you, that they must go to look up their sheep, cut furzes, get their cow out of the pound, or perhaps say they must take their horse to be shod, that he may carry them to a horse-race or cricket-match. The first is plausible; but I am sorry to say merely so, because the benefit which the sheep are either to himself or the country is not an object worth notice; the little care that such people can take of them, frequently occasions the loss of their lambs, and the difficulty, nay the impossibility, of supporting them in the winter, is the death of the few scrubby things which have been eating the grass that would have maintained an useful flock."[39]

The accusation of workshyness in this passage is obvious; but note also the implication of a luxurious lifestyle, probably involving the extravagance and immorality of betting, combined with incompetence in farming and the neglect of livestock.

John Billingsley developed the theme.

"Moral effects of an injurious tendency accrue to the cottager, from a reliance on the imaginary benefits of stocking a common. The possession of a cow or two, with a hog, and a few geese, naturally exalts the peasant, in his own conception, above his brethren in the same rank of society. It inspires some degree of confidence in a property inadequate to his support. In sauntering after his cattle, he acquires a habit of indolence. Quarter, half, and occasionally whole days are imperceptibly lost. Day-labour becomes disgusting; the aversion increases by indulgence; and at length the sale of a half-fed calf, or hog, furnishes the means of adding intemperance to idleness. The sale of the cow frequently succeeds, and its wretched and disappointed possessor, unwilling to resume the daily and regular course of labour, from whence he drew his former subsistence, by various modes of artifice and imposition exacts from the poor's-rate that relief to which he is in no degree intitled."[40]

Commons were portrayed as the actual cause of poverty, which was to be remedied by enclosure.

"At Chailey in Sussex, they have miles of commons on which the poor have flocks and herds; ought not this to maintain them free from rates? So much the contrary, that they are 9s in the pound there, and owing to that very cause. Give the poor a thousand pounds a year, do you make them *less*

---

36 Arthur Young. Six Weeks' Tour through the Southern Counties of England and Wales. Introduction to second edition.
37 Arthur Young. Farmers Letters. P. 91. Yes, he really wrote that!
38 Arthur Young. General View of the County of Oxfordshire. Pp. 35-6.
39 John Arbuthnot. An Inquiry into the Connection between the present advanced Price of Provisions and the Size of Farms. P. 81.
40 J. Billingsley. General View of the County of Somerset. P. 52. Which he wrote without visiting the county.

poor? By no means; but much *more* so. Lessen the spur to industry in a class that must be maintained by industry, and you take away what nothing can recompense."[41]

John Howlett wrote in support.

"Seldom have I passed over an extensive waste, but I have been shocked with the sight of a proportionable number of half-naked, half-starved women and children, with pale meagre faces, peeping out of their miserable huts, or lazing and lounging about after a few paltry screaming geese, of scabby worthless sheep; and as seldom have I found, upon enquiry, that the parochial assessments were not excessively high."

Howlett answers his own argument. He mentions the inspired management of the common at Sutton Coldfield, where the poor were allowed plots to cultivate themselves; in spite of which parish rates quintupled between 1740 and 1785.

"Part of this prodigious increase is, perhaps, to be ascribed to the increase of population, which is now almost twice as great as in the year 1740; I am strongly apprehensive, however, that it has chiefly arisen from the very great and unusual privileges above described. Servants, etc. in the neighbourhood allured by these temptations, try every stratagem in order to gain a settlement in so flattering a situation. Hence an influx of inhabitants more than adequate to the increased employment; the want of which the rights of common cannot compensate."[42]

Commons became flooded with refugees from neighbouring enclosures; and the distress of these refugees was used by the propagandists to suggest that it was the common that caused the poverty.

Yet most of these writers conceded that much agricultural improvement displaced the inhabitants.

"That laying down many of these enclosures to grass has prevailed, I shall not disallow; and such tracts must consequently bear the face of depopulation...."[43]

So what was to happen to the rural population, according to the prevailing orthodoxy?

Some points of view are so shameful, although perhaps not uncommonly held, that they appear only in conversation, and never in print; and the historian only becomes aware of them when some decent soul attempts to refute them.

"Some indeed say, 'Let the farmers starve'."

This solution to the problem of the newly-created rural poor was reported for us by Stephen Addington in 1772. However, the written propaganda needed something less drastic, and the argument that agricultural change did not lead to poverty – indeed that it was the remedy for pre-existing poverty – turned essentially on the question of job-creation.

That the enclosure of open-field parishes, involving the consolidation of holdings, and considerable conversion of arable to grass, drastically reduced employment for the poor, was a commonplace which few writers directly challenged. Arguments were nevertheless found.

"The following has been an objection to inclosing, that when an inclosure is finished, there is but little work left for the poor, a few hands being then sufficient to do the work; but then, this objection is commonly made by those people that live near inclosures made of good land, that is more fit, and consequently more employed for pasture than for tillage; and besides, those people making such complaints and objections, have not seen perhaps any large commons, heaths and wastes, thinking the whole kingdom to be of the same quality with the spot on which they were bred and now live upon....What a number of hands would be employ'd in improving the barren *wastes* in this kingdom

---

41   Arthur Young. Annals of Agriculture. Vol. V. P. 222.

42   J. Howlett. Enclosures a Cause of improved Agriculture, of Plenty and Cheapness of Provisions, of Population and of both private and national Wealth. Pp. 80-82.

43   John Arbuthnot. An Inquiry into the Connection between the present advanced Price of Provisions and the Size of Farms. P. 136.

if they were *taken in*, which now employ few or hardly any….An inclosure then is certainly….the best remedy against idleness and beggary; the poor being employed by the continual improvements and labour bestowed thereon….and will also maintain double the number of inhabitants than the champion grounds can do."[44]

This argument, from John Mordant, involves the deliberate confounding of the enclosure of almost uninhabited wastes on poor soils, with the destruction of long-established rural communities; and tries to imply that if the one is beneficial, then so must the other be. This became standard fare amongst writers favouring the new agriculture.

Arthur Young was conspicuously guilty of the same sleight of hand. Young's archetypal enclosure was that of the Norfolk sands.

"All the country from Holkham to Houghton was a wild sheepwalk before the spirit of improvement seized the inhabitants, and this glorious spirit has wrought amazing effects; for instead of boundless wilds and uncultivated wastes inhabited by scarce anything but sheep, the country is all cut into enclosures, cultivated in a most husbandlike manner, richly manured, well peopled, and yielding a hundred times the produce than it did in its former state."[45]

Unsurprisingly, all of this had a beneficial effect on employment opportunities.

When a tract of land is enclosed, "the whole neighbourhood is benefited, vast numbers of poor people are set to work, at hedging, ditching, and planting – farm-houses, barns, and offices are built – the makers of all kinds of implements of agriculture employed, and where there were formerly one person at work, in consequence of sheep, twenty will be regularly kept by tillage."[46]

Let us leave aside the contradiction to the normal propagandist argument that more people were employed by the manufacture of wool than by tillage. Let us just see what conclusion Young tries to base on his assertion.

"Having, as I think, sufficiently proved that it would be the most politic conduct to turn all <u>the commons</u> and sheep-walks in the kingdom into arable farms; and there being, as I have observed, many millions of acres of such…."[47]

But just how did commons get in there? There was a world of difference between enclosing a sandy uninhabited waste, and a fertile common which formed an essential part of the agricultural system of a populous parish. The sands of Norfolk were brought into cultivation on the basis of long leases and nominal rents; open-field villages were turned over to tenants-at-will paying double the previous rent. Young was including chalk and cheese in the same category, and attempting to justify one on the basis of the other. The classification of commons as waste was standard fare in pro-enclosure tracts; and on the pretext of sophistical tricks such as this the subsistence of thousands of rural families was destroyed.

The intellectual fraudulence of this argument is obvious enough, and could never have been got away with in the face of a critical readership. But Young and his colleagues were preaching to the converted; to an audience of rich landlords and agriculturalists eager to hear that their improvements not only did not hurt the poor, but actually benefited them.

So however dubious the connection with the premise, the desired conclusions were drawn. Enclosures benefitted the rural community by creating more employment.

"Great quantities of the newly enclosed common fields have been *laid down*[48]….For every acre of common field land that has been enclosed, there have been enclosed two acres of commons, and

44 J. Mordant. The Complete Steward. Pp.167-168.
45 G. E. Mingay. Arthur Young and his Times. P. 59.
46 Arthur Young. The Farmer's Letters to the People of England. 1771. Vol. I. P. 14.
47 Ibid. P. 17.
48 I. e. to grass.

other waste ground; almost every acre of which has necessarily had the plough thrown into it, in order to cultivate and improve it….Hitherto, inclosures have been so far from lessening employment, that they must have greatly increased it. The enclosed common and waste land, being so much more in quantity than the common fields which have been taken in; and requiring, at the same time, so much more labour, to bring them into order, than it required to work lands, already cultivated, must greatly have increased employment. We may add the great increase of labour in fencing, and dividing both sorts of enclosures, as well as the additional employment of keeping them continually in repair, and in cultivating continually a quantity of land so much greater than was under cultivation before….

"In short, the whole inconvenience which has arisen from enclosing, and which has given rise to all these complaints, is, that where the enclosures have been chiefly, or wholly, of common fields, employment has declined; whilst it has increased in a much greater proportion, in those parts where the enclosures have been chiefly ,or wholly, waste lands; and, consequently, the people have been obliged to remove from one place to another, after their employment."[49]

Unemployment, then, was just a local phenomenon; a mere momentary misfortune.[50] Wales's argument could possibly be sustained if there had been a vast migration of people form the open-field areas to the sands of Norfolk, the moors of Yorkshire, ot even the forested areas of Nottinghamshire and Leicestershire. But the indications seem to be that for the most part displaced peasants set out for other, so far unenclosed, villages with commons; or else for industrialised villages or manufacturing towns; many thousands, as we have seen, becoming marooned without resources en route.

Henry Homer, writing in 1766, conceded that over a twenty year period after enclosure, agricultural employment might gradually decrease. But enclosure provided an array of alternative opportunities.

"It behoves those, who are disposed to be industrious, to seek out other Methods of Employment; such as the getting of Brake, or raising Nursery Sets, the planting or weeding of Quicksets, hoeing Turnips, morticing and hewing out Posts, cleaving Rails, setting down Hedges, or other Mounds, making Drains, sinking Pits, forming and getting Materials for the repair of Roads; and if none of these offer at home, to strike out into other Parishes; and such Persons as can form their Hands to any Variety of Labour, and will be at the Pains to enquire after it, will very rarely be at a Fault for Employment."

Homer actually went so far as to assert that enclosure brought an increase of wage rates. Unfortunately, however, because of their improvidence, the poor were actually worse off when better paid. Whatever they got, they spent….

"To such Persons as these the extraordinary Profits of one Season are no Counterballance to the Defects of another. Nay indeed they are rather a misfortune to them, as they only furnish them with the Means of living better for a while, and consequently of feeling more sensibly the Alteration, when the Necessity of their Affairs obliges them to retrench….When their Work is over, they consider themselves and their Families as the Victims of Poverty, to be supported by the Parish; and in the mean Time make no Use of Foresight to prevent it."

According to Homer, no one needed to be poor on account of enclosures.

"Those who have Capacity enough to undertake Business, Inclination to seek after it, and Steadiness to attend closely to it, and who are also endued with such a Share of Oeconomy as to confine themselves, when they get fourteen, sixteen or eighteen Pence a Day, to the same Diet, as they found sufficient when their Gains amounted to no more than eight or nine Pence….if it should

---

49   W. Wales. An Inquiry into the Present State of Population. Pp. 71-72.
50   H. S. Homer. An Essay on the Nature and Method of Ascertaining the Specifick Shares of Proprietors upon the Inclosure of Common Fields. P. 27. J. Arbuthnot. An Inquiry into the Connection between the present advanced Price of Provisions and the Size of Farms. P. 133.

happen that they are now and then at a Fault for Employment, will nevertheless in the long Run find themselves considerable Gainers, and secure to themselves the Means of Subsistence not only against casual Defects, but also against the necessary Approaches of old Age, when Health, Strength and Ability must fail.

"Thus far then it appears that the Understanding and industrious Labourer may derive Advantage, if He pleases, from Inclosures; and that the Improvident, if He is a sufferer by them, is so by his own Fault."

Enclosure, in fact, was a form of beneficial social engineering; by reducing the population of a village to the level required by the new organisation of it.

"When a Parish or Country becomes inclosed, the Children of the Inhabitants, whose Business was before to attend Cows or Sheep at home, or to drive Plough, are necessarily constrained to seek Subsistence elsewhere by Service or Apprenticeship....And thus there is a natural Transition of the inhabitants of Villages, where the Labour of Agriculture is lessened, into Places of Trade, where our Naval Superiority, as long as it lasts, will furnish Sources of perpetual Employment."[51]

Service and apprenticeship, as we have seen, were rather features of the traditional village organisation, than of the modern, enclosed one.

Enclosure, then, was portrayed as a great benefit to the rural classes. John Arbuthnot thought small farmers much better-off as day-labourers.

"The certain weekly income of the husband's labour (sic), not attended with the anxiety of the little farmer, will procure more real comfort in his little cottage....If by converting the little farmers into a body of men who must work for others more labour is produced, it is an advantage which the nation must wish for; the compulsion will be that of honest industry to provide for a family, which by that means is less liable to become a burden to the parish, than that of the little farmer, whose labours, being attended with constant anxiety and distress, seldom prosper."

As for day-labourers, they, thanks to enclosure, found themselves in a very desirable situation indeed.

"With regard to the class called Hirelings, I believe they are mostly in the state as they were, with the benefit of work at present, instead of being prowling about commons and wastes; luxury.... has been and ever will be an attendant on a wealthy free people, and, with the riches, diffuses itself through all ranks of people.

"An industrious life leads them to a knowledge of those real and reasonable comforts which I wish them to enjoy; such as a good dwelling decently furnished, they and their children well fed and clad; and if these last are early brought up to honest labour, instead of pilfering, there cannot be a better security for their not becoming a burden to the parish."[52]

John Arbuthnot was a gentleman farmer who had close contacts with government and high society; and in this line of argument, as in so many others, he foreshadowed the establishment propaganda of the 1790s. It was with an increasing air of absurdity and unreality that pro-enclosure pamphleteers responded to the challenge of the connection between agricultural change and poverty, by pretending that after enclosure, the poverty and dishonesty, that were portrayed as characteristic of the peasant class, simply no longer existed.

In 1787, John Howlett described an honest farm labourer whom he professed to know. He came to his calling without any flocks, or herds, or any "paradisiacal common", but supported his family on the proceeds of day-labour alone; indeed, these funds enabled him also to build a house by the

51 H. S. Homer. An Essay on the Nature and Method of Ascertaining the Specifick Shares of Proprietors upon the Inclosure of Common Fields. Pp. 31-35.

52 John Arbuthnot. An Inquiry into the Connection between the Present Advanced Price of Provisions and the Size of Farms. Pp. 128, 139, and 84.

highway, with outbuildings, a brewhouse, a pig-sty; and to invest in spinning-wheels and bee-hives; he fenced his yard, planted fruit trees, peas and beans, potatoes and grape-vines. After all this, he still had enough left over to build another house.

"Heartfelt joy appeared in every face, and their wholesome supper was eaten with a relish....which the rich and the great but seldom know. No more let us hear of *happy commoners* and the wondrous *rights of commonage*."

By way of conclusion, Howlett quoted a letter from Thomas Davis, of Longleat, Steward to Lord Weymouth.

"Is it not evident that the inhabitants of this kingdom are greatly increased? Is it not equally manifest that the consumption of all kinds of provisions is increased still more than our people? Is not wheaten bread the universal food of the lowest orders of men in counties where it used to be confined to the middle and higher ranks? Is not that bread made of the finest flour? Is not the consumption of cheese and butter, in many places almost trebled? Are not beef and mutton now eaten almost daily in villages where formerly the use of them was hardly known, or not more than once a week? Do not the farmers, in most parts of the nation, allow their servants, and workmen three times as much strong beer as heretofore?" This was not possible "unless the common fields and pasture had been divided and allotted in specific shares to every proprietor."[53]

We have heard of this Thomas Davis before. It was the very same Thomas Davis who reported to the Board of Agriculture on the county of Wiltshire, and made the following comments about the poor.

"Although the wages of labourers have increased considerably within these few years, yet it is now barely sufficient for their subsistence, and a few days illness brings them to the parish....It is a melancholy fact, that....the labourers of many parts of this county....may be truly said to be at this time in a wretched condition."[54]

As, indeed, was it also the very same John Howlett, who, in 1796, wrote of the labourers as being in "a state of wretched and pitiable destitution....The father and mother are covered with rags; their children are running about, like little savages, without shoes or stockings to their feet; and by day and night, they are forced to break down the hedges, lop the trees, and pilfer their fuel, or perish with cold."[55]

In the end, the argument, about enclosure and poverty, came around full circle. The General Report on Enclosures was published in 1808 by the Board of Agriculture, the advocates of enclosure, and written by Arthur Young himself.

"Many arguments have been framed, as well as assertions advanced, to prove that enclosing commons has been *universally* beneficial to the poor; but this is directly in the teeth of their own feelings and positive assertions, as well as many other most respectable eye-witnesses...."

Young went back to the argument advanced by Joseph Lee in 1656 that the "evils which do too usually accompany Inclosure of Commons, are not the faults of Inclosure, but of some Inclosers only." Young commented;-

"That the injury, which, seems really to have been received, flowed from inattention to the property or customs of the poor, and by no means of necessity from enclosure, appears from the following cases...." And he subjoins a list of parishes in which the poor were supposed to have benefited. Young was reduced to waffle in order to maintain some semblance of his previous position.

---

53 John Howlett. Enclosures a Cause of improved Agriculture, of Plenty and Cheapness of Provisions, of Population, and of both private and national Wealth. Pp. 77-79 and 98-99.
54 Thomas Davis. General View of the County of Wiltshire. Pp. 154-155.
55 J. Howlett. An Examination of Mr. Pitt's Speech. Pp. 48-49.

"It should therefore seem, that notwithstanding the increase of employment, yet there has been some contrary current which has been bearing heavily against the force of such employment."[56]

Contrary currents explain little. The fact was - and it is surely no more than logic should teach us to expect – that where the object of agricultural change was a big increase of rent, the rural community was almost bound to suffer. "It follows", wrote John Moore, in answer to Joseph Lee in 1656. "We see it with our eyes; It is so…."

✻

We have already seen that a major factor in the deterioration of living conditions in England in the 18th century was the great rise in the cost of living which began around mid-century. The crucial times were the poor harvests of 1756 and 1757, and of 1765 and 1766. But in times of normal crops, between and after these crisis years, it became observable that, though prices dropped, they failed to fall to their previous normal levels.

"It has pleased God to bless this nation, this year, with as large a crop of almost all sorts of corn, as has been known for many years past; and yet, how is the price kept up beyond every man's expectation?"[57]

So wrote a correspondent to the Gentleman's Magazine in 1758. A similar observation was made in 1772.

"The hand of Providence was exceedingly bountiful in the harvest of last year, yet some baneful influence robbed us of the blessing – Corn was still scarce and dear."[58]

It was becoming clear that here was emerging a long-term trend.

The distress engendered by these dearths produced serious disturbances in the crisis years, and simmering discontent in the intervals. In August 1756, hungry crowds rioted in the Midlands and north; farmers and traders were attacked; mills and farmhouses damaged or destroyed; markets occupied and flour carried off. The crisis recurred in 1766, with summer riots particularly serious in Berkshire and the West Country, and further extensive and serious disturbances in September. Coinciding with poor harvests and food rioting was a flood of pamphlets analysing the causes of the crisis that was unfolding; but what started off as analysis ended up as controversy.[59]

Nearly all the writers on the subject, especially in the early years, connected the rise in the price level, in one way or another, directly or indirectly, with the changed condition of rural England. The enclosing and consolidating of holdings, the conversion of tillage to pasture, the ploughing up of poorer, lighter soils, the massive increases in rent and the changing personnel of the tenantry – all this constituted such a radical alteration that it affected just about everything. The widespread conversion of the mixed culture of common fields into enclosed grazing land had an obvious tendency to produce scarcity, and raise prices, which even the advocates of enclosure could not deny. This complaint was particularly frequent in the Midland counties.

"Many lordships have not fifty acres plowed yearly since they were inclosed, in which fifteen hundred, or at least a thousand, were plowed before; and scarce an ear of corn is now to be seen, in some that bore hundreds of quarters.

---

56 Board of Agriculture. General Report on Enclosures. Pp. 155-157.

57 Gentleman's Magazine. 1758. Pp. 509-511.

58 A Letter to the Right Honourable LORD NORTH Attempting to show The Cause and the Remedies of the High Price of Provisions. P. 5.

59 D. G. Barnes. History or the Corn Laws. P. 32. W. J. Shelton. English Hunger and Industrial Disorder. Pp. 32-36.

"The consequences of this are felt severely already in the inland counties; so severely in Northamptonshire and Leicestershire, as that worse wheat has lately been sold there on an average at 7s and seven and six-pence the Winchester bushel, for many months together, than they have been used to buy at three and six-pence and four shillings; and they have given five shillings and five and six-pence for malt, that has usually been bought there at little more than half a crown. In these counties, inclosing has greatly prevailed, and most of their new-inclosed lordships are laid down for pasturage."[60]

Agricultural change could produce this scarcity without enclosures taking place. In Devon, enclosed centuries before, the complaint was the same.

The "monopolising Farmer, who having several Farms united in One, and being by express Covenants, with his provident Landlord, restrain'd from the Tillage of any of his *arable* or other Land, except perhaps with a few Turnips and Oats for his Cattle, and these in limited Quantities; of which (incredible as it may seem, when a general Dearth requires a contrary Conduct) we have lately had, and still have too many Instances in this County! And this in Parishes which heretofore produced corn sufficient, not only for their Home Consumption and the neighbouring Markets, but also for Exportation."[61]

It was not only corn that was said to have become scarce and dear on account of the new agriculture. Many of those foodstuffs which rural communities had traditionally produced for themselves were disappearing from the markets.

"The vast number of poultry, the quantity of pork, and a variety of other small articles of provision, are no longer supplied in their former abundance. The great farmer raises no more of these than are necessary for his own consumption; because his wife, and children, will not take the trouble, and care of them, or condescend to attend the market, like the wives, and children, of little farmers. His views are formed upon a large scale, and everything flows from him in a wholesale channel. And as no man can execute any very extensive business, so well as that which lies within a more contracted space, he must, when he has a great deal more upon his hands, neglect many small objects, partly for want of time, and partly because they appear trivial in their nature; and many trifles added together make a large deficiency upon the whole."[62]

This was in marked contrast to the farmers of the traditional village.

Small farmers, "were not opulent, and were obliged to make money of everything they could sell; therefore the markets were fully stocked; and to supply the markets, the farmers' wives used all their industry and care to raise all manner of poultry and eggs, and to make the most of their dairies, out of which they used to supply the house with all manner of goods from the shops."[63]

Under the new regime, however, the wives and daughters of opulent farmers considered themselves as of an elevated social position. Luxury, it was said, led to indolence; and the making of cheese, butter, and the rearing of poultry, were all given up.[64]

That produce which did reach market did so at a vastly inflated cost. The great farmer probably paid double the rent for his farm that his less opulent predecessors had done. This, according to some writers, was bound to have an effect on prices. Rent increases could not normally be recovered by increased production.

---

60 S. Addington. An Inquiry into the Reasons for and Against Inclosing Open-Fields. Pp. 50-51.
61 William Chapple. Risdon's Survey of Devon. P. 43.
62 Nathaniel Kent. Hints to Gentlemen of Landed Property. 1799 ed. Pp. 193-194.
63 A Country Farmer. Cursory Remarks on Inclosures. P. 19.
64 A Society of Farmers. A Political Enquiry into the consequences of Enclosing Waste Lands. P. 75.

"The improvements of modern husbandry are frequently mentioned as a counter-balance to the rack of rents. I am afraid they consist more in theory than in general use...."[65]

So increased burdens such as rent had to be paid for in other ways.

"Whether the landlord raises the land, and the farmer the price of produce; or the farmer is enriched by the generosity of the landlord, the *labouring part of the people*, and the *public*, may suffer equally."[66]

Other burdens weighed equally heavily on the great farmer of the new agriculture. The new and increased taxes imposed upon him as a result of the wars and the national debt; the greater expence of the articles of his own consumption; and the higher standard of opulence which he was expected to maintain; all of these would have had an effect on the price level.[67] The pamphlet published by 'A Society of Farmers' in 1785 puts forward the theory that production costs have a more permanent influence over the price level than temporary plenty or scarcity.

"*Plenty* abstractedly considered, may not always produce *cheapness*."[68]

It attributes the "exorbitant price of butcher's meat....to the prodigious number of inclosures made in England over thirty years." As a result, not only rents, but the costs of production had shot up. Many poorer soils had been brought into cultivation which were expensive to work. Cottagers could rear sheep for 10s per head with the help of common land, where it cost a farmer a guinea on high-rented, enclosed land. Heifers in 1785 were said to cost between £4 and £5 which twenty years previously could be bought for 50s or 60s. There were no complaints about a scarcity of animals, just of their dearness.[69]

The very opulence of the farmers of the new agriculture, it was asserted, itself distorted the market. Having greater financial reserves, "they can keep corn one month after another, for dearer times, without being obliged to thresh it out, and bring it to market, as poorer farmers must do, in order to pay their rent, and support their families."[70]

The engrossing of farms, it was claimed in 1758, put it "too much in the power of these great growers, in a time of scarcity, to distress the county, by withholding their corn from market, and thereby to occasion an artificial famine. This we know has been the case lately."[71]

"The wealthy monopoliser can sell or withhold, and go to this or that market as is most convenient and advantageous. He seldom chuses to draw a load of grain with him to market, and there expose it to sale; but when it suits him to take a ride, he can put a handful or two in his pocket by way of sample, and so keep the markets thin, and make an artificial scarcity around him, even when his barns are filled with plenty at home. This is certainly one occasion of the high price of grain, and the necessary consequence of that monopoly and ingrossing of land which is encouraged by inclosing."[72]

During the scarcity of 1757, or so it was claimed, "these merciless withholders of their corn kept up the price at such an exorbitant rate, that the poor in most parts of the kingdom were almost starved."

---

65 A Letter to the Right Honourable LORD NORTH Attempting to shew The Cause and the Remedies of the High Price of Provisions. P. 10.

66 Jonas Hanway. Letters on the Importance of the Rising Generation. P. 209.

67 E. g. Letter to Lord North. P. 10.

68 A Society of Farmers. A Political Enquiry into the Consequences of Enclosing Waste Lands. P. 71.

69 Ibid. P. 59.

70 S. Addington. An Inquiry into the Reasons for and Against Inclosing Open-Fields. P. 39.

71 Gentleman's Magazine. 1758. Pp. 509-511.

72 S. Addington. An Inquiry into the Reasons for and Against Inclosing Open-Fields. P. 39.

In 1758, plenty returned; "yet how is the price kept up beyond every man's expectation? Why, truly, our great growers thrash out little, or none; for, they say, after Christmas the ports will be opened for exportation, and the distillers permitted to distill from grain again."[73]

Wealthy farmers were even said to have turned speculators in their own product, by actually buying in grain from outside.[74]

The changed system of agriculture brought with it a whole new system of marketing, which many writers held responsible for the rising cost of living. Here is Joseph Massie again.

"The modern state of *England*....differs as much from the State thereof in the Reign of Queen *Elizabeth*, as the *Sea in a* STORM doth from the *Sea in a* CALM. The Inhabitants of most Counties and even Neighbourhoods, did then grow their own *Corn*, breed their own *Cattle*, made their own *Linen Cloth*, manufactured *Wool* for their own Cloathing, &c.....but of late Years, *Corn* is grown in one County, *Cattle* bred in another, *Cheese* made in a third, *Butter* in a fourth, *Woollen Manufacturies* confined to a few Counties, but no *Linen Manufactury* in any County...."

Everywhere there was an "EQUAL PLENTY of the common Necessaries of Life", and this provided "SECURITY against *Forestallers, Regrators,* and *Ingrossers of CORN, CATTLE, WOOL, &c.*"[75]

Engrossing was the practice of buying up large quantities of grain with a view thereby to produce a rise in price; regrating meant the reselling of such grain in the same market in which it had been bought, after the desired price rise had taken place; and forestalling was buying the grain before it reached the open market; this could happen on the farms, from the rickyard or even while the corn was still standing in the field; on the road between farm and market; or, increasingly, in private rooms in the inns of the market towns, on the basis of samples provided by the farmer; this was designed to keep the markets under-supplied, and to disguise the amount of supply available; and so bolster the price. These were all speculative practices designed to manipulate price, and they were illegal. It was the common contravention of these marketing laws which very many pamphleteers thought to be the cause of the increasing cost of living.

When most areas were largely self-sufficient in the necessaries of life, opined Massie, "there were not then any *Pretences* for buying great Quantities or Numbers thereof in one County, to sell them in other Counties." The breakdown of mixed farming "furnished *Pretences* for FORESTALLING *Corn, Cattle, Wool* &c., which have been increasing ever since, and wickedly practised for near Two Years last past, in Defiance of Law and Justice, and without the least Regard to the Miseries and Distresses of Fellow-Creatures."[76]

The theme was a common one; and Stephen Addington provided a glimpse of the process in action. He wrote of the rising price of bacon.

"This has been for many years, and (perhaps) ages, the principal support of the country-people; almost the only flesh many families tasted of for eight or nine months in the year. Some hundreds of hogs were kept in open-field parishes in *Leicestershire*, which, since they have been inclosed, have not kept twenty; in consequence of this, such store-pigs as were bought a few years ago for four or five shillings, are now sold readily at fifteen or sixteen; nor are many to be bought at all, but out of the hands of jobbers. Every thing, from the sucking pig to the fattest bacon, is advanced in proportion; and this is the necessary consequence of laying down those fields for pastures in the inclosures, which afforded these animals a variety of sustenance when they were upon tillage and open."[77]

73 Gentleman's Magazine. 1758. Pp. 509-511.

74 W. J. Shelton. English Hunger and Industrial Disorder. P. 43.

75 Joseph Massie. Considerations Relating to the Poor. Pp. 61 and 87.

76 Ibid. P. 87.

77 S. Addington. An Inquiry into the Reasons for and Against Inclosing Open-Fields. P. 29.

The opportunities for buying and selling in a wholesale way provided by the new agriculture produced a whole crop of middlemen in the provisions trade who had never been heard of before, and to these was imputed the responsibility for the rising cost of living.

"Monopoly is an epidemical distemper, it has produced an infinite number of agents, corn-jobbers, meal-men &c. &c. persons who neither grew corn themselves, or in any shape manufactured it; but whose whole study, and whose whole profits depended on employing every art to raise the price of it…."[78]

Especially on the receiving end of denunciation by pamphleteers and newspaper writers were the overlapping occupations of millers and flour-dealers. Traditionally, millers were not participants in the grain market at all. Their function had been to grind into flour whatever corn was brought to them, in return for payment. By the middle of the 18th century, it was said, many no longer performed this function.

"Now, do these gentlemen condescend to take poor man's grist? Do not the greatest part, and those of the largest dealings, grind wholly for themselves?"[79]

By this time, many had become powerful capitalists in their own right. Many came to dominate the agriculture of their district, with farmers dependent upon them for sales, advice, and ready cash. At the same time, they were accused of maintaining an anti-competitive correspondence with other millers, dividing up the trade between themselves, and regulating prices. In times of low prices, it was said, they were nowhere to be found. However;-

"Let there be but a bad season, and thin crops….this herd of dealers in the dark are incessantly busy to increase the calamity. By large contracts with the farmers; by changing of hands, and such concealments as are exceedingly difficult, if not impossible to detect; they can monopolise the corn, introduce an artificial scarcity, and dispense the necessaries of life upon their own terms. – Hence, the bitter complaints of starving the poor; Hence, in populous towns, those grievous parish rates."[80]

The flour-dealer, or meal-man, was a middleman who interposed himself between the miller and the baker; he was similarly roughly treated by the pamphleteers.

"The flourman….who is an engrosser by profession, having first bought a stock of corn on as good terms as he can, employs himself in the next place to raise the price of it, sometimes bidding, as this writer has been a witness, more than the farmer asks him in the market."[81]

"What general good end the meal-man's business has answered, has hitherto been undiscovered; the bad effects thereof have frequently and publicly appeared."[82]

The decline of open retail markets meant that agricultural and industrial labourers could no longer buy their own grain; and had few opportunities to get it ground even if they could.

"Bread is not only enhanced in price by these means, but is made still dearer; and much debased in quality, since the disuse of making it at home, and the almost universal custom in the country, as well as in the towns, of receiving it through the hands of the flourman and baker.

"The baker….practises all the arts of adulteration, in which bean-meal, plaister, whiting, and alum, are the usual ingredients."[83]

Similar complaints were made about the markets for meat and fish. The meat-salesmen and wholesale butchers in Smithfield market in London were said to be forestallers and engrossers, who owned large numbers of livestock, and could afford to withhold them from sale on a rising market.

---

78 Michael Combrune. An Enquiry into the Price of Wheat, Malt etc. P. 119.
79 Gentleman's Magazine. 1758. Pp. 424-425.
80 Ibid. Pp. 424-425.
81 Letter to Lord North. P. 13.
82 M. Combrune. An Enquiry into the Price of Wheat, Malt etc. P. 119.
83 Letter to Lord North. P. 13.

Complaints were made of both Smithfield and Billingsgate markets; they were too small to hold everyone who had business there; leading to a degree of bustle and confusion which resulted in transactions being confined to a few large participants. Consequently, there was a massive difference between the price of fish on the coast of Sussex and in the London market. Retail butchers were alleged commonly to make a profit of 50 per cent. Though 1765 was said to have been an excellent season for the growth of grass, which ordinarily would have made cattle cheap, yet, at Smithfield, they had never been dearer.[84]

Some of the pamphleteers saw taxation as a further major cause of the rising cost of living.

"The general tendency of taxes of all kinds to enhance the price of every thing brought to market is too obvious to need a proof. That a tax upon any article must have this effect upon that single article is self-evident. That it will also in some degree affect the prices of all other commodities is equally clear."

Consequently, Nathaniel Forster thought, the art of taxation was an important one to perfect, in order to achieve a just distribution of the burden. "The security of the state, as well as the happiness of the people, turns upon this point." Taxes on luxuries he thought the most equitable, because "least prejudicial to the body of the people."

"Whence happens it then, that the practice is so little governed by this principle? Whence happens it, that in some instances of taxation the burthen falls almost entirely upon the labouring poor?" [85]

Such taxes were the excises on soap, leather, beer and candles. Being paid immediately by the retailer, they caused a disproportionate rise in prices. In the case of candles, a tax of 1d per pound resulted in a retail price hike of 40 per cent. One penny per pound put on leather caused the price of a pair of shoes to rise by a whole shilling. As a result of this, it was complained, for every £6 millions which reached the Exchequer from this source, consumers paid over £10 millions.[86]

There was one more important, long-term, underlying cause of rising prices which exercised the pamphleteers. It had long been known that prices were affected by the amount of currency in circulation. Already in 1740, David Hume put it like this;-

"It seems a maxim almost self-evident, that the prices of every thing depend on the proportion between commodities and money, and that any considerable alteration on either has the same effect, either of heightening or of lowering the price. Encrease the commodities, they become cheaper; encrease the money, they rise in their value. As, on the other hand, a diminution of the former, and that of the latter, have contrary tendencies."[87]

William Chapple, writing about Devon in 1785, noted the process at work.

"The great Dearness of the Value of Money….whether occasioned by the Wealth of *Indian* Nabobs circulated here, and increasing the Quantity of current Cash, whilst the *whole* Produce of our Lands, Manufactures, etc, to be purchased therewith, continue much the same,…or whatever else may be the Cause, is sufficiently evident from its Effects; having within 20, or 25 Years at most, rais'd the Price of Provisions and Rents of Estates….by at least *One Third*…."[88]

Perhaps the subject was best treated of by Nathaniel Forster, writing in 1767. Increasing amounts of money, according to Forster, were flowing into circulation in a number of ways. It was brought into the country by shipping; or by foreign travellers, or by natives whose wealth had been acquired abroad. It also came in as a result of the type of overseas commerce, where exported goods were paid

---

84 Letter to the House of Commons On the Nature of Certain Abuses Relative to the Articles of Provisions. P. 6-7. Political Speculations on the Dearness of Provisions. P. 12.

85 Nathaniel Forster. An Enquiry of the General Causes of the High Price of Provisions. Pp. 49-50.

86 Political Speculations on the Dearness of Provisions. P. 4.

87 David Hume. Of Money. In Writings on Economics ed. E. Robinson. P. 41.

88 William Chapple. Risdon's Survey of Devon. P. 52n.

for in specie, and not by returned commodities. But, perhaps most importantly, and ultimately most controversially, the circulation was increased "by notes issued from a public bank, or by any other paper passing current as coin. This is indeed properly speaking a creation of money....and is just so much added to the circulating cash of the kingdom, and that without adding to the real wealth of a single person in it. I suppose the money paid into the bank for which notes are given, to be constantly upon the wing from thence."

Intimately connected with this was the subject of the funding system – the money lent to government. The money subscribed, asserts Forster, "does not remain a moment in the Exchequer, but flies immediately a thousand ways." And where that money was supplied by foreigners – and the Dutch lent a high proportion in those days – it represented a double increase in the circulation.

But, according to the perceptive Forster, it was not the increase in the circulating medium itself which exacerbated the poverty of the people. It was the unevenness of its distribution.

"If....this increase of money was equally diffused throughout the community, it is evident at first sight, that the high prices of commodities in consequence of it would not in this single view prejudice any particular members. For money being representative merely; and a conventional contrivance for the easier exchange of goods, it is certain, that the greater or lesser quantity of it cannot in this way have the least effect. Supposing, for instance, in any period of time, the circulating money be double what it is in another period; be double upon the whole, and double in the hands of each individual; and supposing the labour, produce, merchandise, and everything else which is exchanged or brought to market to be the same; what will be the consequence? The absolute and nominal prices will be doubled; but the relative and real ones will be the same. As a buyer I shall pay double, and as a seller I shall receive in the same proportion."

The trouble was that no steps were being taken to diffuse that new money. Forster thought that the object of trade and industry ought to be the employment of the greatest possible number of hands. That commerce which brought immense wealth to a few he deemed detrimental.

"The employment of the people and their plentiful enjoyment of the necessaries of life are the great objects which the public eye ought to have in view, in respect to the encouragement and exportation both of its produce and manufactures. No particular interest ought to be attended to when in competition with these capital objects....the temporary riches acquired by one or both....interests (landed and trading), when acting at all in opposition to these views of more general importance, are the real poverty of the people."[89]

And this, or so Forster thought, was the problem – "the influx of wealth generally into few hands, in comparison to the whole body of the people". It was this concentration of excess circulating medium into the hands of the few that connects this subject with the previous ones of monopolistic marketing practices and agricultural change. Wealth failed to diffuse itself through society, and so altered the whole balance between funds available for investment and investment opportunities. Investment hunger and speculation were the inevitable results.

"That penury grows out of opulency is beyond dispute...." We prey on each other "by running up the value of things."

That is how Jonas Hanway summed up the arguments for us. A Letter to the House of Commons, written in 1765, attributed the raised cost of living to ambition, avarice, the extravagance of men

---

89 Nathaniel Forster. An Enquiry of the General Causes of the High Price of Provisions. Pp.2, 13-
    14, 20-26, 31. Even William Cobbett never fully understood this point. Why is it that we have
    all heard of Adam Smith, but nobody has heard of Nathaniel Forster? Because Forster was on the
    unorthodox, unprogressive, unfashionable side of the argument?

of affluence, and combinations; there being "no limit to the avarice of mean and sordid minds." Remember this.[90]

❋

This attribution of the causes of the rising cost of living to the changed social and economic circumstances in which the country found itself met, at first, with few challenges. A few murmurs came there, unsurprisingly, from corn traders, who did not emerge with much credit from the flood of pamphlets. The respected corn merchant, Charles Smith, wrote a series of papers on the corn trade during the late 1750s, in which he defended opulent farmers and middlemen. Very few farmers, he contended, were actually wealthy enough to withhold their produce from sale, still less to speculate in corn. He argued for a continuation of the current state of affairs, which, he thought, rather perversely, kept corn at a moderate price, and enabled traders to perform their proper function of transferring corn from producing to consuming areas. The laws against engrossing, regrating and forestalling, in his opinion, needed, not rigorous enforcement, but repeal.

The analysis of the corn traders differed radically from that of the pamphleteers already cited. These latter writers were said to be "mistaken in their sentiments, and quite strangers to the question; they abounded with false and idle stories invented with the most villainous design, or proceeding from the most profound ignorance and prejudice."

"I cannot think that engrossing is ever a crime," wrote a flour-merchant in 1756. "No person would buy corn merely upon speculation, when the price is at 10l. or 12l. per load, to keep it by him in expectation of a farther advance. When corn is engrossed, (if I may use the term in a good sense) it is at a time when there is a great plenty, and the price low; which corn, if it be kept till a time of scarcity, and then sold out, is really of service to the poor."

The idea of speculators being willing to tie up their capital without any prospect of a rising market is a curious one.

The accusation that speculators combined for the purpose of raising the price was "so very idle and ridiculous, as not to deserve a serious refutation."

"The news-papers are filled with complaints against forestallers and engrossers....taking it for granted, that there are in reality such men to whose account the high price of provisions is to be charged. But, I take it upon me to aver, that this is false in fact; it is merely an imaginary evil, and it might as well be charged on the inhabitants of the moon."

The miller, it was asserted, could not possibly raise the price of corn, as he did not buy or sell on his own account. In fact, he was an altruist, who "never refuses to grind wheat for the poor at three-pence per bushel let the price be what it will; and for the industrious poor, when wheat is at a high price, he will often grind it toll-free."

"As it cannot be made appear how grinding wheat, and dressing meal into flour, any wise contributes to rise the price of it; the mob and their advocates dwell chiefly on the adulteration."

This flour-merchant then proceeded to defend bakers and mealmen from the charge of adulteration.

"One of these writers....tells you a tale, or quotes a secret, which, for the life of me I cannot conceive how he came at the knowledge of, unless he has been bribing one of our men; or, as I am rather inclined to think, been tampering with one of our girls. This slut has told him, that two thirds of what is commonly called sack flour, is made from wheat....What a pity it is, when he was upon it,

---

90 Jonas Hanway. Letters on the Importance of the Rising Generation. P. 176. A Letter to the House of Commons in which is set forth the Nature of certain Abuses Relative to the Articles of Provision. P. 34.

that he had not gone one step further, and told the world what the other third was made of? – Not, surely, of an author's brains; for if no one had more than himself, all the authors in the universe would not furnish a sufficient quantity to make good the sack...."

Later on, this flour-merchant relates a conversation in a coffee-house, involving an apothecary.

"Lord have mercy upon us! We shall all be poisoned; *this flour* will destroy half the nation. I declare against using a dust more of it. Upon examining my stools with a glass, I have discovered certain moleculae, like bits of chalk, in the feces. On my conscience, it was arsenic; and I am confirmed in this opinion by what the learned Dr. Manning has lately published to the world. He has proved, as plainly as words can do, That not one man in the kingdom, who has lived upon bakers bread, or meal-mans flour, has, for these seven years past, died a natural death; but has been sent out of the world by alum, or whiting, or chalk; or by bones picked up in the streets, or taken from dunghills. – Nay the very graves and charnel-houses, have been ransacked for bones, which, being dried and ground to powder, the bakers have mixed with flour, and made into bread! It is for this reason, continues the doctor, we hear of so many sudden deaths; so many new, and till lately, unheard-of distempers, for which we have no name; which puzzle all the gentlemen of the faculty, and elude their art."

The decline and disappearance of the open market in corn, according to this same merchant, was driven by the poor themselves; when they found by experience that they were better off financially buying flour from the mealman than wheat in the market. Farmers no longer sold wheat to their labourers because there was simply no demand for it.

"In all markets where I have been concerned, the farmers never left off to bring wheat for this purpose, 'till the poor, finding the benefit of buying flour, left off to purchase it."[91]

So if the changes in marketing practice had no effect on the price of wheat, what, in the opinion of the corn-traders, was the cause of the rise? Although middlemen, of course, would never themselves manipulate price, they were not averse to blaming farmers for withholding corn and speculating. Lip service was paid to the widespread conversion of arable to pasture; and to the depreciation of the currency. But if prices were high, the main cause was, quite simply, scarcity caused by a deficient crop.[92]

"The sudden rise which we now feel, and which is so generally complained of, as the consequence of forestalling, is absolutely, and beyond doubt, chiefly owing to the shortness of the late crops, and smallness of quantity at market.

"We have had extremes of wet and extremes of dry weather for four or five years past; some of the seasons have been of the longest continuance ever known within the memory of man."[93]

The most extreme weather ever is not a modern invention.

But there was another altogether more sinister strand of argument underlying the corn-dealers' pamphlets. The scarcity and high prices, it was said, were actually caused by the food riots. High prices formed merely the pretext for ill-disposed persons to cause riot and confusion.

"The alarm given of imaginary dearths, and the usual madness and violences attending them in destroying mills, and other repositories of corn, when there is any pretence of its high price, are capable of producing most of the ill effects of real dearths.

"The usual motives to violent and desperate actions, in at least the contrivers of them, are resentment and revenge on account of some real or supposed injury."[94]

91 Two Letters on the Flour Trade and the Dearness of Corn. Pp. 4-24.
92 Ibid. P. 19. Gentleman's Magazine 1757. Pp. 129-131. Reflections on the Present High Price of Provisions. P. 17.
93 Reflections on the Present High Price of Provisions. P. 18.
94 Gentleman's Magazine 1757. Pp. 129-131.

"Mobs are made up of the drunken, the lazy, and most abandoned part of the people, whose case is misrepresented, and whose distresses are greatly aggravated, or rather created, by certain senseless and injudicious writers in the common news-papers....who endeavour to justify those incendiaries in their violent practices; they are poor and wretched, no matter by what means; though they refuse to work, or immediately spend what they earn in strong beer and spirituous liquors, their poverty, it seems, gives them a right to plunder; and (altho' an apostle has determined otherwise) to feast on the fruits of other people's labour."[95]

Victim-blaming and anti-poor propaganda, as we have seen, go back into the seventeenth century. But the vilification also of those who wrote on the subject of the rising cost of living was a new trend, which was to become prominent in later years.

There were many ways in which high prices were blamed on the poor themselves. The high wages of labourers in flourishing manufactures, it was said, enabled them to spend more on food, and so increased overall consumption. The operation of the poor law also increased prices.

"The hand that is idle....steals from the hand which is employed....The nourishment which should support the industrious is drained away to feed the lazy....They generally rely upon the parish for a maintenance on every frivolous pretence....No misconduct, extravagance, or debauchery that poor persons have been guilty of, is to be alledged against them....The poor must be maintained."

The dishonesty of the poor in running up small debts with shopkeepers which were not recoverable at law, and then refusing to pay them, was apparently a major factor in forcing up prices; as traders were obliged to increase their profit margins in order to cover the losses.

But riots, and the lack of protection afforded corn-dealers by the authorities, were designated one of the chief causes which "enhance the price of commodities."

The solution to the problem, according to this literature, was to overcome "the indolence and weakness of those in power", and to find ways to keep the people "in due order and subjection". There were very few laws, complained a corn-dealing pamphleteer, "made for keeping the common people within the bounds of morality or temperance....no punishments on them for adultery, incest, lying and other vices". Another writer suggested enacting a law to make it a felony to abet or assist in any disturbances. Those convicted of the offence were to have no possibility of pardon or reprieve, and the costs of prosecution were to be borne by the county. Any losses sustained by corn-dealers as a result of riots were to be compensated within a month.[96]

Most importantly, the subsistence of the people was to be considered as the private property of individuals. And it was the duty of government to defend those individuals in the possession of their property – "otherwise we recur to the savage laws of force." The implication was fairly clear that the army ought to be deployed against food rioters. Moreover, corn-dealers should be left alone to deal with the market however best suited them.

"The legislator cannot, by interposition in these matters, attempt a remedy without invading the property of one subject in favour of another." All these writers thought it necessary to repeal "the oppressive and narrow-spirited regulations" against engrossing, regrating and forestalling.[97]

The perniciousness of this literature hardly needs pointing out. To begin with, the pamphlets of the corn-dealers were very much in the minority. Numerically, they were overwhelmed by the pamphlets written by clerics, merchants, agricultural experts and others who took a much more widely ranging and long-term view of the crisis. The flimsiness of the arguments presented amounts, in many areas, to lack of any argument at all; some are in the teeth of established historical fact. The abuse of

---

95 Two Letters on the Flour Trade and the Dearness of Corn. Pp. 18-19.
96 Reflections on the Present High Price of Provisions. Pp. 9-13. Gentleman's Magazine 1757. Pp. 129-131.
97 Reflections on the Present High price of Provisions. Pp. 5-7.

those suffering in the famines needs no comment. And their advocacy of the use of legal and military force to ensure to one small section of the nation a profit which the vast majority of consumers saw as made at their expence is surely the essence of totalitarian opinion.

The constant demand for the repeal of the laws against the marketing offences is telling. Corn-dealers claimed to be doing nothing illegal, and, indeed, the practice of buying corn where it was cheap and plentiful and selling it where it was scarce was already legal under most circumstances, and was widely recognised as the legitimate business of the middleman. The laws against engrossing, regrating and forestalling were directed against the speculative practices which manipulated price. Why, then, were the dealers so keen on repeal?

Not many were convinced by this special pleading. Indeed, three parliamentary committees investigated the rising price of provisions between 1764 and 1766, and took evidence from corn-dealers and others, and all came to the conclusion that the crisis was being exacerbated by speculative manipulation. Middlemen raised the prices, it was said in 1765, "to get an estate". The most common complaint to the House of Lords committee of 1765 was of secretive sample sales forestalling the market. The claims of the corn-dealing pamphleteers were simply not believable.[98]

However, in the upper echelons of government, the arguments of the corn-dealers won the day. And from this period, perhaps, we can date the emergence of an establishment viewpoint on the causes of poverty. An orthodoxy was in the process of formation.

The 1760s were the era of the King's Friends. These were a cabal of aristocratic politicians led by the Earl of Bute, who interposed themselves between the king and the government, ostensibly to protect the court from the ravages of factional politics. Their position depended entirely upon the royal favour. They formed an elitist clique, who, according to Edmund Burke writing in 1770, set themselves against any influence which popular or public opinion might have on the policies of government. They deplored "the monstrous evil of governing in concurrence with the opinion of the people".

"For it seems to be laid down as a maxim, that a King has some sort of interest in giving uneasiness to his subjects; that all who are pleasing to them, are to be of course disagreeable to him; that as soon as the persons who are odious at Court are known to be odious to the people, it is snatched at as a lucky occasion of showering down upon them all kinds of emoluments and honours. None are considered as well-wishers to the Crown, but those who advised to some unpopular course of action...."[99]

Between this elitist government and the large-scale players in the grain trade there seems to have grown up, in these years, an alliance, shadowy indeed, but lasting for many decades, and exerting such a formidable influence over government policies, that it is rather surprising how it has largely escaped the notice of historians.[100] We might surmise that it was natural enough for the major landowners, whose agricultural reorganisation was dependent for its viability on the high price of agricultural produce, to form an alliance with those who speculated in that produce, and to exert the powers of the state on their behalf. Whatever the cause, the alliance was clear enough in its consequences; for the government seems to have accepted the analysis of the causes of the rise in prices, and the resulting disturbances, as set out in the pamphlets of the corn-dealers. Just how out of touch with reality ministers were was well demonstrated for us by Edmund Burke.

---

98 W. J. Shelton. English Hunger and Industrial Disorder. P. 72.

99 Edmund Burke. Thoughts on the Cause of the Present Discontents. In Select Works ed. E. J. Payne. Pp. 49-50.

100 Largely, but not completely. See R. Wells. Wretched Faces.

"Our Ministers are of opinion, that the increase of our trade and manufactures, that our growth by colonisation and by conquest, have concurred to accumulate immense wealth in the hands of some individuals; and this again being dispersed among the people, has rendered them universally proud, ferocious and ungovernable; that the insolence of some from their enormous wealth, and the boldness of others from a guilty poverty, have rendered them capable of the most atrocious attempts; so that they have trampled upon all subordination, and violently borne down the unarmed laws of a free Government; barriers too feeble against the fury of a populace so fierce and licentious as ours. They contend, that no adequate provocation has been given for so spreading a discontent; our affairs having been conducted throughout, with remarkable temper and consummate wisdom. The wicked industry of some libellers, joined to the intrigues of a few disappointed politicians, have, in their opinion, been able to produce this unnatural ferment in the nation." In short, "that we have a very good Ministry, but that we are a very bad people; that we set ourselves to bite the hand that feeds us; that with a malignant insanity we oppose the measures, and ungratefully vilify the persons, of those whose sole object is our own peace and prosperity."

The "confused and disturbed state of the nation", which began around mid-century – "beyond the disorders of any former time" – were imputed, not to excessive penury, but to excessive well-being![101]

Just as the government fell in with the corn-merchants' explanations of the crisis, so also it followed their agenda for dealing with it.

During a major subsistence crisis, such as occurred in England in the mid 1760s, it was clearly not justifiable to allow large-scale exports of corn. The movement of grain towards the ports was provocative, and most of the food-rioting of 1766 was connected with such movements. Yet the government did all it could to facilitate the continued operations of the merchants. Early in 1766, shipments were still leaving the country. At the grain port of Lyme, this was provoking riots, but the exportation was maintained by the use of the army. Eventually, at the end of February, exporting was banned for six months, and rioting ceased.[102]

The movements of corn, however, did not. Even apart from smuggling by merchants, the loading of ships for export continued in anticipation of the ending of the embargo at the end of August. Public opinion believed this to be wrong, and pressure was put on the government to prevent it. But it did not. Indeed, these grain movements would hardly have occurred at all had there not been some degree of certainty among the merchants that exporting would be allowed; and interesting questions could be asked about the source of such certainty. However that may have been, when the embargo finally expired, massive amounts of grain flooded out of England on to the Continent. There followed the extraordinary and astonishing decision to delay for two months the meeting of parliament, which alone was constitutionally capable of re-imposing the ban on exports. Not only were the merchants given a whole month in which to get their cargoes shipped – they were even paid the export bounty for doing so. The Corn Law was so formed that the export bounty could not be claimed during times of high prices of corn, and that it was paid in 1766 can only have been as a result of price manipulation at Bear Key in London and at the outports, whilst prices inland remained high. The payment of the export bounty during a famine was something which even the corn-dealing pamphleteers professed not to think justifiable.

The resumption of exports, and the resulting huge movements of grain across the countryside, led also to the resumption of rioting in September 1766. Faced with a choice between the re-imposition

---

101 Edmund Burke. Thoughts on the Cause of the Present Discontents. In Select Works ed. E. J. Payne .Pp. 4-5.

102 Most of the rest of this segment, except where stated, is taken from W. J. Shelton. English Hunger and Industrial Disorder. Pp. 1-157.

of the embargo on exports, and the military suppression of the riots, the government chose the latter. The military solution to the problem of poverty was something of an innovation. It was introduced by the government in a way which suggested that criticism and opposition were expected; but at that crucial time, September 1766, the opening of parliament had been unaccountably deferred. Nevertheless, the use of "that dreaded monster, the military", was criticised by Whig politicians. In the militia, officers objected to being employed to quell rioters, and an M. P. declared, reasonably enough, that it was not the purpose of the military "to war on the people". In spite of all misgivings, the minister at the War Office, Lord Barrington, was given responsibility for dealing with the rioting that resulted from grain movements and exports at a time of scarcity, and the military solution pressed upon reluctant local authorities.

Out in the real world, conscientious magistrates attempted to deal with the crisis in the time-honoured ways. Gentlemen formed associations for providing the poor with corn at below cost price. In Gloucestershire, magistrates refused to employ military force, and instead put pressure on farmers to reduce the prices they asked for their grain. Many petitioned for the control of corn exports, and for a prohibition on the use of corn in distilling and starch-making. The duty of prosecuting forestallers of the market, which should have been the responsibility of government, was abdicated to the local gentry, who formed themselves into groups for the purpose.

For all their efforts, the magistrates were roundly abused by the ministers responsible for dealing with the disturbances, who deemed military force the only option. Lord Barrington at the War Office complained the troops which had been sent "to aid the civil power had not been used. The magistrates at this juncture have less spirit or prudence than usual".

The rationale of decision-making at the heart of government which resulted in the government's use of the army against its own citizens is revealed for us by Edmund Burke.

"If the Administration seems now and then, from remissness, or from fear of making themselves disagreeable, to suffer any popular excesses to go unpunished, the Cabal immediately sets up some creature of theirs to raise a clamour against the Ministers, as having shamefully betrayed the dignity of Government....After having first vilified them with the higher orders for suffering the laws to sleep over the licentiousness of the populace, they drive them (in order to make amends for their former inactivity) to some act of atrocious violence, which renders them completely abhorred by the people."[103]

In consequence, rioters were increasingly confronted by armed troops, detachments of which were shifted around the country to wherever the danger appeared to be greatest. Many of these were said to be collected up from "the scum of the towns". The severity with which they were disciplined, and the frequent movement of them around the country, to prevent the formation of local ties, ensured that troops would fire on civilians when ordered. In the weeks following the suppression of the riots, the ringleaders were rounded up, and Special Commissions sent out into the localities to mete out justice. Many were capitally convicted; some hanged; some transported; some condemned to serve in the forces; and others left subject to suspended sentences, the threat remaining in place as a deterrent against future commotions. Government methods plumbed the depths of the suborning of magistrates and the use of informers to infiltrate and manipulate rioters. Brutality succeeded in overawing the populace, and in the years following, the hungry hungered largely in silence.

By contrast, corn-dealers of all sorts achieved their objective of being left alone in command of the market. The view gained an increasing acceptance that trade would prosper best if left unregulated. This was known as Free Trade; but how a trade could be called free which was so totally dominated by a small number of highly capitalised participants who could control price was never explained; nor

---

103 Edmund Burke. Thoughts on the Cause of the Present Discontents. In Select Works ed. E. J. Payne. P. 27.

ever has been since. It was, I suppose, free for them. Finally, in 1772, the laws against the speculative marketing offences of engrossing, regrating and forestalling were repealed....

❋

"Whatever be the road to power, that is the road which will be trod."[104]

As it was with politics, so was it also with writers and pamphleteers. The orthodoxies about the poor had been established, and it behoved every writer who aspired to popularity or profit to conform to them.

"I know it to be too much the modern system of writing to flatter the prejudices of mankind," wrote an agricultural dissident in 1785.[105] The anti-democratic strand of thought manifested itself henceforth in most works aimed at those connected with the establishment. In many cases, it has passed unnoticed by historians.

It is, for example, striking, how frequently the arguments of the corn-dealing pamphleteers turn up in the writings of those who advocated and defended the new agriculture. Arthur Young, in his earlier works, was keen to attract a readership of landed aristocrats and gentleman farmers. Not surprisingly, he defended large farms against the charge of raising the cost of living.

"That the turning small farms into large ones, *does not* occasion a scarcity of corn; I flatter myself I have proved sufficiently....in shewing that their produce is much less considerable, acre for acre, than that of large ones."[106]

John Arbuthnot, a friend of Young's, agreed.

The large farmer "with a proportionate capital and number of horses, is able to do more than his proportion of work in the same time; and the doing of it at the critical juncture, is of so much the greater consequence; thus his ground is naturally in better tilth, his fallows, feed-time, dung-cart, in short, every operation performed better because they can be dispatched; and his ground being in better order, it will not be denied but that his produce must be greater."

A concentrated capital, according to Arbuthnot, in the hands of one man, would produce more than if divided between several. And the consolidation of farms into few hands he asserted to have a similar effect.[107]

It was small farms that were responsible for dearth; small farms, according to Young, which did not produce butter, cheese or pork. "Cattle....are scarcely ever kept by *little* farmers." (sic) As for eggs and poultry, "of what national good is the cheapness of poultry?...Nothing can be more truly the language of prejudice."[108]

Arbuthnot agreed again.

Pigs and poultry "are not objects worthy of the attention of the legislature." Small farmers could not rear either to advantage. Pigs could only be profitably kept by large farmers and cottagers; the latter "by letting a sow with her litter of pigs run in the lanes, or rather, under that pretence, in the fields and meadows of the neighbouring farmers. Yet this cannot be deemed a national benefit."

Pigs, asserted Arbuthnot, rather unusually, require fields full of clover.

---

104 Ibid. P. 36.
105 A Society of Farmers. A Political Enquiry into the Consequences of Enclosing Waste Lands. P. 12.
106 A. Young. Farmer's Letters. 1771 ed. P. 180.
107 J. Arbuthnot. An Inquiry into the Connection between the present Price of Provisions and the Size of Farms. Pp. 7-13.
108 A. Young. Farmer's Letters. 1771 ed. P. 183-184.

Arbuthnot thought pigs, poultry, butter, and eggs such insignificant subjects that he was almost ashamed to be discussing them.[109]

If the consolidation of farms was absolved from responsibility for the rising cost of living, so too were the dealers in corn. Arthur Young lamented the amount of abuse heaped on jobbers in corn, and declared that "this species of traders are excellently useful." He defended secret sales by sample, on the ground that it reduces transport costs – an argument straight out of the Letters on the Flour Trade of 1756. Both Young and Arbuthnot put forward the seemingly contradictory argument that the monopolising of corn in order to enhance the price was both impossible and beneficial. For Young, arguments based on the speculative marketing offences were "a collection of mere vulgar errors and low prejudices....As to engrossing of corn, it is mere idle talk; the thing is impossible to be done in any degree, that can raise or fall the price one farthing a quarter."

And yet, Young goes on, "corn would be engrossed while cheap, to sell again when dear....Much engrossing should *lower* the price in dear times."

Young knew perfectly well that the stores of grain accumulated when the price was low were exported under the bounty scheme.

"Great farmers are the only people, who are, what are called engrossers. All engrossing to such, or any degree, is impossible. The magazines which individuals form in good years, are a ready supply in bad ones."[110]

Arbuthnot was guilty of a similar contradiction.

"The dread which some may have of monopolies, cannot bear an argument....The yearly produce of wheat alone is said to be 4, 000,000 of quarters, which I believe far short of the reality; but even that quantity, at 30s. a quarter, would amount to 6,000,000l. *per annum*. Will any man, or set of men, dream of such a monopoly?"

Yet this assertion follows a paragraph in which Arbuthnot complains, quite rightly, of the artificial manipulation of the price at Bear-Key in London, for the sole benefit of a small number of dealers; and precedes one lamenting the present breed of speculators with whom farmers are forced to deal, "of whom they are ever jealous, and always suspicious that when such buyers appear in markets, some sudden rise is expected."

That the great farmers withheld their corn from market was actually supposed to be fortunate for the poor. "Was it otherwise, as the corn laws now stand, we might often, even with a most plentiful harvest, be in the utmost danger of famine."[111]

Did farmers, therefore, refrain from selling during times of falling prices?

John Howlett, writing in 1787, reveals for us the altruism to the poor shown by the dealers in the provisions trade. For during scarcities they would fetch food from all parts, even to their own disadvantage, "that the ungrateful murmurers might not be starved."

If neither modern agriculture, nor modern marketing, was responsible for the rising cost of living, what was? The writers of this literature display a degree of reluctance to concede that prices were rising at all.

"I have never known wheat uncommonly dear", surprisingly asserted John Howlett in 1787.[112]

According to Arbuthnot, the advance in the price of provisions was "not so great as is generally believed, nor such as ought to alarm this nation." To the extent that prices were rising at all, Arbuthnot

---

109 J. Arbuthnot. An Inquiry into the Connection between the present Price of Provisions and the Size of Farms. Pp. 18-23.

110 A. Young. Farmer's Letters. 1771 ed. Pp. 186-193.

111 J. Arbuthnot. An Inquiry into the Connection between the present Price of Provisions and the Size of Farms. Pp. 89-90 and 14.

112 Rev. J. Howlett. Enclosures a Cause of Improved Agriculture etc. P. 56.

was willing to ascribe some causative influence to the plentiful currency, the great wealth of society, and forestallers. But, in general, there was only one cause – the weather. "For these five years past, we have had, at one time or another of the year, the most unfavourable seasons for corn that have been known for a long while past," he declared, not altogether accurately.

"It is the hand of God, which has visited us."[113]

God's shoulders, of necessity, were broad.

By 1787, after over twenty years of escalating prices, John Howlett was still blaming the weather. He cited a series of severe winters followed by cold, backward springs, which took a toll on the body condition of cattle and prevented their breeding; and which caused the starvation of multitudes of sheep. The resulting deficiency of the barley crop prevented the fattening of huge numbers of pigs. The effects of the severe winter of 1739, he asserted, rather oddly, were still being felt forty years later.[114]

The obvious logical conclusion to be drawn from all this was that the increasing hardships and distresses of the people of England were being caused by the weather. But neither Young nor Arbuthnot went this far; because neither was really willing to acknowledge that such hardships and distresses existed at all. Instead, they promoted an alternative reality in tune with, if not directly derived from, the prevailing establishment orthodoxies.

Arthur Young composed a menu for the poor upon which, he claimed, they could live comfortably, and still have a significant cash surplus at the end of the year. It included mixed-grain bread, but not every day; cheese three times a week; home-brewed beer; fat meat; potatoes. On some days, the poor were to subsist on soup or rice pudding only. This would leave £13 8s. annually in reserve. Here are Young's comments.

"Some of my readers, will, I suppose, cry out, 'This calculation is all romance! Shew me a family that lives so cheap! But is their not living so cheap any fault in the price of provisions? Let me ask in return, where the poor family is to be found, that do not drink tea once a day at *least*? Can they live so cheap, as if they desisted from their tea-sipping? Or are they to complain of prices, when they will not allow them to trifle at the tea-table? Is there any necessity that they should eat nothing but the best wheaten-bread, when other kinds are to be had much cheaper, but equally wholesome? Whenever, therefore the price of provisions is complained of let an explanatory expression come in, 'as we chuse to live'."

Here is Young again on the rosy and idyllic situation of the English poor.

"The labouring poor, in general, earn *now* sufficient to live decently cloathed, and in good health....sufficient in these dear times to support themselves, their wives, and their families, and provide for all extraordinaries; besides laying by no inconsiderable sum; and I am sure I know no difference, in point of health, vigour, and strength, between them and their families now, and years ago, when provisions were much cheaper....

"What was the effect of such cheapness? If the present dearness is so afflicting, sure the former good times were attended with no trifling effects? Instead of laying up three or four pounds; they then, doubtless, saved twice as much! No such matter; whatever was gained by such cheapness, was constantly expended by the husband in a proportionable quantity of idleness and ale, and by the wife in that of tea; as to health, strength, cloathes, and money in pocket; I well know there was no difference in those cheap times, from the present dear ones....

"The present prices of the necessaries of life are only *dear* on comparison with those of *some* preceding years; but not intrinsically so; since a commonly industrious man may considerably more than maintain himself, his wife, and family....It may be said, that wheaten-bread, that beef, that

113 J. Arbuthnot. An Inquiry into the Connection between the present Price of Provisions and the Size of Farms. Pp. 53-55.
114 J. Howlett. Enclosures a Cause of Improved Agriculture etc. Pp. 46-48.

mutton, that tea, that sugar, that butter are dear; but do not in the height of an argument, jumble these and *the necessaries of life* together…."[115]

If the poor were not distressed, therefore, why did they riot in years of scarcity? Young asserted that it was the labourers on higher pay who rioted. He was perhaps mistaken, and certainly wrong. But he drew his own conclusions.

"Very far is it from my thoughts, to assert or hint, that our poor are too well paid….but I must…. assert, riots and public disturbances form no just rules to judge by.

"It was always my opinion, and experience confirms it; that sober and industrious workmen, of any sort, *never* riot. In all occupations, there will be idle, drunken, unsettled and disorderly persons; a few of these getting together and talking over the *dearness of provisions* (which frequently becomes a cant term among them) inflame each other, and all of their own stamp; they know a riot is their best diversion; to stroll in a party about the country, eating and drinking at free cost, and having no work to do but mischief, suits such geniuses to a hair…."[116]

John Arbuthnot's version of the well-being of the poor owed even more to establishment orthodoxy, as set out by Edmund Burke in 1770. The great and increasing wealth of the nation diffused itself, through the luxurious consumption of the rich, to all ranks of society, including the lowest, who all partook of their portion.

"In every instance, the poor receive their share of this scattered wealth; and in proportion to the luxury of the spot, the poor who inhabit are, by the diffused riches, enabled to bear their share in the price of provisions….I do not speak of the worthless abandoned poor; they always flock to large cities, and subsist by charity and theft, where they are not so easily detected as in the country…."

As a result of this luxury descending to the lowest class, "the tradesman who formerly was contented with a shoulder of mutton, must now have his fillet of veal….The chimney sweeper's boy, who, instead of the crust of bread which used to be his fee, now receives a morsel of meat."[117]

John Arbuthnot was a gentleman farmer who had strong links to government and high society. His pamphlet, written in 1773, is an extremely important one in the history of establishment propaganda; being strongly linked to contemporary orthodox thinking, in all its contradictoriness and muddle-headedness. It is also seminal; many of its ideas formed the basic tenets which became enshrined in economic thought through Adam Smith's Wealth of Nations. But in its portrayal of the well-being of the poor, and its assumption that discontent was merely something stirred up by writers for their own evil purposes, it shows the way official thinking was tending, and foreshadows the propaganda of the 1790s.

Arbuthnot was perhaps the first to abuse, not just the poor, but those who wrote on the subject of the poor. It was to the evil designs of such writers that Arbuthnot attributed the disturbed state of the country.

"There now prevails among the lower class of people a licentiousness which has been, in a great measure, occasioned by the numberless publications on the causes of scarcity, too evidently calculated to inflame their minds."

And he clearly implies the need for some kind of legal censorship; and an official campaign of propaganda.

"Most of those publications have appeared to me big with mischief, as blowing the trumpet of discontent among every rank of people; and, however inadvertently they may have been suffered to

115 Arthur Young. Farmer's Letters. 1771 ed. Vol. I. Pp. 196-205.
116 Arthur Young. A Six Weeks Tour through the Southern Counties of England and Wales. 1769.
      Pp. 331-332.
117 John Arbuthnot. An Inquiry into the Connection between the present Price of Provisions and the
      Size of Farms. Pp. 139, 46, and 55-57.

creep into the world, they cannot fail to breed, especially among the lower class, that rancour and jealousy which are the mother of riot and confusion, and which may, if thus fomented, carry them to such lengths as may seriously increase the misfortunes we complain of. My only motive for thus offering to the public my opinion on this head, proceeds from an ardent desire to rectify, if I can, the strangely misconceived notion of my countrymen, by proving to them, that it is not to any individual, or set of individuals, that we ought to ascribe this calamity; but that it is the hand of God, which has visited us...."[118]

The future was with John Arbuthnot.

Meanwhile, perhaps the best known piece of establishment propaganda of the period, which still influences our modes of thought today, was by Adam Smith, and was entitled the Wealth of Nations. On all those topics which concerned the well-being or otherwise of the populace, Smith followed the establishment line as set out by Young, Arbuthnot, and the corn-dealing pamphleteers.

Any suspicion that a moral philosopher leading a sheltered life in a Scottish university might not be the person best qualified to pronounce upon the condition of the English poor is amply confirmed by the arguments he put forward. He saw the labouring poor as enjoying, in general, a good standard of living; and he based this perception on the fact that real wages varied. They varied between seasons; between years of plenty and scarcity; and from place to place. If the poor could live when real wages were low, reasoned Smith, they must be in very comfortable circumstances at other times and in other places.

The fragility of this logic was no problem in the face of an indulgent readership.

"It is certain that....grain was somewhat dearer in the last century than in the present, it is equally certain that labour was much cheaper. If the labouring poor, therefore, could bring up their families then, they must be more at their ease now.[119]

Smith follows Arbuthnot in seeing the greater wealth of the higher classes diffusing itself through society – the "universal opulence which extends itself to the lowest ranks of the people." As a result, the English poor were enjoying a rising standard of living.

"The real recompense of labour, the real quantity of the necessaries and conveniences of life which it can procure to the labourer, has, during the course of the present century, increased perhaps in a still greater proportion than its money price. Not only grain has become somewhat cheaper, but many other things from which the industrious poor derive an agreeable and wholesome variety of food have become a great deal cheaper....The great improvements in the coarser manufactures of both linen and woollen cloth furnish the labourers with cheaper and better clothing; and those in the manufactures of the coarser metals, with cheaper and better instruments of trade, as well as with many agreeable and convenient pieces of household furniture....The common complaint that luxury extends itself even to the lowest ranks of the people, and that the labouring poor will not now be contented with the same food, clothing, and lodging which satisfied them in former times, may convince us that it is not the money price of labour only, but its real recompense, which has augmented."[120]

Like Young and Arbuthnot before him, Smith defended the corn-merchants against the charge of raising the cost of living. His famous Digression concerning the Corn Trade is perhaps the weakest part of the whole performance. Apart from its lack of consistency with the tenor of much of the rest of the work, it amply displays Smith's lack of understanding both of agriculture and of marketing. For example, he clearly had no idea what was meant by forestalling. Nevertheless, he confidently put forward the paradoxical view, already made respectable by Young and Arbuthnot, that monopolising grain in order to enhance the price was both impossible and beneficial. At one point he assures us;-

118 Ibid. Pp. 130 and 52.
119 Adam Smith. The Wealth of Nations. Penguin ed. Pp. 176-179.
120 Ibid. Pp. 115, 176, and 180-181.

"It is scarce possible, even by the violence of law, to establish such an extensive monopoly with regard to corn....It is of all commodities the least liable to be engrossed or monopolised by the force of a few large capitals, which buy up the greater part of it. Not only its value far exceeds what the capitals of a few private men are capable of purchasing....but....the manner in which it is produced renders this purchase altogether impracticable."

Yet previously Smith had extolled the benefits of the raising of the price by the corn-dealer.

"It is his interest to raise the price of his corn as high as the real scarcity of the season requires, and it can never be his interest to raise it higher. By raising the price he discourages the consumption, and puts everybody more or less, but particularly the inferior ranks of people, upon thrift and good management....Though from excess of avarice....the inland corn merchant should sometimes raise the price of his corn somewhat higher than the scarcity of the season requires, yet all the inconveniences which the people can suffer from this conduct, which effectually secures them from a famine in the end of the season, are inconsiderable in comparison of what they might have been exposed to by a more liberal way of dealing in the beginning of it."

Surely the most cursory reading of this Digression must reveal the fundamental incompatibility of the views expressed within it.[121]

Thus far, Smith was on the well-trodden path of establishment thought. But he went on to break new ground. He was, perhaps, the first openly to assert that the taxation of the necessaries of life did not harm the poor, or actually benefited them. All such taxes, including the tax on salt, and the big excises on leather, soap, candles, etc. as well as the heavy tax on the coastwise shipment of coal, were compensated to the poor by the increase of wages, and paid ultimately by landlords in diminished rents, or by wealthy consumers.

"As the wages of labour are everywhere regulated....partly by the average price of the necessary articles of subsistence, whatever raises this average price must necessarily raise those wages so that the labourer may still be able to purchase that quantity of those necessary articles which the state of the demand for labour....requires that he should have."[122]

Taxes on those articles denoted the luxuries of the poor, on the other hand, were said not to be compensated by wage rises. Such luxuries included not just tobacco, tea and sugar, but also beer and meat.

"Upon the sober and industrious poor, taxes upon such commodities....dispose them either to moderate, or to refrain altogether from the use or superfluities which they can no longer easily afford. Their ability to bring up families, in consequence of this forced frugality, instead of being diminished, is frequently, perhaps, increased by the tax....The dissolute and disorderly might continue to indulge themselves in the use of such commodities after this rise of price in the same manner as before, without regarding the distress which this indulgence might bring upon their families. Such disorderly persons, however, seldom rear up numerous families, their children generally perishing from neglect, mismanagement, and the scantiness or unwholesomeness of their food."[123]

It was not only the taxman whom Smith attempted to bring into the shelter of establishment respectability. The banker and the financier were similarly favoured. Arbuthnot had conceded that

---

121 Ibid. Vol. II. Pp. 102-104 and 112-113. One cannot refrain from asking how a writer of such utter nonsense came to be respected as an economic thinker.

122 Compare this statement with that contained in Vol. I. P. 177 – "The wages of labour do not in Great Britain fluctuate with the price of provisions....The high price of provisions during these ten years past has not in many parts of the kingdom been accompanied with any sensible rise in the money price of labour."

123 Ibid. Vol. II. Pp. 466-469. Was there any pernicious absurdity that promoters of establishment orthodoxy could not get away with?

the rise in the cost of living might, in part, be caused by the "cheapness of money". The corn-dealing pamphleteers also nodded in this direction. Smith was perhaps the first to challenge the idea that an increase of circulating currency leads to an increase in prices.

"Any rise in the money price of goods which proceeded altogether from the degradation of the value of silver would affect all sorts of goods equally."

From our own recent experience we know well that a reduction in the value of money can affect some commodities differently from others.

"As to the high price of corn during these last ten or twelve years, it can be sufficiently accounted for from the badness of the seasons, without supposing any degradation in the value of silver."

Nor were the issues of paper money to be blamed.

"The increase of paper money, it has been said, by augmenting the quantity and consequently diminishing the value of the whole currency, necessarily augments the money price of commodities. But as the quantity of gold and silver, which is taken from the currency, is always equal to the quantity of paper which is added to it, paper money does not necessarily increase the quantity of the whole currency."[124]

Rising prices, according to Smith, were all caused solely by the "badness of the seasons". Demonstrably, it was all nonsense, but that did not prevent such arguments as these from forming a bankers' charter, or literally a licence to print money, for many years to come.

From this point, Smith entered some seriously totalitarian territory. He recycled the complaints of the corn-dealers about being victimised by rioters, and having their property plundered or destroyed.

"No trade deserves more the full protection of the law, and no trade requires it so much, because no trade is so much exposed to popular odium."

With respect to that law, Smith gave vent to some very authoritarian views indeed. The purpose of that law, and of the civil magistracy, was to enable the owner of valuable property to sleep in security.

"Civil government, so far as it is constituted for the security of property, is in reality constituted for the defence of the rich against the poor, or of those who have some property against those who have none."

Obliquely but unmistakeably, Smith commended the use of the army against the starving. The art of war he proclaimed "the noblest of all arts", and a standing army, that widely recognised abuse of the people's rights and of the constitution, as favourable to liberty and a force for civilisation. Firearms, far from being pernicious, afforded an evident advantage to the opulent and civilised against the poor and barbarous.[125]

To those of the elitist, authoritarian, anti-democratic mindset, the views set out in the Wealth of Nations would clearly have been welcome, and it is not difficult to account for the indulgence shown to Smith by certain sections of contemporary opinion.[126] Invited to dinner with a group of eminent politicians at the house of Viscount Dundas, Smith arrived late. As he did so, the guests rose to their feet. When Smith asked them to sit, William Pitt replied;-

"No, we will stand till you are seated, for we are all your scholars."[127]

Of course, the reality was entirely the other way around, and Smith duly received his reward. Two years after publication, rather perversely for a professed free-trader, he accepted the post of Commissioner of Customs in Edinburgh – a post which enabled him to live out his days in some degree of opulence.

124 Ibid. Vol. I. Pp347-348 and 424.
125 Ibid. Vol. II. Pp. 106 and 294-302.
126 William Cobbett, however, recommended throwing his work on the fire.
127 F. W. Hirst. Adam Smith. P. 228.

The respect accorded to Adam Smith by the economists and historians of our own day, however, is a conundrum altogether more difficult to solve; but one none the less interesting for that.

✱

Despite the obviously and increasingly yawning chasm that was opening up between much of the literature on the causes of poverty, representing, on the one hand, in one way or another, orthodox establishment thought, and on the other, the actual circumstances in which the poor were coming to find themselves; there was nevertheless one respect in which the whole controversy faithfully represented the reality. The great dichotomy of society, by which rich and poor now stared at each other across an ever wider divide, which had come to replace the fluid, graduated, hierarchical society in which all classes had their place, was reflected in the arguments put forward concerning the causes of poverty. The dichotomy in these arguments was so great, that it is scarcely possible to believe that the authors were writing about the same set of circumstances. By way of illustration, and in order to set the scene for the controversies of the 1790s, let us compare John Scott with Joseph Townsend.

Here is Scott, writing in 1773.

"Much hath been said on the effects of poverty, something, it may be expected, should be said on its causes; and as prevention is better than cure, it may be thought more necessary to attempt the removal of the latter, than the relief of the former. Poor there have always been, and notwithstanding every possible provision and regulation, always will be….That poverty, however, is more prevalent in the same place, at one time than at another; and that it is more so, in this nation, in the present age, than in the past, is generally apprehended; and supposing this to be the case, the origin of its prevalence must be sought for in the conduct of the great, a conduct which has unhappily formed the national character, and that character is *Extravagance*….

"The avarice of the present age is not the Avarice of the past; an Avarice, which sneakingly pilfered from the wants of its own back and its own belly, to replenish its coffers; but a monster composed…. of two halves, more nearly related in reality than in appearance, a bold rapacity and a lavish Prodigality; snatching with one hand and dispensing with the other, and unpropitious to the poor only. The universality of the prejudice against poverty is astonishing; even those characters, who squander their money with the most unthinking profusion, who will lend, or give, or throw away, will rarely bestow alms on a beggar.

"In the days of our ancestors, luxury was in a manner confined to the peerage….But the case is now very different….The influx of money to the hands of individuals has proved so disproportionate to all common expences, that the possessors have racked their invention for new methods of expending….

"Where are the princes of the people, the lords of villages, the patrons and employers of the poor? – All fled to that favourite scene of riot and dissipation. If they vouchsafe to a transient visit to their paternal domains, to view their rural improvements, those transpositions of wood, earth, and water, which some arbiter of modern taste has told them they must make to be completely fashionable; what are the advantages derived from this temporary presence? The inclosure of commons for the pasturage of horses, designed for exportation to our enemies; the demolition of cottages; and the accumulation of farms, *adding house to house, and field to field, till there be no* PLACE FOR THE POOR IN THE EARTH.

"If, then the conduct of the great be thus injurious to the poor, to whom but the great can the poor look up for assistance? Should not those who have laid a burthen on the shoulders of the people with one hand, endeavour to remove it with the other? Can power and affluence be employed to better purpose, than in alleviating the miseries of the impotent and needy? But the great have other avocations. – AMUSEMENT is the grand business of life! And amid the tempest of amusement, the cry of distress is too feeble to be heard. But what, O ye triflers, or worse than triflers, of the age! are these indispensable engagements, which must supersede your duty to your maker, your country, your fellow-creatures and every other consideration?...

"Have ye not your farces and burlettas, your dialogue without nature, and your music without sentiment; your puppet shews and your pantomimes, with their monstrous incongruities and insufferable indecencies....? Have ye not your midnight masquerades, and your morning dances.... your public scenes of levity and whim, and your private retreats for lewdness? Have ye not your sports of the turf, where vanity and avarice unite to produce cruelty...: and, to compleat all, your gaming tables where vanity and avarice unite to stretch the human heart on the rack of anxiety, and the sudden vicissitudes of fortune distort your countenances with the malignant triumph or despondence of infernals?

"But, in active wickedness, there must be satiety and weariness; and to preclude the intrusion of thought in the moment of solitude, amusements of a character more neutral, but not more consistent with reason or productive of advantage, are in readiness to relieve you. For this, you have your auctions and exhibitions; your professors of manual dexterity; your equestrian posture masters; and your mechanical Museum, where an ingenuity....has been misapplied to the service of false taste, and extravagant flattery....For this, you have your monthly chronicles of scandal and debauchery; your romances and novels....Such are the objects of your pursuit! and is not the public proffer of such objects to your notice, a sarcasm on your intellects and on your conduct, severer than any the pen of satire could have produced?

"The hand of Time must write *Finis* on the page of Life and a retrospect of its contents taken, and if he, whose history is the History of inoffensive indolence, does not escape condemnation; and if he whose few crimson periods relate only a few instances of injury to his neighbour, must repent with anguish of remorse unspeakable; what must be the portion of continual ridiculous and mischievous Activity!"[128]

Joseph Townsend's pamphlet was written in 1786. It enjoyed considerable, if short-lived popular success; but it is in its long-term influence over future thought and writings that its importance lies. Viewing the same national situation as John Scott, Townsend saw things in a completely different light.

Townsend followed Smith and Arbuthnot in positing an actual improvement in the financial circumstances of the poor. Distress, he thought, could not arise from high prices, because wheat was dearer, on average, during the seventeenth century than during the eighteenth; and because a "superior advance" had taken place in the price of labour, "in the proportion of six to four within a century".

But it was this very improvement in their situation which was the cause of their increasing poverty.

"Where the price of labour is the highest and provisions are the cheapest, there the poor rates have been the most exorbitant."[129]

The paradox that material deprivation was greatest where wages were the most generous became a commonplace in the 1790s.

Much of the blame lay with the poor law.

"There never was greater distress among the poor; there never was more money collected for their relief....poverty and wretchedness have increased in exact proportion to the efforts which have been made for the comfortable subsistence of the poor; and that wherever most is expended for their support, there objects of distress are most abundant; whilst in those counties and provincial districts

---

128 John Scott. Observations on the Present State of the Parochial and Vagrant Poor. Pp. 119-129.
129 Joseph Townsend. A Dissertation on the Poor Laws. Pp. 19-22

where the least provision has been made for their supply, we hear the fewest groans. Among the former we see drunkenness and idleness cloathed in rags; among the latter we hear the chearful songs of industry and virtue."

Townsend's Dissertation on the Poor Laws, however, was really a dissertation on the poor. Poverty was the inevitable result of the idleness, drunkenness, debauchery, and, above all, the improvidence of the poor themselves.

"It must be confessed that too many of them have some little resemblance to the animal described by travellers under the name of Nimble Peter; a creature so inactive, that, when he has cleared one tree, he will be reduced to skin and bones before he climbs another, and so slow in his motions, that even stripes will not make him mend his pace. Drunkenness is the common vice of poverty; not perhaps of poverty as such, but of the *uncultivated* mind; for it is the characteristic of unpolished nations to be fond of intoxicating liquors. Whatever be the cause, it is notorious, that with the common people the appetite for strong drink is their prevailing appetite. When therefore, by the advance of wages, they obtain more than is sufficient for their bare subsistence, they spend the surplus at the alehouse, and neglect their business. Is a man drunk one day? He will have little inclination to work the next. Thus for every drunken fit two days are lost. By frequent repetition the habit is confirmed, and, by reducing the number of working days, their value is enhanced."[130]

Townsend arrives almost at a genetic explanation of poverty; an in-group/out-group dichotomy, which approaches categorising the poor as being of a different race from the rich.

"If a new and equal division of property were made in England, we cannot doubt that the same inequality which we now observe would soon take place again; the improvident, the lazy, and the vicious, would dissipate their substance; the prudent, the active, and the virtuous would again increase their wealth."[131]

The rich were rich because they were virtuous; the poor were poor because they were vice-ridden. The rich were good people; the poor were bad people.

Townsend's solution to the problem of poverty was to increase the pressure upon the poor; remove the cushion of the poor law; and confront them with the fear of starvation, in order to compel them to greater honest exertions on behalf of their employers.

John Scott said "Good morning" to the elephant. But the future lay with Townsend.

---

130 Ibid. Pp. 29-30.
131 Ibid. P. 40.

The Elephant on the Sofa

Part Two

The causes of poverty and the Malthusian tendency

"I ca'n't believe that!" said Alice

"Ca'n't you?" the Queen said in a pitying tone. "Try again; draw a long breath, and shut your eyes."

Alice laughed. "There's no use trying," she said; "one *ca'n't* believe impossible things."

"I daresay you haven't had much practice," said the Queen. "When I was your age, I always did it for half-an-hour a day. Why, sometimes I've believed as many as six impossible things before breakfast." Lewis Carroll. Through the Looking Glass. Pp 86-87.

During the 1790s, poverty became a major political issue. All things considered, it was probably bound to become so; but the trigger was the controversy in England concerning the French Revolution, and, in particular, the political disagreement between Edmund Burke and Thomas Paine. The first part of Paine's Rights of Man, written in answer to Burke's Reflections, appeared in February 1791.

The Rights of Man is perhaps best known for its exposition of the author's anti-monarchism, his democratic views, and his opposition to church establishment. His contemporary critics answered him largely in these terms, and modern historians seem, in general, to have followed them in seeing the book as an expression of political principle. But it is perhaps here that Paine was at his most vulnerable; his assertion that the replacement of monarchies by republics would put an end to the warlike tendencies of governments was especially unfortunate in view of subsequent history. Even Paine's most enthusiastic supporters did not necessarily accept the political principles put forward in his book.

The burden of much of the two pamphlets in fact concerned the ways in which the poverty of the mass of the people of Europe was brought on directly by their governments. The logical conclusion to be drawn from this was that the solution to the problem of poverty was political reform; and it was this, undoubtedly, that sparked the outpourings of mass support which followed publication.

For Paine, the most important instrument of oppression and exploitation used by the governments of old Europe was warfare. What the Rights of Man amounts to, perhaps first and foremost, is a treatise against war; surely a fairly unexceptionable subject, and one which he had already expounded upon in 1787, in "Prospects on the Rubicon."

"When we consider, for the feelings of nature cannot be dismissed, the calamities of war, and the miseries it inflicts upon the human species, the thousands and tens of thousands of every age and sex who are rendered wretched by the event, surely there is something in the heart of man that calls upon him to think!"[1]

---

1 Thomas Paine. Prospects on the Rubicon. In the Complete Writings of Thomas Paine ed, Philip S. Foner. Vol. II. P. 624

"With the Revolution of 1688, and more so since the Hanoverian succession, came the destructive system of continental intrigues, and the rage of foreign wars and foreign dominion."

Warfare, according to Paine, had become institutionalised.

"War....from its productiveness, as it easily furnishes the pretence of necessity for taxes and appointments to places and offices, becomes a principal part of the system of old Governments; and to establish any mode to abolish war, however advantageous it might be to Nations, would be to take from such Government the most lucrative of its branches. The frivolous matters upon which war is made, shew the disposition and avidity of Governments to uphold the system of war, and betray the motives upon which they act....

"As war is the system of Government on the old construction, the animosity which Nations reciprocally entertain is nothing more than what the policy of their Governments excites to keep up the spirit of the system. Each Government accuses the other of perfidy, intrigue, and ambition, as a means of heating the imaginations of their respective Nations, and incensing them to hostilities. Man is not the enemy of Man, but through the medium of a false system of Government."[2]

There were many people, in and around government, who profited greatly from war.

"It will always happen, that any rumor of war will be popular among a great number of people in London. There are thousands who live by it; it is their harvest; and the clamor which those people keep up in newspapers and conversations passes unsuspiciously for the voice of the people, and it is not till after the mischief is done, that the deception is discovered."[3]

In this way, Paine explained the warmongering of the English government; "it is in search of a war that will serve as an excuse for its insane prodigality."

"That there are men in all countries who get their living by war, and by keeping up the quarrels of Nations, is as shocking as it is true; but when those who are concerned in the Government of a country, make it their study to sow discord, and cultivate prejudices between Nations, it becomes the more unpardonable."[4]

War, says Paine, "has but one thing certain, and that is the increase of TAXES."

Taxation was not just the inevitable consequence of war....

"What has been the event of all the wars of England, but an amazing accumulation of debt, and an unparalleled burden of taxes? Sometimes the pretence has been to support one outlandish cause, and sometimes another....but the consequence has always been TAXES. A few men have enriched themselves by jobs and contracts, and the groaning multitude bore the burden."

....it is often even the purpose.

"It is the art of *conquering at home*; the object of it is an increase of revenue; and as revenue cannot be increased without taxes, a pretence must be made for expenditures. In reviewing the history of the English Government, its wars and its taxes, a bystander, not blinded by prejudice, nor warped by interest, would declare that taxes were not raised to carry on wars, but that wars were raised to carry on taxes."[5]

Paine compares the relatively trifling expence of the United States government, with the endless extravagance practised in England.

"I see in America, a Government extending over a country ten times as large as England, and conducted with regularity, for one fortieth part of the expence which Government costs in England....I

2 Thomas Paine. The Rights of Man. Everyman ed. Pp. 236, and 136-137.
3 Thomas Paine. Prospects on the Rubicon. P. 632
4 Thomas Paine. The Rights of Man. Everyman ed. P. 6.
5 Thomas Paine. Prospects on the Rubicon. Pp. 623-624. The Rights of Man. Everyman ed. P. 55.

see in America the generality of the people living in a style of plenty unknown in monarchical countries."[6]

The expences of government in America amounted to just £130,000; just one eighth of the sum devoted to the English civil list! By contrast, in 1791, the English government collected £17 millions in taxes, according to Sir John Sinclair. And yet less than one thirtieth part of this was actually applied to government.

"In America", observed Paine, "every department in the Government is decently provided for; but no-one is extravagantly paid."

In England, on the other hand, "we have two distinct characters of Government; the one civil Government, or the Government of laws, which operates at home, the other Court or Cabinet Government, which operates abroad....the one attended with little charge, the other with boundless extravagance."

"It appears impossible to account for the enormous increase of expenditure, on any other ground than extravagance, corruption and intrigue."[7]

"What", asks Paine, "are the present governments of Europe, but a scene of iniquity and oppression? What is that of England? Do not its own inhabitants say, It is a market, where every man has his price, and where corruption is common traffic, at the expense of a deluded people?"

So much of the revenue was devoted, not to the expences of government, but to the enrichment of individuals. It became a sort of poor rate for aristocrats.

"All the children which the Aristocracy disowns (which are all except the eldest) are, in general, cast like orphans on a parish, to be provided for by the public, but at a greater charge. Unnecessary offices and places in Governments and Courts are created at the expence of the public to maintain them."[8]

And this system of unnecessary offices and places was keenly exploited by the ruling elite of the House of Lords.

"There are but a few of its members, who are not in some mode or other participators, or disposers of the public money. One turns a candleholder, or a lord in waiting; another a lord of the bed-chamber, a groom of the stole, or any insignificant nominal office to which a salary is annexed, paid out of the public taxes, and which avoids the direct appearance of corruption. Such situations are derogatory to the character of man; and where they can be submitted to, honour cannot reside. To all these are to be added the numerous dependants, the long list of younger branches and distant relations, who are to be provided for at the public expence."[9]

And, of course, those who benefited from the system were keen to support it; even to extend it.

"It is easy to conceive that a band of interested men, such as placemen, pensioners, lords of the bed-chamber, lords of the kitchen, lords of the necessary-house, and the Lord knows what besides, can find as many reasons for Monarchy as their salaries, paid at the expence of the country, amount to...."[10]

Paine held up the Duke of Richmond as an example. The produce of the tax on coals was devoted to His Grace, and it amounted annually to a sum of £20,000!

"By what right, moral or political, does any Government assume to say, that the person called the Duke of Richmond, shall be maintained by the public? Yet, if common report is true, not a beggar

---

6 Thomas Paine. The Rights of Man. P. 113.
7 Thomas Paine. The Rights of Man. Everyman ed. Pp. 208, 214 and 236.
8 Ibid. Pp. 99 and 61.
9 Ibid. P. 233.
10 Ibid. P. 113.

in London can purchase his wretched pittance of coal, without paying towards the civil list of the Duke of Richmond."[11]

There were probably many other cases which Paine could have cited with as much effect as the example of the Duke of Richmond. Given which, "is it, then, any wonder that under such a system of Government, taxes and rates have multiplied to their present extent?" In just a hundred years, the amount taken by government out of the English economy had increased tenfold.[12]

"Whatever the Constitution may be in other respects, it has undoubtedly been *the most productive machine for taxation that was ever invented.*"[13]

It was not just the amount of taxation that was so burdensome to the people. There had been a shift of emphasis towards taxing the poorer sections through consumption. Paine tells us that at the start of the century taxes were divided more or less equally between land and consumption. By 1788, the yield of the land tax had fallen by £500,000, even though rents had doubled, whilst taxes to the annual value of £12 million had been added to the price of articles of consumption. This had come about, according to Paine, because the House of Lords had the power to ward off taxes from itself, and throw the burden upon the consuming public. Many of the excises failed to tap the resources of the upper classes equally with the lower. Paine singled out the tax on beer, which the rich avoided by brewing their own.

"What will mankind think of the justice of taxation when they know that this tax alone, from which the Aristocracy are from circumstances exempt, is nearly equal to the whole of the land-tax.... and with its proportion of the taxes on malt and hops, it exceeds it. That a single article, thus partially consumed, and that chiefly by the working part, should be subject to a tax, equal to that on the whole rental of a Nation, is, perhaps, a fact not to be paralleled in the histories of revenues."

"It is from the power of taxation being in the hands of those who can throw so great a part of it from their own shoulders, that it has raged without a check."[14]

The ever-increasing hardships and distresses visible the country over were being actively caused by government; by the combination of an aggressive foreign policy and resulting excessive and partial taxation. Their source was the greed of government.

"If, from the more wretched parts of the old world, we look at those which are in an advanced stage of improvement, we still find the greedy hand of Government thrusting itself into every corner and crevice of industry, and grasping the spoil of the multitude. Invention is continually exercised to furnish new pretences for revenue and taxation. It watches prosperity as its prey, and permits none to escape without a tribute."

"In the present state of things a labouring man, with a wife and two or three children, does not pay less than between seven and eight pounds a year in taxes. He is not sensible of this, because it is disguised to him in the articles which he buys, and he thinks only of their dearness; but as the taxes take from him, at least, a fourth of his yearly earnings he is consequently disabled from providing for a family, especially if himself or any of them are afflicted with sickness."[15]

"By....engrafting the barbarism of Government upon the internal civilisation of a country, it draws from the latter, and more especially from the poor, a great portion of those earnings which should be applied to their own subsistence and comfort. Apart from all reflections of morality and

---

11 Ibid. P. 205.
12 Ibid. P. 233.
13 Ibid. P. 193.
14 Ibid. Pp. 229-232.
15 Ibid. Pp. 153 and 246

philosophy, it is a melancholy fact that more than one-fourth of the labour of mankind is annually consumed by this barbarous system."[16]

The Rights of Man was a massive popular success, and Paine's views spread rapidly through the country, largely through the offices of the Society for Constitutional Information. The simplicity of his explanation of escalating distress was perhaps what underlay its effectiveness. The main burden of its argument was the direct causal connection which Paine drew between the increasing hardships of the people and the abuses of government. If the abuses of government were the problem, then political change was the solution. Thus, poverty had become politicised. Traditional reforming politicians used poverty more and more as an important plank in a political platform that was coming to be known as radical. On the other hand, working class leaders began to see the corruption of government as the mainspring behind a wide range of popular grievances, and also began to agitate for parliamentary reform.

The Sheffield Constitutional Society was perhaps the first society of its type, founded in late 1791. The wide range of local issues out of which it grew demonstrates both the over-simplicity of Paine's explanations of poverty, and the general truth of his indictment of government and the ruling classes as the prevailing cause. Against a background of spiralling food prices and the increasing pauperisation of artisans, industrial relations in Sheffield were bitter and turbulent. There were loud complaints about apprenticeship restrictions and combinations among employers to keep wages low, and a long-running dispute between the cutlers and their masters. Sensitivity over prices roused concerns about the proposed Corn Bill of 1791, which set out new export bounties and import duties, and looked set to enhance the price of corn yet again. Then, in June 1791, the townsfolk of Sheffield lost their large common. Six thousand acres were placed in private ownership, with totally inadequate compensation. The commissioners for the enclosure included the agent of the Duke of Norfolk, the chief landowner, and the wealthy vicar of Sheffield, James Wilkinson. The main beneficiaries were, unsurprisingly, the Duke of Norfolk and James Wilkinson. Such flagrant abuse, it was pointed out, was only possible with the active connivance of the House of Commons.[17]

William Broomhead was a prominent member of the society. Its purpose, he asserted in 1794, was "to enlighten the people, to show the people the reason, the ground of all their complaints and sufferings; when a man works hard for thirteen or fourteen hours of the day, the week through, and is not able to maintain his family; that is what I understand of it; to show people the ground of this; why they were not able."

The complaints and sufferings were economic; but the causes were coming to be seen as political, as were the remedies.

At the society's meetings, the reasons for the "enormous high price of provisions" were the major topic of debate. This was attributed to general corruption; to oppressions by all types of monopolist; to the devoting of the public revenue to "Placemen and Pensioners"; and to the "Mock Representation of the People."[18]

A similar society was founded in London by Thomas Hardy early in 1792 – the London Corresponding Society. Membership was open to all, for a subscription that most could afford. There was a resulting huge and rapid accretion of members, consisting largely of distressed artisans and small tradesmen, immersed in pauperism and struggling with the spiralling costs of living. Once again, economic grievances were attributed to political causes, and led to demands for political remedies. They asserted "that they were oppressed, that the fruits of their honest industry were taken from them, either by force or fraud, to support *idle drones* in *useless* places and unmerited pensions." Complaints

16 Ibid. P. 213.
17 A. Goodwin. The Friends of Liberty. Pp. 159-163.
18 Ibid. Pp.166-7.

of "oppressive taxes, unjust laws, restrictions of liberty and wasting of the public money", as well as of unjust enclosures, were to be answered with universal male suffrage, annual parliaments, and a crackdown on abuses of power.[19]

The same types of argument were being heard from all over the country; William Ward, for example, founder member of the Derby Society for Political Information, connected social distress and deprivation with the abuses of government; and over all types of issue. John Baxter of London criticised landlords who enclosed and engrossed farms, converting arable into pasture, and impoverishing their tenants by extracting ever-increasing rents. This was done through the support of parliament, and through "the whole power of the state" being "confined to men of landed property".[20]

Traditional radicals used the economic grievances of the nation to drum up support for their demands. The Society for Constitutional Information suggested to John Andrew of Stockport that "a temperate and dispassionate relation of the immense number of sinecure places and useless offices, in which the corrupt and prostituted favourites, Agents and Dependents of the rich and Great, riot in the spoils and plunder, wrested from the sweat of the Brow, and continual labour of body of the Husbandman, the Mechanic, the Labourer and Artificer" would generally gain support for the cause. But it was a symbiotic relationship; working class societies looked to aristocratic politicians to put their case in parliament. In 1792, the Norwich delegates, in a resolution addressed to the aristocratic Friends of the People, "humbly recommended the said gentlemen to use their utmost endeavours towards the procuring, as speedily as may be, a smaller and more equal division of all the lands of the kingdom, as a reasonable means both of lowering the price of provisions, and also furnishing employment, and a decent maintenance for a multitude of labourers and mechanics, who are at present groaning under hard labour and the want of necessaries."[21]

The opening of hostilities with France in 1793 added another grievance to the repertoire of the radicals. The connection with the writings of Paine is obvious enough. But once again the statements of the working class societies reflected rather more realistically the complexities of the situation, than Paine's somewhat simplified model of one class benefiting from war by imposing ever more oppressive taxes. War worsened the condition of the poor in many ways. Forcible recruitment by crimping gangs and press gangs was an ever-present grievance, which left many families reliant on parish relief. The destructive economic consequences of war were much emphasised, for example, in a pamphlet by Thomas Cooper of Manchester. Cooper forecast the depression of overseas trade, the degradation of the local weavers, and the forced enlistment of the local poor into the army and navy. William Frend dwelt on much the same theme in December 1792. The spinners around St. Ives had their wages lowered even before the war began. "We are to be scotched 3d in the shilling – a fourth part of our labours. What is all this for?" What indeed? Of what moment were the issues which supposedly took England to war, in the face of the manifold sufferings of the poor? And all the while war contractors and those benefiting from the system of finance and government were amassing huge fortunes, whilst themselves contributing very little. The theme recurred time and again. An address of the London Corresponding Society in January 1794 condemned the "fruitless crusade to re-establish the odious despotism in France", as a result of which trade and industry had been damaged, many poor families brought into misery, and ancient political rights destroyed.[22]

Norwich, for example, suffered grievously as a result of the "unprincipled war". Thomas Holcroft recorded that the money paid to the villages for spinning, before the war, was £1,000 a week. "It is at this time not quite half the sum; and the quantity of spinning that used to be done for a shilling

---

19 Ibid. P. 191-198.
20 Ibid. P. 230.
21 Ibid. Pp. 228 and 213.
22 Ibid. Pp. 268-269 and 309.

is now done for sixpence; so that the poor spinners are doubly distressed." As a consequence of the depressed trading conditions the poor-rate in the city was said to have doubled, and over half the population had become dependent upon charity.[23]

The further distresses brought upon the poor by the below-average harvest yields of 1794 and 1795 have already been described; a sudden deterioration in an already steadily worsening situation. The unprecedented price of corn re-ignited the long-standing controversy over whether scarcity was of natural or man-made origin. The question, as discussed at a meeting of the London Corresponding Society in October 1795, was;-

"Ought the present high price of bread be attributed to a scarcity of grain, a secret monopoly, or the unavoidable consequence of war?"

The answer, without doubt, was that all three played their part, and which aspect you emphasised depended upon who you were. Whilst it may be tempting to blame the government for the weather, it remains a fruitless exercise, and government spokesmen endeavoured to lay the whole blame for the distress on the poor crops, and ultimately on God.[24] But scarcities were not new; the levels to which prices rose, however, were new. And many people attributed this to speculation, and to the secretive and monopolistic marketing practices of capitalist millers, large-scale corn-dealers and opulent farmers. This was the view held by the radical Robert Lowry, when faced with demands for bread from a starving family which he was unable to satisfy.

"Were it pestilence or famine, plainly sent by our Heavenly Parent, faith in His wisdom and goodness might be summoned up to bear the chastisement….But when you know it is man made, and therefore to remove it is manhood's duty, then to rest idle contented under it becomes a sin. You turn with disgust from a system of which the Word of God says 'He that witholdeth corn, the people shall curse him'."[25]

It was a view echoed popularly across the country in times of famine. During rioting in London in 1800, posters were placed on London Bridge and the Monument claiming that the authors of the famine were corn-dealers with "extensive monopolies". The remedy for this problem was once again political. It was the more efficient enforcement of the traditional laws against the marketing offences of engrossing, regrating and forestalling.[26]

Most of the radical politicians, however, preferred to emphasise the third option – the war. This enabled them to attach their demands for reform to a burgeoning movement for peace, which resulted in a great deal of weight being given to the role of the war in raising prices, both in London and the provinces. At a meeting of the London Corresponding Society at St. George's fields in June 1795, it was resolved that the sharply rising cost of living was owing entirely to "the cruel and unnecessary war." The sentiment was echoed in Sheffield, where a meeting petitioned for bread and peace. The war, it was said, destroyed commerce and impoverished families. Here, it was resolved, more specifically but less believably, that the famine was caused entirely by the export of food to armies in Europe, which were "fed with that bread which our famished Peasantry have long cried for in vain."[27]

Once again, following Paine, the remedy for the warlike tendencies of government lay in a political reform which would make government more responsive to the wishes of the people. The St. George's Fields meeting saw the answer in manhood suffrage and annual parliaments. The Norwich Patriotic Society put it like this;-

---

23 Ibid. P. 374.
24 Poor God!
25 R. Wells. Wretched Faces. P. 74.
26 Ibid. P. 128.
27 A. Goodwin. The Friends of Liberty. Pp. 377 and 383. R. Wells. Wretched Faces. P. 138.

"Any inquiry into the cause of your distress would reveal that the present unjust and unnecessary war has hastened that crisis of misery which a defective representation must necessarily produce."

The severe economic hardships of these years brought a spate of publications on the subject of the poor; some overtly political, like the works of George Dyer and John Thelwall; many others investigations of a non-political nature. Pamphlets, books and reprints were brought out by Nathaniel Kent, Thomas Ruggles and John Howlett. Foremost among these was the Case of the Labourers in Husbandry, already extensively quoted, written by Berkshire clergyman David Davies. This was a detailed, scientific and comprehensive account of the conditions under which his poor parishioners existed, even before the famine of 1795; written by a man who lived amongst them, and saw their hardships for himself. Davies could see that poverty was a complex and multifactorial phenomenon, and produced a lengthy explanation.

The harmful effects of war, so prominent in radical propaganda, find their place also in Davies's work; so do the ills resulting from the associated burdens of taxation. Taxes raised the price of the articles of consumption needed by the poor, and a tax on one commodity could raise the price of many. The malt tax was singled out as especially damaging. Davies observed that the national debt, the amount of interest payable on it, and the poor-rates, all rose together. Many other factors contributed to the rise in the cost of living. Davies discussed the changes in the corn trade, together with the greater prevalence of wholesaling. The poor now had to pay retail prices for their provisions. The new luxurious tastes of the rich raised prices. So did the depreciation of the currency. Less corn was being grown for consumption, as arable fields were turned over to pasture. Gentlemen farmers preferred grassland farms, as they entailed less trouble and expence, and increasing numbers of horses were consuming the produce of many acres, which before had been devoted to human subsistence. Roads, parks and canals were all occupying land where previously food had been grown. Where corn was still being raised, an immoral amount of it was being distilled into strong liquor. All of these factors were causing a long-term rise in prices, with which a marginal rise in wages totally failed to keep pace. The changes in agriculture which were concerning the radicals were also given prominence by Davies. Throwing numbers of small farms together into large farms, and the accompanying destruction of cottages and gardens, were depriving the peasantry of any support to be gained by their own cultivations. The poor were being forced to give up their cows to larger farmers. Farmers were being turned into labourers, and as farming families became less in number, the poor proliferated. Too many hands were now chasing a diminishing amount of work, and employment for women and children, except at harvest-time, had all but disappeared.

Many of Davies's observations more or less supported Paine's contention that distress was caused by the abuse of power and the greed of the rich, but it was not in every case as simple as that. Davies's work was not political; he drew no conclusions from it as to the faults of the constitution or the need for political reform. He did, however, assert that a remedy needed to be speedily found by parliament.

Davies almost got his wish. In December 1795, amidst ever-increasing distress, Samuel Whitbread M.P. introduced a bill to allow the magistrates to set a minimum wage. The debate brought the state of the poor forcefully to the attention of the Commons. During the debate on the second reading, in February 1796, Whitbread told the House that "every inquiry he had instituted convinced him of the necessity of remedying the grievances of the industrious poor by some legislative provisions."

"He did not mean that the wages of the labourer were inadequate for his subsistence and comfort in times of temporary scarcity and unusual hardship; but even at the period preceding such distress, the evil had prevailed. In most parts of the country, the labourer had long been struggling with increasing misery, till the pressure had become almost too grievous to be endured, while the patience of the sufferers under their accumulated distresses had been conspicuous and exemplary."[28]

These, then, were the types of message being sent to the king and his ministers from all parts of the country. In books and pamphlets, speeches and lectures, addresses and petitions, mass meetings and resolutions, and even in speeches in parliament, by the dark days of 1795 the cry had become deafening. Poverty and politics had become inextricably intertwined. Working class protests about food prices and scarcity were more and more connected with political issues. "Cheap Bread or No King" was a proposition posted on the church door at Banbury; and in Yorkshire Earl Fitzwilliam spoke of how the people saw revolution as a remedy for their social distress. At an election at Ipswich, candidates were heckled with cries of "No Barley Bread". Radical politicians everywhere were using social and economic distress as the central item in their agenda of political reform. Norwich radicals, complaining of "numerous burdensome and unnecessary taxes and unprincipled, ruinous and unnecessary wars", together with exorbitant food prices, connected the whole train of evils with the unrepresentative nature of the House of Commons, and suggested, as remedies, universal suffrage and annual parliaments.

"Were you determined legally to correct the errors of the delinquents, you would not be reduced to the dire necessity of eating bran; your table would be furnished with the bounties of Providence, and the guilty authors of your distress would be sent to Germany to eat straw."

At a mass meeting held by the Sheffield Constitutional Society in August 1795, parliamentary reform was put forward as a panacea to a wide range of issues, from war and taxes, to the national debt, through to trade dislocation and spiralling poor-rates.

John Thelwall, the radical London lecturer, used social distress as his central theme.

"All the miseries to which the poor are subject proceed from unnatural and impolitic wars, and war proceeds from corrupt and vicious parliaments."[29]

Such themes as these, however, could only be maintained up until the passing of the Gagging Acts late in 1795; which brings us to the reaction of the establishment.

We have already seen how, during the 1760s, a conflict arose within the establishment between the traditional type of administration based partly on public opinion, and government by royal prerogative, based on a small elitist group of King's Friends, whose position depended entirely upon royal favour. By this group, as Edmund Burke pointed out in 1770, any popular opinion was looked upon with disfavour, merely because it was popular.

The elitist mindset is an extremely complex phenomenon; which was crucial to the formation of the establishment view of poverty. One of its principal characteristics was an unquestioning acceptance of received orthodoxies, and an intolerance of any kind of divergence from accepted norms of behaviour or belief. An exaggerated reverence for the monarchy is an unsurprising feature of a faction depending, or wishing to depend, entirely upon the royal favour. But, perhaps most importantly, the adherents of this world view displayed a fervent high church Anglicanism, which was highly intolerant of other religions, especially non-conformist ones.

The whole constituted a gradually hardening anti-democratic strand of opinion, which, as the distresses of the people increasingly called for political reform, came to set its face against change of any description, either in church or state. Lord North gave vent to this view in 1785. For him, the British constitution was "the most beautiful fabric that, perhaps, had ever existed from the beginning

---

28   Parliamentary History. 1796. P. 703.
29   R. Wells. Wretched Faces. Pp. 138-152.

of time. He never would consent to any attempt to tamper with such a fabric."[30] In religion, a similar attitude was manifested. In 1772, North told the House of Commons that any concession over the thirty-nine articles of religion would destroy the Church of England, and in 1787 he called the Test Acts, which disqualified religious dissenters from political office, "the cornerstone of the constitution, which should have every preservation."

By the possessors of this mindset, the popular clamour for reform was stoutly resisted; but the clamour itself was so eminently reasonable that it could only be resisted by questioning the aims and motives of the clamourers.

"The reforming notions of this age are dangerous in their tendency; something more than reformation is intended; something that deserves a harsher appellation; and to which if we give way, adieu to religion, adieu to everything dear to us as men and Christians."[31]

Elitists are good haters, and need enemies. This role was variously filled by radicals, atheists, and French philosophers. But perhaps foremost among the foes of the Anglican elite were the low church dissenters, who were accused, *en masse*, of republican tendencies, and about whom conspiracy theories were woven, concerning long-term plots to destroy the monarchy.[32]

It was perhaps a fascination with the power conferred by money that was probably one ground of the connections forged by this elite with wealthy corn merchants and financiers. Arising partly from those connections was the increasingly intolerant attitude displayed towards poverty; and the greater severity shown towards the poor, as in, for example, the use of the army as the response of first resort to the distresses of the populace.

In mid-century, this mindset was prevalent among a tiny group at the centre of public life, and its most notable exhibitors were perhaps the Earl of Bute and Dr. Samuel Johnson. It is observable among the upper echelons of the legal profession; but more especially in the Church of England, where a high Anglican group led by Bishop Horne of Norwich eventually came to set the tone for the whole church.[33]

Yet for much of the second half of the eighteenth century, the elitist tendency was in eclipse. The loss of the American colonies convinced many of the need for change, and William Pitt came to power in 1784 as a reforming minister. He forged links with the Yorkshire Movement for economical reform, and brought in, or attempted to bring in, a number of reforms aimed at achieving greater efficiency and economy in government, and reducing the opportunities for corruption.

But anti-democratic attitudes were hardening all the while, and the watershed came, perhaps, in 1787. In that year, a bill came before parliament to repeal the Test and Corporation Acts, and so to remove some of the disabilities and disqualifications under which non-conformists suffered. The proposed reform enjoyed wide support at first, including that of Pitt himself, but the Church of England finally decided to exert its powerful influence to block the repeal.

It seems clear, then, that the renewed growth of this more uncompromising attitude originated within the church. But it strayed also into politics. Its adherents included, to be sure, the remaining survivors of Lord North's Tory party, like Lord Loughborough; but opinion within a section of the Whig party became even more extreme. This faction was led by the Duke of Portland, and included William Windham, and Earls Fitzwilliam and Spencer.

A further issue then strengthened this anti-democratic tendency – the controversy over the revolution in France in 1789. Widely welcomed in England at first, including by Pitt himself, it was especially so by all those elements who had supported reform throughout the 1770s and 1780s, non-

---

30 J. J. Sack. From Jacobite to Conservative. P. 149
31 Ibid. P. 80.
32 Ibid. Pp. 37, 31 and 199.
33 Ibid. P. 78.

conformists foremost among them. Leading dissenting minister Dr. Richard Price made a laudatory speech to the Revolution Society in November 1789. Charles James Fox extravagantly eulogised the whole event. And constitutional clubs and societies sprung up the country over.

Edmund Burke was a Whig politician and dependent of Earl Fitzwilliam, who was less favourably impressed by events in France. His Reflections on the Revolution in France, published in November 1790, constituted a savage condemnation of the revolution. He stressed the tyranny that was bound to result, or so he thought, from the new democracy, inspired by the French financial interest. He expressed his horror at the destruction of the established church, and at the dispossession of the clergy and aristocracy. He mercilessly criticised the new institutions, and forecast, correctly if not necessarily perceptively, the collapse of the new paper currency. Chaos, anarchy and bloodshed were bound to follow.

On balance, most of the published criticism of the Reflections was unfavourable to Burke, and some was positively hostile. But it seems safe to assume that there was, within the political establishment, a strong underlying current of opinion, not necessarily expressed in print, which agreed with him; and that, inside parliament, besides the bishops, this was to be found among the surviving Northite Tories, and the group of Whig politicians surrounding the Duke of Portland.

The revolution in France had not yet run its course. With the flight of the French royal family in June 1791, the tide of opinion began to turn in Burke's favour. As the events of the revolution became ever bloodier, with the execution of the French king and the September massacres, Burke's prophecies and assertions began to seem percipient. Those of the anti-democratic tendency were beginning to find themselves in a much more convivial atmosphere for voicing their views and for pressing for measures of popular repression.

So at the time of the popular ferment caused by the publication of Thomas Paine's Rights of Man, the anti-democratic tendency was gradually taking over the administration. Pitt needed the Portland Whigs in government in order to counter the popularity of Fox, Grey and the Friends of the People. The Whig magnates, in their turn, saw Pitt as the man to lead Britain into a war against the expressers of popular discontent both at home and in France. Portland held all the trumps, and he had his price. He demanded that Pitt change his position on all the major issues, including parliamentary reform. Earl Fitzwilliam made it clear that Whigs of his persuasion were keen to see the passing of measures of repression against the people.

Pitt allowed himself to be manipulated, and, early in 1792, he responded to the pressure. The government became openly critical of the French revolution, and the ideas that it promoted. Home Secretary Dundas declared that all parliamentary reformers were, in reality, revolutionaries. In February was published the second part of Thomas Paine's Rights of Man, and, before a week had passed, it was condemned by the government as seditious, Paine himself was outlawed and forced to take refuge in France.

Pitt announced to the world his conversion to the anti-reform strand of thought in the spring of 1792, during a debate on Charles Grey's motion for parliamentary reform. He recycled the old Northite line; Grey's motion, Pitt asserted, was born out of the impractical ideas of the French revolution, and any attempt to implement it could only have chaos and anarchy as its outcome.

The issue of a royal proclamation followed, condemning seditious publications, and exhorting magistrates to take all necessary steps to suppress them. That same month, Pitt announced to the Duke of Portland that he had royal permission to consult with Portland on "such measures as may on due consideration be thought necessary for checking any attempts dangerous to public order and tranquillity."

Of course, there were no attempts dangerous to public order and tranquillity. It was all elitist mythology – the anti-democratic response to popular demands for reform, which grew out of the increasing economic distress and deprivation of the people. But this mythology had now become the official government line.

Pitt continued to reinforce his anti-democratic credentials. The war with France, from its commencement in 1793, had been presented as a defensive one with limited objectives. Most of these were quickly achieved, yet the war went on and on. At the opening of parliament in 1794, Pitt stunned observers by asserting that his war objective had now become "the destruction of the atrocious system now prevalent in France", and by presenting the war as a Europe-wide struggle against the reforming tendencies of radicals and dissenters, who were now stereotyped as conspirators and revolutionaries.

At home, Pitt began his campaign against radicalism and dissent by publicly equating demands for reform with French subversion.

"The fraud was too gross and palpable; it was obvious from what quarter they came....The French had disclosed a system of procuring proselytes in every part of Europe, – a system which they had particularly followed up with respect to this country." The popular radical societies were not agitating the grievances of the poor at all – merely the interests of the enemy across the Channel.[34]

Here was Lord North's line of reasoning brought up to date – the most moderate reformer had a hidden revolutionary agenda. Radicals "aspired at something more than a radical reform – the introduction of those French principles which from their consequences I could not but regard with horror."

Of course it was all nonsense, but the train of logic was followed. On the presumption that all those protesting about deteriorating conditions of life were, actually, bent only on the overthrow of the government, Pitt, in May 1794, persuaded parliament to suspend the Act of Habeas Corpus, the law which set out the procedure for redress in cases of illegal imprisonment by the government. This was done on the flimsiest of pretexts, and the conspiracy here spoken of was, in fact, a figment of the official imagination.

"Even supposing the executive government to have been guilty of every neglect of duty, the conspiracy would have failed; it was still right to prevent, by timely interference, the misery which a small struggle might necessarily produce."

Pitt wished to prevent the hypothetical misery of a fictional small struggle, whilst living perfectly equably with the mass degradation brought on by lengthy wars, hefty taxation, currency manipulation and monopolistic trading practices. The suspension of Habeas Corpus was the occasion of the Whig magnates entering the cabinet. Portland himself became Home Secretary, whilst William Windham became the government's chief spokesman in the House of Commons. By this time, Portland was declaring that he "now considered the expulsion of the soul and spirit of Jacobinism as a point of union for us all", which "might make us act as one great family." By which he meant that, come what may, the small establishment in-group of which he was a part would continue to feast on the wealth created by the productive classes of the nation; and that the arguments of those who dared to protest were to be met with the dungeon, the hulk and the gallows.

Thus, the series of psychological propensities which I have described as the anti-democratic tendency came to be ensconced at the heart of government, forming the basis on which were taken decisions which profoundly affected the lives, livelihoods and general well-being of millions of people. And nowhere was this tendency more pronounced, or more damaging, than in the orthodox, establishment attitude to poverty and the poor.

---

34 J. Mori. William Pitt and the French Revolution. P. 182.

The establishment's reaction[35] to Thomas Paine, and the connection which he made between the abuses of government and the sufferings of the people, along with the outpourings of popular discontent which this triggered, was to pump into circulation vast quantities of propaganda. Propaganda could take many forms. The Royal Proclamations of 1792 had a public relations function. That of May of that year put forward the view that radical and seditious literature was inciting the people to violence, and it stimulated a massive response of loyal addresses from all over the country, largely organised by the government itself. That of December embodied much of the militia on the basis of a threat of insurrection which barely existed, and succeeded in arousing much hostility against France. Government statements were constantly endeavouring to connect those who dwelt on the distresses of the poor with revolutionaries, or radical societies with French agents and violent conspirators. The engendering of fear was an important aim. Parliament itself could become one vast engine of propaganda, whose endorsement could lend credibility and respectability to ministerial statements, no matter how far-fetched they may have been.

The Church of England served similar purposes, with clergymen preaching regularly to the populace from pulpits the country over. For some time before the French Revolution, many Anglican clergy were embracing elitist anti-democratic views, and were preaching to the poor on the need for submission and forbearance in the face of whatever suffering may come, and on the God-given privileges of the wealthy. A large proportion of the clergy of all denominations were supporters of Pitt, but the High Anglican churchmen were especially loyal. Notable among these were George Horne, Bishop of Norwich, who owed his preferment to Charles Jenkinson; his clerical associates in the work of anti-radical propaganda, most notably the prolific William Jones of Nayland; and their friends among the press and the pamphleteers – Reeves, Bowles and Gifford.[36]

In 1792, John Reeves founded his famous 'Association for Preserving Liberty and Property against Levellers and Republicans'. Government almost certainly was involved in its establishment – two ministers were actually members. Pitt lent his weight to the society's publicity, and Reeves duly received his reward. This spawned huge numbers of similar organisations throughout the country, which became a vast network for the publication and distribution of tracts and pamphlets supportive of Pitt and his government. Reeves's Association, for example, published about fifty tracts of its own, and paid for many thousands of pamphlets to be distributed through its offspring associations in the provinces. The Bull's Head Association in Manchester performed much the same function, said to have circulated over 16,000 pamphlets. It was these societies which were largely responsible for sending in loyalist petitions from all parts, mostly modelled on a pattern sent out by Pitt and Grenville.[37]

The use of the press as an instrument of official propaganda was not entirely unprecedented. Lord North utilised the journalistic services of Henry Bate Dudley during the American War. Fox and North had used it again at the time of the India Bill. And Pitt himself, during his electoral triumph of 1784, paid £100 each to five different newspapers. But it had never been done before on the scale of the 1790s. The New Monthly Magazine put it like this;-

"When Mr. Pitt, to find a constant instrument for the inoculation of his views indispensable to bear along with him the force and currency of popular sentiment, a public officer was instructed to open a communication with the proprietors of journals of large circulation and the result was that

---

35   This section, except where stated, is based on the following secondary works. J. Mori. William Pitt and the French Revolution. S. Watson. The Reign of George III. Colin Jones ed. Britain and Revolutionary France. A. Aspinall. Politics and the Press. J. J. Sack. From Jacobite to Conservative. H. T. Dickinson. Britain and the French Revolution. Robert Hole. Pulpits, Politics and Public Order.

36   H. T. Dickinson. Britain and the French Revolution. P. 18.

37   Ibid. P. 111.

a vast majority of them two or three London papers were sent gratuitously certain articles of which were marked with red ink, and the return made was the insertion of as many of these as the space of the people would allow. Thus was the whole country directed by one mind, as it were; and this fact accounts in no small degree for the origin, propagation and support of that public opinion which enabled the minister to pursue his plans with so much certainty of ensuring general approbation."

The press was heavily taxed to make it susceptible to bribe and subsidy; which were subsequently forthcoming. £5,000 per year is said to have been paid to newspapers during the 1790s, and a shady business it was. The money had to be taken from the secret service fund, in order to prevent Parliament having any say or knowledge in the matter; and the money often reached its destination by roundabout routes. Thomas Harris was proprietor of Covent Garden Theatre, and he seems to have acted as a government agent, as many subsidies were paid to him for subsequent distribution to editors. Bate Dudley, for example, received £600 from Harris during the 1790s. Strangely, or not so strangely, the secret service accounts from 1793 onwards have not come down to us!

Whilst from 1792 most of the press was becoming more staunchly anti-democratic and pro-Pitt, an absurd belief was expressed in official circles that most newspapers were in the pay of the French. New newspapers, urged Burke and others, needed to be set up, to support the government and oppose the contrary influence. And so it was done in 1792. The Sun came out in the evening, perversely, and the True Briton in the morning. They were founded with Pitt's encouragement by government officials, and were even said to be owned by members of the administration. The editorship of both went to John Heriot, who had by 1790 already been receiving £50 a quarter from the government "for writing in the papers", and subsequently went on to make a fortune. Both papers were a success; the Sun had the largest circulation of any London newspaper. A periodical was also set up – the British Critic – probably with government sponsorship, though in this shadowy world it is difficult to be sure. It was initiated by high Anglican William Jones, and the editors were two other high church clergymen. Not only were these publications successful in themselves; they also initiated a vast explosion of anti-reform pro-government journalism during the 1790s.

Many writers were directly paid by government, or else patronised by ministers, for writing and publishing pamphlets. Charles Jenkinson, said to be behind every repressive measure, was Reeves's greatest patron, whilst William Windham patronised, as well as Reeves, John Bowles, William Playfair, and William Cobbett in his early loyalist days. Many others wrote in the hope of reward, or merely to support the cause. In addition, from 1792, the Treasury itself was directly publishing and distributing many tracts by various authors, real or pseudonymous. As a result of all this, in the early 1790s, the country was awash with pamphlets, tracts, and broadsheets, all aimed at divers sections of the population.

William Pitt's campaign of propaganda, in which he himself took a great personal interest, was a huge and resounding success. Those newspapers which were supportive of the government turned out far more numerous and successful than their opponents. The Sun was the most widely read newspaper in London, and its glory was reflected in the provinces by such journals as the Manchester Mercury, the Leicester Journal, and the York Courant. With pamphlets and periodicals, the story was the same. George Canning's Anti-Jacobin achieved weekly sales of 2,500. The sales of Paine's Rights of Man, though great, were completely eclipsed by the Cheap Repository Tracts, many of them written by Hannah More; the sales of these tracts were supported by a wide system of distribution, and customers who were prepared to buy wholesale and distribute free.

Inaction and reaction, then, characterised the government's response to the widespread agitation over social and economic hardship, and to the popular clamour for change. But how did the government justify this response? What, in other words, was the substance of the masses of verbiage released so liberally upon the people?

Edmund Burke set the tone. His answer to Paine's Rights of Man was called An Appeal from the New to the Old Whigs; and this became the fountainhead for all the propaganda issuing from establishment pens right down until the time of Malthus.

Burke's answer to radical complaints about the increasing hardships caused by the abuses of the governing classes was – blithely to ignore them. Incredibly for one who claimed conscientiously to have studied all the radical propaganda, Burke publicly reprobated "the conduct of those societies in England, who, alleging no one act of tyranny or oppression, and complaining of no hostile attempts against our ancient laws, rights, and usages, are now endeavouring to work the destruction of the crown of this kingdom, and the whole of its Constitution."[38] And yet, the works of the radical writers were filled with complaints about never-ending pointless wars, ever-increasing and partial taxation, dispossession by enclosure act, the engrossing of farms, spiralling interest on the national debt, monopolies in the corn trade, and the ravages of crimp-gangs and press-gangs. All of these, surely, could be categorised as acts of tyranny and oppression which were being complained of. But, in Burkean mythology, whether arising from deliberate falsehood, or from psychologically inculcated self-deception, there were no grievances, either social or economic. For Burke, the radicals were acting solely on the basis of abstract political principles, and were all the more dangerous for that.

"If I were to form a prognostic of the effect of the present machinations on the people from their sense of any grievance they suffer under this Constitution, my mind would be at ease. But there is a wide difference between the multitude, when they act against their government from a sense of grievance or from zeal for some opinion. When men are thoroughly possessed with that zeal, it is difficult to calculate its force. It is certain that its power is by no means in exact proportion to its reasonableness. It must always have been discoverable by persons of reflection, but it is now obvious to the world, that a theory concerning government may become as much a cause of fanaticism as a dogma in religion. There is a boundary in men's passions when they act from feeling; none when they are under the influence of imagination. Remove a grievance, and, when men act from feeling, you go a great way towards quieting a commotion. But the good or bad conduct of a government, the protection men have enjoyed or the oppression they have suffered under it, are of no sort of moment, when a faction, proceeding upon speculative grounds, is thoroughly heated against its form."[39]

In spite of unreality thus spilling over into patent absurdity, Burke's views permeated establishment pronouncements. In his speech on Grey's reform motion, Prime Minister Pitt spoke of "the principles of the French Revolution" and of "imaginary grievances".[40] Here is Burke's tacit dismissal of the existence of any genuine complaints concerning the connection between the distresses of the people and the corruption of government. Similar thinking finds its way into the Royal Proclamations. That issued in May 1792, for example, condemned "divers wicked and seditious writings" which, it complained, excited "tumult and disorder by endeavouring to raise groundless jealousies and discontents in the minds of our faithful and loving subjects, respecting the laws and happy constitution of government civil and religious, established in this kingdom."[41]

The deepening poverty of the people, which the radicals wished to remedy with parliamentary reform, was not a genuine grievance at all, but a groundless jealousy. The phrase turns up again and again, in the Royal Proclamation of 1795, as well as in later ones. Here, once again, even in the midst of a famine, the discontent of the people was not the result of material deprivation at all, but was deliberately stirred up by evil disposed persons for their own wicked and violent purposes.

---

38 Edmund Burke. An Appeal from the New to the Old Whigs. In The Writings and Speeches of Edmund Burke. Vol. 4. P. 104.

39 Ibid. P. 192.

40 Parliamentary History. Vol. 31. P. 1792.

41 Parliamentary History. Vol. 29. P. 1476.

"Divers inflammatory discourses were delivered,....and divers proceedings were had, tending to create groundless jealousy and discontent, and to endanger the public peace, and the quiet and safety of our faithful subjects...."[42]

Meanwhile, out in the real world, there was misery, and wretchedness, and impoverishment. In Parliament, in 1795, Samuel Whitbread told the House of Commons that;-

"The poor in this country are in a state scarcely consistent with the character of a civilised country."[43]

The observation was plainly out of step with the picture of the King's faithful and loving subjects, totally without grievance or complaint. How did the propagandists reconcile the discrepancy?

Many tracts depict the situation of the poor as one of almost idyllic good fortune. The tone was set by Archdeacon William Paley, in his "Reasons for Contentment". Here, Paley actually tried to make out that the poor were better off than the rich. The poor have "a constant train of employment both to body and mind. A husbandman, or a manufacturer, or a tradesman, never goes to bed at night without having his business to rise up to in the morning. He would understand the value of this advantage, did he know that the want of it composes one of the greatest plagues of the human soul; a plague by which the rich....are exceedingly oppressed."

"Some of the necessities which poverty....imposes, are not hardships but pleasures. Frugality itself is a pleasure....This is lost amidst abundance. There is no pleasure in taking out of a large unmeasured fund."

Paley goes on to speak of the "difficulty experienced by the rich in finding suitable situations for their children, from which great and oftentimes distressing perplexity the poor are free." Industry and innocence can be provided by every poor parent without expence.

The poor should not envy the rich for the sensual pleasures of eating, drinking, and so forth. For "the rich who addict themselves to indulgence lose their relish. Their desires are dead. Their sensibilities are worn and tired. Hence they lead a languid, satiated existence. Hardly anything can amuse, or rouse, or gratify them."

The perceived ease of the rich is similarly just a trying burden. For "no man can rest who has not worked....The rich see, and not without envy, the refreshment and pleasure which rest affords to the poor."

Paley's contentment seems to have consisted in his complete unconsciousness of the absurdity of his argument. For he compounds it with the following rural idyll.

"If the face of happiness can any where be seen, it is in the summer evening of a country village. Where, after the labours of the day, each man, at his door, with his children, amongst his neighbours, feels his frame and his heart at rest, every thing about him pleased and pleasing, and a delight and complacency in his sensations far beyond what either luxury or diversion can afford. The rich want this."

Paley repeatedly demonstrates his detachment from the reality of the deteriorating condition of ordinary people; as in the following passage about "that gradual and progressive improvement of our circumstances, which is the natural fruit of successful industry; when each year is something better than the last; when we are enabled to add to our little household one article after another of new comfort or conveniency, as our profits increase, or our burthen becomes less; and, what is best of all, when we can afford, as our strength declines, to relax our labours, or divide our cares. This may be looked forward to, and is practicable, by great numbers, in a state of public order and quiet...."

The reality was that increasing numbers were being forced to work into old age, until they could work no longer. At which point, many had no choice but the parish, or even the workhouse, their

---

42 Parliamentary History. Vol. 32. P. 243.
43 Parliamentary History. Vol. 32. P. 714.

families now being too poor to support elderly relatives. But Paley wrote as if he was unaware of this; perhaps, even, he was.

"The man who murmurs and repines, when he has nothing to murmur and repine about, but the mere want of independent property, is not only irreligious, but ill founded and unreasonable in his complaint….a life of labour, such I mean as is led by the labouring part of mankind in this country, has advantages in it, which compensate all its inconveniences. When compared with the life of the rich, it is better in all these important respects….It is free from many heavy anxieties which rich men feel; it is fraught with many sources of delight which they want…."[44]

The ideas put forward by Paley were a logical consequence of Burke's contention that no genuine grievances were being agitated for. Paley sub-titled his work "Addressed to the labouring part of the British public". Clearly it was not. It was too expensive. It was couched in terms which the poor might not have understood. And it depicted a situation which no ordinary person in England at the time would have recognised. It was directed largely at potential pamphleteers; and it projected an argument which could be, indeed was, used by them, to counter the claims of the radicals. Many writers followed Paley in painting a rosy picture of the condition of the English poor.

Arthur Young was one. Although Paley may have been genuinely ignorant of the true state of the poor, Young demonstrably was not. Yet still he chose to write on "the ease, happiness and security of all the lower classes". It is impossible to class this as anything other than a deliberate and premeditated falsehood. And he stands unanswerably accused of the following passage on the situation of the working poor in the manufacturing towns.

"Industry here meets its reward; you are paid in hard cash every Saturday night; you have something better, for your Sunday dinner than an assignat; a warm house covers you better than a branch of the tree of liberty; a good coat, or stout pair of shoes, would be ill exchanged for a three coloured cockade; whatever evil you have to complain of would be very ill remedied by any measures that tended sooner or later to change your beef and pudding for frogs and soup meagre; your coal fires for the pillaged sticks of a national forest; your shuttles for a hatchet; or your hammer for a pike; and the shillings and guineas (sic) of Old England for the paper assignats of Jacobin philosophers."[45]

In the tracts, the wages of labour are universally represented as generous. Dr. Vincent maintained that "industry….in this country, at least,…will never fail of obtaining bread and maintenance, and rarely miss of competence and comfort." In A Serious Caution to the Poor, written in 1792, wages are said to be "extremely liberal". And Job Nott wrote of the great rewards for industry available in Nottingham.

"In this town particularly, where the industrious poor constitute so great and useful a part of the community, and where labour is so well rewarded, nothing but health is necessary to procure an ample subsistence."[46]

Wages, in fact, were so high, as to prompt the following comment from John Bull, alias the Rev. William Jones of Nayland.

"I can see many a rare hard fellow who can afford to drink three days in the week with the money he gets in the other three, and see many others very wise and good, who quietly treasure up their gains, and presently set down to enjoy a comfortable rest in their declining years."[47]

---

44 W. Paley. Reasons for Contentment. Pp. 8-21.

45 Arthur Young. The Example of France. Pp. 75 and 95.

46 Dr. William Vincent. Short Hints upon Levelling. P. 10. A Serious Caution to the Poor. Job Nott. Advice to Sundry Sorts.

47 Rev. William Jones. John Bull's Letter to his Countrymen. P. 11.

John Bull writes of the comfortable cabins which his family inhabited, following Young's "warm house". If they fell into disrepair, it was only necessary to ask the landlord.[48] In the real world, the disrepair and squalid condition of the cottages of the poor, under the system of sub-letting by farmers, where both landlord and tenant avoided the responsibility of maintenance, were so notorious that the subject found its way into Samuel Whitbread's speech to the House of Commons in 1795.

Nothing daunted, John Bull continued.

"How would the numerous family of the Bulls (who have been admired for their fat, jolly, rosy faces and round bellies) like to change roast beef and plum pudding for bran and garden stuff; and to be all made by changing their round faces and paunches for thin jaws and lank guts."[49]

The meat consumed by the poor was a recurring theme in this sort of propaganda. "How pleasant would it be", asked the writer of A Cordial Drop, "when you set down to your four ribs of mutton, to see another come without restraint and take away two of them?" In Village Politics, Hannah More's protagonists end their conversation by singing "O the roast beef of Old England!"[50] But old England was passing. Bacon and mutton had all but disappeared from the diets of the poor. Roast beef was long gone.

Not only were the poor supremely fortunately placed; their condition was continually improving. "With all these taxes of which they complain", wrote John Bull, "I beg you to observe that there is scarcely one man in a hundred but what lives better than his father or his grandfather did...." In a Pamphlet written in 1792, an eighty year old man sees his son's white bread, tea and sugar, and cotton clothes as the signs of great improvement since his youth.[51]

Opportunities abounded, so it was said, for the poor to rise up the social scale. "You daily see numberless Instances of Individuals rising very honourably from Poverty to great Wealth." The tracts were full of characters who had done just that. "The road to honour, rank and dignity is open to all."[52]

And to what did the poor owe all this good fortune? Why, of course, to the rich. Here is Thomas Bull, alias William Jones.

"The poor of this country....do better under the benevolence of the rich, than they would do if they were stewards for themselves. It is the interest of the poor that all gentlemen should be rich where all gentlemen are charitable. On every occasion of scarcity and distress, they take delight, and even vie with one another in relieving their poor neighbour." Hannah More used the fable of the hands and feet rebelling against the lazy belly, to imply that the subsistence of the poor was available only by courtesy of the rich. But it was not only subsistence. The rich provided protection, and security, and good law, which "secures your Property, Persons, and every possible Liberty." The poor, it was alleged, had no cause to fear their property being taken from them by an unjust arm.[53]

In short, according to Dr. Vincent, "the superior orders of this Country might walk through the streets of this Metropolis, and challenge the poor with having nothing to complain of, except a life of labour; 'and that', they might say, 'is not allotted you by the ordinance of Man, but by the will of God'."[54]

---

48 Rev. William Jones. One Pennyworth of Answer. P. 2.
49 Rev. William Jones. John Bull's Second Answer to his Brother Thomas. P. 7.
50 The Works of Hannah More. Vol. II. P. 236.
51 Rev. William Jones. John Bull's Letter to his Countrymen. P. 10.
52 A Serious Caution to the Poor. P. 10. Dr. William Vincent. Short Hints on Levelling. P. 9.
53 Rev. William Jones. A Letter to John Bull from his second cousin Thomas. P. 39. A Serious Caution to the Poor.
54 Dr. William Vincent. Short Hints on Levelling. P. 11.

The fruits of this line of argument fell back to the soil in which they had germinated. Amidst the suffering of the famine of 1795, Edmund Burke demonstrated his complete lack of awareness of the outside world. He was writing with the intention of scuppering Samuel Whitbread's minimum wage proposal. Philosophical happiness, according to Burke, was all in the mind – it was to want little, and to be contented with what you have.

"If the happiness of the animal man (which certainly goes somewhere towards the happiness of the rational man) be the object of our estimate, then I assert, without the least hesitation, that the condition of those who labor (in all descriptions of labor, and in all gradations of labor, from the highest to the lowest inclusively) is, on the whole, extremely meliorated, if more and better food is any standard of melioration. They work more, it is certain; but they have the advantage of their augmented labor….But as to the fact of the melioration of their diet, I shall enter into the detail of proof, whenever I am called upon; in the mean time, the known difficulty of contenting them with anything but bread made of the finest flour and meat of the first quality is proof sufficient.

"I further assert, that, even under all the hardships of the last year, the laboring people did, either out of their direct gains, or from charity (which it seems is now an insult to them,) in fact, fare better than they did in seasons of common plenty, fifty or sixty years ago, - or even at the period of my English observation, which is about forty-four years. I even assert that full as many in that class as ever were known to do it before continued to save money; and this I can prove, so far as my own information and experience extend.

"It is not true that the rate of wages has not increased with the nominal price of provisions…. Wages have been twice raised in my time; and they bear a full proportion, or even a greater than formerly, to the medium of provision during the last bad cycle of twenty years. They bear a full proportion to the result of their labor."

The minimum wage, asserted Burke, would constitute an arbitrary tax on the farming interest. No farmer would oppress his labourers, because it was in his interest to keep them fit and happy. And the more avaricious the farmer, the better he would treat his workforce.

Burke then contradicted himself. Labour was merely an article of trade.

"The impossibility of the subsistence of a man who carries his labor to market is totally beside the question….The only question is, What is it worth to the buyer?" And he strongly implied that the wages of agricultural labour were already too high for the profitability of farmers.

To Burke, there were no able-bodied poor.

"Nothing can be so base and so wicked as the political canting language 'the labouring *poor*'…. It is horrible to call them 'the *once happy laborer*'."

And he concluded.

"In our history, and when 'the laborer of England is said to have been once happy', we find constantly, after certain intervals, a period of real famine, by which a melancholy havoc was made among the human race. The price of provisions fluctuated dreadfully, demonstrating a deficiency very different from the worst failures of the present moment. Never, since I have been in England, have I known more than a comparative scarcity. The price of wheat, taking a number of years together, has had no very considerable fluctuation; nor has it risen exceedingly until within this twelvemonth. Even now, I do not know of one man, woman, or child that has perished from famine; fewer, if any, I believe, than in years of plenty, when such a thing may happen by accident. This is owing to a care and superintendence of the poor, far greater than I ever remember."[55]

---

55 Edmund Burke. Thoughts and Details on Scarcity. In The Writings and Speeches of Edmund Burke. Vol. 5. Pp. 135-170.

It seems safe to assume that Burke's alternative reality was that generally entertained by the members of the anti-democratic elite. Burke never dared to publish this during his lifetime. But he sent it to Prime Minister Pitt before the second reading of Samuel Whitbread's bill. After Whitbread's opening speech, Pitt got up to oppose.

"He would not argue how far the comparison of the state of the labourer, relieved as it had been by a display of beneficence never surpassed at any period, with the state of this class of the community in former times, was just, though he was convinced that the representations were exaggerated. At any rate, the comparisons were not accurate, because they did not embrace a comprehensive view of the relative situations....Corn, which was then almost the only food of the labourer was now supplied by cheaper substitutions and it was unfair to conclude that the wages of labour were so far from keeping pace with the price of provisions, because they could no longer purchase the same quantity of an article for which the labourer had no longer the same demand."[56]

Pitt was supported by a Mr. Burdon. He "did not think that the industrious poor were in that wretched situation stated by some gentlemen. The industrious labourer, in many instances, was able to support his family, and lay up something for his old age. From the average price of labour for some years, the House must perceive, that the wages of the labourer were considerably increased...."[57]

Whitbread's bill was thus voted out; and the vote was of monumental significance, because it sent out the message to employers the country over that there was no need to raise wages to a level that would keep their workforces from starving. That function was now taken over by the parish. It led to a vast extension of the system whereby labourers received part of their wages out of the rates.

If the poor, then, were not poor; if, on the contrary, they were so fortunate and prosperous, why were they so discontented? In Village Politics, by Hannah More, Tom Hod is found reading the Rights of Man.

"I find here that I am very unhappy, and very miserable; which I should never have known, if I had not the good luck to meet with this book. Oh! 'tis a precious book!"[58]

According to establishment propaganda, the populace was being stirred up to discontent and rebelliousness by the seditious publications of radical politicians, for their own evil and wicked purposes.

John Bowles professed to think it the objective of the Rights of Man "to create restlessness and dissatisfaction, and to persuade mankind, that they suffer injuries which they do not perceive, that they sustain hardships which they do not feel, that their comforts are visionary and their happiness mere delusion; in short, these doctrines find men happy, prevail on them to believe that they are not so, and in the end render them miserable."[59]

Establishment propaganda of the early 1790s, therefore, tended to focus not on the poor at all, but upon those who agitated their grievances – the radical writers. Edmund Burke's principal method of refuting their arguments was by vilification, and by imputing to them motives which they did not profess. They were members of a wicked faction, allied with the perfidious usurpers of France, whose audacity grew with their impunity. The leaders of these factious societies might be thought wild and absurd; their writings contemptible and inconsequential, except insofar as "they show the evil habit of the bodies whence they came."[60]

According to Burke, these men were dangerous subversives, influenced by, even in league with, French revolutionaries. They were said to be "taking a factious interest in the proceedings of France"

---

56 Parliamentary History. Vol. 32. Pp. 705-706.
57 Ibid. P. 713.
58 The Works of Hannah More. Vol. II. P. 221.
59 John Bowles. A Protest against Thomas Paine's Rights of Man. P. 7.
60 Edmund Burke. An Appeal from the New to the Old Whigs. Pp69-71 and 199-201.

and planning "the subversion of nothing short of the whole Constitution of this kingdom....for the utter overthrow of the body of its laws, civil and ecclesiastic, and with them the whole system of its manners, in favour of the modern usages of the French nation."[61]

None of the radicals openly avowed any such intentions; indeed, they were generally inclined to act with moderation, and to disown republican and egalitarian theories. Yet Burke managed to assert, quite paradoxically, not only that their motives were more sinister than appeared; but also that they openly advocated subversion.

"The members of this faction leave no doubt of the nature and the extent of the mischief they mean to produce. They declare it openly and decisively. Their intentions are not left equivocal."[62]

Burke missed no opportunity of connecting British radicals with the French....

"What men admire and love they would surely act. Let us see what is done in France; and then let us undervalue any the slightest danger of falling into the hands of such a merciless and savage faction!"[63]

....and no opportunity of abusing the French, with whom he connected them.

"What was done in France was a wild attempt to methodize anarchy, to perpetuate and fix disorder....It was a foul, impious, monstrous thing, wholly out of the course of moral Nature....It was generated in treachery, fraud, falsehood, hypocrisy, and unprovoked murder."[64]

Where Burke led, others followed. The vilification of those who agitated the distresses of the poor was an especial aim of both government and pamphleteers. Thomas Paine himself fared particularly badly. An alleged 'Life of Paine' was published, written by George Chalmers, a government official, under the pseudonym of Francis Oldys, a fictitious graduate of the University of Pennsylvania. Paine's basic premise about war and corruption raising taxes to a level which impoverished the labouring classes was totally ignored, and Paine treated as a 'metaphysical reformer', whose political principles were, in reality, just a mask for his criminality.

"We are thus led to suspect, that the ultimate object of Mr. Pain, and of those who circulate his tract, must be, to give themselves little trouble about the constitution and laws of Great Britain when they can collect numbers enow to annihilate all by a tumult."[65]

A criminal who denies the authority of laws which society has enacted; who considers himself not bound by laws passed before he was born, or to which he did not give consent, could easily justify to himself all the roguery which Chalmers imputes to Paine; the whole intermingled with various allegations about Paine's dishonesty, perjury, lack of diligence and regard for the future, laziness, the outrageous treatment of his two wives, with a dose of sexual innuendo thrown in for good measure.[66] A vigorous campaign to blacken the character and undermine the credibility of Paine, without actually addressing the main arguments which he put forward, was reflected in propaganda nationwide. William Jones of Nayland, writing as John Bull, asserted that radical ideas came from the Devil, in the shape of Thomas Paine – Mad Tom, writer of the Rights of Rogues. He was too idle to earn his bread, so he sold the goods from his furnished lodging and ran away with the money. He was said to have had two wives at once, one of whom died of a broken heart, whilst the other was left to starve. He was kicked out of the Excise for roguery, and betrayed his country over the American Revolution. By all this roguery, he hoped to be given an estate in France. The poor mad wretch,

---

61 Ibid. Pp. 68-69.
62 Ibid. P. 69.
63 Ibid. 198.
64 Ibid. Pp. 70-71.
65 George Chalmers. Pseud. Francis Oldys. The Life of Thomas Pain. P. 120.
66 Ibid. Pp. 14-15, 25-26 and 33-34.

according to John Bull, ought to have been in Bedlam, or Newgate.[67] John Bowles refers to Paine as an "envious and malignant *Fiend*" with "an implacable animosity to this country"; and Arthur Young calls him the "Prince of Incendiaries".[68] The Rights of Man was similarly roughly treated. Hannah More, in Village Politics, defines it as "battle, murder and sudden death", which seems a little odd for a work whose near-pacifism was, perhaps, its leading feature. John Bowles asserts that Paine's "*Mob Government*" – in fact Bowles's own invention – assumes "the name of *Freedom*....because it leaves people *free* to do all the mischief they please, and restrains them merely from doing good". It was "a deliberate plan to sap and undermine the happiness and prosperity of Great Britain".[69]

The radical followers of Paine fared little better. Radicalism, asserted Hannah More, was the operation of fraud upon folly; whilst Arthur Young professed to see the whole argument as a contest between honest men and wicked men.[70] The evil and wickedness and criminality of the radicals is a constant theme; evil-minded persons a recurring epithet. John Bull, alias William Jones, calls them Revolutionaries and Republicans; wolves in sheep's clothing; hypocrites; robbers; murderers; fellows void of principle; incendiaries who would set fire to a house that they might plunder the property in the confusion; a nest of rascally levellers with mouths of envy. "How", asks John Bull, "do they settle such crimes with their consciences? – The robbery of their Neighbours! Murder of their fellow Creatures! Treason to their King, and Ruin to their Country!"[71]

The lack of any material grievances or complaints among the poor, then, was combined in establishment propaganda with the criminality of those writers and orators who would stir them up to rebellion, for their own wicked purposes. The government's response to growing social distress became, increasingly, to prevent anyone from talking about it. From within the establishment, there was constant pressure for harsher measures of repression, both legal and physical; and so, during most of the years of the 1790s, repressive measures passed through parliament.[72]

Suspending the Act of Habeas Corpus in 1794 allowed the authorities to arrest and imprison without trial anyone they chose. This opened the way to move against the leaders of the London Corresponding Society and the Society for Constitutional Information. Thomas Hardy, Horne Tooke, John Thelwall and others were charged with high treason, an offence which carried the death penalty. The case against them was weak, even with a rigged jury, and when Hardy was acquitted the cases against the others were dropped. In a political sense, however, the show trials were a success for the government, as they intimidated the radicals and drove them somewhat back into their shells.

So much so that the famine of the following year saw no great surge of support for the radical organisations, whose methods remained peaceful and restrained. The Act of Habeas Corpus was restored, and Dundas commented;-

---

67 Rev. William Jones. John Bull's Second Answer to his Brother Thomas. P. 6.

68 John Bowles. A Protest against Thomas Paine' Rights of Man. Pp. 3 and 5. Arthur Young. The Example of France. P. 50.

69 The Works of Hannah More. P. 233. John Bowles. A Protest against Thomas Paine's Rights of Man. P. 31.

70 The Works of Hannah More. P. 232. Arthur Young. The Example of France. P. 101.

71 Rev. William Jones. John Bull's Answer to his Brother Thomas.

72 This section, except where stated, is based on the following secondary works. J. Mori. William Pitt and the French Revolution. S. Watson. The Reign of George III. Colin Jones ed. Britain and Revolutionary France. A. Aspinall. Politics and the Press. H. T. Dickinson. Britain and the French Revolution.

"As for the feelings of the country, they are infinitely better than one could expect considering the price of provisions."

Even William Pitt conceded that the riots of that year were caused by social distress and disillusionment with the war. Nevertheless, in the midst of the increasing sufferings of the people, pressure came from within the governing elite for further repressive measures. As if to prepare the way, a Select Committee of the House of Commons announced, seemingly out of the blue, that the evil design "to overturn the laws, constitution and government in concert with a foreign enemy has never been abandoned". An apparently premeditated campaign to bring in the Gagging Acts came to fruition when a stone was thrown at the King's Coach in October.

The Seditious Meetings Act prohibited meetings of over fifty people, whether seditious or not, and forbade lectures unless licensed and supervised by magistrates.

The Treasonable Practices Act changed the definition of treason to include the spoken and written word. Criticising the government became virtually a capital offence, if under one of the classifications of attempting to coerce parliament or attacking the constitution. Orators, writers and publishers could all now be severely punished for their opinions.

The following year, the stamp duty on newspapers was raised. This was aimed at raising not revenue, but the price of newspapers in order to restrict their circulation; and at reducing the profits of newspapers in order to make them more dependent upon patronage. Henceforth, the law required that all printing presses should be registered, along with the names and addresses of printers and publishers, so that legal action could be taken if they stepped out of line. Printers, publishers and journalists could all fall foul of the law on libel, or the Gagging Acts. Charges could be laid, but not brought to court; and left in suspension as a sort of security for future good conduct. Journalists could be ruined financially by legal action even if innocent; even, indeed, if found innocent. Even the very fundamental and traditional right of petitioning parliament came to be in doubt. When asked by the Opposition if he intended making petitioning illegal, Pitt replied that it was necessary to distinguish between "true" and "false" petitions.

"Those men were not, in his opinion, the best friends either to the Constitution or to the lower ranks of the people, who endeavour to habituate them to petitioning; who encourage those to frequent deliberations on public affairs….who, of all men, by education and habits of life, and means of information, were the least capable of exercising a sound judgment on such subjects, and who are most likely to be imposed upon by others."[73]

And, increasingly, petitions to parliament were left to "lie upon the table", if not believed to come from "the right sort of people".

Fear was a potent weapon for enforcing silence about the distresses of the populace, and was extensively used. The fear of spies and secret government agents dissuaded people from voicing their opinions in public. The sinister Alien Office, described as "almost a mirror image of the much despised French system of secret police", became an important engine of internal state espionage. There were constant rumours, not entirely unfounded, about the landing of mercenaries from Hesse or Hanover, brought by government to enforce martial law. The lingering memories of the state trials of the leading English radicals were reinforced by the savage sentences actually handed down to radicals in Scotland; and by an awareness that, as the law had now become, a similar fate, or worse, would have befallen the English radicals.

At times, militant loyalism became paramilitary. In many cities, violent loyalist demonstrations were connived at by magistrates, or even actively organised by them. Political Clubs and associations covered the country; many had links with the Reeves Association; others were set up by the Church of England. These came to have a military purpose, ostensibly in case of invasion, but in reality

---

73 J. Mori. William Pitt and the French Revolution. P. 253.

largely with a view to prevent the expression of unsound opinions. Speeches and military parades had an intimidatory purpose, and violent attacks on radicals became common – at least twenty-five are recorded in the north-east of England between 1792 and 1795; and many also in other parts of the country, from Exeter to Sheffield.

The propaganda war over the worsening poverty of the people, therefore, was won by the elitist tendency, because the resources of government were brought to bear in its support. Voicing sympathy for the poor became, not just illegal, but dangerous and socially unacceptable. When, in 1794, David Davies brought out his study of the conditions in which his parishioners lived, he was careful to make it entirely non-political. He addressed the legislature with respect; and even inserted, towards the end, some surprising criticisms of the poor, which, one suspects, were designed to conciliate the elitist tendency. In spite of everything, Yorkshire gentleman Sir Christopher Sykes, writing to William Wilberforce, labelled this innocuous study as pernicious as the Rights of Man; and presumably its author as deserving a similar fate.[74] Already by 1793, a man of radical opinion found it "prudent to say as little as possible upon political subjects, in order to keep myself out of Newgate."

Conversely, expressing contempt for the ordinary people of this country was becoming much more frequent, acceptable and open; in some social circles it was becoming *de rigueur*, if acceptance and respectability were the goals aimed at; and if the social stigma of sympathy for the poor was to be avoided. Many writers wishing for an upper class audience laced their works with liberal dosings of abuse for the labouring classes. Poverty, and the causes of poverty, had become taboo.

Meanwhile, on the 5th November 1795, in the parish church of Heacham in Norfolk, a large meeting took place of the agricultural labourers of the parish and those surrounding.

"In order to take into consideration the best and most peaceable mode of obtaining a redress of all the severe and peculiar hardships under which they have for so many years so patiently suffered, the following resolutions were unanimously agreed to;- 1st, That – *The labourer is worthy of his hire*, and that the mode of lessening his distresses, as hath been lately the fashion, by selling him flour under the market price, and thereby rendering him the object of a parish rate, is not only an indecent insult on his lowly and humble situation (in itself sufficiently mortifying from his degrading dependence on the caprice of his employer) but a fallacious mode of relief, and every way inadequate to a radical redress of the manifold distresses of his calamitous state. 2nd, That the price of labour should, at all times, be proportioned to the price of wheat, which should invariably be regulated by the average price of that necessary article of life."

The report, from a Norwich newspaper, goes on to detail the comprehensive arrangements made for presenting a petition on the subject to parliament, and for financing it. But the petition was never presented; and that, presumably, because it was thought to fall within the scope of the Gagging Acts, passed around the same time. We do not know, but might strongly suspect, that meetings such as this were taking place around the country, in order to petition in support of Samuel Whitbread's Minimum Wage Bill. The governing elite would certainly not have welcomed a surge of popular support for Whitbread; they would not have wished the public at large to believe that the poor, contrary to official propaganda, had any grievances which could be to any extent addressed by the legislature, or, indeed, any genuine grievances at all; and they would not have wished anyone to suspect that those who raised those grievances might be anything other than raging Jacobins wishing to cut all their throats and seize their property.[75]

The voice of the ordinary man was thus silenced by the Gagging Acts; and it seems highly likely that that, specifically, was their purpose.

---

74 R. Wells. Wretched Faces. P. 292.
75 J. L. and B. Hammond. The Village Labourer. Pp. 113-115.

The poor harvests of 1794 and 1795, and of 1799 and 1800, and the resulting distresses of huge sections of the population, brought to the fore once again the long-running controversy over the extent to which rapidly rising prices were exacerbated by the manipulations of the more opulent participants in the corn trade.[76] Hungry consumers expected and understood that when harvests were deficient, prices would rise. But when the increase of price seemed greater than could be accounted for by the shortness of yield, widespread disturbances were the result. It was only during the summer of 1795 that people believed that starvation was possible through actual scarcity; and then, understandably enough, disturbances stemmed from the transportation of grain, as the consumers of producing regions attempted to prevent their localities being drained of corn by dealers wishing to sell in more distant markets. At all other times, riots hinged, not on movements, but on prices. If prices were perceived as behaving abnormally, commercial malpractice was immediately suspected. A belief arose in a "spirit of profiteering and extortion". And price riots were the result, in which were targeted those farmers, millers and dealers who were thought to be hoarding grain with a view to raising its price. Stocks were seized and sold at prices perceived as reasonable, perhaps those of 1794. Angry crowds imposed price ceilings at markets, aided by injunctions from sympathetic magistrates. Such was the case in the spring of 1795, when commotions broke out all around the country; perhaps most notably at Lewes in Sussex, spreading out into Kent. A similar scenario occurred in the spring of 1800. That summer, prices remained high, when the popular opinion was that they ought to have been falling, and manipulation by dealers was again suspected. Finally, and perhaps most seriously, after the harvest of 1800, at a time of year when prices always fell, they were on the increase again. A sudden increase in the price of flour provoked rioting at Sheffield at the end of August; and violence spread into Nottinghamshire, Derbyshire, Leicestershire, and throughout the West Midlands. Particularly serious rioting in Nottingham led to the imposition of a maximum price of flour in September 1800; and by the spring of 1801 the whole of the south-west of England was in open revolt. It was prices that were seen as being abnormally and artificially high or rising that led, at these times, to the country being in a state of violent and chaotic disorder.

As might be expected, this popular analysis of the causes of distress was not shared by William Pitt's anti-populist government. We have already seen how, in mid-century, the economic doctrines, if such they can be called, of a small number of corn-dealing pamphleteers seeped into government thinking, in what was probably a coincidence of financial interest; and from there spread into establishment propaganda, culminating in Adam Smith's Wealth of Nations. According to these writers, the rise in prices was caused by the shortness of crops; in spite of a few subsidiary causes, like the plenty of money, or the withholding of corn by opulent farmers, the bulk of the blame was attached to unfavourable seasons, and through them to God. By the time of Adam Smith, price manipulation by wealthy dealers of all sorts was said to be both impossible and beneficial at the same time. In the face of this explanation of the material hardships of the people, corn-traders saw food-rioting as an unwarranted attack on their property and profits, and called for the army and the law to be employed for their protection. This approach was eagerly acquiesced in by an elitist government, and endorsed by the authority of Adam Smith.

By the 1790s, establishment thinking was permeated with this explanation of hunger and food rioting. Politicians of all persuasions seem to have had more or less close links to the foremost participants in the grain trade – a subject greatly in need of further historical investigation. Faced, therefore, with widespread disturbances caused by the popular perception of abnormal prices being caused by profiteering at the expence of consumers, the elitist reaction was to send in the troops.

---

76 This whole section owes an obvious debt to R. Wells. Wretched Faces.

The elite, however, constituted only a very tiny section of opinion; out in the real world, landowners, gentlemen, clergy and magistrates of all sorts doubted whether this was the best approach. Here is the Rev. Haden, writing audaciously to Home Secretary Portland.

"As a Conservator of the Peace, I shall always stand forward to protect it, but I can never attempt it, at the hazard of my Life, for enriching one part of the Community and supporting them in the most glaring Acts of Oppression at the Expense of the Comforts, Happiness and even the Existence of the other."[77]

Consequently, the use of military force against the starving needed an intensive campaign of propaganda, aimed largely at local authorities, discrediting popular explanations of spiralling prices, and providing a justification for using the resources of the state to defend the sectional interests of the grain traders.

To begin with, official sources played down the seriousness of the crisis. This is how Portland replied to an angry letter from a magistrate.

"It would....be absurd in the extreme to suppose that what is stated in your letter....namely 'that the Poor are Starving in the midst of Plenty' is a matter of fact."[78]

Here was brought to bear the putative authority of Adam Smith.

"In an extensive corn country, between all the different parts of which there is a free commerce and communication, the scarcity occasioned by the most unfavourable seasons can never be so great as to produce a famine."[79]

On this subject, as on so many others, Smith was not only proved wildly wrong by subsequent events; he was even wide of the mark for his own time. What occurred in England between 1794 and 1796, and between 1799 and 1801, were famines by any definition. Yet ministers sheltered behind Smith to label what was happening merely a scarcity. The word famine was never used, except in a hypothetical sense. The unfettered operation of the grain trade would avert a "very real famine". Unsuppressed riots would see "famine substituted in place of Scarcity". Privately it was different. Lord Auckland, writing to Pitt, defined famine as "the want of Wheat sufficient to furnish the lower & labouring classes....with the species of food which long usage has made a necessary of Life to them." Colonel Clinton, writing to Lord William Bentinck in Austria in 1800, remarked that such conditions "in any other Country than this....would be called Famine". Thus, there was a deliberate attempt to belittle, in the eyes of the political classes, the sufferings of the poor. The scarcity, it was alleged, was merely "the pretext for their outrages", committed for sinister reasons of their own by "the deluded and ill-disposed part of the community." There, or so ministers hoped, discussion ended.[80]

The realistic discussion of the conditions under which people lived, suffered and died was made virtually illegal, a capital offence in fact, by the Gagging Acts passed in the autumn of 1795.

For a while, government seemed to have nothing to say on the subject. A request from the corporation of London, for "decisive and vigorous measures to procure a very considerable importation of wheat", remained unanswered. The Mayor's demand for legislation to ensure a supply of grain was rejected by Portland, on the grounds that it "might....create an immediate alarm." And discussion in Parliament was discouraged. When the opposition broached the subject of the scarcity of wheat, Pitt retorted that "such discussion was very disorderly and calculated to do no good. It might provoke an unspecified mischief." The Foxites, whose links with the grain trade were perhaps even closer than the government's, acquiesced; and when one of their number, a Mr. Jeckyll, demanded "official inquiries

---

77 R. Wells. Wretched Faces. P. 230.
78 Ibid. P. 237.
79 Ibid. P. 35.
80 D. Wilkinson. The Duke of Portland. P. 122.

into commercial malpractices in the grain trade", it was a colleague from his own side of the House who buried the entire subject in an important discussion of the debts of the Prince of Wales!![81]

But when, after the harvest of 1795, prices rose yet again, suspicions about market manipulation once more provoked anger amongst hungry consumers. Of the letters reaching the Home Office on the subject, a clear majority placed the blame on abuses in the grain trade. The government's reaction to the crisis was to attempt to alter people's perceptions[82]

Throughout both the famines, the monofactorial role of harvest failure was emphasised by government, and by Home Secretary Portland in particular, in its justification of the use of military force against starving rioters. Deficient crops were a constant theme.

"I am sorry to say that according to the most sanguine estimations, the produce of (the harvest)... is not likely to amount to more than three fourths of an average crop, and it is thought by many that it will not exceed three fifths."[83]

In 1799, the government used the authority of Parliament to give weight to its propaganda; by confirming ministers' opinions of the shortness of yields.

Somehow, the fact of a deficient harvest was supposed to preclude the possibility of price manipulation. Grain traders, asserted Portland, were not engrossers, but "the purveyors and provident stewards of the people." Without them, consumers would want the "regular succession of supplies which is to carry them through the year."

Engrossers, "as they increase in number, counteract the mischief which it is supposed they are the cause of, and make....combinations impossible."[84]

To emphasise the point, some of the leading corn-dealers were summoned to appear before the parliamentary committee and questioned.

"Have you any Idea of the Supply of Wheat being withheld from the Market in Consequence of Combination?"

The answer was as you might expect. One cornfactor replied;

"I have no such Idea. I believe the Thing to be impossible....Rich Farmers will of course keep up the Wheat in Expectation of high Prices."[85]

Everything, therefore, was just as it should have been.

The absurdity of this exercise must have been plain to all. Yet the parliamentary outcome was a consensus that high prices were entirely the product of natural scarcity; artificial causes playing no part. Further, the report of the committee on high prices completely acquitted grain traders of any wrong-doing. Corn-jobbers were praised for taking supplies of corn from producing to consuming areas. The problem of speculation was not addressed. And combinations between dealers were said to be impossible. Famine, it was said, had been averted thanks to the practice of opulent farmers of holding their corn back from market. What started out as an enquiry into the distresses of the poor ended up as a hymn of praise to wealthy traders and producers.[86]

Popular explanations of the crisis could now be dismissed with contempt. They were merely, according to Portland, popular prejudices which led to riots and disturbances.[87] When some M.P.s raised the question once again of combinations among monopolistic corn-traders early in 1796, Pitt

81 R. Wells. Wretched Faces. P. 185.
82 Ibid. P. 232.
83 D. Wilkinson. The Duke of Portland. P. 122.
84 Ibid. P. 116.
85 R. Wells. Wretched Faces. P. 233.
86 Ibid. P. 234.
87 D. Wilkinson. The Duke of Portland. P. 116.

could afford to be merely dismissive. Would M.P.s, he asked, "lend themselves to confirm vulgar prejudices, to mislead ignorance and inflame discontent?"

The role of harvest deficiency as the sole cause of rising prices was combined in official communications with doctrines of free trade, and an increasing emphasis on the inviolable sanctity of private property, to provide a justification for the use of military force against crowds. Portland himself put it like this.

"Wherever a scarcity of provisions exists, or is seriously to be apprehended, the only means which can tend effectually to obviate it....consists in holding out full security and indemnity to all farmers and other lawful dealers in grain who shall bring their corn....regularly to market, and in giving early notice of a determined resolution to suppress at once....every attempt to impede....the regular business of the markets."

There was, according to Portland, a need for the "religious observation or the respect which is due to private property."[88]

Accordingly, an increasing amount of pressure was brought to bear on the local authorities to summon in military aid as a response of first resort to disturbances, actual or feared. In similar circumstances during the 1750s and 1760s, anti-poor propaganda was used to assuage the misgivings of the political classes. By the 1790s, methods of pumping propaganda into circulation had become much more sophisticated. In this case, the establishment will made itself felt through the Church of England. Bishop Porteus of London put pressure on his friend, the well-known authoress Hannah More, to put pen to paper in support of the cause. The result was the Cheap Repository Tracts. Financed by banker Henry Thornton, this was a long series of parable-like stories by many authors, but principally the work of the genius of More herself. They achieved a massive success, perhaps above any other literature of the period, with More claiming that two million copies had been distributed. Many of them were claimed to be directed towards the poorer classes of the community; but most, in fact were about the poorer classes, for the consumption of the middle and the upper. The analysis of the causes of poverty portrayed allegorically in these stories was clearly designed to engender prejudice and hostility.[89]

More endorsed the official version of the causes of the scarcity.

"I lament both the War and the Taxes together,
Tho' I verily think they don't alter the weather.
The King, as I take it, with very good reason,
May prevent a bad law, but can't help a bad season.
The parliament men, altho' great is their power,
Yet they cannot contrive us a bit of a shower,
And I never yet heard, tho' our rulers are wise,
That they know very well how to manage the skies;
For the best of them all, as they found to their cost
Were not able to hinder last winter's hard frost."[90]

Popular accusations about malpractice in the grain trade were countered by More's ballad of The Honest Miller of Gloucestershire.

"Of all the callings and the trades
    Which in our land abound,
· The miller's is as useful, sure,
    As can on earth be found."

---

88 D. Wilkinson. The Duke of Portland. P. 115.
89 W. Roberts. Memoirs of the Life and Correspondence of Mrs. Hannah More. Vol. II. Pp. 365-367.
90 Hannah More. The Riot.

This miller found himself in a monopoly position during the hard winter of 1795, when the stream which drove his mill was the only one in the locality not to freeze up. His neighbours urged him to take advantage and make his fortune. But the miller, who was intended to represent the generality of middlemen in the corn trade, was much too upright a man to stoop to this.

"Our miller scorn'd such counsel base,
  And when he ground the grain,
With steadfast hand refus'd to touch
  Beyond his lawful gain.
"When God afflicts the land", said he,
  "Shall I afflict it more?
And watch for times of public wo,
  To wrong both rich and poor?"

Like ministers, More tried to play down the disastrous effects of famine on the well-being of the people. Scarcity, she asserted, was a trial sent by God to prove us, to promote penitence and cheerful submission. It could even be beneficial.

"A bad season may thus be made a lasting benefit to us, by putting us upon new habits of temperance and oeconomy, and this visitation of which we have been so much afraid may be turned into a blessing to the whole land."[91]

To More, famine was a storm in a teacup.

"What trembling and complaining have we lately seen, what calling of vestries, and advertising, and bustling, and subscribing, because one of the articles of our food has become dearer for a few months than it is in common."[92]

The lot of the poor was in reality a truly happy one.

"God is pleased to contrive to make things more equal than we poor, ignorant, short-sighted creatures are apt to think." David was happier when he tended his father's sheep than he was as king. "A laborious life is a happy one....and more so especially, as it exposes a man to fewer sins."

"A man with ever so small an income, if he had but frugality and temperance, and cast off all vain desires was richer than a lord who was tormented by vanity and covetousness."

On Salisbury Plain Mr. Johnson met with a shepherd, who earned but a shilling a day. This had to keep eight children and a sick wife. He lived in a two-roomed hovel, with rain coming through the thatch. Often they had little to eat, but the shepherd claimed not to be distressed, because he possessed the inner contentment which came from religion. When he and his family dined on just potatoes and salt, they were thankful.

"What must poor people do, who have no salt to their potatoes, and do but look, our dish is quite full....A good dinner....was not to be compared to *a contented Mind, which, as the Bible truly says, is a continual feast.*"

Miraculously, the shepherd's daughter was "a fine plump cherry-cheek little girl....with a smile on her happy young face.[93]

Hannah More was perfectly well aware of the true consequences of dependence on a daily wage of one shilling from her philanthropic works in Somerset, as we know from her private letters.

More's economic theory of the infinite elasticity of the daily wage found expression in The Happy Waterman. The economic genius who was the subject of this parable, on daily labour and the occasional earnings of his wife, managed to support an increasing family, as well as his wife's ageing parents; contribute generously to the local poor; and still had surplus cash each week to save up!

---

91 Hannah More. Hints to All Ranks of People. P. 17.
92 Ibid. P. 30.
93 Hannah More. Tales for the Common People. Pp. 34-35, 18, 36, 43-45 and 37.

The happy situation of the poor was made more fortunate still by the constant stream of kindnesses which they received at the hands of the rich. Thanks to the rich, proclaimed the Wiltshire shepherd, the poor possessed the advantages of law and order.

"The house is very well, Sir, and if the rain did not sometimes beat down upon us through the thatch when we are a-bed, I should not desire for a better; for I have health, peace, and liberty, and no man maketh me afraid."

In hard times, they had charity; as Farmer White remarked.

"The rich have been very kind, and I don't know what we should have done without them."

Previously, as plain Tom, Farmer White had recovered from his injuries "by the blessing of God and the skill of the surgeon.

"What a mercy it is that we live in a Christian country, where the poor, when sick, or lame, or wounded, are taken as much care of as any gentry; nay, in some respects more, because in hospitals and infirmaries there are more doctors and surgeons to attend."

Education was another blessing. Unfortunately for her, Betty Brown, the St. Giles orange girl, "came into the world before so many good gentlemen and ladies began to concern themselves so kindly that the poor might have a little learning." The Salisbury Plain shepherd, mentioned earlier, had suffered under a similar disadvantage.

"Reading was not so common when I was a child, as I am told, through the goodness of Providence, and the generosity of the rich, it is likely to become now-a days."[94]

Under such circumstances as these, there was clearly no need for anybody to be distressed. The riots and disturbances, therefore, were not caused by hunger at all. Part of the problem was envy of the rich.

"You are hurt possibly through your having heard or seen much of the luxury of the rich around you, and you have thus learnt to condemn them altogether as a body of most unchristian and wicked people."

Many a poor man was "fretful and discontented with your lot, you are always talking against the rich and great, your whole thought is engaged not about your own faults but about their pomp, and luxury, and sin."

In general, riots were stirred up by "evil-minded people, who are on the watch for public distresses, not that they may humble themselves under the mighty hand of God (which is the true use to be made of all troubles) but that they may benefit themselves by disturbing the public peace. These people, by riot and drunkenness, double the evil which they pretend to cure."

Rioting was just such a desirable way of life.

"It seems both easier and pleasanter to plunder a mill or even to pull down a kingdom, than to rise by the slow means of patient industry, trusting in God."[95]

Life, then, was good for the poor, if they were sober, frugal, industrious, and contented under every difficulty. Distress was unnecessary. But distress there undoubtedly was, and More felt constrained to explain it.

Much of it was just a charade – not real at all. Black Giles lived in a mud cottage, with broken windows stuffed with dirty rags. There were ragged tiles on the roof, and loose stones ready to drop out of the chimney. It would have been easy to repair it but "Giles fell into that common mistake, that a beggarly looking cottage, and filthy ragged children raised most compassion, and of course drew most charity."[96]

Where distress was real, it was the fault of the poor themselves.

---

94 Ibid. Pp. 36, 28, 8, 55 and 35-36.
95 Hannah More. Hints to All Ranks of People. Pp. 25-29.
96 Hannah More. Tales for the Common People. P. 67.

"If every poor man….would try to trace the evils which have befallen him to their proper source….he would perhaps find that more of the hardships he now suffers are owing to his own fault than he would imagine….Either want of industry when he was young, or want of oeconomy when he was a little older, and might easily have laid up money; want of temperance, chastity, sobriety, want of character for strict truth and exact integrity; want of prudence in some of the important steps of his life and above all want of religion, which is the root indeed of all the other sins I have named."[97]

Idleness and drunkenness were said to be the prevailing causes of poverty. Dick Guzzle the smith only worked two or three days in the week, and spent the rest at the Red Lion. Consequently, he lost most of his employment. Tom the thatcher complained that meat was so dear that he could not afford it. Yet Tom took a holiday on Easter Monday and Tuesday, by which he lost 4s. in wages, and spent 3s. at the alehouse.

"Tom, you often tell me times are so bad that you can never buy a bit of meat. Now here is the cost of two joints at once, to say nothing of the sin of wasting time and getting drunk." And the farmer suggested the purchase of a shoulder of mutton, to be baked in a deep dish full of potatoes.

"Aye, but I've got no beer, master."

"Times are bad, and malt is very dear, Tom, and yet both don't prevent your throwing away seven shillings in keeping holiday."[98]

Much distress was caused by what Hannah More labelled bad management; by which she meant profusion and extravagance. The reason why the poor could not afford meat was that they drank gin; the reason why they could not afford to brew beer was that they spent their money at the alehouse.

"The number of public-houses in many a parish brings on more hunger and rags than all the taxes in it….All the other evils put together hardly make up the sum of that one."[99]

The practice of eating wheaten bread was a common target. Jesus Christ's five loaves were apparently made from barley.

"How many of you are there….who, if the same barley bread was presented to you which was presented to the Saviour of the world, instead of giving thanks as he did, would be ready rather to complain; not chusing, even in a time of scarcity, to eat any bread that is not wheaten."[100]

Wheaten bread, tea, sugar and butter were all portrayed as hopeless and pernicious extravagances.

"My good woman…." says the vicar addressing one of his parishioners, "one half of your present hardships is owing to BAD MANAGEMENT. I often meet your children without shoes and stockings, with great luncheons of the very whitest bread, and that three times a day."

"A poor man gets 7s. to 8s. per day", says Mrs. White. "If he is careful he brings it home." (Note the subtle implication here that many spend it at the alehouse.) "I dare not say how much of this goes for tea in the afternoon, now sugar and butter are so dear, because I should have you all upon me; but I will say, that too much of this little goes for bread, from a notion that it is the hardest fare."

Amy Grumble looked as dirty as a cinder-wench, with her face and fingers all daubed with snuff, another supposed luxury of the poor. She complained that rice was of no use to her without fuel to cook it with. And yet, remarked the vicar, "I see your tea-kettle boiling twice every day as I pass by the poor-house, and fresh butter at eleven-pence a pound on your shelf."[101]

According to More, virtue was what led to wealth in this world; and the lack of it was what led almost inevitably to poverty. Young Tom White made good in the world.

---

97   Hannah More. Hints to All Ranks of People. P. 29.
98   Hannah More. Tales for the Common People. Pp. 19-20.
99   Ibid. P. 28.
100   Hannah More. Hints to All Ranks of People. P. 8.
101   Hannah More. Tales for the Common People. Pp. 25-26.

"Being diligent, he *got* a great deal of money; being frugal, he *spent* but little; and having no vices, he *wasted* none.

"The same principles which make a man sober and honest, have also a natural tendency to make him healthy and rich; while a drunkard and a spendthrift can hardly escape being sick and a beggar in the end. Vice is the parent of misery here as well as in the hereafter."[102]

More is close to asserting here that the rich are good people and the poor are bad people. And with what a catalogue of vices she damns those who were suffering in the famines of the 1790s! Menfolk drink away their wages at the alehouse, and leave their families ragged and starving. Or if the men manage not to squander their money, they have wives who do it for them.

"It is little encouragement to an honest man to work hard all the week, if his wages are wasted by a slattern at home....A poor woman, who will be lying-a-bed, or gossiping with her neighbours when she ought to be fitting out her husband in a cleanly manner, will seldom be found to be very good in other respects."[103]

More does not resist the usual sideswipe at the traditional agricultural classes. In The Two Shoemakers, Jack Brown was the son of a farmer. Spoilt by his mother, he was wild and giddy, and preferred bird-nesting and marbles, or idling away his time, to working on the farm or going to school. James Stock, on the other hand, was the son of an honest day-labourer; he, by contrast, was a modest, industrious, pious youth. Black Giles the poacher was a commoner.

"The right of Common....was converted by Giles into the means of corrupting his whole family, for his children, as soon as they grew too big for the trade of begging at the gate, were promoted to the dignity of thieving on the Moor. Here he kept two or three asses, miserable beings, which, if they had the good fortune to escape an untimely death by starving, did not fail to meet with it by beating. Some of the biggest boys were sent out with these lean and galled animals to carry sand or coals about the neighbouring towns. Both sand and coals were often stolen before they got them to sell, or if not, they always took care to cheat in selling them. By long practice in this art they grew so dextrous, that they could give a pretty good guess how large a coal they could crib out of every bag before the buyer would be likely to miss it.

"All their odd time was taken up under the pretence of watching their asses on the moor, or running after five or six half-starved geese; but the truth is, these boys were only watching for an opportunity to steal an odd goose of their neighbour's. They used to pluck the quills or the down from these poor live creatures, or half milk a cow before the farmer's maid came with her pail. They all knew how to calculate to a minute to be down in a morning to let out their lank, hungry beasts, which they had turned over night into the farmer's field, to steal a little good pasture...."[104]

But perhaps the ultimate insult offered to the poor is contained in The Story of Sinful Sally. In an age when the growing lack of employment opportunities for women, combined with poverty and desperation, was driving thousands of girls and young women into prostitution, and from thence to an early grave, Hannah More came out with a ballad about a young lady whose vices led her voluntarily into that style of life.

"Ah how many youths so blooming
By my wanton looks I've won;
Then by vices all-consuming
Left them ruin'd and undone!
Now no more by conscience troubled,
Deep I plunge in every Sin;

---

102 Ibid. P. 10.
103 Hannah More. The Cottage Cook. P. 13. Tales for the Common People. Pp. 33-34.
104 Hannah More. Tales for the Common People. Pp. 68-69.

True; my sorrows are redoubled,
But I drown them all in Gin.
See me next with front so daring
Band of ruffian Rogues among;
Fighting, cheating, drinking, swearing,
And the vilest of the throng."[105]

It is not conceivable that More believed very much of her own propaganda. She was, under duress, presenting an account of poverty and the poor which had become orthodox to a relatively small elitist clique at the heart of government, the legal profession, and the established church; which, for their own reasons, they wished to propagate amongst the political classes of the provinces and the localities. That More really was presenting the mindset of the establishment is well demonstrated by comparison with the influential, and widely read, State of the Poor, published in 1797. This was written by F, M. Eden, brother of Lord Auckland who was a member of the government and a friend of William Pitt. Eden himself was a prominent businessman, with interests in insurance and friendly societies.

In the introduction to his comprehensive survey, Eden reiterates many of the points that were portrayed allegorically by Hannah More and her colleagues in the Cheap Repository Tracts. The desirable and improving situation of the poor is emphasised also by Eden. After presenting the accustomed catalogue of writings on the Poor Laws, he concludes from it that "not only the aggregate body of the nation must have advanced to wealth and independence, but that the portion of the community, which consists of those who are emphatically called the *labouring* classes, must have considerably bettered its condition in the course of the present century."[106]

It has to be said that there is nothing in the survey of writings presented by Eden that could possibly justify any such conclusion. Nothing daunted, Eden maintains his theme.

"From the information which I have received from various parts of England, I have reason to think, that the price of labour, in most parts of England, except in the vicinity of great towns, has been nearly doubled within the last 60 years."[107]

Indeed, there appears in this introduction that long-forgotten custom – the "labourer's Sunday roast", by this time only to be found in the tracts of establishment propagandists.[108]

It is inaccurate, asserted Eden, to attempt a comparative assessment of the labouring classes during a period of scarcity, such as the nation had just suffered during 1794 and 1795.

"If we, however, except the late period of scarcity (which was such as had not occurred for near a century before) I believe no period during the present reign can be adduced, in which the condition of day-labourers was not much more comfortable than that of the same class of people in what are often called the 'good old times' of former reigns."[109]

Even during the famine, the poor were well-off, thanks to the kindnesses of the rich.

"The situation of the labouring Poor in Berkshire was never better than during the last hard winter; but they received these advanced wages in the way most prejudicial to their moral interests; they received it as charity; as the extorted charity of others; and not as the result of their own well-exerted industry."

Yes, that was Berkshire, the same county of which David Davies was writing in 1794.

In the face of such a rosy picture as this, it seems surprising that Eden felt the need to account for poverty and distress at all. But he did, and the reasons he adduces bore great similarity to the reasons

---

105 Ibid. P. 134.
106 F. M. Eden. The State of the Poor. Vol. I. P. 404.
107 Ibid. P. 385.
108 Ibid. P. 547.
109 Ibid. P. 560.

put forward in Hannah More's stories. Like More, he finds very little room for explaining conditions of life in terms of social and economic change. He mentioned the ending of the feudal system, and claims that poverty is the necessary concomitant of liberty. Beyond that, poverty was, of course, the result of the vices of the poor.

Among which, idleness, of course, takes pride of place. Eden flatly discounts John Howlett's assertion that the conditions of life permitted by poor relief were not such as to encourage people to submit to it voluntarily.

"The real case, however, is that, in every part of England, (I had almost said every parish) instances may be found of persons preferring a pension from the parish, and a life of idleness, to hard work and good wages. I could even particularize instances of stout able-bodied men having been desirous of obtaining, and of their having actually obtained, admission into poor-houses, and resided there very contentedly....Any permanent establishment for the relief of the Poor has a tendency to increase the number wanting relief."[110]

The extravagance of the poor was also a great contributor to their sufferings.

"The miseries of the labouring Poor arise less from the scantiness of their income than from their own improvidence and unthriftiness....The misfortune....does not arise from his being obliged to purchase the few articles he has occasion for, from petty retail shops, and consequently to pay a larger price for them than his more opulent master; but....because, either through ignorance, custom or prejudice, he adheres to ancient improvident systems in dress, in diet, and in other branches of private expenditure."[111]

Eden even goes so far as to assert that labourers on moderate wages are more comfortable than those whose wages are exorbitant. That is because they had less opportunity for profligate living.

Foremost among the extravagances of the poor was wheaten bread. In Oxfordshire, it was the consumption of this which left little money over with which to purchase clothing. Alcoholic drink and tea were among the usual suspects.

"It may....be doubted, whether the same quantity of fuel, which is required to boil a tea-kettle twice a day, is not more than sufficient, with proper management, to dress a potato soup, or an hodge-podge."[112]

By way of conclusion, Eden puts forward the idea that only the poor could remove their own distresses, not by earning more, but by spending less. Their well-being was entirely dependent "on good management and economy". Eden quoted approvingly from Arthur Young's annals of Agriculture.

"There is more difference, comparatively, in the mode of living from economy, than from income; the deficiency in income may possibly be made up by increase of work or wages; but the want of economy is irremediable, and the least income in question *with it* will do more than the greatest *without it*.

"If the poor do not prudently serve themselves, none can effectually assist them; if they are not their own friends, none can sufficiently befriend them; the idle in procuring, or the wasteful in using, the means of subsistence, have neither merit in themselves to deserve, nor have others power to grant them, that supply, which alone is due, and can alone be afforded, to the honest, industrious and prudent....It is far more useful to teach them to spend less, or to save a little, than to give them much more."[113]

Of course, it was all absurd. How did Eden come to know more about the daily struggle for existence in England in the 1790s than those who were confronted by it day after day? How do you

110 Ibid. Pp. 449-450.
111 Ibid. P. 491.
112 Ibid. Vol. II P. 587. Vol. I. P. 548.
113 Ibid. Vol. I. P. 587.

teach starving families to economise? It should be noted that in the huge amounts of material which Eden presented later in The State of the Poor, there is very little to support the contentions which he made in the introduction, and much to contradict them.

So it was in such ways, and with such arguments, that the government of the 1790s attempted to manipulate public opinion. Issuing forth from ministers themselves, and endorsed by Parliament, were lectures on the monofactorial role of weather and harvest failure as the cause of rising prices; connected with this were eulogies on what was called freedom of trade, and the sanctity of private property; and the whole complemented by large amounts of anti-poor propaganda, written and financed by those closely connected with the establishment. This emphasised the comfortable circumstances of the virtuous poor; the consequent lack of justification for riot and tumult; the selfish and sinister motives of those who took part in them; and the vices and the extravagances which were virtually the only causes of poverty and distress. Whatever professions were made about the intended target audience for these works, the thrust and burden of the campaign was clearly aimed at those who held power in the localities. And the object of it all was to massage public opinion into the acceptance of the new marketing systems of the speculative capitalist, and to justify the use of military force against the starving – still something of a novelty in the 1790s – in defence of the profits and property of those speculators, who, behind the scenes, or so it seems, had now become closely allied to the political establishment.

The Duke of Portland, as Home Secretary, thus felt enabled to push ahead with his military campaign against his own people.

"The possession of an adequate and commanding military force is unquestionably the first step to be taken to enable the civil power to resume its authority and give that energy to the law by which alone private property can be protected and any permanent hopes of relief be secured for the distresses which the common people experience….I trust that every possible care will be taken to avoid giving any encouragement to any description of persons to expect that their wants will be relieved at the expense of private property, or that any right can accrue to them by any means whatever to call upon the farmers or dealers in corn or any other article of provision to part with it at a fixed price, or even at all, except by their own free will and consent."[114]

Throughout the two famines, Portland became ever bolder and more strident in his demands for the use of force, and increasingly out of step with custom and usage. Pressure was stepped up on local dignitaries to call in the army at the first sign of unrest, and those who thought that other methods would yield better results were roundly criticised. One such was the Mayor of Banbury, to whom Portland wrote;-

"When you found that the power of the Magistrates and the reading of the Riot Act were alike disregarded, it became your duty, how painful soever it might be, to enforce your Authority and to compel an obedience to the Laws, by the Military Force under your direction." In future, he was "to have earliest recourse to troops."[115]

In response to requests for assistance with supplying the needs of the poor, the Home Office simply ordered swift military intervention against the populace. Indeed, in some instances, detachments were sent to escort the corn through or out of the areas needing that assistance!

During the first famine, the Home Office relied mainly on the various paramilitary volunteer associations to quell unrest. By 1800, however, Portland was exceeding the boundaries both of legality and accepted practice, and deploying the regular army both to avert apprehended disturbances as well as to suppress actual riots. An intensive programme was under way of building army barracks close to all the major centres of population. The barrack system, as William Cobbett dubbed it, became

114 D. Wilkinson. The Duke of Portland. P. 114.
115 R. Wells. Wretched Faces. P. 255.

a major pillar of support for governments throughout the early 19th century. The almost complete silence of historians on this subject, therefore, requires some explanation.

By customary usage, in the case of rioting, military force would only be employed when requested by the local authorities. But increasingly Portland rode roughshod over their wishes. Even so well respected an aristocrat, landowner and local dignitary as the Duke of Grafton could make no impact. He wrote;-

"In many parishes poor families have not been able to procure bread for their Money. The bench was endeavouring to relieve them by every means....but....all our Efforts will prove ineffectual; if it should be true, what is circulated here, but which I will not believe, that some wealthy farmers are to be supported by a military force, in conveying from hence the Corn, we would be happy to pay for, Even at the unconscienable Price, at which....some of our shamefully interested Farmers have sold it for at a Distance."[116]

It was to no avail; the troops arrived, and the corn, presumably, departed. This was becoming common practice. In London, Portland used troops against rioters without the agreement of the Mayor and Corporation. In Nottingham, the army was sent in uninvited. Birmingham and the West Midlands were overrun with regular troops merely on the basis of the correspondences of individuals with the Home Office. And the military intervention in Devon and Cornwall in the spring of 1801 has led the historian of the famines to refer to Portland as waging war on the south-west.[117]

Portland ventured ever further in the exceeding of law and of his constitutional authority. A Proclamation issued in September 1800 demanded the officials resort at the earliest opportunity to the reading of the Riot Act. "The moment....the authority of the Civil Power is disregarded," wrote the Home Office, "resort cannot be had too soon to the Military." The Riot Act only allowed civil force to be used against crowds which refused to disperse after the reading of the Act. But Portland told his officers that they were to dispense with the Riot Act in the face of any kind of disturbance, and were to proceed on their own authority against all crowds, whether peaceful or riotous. The extent to which Portland was prepared to act outside the law is well demonstrated by his assurance to Colonel Bastard, a military commander in Devon.

"Whatever Acts of Power he may have found it necessary to have recourse to in the course of the....Contest will be most readily sanctioned and confirmed and no time will be lost in taking whatever Steps may be necessary for that purpose."[118]

In addition, after the riots had been quelled, the Home Office agitated for the full force of the law to be used against the culprits.

"It is absolutely necessary that the people should be made to feel....that private property of all descriptions has equal rights, and that they can not be violated without subjecting those who are parties to the violation of those rights to certain and capital punishment."

Portland wanted prosecutions; he wanted examples made; he wanted hangings.[119]

Not surprisingly, the policy of punishing the hungry produced much uneasiness amongst those who possessed power in the provinces, which was greatly aggravated by Portland's insensitive approach, arbitrary acts, and heavy-handed tactics. Even the loyalty of the military was being put under strain by the ferocity of the demands of central government. Holland Watson, a volunteer officer from Stockport, wrote to Windham that the distresses of the people meant that "every one feels an unwillingness to proceed hastily to extremities, even against rioters."[120]

---

116 Ibid. P. 231.
117 Ibid. P. 256.
118 Ibid. P. 257.
119 D. Wilkinson. The Duke of Portland. Pp. 114-115.
120 R. Wells. Wretched Faces. P. 264.

The loyalty of the military was not, in general, robust enough to withstand the deaths and injuries of civilians. Magistrates also preferred a cautious approach; the traditional methods of treating with food rioters quelled disturbances, in most cases, far more successfully than the heavy-handed use of force, which could, of itself, provoke further violence.[121]

Every aspect of the government's handling of the subsistence crisis of 1799-1800 was bringing it into disrepute in the country; but especially the conduct of the Duke of Portland. The crisis of confidence was such that ministers felt compelled to recall Parliament. But whilst a starving people saw Parliament as a means of bringing in measures to relieve their distresses, ministers saw it purely as a public relations exercise; as a means of re-affirming once again the monofactorial role of unfavourable seasons and harvest deficiency in raising prices, and the related doctrines of the freedom of trade and the sanctity of private property. Grenville saw Parliament as a way of countermanding the "torrent of ignorance and mischief" concerning commercial malpractice.[122]

The government's assertion that harvest failure was solely to blame has been treated with a very uncritical indulgence by modern historians, which is both surprising and unaccountable. It is, after all, a very weak and inadequate explanation. On a logical level, it is obviously flawed, because the demonstration of the shortness of the crop does not preclude the possibility of price manipulation by traders and speculators; indeed, it makes it more likely, as the price of a short crop is easier to affect than that of a plentiful one; and speculators will only buy heavily on a rising market. It is made the more likely by the investment hunger that was evident at times throughout the 1790s. No one really doubted that the harvests of these years were below par; what troubled the authorities in the provinces was that prices rose completely disproportionately to the scale of the shortage; and the lectures on free trade which the Home Office seemed to append to most of its communications were not really a rational or satisfactory response to those misgivings. The government explanation was also inadequate on a factual and historical level, because it ignored completely the whole host of changes that had taken place during the 18th century in agricultural production, marketing and trade. It was an explanation *ceteribus paribus*, as they used to say; but circumstances had changed beyond recognition.

The whole 'natural scarcity' theory would have been far more credible had ministers believed in it themselves. Demonstrably, they did not. Even during the first famine, there was a clear gap between pronouncement and belief. At the very time when the government was setting out on its programme of re-education after the harvest of 1795, letters were flooding in complaining of the manipulation of prices by grain traders. In private, Pitt told a committee headed by Walter Boyd that the diminution of the money supply by the Bank of England had become necessary on account of damaging monopolies, particularly in grain; and that, as a result of that diminution, the price of wheat had dropped from 120s. a quarter to 80s.[123]

By March of 1796, when Pitt, in the House of Commons, dismissed concerns about price manipulation as "vulgar prejudices" and "ignorance", government had, for some months, already been trickling its own imported corn on to a rising market in such a way as not to cause the price to fall![124]

During the second famine, the credibility gap widened further. This time, concerns centred around imports. In 1799 and 1800, massive and unprecedented amounts of grain were imported by the wealthy corn merchants of London. By May 1800, all the granaries along the Thames were full of imported grain, and 300 ships were lying in the river which could not be unloaded. By the summer,

---

121 Ibid. Pp. 262-263.
122 Ibid. P. 244.
123 S. Cope. Walter Boyd. P. 97.
124 R. Wells. Wretched Faces. P. 193

there was no longer a shortage, yet prices continued to rise. This triggered various investigations on the part of government. George Rose questioned Alderman Shaw of the Corporation of London, "who stated the price of wheat to have been raised form 105s. to 122s. by a principal factor and alluded to Mr. C(laude) S(cott)." At the Board of Trade, the President, Lord Liverpool, instigated his own enquiry, and this confirmed suspicions of price manipulation by the larger dealers.[125]

"A few of the principal Corn-Factors in Mark Lane have it....in their Power to set the Price of Wheat, as it may answer their Interests....they have augmented the Evils arising from real Scarcity, by producing an artificial Scarcity....The Fortunes made by Corn factors....have of late been very great."[126]

The millers, said the report, formed a cartel, the members of which were making unreasonable profits at the expence of consumers. What was happening was that importers were managing to unload their corn on to the market whilst using their control of that market to keep prices high and rising, even after the harvest of 1800. Ministers were well aware of this, and not just Rose and Liverpool. John Kay was under-secretary at Portland's home Office. On the subject of prices which refused to fall, he wrote;-

"I feel myself at a loss on a subject which eludes investigation and appears at least to submit to no rule."

Even the Prime Minister had to admit the reality of "speculations....for the purpose of unduly and artificially raising the price"; but was criticised by his colleagues for doing so.

Finally, even the Duke of Portland, in the face of the Board of Trade enquiry, was forced to concede that prices remained high because of the "speculations of the Importers whose Cargoes are actually in the River."[127]

None of this, of course, was for public consumption. The report of the Board of Trade, needless to say, was not published, and ministers' public statements continued to be at odds with their private beliefs. In public, Portland maintained that traders were not engrossers, but "the purveyors and provident stewards of the people". But privately, in Cabinet, the story was different. There, Portland opined that people needed to be instilled with the idea "that without the aid of Monopolists & Engrossers they must starve."[128]

By January 1801, there were 700 ships full of grain clogging up the Thames, and still the price refused to fall.

Parliament assembled, then, in the autumn of 1800, with the life-guards on the alert at their barracks nearby. In the House of Commons, a few brave members attempted to pressurise the government into taking remedial measures. Scarcity was illusory; "the great evils to which it alone could be attributed, monopoly and extortion, were still without a remedy" even being proposed. But they came up against a comprehensive speech on the subject by Pitt, who warned that members should "guard against the influences of popular prejudices"; and the bulk of the House united in his support.

In the Lords, the story was the same. The Earl of Warwick mounted a doughty attack on monopolists, secretive marketing practices, withholding of corn by opulent farmers, and the astronomical profits of provisions traders. But he, too, was roughly treated by members of the government.[129]

---

125 Ibid. Pp. 196, 88 and 217.
126 Ibid. Pp. 196-197.
127 Ibid. p. 87-88.
128 R. Wells. Wretched Faces. Pp. 40 and 244. D. Wilkinson. The Duke of Portland. P. 116.
129 R. Wells. Wretched Faces. PP. 245-247.

Out in the real world, the influential members of provincial society remained convinced of the role of commercial malpractice in raising prices. In private, aristocrats bitterly criticised ministers and their actions. During the revolt of the south-west in the spring of 1801, clergymen sent in numerous complaints of market manipulation by farmers and grain-traders, which, they said, urgently required the attentions of government and Parliament. The Reverend Henry Davis expressed the "wish that speculation in bread was finally abolished."[130]

But in Parliament it was different. Both houses placed the entire blame for the crisis on deficient harvest yields. The Select Committee of the House of Lords, which had been hand-picked by Lord Grenville, affirmed the desirability of allowing grain traders to operate unfettered, and dismissed monopolistic malpractice as the visionary results of "suspicions and vague reports as usually prevail in times of scarcity." The market was said to be pure, and the operations of wealthy merchants "highly useful".

The Commons Select Committee, at least, proposed some degree of regulation of the London corn market at Mark Lane. But their report was not published until after the crisis was over, and its recommendations were ignored.

Those who dared to dissent from this line were hounded. Some seem to have been disciplined by party leaders on both sides; the Earl of Warwick was threatened with the loss of his Lord Lieutenancy; Lord Kenyon, the judge who had been active in prosecuting market offences under the common law, was silenced by unconstitutional pressure.[131]

The whole formed, perhaps, one of the most shameful episodes in our parliamentary history. The Emperor had no clothes; the Emperor knew that he had no clothes; everybody knew that he had no clothes; but no-one, in public at least, could say so. Such is the power of an orthodoxy.

1797 was a momentous year. Pitt's government was waging an unpopular war, with little competence and less success. An invasion scare enabled ministers to pass unpopular new laws concerning the militia. The radical societies were finally proscribed by law, forcing a minority of their more determined members underground to produce, in miniature, the revolutionary threat that ministers had always dreamed of. There were two naval mutinies. And in February, the Bank of England went bankrupt, largely through the ineptitude of government. In these circumstances, it was hardly surprising that petitions were reaching parliament "for the removal of the king's ministers."[132]

How did the government react to these multiple crises? As, by now, we would expect, it set in train yet another campaign of propaganda; and out of this campaign arose the establishment orthodoxy on the causes of poverty which was finally to win over most of the upper echelons of English society, and to remain as a force and an influence for many decades to come. Indeed, we are not free of it today, as it still affects our thinking on the poor.

The object of hatred at which this campaign was directed was called William Godwin. He was a philosopher and the author of many rather esoteric works, the best known being his Enquiry Concerning Political Justice, and its influence on General Virtue and Happiness. This was published in 1793, and can probably be considered as part of the radical reaction to the works of Edmund Burke. It was a long and involved political speculation, endorsing the French Revolution, democratic principles, general philanthropy, and taking an optimistic view of man and society's capacity for

130 Ibid. P. 248.
131 Ibid. Pp. 243-248.
132 William Godwin. Thoughts Occasioned by the Perusal of Dr. Parr's Spital Sermon. P. 4.

improvement. Godwin was a mild and studious type, for whom the cultivation of the intellect seems to have been the ultimate goal in life, and who always professed himself against violence and against revolution. But the explanation he gives of the causes of human misery was quite revolutionary under the circumstances of the time.

In spite of his sheltered existence, Godwin seemed quite well-informed about the poverty around him.

"In the most refined states of Europe, the inequality of property has arisen to an alarming height. Vast numbers of their inhabitants are deprived of almost every accommodation that can render life tolerable or secure. Their utmost industry scarcely suffices for their support....The peasant and the labourer work, till their understandings are benumbed with toil, their sinews contracted and made callous by being forever on the stretch, and their bodies invaded with infirmities and surrendered to an untimely grave. What is the fruit of this disproportioned and unceasing toil? At evening they return to a family, famished with hunger, exposed half-naked to the inclemencies of the sky, hardly sheltered, and denied the slenderest instruction, unless in a few instances, where it is dispensed by the hands of ostentatious charity, and the first lesson communicated is unprincipled servility."[133]

The responsibility for this disastrous state of affairs Godwin placed squarely upon the shoulders of the rich. The administration of property, as Godwin called it, was in reality a system of robbery and fraud, which took the fruits of industry from the peasant and the labourer, and bestowed them upon the idle rich. The problem was particularly acute, in those countries which most abounded in counsellors, nobles, wealthy commoners who aspired to aristocratic values, and all their kindred and dependents.[134]

"Is it any wonder", asked Godwin, "that in such countries the lower orders of the community are exhausted by all the hardships of penury and immoderate fatigue? When we see the wealth of a province spread upon a great man's table, can we be surprised that his neighbours have not bread to satiate the cravings of hunger?....In civilised countries the peasant does not consume more than the twentieth part of the produce of his labour, whilst his rich neighbour consumes perhaps the produce of the labour of twenty peasants."[135]

Poverty became institutionalised, when the rich, as legislators, reduced "oppression into a system". Laws were passed which patently favoured the rich. The Game Laws were a glaring example. Increasingly the legislature threw the burden of taxation from the lands of the rich on to the consumption of the poor. And whilst the rich associated in pursuit of partial and oppressive laws, and monopolistic trading practices, a "vigilant policy" was employed "to prevent combinations of the poor to fix the price of labour". This was what Godwin termed a "direct despotism".[136]

Godwin's definition of justice was that "no man would be pressed to the earth that another might enjoy immoderate luxury."[137]

"Will it often come out to be true, that hundreds of individuals ought to be subjected to the severest and most incessant labour, that one man may spend in idleness what would afford to the general mass ease, leisure, and consequently wisdom?....Is it well that so large a part of the community should be kept in abject penury, rendered stupid with ignorance and disgustful with vice, perpetuated in nakedness and hunger, goaded to the commission of crimes, and made victims to the merciless laws which the rich have instituted to oppress them? Is it sedition to enquire whether this state of things may not be exchanged for a better? Or can there be anything more disgraceful to ourselves than to

---

133 William Godwin. Enquiry Concerning Political Justice. Pp. 34 and 806-807.
134 Ibid. Pp. 484-485.
135 Ibid. P. 792.
136 Ibid. Pp. 39-40.
137 Ibid. P. 471.

exclaim that 'All is well', merely because we are at our ease, regardless of misery, degradation and vice that may be occasioned in others?"[138]

Given the political climate in which he was writing, Godwin feared that he would be prosecuted for his views by the authorities. In the event, in spite of a few predictable condemnations from establishment sources, the Enquiry was well received by the critics and sold well to the public; until, that is, the spring of 1797. From that time, Godwin tells us;-

"I was at length attacked form every side, and in a style which defied all moderation and decency. No vehicle was too mean, no language too coarse and insulting, by which to convey the venom of my adversaries. The abuse was so often repeated, that at length the bystanders, and perhaps the parties themselves, began to believe what they had so vehemently asserted. The cry spread like a general infection, and I have been told that not even a petty novel for boarding-school misses now ventures to aspire to favour, unless it contains some expression of dislike and abhorrence to the new philosophy, and its chief English adherent."[139]

The attack was begun by two pamphlets published in 1797, probably by Thomas Green and W. C. Proby. In the same year, Hannah More threw in her contribution. This was called the History of Mr. Fantom, and concerned a man who was "tormented with a longing desire to draw public notice, and to distinguish himself." So he became a philosopher of the new benevolent school.

To "see himself at the head of a society of his own proselytes" was "the supreme object of a philosopher's ambition."

Fantom sighed for the reign of universal benevolence.

"I want to make all mankind good and happy….Every thing is bad, as it now stands. I would alter all the laws, and do away with all the religions, and put an end to all the wars in the world. I would every where redress the injustice of fortune, of what the vulgar call providence. I would put an end to all punishments. I would not leave a single prisoner on the face of the globe."

In practising the new philosophy "on a great field", he neglected the well-being of his neighbours and family, and instilled his principles so thoroughly into his footman, William, that the latter was inspired by them to become a drunkard, a thief, and a murderer, and in consequence ended his life on the gallows.[140]

The campaign continued with a series of thirty-nine lectures delivered by Sir James Mackintosh, previously a friend of Godwin's, at Lincoln's Inn, before an audience which included M. P.s and peers of the realm. Godwin was particularly upset by the virulence of personal invective contained in Mackintosh's lectures.

"Gentlemen may be assured that, if these self-called philosophers once came to have power in their hands, it would speedily be seen that the consequences I draw from their doctrines, are not, as they would have us believe, far-fetched inferences; they would be seen to be realised in action; and those who maintain them would be found as ferocious, as blood-thirsty, and full of personal ambition, as the worst of those men who sheltered themselves under similar pretensions in a neighbouring country."[141]

Next in the sequence of attacks came the Rev. T. R. Malthus. "A book was published about the same time professing to contain remarks upon some speculations of mine, entitled an Essay upon Population."

"Soon after followed a much vaunted Sermon by Mr. Hall of Cambridge, in which every notion of toleration or decorum was treated with infuriated contempt. I disdain to dwell on the rabble of

---

138 Ibid. 432 and 467.
139 William Godwin. Thoughts Occasioned by the Perusal of Dr. Parr's Spital Sermon. P. 21.
140 Hannah More. The History of Mr. Fantom. Pp. 3, 6, 9 *et seq.*
141 William Godwin. Thoughts Occasioned by the Perusal of Dr. Parr's Spital Sermon. P. 17.

scurrilities which followed; the vulgar contumelies of the author of the Pursuits of Literature, novels of buffoonery and scandal to the amount of half a score, and British Critics, Anti-Jacobin newspapers and Anti-Jacobin Magazines without number. Last of all, for the present at least….Dr. Parr, with his Spital Sermon before the Lord Mayor, brings up the rear of my assailants."[142]

Godwin makes it clear, then, that there was a concerted campaign of propaganda afoot from the spring of 1797, in which his Enquiry became the principal object of "ribaldry, invective and intolerance." But why, he asks, did it happen then? After all, many of those who welcomed the French Revolution continued to be sympathetic throughout all the violent outrages, and right up until 1797. By that time, the atrocities had ceased. In England, the radical societies were in retreat, and democratic views no longer to be heard. "Yet it is now that these persons come forth to sound the alarm; now that they tread upon the neck of the monster, whom they regard as expiring; now they hold it necessary to show themselves intemperate and incessant against the spirit of innovation."[143]

Godwin seems to have connected this phenomenon with the unpopularity of the king's ministers. He treads rather delicately over the issue, but it seems likely that what was afoot was a deliberate programme instigated by government. This succeeded so well because "recent events have tended to confirm and give stability to the old governments of Europe, and that of our own country in particular….so these persons are willing to make their peace." There was a large element of self-interest in this, but also; "It is not in the nature of man to like to stand alone in his sentiments or creed. We ought not to be too much surprised, when we perceive our neighbours watching the seasons and floating with the tide."

The result was that "persons who, without any fresh reasons to justify their change, think it now necessary to plead for establishments, and express their horror at theories and innovation, though I recollect the time when they took an opposite part."[144]

A sort of political correctness had arisen. "Discussion is no longer regarded as one of the great sources of benefit to man. The principle and practice of toleration among us hang by a very slender thread. All declamation, and all licensed argument, must be on one side." Discussion had been banished by "abhorrence and obloquy."

Once again, Godwin implies, though falls short of stating, that the campaign had an official origin. "There is nothing singular in my case. It is part of a great plan." He speaks of "the present deep-laid project of despotism and intolerance." And he views the whole situation with foreboding.

"It is a serious thing to say, that men must neither argue nor write, till they have first subdued the free-born nature of their souls to the trammels of some fortunate and highly patronised creed, which is to be perceived as orthodox."[145]

By far the most significant contribution to this outpouring of establishment orthodoxy was the Essay on Population by T. R. Malthus; which seems to have been a spontaneous contribution, not directly inspired by government, but nevertheless in the hope of some "mark of public gratitude and private sympathy from the members of a government in whose political creed he perfectly agreed."[146] Malthus took his turn, in his own way, to set about William Godwin.

"The great bent of Mr. Godwin's work on *Political Justice*, if I understand it rightly, is to shew that the greater part of the vices and weaknesses of men proceed from the injustice of their political and

---

142 Ibid. P. 10.
143 Ibid. Pp. 1-7.
144 Ibid. Pp. 8-9.
145 Ibid. Pp. 77-79.
146 William Empson in the Edinburgh Review. January 1837. P. 502.

social institutions, and that if these were removed, and the understandings of men more enlightened, there would be little or no temptation in the world to evil."[147]

Malthus quotes Godwin.

"The spirit of oppression, the spirit of servility, and the spirit of fraud, these are the immediate growth of the established administration of property. They are alike hostile to intellectual improvement. The other vices of envy, malice, and revenge are their inseparable companions."[148]

Godwin looked forward to a time when ever-improving human institutions would lead to an age without hunger, want or misery – in short, to the perfectibility of man. Malthus answered this with his own alternative explanation of the distresses in which a large proportion of mankind seemed constantly to be living.

"I say, that the power of population is indefinitely greater than the power in the earth to produce subsistence for man.

"Population, when unchecked, increases in a geometrical ratio. Subsistence increases only in an arithmetical ratio….This implies a strong and constantly operating check on population from the difficulty of subsistence. This difficulty must fall somewhere and must necessarily be severely felt by a large portion of mankind….

"Nature has scattered the seeds of life abroad with the most profuse and liberal hand. She has been comparatively sparing in the room and nourishment necessary to rear them….The race of plants and the race of animals shrink under this great restrictive law. And the race of man cannot, by any efforts of reason, escape from it."

It is for this reason, says Malthus, that Godwin's vision of a social system without poverty can never be realised.

"This natural inequality of the two powers of population and of production in the earth, and that great law of our nature which must constantly keep their effects equal, form the great difficulty that to me appears insurmountable in the way to the perfectibility of society. All other arguments are of slight and subordinate consideration in comparison of this. I see no way by which man can escape from the weight of this law which pervades all animated nature. No fancied equality, no agrarian regulations in their utmost extent, could remove the pressure of it even for a single century. And it appears, therefore, to be decisive against the possible existence of a society, all the members of which should live in ease, happiness, and comparative leisure; and feel no anxiety about providing the means of subsistence for themselves and families."[149]

Malthus then used this argument to counter Godwin's contention that it was artificial causes, social and political, that produced most of the poverty and distress in society. Poverty cannot be caused by man, because it is caused by nature. Clearly, this is a *non-sequitur*. But it is precisely the type of *non-sequitur* employed by ministers to absolve the grain-traders from responsibility for raising prices. The high cost of living was not caused by commercial malpractice, because it was caused by bad weather and deficient harvest. It is the type of argument you can only get away with when your target audience already has its own reasons for wishing to believe what you have to say,

"The great error under which Mr. Godwin labours throughout his whole work is the attributing almost all the vices and misery that we see in civil society to human institutions. Political regulations and the established administration of property are with him the fruitful sources of all evil, the hotbeds of all the crimes that degrade mankind. Were this really a true state of the case, it would not seem a hopeless task to remove evil completely from the world….But the truth is, that though human institutions appear to be the obvious and obtrusive causes of much mischief to mankind, yet in reality

---

147 T. R. Malthus. An Essay on the Principle of Population. Penguin ed. P. 169.
148 Ibid. P. 133-4.
149 Ibid. Pp. 71-72.

they are light and superficial, they are mere feathers that float on the surface, in comparison with those deeper seated causes of impurity that corrupt the springs and render turbid the whole stream of human life."[150]

"Independent of any political or social institutions whatever, the greater part of mankind, from the fixed and unalterable laws of nature, must ever be subject to the evil temptations arsing from want, besides other passions."[151]

The whole tendency of the Essay was to absolve both government and the wealthy in general from any responsibility for the poverty and distresses of the time. Poverty, by Malthus's reasonings, was natural and inevitable, and there was simply nothing that anybody could do about it.

"No possible contributions or sacrifices of the rich, particularly in money, could for any time prevent the recurrence of distress among the lower members of society whoever they were. Great changes might, indeed, be made. The rich might become poor, and some of the poor rich, but a part of the society must necessarily feel a difficulty of living, and this difficulty will naturally fall on the least fortunate members.

"I cannot by means of money raise a poor man and enable him to live much better than he did before, without proportionably depressing others in the same class....If the rich were to subscribe and give five shillings a day to five hundred thousand men without retrenching their own tables, no doubt can exist, that as these men would naturally live more at their ease and consume a greater quantity of provisions, there would be less food remaining to divide among the rest."[152]

"The truth is that the pressure of distress on this part of a community is an evil so deeply seated that no human ingenuity can reach it....It has appeared, that from the inevitable laws of our nature some human beings must suffer from want. These are the unhappy persons who, in the great lottery of life, have drawn a blank."[153]

People should therefore stop blaming the government.

"It is the lot of man, that he will frequently have to choose between two evils; and it is sufficient reason for the adoption of any institution, that it is the best mode that presents itself of preventing greater evils. A continual endeavour should undoubtedly prevail to make these institutions as perfect as the nature of them will admit. But nothing is so easy as to find fault with human institutions; nothing so difficult as to suggest adequate practical improvements. It is to be lamented, that more men of talents employ their time in the former occupation than in the latter."[154]

So radicals could cease agitating, and politicians could continue to abuse their position, in the certain knowledge that no amount of reform could significantly help the poor.

"This argument appears to be conclusive, not only against the perfectibility of man, in the enlarged sense in which Mr. Godwin understands the term, but against any very marked and striking change for the better, in the form and structure of general society; by which I mean any great and decided amelioration of the condition of the lower classes of mankind, the most numerous, and, consequently, in a general view of the subject, the most important part of the human race....No possible sacrifices or exertions of the rich, in a country which had long been inhabited, could for any time place the lower orders of the community in a situation equal, with regard to circumstance, to the situation of the common people about thirty years ago in the northern States of America."[155]

---

150   Ibid. P. 133.
151   Ibid. P. 169.
152   Ibid. Pp. 95-96.
153   Ibid. Pp. 101 and 143.
154   Ibid. P. 165.
155   Ibid. P. 172.

To nature, we owe all the distresses of mankind; to government, we are obliged for all the blessings!

"It is to the established administration of property and to the apparently narrow principle of self-love that we are indebted for all the noblest exertions of human genius, all the finer and more delicate emotions of the soul, for everything, indeed, that distinguishes the civilized from the savage state."[156]

Such extravagant claims for government as established at the end of the 18th century seem to us obviously ludicrous. But the approach brought success. Malthus himself might have been nervous about the reception which his book might get; but his friend William Otter tells us that "the book was received with some surprise, and excited considerable attention….the minds of the generality were in suspense…."[157] It sold rapidly, and by 1800 Malthus was remarking that it was impossible to get hold of a copy.

The reasons for the popularity of Malthus's Essay among supporters of the establishment, and the holders of anti-democratic, loyalist views, therefore, are obvious enough, and were pointed out by many authors. Here, again, is William Godwin.

"The author very truly says, that his inferences are in a state of open war against every 'extraordinary improvement in society'. Not only what Mackintosh styles the 'abominable and pestilential paradoxes' of Political Justice, but every generous attempt for any important melioration of the condition of mankind, is here at stake. The advocates of old establishments and old abuses, could not have found a doctrine, more to their hearts content, more effectual to shut out all reforms and improvement for ever."[158]

By jumping aboard the anti-Godwin bandwagon, Malthus had gone much further than a mere refutation of Godwin. He had, wittingly or unwittingly, produced a pseudo-scientific explanation of poverty and distress which completely absolved the governing classes from responsibility; and placed the whole burden of blame on inevitable natural processes which man was powerless to remedy. This line of reasoning was lifted directly from government propaganda about famine and high prices, and was to serve Malthus well in his subsequent works for many years to come.

Indeed, in 1800, at the height of the second famine, Malthus himself waded into that very controversy. In his Investigation of the Cause of the Present High Price of Provisions, he endorsed the government line, and asserted that the scarcity was, in fact, natural, and caused by deficient harvests. In answering the cry of the common people that "there must be roguery somewhere", Malthus revealed his motivation, and the way his mind was working.

"I cannot but think, therefore, that I should do an acceptable service, if I could succeed in accounting for the present high price of the necessaries of life, without criminating a class of men, who, I believe, have been accused unjustly, and who, every political economist must know, are absolutely necessary in the complicated machinery that distributes the provisions and other commodities of a large nation."[159]

It was important, he thought, not to "lay the blame on the wrong persons".[160]

Malthus echoed Adam Smith. Price manipulation was both impossible and beneficial at the same time.

---

156 Ibid. P. 176.

157 W. Otter. Memoir of Robert Malthus. P. XXXVI. Prefaced to T. R. Malthus. Principles of Political Economy.

158 William Godwin. Thoughts Occasioned by the Perusal of Dr. Parr's Spital Sermon. P. 63.

159 T. R. Malthus. An Investigation of the Cause of the present High Price of Provisions. P. 4.

160 Ibid. P. 21.

"In an article which is in so many hands as corn is, in this country, monopoly to any pernicious extent, may safely be pronounced impossible....There had been no speculations in corn that were prejudicial to the country. All that the large farmers and cornfactors had done, was to raise the corn to that price which excluded a sufficient number from their usual consumption, to enable the supply to last throughout the year."

"The man who refuses to send his corn to market when it is at twenty pounds a load, because he thinks that in two months time it will be thirty....is a positive and decided benefactor to the state."[161]

And he condemned the popular clamour which kept "farmers and corn-dealers in perpetual fear for their lives and property."[162]

Malthus concluded;-

"I own that I cannot but consider the late severe pressures of distress on every deficiency in our crops, as a very strong exemplification of a principle which I endeavoured to explain in an essay published about two years ago, entitled, *An Essay on the Principle of Population*."[163]

In his pamphlet, Malthus leapt to the defence of two groups of wealthy and powerful traders that were inextricably bound up with the political establishment. Not only corn-dealers, but bankers also benefited from his protection.

The idea that one of the causes of persistently rising prices was the excessive issue by bankers of paper currency runs as a sub-text throughout the propaganda war on the causes of poverty. It appears on both sides of the argument. David Hume put forward the idea, writing in the 1740s. It was conceded by the corn-dealing pamphleteers of mid-century, who were unsympathetic towards the poor; it appears in the work of Joseph Massie, and in the account of the Devon poor by William Chapple, both of whom were sympathetic. For the establishment, John Arbuthnot used it in 1771; for the poor, David Davies did so also in 1794.

Adam Smith, however, tried to discredit the whole idea; and Malthus followed him.

"There was undoubtedly great reason for apprehension that when, by the stoppage of the Bank to pay in specie, the emissions of paper ceased to have its natural check, the circulation would be overloaded with this currency; but this certainly would not have taken place to any considerable extent without a sensible depreciation of bank notes in comparison with specie. As this depreciation did not happen, the progress of the evil must have been slow and gradual, and never could have produced the sudden and extraordinary rise in the price of provisions...."[164]

It is perhaps worth noting that the paper price of gold had shot up to £4 6s. 0d. by January 1801.

Throughout most of his writing career, Malthus tended to deny the effects of excessive circulating medium in raising prices. He wavered considerably at the time of the Bullion Committee in 1810; but in general maintained that it was prices that rose from causes outside the control of bankers that determined the level of paper currency necessary for the transactions of the country.

Malthus's "Investigation" was received with unthinking approbation by the political classes, and in particular drew down the praises of the Lord Chancellor and the Prime Minister.

A pattern of thought was emerging which was to run through much of Malthus's work, from the Essay of 1798, to the Principles of 1821. Take a powerful vested interest group, whose activities were widely considered parasitic and damaging to the productive classes of the community. Explain those activities; justify them as natural and necessary and part of the progressive improvement of

161 Ibid. Pp. 13-15.
162 Ibid. P. 21.
163 Ibid. P. 27.
164 Ibid. P. 23.

society; perhaps even eulogise them; and portray the damaging consequences of those activities as beyond human control. In this way Malthus gained the ear of the political classes; and great respect and approval from the establishment and the orthodox.

This line of reasoning, which Malthus borrowed from the official famine propaganda of the 1790s, and greatly developed, served him well over a period of many years. He used it first to counter Godwin's claims that human misery was caused by government and society. He used it to defend corn-dealers and withholding farmers; employers; bankers; landlords; and even the notorious Irish middleman class. But although it continued to permeate his writings on many subjects, when writing about the poor themselves, Malthus moved on. A great and radical change came about between publishing the first Essay in 1798, and the second edition of 1803.

Depicting poverty as the inevitable and irremediable effect of natural causes, as Malthus did in the first Essay, may have neatly absolved the governing classes from responsibility. But, from the logic of the argument, it also portrayed the poor as being in a pitiable condition from circumstances beyond their control also; and as such worthy of the sympathy of the classes above them. Indeed, the first Essay abounds in sympathetic references to the poor.

Whilst Paley, and More, and Burke, and Young, were all eulogising the happy and enviable situation of the English poor, Malthus faced the reality. It was well known, he wrote, that the "nominal price of labour….frequently remains the same, while the nominal price of provisions has been gradually increasing". And this represented a gradual worsening of the conditions of life of the lower classes.[165]

"The great increase of the poor rates is, indeed, of itself a strong evidence that the poor have not a greater command of the necessaries and conveniences of life, and if to the consideration, that their condition in this respect is rather worse than better, be added the circumstance, that a much greater proportion of them is employed in large manufactures, unfavourable both to health and virtue, it must be acknowledged, that the increase of wealth of late years has had no tendency to increase the happiness of the labouring poor."[166]

Malthus noted the low physical condition of the poor, even in the country.

"The sons and daughters of peasants will not be found such rosy cherubs in real life as they are described to be in romances. It cannot fail to be remarked by those who live much in the country that the sons of labourers are very apt to be stunted in their growth, and a long while arriving at maturity. Boys that you would guess to be fourteen or fifteen are, upon inquiry, frequently found to be eighteen or nineteen. And the lads who drive plough, which must certainly be a healthy exercise, are very rarely seen with any appearance of calves to their legs, a circumstance which can only be attributed to a want either of proper or of sufficient nourishment."[167]

Whilst acknowledging that inequality can never be eradicated, Malthus denied that "the present great inequality of property is either necessary or useful to society. On the contrary, it must certainly be considered as an evil."[168]

"We cannot possibly expect to exclude riches and poverty from society, yet if we could find out a mode of government by which the numbers in the extreme regions would be lessened and the numbers in the middle regions increased, it would undoubtedly be our duty to adopt it."[169]

Malthus complained that when prices were rising, the rich got together to ensure that wages did not follow.

---

165 T. R. Malthus. An Essay on the Principle of Population. 1798. Penguin ed. P. 78.

166 Ibid. P. 189.

167 Ibid. Pp. 93-94.

168 Ibid. P. 177.

169 Ibid. P. 207.

"The rich by unfair combinations contribute frequently to prolong a season of distress among the poor."[170]

And he condemned unreservedly attempts by some to stimulate population with a view to creating a labour surplus. These were "vicious, cruel and tyrannical, and in any state of tolerable freedom cannot therefore succeed."

"It may appear to be the interest of the rulers, and the rich of a state, to force population, and thereby lower the price of labour, and consequently the expense of fleets and armies, and the cost of manufactures for foreign sale; but every attempt of the kind should be carefully watched and strenuously resisted by the friends of the poor."[171]

At this point, Malthus still considered himself a friend of the poor. The trouble was, that by representing the sufferings of the poor as natural, inevitable and irremediable, and by the sympathetic approach to the poor that was the logical consequence of this, though Malthus shifted the blame from the shoulders of ministers and the upper echelons of society, he had done nothing whatever to justify repressive laws against the poor, draconian punishments, the building of barracks, and the use of the military against hungry rioters. For Malthus's own purposes, the first Essay on Population had not gone nearly far enough.

Historians in general have tended to treat the second edition of the Essay as a development of the first. In fact, it is a completely different book, as Malthus himself tells us.

"In its present shape it may be treated as a new work, and I should probably have published it as such, omitting the few parts of the former which I have retained, but that I wished it to form a whole of itself, and not to need a continual reference to the other."[172]

Malthus wrote the second edition as he was planning to marry. He had previously observed how the expences of married life resulted in a fall of several steps in social status; the edition of 1803 was clearly intended to finance family life. It was written, not just for the approval of the governing classes, but for profit. It needed to be popular amongst those who were its intended readership. Malthus made a judgment of that readership, and came to the conclusion that a much sterner line was required. Somehow or other, the poor had to be made blameable.

As a consequence, gone were virtually all the sympathetic references to the poor. A comparison of texts will reveal that much even of the first Essay was taken from the virulently anti-poor tract written by the eccentric Joseph Townsend in 1786, which saw the poor as an inherently, perhaps even genetically, inferior race of human beings whose sufferings were brought on by their own idleness, improvidence, and numerous other vices. In the second edition, Malthus acknowledged Townsend openly, and referred to "Mr. Townsend's excellent dissertation". This was entitled a Dissertation on the Poor Laws", but was more accurately a dissertation on the poor themselves, in which Townsend used the Poor Laws as a stick with which to beat them. In this, in 1803, Malthus followed Townsend. In the second edition, the issue of the Poor Law became a vehicle of anti-poor propaganda, in an attempt to drive a wedge between the poor and other sections of the community; and to divert attention from the methods of exploitation used, for example, by bankers and corn-dealers. The incoherent and venomous ramblings of Joseph Townsend, an eccentric country parson to whom even his own parishioners would not listen, were thus enabled to enter mainstream orthodox thinking.

In the first Essay, Malthus was at pains to insist that no more than a tiny fraction of the distresses suffered by mankind could possibly be attributed, as Godwin had said, to social and political institutions. In the second edition, he accuses the Poor Law. This seems like quite a radical reversal of opinion, yet Malthus never accounted for it; and modern historians seem scarcely to have noticed.

---

170 Ibid. P. 79.
171 Ibid. P. 116-117.
172 T. R. Malthus. An Essay on the Principle of Population. Second ed. Ed. P. James. P. 2.

Already, in his anonymous pamphlet of 1800, Malthus was indicting the Poor Law as a cause of increasing poverty. He acknowledged, what the government did not, that the price of corn had climbed "higher than the degree of that scarcity would at first sight appear to warrant."[173] And his explanation was novel.

"The attempt in most parts of the kingdom to increase the parish allowances in proportion to the price of corn, combined with the riches of the country, which have enabled it to proceed as far as it has done in this attempt, is, comparatively speaking, the sole cause, which has occasioned the price of provisions in this country to rise so much higher than the degree of scarcity would seem to warrant….It never could have reached its present height, but from the system of poor laws and parish allowances….With this additional command of money in the lower classes, and the consequent increased consumption, the number of purchases at the then price would naturally exceed the supply….Some of the poor would naturally make use of their additional command of money to purchase butter, cheese, bacon, pickled pork, rice, potatoes etc…..These commodities, therefore, rose as naturally and as necessarily as the corn."[174]

At a time when it is well known that the system of parish allowances did not always succeed in its very limited aim of keeping the poor from starvation; when most family budgets would not even purchase a sufficient quantity of bread alone; Malthus painted a picture of them luxuriating on butter, cheese and bacon. The poor were starving because they were eating too much!

Despite its obvious absurdity, this argument reappeared in the second edition of 1803. But here it was given a sinister new twist, which undoubtedly owed quite a lot to Joseph Townsend.

"The price of corn, in a scarcity, will depend much more on the obstinacy with which the same degree of consumption is persevered in, than on the degree of the actual deficiency. A deficiency of one half of a crop, if the people would immediately consent to consume only one half of what they did before, would produce little or no effect on the price of corn….the more is given in parish assistance, the more power is furnished of persevering in the same consumption; and, of course, the higher will be the price before the necessary diminution of consumption is effected."[175]

William Pitt's government was keen to encourage ordinary people to take to a diet less expensive than wheaten bread; and one must strongly suspect that it was attempting to use the famine to accomplish this on a permanent basis. Here, Malthus joined in the official condemnation of the popular reluctance to comply. But he went further.

"High prices do ultimately diminish consumption; but, on account of the riches of the country, the unwillingness of the people to resort to substitutes, and the immense sums which are distributed by parishes, this object cannot be attained till the prices become excessive, and force even the middle classes of society, or at least those immediately above the poor, to save in the article of bread from the actual inability of purchasing it in the usual quantity. The poor who were assisted by their parishes had no reason whatever to complain of the high price of grain; because it was the excessiveness of this price, and this alone, which, by enforcing such a saving, left a greater quantity of corn for the consumption of the lowest classes, which corn the parish allowances enabled them to command. The greatest sufferers in the scarcity were undoubtedly the classes immediately above the poor; and these were in the most marked manner depressed by the excessive bounties given to those below them…. Giving to the poorer classes a command of food so much greater than their degree of skill and industry entitled them to,….diminished,…that command over the necessaries of life which the classes above them, by their superior skill and industry, would naturally possess; and it may be a question whether

---

173 T. R. Malthus. An Investigation of the Cause of the present High Price of Provisions. P. 2.

174 Ibid. Pp. 8 and 11-12. How can something be comparatively speaking the sole cause?

175 T. R. Malthus. An Essay on the Principle of Population. Second ed. Ed. P. James. Vol. I. Pp. 350-351.

the degree of assistance which the poor received, and which prevented them from resorting to the use of those substitutes which, in every other country on such occasions, the great law of necessity teaches, was not more than overbalanced by the severity of the pressure on so large a body of people from the extreme high prices, and the permanent evil which must result from forcing so many persons on the parish, who before thought themselves almost out of the reach of want."[176]

Malthus was at least correct in his assumption that the distresses produced by the famine of 1800 spread themselves throughout much of the social spectrum. But here he was attempting to influence the minds of those who had suffered in the famines, but who were normally to be considered above the level of the poorest. Shielding from blame the traders in grain, the issuers of currency, and the supporters of a pointless war, Malthus pointed an accusing finger at the parochial poor; he attempted to prejudice society against those poor; and to stereotype them as lacking in "skill and industry".

The Poor Law, he claimed, "diverted a considerable share from the support of the diligent and careful workman to the support of the idle and negligent", and depressed the condition of all those who were not normally recipients of parochial relief.

Furthermore, the Poor Laws "contributed to generate that carelessness and want of frugality observable among the poor, so contrary to the disposition generally to be remarked among petty tradesmen and small farmers."

Malthus made the astonishing claim that a man on relief still had 2s. to spare for wants other than food. Yet, "even when they have an opportunity of saving, they seldom exercise it; but all that they earn beyond their present necessities goes, generally speaking, to the alehouse."[177]

The section in the second edition on the Poor Laws represents a clear attempt to bring them into discredit with general public opinion, and through the Poor Laws to blacken and vilify the poor themselves, and to eradicate that sympathy for them which might otherwise be felt.

There seemed to be no end to the perniciousness of the laws for relieving the poor. The depreciation of the currency, which many writers attributed to excessive issues of paper currency by the Bank of England, Malthus ascribed to very different causes. The huge amount of cash being spent by the poor during the years of high prices necessitated a big increase in the circulating medium. The main culprit, of course, was "the single article of the weekly payment of labourers' wages, including the parish allowances." To satisfy this demand, it was the private country banks that had pumped paper into circulation.

"The very great issue of country bank paper during the years 1800 and 1801 was evidently, therefore, in its origin, rather a consequence than a cause of the high price of provisions; but being once absorbed into the circulation, it must necessarily affect the price of all commodities, and throw very great obstacles in the way of returning cheapness. This is the great mischief of the system."[178]

So the Poor Laws were the cause of the excessive price of grain during the years of scarcity; of depressing the condition of the worthy classes of petty traders and small farmers during those years; and of sucking into circulation vast quantities of country bank paper, which, long-term, could have such disastrous consequences.

But the damage did not stop even there. The Poor Laws increased population without increasing food, and it was this disproportion, according to the first Essay, which was responsible for all the distresses of mankind.

"Among the lower classes, where the point is of the greatest importance, the poor laws afford a direct, constant, and systematical encouragement to marriage, by removing from each individual that

---

176 Ibid. Vol. I. Pp. 351-352.
177 Ibid. Vol. I. Pp. 364, 359 and 352.
178 Ibid. Vol. I. Pp.353-354.

heavy responsibility, which he would incur by the laws of nature, for bringing beings into the world which he could not support."[179]

The customs of marriage among the lower classes, and in particular the age at which marriages took place, were at the crux of Malthusian theory. Clearly, the lower the age at marriage, the more numerous the family that was likely to result.

After the publication of the first Essay, Malthus decided to travel abroad in order to collect the evidence, about this issue as well as others, with which to substantiate his theory. His friend, William Otter, gave a short account of his wanderings.

"In 1799 he sailed for Hamburg with three other members of his college…; the party separated in Sweden, and Dr. Clarke and Mr. Cripps having proceeded rapidly to the north, Mr. Malthus with Mr. Otter continued leisurely their tour through Sweden, Norway, Finland, and a part of Russia, these being the only countries at the time open to English travellers.…During the short peace of 1802, he again left England, and visited with some of his relatives, France and Switzerland; exploring with them, all that was most interesting in nature or art in those countries, but always continuing, wherever he went, to collect facts and documents for the illustration of the principle he had announced, and for the completion of his work."[180]

This egregious placing of the cart before the horse resulted, in the second edition, in a lengthy section on the relative situation of population and subsistence in the countries which he had visited. Of particular interest were his comments on marriage in Norway and Switzerland.

In Switzerland, Malthus observed that those regions which could be considered the healthiest, according to the criteria of child mortality and life expectancy, had the lowest birth rates. In the Alpine village of Leyzin, for example, in the wholesome air of mountain pastures, there was no scope for emigration or extended cultivation, and yet life expectancy was fully sixty-one years. The number of births equalled the number of deaths, and the population remained static. This occurred because it was impossible for the young people to contemplate marriage until a position as a herdsman became available; and, given the high life expectancy, this did not happen very frequently. Marriages, therefore, occurred perforce late in life, and families were small. This delaying of marriage Malthus termed the preventive check to population; in fact, it was a self-regulating demographic mechanism that seems to have been inherent in traditional agricultural societies. And as a result of this social system, of which the 'preventive check' was a part, Swiss peasants were known for their wealth, and all foreign travellers observed "the state of the Swiss peasantry as superior to that of other countries."[181]

Similarly in Norway. Here are Malthus's interesting remarks on the people of that country.

"There is but little division of labour in Norway. Almost all the wants of domestic economy are supplied in each separate household. Not only the common operations of brewing, baking and washing, are carried on at home, but many families make, or import, their own cheese and butter, kill their own beef and mutton, import their own grocery stores; and the farmers and country people in general spin their own flax and wool, and weave their own linen and woollen clothes."

There was not much good ground in Norway where corn could be grown, and scarcity was normally felt for a couple of months before harvest. However, all the independent labourers kept cows – even the poorest had two or three and many had up to six. The milk filled the hungry gap.

---

179 Ibid. Vol. II. P. 120.

180 W. Otter. Memoir of Robert Malthus. Pp. XXXVI-XXXVII. Prefaced to Principles of Political Economy.

181 T. R. Malthus. An Essay on the Principle of Population. Second ed. Ed. P. James. Vol. I. Pp.218 *et seq.*

"The hardship of being obliged to mix the inner bark of pine with their bread is mitigated by the store of cheese, of salt butter, of salt meat, salt fish and bacon, which they were enabled to lay up for winter provisions."

Clearly Malthus was describing here the traditional agricultural society of Norway; the similarity to the village life of Wigston Magna needs hardly to be pointed out; nor the contrast with the proletarian day-labourers of Malthus's own day.

As in England, the Norwegian peasantry operated their own system of farm service. A young single labourer would live in with the farmer's family.

"It is not uncommon for a farmer in the country who, in his appearance is not to be distinguished from any of his labourers, to have a household of twenty persons, including his own family."[182]

When employment with a house became available, and not until then, the single man could marry. This delay in marriage led to smaller families, and kept the population equal to what the land could support.

Unsurprisingly, Malthus remarked on the well-nourished appearance of Norwegian peasant children, compared with the sons of labourers in England. The inhabitants were healthy; mortality was low; and during the summer of 1799, "the Norwegians appeared to wear a face of plenty and content."

Malthus's observations about the traditional rural communities of Switzerland and Norway were profoundly destructive of his theory of population as presented in his first Essay. Instead of inevitably increasing numbers of people putting a constant pressure on food supplies, and resulting in an irremediable degree of poverty and misery, here were societies which contained inherently within them mechanisms which equalised population and subsistence; where people were prosperous, well-nourished and happy.

The theory of the natural, unavoidable and irremediable nature of poverty had been blown out of the water.

The proper and valid conclusion to be drawn from this evidence was that, in England, it was the destruction of traditional rural society that was a foremost cause both of poverty and misery, and of the soaring population. Village life, with its systems of service for the young and unmarried, and of social mobility throughout the village hierarchy, would have had much the same effect in delaying marriage and maintaining prosperity, as the systems which Malthus remarked upon in Switzerland and Norway. Indeed, Malthus saw for himself, at first hand, the deleterious effects of the disruption of this system. At the Lac de Joux, in the Jura in Switzerland, Malthus found the people miserable and in a starving condition, with boys and girls marrying "who ought still to be at school". What had happened was that a stone-polishing industry had become established in the area, which for a time had provided regular employment and good wages. But from "change of fashion, accident, and other causes", manufacturing ceased, leaving the country people to manage as best they could.[183] Once the traditional social system failed, whether in Switzerland or England, social mobility ceased and poverty prevailed. There was no longer any reason or incentive to delay marriage. It is well known today that the impoverishment of communities leads to a rapidly rising birth-rate.

Logically, Malthus's discoveries in Switzerland and Norway should have led him to condemn the agricultural changes of the 17th and 18th centuries as the primary causes of the sufferings of the English poor. This, however, would have been very far from his purpose, and would have won him few friends among the rich and powerful. Throughout his works, Malthus seldom mentions agricultural change as a possible factor in the deteriorating condition of the English poor, or as a determinant of demographic change. It was, conspicuously, the elephant on the sofa.

---

182 Ibid. Vol. I. P. 151.
183 Ibid. Vol. I. Pp. 226-228.

Indeed, Malthus propagated a rather different conclusion. In the first Essay of 1798, Malthus portrayed poverty as unavoidable and totally beyond human control. In the second edition of 1803, he reversed this position and depicted poverty as the direct result of the poor reproducing themselves too quickly. As Malthus put it in a private letter to William Godwin;-

"The very admission of the necessity of prudence, to prevent the misery from an overcharged population, removes the blame from public institutions to the conduct of individuals."[184]

Poverty, in short, was the fault of the poor.

"Natural and moral evil seem to be the instruments employed by the Deity in admonishing us to avoid any mode of conduct which is not suited to our being, and will consequently injure our happiness. If we be intemperate in eating and drinking, we are disordered; if we indulge the transports of anger, we seldom fail to commit acts of which we afterwards repent; if we multiply too fast, we die miserably of poverty and contagious diseases. The laws of nature in all these cases are similar and uniform. They indicate to us that we have followed these impulses too far, so as to tread upon some other law, which equally demands attention. The uneasiness we feel from repletion, the injuries that we inflict on ourselves or others in anger, and the inconveniences we suffer on the approach of poverty, are all admonitions to us to regulate these impulses better; and if we heed not this admonition, we justly incur the penalty of our disobedience, and our sufferings act as a warning to others."

"There are perhaps few actions that tend so directly to diminish the general happiness as to marry without the means of supporting children. He who commits this act, therefore, clearly offends against the will of God; and having become a burden on the society in which he lives, and plunged himself and his family into a situation in which virtuous habits are preserved with more difficulty than in any other, he appears to have violated his duty to his neighbours and to himself, and thus to have listened to the voice of passion in opposition to his higher obligations."

"This duty is express, and intelligible to the humblest capacity. It is merely that he is not to bring beings into the world for whom he cannot find the means of support. When once this subject is cleared from the obscurity thrown over it by parochial laws and private benevolence, every man must feel the strongest conviction of such an obligation. If he cannot support his children, they must starve; and if he marry in the face of a fair probability that he shall not be able to support his children, he is guilty of all the evils which he thus brings upon himself, his wife and his offspring."[185]

Under the circumstances of Malthus's time, the number of the labouring classes who were entitled to marry according to Malthus's criteria, at any stage of their lives, must have represented a very small proportion indeed.

What Malthus's new theory had in common with his previous one, was that they both absolved the governing classes, both from the blame for the poverty prevailing in society, and for the responsibility for alleviating it.

According to Malthus, the poor needed to understand "that they are themselves the cause of their own poverty; that the means of redress are in their own hands, and in the hands of no other persons whatever; that the society in which they live, and the government which presides over it, are totally without power in this respect; and that however ardently they may desire to relieve them, and whatever attempts they may make to do so, they are really and truly unable to execute what they benevolently wish, but unjustly promise; that when the wages of labour will not maintain a family, it is an incontrovertible sign that their king and country do not want more subjects, or at least that they cannot support them; that if they marry in this case, so far from fulfilling a duty to society, they are throwing a useless burden on it, at the same time that they are plunging themselves into distress; and that they are acting directly contrary to the will of God, and bringing down upon themselves various

184 P. James. Population Malthus. P. ?
185 Ibid. Vol. II. Pp. 88, 101 and 105.

diseases, which might all, or in a great part, have been avoided, if they had attended to the repeated admonitions which he gives, by the general laws of nature, to every being capable of reason."

"Nothing perhaps would tend so strongly to excite a spirit of industry and economy among the poor, as a thorough knowledge that their happiness must always depend principally upon themselves; and that, if they obey their passions in opposition to their reason, or be not industrious and frugal while they are single men, to save a sum for the common contingencies of the married state, they must expect to suffer the natural evils which Providence has prepared for those who disobey its repeated admonitions."[186]

It was just five short years since his assertion that poverty was natural and unavoidable. Malthus came to a directly contrary conclusion; that poverty was the consequence of the improvidence, the irresponsibility, and the uncontrolled passions of the poor themselves; who had it manifestly within their power to rectify the situation.

"When the wages of labour are hardly sufficient to maintain two children, a man marries and has five or six. He of course finds himself miserably distressed. He accuses the insufficiency of the price of labour, to maintain a family. He accuses his parish for their tardy and sparing fulfilment of their obligation to assist him. He accuses the avarice of the rich, who suffer him to want what they can so well spare. He accuses the partial and unjust institutions of society, which have awarded him an inadequate share of the produce of the earth. He accuses perhaps the dispensations of Providence, which have assigned to him a place in society so beset with unavoidable distress and dependence. In searching for objects of accusation, he never adverts to the quarter from which all his misfortunes originate. The last person that he would think of accusing is himself, on whom, in fact, the whole of the blame lies."[187]

Malthus had, himself, only very recently formulated his theory of the causes of poverty lying in the failure of the labouring classes to attend to the preventive check to population. Yet straight away he was prepared to condemn the people for their ignorance of this theory. Indeed, the tendency to attribute the causes of suffering to the government and the rich, instead of to the causes pointed out by Malthus, was said to represent a serious danger.

"While any dissatisfied man of talents has power to persuade the lower classes of people that all their poverty and distress arise solely from the iniquity of government, though perhaps the greatest part of what they suffer is totally unconnected with this cause, it is evident that the seeds of fresh discontent and fresh revolutions are continually sowing....A mob, which is generally the growth of a redundant population, goaded by resentment for real sufferings, but totally ignorant of the quarter from which they originate, is of all monsters the most fatal to freedom."[188]

The menace posed by such an uncomprehending mob necessitated strong repressive measures by government. Malthus was attempting to justify the Pittite despotism on the grounds of the popular lack of understanding of population theory!

"The degree of power to be given to the civil government, and the measure of our submission to it, must be determined by....the degree of ignorance and delusion prevailing among the common people....It is more the ignorance and delusion of the lower classes of people that occasions the oppression, than the actual disposition of the government to tyranny."

"The most successful supporters of tyranny are without doubt those general declaimers, who attribute the distresses of the poor, and almost all the evils to which society is subject, to human institutions and the iniquity of governments. The falsity of these accusations and the dreadful consequences that would result from their being generally admitted and acted upon, make it absolutely

186 Ibid. Vol. II. Pp. 107 and 111.
187 Ibid. Vol. II. P. 106.
188 Ibid. Vol. II. P. 123.

necessary that they should at all events be resisted....If I were called upon to name the cause which, in my conception, had more than any other contributed to the very slow progress of freedom, (sic!)....I should say that it was the confusion that had existed respecting the causes of the unhappiness and discontents which prevail in society; and the advantage which governments had been able to take, and indeed had been compelled to take, of this confusion, to confirm and strengthen their power."[189]

And, on these grounds, Malthus commended the Duke of Portland's military campaign against food rioters.

"Had it not been for the organised force in the country, the distresses of the people during the late scarcities, encouraged by the extreme ignorance and folly of many among the higher classes, might have driven them to commit the most dreadful outrages, and ultimately to involve the country in all the horrors of famine."[190]

The failure of the populace to submit to or comprehend Malthus's ever-shifting contradictions and convoluted *non-sequiturs* was supposed to justify despotism, oppression, barracks, shootings, hangings....

Malthus ended up where he wanted to be. From a reasonably compassionate (if incorrect) exposition citing natural and inevitable causes of poverty, which Malthus stumbled upon in his confutation of Godwin in 1798, he had moved swiftly on to a totally unsympathetic indictment of the lower classes, which served as a justification not only for whatever oppression might be inflicted upon them, but also for its enforcement by law and physical force. And it laid the blame entirely upon them.

Perhaps Malthus's second edition does not sink quite to the murky depths of prejudice and stereotyping plumbed by Joseph Townsend. Still, it is impossible to classify it as anything other than intentionally socially divisive, and an extreme piece of anti-poor propaganda. As such it is more an indication of Malthus's assessment of the mindset of his target audience, than of his own beliefs.

This assessment proved remarkably percipient; for it achieved all that was required. Quite apart from the success of the book in terms of sales – several more editions were published – Malthus was offered a position. The East India Company had set up a college for training its future recruits to the administration of India; and it invited Malthus to become the Professor of Political Economy there; seeing him, no doubt, as the ideal teacher to prepare these young men for living amongst the barefaced exploitation and abject poverty of the sub-continent with some degree of equanimity. The college was at Haileybury, in Hertfordshire, and here Malthus enjoyed, with his family, income, accommodation and security for the rest of his days.

But perhaps more important to Malthus even than this was the acceptance and acclaim which his work received from the classes whose good opinion he coveted. In a sense, Malthus's work was far more pernicious than Townsend's; for whilst the latter was quickly forgotten, the Principle of Population became the prevailing orthodoxy concerning the poor for many years; indeed, we are not free of it today. It was not an analytical respect that the ruling classes paid to Malthusian theory; indeed, it was a rather unquestioning attachment. One could fill a small volume with all the inconsistencies and contradictions, both implicit and stated, in Malthus works; in fact, it is not an easy task to decipher what Malthusian theory actually is. And it must be open to doubt whether many of his adherents stopped to wonder whether the increase of population was natural and unavoidable, or caused by plentiful subsistence, or high wages only, or the Poor Laws, or the passions, improvidence and imprudence of the poor themselves, all of which positions were confidently asserted by Malthus at different times; or whether they asked themselves why, when according to Malthusian theory population should have been advancing, it was static; and why, when it should have been static, it

189   Ibid. Vol. II. Pp. 129-131.
190   Ibid. Vol. II. P. 123.

was rapidly increasing. It was more an impressionistic adherence that the ruling elite displayed; an opinion that, in a general way, poverty was caused by increasing numbers. A writer in the Quarterly Review put it like this in 1831.

"Politicians saw in it an excuse for the evils, under which the lower classes might at any time be suffering, fully sufficient to be an answer to all reproaches on their score, and to exculpate every government from the blame of causing the misery of the people under their sway. It was exceedingly convenient to an ignorant or idle statesman to be able to *prove*, philosophically and statistically, that poverty and extreme misery are irremediable, - the necessary condition of the lower classes in every country under the sun – and thus to reconcile his conscience to the spectacle of their existence in that over whose destinies he presided. Nay, to many private individuals, rolling in wealth, and environed by starving fellow-creatures, it was not disagreeable to be assured, on high authority, that even though they should literally obey the divine precept 'to sell all their goods, and give to the poor', they could in no way reduce the sum of human calamity, which would increase upon them faster than by any efforts of charity and benevolence it could be diminished. Under this persuasion, they might continue their career of selfish indulgence and wanton luxury, undisturbed by the visitings of self-reproach for their neglect of the wretched victims of famine, to whom the crumbs from their overloaded tables would be as manna from heaven. In one word, the Malthusian theory absolves wealth and power from all responsibility for the misery which may surround them. No wonder, then, that it was favourably received, made many converts, and took its post as the reigning philosophy of the day."[191]

William Godwin had pursued much the same line in 1820.

"Never certainly was there so comfortable a preacher as Mr. Malthus. No wonder that his book is always to be found in the country-seats of the court of aldermen and in the palaces of the great. Very appropriately has a retreat been provided for him by the commercial sovereigns of the regions of the East."[192]

Malthusian influence went right to the very heart of government. When Lord Suffield was canvassing support for his scheme for improving the lot of agricultural labourers in 1830, he had a meeting with the Home Secretary, Lord Melbourne. Melbourne was dismissive.

"I consider it hopeless….the evil is in numbers, and the sort of competition that ensues."[193]

In this way, Malthusian theory became a part of the problem. A theory, evolved to explain the causes of poverty, became, itself, one of those causes, and remained so for decades.

Henry Colman was an American agriculturalist, who undertook a tour of the British Isles in 1843. He enjoyed the hospitality of many of the major landowners, and had frequent occasion to comment upon the close juxtaposition in England of extreme wealth with extreme destitution.

"There is here a vast amount of poverty and vice and misery."

And he assigned a reason why such a state of affairs was suffered to persist.

"Most persons here are Malthusians…."[194]

---

191   Quarterly Review. April 1831. P. 100.
192   P. James. Population Malthus. P. 379.
193   J. L. and B. Hammond. The Village Labourer. P. 299.
194   H. Colman. European Life and Manners. Vol. I. Pp. 43-44.

The Thing

William Cobbett and the Exposition of the Anatomy of a System of Exploitation

"And *who are you*", as the Attorney-General, now Chancellor of the Exchequer, said of me, in *Latin*, when he was pleading against me, in the Court of King's Bench; "*Who are you*, that presumes to tell us we are all in error?" Why, what signifies it who I am? The only question is, *am I right*? If I am not, overset my arguments, and shew the world that I am wrong. <u>Political Register 28/11/1807</u>[1]

Section One; Cobbett's Countrymen

It was with a robustly expressed indignation that William Cobbett witnessed and noted down the continuing deterioration in the conditions of life of the bulk of the English people. In 1806, he pointed to the novelty of the degradation by which they were now faced.

"Upwards of *six millions* a year are now raised upon the parishes to be dealt out in aid of those means by which the labourer obtains his bread; and of persons receiving this aid there are upwards of a million. *All*, all, the labourers, having families, are now *paupers*! This is a new state of things…. Let us not be answered, by the observations, that there must be poor, that there always have been and that there always will be, in every state of society in every country in the world. We know there must be poor; we know that some must be very poor; we know that some must be maintained, or assisted, at least, either by the parish or by voluntary alms; but, is there anyone who will deny, that this is a new and most deplorable state of things, which has rendered all the labourers, having families, paupers? The plain fact is, that a man with a wife, and with four children that are unable to work, cannot now, out of his labour, possibly provide them and himself with the means of living. I do not mean that he cannot live *comfortably*, for, to comfort, such men have long ago bid farewell; but, I assert, and am ready to prove, that he cannot provide them, without parish aid, with a sufficiency of food, not to *satisfy* their cravings, but to *sustain life*. And, will any one say that this state of things is such as England ought to witness?…There are hundreds of thousands of the people of England who never taste any food but bread and vegetables, and who scarcely even know what it is to have a full meal even of these. This is *new*; it was not so in former times; it was not so even till of *late* years…. In his present pining famishing state, it may, almost without a figure, be said, that, 'in the midst of life he is in death'."[2]

Cobbett returned to the theme again and again. In an open letter to William Wilberforce published in the Political Register in 1823, Cobbett impugned the humanity of the renowned campaigner, and berated his indifference.

"A very large portion of the agricultural labourers of England. A very large portion of those <u>who raise all the</u> food, who make all the buildings, who prepare all the fuel, who, in short, by their

---

1 Quoted in The Opinions of William Cobbett. Ed. G. D. H. Cole.
2 Political Register. 8/2/1806. Quoted in The Opinions of William Cobbett. Ed. G. D. H. Cole. Pp. 121-122.

labour, sustain the community. A very large part of these exist in a state of almost incessant hunger. The *size* of the people is diminishing from this cause. They are becoming a feeble race, they suffer from numerous bodily ailments engendered by the poverty of their food. Their dress is fast becoming nothing but rags; and, in short, every hardship and every suffering that labour and poverty and the starvation can inflict, are becoming their lot. You know this as well as I do…."[3]

It never used to be thus. Cobbett attempted to trace the lowering of English standards of living through the centuries.

"England was always famed for many things; but especially for its *good living*; that is to say, for the *plenty* in which the whole of the people lived; for the abundance of good clothing and good food, which they had….Its *good living*, its superiority in this particular respect, was proverbial amongst all who knew, or had heard talk of the English nation."

Cobbett quotes Sir John Fortescue, a distinguished English judge of the 15th century, on the superior condition of his countrymen, which resulted from the practice of parliamentary law-making.

"Every inhabitant is at his liberty fully to use and enjoy whatever his farm produceth, the fruits of the earth, the increase of his flock, and the like; all the improvements he makes, whether by his own proper industry, or of those he retains in his service, are his own, to use and to enjoy, without the let, interruption, or denial of any….the inhabitants are *rich in gold, silver*, and in all the necessaries and conveniences of life. They *drink no water*, unless at certain times, upon *a religious score*, and by way of doing penance. They *are fed in great abundance*, with *all sorts of flesh* and *fish*, of which *they have plenty every-where*; they are *clothed throughout in good woollens*; their bedding and other furniture in their houses *are of wool*, and that *in great store*. They are also well provided with all other sorts of household goods and necessary implements for husbandry. Every one, according to his rank, hath *all things which conduce to make life easy and happy*."

Of course, this passage from Fortescue may well have been political propaganda just as surely as the eulogistic idylls of Paley and Young. But we have seen for ourselves the general direction at least taken by living standards from the early 17th century. Cobbett dug up an ancient act of Parliament, which attempted to fix the price of beef, pork, mutton and veal, "these being THE FOOD OF THE POORER SORT." In Cobbett's day, magistrates declared from their benches "that BREAD AND WATER were the general food of working people on England." A curiosity uncovered by Gilbert White, vicar of Selbourne in Hampshire, whilst researching the history of his parish, was a document recording the punishment of men for disorderly conduct, by being "compelled to *fast* a fortnight on *bread and beer*!" "Go tell the harnessed gravel-drawers in Hampshire", thundered Cobbett, that they may be compelled to "*fast* on *bread and beer*," and not suffered "to continue to regale themselves on nice potatoes and pure water."

At any rate, it seemed evident to Cobbett that a standard of comfort had existed among ordinary people in times past which had disappeared by his own era.

"Good God! How changed! Now, the very worst fed and worst clad people upon the face of the earth, those of Ireland only excepted. *How, then, did this horrible, this disgraceful, this cruel poverty come upon this once happy nation?*"

And he traces the deterioration through his own times.

Writing in 1771, Arthur Young had maintained that 13s 1d was the lowest possible sum on which a family could exist. "Alas! We shall find, that they can be made to exist on little more than *one-half* of this sum!" Along came the American War of Independence.

"This American war caused a great mass of new taxes to be laid on, and the people of England became *a great deal poorer than they had ever been before*. During that war, they BEGAN TO EAT

---

3   G. D. H. Cole. Ed. The Opinions of William Cobbett. P. 136.

POTATOES, as something to 'save bread'. The poorest of the people, the very poorest of them, refused, for a long while, to use them in this way; and even when I was ten years old, which was just about *fifty years ago*; the poor people would not eat potatoes, except *with meat*, as they would cabbages, or carrots, or any other moist vegetable. But, by the end of the American war, their stomachs had come to! By slow degrees, they had been reduced to swallow this pig-meat (and bad pig meat too)[4], not, indeed, without grumbling; but to swallow it; to be reduced, thus, many degrees in the scale of animals."

By 1795, "a new war, and a new series of '*victories and prizes*' had begun. But, who it was that *suffered* for these, out of whose blood and flesh and bones they came, the allowance now (in 1795) made to the poor labourers and their families will tell. There was, in that year, a TABLE, or SCALE, of allowance, framed by the Magistrates of Berkshire….According to this scale, which was printed and published, and also acted upon for years, the weekly allowance, for *a man, his wife and three children*, was, according to present money-prices, 11s 4d. Thus, it had, in the space of twenty-four years, fell from 13s 1d to 11s 4d. Thus were the people brought to the *pig-meat*! Food, fit for men, they could not have with 11s 4d a week for five persons.

"One would have thought, that to make a human being *live upon 4d a day*, and find *fuel, clothing, rent, washing* and *bedding*, out of the 4d, besides eating and drinking, was impossible; and one would have thought it impossible for any-thing not of hellish birth and breeding, to entertain a wish to make poor creatures, and our *neighbours* too, exist in such a state of horrible misery and degradation as the labourers of England were condemned to by this scale of 1795. Alas! this was happiness and honour; this was famous living; this 11s 4d a week was *luxury* and *feasting*, compared to what we NOW BEHOLD! For now the allowance, according to present money-prices, is 8s a week for the man, his wife, and three children; that is to say 2d. and 5/7ths of a 1d. In words, TWO PENCE AND FIVE SEVENTHS OF ANOTHER PENNY, FOR A DAY! There, that is England now! That is what the base wretches, who are fattening upon the people's labour, call 'the *envy* of surrounding nations and the *admiration* of the world'!"[5]

As Cobbett travelled through the Valley of the Wiltshire Avon in 1826, making computations about the produce and the consumption, he composed a diet which, he thought, was the minimum that could keep a labouring family fit for their work.

"Let it be a family of *five persons*; a man, wife and three children, one child big enough to work, one big enough to eat heartily, and one a baby; and this is a pretty fair average of the state of the people in the country. Such a family would want 5lb. of bread a-day; they would want a pound of mutton a-day; they would want two pounds of bacon a-day; they would want, on an average, winter and summer, a gallon and a half of beer a-day."

This diet we can compare with that of David Davies's parishioners at Barkham in Berkshire in the early 1790s. It will be seen that Cobbett allowed a little less bread than they consumed; but considerably more meat than the pitiful amounts eaten at Barkham. Of beer, at Barkham, they had none, or virtually none, as the price of malt had already reduced them to drinking tea. So Cobbett's theoretical allowance represented a small but significant improvement on the diets evidenced by Davies's budgets. Unfortunately, theoretical was all it was.

"What I have allowed in food and drink is by no means excessive. It is but a pound of bread, and a little more than half-a-pound of meat a day to each person on an average; and the beer is not a drop too much….No man can say, or, at least, none but a base usurer, who would grind money out of the bones of his own father; no other man can, or will, say, that I have been *too liberal to this family*; and

---

4 I. e. pig food.
5 All of the above from The Poor Man's Friend. Pt. IV.

yet, Good God! What *extravagance* is here, if the labourers of England *be now treated justly!*...What do *labourers' families get*, compared to this?"

Costing his diet out, Cobbett came upon an annual total of £62 6s 8d; "for *bare victuals and drink*; just food and drink enough to keep people in working condition."

But labouring families in the Avon Valley received, "*at the utmost*, only about 9s a week." And that comes to an annual total of £23 8s; "for food, drink, clothing, fuel and every thing!" The parish allowance locally was about 7s 6d for the family. In the north of Hampshire at the end of 1825, weekly wages were only 8s per week. At Uphusband, in 1822, wages were brought down to 6s, and things were said to be worse still in Wiltshire. Between Warminster and Westbury in 1826, Cobbett chanced upon thirty men digging in a field; their pay was 4s 6d a week. "How are their miserable families to live?" asked Cobbett. How indeed?

But Cobbett rode on.

"In taking my leave of this beautiful vale I have to express my deep shame, as an Englishman, at beholding the general *extreme poverty* of those who cause this vale to produce such quantities of food and raiment. This is, I verily believe it, the *worst used labouring people upon the face of the earth.* Dogs and hogs and horses are treated with *more civility*; and as to food and lodging, how gladly would the labourers change with them!"

Riding through another valley nearby, in Wiltshire, Cobbett found the situation much the same. The labourers looked half-starved.

"For my own part, I really am ashamed to ride a fat horse, to have a full belly, and to have a clean shirt upon my back, while I look at these wretched countrymen of mine; while I actually see them reeling with weakness; when I see their poor faces present me nothing but skin and bone, while they are toiling to get the wheat and meat ready to be carried away....I am ashamed to look at these poor souls, and to reflect that they are my countrymen; and particularly to reflect, that we are descended from those amongst whom 'beef, pork, mutton and veal, were the food of the poorer sort of people'."

But the worst poverty of all, as witnessed by Cobbett, was to be found in his favourite village of Uphusband, in Hampshire.

"I wish, that in speaking of this pretty village (which I always return to with additional pleasure), I could give *a good account* of the state of *those, without whose labour there would be neither corn nor sainfoin nor sheep.* I regret to say, that my account of this matter, if I gave it truly, must be a dismal account indeed! For, I have, in no part of England, seen the labouring people so badly off as they are here."[6]

Cobbett was clearly deeply affected by what he found at Uphusband.

"I went to see with my own eyes some of the *'parish houses'* as they are called; that is to say, the places where the select vestry put the poor people into to live. Never did my eyes before alight on such scenes of wretchedness! There was a place, about 18 feet long and 10 wide, in which I found the wife of ISAAC HOLDEN, which, when all were at home, had to contain *nineteen persons*; and into which, I solemnly declare, I would not put 19 pigs, even if well bedded with straw. Another place was shown me by JOB WALDRON's daughter; another by Thomas Carey's wife. The *bare ground*, and that in holes too, was the floor in both these places. The windows broken, and the holes stuffed with rags, or covered with rotten bits of board. Great openings in the walls, parts of which were fallen down, and the places stopped with hurdles and straw. The thatch rotten, the chimneys leaning, the doors but bits of doors, the sleeping holes shocking both to sight and smell; and, indeed, everything seeming to say; '*These* are the abodes of wretchedness, which, to be believed possible, must be seen and felt'."[7]

---

6 Rural Rides. Penguin ed. Pp. 283-286, 241, 28, 296, 312, and 405.
7 The Poor Man's Friend. Pt. IV.

It was a constant theme of Cobbett's that the working people of England were worse looked after than even the lowest ranks in the army. At Rogate, in Hampshire, a single working man was allowed just 7d per day, for six days. "It is just *seven-pence less than one half* of what the meanest foot soldier in the standing army receives; besides that, the latter has clothing, candle, fire, and lodging into the bargain." In England, the millions were "fed upon less, to four persons, than what goes down the throat of *one single common soldier!*"[8]

The working people of England were worse fed than the patients in the hospitals, even those, for example, with broken limbs, who were not able to work, and were virtually incapable of taking any exercise. In Guy's Hospital, in London, the daily allowance prescribed by the surgeons, who, as Cobbett pointed out, were "*competent judges* of what nature requires in the way of food and drink", comprised six ounces of meat, twelve ounces of bread, one pint of broth, and two quarts of good beer. In addition, twelve ounces of butter were allowed per week. The cost of this diet was 6s 9d. But to the working man was allowed only 1s 7d! "For, he cannot and he will not see his wife and children actually drop dead with hunger before his face; and this is what he must see, if he take to himself more than a *fifth* of the allowance for the family."[9]

In England, the working people were even said to be more poorly fed than the slaves of the West Indies, and Cobbett was not the only writer to make this point. He taunted Wilberforce with it. "It is manifest that your '*free* British labourers' are worse off than your Black slaves."[10]

But perhaps the extremity of the degradation of the English people was most forcefully brought home by Cobbett's comparison of their conditions of life with those of the prisoners in the gaols.

"We have just seen that the *honest labouring man* is allowed 2d. and 5/7ths of a 1d. a day; and that will buy him *a pound and a half of good bread a day*, and no more, not a single crumb more. This is all he has….A pound and a half of bread a day, and nothing more, and that, too, *to work upon*! Now, then, how fare the prisoners in the gaols? Why, if they be CONVICTED FELONS, they are, say the Berkshire gaol-regulations, 'to have ONLY BREAD and water, *with vegetables* occasionally, from the garden'. Here, then, they are already better fed than the honest labouring man. Aye, and this is not all; for this is only the *week-day* fare; for, they are to have, 'on Sundays, SOME MEAT *and broth.*' Good God! And the honest working man can never, never smell the smell of meat!

"Those Berkshire gaol-regulations make provision for setting the convicted prisoners, in certain cases, TO WORK, and, they say, 'if the surgeon think it necessary, the WORKING PRISONERS may be allowed MEAT AND BROTH ON WEEK DAYS'; and of Sundays, of course!

"The CONVICTED FELON is, if he do not work at all, allowed, on week-days, some vegetables in addition to his bread, and, on Sundays, both *meat and broth*; and, if the CONVICTED FELON work, if he be a WORKING convicted felon….he is allowed *meat and broth every day in the year*, while the WORKING HONEST MAN is allowed *nothing but dry bread*, and of that not half a belly full! And yet you see people that seem *surprised* that *crimes* increase! Very strange, to be sure; that men should like to *work* upon meat and broth better than they like to work on dry bread!"[11]

At Wykham, in Hampshire, Cobbett came across a group of paupers, harnessed like horses, pulling gravel for repairing the roads; a little further on, there was a group of convicts, harnessed in just the same way, and doing the same work. But whilst the convicts were "hale and ruddy-cheeked, in dresses sufficiently warm, and bawling and singing", the labourers were "thin, ragged, shivering, dejected mortals, such as never were seen in any other country upon earth."[12]

---

8 Rural Rides. Penguin ed. P. 242.
9 The Poor Man's Friend. Pt IV.
10 G. D. H. Cole. The Opinions of William Cobbett. P. 137.
11 The Poor Man's Friend. Pt. IV.
12 Rural Rides. Penguin ed. P. 215.

With such a large proportion of the population living permanently on the verge of famishing, one would naturally expect a large number of deaths from that cause. And so it was. Precisely how many it is impossible to determine, but that it was an unpalatable but commonplace part of contemporary life, in some parts of the country, Cobbett leaves us in no doubt. In 1823, he assailed Wilberforce with this fact.

"It is notorious that great numbers of your 'free British labourers' have actually *died from starvation*; and that, too, at a time when the Minister declared from his seat in Parliament, that there was in the country an over-production of food. This is notorious. This can be denied by no one. The devil himself, if he were to come to the assistance of the hypocrites, could not embolden them to deny the fact."[13]

As a general rule, free men do not starve to death. But in England, men did, as Cobbett observed of the crowds of labourers outside Devizes cultivating small pieces of land for potatoes.

"Where honest and laborious men can be *compelled to starve quietly*, whether all at once or by inches, with old wheat ricks and fat cattle under their eye, it is a mockery to talk of their 'liberty', of any sort; for, the sum total of their state is this, they have 'liberty' to choose between death by starvation and death by the halter!"[14]

Death by starvation, evidently, was more common in the north of England.

"At a public meeting of rate-payers, at Manchester, on the 17th August, MR. BAXTER, the Chairman, said, that some of the POOR had been *starved to death*, and that *tens of thousands were on the point of starving*; and at the same meeting, MR. POTTER gave a detail, which showed, that MR. BAXTER'S general description was true. Other accounts, very nearly official, and, at any rate, being of unquestionable authenticity, concur so fully with the statements made at the Manchester Meeting, that it is impossible not to believe, that a great number of thousands of persons are now on the point of perishing for want of food, and *that many have actually perished from that cause*; and that this has taken place, and is taking place, IN ENGLAND."[15]

Section Two; Malthus and Cobbett

William Cobbett was born in 1763, to a farming family, at an inn which now bears his name, in the hop-producing country on the borders of Surrey and Hampshire. Ploughboy, soldier, scholar, farmer, and politician, he was best-known for his weekly journal, the Political Register, which came out, and contained an editorial by Cobbett himself, almost every Saturday, from 1802 until his death in 1835. Cobbett was incomparable; it is impossible to find his like among his contemporaries, and not easy to think of anyone who filled an equivalent role in any other age. He could be thought, perhaps, the English Gandhi. He was the most forceful, the most feared, and the foremost, writer of his day. In terms of numbers of readers, he was the most influential. And it was with a pronounced and robustly expressed indignation that Cobbett observed the sufferings of his countrymen.

"What must that man be made of, who can allow to a *working man*, a man fourteen hours every day, in the open air, one shilling and seven pence worth of victuals and drink for the week! Let me not, however, ask what 'that *man*' can be made of; for it is a monster and not a man; - it is a murderer of men; not a murderer with the knife or the pistol, but with the more cruel instrument of starvation."[16]

---

13 G. D. H. Cole. The Opinions of William Cobbett. P. 136.
14 Rural Rides. Penguin ed. P. 324.
15 The Poor Man's Friend. P. 4.
16 The Poor Man's Friend. Pt. IV.

Cobbett was shocked at the equanimity betrayed by the attitudes of those in authority to the occurrence of death by starvation. The overseers in the north of England, "those who ought to see that the poor do not suffer, talk of their *dying with hunger* as Irish 'Squires do; aye, and applaud them for their patient resignation!"[17]

"I detest the wretch", raged Cobbett, "be he who he may, who can behold the miseries of the people without feelings of indignation."[18]

But indignation was a very long way indeed from the attitude displayed by many of the writers on poverty of Cobbett's own era, as we have seen. Leaving aside the likes of Massie, and Addington, and Scott, we might characterise their attitudes as ranging from denial, through justification, to victim-blaming. And this contrast in attitude arose from the differing causes to which Cobbett and the other writers attributed the poverty and misery of the English people.

Of all these writers, Cobbett had a particular problem with Malthus. He called him a "hardened and impudent Parson", and addressed an open letter to him in the Political Register in 1819.

"You, who are a Protestant priest, have the infamy to affect to believe, that the miseries of the nation are occasioned by the labouring classes, and, accordingly, you propose to *punish them*!

"If you had not been a shallow and muddle-headed man, you never could have supposed, that the increase of the paupers in England had been caused by the practice of affording parish relief.... Anyone but a mud-headed parson, or a perverse knave, would have looked about him for causes of the increase other than the practice of giving parish relief. When any rational and sincere man had seen, that this practice of giving relief had, in the first two hundred years not debased the people and made them improvident....he would have looked out for the real causes in operation....

"As to your notion of *danger* from an increase of the population of this kingdom, it is too absurd to merit serious remark; seeing that, at the end of a thousand years of the kingly government, there remain *six or seven acres of land* to every man, every woman, and every child!"[19]

Cobbett took issue with Malthus over the cause of the rising population. Poverty was the cause; not the effect.

"That shallow and savage fellow, MALTHUS, has his project for what he calls *checking population*....But, what says common sense and the experience of mankind upon the subject? What do these point out as the most effectual means of making the labourer careful; restraining him from indulgences tending immediately to poverty; making him look forward; making him provident in the steps that he takes as to matrimonial connections; what do these point out? Why, to put good wages into his hands; to let his labour bring him something to preserve; to enable him to have a little store; to make him desirous that his wife and children when he have them, shall be well provided for, shall have a sufficiency of food and shall be dressed as well as their neighbours in the same rank of life. These are what wisdom, and justice, too, point out as the only means of *checking population*. The check which these will give is proper and productive of happiness; a check by any other means is unjustifiable, cruel and beastly.

"When a single man sees that he is no better off than the married man; when he sees that, single or married he is to have the bare means of existence and no more; and especially when he sees, that part of his wages is deducted to go to the maintenance of the married man's family; when he sees this, Parson Malthus may preach till he is as hoarse as I was at Coventry; but never will he find a labourer to listen to his doctrines of *moral restraint*.

"....The farmer, from the burthen of the taxes, is compelled to deduct from the wages of his labourer....To be a pauper ceases to be a shame; and the unmarried man, sensible of the injustice

17 Rural Rides. Penguin ed. P. 347.
18 The Poor Man's Friend. Pt. V.
19 Political Register. 8/5/1819.

exercised towards him, and of the utter inutility of the smallest restraint upon his natural inclinations, hastens to become a father, in order to be enrolled upon the poor book, knowing well that, in any case, his lot cannot be worse than it is. Thus, by premature marriages, the number of paupers is increased.

"Those are impostors, who pretend that the misery of the people arises from a falling off of their morals…."[20]

The contrast between Malthus and Cobbett is a stark one. Malthus, the Cambridge educated clergyman, led a relatively quiet, scholarly life. Afflicted with a cleft palate and hare lip which impeded his speech, he devoted his life to his writing and his teaching. Biographically, a relatively small amount has been published about him; but large numbers of volumes have been devoted to the analysis of his theories, and these have ranged from eulogistic, to over-indulgent, to critical. But in all cases, his population theory, and his political economy, have been treated with a seriousness for which it is not always easy to see the justification. Cobbett, on the other hand, was a highly colourful character. As a resolute champion of the poor and the underdog, he conforms to our modern ideas of a hero. Consequently, there are huge numbers of biographies written about his life. But as for his ideas on the causes of poverty; as for the political economy of William Cobbett; very little is actually written. This is partly because his views were not published in a consolidated format, like the works of Malthus, or Ricardo, or Mill, but distributed throughout a vast volume of writings on a wide variety of subjects; and it would be a huge work to bring them all together and give them an integrated form. Related to this is the fact that Cobbett did not spring from an educated background, and was not always addressing an educated audience. His ideas are not, therefore, always treated with quite the seriousness they deserve. But perhaps the main reason for this neglect is that Cobbett's analysis of the economic and social circumstances of his time is just as uncomfortable to modern ears as it was to his contemporaries of the establishment and the elite. Many of his targets have now become the respectable icons of the modern world; the victors, by whom, or for whom, history is written.

Hence it is that we find one modern historian, in a highly dismissive chapter on Cobbett, claim that he was "more persuasive in criticism than in constructive guidance, in exposing evils than in proposing remedies." Malthus's thorough, but rather indulgent and uncomprehending biographer seems more concerned to defend her hero against Cobbett's unkindness and savagery, rather than what he actually said; and she classed Cobbett's writings with those of the likes of Coleridge and Southey, which she calls familiar to students of English literature, and distinguishes from serious discussions of Malthusian theory "familiar to students of the history of economic thought". To her, evidently, if an idea is not broadly in agreement with Malthus, it is not worthy of serious consideration. Malthus himself took a similar view. Another modern Cobbettian critic, writing on the poor law, claimed;-

"As always, it was denunciation he offered, and he made no contribution at all to the debate…."

The same writer also claimed that Cobbett's anti-Malthusianism was emotional rather than intellectual.

"Cobbett was not really a contributor to the Malthusian debate; he was simply anti-Malthusian."[21]

The inanity of the above comments will be immediately apparent to anyone who has read even a small proportion of Cobbett's writings, and is clear evidence of the raw nerve which he continues to touch. That Cobbett denounced; indeed that he fulminated; cannot be denied. But his highly complex and detailed analysis of the causes of poverty was developed through the years, oft repeated,

---

20 Political Register. 24/2/1821.
21 G. Himmelfarb. The Idea of Poverty. P. 207. P. James. Population Malthus. P. 346. J. R. Poynter. Society and Pauperism. Pp. 175-6 and 263.

and self-consciously opposed to Malthus's analysis of the same things. To point to a cause is to suggest a remedy. But it is not necessary to rely on this argument; for Cobbett never tired of telling us what he thought should be done. You do not have to agree with his arguments to recognise that he made them.

The opposing views of Malthus and Cobbett concerning the causes of poverty perhaps epitomise every debate that has ever taken place on this subject, or that ever could take place. Malthus took the view that any challenge to his theories that came from outside the ranks of the establishment was beneath contempt, and required no response. The foremost challenge of this sort came from William Cobbett, a large proportion of whose writings, on the other hand, formed a ceaselessly on-going refutation of Malthus.

It is rather sad, therefore, that we have no idea how Malthus might have responded to Cobbett's description of the valley of the Wiltshire Avon. Riding his horse through this valley in 1826, he wrote;-

"It seemed to me, that one way, and that, not, perhaps, the least striking, of exposing the folly, the stupidity, the inanity, the presumption, the insufferable emptiness and insolence and barbarity, of those numerous wretches, who have now the audacity to propose to *transport* the people of England, upon the principle of the monster MALTHUS, who has furnished the unfeeling oligarchs and their toad-eaters with the pretence, that *man has a natural propensity to breed faster than food can be raised for the increase*; it seemed to me, that one way of exposing this mixture of madness and blasphemy was, to take a look, now that the harvest is in, at the *produce*, the *mouths*, the *condition*, and *the changes that have taken place*, in a spot like this, which God has favoured with every good that he has to bestow upon man."[22]

In this valley, Cobbett came upon the village of Milton. On one of the farms in the parish of Milton, he made a calculation of the total produce, and, finding from the locals that the farm encompassed about a fifth of the parish, he made a rough computation of all the subsistence produced by the parish of Milton. Now, according to the population census, Milton contained 500 people, or 100 families. Thus, it became apparent that, according to Cobbett's diet, mentioned earlier – the minimum required to keep a family in working condition – the 100 families of Milton produced enough subsistence for 502 families. On the actual diet which these families had the misfortune to be living on, they actually produced enough for well over 1500 families.[23]

"And yet *those who do the work are half-starved.*"

Cobbett extended his calculations to cover the entire valley.

"Thus it must be, or much about thus, all the way down this fine and beautiful and interesting valley. There are 29 agricultural parishes....Now according to the 'POPULATION RETURN', the whole of these 29 parishes contain 9,116 persons; or, according to my division, 1,823 families. There is no reason to believe, that the proportion that we have seen in the case of MILTON does not hold good all the way through; that is, there is no reason to suppose, that the *produce* does not exceed the *consumption* in every other case in the same degree that it does in the case of MILTON. And, indeed, if I were to judge from the number of *houses* and the number of *ricks of corn*, I should suppose, that the excess was still greater in several of the other parishes. But, supposing it to be no greater; supposing the same proportion to continue all the way from WATTON RIVERS to STRATFORD DEAN, then here are 9,116 persons raising food and raiment sufficient for 45,580 persons, fed and lodged according to my scale; and sufficient for 136,740 persons according to the scale on which the unhappy labourers of this fine valley are now fed and lodged!"[24]

---

22 William Cobbett. Rural Rides. Penguin ed. P. 277.
23 Ibid. Pp. 282-286.
24 Ibid. Pp. 286-287.

This was not all. Almost incredibly, whilst producing this prodigious surplus, the inhabitants of this valley were actually under-employed!

"The villages down this Valley of Avon, and, indeed, it was the same in almost every part of this county, and in the North and West of Hampshire also, used to have great employment for the women and children in the *carding and spinning of wool for the making of broadcloth*. This was a very general employment for the women and girls; but it is *now wholly gone*...."[25]

The reason for its disappearance was that these operations, instead of being performed in the cottages, were now being done by machines in factories in the towns of Wiltshire. There remained only the agricultural work; and this could be done by the men and the boys, with only occasional help from the womenfolk. For most of the year, then, the women and girls had nothing to do.

Cobbett drew his conclusion.

"The state of this Valley seems to illustrate the infamous and really diabolical assertion of MALTHUS, which is, that the human kind have a NATURAL TENDENCY, *to increase beyond the means of subsistence for them*....Now, look at this Valley of AVON. Here the people raise nearly *twenty* times *as much food and clothing as they consume*. They raise five times as much, even according to my scale of living. They have been doing this for many, many years. They have been doing it *for several generations*. Where, then, is their NATURAL TENDENCY *to increase beyond the means of sustenance for them*?"[26]

No doubt Malthus would have had an answer to this. Sadly, we do not know what it was....

Section Three; The National Wealth

To what causes, then, did Cobbett attribute the poverty and distress of which he was such an acerbic witness?

There is a dominant theme running through much of Cobbett's writing – a theory concerning the suction of resources, away from some sections of the nation, towards other sections. The idea crops up time and again.

Famously, Cobbett labelled the metropolis of London the "Great Wen". A wen is a tumour; and a tumour kills its victim by draining increasing amounts of nutrient away from the vital organs towards itself. So it was, according to Cobbett, with London; as he stated in his open letter to George Canning, published in the Political Register in 1823.

"Let me, Sir, beg of you just to take a ride out round this WEN. When you come back you will tell me that you see the foundations and part structure of about *three thousand new houses*. I shall then ask you, whence can this arise? You will hardly have the face to tell me, that it is a proof of increasing *national prosperity*; and I have the vanity to think, that, after getting you to sit down, to forget, for a quarter of an hour, all the allurements of Whitehall, and all the botheration of its neighbourhood; I am really of opinion, that I should make you confess, that there is something radically wrong....In short, it is to suppose a man an idiot, to suppose him not to perceive, that this monstrous WEN is now sucking up the vitals of the country."[27]

London was the great Wen; but it was not the only one. Cobbett applied the term to any resort where were gathered together the fashionable members of the establishment and the elite. Bath was the classic example; Weymouth, Brighton, Tunbridge Wells and Scarborough all fell under the denomination of "devouring wens". Here is how Cobbett described Cheltenham.

---

25 Ibid. P. 294.
26 Ibid. P. 293.
27 G. D. H. Cole. The Opinions of William Cobbett. P. 88.

"Cheltenham....is what they call a *'watering place'*; that is to say, a place to which East India plunderers, West India floggers, English tax-gorgers, together with, gluttons, drunkards, and debauchees of all descriptions, *female* as well as male, resort, at the suggestion of silently laughing quacks, in the hope of getting rid of the bodily consequences of their manifold sins and iniquities. When I enter a place like this, I always feel disposed to squeeze up my nose with my fingers. It is nonsense, to be sure; but I conceit that every two-legged creature, that I see coming near me, is about to cover me with the poisonous proceeds of its impurities. To places like this come all that is knavish and all that is foolish and all that is base; gamesters, pickpockets, and harlots; young wife-hunters in search of rich and ugly old women, and young husband-hunters in search of rich and wrinkled or half-rotten men, the former resolutely bent, be the means what they may, to give the latter heirs to their lands and tenements. These things are notorious."[28]

This draining away of the resources of the country led to a rapid expansion of the capital outwards from the centre in nearly every direction. One of the places being built up that was encountered by Cobbett in his travels was Windsor Forest, "as bleak, as barren, and as villainous a heath as ever man set his eyes on".

"Here are *new enclosures* without end. And here are *houses* too, here and there, over the whole of this execrable tract of country. 'What!' Mr. CANNING will say, 'will you not allow that the owners of these new enclosures and these houses *know their own interests*? And are they not a proof of *an addition to the national capital?*'"

Cobbett would not concede that a transfer of resources from one part of the country to another could constitute an increase of national wealth. To Cobbett, the increase of national wealth resulted from production; the acacia plantations, which Cobbett thought should be laid out all over England, would represent "a prodigious creation of real and solid wealth....it would be a creation of money's worth things". But he deprecated the kind of wealth that was not a production, but merely a transfer, "which only takes the dinner from one man and gives it to another, which only gives an unnatural swell to a city or a watering place by beggaring a thousand villages."

To this latter class of wealth belonged the "improvements" on Windsor Forest.

"These new enclosures and houses arise out of the beggaring of the parts of the country distant from the vortex of the funds. The farm-houses have long been growing fewer and fewer; the labourers' houses fewer and fewer; and it is manifest to every man who has eyes to see with, that the villages are regularly wasting away. This is the case all over the parts of the kingdom where the tax-eaters do not haunt. In all the really agricultural villages and parts of the kingdom, there is a *shocking decay*; a great dilapidation and constant pulling down or falling down of houses....And all the *useful* people become less numerous. While these *spewy sands* and *gravel* near London are enclosed and built on, good lands in other parts are neglected. These enclosures and buildings are a *waste*; they are means *misapplied*; they are a proof of national decline and not of prosperity. To cultivate and ornament these villainous spots the produce and the population are drawn away from the good lands....As to this rascally heath, that which has ornamented it has brought misery on millions....A set of men who can look upon this as 'improvement', who can regard this as a proof of the *'increased capital of the country'*, are pretty fit, it must be allowed, to get the country out of its difficulties."

The same applied to the barracks which Cobbett found built upon Hounslow Heath.

"What an *'improvement'*! What an 'addition to the national capital'! Do you pretend that the nation is *richer*, because the means of making this barrack have been drawn away from the people in taxes?"[29]

28 Rural Rides. Penguin ed. P. 370.
29 Rural Rides. Penguin Ed. Pp. 35-37.

Cobbett, by this time, had clearly not understood what was meant by national wealth. The doctrine of national wealth can be traced far back into the seventeenth century, and there was a massive literature on the subject. Cobbett, in his busy life, was not up to date with his reading.

Let us, then, attempt to scratch the surface of this enormous subject of the national wealth; or, at least, that part of it which appears to have a bearing on Cobbett's description of the Avon valley.

At base, most of the writers on this subject purported to place subsistence farming in opposition to capitalist farming, with regard to the benefit accruing to "the nation" or "society". Here is Arthur Young, writing in 1774.

"Let us grant the fact, that when a family has just land enough for its subsistence, that portion will be well cultivated; what useful deductions are to be drawn from it relative to modern policy? Of what use in a modern kingdom would be a whole province thus divided, except for breeding men, which, singly taken, is a most useless purpose....

"It is of no consequence to say, that the little portion of land is perfectly cultivated, if its perfection is of no benefit to the state. Hence arises the necessity of distinguishing between the practice of agriculture as a mere means of subsistence – and practising it as a trade. The former is of no benefit to a modern state, the latter of infinite importance."

What was being aimed at was the introduction of the money economy.

"As money flows in, such little portions of land must disappear, by becoming united in large parcels, wherein agriculture is exercised as a trade – wherein products are raised in surplus – carried to market – sold – taxes paid – and the circulation of money active. Upon what consistent principles, therefore, can that cause be condemned, which works just the effects that are essentially necessary in a modern kingdom?"[30]

Writers on the national wealth lost few opportunities to blacken and vilify traditional agriculturalists, in order to justify the changes which they wished to see taking place.

"While the land-rents of Europe were very low," wroth Sir James Steuart in 1766, "numbers of the inhabitants appeared to be employed in agriculture; but were really no more than idle consumers of the produce of it." It was necessary "to remove the unnecessary load upon the land; those idle people, who eat up a part of the produce of labour without contributing to it."

A subsistence farmer, according to Steuart, is only useful to himself. "The state would lose nothing though (he) and his land were both swallowed up by an earthquake. The food and the consumers would both disappear together, without the least political harm to any body; consequently, such a species of agriculture is no benefit to a state.....Idle mouths are useful to themselves only, not to the state; consequently are not an object of care to the state, any farther than to provide employment; and their welfare (while they remain useless to others) is, in a free country, purely a matter of private concern."[31]

Arthur Young pursued much the same theme.

"You had before a population useless, because not industrious; who, instead of adding to the national wealth, only eat up the earth's produce. A province of such farmers would live only to themselves – they would consume nothing but the produce of their lands – they would not be able to buy manufactures – and they could pay no taxes, without an oppression which would reduce them to indigence and misery....Population, which, instead of adding to the wealth of a state, is a burthen to the state, is a pernicious population."[32]

Of course, it was all nonsense. We have seen the members of the agricultural community of Wigston Magna at their work. We have seen the massive variety of agricultural produce raised by

30   Arthur Young. Political Arithmetic. Pp. 48-49.
31   Sir James Steuart. An Inquiry into the Principles of Political Oeconomy. Pp. 55 and 92-93.
32   Arthur Young. Political Arithmetic Pp. 71 and 123.

them. Their village supported numerous tradesmen of various descriptions. They were able to bring in commodities from outside the village, notably salt and metal. They paid entry-fines and rents in many cases; they paid tithes; they no doubt paid their share of the land tax and the excise. And from the late 17th century they worked at framework-knitting in their cottages. The traditional agriculture, the destruction of which was being advocated by Young, Steuart, and many others, can hardly be considered an example of purely subsistence farming.

It was, however, a part of a largely locally-contained economic system, and it was this that frustrated the purposes of those whose concern was the wealth of the nation. Under the traditional systems, the bulk of the produce was consumed close to where it was produced. Before the Highland clearances, complained the Earl of Selkirk, the "produce was almost entirely consumed on the spot"; but, afterwards, "the produce of the country, instead of being consumed by a set of intrepid but indolent military retainers, is applied to the support of peaceable and industrious manufacturers." (sic) [33] Steuart could see a number of advantages in consumers living at a distance from where their food was produced. Transportation implies the necessity of converting produce into money; a proportion of which could then be drained off by the government in taxation.

"As long as the earth nourishes directly those who are upon her surface, as long as she delivers her fruits into the very hand of him who consumes them, there is no alienation, no occasion for money, consequently no possibility of establishing an extensive taxation."

Gathering people together into cities and feeding them from a distance was what gave the opportunity to tax.

The conversion of produce into money also allowed a greater proportion of it to be taken as rent.

"The raising of rents shows the increase of industry, as it swells the fund of subsistence consumed by the industrious, that is, by those who buy it."[34]

The idea that a greater proportion of the produce of an estate could be turned into a money rent, which could then be taxed, went back a long way. In the high taxing days of the Protectorate, such a scheme was already being put forward by agricultural writer Samuel Hartlib; and he was rewarded by Cromwell with a pension of £100.[35] It became a commonplace with writers on the national wealth that if agriculture were differently organised, a much greater cash surplus could be drawn from it. In those days, it was deemed both possible and desirable for the state to re-organise economy and society along lines more favourable to itself.

"It is the business of a statesman to judge of the expediency of different schemes of oeconomy, and by degrees to mould the minds of his subjects[36] so as to induce them, from the allurement of private interest, to concur in the execution of his plan."

"Every method" should be used "to prepare the people to relish the innovation."[37]

The innovation in question was nothing less than the re-organisation of the landscape. Steuart explained. Quoting Davenant, he states that the gross product of the corn lands of England amounted to £9 millions, whilst they were rented at only £2 millions. The gross produce of the pasture lands, on the other hand, was £12 millions, of which £7 millions were paid in rent. Rent Steuart defines as what is left of the gross produce after the deduction of the subsistence of the farmer, his family and his servants; the family's expences in manufactures and implements; and the profits of the farming operation. On grassland farms, this consumption amounted to only £5 millions out of £12 millions.

33 Earl of Selkirk. Observations on the Present State of the Highlands of Scotland. P. 131.
34 Sir James Steuart. An Inquiry into the Principles of Political Oeconomy. Pp. 59 and 55.
35 Walter Harte. Essays on Husbandry. P. 2.
36 Statesmen do not have subjects.
37 Sir James Steuart. An Inquiry into the Principles of Political Oeconomy. Pp. 17 and 25.

On arable however, out of the gross produce of £9 millions, £7 millions were consumed on the spot. Grazing, therefore, was far more conducive to national wealth than tillage.

The difference between the rent of corn land and pasture "must proceed from the greater proportion of labouring and other inhabitants employed in consequence of tillage; which make the expences of it far greater than that of pasture."

The idea of national wealth, then, was largely about the surplus produce of the countryside.

"Must not this of necessity be employed in the nourishment, and for the use of those whom we have called the *free hands*; who may be employed in manufactures, trades, or in any other way according to the taste of the times?.... The more a country is in tillage, the *more* it is inhabited, and the smaller is the proportion of *free hands* for all the services of the state. The more a country is in pasture, the *less* it is inhabited, but the greater is the proportion of *free hands*."

Steuart provides an illustration.

"I have a corn farm where I maintain ten horses and four servants for the cultivation alone; at the end of the year I find my surplus equal to 40l. sterling. If, by throwing my grounds into grass, I can dismiss three servants and eight horses, and at the end of the year raise my surplus to 50l. sterling, who doubts of my doing it?"[38]

The other method frequently used to reduce the number of hands and mouths necessary for a farming operation was to throw the small farms into large ones – something which was greatly favoured by Arthur Young.

"In a great farm there is but one idle person, in a small one there is the same. Sure, therefore, the supernumerary farmers are a mere burthen to the state; an idea applicable to everyone who stands in the place of a labourer without performing his office, but consumes those products that ought to go to market....I have before mentioned that application of the soil to be most beneficial, which yields the greatest neat profit in the market."

For this reason it was necessary to clear the human dross from the countryside.

"The fewer employed (consistent with good husbandry) the better; for then the less product is intercepted before it reaches the markets, and you may have so many the more for manufacturers, sailors and soldiers."[39]

Young, the arch defender of the modern agriculture on the grounds that it provided more employment, was, in reality, in favour of it because it provided less employment.

Here is a revealing passage from Sir James Steuart.

"A Machiavelian stands up (of such there are some in every country) and proposes, instead of multiplying the inhabitants, by rendering agriculture more operose, to diminish their number by throwing a quantity of corn-fields into grass. What is the intention of agriculture, says he, but to nourish a state? By our operose method of plowing and sowing, one half of the whole produce is consumed by those who raise it; whereas by having a great part of our island in pasture, one half of the husbandmen may be saved. Pray what do you propose to do with those whom you intend to make idle? replies a citizen. Let them betake themselves to industry. But industry is sufficiently, nay more than sufficiently, stocked already. If, says Machiavel, the supernumerary husbandmen be thrown out of a way of living, they may go where they please; we have no occasion for them, nor for anyone who lives to feed himself alone....If I propose a reform, it is to augment only the surplus, upon which all the state, except the husbandman, are fed; if the surplus, after the reform, is greater than at present, the plan is good, although 250 of our farmers should thereby be forced to starve for hunger."

Steuart paid a very feeble lip service indeed to humanity.

---

38 Sir James Steuart. An Inquiry into the Principles of Political Oeconomy. Pp. 53-55 and 135.
39 Arthur Young. Political Arithmetic. Pp. 293 and 296.

"Though no man is, I believe, capable to reason in so inhuman a style, and though the revolution here proposed be an impossible supposition, if meant to be executed all at once, the same effects however must be produced, in every country where we see corn-fields by degrees turned into pasture; the change is gradual only, industry is not overstocked anywhere, and subsistence may be drawn from other countries."[40]

On the contrary, there were those, as we have seen, who did indeed reason thus, and there have been many more since in various parts of the globe. Full employment outside agriculture had always been the chimera of the propagandist. Even Samuel Fortrey, as early as 1669, admitted that manufacturing was not soaking up all the hands set adrift from the farms, though it did not help his argument. Even Daniel Defoe, in 1704, admitted the same thing. By Steuart's time, it was already becoming obvious that the trades in many towns, like Exeter and Nottingham, were saturated with displaced countrymen; the limits of a trade being prescribed by the market and not the supply of labour. John Arbuthnot's statement that unemployment was nothing more than a momentary misfortune was a patent absurdity.[41] So whether starving the husbandman slowly and out of sight was any less inhuman than starving him on the spot becomes the question.

Such arguments as these were used by a plethora of writers. It hardly needs pointing out that Adam Smith's *magnum opus* was entitled the Wealth of Nations. But perhaps the theory of the agricultural surplus was most openly and explicitly stated in the Earl of Selkirk's work on the Highland clearances;[42] which Francis Horner, its reviewer in the Edinburgh Review of 1805, thought had "claims to a permanent reputation and utility", being "a large contribution to the theory of political economy, of most satisfactory deductions and general conclusions." Malthus himself, no less, eulogised this agricultural surplus which, when extracted from the countryside, constituted the national wealth; though it is not easy to see how he might have reconciled this with his theory of the permanent pressure of population on subsistence. He writes of "the very great benefit which society derives from that surplus produce of the land which, in the progress of society, falls mainly to the landlord in the shape of rent...." This, Malthus calls "a bountiful gift of Providence."

"Must we not....allow that rent is the natural result of a most inestimable quality in the soil, which God has bestowed on man – the quality of being able to maintain more persons than are necessary to work it? Is it not a part....of that general surplus produce from the land, which has been justly stated to be the source of all power and enjoyment; and without which, in fact, there would be no cities, no military and naval force, no arts, no learning, none of the finer manufactures, none of the conveniences and luxuries of foreign countries, and none of that cultivated and polished society, which not only elevates and dignifies individuals, but which extends its beneficial influence through the whole mass of the people?"[43]

So, whatever William Cobbett may have thought, when Canning and his like looked at the thousands of houses under construction in the Great Wen, or the enclosures on the "execrable tract" of Windsor Forest, or the barracks on Hounslow Heath, and saw them as additions to the national wealth; even though built with resources sucked out of the countryside, or rather, perhaps, for that very reason, they were right; at least in the sense in which the term had been used by the writers of the previous century and a half.

At length, Cobbett cottoned on; discussing the subject of national wealth during his account of the Avon Valley from 1826.

---

40 Sir James Steuart. An Inquiry into the Principles of Political Oeconomy. Pp. 132-133.
41 John Arbuthnot. An Inquiry into the Connection between the present advanced Price of Provisions and the Size of Farms. P. 133.
42 Earl of Selkirk. Observations on the Present State of the Highlands of Scotland.
43 T. R. Malthus. Principles of Political Economy. Pp. 207 and 147-148.

"I have never been able clearly to comprehend what the beastly Scotch *feelosophers* mean by their '*national wealth*'; but, as far as I can understand them, this is their meaning; that national wealth means, that which is *left* of the products of the country over and above what is *consumed*, or *used*, by those whose labour causes the products to be. This being the notion, it follows, of course, that the *fewer* poor devils you can screw the products out of, the richer the nation is."

Cobbett atoned for his slowness of comprehension by his acuteness in asking the question studiously avoided by all the writers on national wealth. If the surplus removed from the countryside constitutes the national wealth, where does it go? Where does it reside? In whose hands is it and who has the benefit of it? Clearly not the state, for the government was chronically insolvent, dragging out a hand to mouth existence, and surviving only because of the certainty of incoming taxes to pay the next instalment of the interest on the national debt. The government only acted as a channel through which this national wealth was directed to its recipients.

"What, then, is to be done with this *over-produce*? Who is to have it? Is it to go to pensioners, placemen, tax-gatherers, dead-weight people, soldiers, gendarmerie, police-people, and, in short, to whole millions *who do no work at all*? Is this a cause of '*national wealth*'? Is a nation made *rich* by taking the food and clothing from those who create them, and giving them to those who do nothing of any use? Aye, but, this *over-produce* may be given to *manufacturers*, and to those who supply the food-raisers with what they want besides food. Oh! but this is merely an *exchange* of one valuable thing for another valuable thing; it is an exchange of labour in Wiltshire for labour in Lancashire; and, upon the whole, here is *no over-production*. If the produce be *exported*, it is the same thing; it is an *exchange* of one sort of labour for another. But, *our course* is, that there is not an *exchange*; that those who labour, no matter in what way, have a large part of their labour *taken away*, and receive nothing *in exchange*. If the over-produce of this Valley of Avon were given, by the farmers, to the weavers in Lancashire, to the iron and steel chaps in Warwickshire, and to other makers and sellers of useful things, there would come an abundance of all these useful things into this valley from Lancashire and other parts; but if, as is the case, the over-produce goes to the fundholders, the dead-weight, the soldiers, the lord and lady and master and miss pensioners and sinecure people; if the over-produce goes to them, as a very great part of it does, nothing, not even the parings of one's nails, *can come back to the valley in exchange*. And can this operation, then, add to the '*national wealth*'? It adds to the '*wealth*' of those who carry on the affairs of state; it fills their pockets, those of their relatives and dependants; it fattens all tax-eaters; but it can give no *wealth* to the 'nation', which means, *the whole of the people*....DEVIZES is the market-town to which the corn goes from the greater part of this Valley. If, when a wagon-load of wheat goes off in the morning, the wagon came back at night loaded with cloth, salt, or something or other, *equal in value to the wheat*, except what might be necessary to leave with the shopkeeper as his profit; then, indeed, the people might see the wagon go off without tears in their eyes. But, now, they see it go *to carry away*, and to bring *next to nothing in return*."[44]

Section Four; The Muck-worm and the Blood-sucker

The system that was responsible for carrying away the so-called surplus from the productive parts of the country Cobbett denominated "The Thing". Of this "Thing", he was no admirer.

"The taxing, funding and paper-money system has always, with me, been an object of hatred. From the moment I understood it, I detested it. It was in 1803 that I began to examine into it. In that very year I predicted that, unless it were put a stop to in time, it would make this the most miserable, enslaved and contemptible nation in the world. From that day to this, I have been at war against this all-corrupting and all-degrading system. And I have lived to see the system pushed along to its utmost

44 Rural Rides. Penguin ed. Pp. 291-292.

extent, and to see the consequences in a greater mass of ruin and of human wretchedness than was ever before witnessed."[45]

Here is Cobbett's account of the origins and progress of this system, contained in his Letters to the People of Salisbury, which he entitled Paper against Gold.

"Some people seem to regard the Bank of England as being as old as the Church of England, at least, and some appear to have full as much veneration for it. The truth is, however, that the Bank of England is a mere human institution, arising out of causes having nothing miraculous, or supernatural, about them; and that both the institution and the agents who carry it on, are as mortal as any other thing and any other men, in this or any other country. THE BANK, as it is called, had its origin in the year 1694, that is, a hundred and sixteen years ago; and it arose thus; the then King, WILLIAM III, who had come from Holland, had begun *a war* against France, and, wanting money to carry it on, an act was passed....to invite people to make voluntary advances to the government of the sum of 1,500,000 pounds, and for securing the payment of the interest, and also for securing the re-payment of the principal, *taxes* were laid upon beer, ale, and other liquors. Upon condition of 1,200,000 l. of this money being advanced within a certain time, the subscribers to the loan were to be incorporated; and, as the money was advanced in due time, the incorporation took place, and the lenders of the money were formed into a trading company, called 'THE GOVERNOR AND COMPANY OF THE BANK OF ENGLAND'. In time, when more and more and more money had been borrowed by the government, in this way of mortgage upon the taxes, there grew up a thing called the *Stocks*, or the *Funds*....but the Bank Company remained under its primitive name, and as the *debt* of the nation increased, this Company increased in *riches* and in consequence.

"Thus, you see, and it is well worthy of your attention, the Bank had its rise *in war* and *taxation*."[46]

Similar considerations applied to what became known as the funding system, according to Cobbett merely another name for the national debt. The origin of this system pre-dated the founding of the Bank of England by just two years; and the Bank quickly became its central feature. Here is Cobbett's description of its origin and of its workings.

"Soon after the ENGLISH REVOLUTION; that is to say, soon after our ancestors, who had too much spirit to be *dragooned* out of their liberty and their property, had driven away king James the Second, and had brought over the Prince of Orange and made him king in his stead, and had, at the same time, taken measures for stripping the family of Stuart of the crown for ever and putting it on the head of his present Majesty's family; soon after this Revolution, the existence of Funds, Stocks, and a National Debt began, under the auspices of this same Prince of Orange, who was then become our king William III, and who appears to have lost but very little time in discovering, the effectual way of obtaining money from the English, without resorting, as the Stuarts had, to those means, the use of which had ever and anon, excited commotions against them; which had brought one of them to the scaffold; which, at last, after driving another from the land, had for ever stripped them of their crown....

"William the Third was hardly seated upon the throne before a war was begun against France, and in the 4th year of his reign, being the year 1692, an act of parliament was passed imposing 'certain Rates and Duties upon Beer, Ale and other Liquors, for *securing certain Recompences and Advantages* in the said Act mentioned, to such Persons as shall voluntarily advance the sum of *Ten Hundred Thousand Pounds* towards carrying on the *War against France*'....These are the very words; and fatal words they were to England.

---

45 Political Register. 17/5/1820
46 Political Register. 1/9/1810.

"In the body of this Act, it is enacted, that the persons, who shall advance the million of pounds shall, out of the rates and duties imposed by the act, receive a certain *interest*, or annual payment, for the use of the money so advanced. They were to have, and they had, their money secured to them by way of *annuity for life or lives*; and, they were to have certain advantages in cases of survivorship; and the annuities were to be redeemed upon certain conditions and at certain times. But, it will be quite useless for us to load our subject with a multitude of words, to ring the changes upon all the quaint terms, which, as appertaining to these matters, have, one would think, been made use of for no other purpose than that of confusing the understandings of plain men. The light wherein to view this transaction is this; The Government was....got into a war with France; and for the alledged purpose of pushing on the war with '*vigour*' (it is odd enough that the very word was made use of, just as it is now) they borrowed a million pounds of individuals, and, at the same time, imposed taxes upon the whole nation for the purpose of paying the interest so borrowed; or, in other words, the nation's taxes, or property, were *mortgaged* to the lenders of the million pounds.

"The lenders of the money, who, in time, came to be called *fund-holders*, or *stock-holders*, did, as the work of lending and fund-making advanced, make their loans in various ways, and the bargains between them and the government were of great variety in their terms, and in the denominations made use of; but it was always the same thing in *effect*; the government borrowed the money of individuals; it mortgaged taxes for the payment of the interest; and those individuals received for their money, promises, or engagements, no matter in what shape, which enabled them to demand annually, or quarterly, the share of interest due to each of them; and any single parcel of interest, so received, is what is, in the queer language of the funding trade, called a '*dividend*'."[47]

On the one side, governments were seldom in a position to repay these loans; on the other, lenders soon found it more to their advantage, especially during the many periods of plentiful money and investment hunger, to leave their money out at interest at the taxpayer's expence, than to have it back. One of the consequences of this is that we are still paying today for William III's pointless and unnecessary personal vendetta against the French king. Another is that, over a long period, the national debt accumulated, at times gradually, at other times rapidly, as Cobbett demonstrated in the following table.

On the increase of the debt

When Queen Anne succeeded to the throne	1701.	£16,394,702
When George I succeeded to the throne	1714.	£54,145,363
When George II succeeded to the throne	1727.	£52,092,235
When George III succeeded to the throne	1760.	£146,682,844
After the American War.		£257,213,043
After the Anti-Jacobin War	1801.	£579,931,447
January last.	(1810)	£811,898,082

Cobbett commented;-

"PITT, it is well known, grew into favour with the nation in consequence of his promises and his plan to pay off the National Debt; and this same PITT, who found that Debt 257 millions, left it upwards of 600 millions, after having, for twenty years, had the full power of managing all the resources of the nation; after having, for nearly the whole of that time, had the support of three fourths, if not more, of the Members of the House of Commons; after having, of course, adopted whatever measures, he thought proper, during the whole of that time. He found the Debt *two hundred*

---

47 Political Register. 8/9/1810.

and fifty odd millions, and he left it *six hundred* and fifty odd. This was what was done for England by that PITT."[48]

Here is William Cobbett's account of the raising of a government loan.

"Let us take a plain common-sense view of one of these *loaning* transactions. Let us suppose, then, that the Government wants a *loan*, that is, wants to *borrow money*, to the amount of a million of pounds. It gives out its wishes to this effect, and, after the usual ceremony upon such occasions, the loan is made, that is, the money is lent, by Messrs. Muckworm and Company....Well; what does Muckworm get in return? Why, *his name is written in a book; against his name is written that he is entitled to receive interest for a million of money*; which book is kept at the Bank Company's house, or shop, in Threadneedle Street, London. And thus it is that Muckworm '*puts a million of money into the Funds*'. 'Well', you will say, 'but *what becomes of the money?*' Why the Government *expends it*, to be sure, what should become of it? Very few people borrow money for the purpose of locking it up in their drawers or chests. 'What? Then, the money all *vanishes*; and *nothing remains in lieu of it but the lender's name written in a book?*' Even so; and this, my good neighbours, is the way that '*money is put into the Funds*.'

"But the most interesting part of the transaction remains to be described. Muckworm, who is as wise as he is rich, takes special care not to be a fund-holder himself; and, as is always the case, he loses no time in *selling his stock*, that is to say, his *right to receive the interest of the million of pounds*. These funds, as we have seen, have no bodily existence, either in the shape of money or of bonds or of certificates or of anything else that can be seen or touched. They have a being merely in *name*. They mean, in fact, a *right to receive interest*; and, a man, who is said to *possess or to have, a thousand pounds' worth of stock*, possesses, in reality, nothing but *the right of receiving the interest of a thousand pounds*. When, therefore, Muckworm *sells* his million's worth of stock, he sells the right of receiving the interest upon the million of pounds which he lent to the government. But, the way in which sales of this sort are effected is by parcelling out the stock to little purchasers, every one of whom buys as much as he likes; he *has his name written in the book* for so much, instead of the name of Muckworm and Company; and, when Muckworm has sold the whole, his name is crossed out, and the names of the persons, to whom he has sold, remain in the book."[49]

What Cobbett forgot to mention in this account, was that the sum of a million was only a nominal sum. Muckworm would offer a price, somewhat below a million, for a million's worth of stock, or the right to receive interest on a million. By the time Muckworm sold his stock, the price would normally have risen to a premium. This was planned, or even engineered; and massive profits were the usual, though not the invariable, result. Under these circumstances, with public money, collected by taxation, being funnelled through government, by this and other related methods, into the pockets of individuals, and often in return for very little; it would have been surprising indeed had an industry not grown up based upon it.

The industry, centred on the City of London, came to be known as the monied or financial interest; and Cobbett described it as comprising the "numerous and powerful body of loan-jobbers, directors, brokers, contractors and farmers-general, which has been engendered by the excessive amount of the public debt". At its centre was the Bank of England, with its board of directors, most of whom were members of the wealthy merchant houses in the City. There were other, similar, incorporations, such as the East India Company, whose headquarters were in Leadenhall Street; the South Sea Company and the Sierra Leone Company. There were seventy other banks in London, some specialising in financing trade, whilst others, mainly in the West End, acted as the repositories for the surplus funds of the great landlords. These London banks maintained close contacts with the

---

48 Political Register. 12/9/1810.
49 Political Register. 8/9/1810.

202

hundreds of banks in the provinces – the country banks. Banking owed its existence largely to the investment opportunities afforded by the national debt, and the increasing amount of liquidity in the country, the consequence of agricultural change, rising rents, and taxation; and the proliferation of banks went hand in hand with the augmentation of the debt. Working in the City also were 700 licensed brokers, and probably many unlicensed ones, who acted as financial middlemen at the Royal Exchange; whilst the great dealers in shares and government debt operated at Capel Court. The business of the City included bullion dealing, bills of exchange, foreign transactions, the stocks of the great companies, insurance, and contracting to supply government with the provisions necessary for the army, the navy, and the civil service.[50] All the most profitable business was connected with the British government. The buying and selling of government securities went on at all times. But the jewel in the crown was the contracting of new loans; and although there occurred attempts to continue this system in peace time, it mostly happened during wars. The great financial middlemen who were allowed to interpose themselves between the government and the lenders became the stars of the City.

In this way there came about an inextricable intertwining of the financial interest with the government. Those who were obsessed with money latched themselves on to those who were obsessed with power. Edmund Burke, quoted by Cobbett, noted that avarice was a very destructive public vice, but that it was only the vice of ambition that allowed avarice to operate.[51] The whole process can be well illustrated by the dealings of Prime Minister William Pitt, who represents ambition, with merchant bankers Boyd, Benfield and Company, who represent avarice.

Paul Benfield was an East India adventurer, who made a fortune by dubious means in India. For his misconduct there, even the East India Company had occasion to punish him more than once. He was described as "exacting, dissatisfied and ambitious", and that by a friend of his. Edmund Burke, who was no friend, called him "a criminal, who, long since, ought to have fattened the region kites with his offal". Benfield became the chief creditor of the Nawab of Carnatic; the latter defaulting, Benfield became unable to satisfy his own creditors, and, returning to England, sought help and protection from William Pitt and his government.[52]

The resulting deal which was struck between Benfield and the government, by which the latter agreed to take over the debts owed to Benfield, was fulminated against by Edmund Burke in a speech to the House of Commons in February 1785, and the fulminations were later quoted by Cobbett in the Political Register.

What Benfield gave to Pitt in return, according to Burke, was the support of his enormous wealth and influence in the general election of 1784. Benfield, by the judicious use of his wealth, had himself, the nomination of eight M.P.s. But in addition to that, he lent the services of his agent, a Mr. Atkinson,[53] who, "for your minister….submitted to keep a sort of public office or counting house, where the whole business of the last general election was managed by the direct agent and attorney of Benfield." Benfield became very rich in the process, and was "enfeoffed with an estate, which, in the comparison, effaces the splendour of the nobility of Europe."[54]

---

50 E.g. S. R. Cope. The Goldsmids and the Development of the London Money Market. In Economica 1942. P. 181.

51 Political Register. 28/4/1810

52 S. R. Cope. Walter Boyd Merchant Banker. Pp. 37-39. Political Register. 12/12/1807.

53 Was this Mr. Jasper Atkinson, shadowy financial figure and one of Castlereagh's backroom boys? Or a relative?

54 Edmund Burke quoted in the Political Register. 28/4/1810 and 12/12/1807.

Cobbett explained the process in terms of the "seats bought by Benfield for insuring the Minister votes, in return for which the Minister was giving him the public money by hundreds of thousands of pounds, part of our enormous debt."[55]

Pitt, to a large extent therefore, owed his position to Paul Benfield.

Walter Boyd was a Scottish banker, operating in Paris. By 1792, the situation in revolutionary France had become too hot to handle, and Boyd moved to London. There, a partnership was formed between the financial expertise of Boyd, and the capital wealth of Benfield; and the result was the merchant bank of Boyd, Benfield and Co. But it was not just his wealth which Benfield brought to the partnership; it was also his influence in government. And the support of William Pitt allowed the new company aggressively to displace the established loan-contractors of the early 1790s. Government backing and financial guarantees enabled Boyd to conclude a lucrative loan agreement with the Austrian government. A scrupulous adherence to law was not a feature of the dealings between Boyd, Benfield and Co. and the government of William Pitt. There were rumours of secret loans to Pitt without parliamentary authority already by 1795. Later that year the contract for the new loan was awarded to Boyd and his partners without any competition being allowed from other houses. A bribe presented to Daniel Giles, Governor of the Bank of England, facilitated the process. Whilst Boyd was in possession of the stock, before he had the opportunity of selling it on, Pitt delivered to the House of Commons a message from the king that the government intended to negotiate peace-terms with France. Of course, the negotiation came to nothing; but any rumours of peace were bound to raise the price of the funds, and the premium on Boyd's loan, already seven per cent, rose to thirteen per cent. As if this were not enough, the Morning Post reported the strange behaviour of the Commissioners for the reduction of the National Debt, whose job it was to buy stock on behalf of the British government, in order to keep up the price of the funds. At the time the loan was making, the Commissioners held off from buying the principal stock, resuming before Boyd sold his stock, and thereby greatly increasing his profits. One of the Commissioners was Daniel Giles, Governor of the Bank of England.

The Morning Post made the following observation.

"The annual subsistence of one hundred and fifty thousand inhabitants of Great Britain has been at one blow, given by Mr. Pitt to gorge the voracious maw of a gang of Loan Contractors."

A committee of the House of Commons, in February 1796, put the same thing rather differently in the following resolution.

"That in every part of the Transaction of the late Loans, the Public Interest has been sacrificed by the Chancellor of the Exchequer; and that the Profit to the contributors, at the Expense of the Nation, has been so exorbitantly swelled, as to have risen....to the enormous and incredible Sum of Two Million One Hundred and Sixty thousand Pounds Sterling."

Despite the obvious truth of most of this resolution, Pitt used his influence in the House of Commons, of which both Boyd and Benfield were members, to get it heavily defeated.[56]

Nothing daunted, Pitt granted the loan of the following year also to Boyd, Benfield and Co., again without allowing any competition. In the House of Commons, a merchant M.P. objected.

"It was, to all intents and purposes, a shut up Loan, and competition, to his knowledge, had been offered by 15 or 16 respectable Houses in the City, but they had received no answer nor any reason why....He wished to know....why this exclusive right to all Government Loans was invested in the present Contractors."[57]

---

55   Political Register. 28/4/1810.
56   S. R. Cope. Walter Boyd, Merchant Banker. Pp. 75 and 81-6.
57   Ibid. P. 102.

An impartial observer might be forgiven at this point for thinking that Pitt's government was in existence for the sole purpose of channelling the national wealth into the coffers of Boyd, Benfield and Co.

But Boyd allowed his avarice to drive him on too far. The loan of 1796 did not sell as well as previous ones, and instead of drawing in his horns Boyd acted the bull. He hung on to his stock in the confident belief that Pitt would be induced to make peace with the French, and so raise the price of the funds. He reckoned without the Portland Whigs, whose support for Pitt was conditional upon a vigorous campaign being conducted against French democratic principles. Pitt, therefore, could not, in 1796, conjure enormous profits for his client bank; but he nevertheless did all he could to help it out of its resulting difficulties. Amongst a series of the most outrageous improprieties and illegalities, there stands out the curious incident of the secret loan. The government took out the loan of 1796 supposedly because it could not conduct the war without it. Boyd, who was lending the money, was now in financial difficulties, and was unable to pay a contracted instalment of £40,000. Pitt and Dundas took this sum illicitly from the Navy Fund; they lent it to Boyd interest-free, who was then enabled to lend it, at interest, to the government.[58] But the scam came to light, and here are Cobbett's later comments upon it.

"We have seen a minister lending the public money, *without interest*, to members of parliament, without the approbation of parliament or of the king, without consulting his colleagues in the cabinet, and without making any minute or leaving any record or trace of the transaction; and when the deed was, by accident, detected, we heard not, in the House of Commons, a single voice to censure him, but, on the contrary, we heard those holders of the purse-strings; those faithful 'guardians of the people's rights and property'; we heard them unanimously join in passing, almost by acclamation, an act, a *law*, to declare that the minister should be, for ever after, held to be perfectly innocent of what it was notorious that he had done!"[59]

"Ours is a stock-jobbing government", raged Cobbett, yet again. "All its favours are reserved for the crew who deal in money."

Just as a rotting carcase attracts large numbers of a certain species of fly; so the easy availability of public money for private purposes attracted large numbers of a certain species of man.

In banking, any wealthy man with moderate talents could rapidly increase his fortune with ease; and the greatest obstacle to this accretion was his own avarice, if it became excessive. Henry Thornton went into banking because it was physically easy, and took up little time; his fragile health rendering him incapable of the routine exertions of proper mercantile work. Cobbett was supremely disparaging about the talents of the founder of Coutts' Bank.

"COUTTS appears to have been a Scotchman, who came to London about sixty or more years ago. The means by which he became a banker; how he came to be a banker to the King and Family; how he got his money together; these are matters of little interest; for we daily, under this system of frauds and loans and jobs and taxes, see beggars, and stupid beggars too, become richer than nobles, in a much shorter space than it took Coutts to get his mass of money together."[60]

Though eulogised in certain quarters, in general, those who made up the monied interest were not well thought of.[61] This is what the Earl of Chatham, ironically William Pitt's father, told the House of Lords, already in 1770.

"There is a set of men, my Lords, in the City of London, who are known to live in riot and luxury upon the plunder of the ignorant, the innocent, the helpless; upon that part of the community which

---

58 Ibid. Pp. 121-122.
59 Political Register. 13/12/1806
60 Political Register. 30/3/1822.
61 N. Ferguson. The World's Banker. Pp. 11-15.

stands most in need of, and best deserves, the care and protection of the legislature. To me, my Lords, whether they be miserable jobbers of 'Change Alley, or the lofty Asiatic plunderers of Leadenhall Street, they are all equally detestable. I care but little whether a man walks on foot, or is drawn by eight horses, or six horses, if his luxury be supported by the plunder of the country, I despise and detest him. My Lords, while I had the honour of serving his Majesty, I never ventured to look at the Treasury but at a distance; it is a business I am unfit for, and to which I never could have submitted. The little I know of it has not served to raise my opinion of what is vulgarly called the 'Monied Interest'; I mean, that blood-sucker, that muck-worm that calls itself the friend of government; that pretends to serve this or that administration, and may be purchased, on the same terms, by any administration; advances money to government and takes special care of its own emoluments. Under this description, I include the whole race of commissaries, jobbers, contractors, clothiers and remitters...."[62]

It was the business of Isaac Barre, Paymaster-General at the end of the American War, to deal with the whole race of contractors who supplied the armed services. He described them as "animals of a greedy nature, always craving and never satisfied, their appetites for dishonest lucre and foul gain were as insatiable as their consciences were easily satisfied."[63]

But the great loan-makers were a race apart. Cobbett's charge of lack of talent will not stick here, for they were all possessed of a profound and compendial knowledge of financial affairs, and the most extensive expertise in profiting from it. Nathan Rothschild, for example, was remarkable for his mental capacity; he knew the currency exchange rates from every nation, and was said to be able to retain in his head the figures from all his past transactions.[64]

But, abilities apart, what all the great contractors possessed in common was an overriding obsession with making money, which bordered on derangement. Discussing Alexander Baring, Cobbett percipiently explained this obsession in terms of upbringing and psychology.

"I can easily conceive an apology for Mr. Baring. Men brought up from their infancy, to count their gains, must be expected to feel most sensibly any measure by which their gains are diminished. They may write and advise what is hostile to the interests of their country, and yet be very honest men; because they see things through a false medium. Their gains they identify with their country's good; and when their gains are diminished by any measure, they naturally conclude that such measure is injurious to the country."[65]

The paramount importance of money to these people is well demonstrated by the suicide of Abraham Goldsmid. Goldsmid's firm was one of the principal contractors for the loan of 1810. Unusually, for various reasons, the loan went wrong, and the stock fell to a discount of six per cent.

"Goldsmidt was losing 6 per cent upon his part of so immense a transaction as that of a loan of 14 millions....The thought of such a loss was more than his mind could bear; which latter is by no means wonderful, seeing that his soul was set upon gain; that all his views and notions of happiness centred in wealth. The lover, whose passion is too strong for his reason, destroys himself, because the object of that passion is dearer to him than life. Goldsmidt destroys himself, because wealth is dearer to him than life."[66]

Nathan Rothschild's single-minded pursuit of financial gain clearly had its origin in the Jewish ghetto of Frankfurt, where he was brought up. The Jewish quarter was squalid and overcrowded, and its inhabitants suffered a number of degrading civil disabilities and disqualifications. Rothschild's father, for example, was not permitted to own any property outside the ghetto. One merchant in

---

62 Quoted in Political Register. 25/1 1806.
63 P. Ziegler. The Sixth Great Power. P. 40.
64 N. Ferguson. The World's Banker. P. 281.
65 Political Register. 20/2/1808.
66 Paper against Gold. P. 153.

particular thought it beneath his dignity to do business with Nathan Meyer Rothschild.[67] The humiliations of his formative years, one might strongly suspect, were what gave Rothschild his unrivalled drive and desire to succeed. For him, the acquisition of wealth equalled happiness. At a dinner at Ham House, in Surrey, in 1834, a fellow guest remarked to Rothschild;-

"I hope that your children are not too fond of money and business, to the exclusion of more important things. I am sure you would not wish that."

"I am sure I should wish that", replied Rothschild. "I wish them to give mind, and soul, and heart, and body, and everything to business. That is the way to be happy."[68]

What was true of Goldsmid was true of Rothschild also. Outside of money-making, there was simply no life worth living.

"After dinner I usually have nothing to do. I do not read books. I do not play cards. I do not go to the theatre, my only pleasure is my business...."[69]

The suspicion that Rothschild's business drive resulted from feelings of inferiority is reinforced by the pronounced competitive edge of his psyche.

"My success all turned on one maxim", he told his fellow-diners at Ham House. "I said, I can do what another man can, and so I am a match for the man with the patterns (the Frankfurt merchant who refused to do business with him), and for all the rest of them."[70]

"His aim", wrote an observer, "was to arrive at his aim more quickly and more effectually than all others and to steer towards it with all his energy."

There was something less than human about this single-mindedness.

"There is a rigidity and tension in his features....Eyes are usually denominated the windows of the soul, but here you would conclude that the windows are false ones, or that there was no soul to look out of them. There comes not one pencil of light from the interior, neither is there one scintillation of that which comes from without reflected in any direction. The whole puts you in mind of a skin to let, and you wonder why it stands upright without at least something in it."[71]

To Rothschild, and to his colleagues and competitors of the financial interest, money occupied that very personal place in the psyche more usually taken up by religion. It was said of Alexander Baring that "he would much rather be summoned before the bench of bishops to be questioned about his belief in the doctrinal points of religion than appear before the commissioners under the property tax."[72]

"A businessman's religion is the same the world over. The businessman's....office is his church; his desk is his pew, his copybook is his bible, his warehouse his holiest of holies, the bourse bell his bell, his gold his God, his credit his faith."

"Money is the God of our time and Rothschild is his prophet."[73]

So wrote Heinrich Heine in 1841. The almost religious zeal of this competitive acquisitive drive transcended considerations of national interest and patriotism. The financial interest was, in any case, largely cosmopolitan. Few of the great contractors considered themselves as owing allegiance to England, either by origin or religion. The Barings were originally from Holland. The Goldsmids were Jews from Amsterdam. Walter Boyd was a Scotsman who set up his banking operation in Paris. And the House of Rothschild, Jews from Frankfurt, was already a multinational concern at the time

---

67 N. Ferguson. The World's Banker. P. 8.
68 Memoirs of Thomas Fowell Buxton. Pp. 160-162.
69 N. Ferguson. The World's Banker. P. 115.
70 Ibid. Pp. 160-2.
71 Ibid. P. 281.
72 P. Ziegler. The Sixth Great Power. P. 90.
73 N. Ferguson. The World's Banker. Pp. 190 and 18.

when Nathan was coming to prominence in England. For all of these and many more, England was merely the prey, to which they were attracted because of the funding system, and the resulting ease with which massive profits could be made.

"It is always the same game that these Rothschilds play, in order to enrich themselves at the cost of the land they exploit. The financiers are the nation's worst enemies."[74]

So wrote Ludwig Borne. The Rothschilds themselves put the same thing rather differently.

"There is luck attached to everything English. Everything touching them turns out happily.... England is our breadbasket."[75]

This tendency did not escape William Cobbett.

"Men engaged in commerce, that is to say, in close and interested connections with foreign countries, must have their local affections divided; and, it would be marvellous indeed, if *some* out of a great number, did not prefer the safety of another country to that of their own, especially when their profession is such as necessarily to have narrowed their minds to questions of individual and immediate profit and loss. These are very fit advisers in matters relating to war, or to treaties...."[76]

The financiers of the British government thought little of financing its enemies at the same time. The firm of Boyd, Benfield and Co. was originally capitalised in 1793, in a way which provided funding to the French government. In 1802, Cobbett sent the following complaint to William Windham.

"The French fleet and army in St. Domingo continue to be supplied with provisions and other necessaries by Willings and Co. of Philadelphia who draw on Barings and Co. for payment."[77]

More conspicuously, the sale of the state of Louisiana by France to the United States was handled by the Barings, who, in consequence, were sending two million francs a month to the French government, through the firm of Hopes of Amsterdam.

Many of the extensive financial operations of these firms, even where they did not directly finance the enemy's war effort, nevertheless led to considerable economic dislocation in England. The resources sent abroad by Boyd, Benfield and Co. by way of loans to allied powers must have been a contributory factor in the bankruptcy of the Bank of England in 1797. During the war, the Rothschilds' massive exports of specie did much to enhance the economic prosperity of France, and might well have secured her military success as well; had not Rothschild gone across to the Continent, collected up all the coins once more, and shipped them off for the use of the Duke of Wellington. After the war was over, the Barings' French loans were accused of overburdening credit in England, and the Commercial Chronicle commented upon "the base and wretched avidity of the Monied Interest, which at the prospect of gain, is ready to forget all the claims of patriotism."[78]

This acquisitive drive transcended also all considerations of scruple and legality. Many financial operations sailed close to the wind; many more were clearly illegal. We have already noted the shady dealings which took place between William Pitt and the firm of Boyd, Benfield and Co. The Goldsmids were little better. William Cobbett tells the story of the preferential treatment accorded by the Exchequer to Abraham Goldsmid and two other financiers in the funding of Exchequer bills. Goldsmid jumped the queue by using a private side entrance to the Exchequer, and presented bills worth £350,000. The clerks, obligingly, altered the book, to show the name of Goldsmid at the head of the list! Walter Boyd dissipated his partner's fortune in speculations without his knowledge; obtained a loan from government on the basis of a false statement of his partner's Indian fortune; and contributed

---

74 N. Ferguson. The World's Banker. P. 244.

75 Ibid. Pp. 165 and 109.

76 Political Register. 12/12/1807.

77 P. Ziegler. The Sixth Great Power. P. 57.

78 Ibid. P. 81.

to his own bankruptcy by appropriating £294,000 out of his business for his own use, whilst asking for support from the taxpayer.[79] Both Boyd and Rothschild failed to keep proper accounts. Irregular dealings between Rothschild and Herries became the subject of parliamentary concern, and records were demanded which did not exist. The fact was that Rothschild had benefited himself to a considerable extent without Herries's knowledge. The resulting need for secrecy led to numbers of omissions and fictions in the accounts. Eventually, a Rothschild employee named Davidson put together a piece of creative accounting which disguised all the frauds on the taxpayer, and showed the profits of all the operations as being derived by government. Baring was a financial smuggler; and Rothschild well-known as a smuggler of goods of all sorts. Rothschild was also an illegal exporter of specie on a massive scale. The accumulation of huge fortunes was simply too important a concern to allow the petty considerations of probity and law to stand in the way.[80]

The acquisitive drive also transcended principle and morality. Politically, the financiers tended to support whichever party was actually in power. The muckworm, according to Chatham, was "the friend of government; that pretends to serve this or that administration, and may be purchased, on the same terms, by any administration." The Baring family took care to have members on both sides of the House of Commons; and Alexander Baring, dubbed "see-saw Baring", was said always to be able to see both sides of every issue. "He always gave his speech one way and his vote another." Nathan Rothschild transferred his allegiance from the Duke of Wellington to the Whigs, when the former resigned and the latter were voted in.[81]

It is surely not difficult to see the many moral issues that are raised by the operations of these firms, but they were clearly not apparent to Nathan Rothschild, for one. On one occasion, Rothschild was the guest of Wilhelm von Humboldt. Humboldt reported the occasion to his wife.

"Yesterday, Rothschild dined with me. He is quite crude and uneducated, but he has a great deal of intelligence and a positive genius for money. He scored off Major Martins beautifully once or twice. Martins was dining with me, too, and kept on praising everything French. He was being fatuously sentimental about the horrors of the war and the large numbers who had been killed. 'Well', said Rothschild, 'if they had not all died, major, you would probably still be a drummer'."[82]

Rothschild himself, of course, had amassed a huge fortune as a result of many years of bloodshed and slaughter, and this comment is a telling revelation of his own mindset. Was there anything so atrocious that it could not be justified by the profit accruing thereby to the House of Rothschild?

One could call to mind here the observation of Isaac Barre on the easy satisfaction of the consciences of the contractors to the government.

Nathan Rothschild seems to have been completely oblivious to any possibility that his operations may have had destructive consequences. In 1821, he was told of a threat of assassination made against him. He replied "with a smile, and after returning thanks for the intelligence, with the observation, that as he felt he had never done wrong to any individual, he could not entertain the idea that any persons could have formed so atrocious a design as that described, and that he really thought the affair unworthy of his attention."

Even on his death-bed, in 1835, even on the point of meeting his maker, Rothschild told the attending rabbi that "it is not necessary that I should pray so much, for, believe me, according to my convictions, I have not sinned...."[83]

---

79 Paper against Gold. P. 147. S. R. Cope. Walter Boyd, Merchant Banker. P. 189.
80 N. Ferguson. The World's Banker. Pp. 109-111. P. Ziegler. The Sixth Great Power. P. 53.
81 Quoted in Political Register. 25/1/1806. P. Ziegler. The Sixth Great Power. Pp. 113 and 59.
82 E. C. Corti. The Rise of the House of Rothschild. Pp. 215-6.
83 N. Ferguson. The World's Banker. P. 282.

This all-pervading drive, this aggressive competitive acquisitiveness, which characterised probably most of the participants in the monied interest, moulded their entire *modus operandi*. The methods employed by all the great contractors displayed remarkable similarity.

Since government was the main channel by which "the national wealth" was directed towards the financial institutions, a strong influence with government was the *sine qua non* of all their operations. It was invariably the object of the ambitious would-be financier to latch himself on to some great statesman.

"You know, dear Nathan, what father used to say about sticking to a man in government", wrote his brother, Salomon, in1815. "You remember father's principle that you have to be ready to try everything to get in with such a great government figure."[84]

Nathan, for sure, did not need reminding.

Francis Baring's first connection with government was through fellow-Devonian Richard Dunning, said to have been the most able lawyer of his day, who was appointed first Solicitor-General, and then Chancellor of the Duchy of Lancaster. Baring, to cement the alliance, married off his sister to Dunning. One of Dunning's closest associates was Isaac Barre, who, as Paymaster-General, had numberless lucrative contracts in his gift during the American War, one of which was awarded to Baring in 1782. The patron of this group of three was the Earl of Shelburne, Prime Minister in 1783, later Lord Lansdowne. Baring achieved his advancement, according to Cobbett, by "having become a *handy city-man* to the father of the present Marquis of Lansdowne".[85]

We have already seen the nature of the connections between Boyd and Benfield on the one hand, and Pitt and Dundas on the other; and the consequences that flowed from that.

But perhaps the supreme practitioners of this art were the family of Rothschild; and they used a wide variety of method. J. C. Herries was perhaps the first Rothschild man in government, and there is a strong suspicion that an element of blackmail over an illegitimate child played its part in making him so. However that may be, Herries was in permanently close contact with Nathan Rothschild from 1813, from which time the latter was said to be "almost continually in Herries's office". In the early years, Herries was the Commissary-General, whose job it was to finance the Duke of Wellington's Peninsular campaign and subsequent invasion of France. The opportunities for mutual enrichment in this arrangement are obvious enough, and were realised to an extent which we will never be able to ascertain.[86]

Bit by bit, Rothschild became close to even more senior members of the government. He befriended Lord Stewart, brother of Foreign Secretary Castlereagh, and Nathan's brothers invested money for him in the French funds. In time, Chancellor of the Exchequer Vansittart and Prime Minister Liverpool also became Rothschild men; so much so that Salomon Rothschild could comment that "Nathan's relations with these gentlemen (of the Treasury) is such as between brothers."

Rothschild, in fact, was receiving insider information from Nicholas Vansittart.

"Van is a very fine man, insofar as he gave you a hint of a forthcoming funding operation."[87]

Lending money to prominent or usefully placed public figures was standard fare in the methodology of the great financiers. Salomon wrote to his brother Nathan that "our late father taught us that if a high-placed person enters into a (financial) partnership with a Jew, he belongs to the Jew." The big-spending and lavish living Prince of Wales was an easy target. The Goldsmid brothers organised loans from abroad for him; and in 1805 Rothschild senior purchased all the debts of the Prince and of his ducal brothers. "This makes me a very powerful man", remarked Salomon. Treasury official George

---

84 Ibid. P. 82.
85 P. Ziegler. The Sixth Great Power. Pp. 34-35.
86 N. Ferguson. The World's Banker. Pp. 9, 92-93, and 160.
87 Ibid. Pp. 164, 9, and 127.

Harrison borrowed money from the Rothschilds; he was still in their debt for £3,000 by 1825. He was an important official in the negotiation of many government loans, and a useful channel through which to exert influence on the King. Charles Arbuthnot was another official recipient of Rothschild loans, to the tune of £12,000; and the Rothschilds themselves regarded this as bribery. The Duke of Wellington himself banked with the Rothschilds for a while.[88]

No way was neglected by the great financiers of ingratiating themselves with powerful men. Carl Rothschild, of the Naples bank, wrote;-

"One must have something when going to see the great and the good, either gossip or something to show them." This was one reason why the Rothschilds famously collected objects of art and of interest. The throwing of dinner parties was a useful tool. Dinners were recognised by the Rothschilds as being "as good as bribes", but it was the Goldsmids who were famed for this method of ingratiation. George III and his Queen are known to have visited Benjamin Goldsmid at Roehampton; and here is what William Cobbett had to say about the lavish dinners given at Morden, in Surrey, by his brother Abraham.

"The public, if it has any memory at all, must remember the accounts that were given of his *entertainments*, at which even princes were present; and at which, probably, as much was consumed in an evening as would have maintained the whole village of Morden for a year. Of these entertainments the most pompous accounts were published in all the news-papers of the day; and, from the manner of the publication, there can be little doubt of its having been *paid for*. As to his having shewn his hospitality to men of *all persuasions*, that is precisely what a man does, who is more intent upon *securing the favour of men in power*, than upon cultivating real friendship; and, indeed, I have, for my part, very little doubt, that the cost of the entertainments of Goldsmidt was always put down amongst the necessary out-goings of his trade."[89]

Direct bribery was unashamedly used. Many of the leading politicians on the continent were in the pay of the Rothschilds, upon whom there came to be centred a Europe-wide system of suborning and peculation. Much to the outrage of the Rothschild brothers, the Barings played the same game!

"He is quite a crook this Baring," wrote Salomon Rothschild to his brother in England. "We must certainly watch our step as far as he is concerned. The Baring lot is and was well versed in the way of using influence, as we are. There is not a single man of importance among the authorities here who would not work with Baring hand-in-glove....Baring and the French authorities are sharing the profit. The Minister is reported to be one of the most corrupt of all."[90]

Here in this country we are a little shy of acknowledging the part which corruption plays in the business dealings of our government. But certain it is that many of those who helped to facilitate the loans profited very greatly from them. Abraham Newland was chief cashier of the Bank of England. As such, he was befriended by the Goldsmid brothers; and from one of the loans in which the Goldsmids were the prime movers, Newland is said to have profited to the tune of £200,000. J. C. Herries, Rothschild's man at the centre of government, was even possibly rewarded with a share in the House of Rothschild during the Napoleonic War, and certainly benefited from Rothschild loaning operations after it. Even the Duke of Wellington was portrayed by the cartoonists as being

---

88 S. R. Cope. The Goldsmids and the Development of the London Money Market. In Economica 1942. P. 185. N. Ferguson. The World's Banker. Pp. 9, and 164-5.
89 Paper against Gold. P. 145.
90 N. Ferguson. The World's Banker. Pp. 163, 93 and 99. P. Ziegler. The Sixth Great Power. P. 82.

bribed by Rothschild, and, whatever the truth may have been, it seems undeniable that he behaved in such a way as to give ground for the suspicion.[91]

Should inducements such as these fail to achieve the desired result, there was always intimidation. James Rothschild wrote;-

"Father used to say, If you can't make yourself loved, make yourself feared."

All the financiers were aggressive, and none more so than Nathan Rothschild.

"Rothschild is the high priest of fear", observed a German writer, and, for sure, Nathan Meyer was known as a bully who was intolerant of opposition, and as someone whose mood could swing unpredictably from one of cool calculation to a state of aggression and bombast.[92] But it was his sheer political power, perhaps, that was the most terrifying thing of all. Here is Heinrich Heine.

"Before Nathan Rothschild I tremble with fear. Before you can say Jack Robinson, he could send a few kings, stockbrokers and policemen to my rooms, and have me carried to the fortress prison."[93]

Entering Parliament was another sure means of augmenting ones influence with the political establishment, and thereby ones chances of profit. Financial men enjoyed little public support, and were consequently compelled to seek the patronage of some wealthy aristocratic or financial borough-owner. Paul Benfield was said to have eight parliamentary seats in his gift, so for him it was no problem. Francis Baring, on the other hand, was actually pressed to become an M. P. by his political patron, Lord Lansdowne, and from 1794 until 1806 he sat for a Lansdowne pocket borough. In 1804, William Cobbett commented;-

"The influence which the paper-aristocracy has had, and has now more than ever, in politics, may easily be seen by reference to the list of the present House of Commons."[94]

As a nod towards political propriety, those contractors who supplied the government with naval and military stores, and with all other kinds of commodity, were theoretically banned from sitting in the Commons. But, asked Cobbett;-

"Can the law, as it now stands, prevent a member of parliament from being a contractor in an hour after he has voted supplies for the year?...Can it prevent a member from being a *sleeping* contractor?"

But loan contractors could and did sit in the Commons, as well as all other types of monied men. Directors of the Bank of England sat there, "with whom the minister has so many money bargains to drive during the year." Merchants form the West Indies and East Indies sat there. Does the law prevent them "from assisting to vote, out of the taxes of the nation, loans of money to themselves to aid them in carrying on their speculations, or in preventing the natural and fit consequences of such speculations?"

"Does it prevent such men as Boyd and Benfield from sitting in the House?"[95]

Of course, the above considerations did not apply universally. For Jews were disqualified by their religion from being eligible for election. Eccentric stock-exchange man David Ricardo renounced his religion and thus became eligible to enter Parliament; but the Rothschilds, among others, were much too attached to their Jewishness to adopt such a course; and there were times when they found themselves consequently at a disadvantage. In 1818, for example, the Rothschilds felt restrained from pursuing their rivalry with the firm of Barings, because of Alexander Baring's position in Parliament, and the opportunity which it gave him of asking awkward questions about the irregular dealings of

91 S. R. Cope. The Goldsmids and the Development of the London Money Market. In Economica. 1942. P. 195. N. Ferguson. The World's Banker. Pp. 164 and 159.
92 N. Ferguson. The World's Banker. Pp. 82, 50, 113 and 224.
93 Ibid. P. 227.
94 Political Register. 8/9/1804.
95 Political Register. 13/12/1806.

Herries and Rothschild in financing the war; about the unauthorised secret profits and the lack of proper record-keeping.[96]

The uses to which Alexander Baring himself put his membership of the House of Commons were summed up by Lord Clarendon.

"There was no exploded fallacy, no stupid prejudice, no reference to selfish interests, which this faithful representative of his own breeches pocket did not hash up together in language mainly characterised by spite against those whom he supposed to be meddling with his interests."[97]

These were the ways, then, in which the blood-sucker, as Cobbett called him, following Chatham, got itself "taken to the bosom of government and cherished in preference to and at the expence of every other being in the community. It wormed itself into every department of state"[98] Its power, though largely hidden and behind the scenes, was considerable and growing. The monied interest had the ability to obtain for itself considerable financial favours from government, at the public expence. Somehow, the Goldsmids were permitted to interpose themselves as financial middlemen between the Treasury and the Bank of England in the issuing of Exchequer bills. Between 1797 and 1810, most of these bills came through the Goldsmids. They charged 1/8 per cent commission, and their historian seems at a loss to say what they did for this. A similar situation pertained with Navy bills, issued to the tune of £4.3 millions between 1800 and 1802. When the firm broke in 1810, it petitioned the government to be released from the debts which it owed to the Exchequer; amazingly, but perhaps also predictably, the government, on behalf of the taxpayer, agreed.[99] The following year, a group of merchants, mainly trading from the West Indies, finding themselves in difficulties as a result of over-speculation, petitioned the government for a loan to keep them afloat. Cobbett maintained that under the circumstances pertaining the loan was likely to become a gift. What about the 1,670 bankrupts that appeared in the London Gazette last year? asked Cobbett. What about those who were paying the taxes who were themselves suffering as a result? No matter; Prime Minister Perceval recommended the loan to the House of Commons, and it was passed without a division. Samuel Whitbread wanted an enquiry into how much of the money was going to "Members of this honourable House."[100] Similar generosity was shown to the Barings in 1818, over the French reparation loan. Owing to disappointing sales of stock, the Barings claimed to be unable to meet their financial obligations to the British government. Wellington and Castlereagh, however, simply waived the claims of the British taxpayer, and thus converted the potential bankruptcy of the House of Baring into the biggest commercial profit ever yet known.[101] Senior ministers, it seems, were always ready to use taxpayers' money to save the great merchants and financiers from the consequences of their own actions.[102]

But financial power did not end there. Major political issues could be decided on the nod or the whim of a great monied man. We have already seen how William Pitt refused to save Boyd, Benfield and Co. by making peace with France. But the fact still remains that Boyd believed he would do so. By 1804, Cobbett was complaining of their influence over the major decisions in foreign affairs.

"Indeed, for them and them alone, war appears to be made and peace concluded."[103]

---

96 N. Ferguson. The World's Banker. P. 126.
97 P. Ziegler. The Sixth Great Power. P. 116.
98 Political Register. 25/1/1806.
99 S. R. Cope. The Goldsmids and the Development of the London Money Market. In Economica 1942. Pp. 188, 190 and 206.
100 Political Register. 9/3/1811.
101 P. Ziegler. The Sixth Great Power. P. 84.
102 !
103 Political Register. 8/9/1804

213

By 1807, he was writing of a sort of commercial "under-government, to which official reports, not only of important occurrences in war and peace, are made, but also of intended measures; the heads of that affiliation being consulted with as regularly as if they were of the king's council....Upon almost every occasion, the question has been, not what is just, but what is expedient; the expediency turning solely upon the interests of commerce."[104]

It was, perhaps, the Rothschilds who wielded this power most ruthlessly. In 1827, Rothschild client J. C. Herries was appointed Chancellor of the Exchequer. This was said to be at the insistence of the King, upon whom the Rothschild influence was exerted through the royal surgeon, Sir William Knighton. This was too bare-faced, even for a British government, and the controversy surrounding the appointment led to the collapse of the ministry. But it prompted the following speech in the House of Commons, from Thomas Duncombe, M. P. for Hertford.

"There is....deny it who can, a secret influence behind the throne, whose form is never seen, whose name is never breathed, who has access to all the secrets of State, and who manages all the sudden springs of ministerial arrangement....Closely connected with this invisible, this incorporeal person, stands a more solid and substantial form, a new, and formidable power, till these days unknown in Europe; master of unbounded wealth, he boasts that he is the arbiter of peace and war, and that the credit of nations depends upon his nod; his correspondents are innumerable; his couriers outrun those of sovereign princes, and absolute sovereigns; ministers of state are in his pay. Paramount in the cabinets of continental Europe, he aspires to the domination of our own....Sir, that such secret influences do exist is a matter of notoriety; they are known to have been but too busy in the underplot of the recent revolution. I believe their object to be as impure as the means by which their power has been acquired, and denounce them and their agents as unknown to the British constitution, and derogatory to the honour of the Crown."

Here was another elephant, and Duncombe, rather shockingly, had acknowledged its presence. Home Secretary Sir Robert Peel, rather more conventionally, professed not to know what Duncombe was talking about.[105]

This reverse notwithstanding, the House of Rothschild continued to exert massive influence over government policy. In 1830, with the nations of Europe on the brink of war, Nathan's mother, Gutle, could tell the world;-

"It won't come to war; my sons won't provide the money for it."[106]

Established financiers, who over time had acquired large holdings of government stocks, had a powerful vested interest in peace. It was only ambitious and aggressive interlopers who agitated for war. The war, of course, did not happen.

Even the issue of parliamentary reform seems to have been decided by the Rothschilds. Financiers in general opposed reform. Taxation was the lifeblood of the funding system, and any action which could promote greater economy in government had obvious consequences. Nathan's brother James wanted the government "to put a stop to the progress of the infamous liberal spirit....The supporters of.... reform will almost certainly make further demands later on." But events were moving ahead of him. The intransigence of the Duke of Wellington was having an adverse effect on the price of British stocks, and Nathan feared a financial crisis. Rothschild's bought man in government, Charles Arbuthnot, went to the Duke with the following message.

"Rothschild....came to tell me that if you let it be known, as soon as you meet Parliament that, whatever may be your own opinion of Reform, you are resolved not to disappoint expectations which are

104   Political Register. 12/12/1807
105   N. Ferguson. The World's Banker. Pp. 155-156.
106   Ibid. P. 247.

so greatly raised....you will surmount all your difficulties. He says that among the monied men there is an alarm lest there should be such an opposition to all Reform as would cause commotions...."[107]

Rothschild told the duke to jump and he jumped; two days later he ceased his opposition. The Great Reform Act passed, partly at least, on the nod of a financier. How many measures of government were passed or rejected because of their effects on the profits of the all-powerful financial interest, and the extent to which their support or opposition was instrumental, we will probably never know. Such things tend always to be hidden from view.

But perhaps the most obvious and glaring illustration of the power of these financiers is this; that the mighty Rothschild even William Cobbett never dared assail!

Section Five: The Fiscal Thing.

It is obvious that, under this system of finance, an ever-increasing amount of interest was becoming payable by the government to the monied interest. And this, in part, accounts for the rapid rise in the national expences that took place throughout the 18th and early 19th centuries. But whilst this expence was coming to form an almost unbelievable proportion of expenditure, all other expences were rising in sympathy. Here is Cobbett's table showing the increase of the national expences, including the interest on the National Debt.[108]

When Queen Anne came to the throne 1701.	£5, 610,987	Peace.
When George I came to the throne, after 11 years war. 1714.	£6,633,581	Peace
When George II came to the throne 1727.	£5,441,248	Peace
When George III came to the throne 1760.	£24,456,940	War
After the end of the American War, and at the beginning of PITT's administration 1784.	£21,657,609	Peace
At the latter end of the ANTI-JACOBIN WAR 1801.	£61,278,018	War
For the last year 1809.	£82,027,288 5s. 13/4d	War

Cobbett pointed to the particularly striking increase that had taken place during the reign of George III. In 1760, a year of warfare cost £24 million; in 1800, £62 million; at the time of writing, in 1810, £82 million. Here is Cobbett's table of the taxation which, when combined with government borrowing, had to cover this expenditure.[109]

When Queen Anne came to the throne 1701.	£4,212,358
When George I came to the throne, after 11 years war. 1714.	£6,762,643
When George II came to the throne. 1727.	£6,522,540
When George III came to the throne. 1760.	£8,744,682

---

107 Ibid. Pp. 242-244.
108 Paper against Gold. P. 41.
109 Ibid. Pp. 43-44.

After the end of the American War and at the beginning of PITT's Administration 1784	£13,300,921
At the latter end of the ANTI-JACOBIN WAR. 1801.	£36,728,971
For the last year 1809.	£70,240,226

Cobbett was at pains to point out that he was not against taxation *per se*.

"Now you will observe, that I do not say, that *no taxes* ought to be collected. Our vile enemies impute this to me; but, my friends, I have never said it or thought it. In a large community of men, there must be laws to protect the weak against the strong; there must be administration of the laws; there must be persons to hold communication with foreign powers; there must be, in case of necessary wars, a public force to carry on such wars. All these require taxes of some sort...."[110]

"I am for a system according to which all *necessary* officers should be well provided for; all *real* services to the public should be well rewarded; all *losses* sustained for the sake of the public should be well compensated."[111]

On the other hand, the British system of government finance exhibited countless instances of the most monumental extravagance and waste, some of it legal, much of it not. The problem was that much of the money collected from the people in taxes was channelled straight into the pockets of private individuals; sometimes it was difficult to determine just what useful services these people rendered; sometimes there was no pretence of performing any service at all. The entire amount of the direct assessed taxes, asserted Cobbett, could be taken off "without producing the least injury to the business of carrying on the government and of defending the honour of England."[112]

The most conspicuous promoter of this system of extravagance and waste, of directing the public money into private pockets, was, according to Cobbett, William Pitt.

"During his terrible reign there was more of the public money squandered away, than ever was squandered away in England from the accession of the Stuarts to the year 1784. During the very last year of his destructive power, he laid on pensions which added nearly a million to the public debt. No 200 years of our history afford instances of so much profligate expenditure as are afforded by his 20 years administration; and all the while he was, year after year, imposing taxes such as the people of England had never before heard of, such as their forefathers never would have submitted to, and such as they would not have submitted to, had they not been, little by little, inveigled into the submission by a crafty use of a settled system of alarm."[113]

Many favoured government officials were grossly overpaid.

"I find, Sir, that the *two Sheridans* cost the public annually more than the amount of all the assessed taxes of *twenty parishes* (upon an average). And, pray pause a moment, and reflect, Sir, upon the trouble, the loss of time, the vexation, the real injury to so many persons, and the discontent, which the keeping of only these two men occasion in the country. The Sheridans would, perhaps, say, that they perform *services* for this money....I will leave the public, who pay them, to judge of that....

"What reason can there be for giving the elder Sheridan 4 thousand pounds a year and a palace to live in? What reason can there be for giving 'Billy Baldwin', who is also a member of parliament, from 7 to 900 pounds a year merely for paying the Police Officers their salaries? What reason can there be for keeping still on foot a 'Dutch Property Office', where John Bowles and his brother commissioners

---

110   Political Register. 30/11/1816.
111   Political Register. 13/12/1806.
112   Political Register. 13/12/1806.
113   Political Register. 21/2/1807.

are growing rich as nabobs long after the nation has been saddled with an enormous pension and grant for the Dutch Stadtholder?"[114]

An Irish barrister by the name of Croker, who had energetically defended the Duke of York against (perfectly correct) charges of corruption, received a salary nearly as great as that of the President of the United States. Each of the Commissioners of the British Excise department were paid almost as many pounds as the top American officials were paid dollars!

But if inflated amounts were paid to working officials, a much greater scandal still was the massive payments made to powerful and influential people for doing nothing whatsoever. Cobbett was constantly attacking sinecures and pensions, and the holders of them who lived parasitically off the payers of the taxes; for while a few of these were granted as rewards for services rendered, most were not, and were awarded simply to cement the loyalty of the great and good to the government and to the system.

"It will surely not be pretended, that the Marquis of Buckingham performs any necessary services as a Teller of the Exchequer. In fact, that place is a notorious sinecure; and the annual profit of it is about 30 thousand pounds....more than the average amount of the assessed taxes of *sixty parishes*.... Is this a mere trifle, Sir? Is it a thing not worth talking about? Lord Liverpool's sinecure swallows the assessed taxes of almost *fourteen parishes*; his son's sinecure, the assessed taxes of about *seven parishes*; a sinecure of Lord Hobart, the assessed taxes of about *twenty parishes*; the sinecure of Lord Sidmouth's son, the assessed taxes of about *seven or eight parishes*; a sinecure just fallen into one of the young Eden's (a son of Lord Auckland) the assessed taxes of about eight parishes; Lord Grenville's Auditorship, the assessed taxes of *fourteen* parishes; Mr. Rose's sinecure, the assessed taxes of not less than *ten parishes*; Mr. Huskisson's precious pension, not less than the assessed taxes of *three parishes*; the pension of Lady Louisa Paget, the assessed taxes of nearly *one parish*, and for *what services*, I should really like to ask her ladyship, or her immensely rich and most noble father."[115]

And this was just the tip of the iceberg. Cobbett listed these from memory; if he were to use the official accounts, the list would have taken up all the space in a double edition of the Political Register!

Lord Henry Petty actually stood up in the House of Commons and defended sinecures as a part of Britain's history and of her constitution.

"Does he really believe," asked Cobbett, "that if these titled persons, these persons bearing coronets upon their coaches, were to cease to receive immense sums out of the public money, out of the fruits of the people's labour, under the character of clerks and custom-house officials, that the aristocratical part of the constitution would thereby *receive a wound*? Does he, in good earnest, believe that the aristocracy is rendered *more respectable* by an Earl's being collector of the customs inwards, and by a duke's being a collector of the customs outwards; by one Lord's being a clerk of the pleas and another a clerk in the admiralty court?"[116]

Inside the government, there were some particularly high-profile empire-builders, nepotists, and plunderers of the tax revenues, who were among the staunchest supporters of the system, both by speech and by pamphlet. In 1809, Cobbett was writing about loyalty – not vulgar loyalty, he insists, "but loyalty in the modern sense of the word, as it is understood and passes current at Whitehall and in the neighbourhood." He meant the loyalty to the system that was bought with large amounts of public money. Lord Castlereagh had a salary as Secretary of State of £6,000 a year, and had been in receipt of this for sixteen or eighteen years. His brother, Brigadier General Stewart, held three posts which yielded over £4,000. Three cousins all held lucrative posts; and four uncles belonging to the

114 Political Register. 13/12/1806.
115 Political Register. 13/12/1806
116 Political Register. 21/2/1807.

Seymour family all held various posts as prothonotaries, clerks, filazers, wharfingers and muster-masters, including some in the newly conquered island of St. Croix, which were directly in the gift of Castlereagh himself. Taking into account the length of time during which these posts had been held, Cobbett calculated that "the total amount drawn from the public by the above persons does not fall much, if at all, short of £3 millions."[117]

George Rose displayed a similar aptitude. Rose's salary as Treasurer of the Navy was £4,324 a year. In addition, he held a sinecure as clerk of the Parliaments, which brought him £3,278 a year, or £4,946 as it seems to have risen to by January 1817. This was granted also for the life of his eldest son, young George Rose. Old George Rose was the possessor of a further sinecure, as Keeper of the Records of the Exchequer, of £400 a year. Rose's second son, William Stewart Rose, was a clerk of the Exchequer Pleas, another sinecure, worth £2,137 a year. By January 1817, George Henry Rose was a foreign minister, but previously had been an ambassador to the United States, where his services, Cobbett said, cost the British taxpayer more than the salary of the President. The various Roses had been in receipt of these sums for, perhaps, twenty-four years, and they totalled, with interest, closer to £400,000 than £300,000; and that without George Henry's ambassadorial emoluments, payments to dependents, or "what we have not in the books". The true figure, probably, as Cobbett suspected, was several times higher. In April 1816, it was proposed in the House of Commons to take £2,000 from Rose's annual payments, but on division the House decided that he should remain in possession. At the expence of the taxpayer, the Rose family became the immensely rich owners of fine mansions and estates in Hampshire, surrounded, as Cobbett puts it, by your voters and slaves of Southampton, Christchurch and Lymington.[118]

From top to bottom, the whole of the British government had been turned into a gravy train. Under Pitt, the Civil List increased at such a rate that it doubled during his time in power. In 1816, as ruin, bankruptcy and starvation spread across the country, Cobbett printed in the Register an account of the living expences of the Prince Regent for the quarter up to January of that year. This was the Lord Steward's account, which only included food and drink, and payments to indoor servants and tradesmen, and it revealed a total expenditure of nearly £41,000.[119] The President of the United States, Cobbett pointed out, only received 25,000 dollars in a whole year. In fact, he did not receive as much in twenty years as the Prince of Saxe-Coburg and the Princess Charlotte received in one.

In his New York newspaper, Cobbett dared to describe the profligacy of the Prince Regent.

"It is notorious, that, after having squandered, on his pleasures, more than 5,000,000 of pounds, previously to his being Regent, he has, during the 4 years of his Regency, expended on himself, his pleasures, and his minions, more than 2,000,000 of pounds....that he has frequently filled up apartments, one month, at the expense of many thousands, and turned out the furniture the next month to make way for another suit....He has now in his pavilion some Chinese Waxwork figures, which cost 50,000l. And a man is kept to stand behind a curtain to keep their heads in motion, when company enters the room where they are....which extravagance is practised at a time when hundreds of thousands of the people are plunged into the most shocking distress by the weight of the taxes...."

And the Prince Regent, asserted Cobbett, was just a petty cormorant compared with the boroughmongers themselves.[120]

The army was notoriously a gravy train. In 1805, the cost of this was £18 million, not including the expences of the ordnance. But the pay of the soldiers and officers, even when generously allowed

117 Political Register. 21/1/1809.
118 Political Register. 30/3/1816 and 4/1/1817.
119 Political Register. 21/2/1807 and 13/4/1816.
120 Political Register. New York. 23/3/1816.

for, came nowhere near £4 million, and although there were horses and other expences to be met, this still left an enormous amount of unnecessary expenditure.[121]

"It is not, therefore, the pay of the soldiers and sailors that costs the money. The main part of the money goes into other channels; goes to create fortunes; goes to enrich hundreds, and not to find food, lodging and clothing for thousands."[122]

It was all, in fact, swallowed up by salaries given to placemen and pensioners.

"Nay, when we know what has passed in the Barrack department; when we cast our eyes back upon the famous accounts of Commissaries and Quarter Masters General; when we know that the Apothecary General (who never sees the army) has a place which clears him *ten thousand* pounds a year; when we see what has taken place with regard to the younger Sheridan, whose place of muster-master general is worth three thousand pounds a year, and to make way for whom a large pension has been settled for life, upon his predecessor; when we see and hear all this, need we wonder, that 18 million a year is charged to the account of the *army*?"[123]

Much the same could be said of the tax-collecting departments. The bureaucratic mindset can already be seen emerging during the 1730s, in the Salt Office. In 1730, the duty on salt was abolished. As a result, 438 well-paid officials lost their jobs, and found themselves in much reduced circumstances. Immediately, an agitation was set on foot for their reinstatement; and government was energetically canvassed on the subject of their "distress" and their "sad plight". Just two years later, Prime Minister Walpole re-imposed the duties. He tried to gain support for this measure by pretending that it was done in order to reduce the land tax. But the real reasons, which he concealed from the public, were his need for further sources of patronage, and his desire to provide the bureaucratic class with a livelihood. Privately, he justified this expenditure by pointing out that the money was all to go "to our own people." An "in-group" mentality was already clearly developing in government circles, which saw it as perfectly acceptable to use the power of the state to take money from the nation, the "out-group", in the form of taxation, in order to provide a livelihood for "our friends". During the 1730s, it was still necessary to keep this mentality concealed from view. But by the time pressure for the repeal of the salt duties had become almost irresistible, during the early nineteenth century, the idea had become a commonplace, and officials could openly campaign for the tax to be kept on. This campaign was led by William Carr, solicitor to the Excise department, who from 1817 vigorously opposed repeal on the basis of the large numbers of officials who would lose their jobs. At the time of eventual repeal, a letter in the Times newspaper complained of officials agitating for the retention of the tax – a "very singular attempt to frustrate repeal". When the salt duties were finally removed, a small duty of 2s per bushel was kept on at first, and it was remarked in the Commons that "there could be little doubt that this obnoxious remnant of taxation was retained at the solicitation of the collectors of it." It was now an orthodoxy that the nation owed a livelihood to those who were "our own people". Sir Francis Ommaney gave expression to this orthodoxy in the House of Commons.

"Let the House look at many public servants who had been employed fourteen, fifteen or twenty years; they were reduced to a state of beggary and some of them had actually shot themselves. This was not the way to treat faithful servants and parliament was bound fairly, openly and honestly to support the taxes in order to enable those persons to support themselves."[124]

The idea that it was the duty of parliament to press for taxation in order to support the bureaucratic tendency is a very strange one indeed!

---

121   Political Register. 13/12 1806.
122   Political Register. 16/3/1816.
123   Political Register. 13/12/1806.
124   E. Hughes. Studies in Administration and Finance. Pp. 217, 291-298, 374, 471-473, and 503-507.

It is no matter of surprise, therefore, that the costs of collecting the taxes had spiralled completely out of control. In 1809, according to Cobbett, writing the following year, they amounted to £2,886,201. This sum omitted the expences of the military and naval force necessary for enforcing payment; and also certain great sums paid to persons connected with tax-collection. However, taking it at the above sum, Cobbett calculated that the wages of 92,500 labourers were sunk into the various tax departments.

"Is this *no evil*? Are we to be persuaded, that, to take the means of supporting 92,500 families, consisting, upon the usual computation (5 to a family) of 461,000 souls; that to take away the means of supporting all these, and giving those means to support others whose business it is to *tax* the rest, instead of adding to the stock of the community by their labour; are we to be persuaded that this is *no evil*...?"[125]

By 1814, the total had rocketed to £3,504, 938; and this was nearly as much as the total amount received in taxes by the Treasury of the United States.[126]

There was mismanagement – in employing, for example, the resources of the nation in wars, subsidies to foreign powers, conquests, contracts and salaries. But there was, in addition, actual illegality on a massive scale. Cobbett believed that over a million pounds had been paid to Paul Benfield by Pitt in return for the successful election campaign of 1784, which, if it had not been raised in taxes, "would have been distributed about in supplying the wants and luxuries of those who paid the taxes". Pitt's close associate in government, Dundas, as Lord Melville, was a notorious embezzler of the public money. According to evidence sworn on oath to the House of Commons impeachment proceedings, Melville had taken huge amounts out of the Bank of England, illegally, but with the knowledge of the directors. Pitt knew of it, but connived, and despite Melville's obvious guilt, he was cleared by a majority in the House of Lords. A similar storm of scandal blew up around the Duke of York, who was involved, with his mistress, Mrs. Clarke, in selling offices and commissions in the army. He too, though obviously guilty, was acquitted, this time by the House of Commons. That such fraud against the taxpayer was found acceptable by the ruling elite is clear from the acquittals of these two lordly fraudsters; that other cases of peculation would have been hushed up wherever possible is a further obvious conclusion; that there were many such cases of misappropriation that we know nothing of seems, therefore, a reasonable supposition.[127]

Such a system of corruption and profligacy, as the British government notoriously was, clearly required a sophisticated propaganda machine to support it, and this added to its expence still further.

"Mr. Peel thinks the English press a '*Valuable Engine*'. The truth is, that it ought to be a valuable one, for it costs a great deal of money."[128]

There was a long list of 'hired hacks' who wrote in defence of the government, and a long list of pensions and sinecures by which they were rewarded. William Gifford was a glaring example. Gifford had been the editor of Canning's Anti-Jacobin during the 1790s, and was, by 1816, the scrupulously loyal editor of the Quarterly Review. He held the sinecure of Clerk of the Foreign Estreats, worth £300 a year, and was also, or had been, a Commissioner of the Lottery. In addition, he was paymaster of the Board of Gentleman Pensioners. Cobbett calculated that he had received £9,600 out of the taxes. The cases of Sir Francis D'Ivernois and Mallet du Pan were both conspicuous because their payments were in flagrant breach of the law. Both these writers were Swiss, and foreign nationals were not allowed pensions. D'Ivernois received £200 a year, and had received, Cobbett thought, probably

---

125 Paper against Gold. P. 51. Political Register. 24/6/1809.
126 Political Register. 19/11/1814
127 Political Register. 23/3/1816 and 12/12/1807. Political Register (New York ed.) 13/1/1816.
128 Political Register. 4/5/1816.

between £3,000 and £4,000 "of the money of the people of England". The wife of Mallet du Pan retained a pension of £200 a year after the writer's death, which, despite its illegality, was "put in the pension list and, with all the insolence of office, laid before the Parliament!" Both these writers produced pamphlets in support of the war against France, "the expences of publishing which were defrayed by those whom you may guess at." Edmund Burke was a further example. As a high-profile writer in favour of war with republican France, Burke was in receipt of £20,000 of pension money during his lifetime. After his death, his wife received a further £12,000. In addition, in 1795, two further grants were made to him for terms of lives, so that, by 1816, the nation was still paying £2,500 a year, "on account of this Burke, who did the country more mischief, and who did more injury to mankind, than almost any other man that ever existed in this country."

"I could make the list very long", commented Cobbett.[129]

The purpose of despotism, asserted Thomas Paine, is revenue. And as despotism seems always to produce absurdity, so there were no lengths of absurdity, in terms of expenditure, to which the British government was unwilling to go. In 1823, Cobbett found himself with his horse on the coast of Kent.

"My eye….lighted upon a *great round building*, standing upon the beach. I had scarcely time to think about what it could be, when twenty or thirty others, standing along the coast, caught my eye; and, if any one had been behind me, he might have heard me exclaim, in a voice that made my horse bound, 'The MARTELLO TOWERS by ___!' Oh Lord! To think that I should be destined to behold these monuments of the wisdom of Pitt and Dundas and Perceval! Good God! Here they are, piles of bricks in a circular form, about three hundred feet circumference at the base, about forty feet high, and about one hundred and fifty feet circumference at the top. There is a door-way, about midway up, in each, and each has two windows. Cannons were to be fired from the top of these things, in order to defend the *country against the French Jacobins*!

"I think I have counted along here upwards of thirty of these ridiculous things, which, I dare say, cost *five*, perhaps *ten*, thousand pounds each….There is, they say, a chain of these things all the way to HASTINGS! I dare say they cost MILLIONS. But, far indeed are these from being all, or half, or a quarter of the squanderings along here. Hythe is half *barracks*; and barracks most expensive and squandering, fill up the side of the hill. Here is a CANAL (I crossed it at Appledore) made for the length of thirty miles (from Hythe in Kent to RYE in Sussex) *to keep out the French*; for, those armies who had so often crossed the Rhine and the Danube were to be kept back by a canal, made by Pitt, thirty feet wide at the most! All along the coast there are works of some sort or other; incessant sinks of money; walls of immense dimensions; masses of stone brought and put into piles. Then you see some of the walls and buildings falling down; some that have never been finished…."[130]

Whilst the British taxpayer was being sunk ever deeper into misery and distress, his money was being frivolously spent in the environs of the court and the government. In 1816, Cobbett was complaining about the raree-shows staged in the London parks, the Chinese works at Brighton, and the new street opposite Carlton Street.[131] Ten years later, nothing had changed.

"More money than sufficient to pay all the poor-rates of Wiltshire and Berkshire will, this very year, have been expended on new palaces, on pullings down and alterations of palaces before existing, and on ornaments and decorations in, and about *Hyde Park*, where a bridge is building, which, I am told, must cost *a hundred thousand pounds*, though all the water, that has to pass under it, *would go through a sugar hogshead*; and DOES, a little before it comes to the bridge, go through an arch which I believe to be smaller than a sugar-hogshead! besides there was a *bridge here before*, and a very good

129 Political Register. 27/4/1816 and 17/8/1816.
130 Rural Rides. Penguin ed. Pp. 150-1.
131 Political Register. 17/8/1816.

one too....This bridge alone will cost more money than *half the poor-rates of the County of Sussex*....I am told, that the *triumphal arch project* is now going on at *Hyde Park Corner!*"[132]

The enormity of this problem; the extent to which the British establishment was riddled with a culture of competitive acquisitiveness, dishonesty, and parasitism; is well demonstrated by comparing its expenditure with that of the governments of other countries. "In France", Cobbett asserted, "there are not, and cannot be, many families, comparatively, fattening upon war." The French taxpayer contributed towards the cost of the war about one fifth of what his English counterpart paid.[133] But it was the cheap government of the United States that Cobbett never tired of holding up by way of example and comparison.

The United States of America occupied a territory of much greater extent than Great Britain. Potentially, it was far more difficult to defend. And its population was not far short, numerically. Yet during the year up to January 1814, its expenditure was less than a ninth of what the British government spent. In Britain, the annual expences, as presented to the House of Commons, were £113,968, 610 – 10s. – 10½d; In America, according to a speech delivered by President Madison, they were 47,550,000 dollars. Furthermore, Cobbett asserted that the taxes paid into the British Treasury actually totalled twenty times the amount paid into the American one. This was not all. In England and Wales, most taxpayers had also to pay poor-rates, and in 1814 these added roughly another £7.8 millions to the burden. So that the total amount paid per head in taxes in England and Wales came to £7-16s–0d; in America, each person, on average, had to pay the equivalent of just 12s–6d; and still President Madison found reason to praise the fortitude of the American people, and the cheerfulness with which they bore their burdens![134]

That massive cuts in expenditure could be made by the British government, both easily and usefully, was obvious to all; and, as a consequence, corresponding reductions in taxation. For example, in 1804, the House of Commons was told that the cost of maintaining the navy could be reduced by a third; and that by an admiral of the name of Markham. In 1809, the M.P. who had taken the leading part in exposing the peculation of the Duke of York and Mrs. Clarke, a Mr. Wardle, undertook to demonstrate that £11 millions of public money could be saved, "without the smallest injury to the service of the country, or the smallest diminution of the splendour of the crown". He pointed out possible economies in all branches of the military, as well as the navy; he saw opportunities for savings in the War Office, the Pay Office, and the collection of taxes; he thought the Bank of England might manage the national debt at a less exorbitant profit to itself; he suggested that pensions could be trimmed; and a clampdown on the practice of turning public offices into sinecures by the employment of deputies; and he pointed out that canvas was supplied to the navy by the same person who received a salary as the inspector of canvas. When Mr. Wardle totalled up his economies, they actually came to £16.5 millions. But it was all to no avail. The establishment was determined to resist, as far as possible, any reduction at all in its prosperity. Indeed, much of the history of government in the early nineteenth century is the history of resistance to necessary reductions in expenditure and taxation, and of resort to alternative contrivances to keep the system afloat. In the House of Commons, Mr. Wardle was answered by William Huskisson. He replied that the heavy expences which Mr. Wardle thought could be saved, could not be saved, because Parliament thought them necessary. Mr. Huskisson is certainly a clever man," commented Cobbett, "and the only objection I have to him is that he and his wife have *both fastened themselves upon us* to a very large amount, without my being able to discover any reason for it."[135]

---

132 Rural Rides. Penguin ed. Pp. 331-2.
133 Political Register. 18/4/1812.
134 Political Register. 19/11/1814.
135 Political Register. 17/6/1809 and 8/7/1809.

Out in the real world, not many people thought like William Huskisson.

"There does exist, from one end of the country to the other, a clear and decided opinion, that, to the waste of the public money, on barracks, military academies and asylums, to an immense standing army, a most enormous staff establishment, to innumerable sinecures, pensions, grants, allowances, commissionerships, with all their endless retinue of officers, clerks, messengers, door-keepers, &c.; there does exist, throughout the whole country, a clear and decided opinion, that to these causes are to be principally ascribed all the distresses which the country endures and which are daily and hourly covering it with shame and degradation, and sapping the foundations of its strength and its fame."[136]

Establishment writers contended that taxation did no harm to the payers of it. Adam Smith, as we have seen, thought taxes advantageous to the industrious poor as they enforced an improvement in living standards through frugality and economy; those who were impoverished by these taxes, were so through their own improvidence and extravagance. Malthus, at least, conceded that the imposition of taxes may produce harm; but asserted that the greater evil was the removal of them, as the government would lay out the cash in a way which stimulated demand, whilst the original earners of the cash would merely hoard it up.[137] Modern governments seem to take a similar view. It was, perhaps, Edmund Burke who gave voice to the standard argument, eulogising taxes as "the dews of superfluity, drawn up by the sun of the government, to be sent back in showers to fertilise and bless this country."[138] This argument, which went right back to the early eighteenth century, sees taxes as finding their way to the rich, who would lay them out in luxuries, thereby providing employment for the poor. In Paper against Gold, Cobbett railed against the absurdity of this idea.

"The pretence is, that taxes *return again* to those who pay them. Return again! In what manner do they return? Can any of you perceive the taxes that you pay coming back again to you? All the interested persons who have written upon taxation, have endeavoured to persuade the people, that to load them with taxes does them no harm at all, though this is in direct opposition to the language of every Speech that the King makes to the Parliament, during every war; for, in every such Speech, he expresses deep *sorrow*, that he is compelled to lay new burdens upon his people.

"The writers here alluded to, the greater part of whom live, or desire to live, upon the taxes, always appear to consider the nation as being *rich* and *prosperous* in a direct proportion to the *quantity of taxes* that is raised upon it; never seeming to take into their views of riches and prosperity the *ease* and *comfort* of the people who pay those taxes. The notion of these persons seems to be, that, as there will always be more food raised and more goods made in the country than is sufficient for those who own and till the soil, and who labour in other ways, that the surplus, or super-abundance, ought to fall to *their* share, or, at least, that it ought to be *taken away in taxes*, which produce a luxurious way of living, and luxury gives *employment* to the people; that is to say, that it sets them to work *to earn their own money back again*. This is a mighty favour to be sure."[139]

It was common with establishment writers to proclaim that the poor paid no taxes. A correspondent to the Board of Agriculture in 1816 claimed that particular care was always taken not to lay taxes on the articles of consumption. This echoed a statement made by William Pitt in 1805, as he announced the massive increase of the salt duty, that taxation policy up to that point had unduly favoured the poor at the expence of the rich. But the whole idea was, according to Cobbett, a "monstrous cheat". What was undoubtedly true was that the poor did not pay direct or assessed taxes.

---

136 Political Register. 10/8/1816.
137 T. R. Malthus. Principles of Political Economy. 2nd ed. Pp. 436-7.
138 Political Register. 13/1/1816.
139 Paper against Gold. P. 45. See also Political Register 16/8/1806.

"The tax-gatherers do not, indeed, come to you and demand money of you."[140]

But throughout the eighteenth century the whole emphasis of taxation had been gradually shifting away from the direct taxes towards taxes on consumption – the excises and the salt duty. In theory, these affected all consumers equally. But some of these fell particularly upon the poor. One such was the beer tax, from which many wealthier citizens were exempt as they brewed their own. Of every sixpence that the poor man paid for his ale, more than fourpence went to the government; and the poor man could not escape this; because the high price of malt prohibited him from brewing his own; and the high price of malt was caused by the malt tax.

"Now, if there were no taxation upon malt, I should pay at this time about *three shillings* and *nine pence* a bushel for my malt, and I do pay *nine shillings*."[141]

Another partial tax was the salt duty, salt being an article of much greater use in poor families than in rich.

"In the single article of *salt*, it is very clear to me, that every one of our labourers who has a *family*, pays more than *a pound* every year. The salt is sold in London at 20s. a bushel, wholesale; but, if there were no tax, it would not exceed perhaps 3s. a bushel. Every labourer with a family must consume more than a bushel, which does not amount to more than *the third of half a pint a day*; and you will bear in mind, there is salt in the bacon, the butter, and the bread, besides what is used in the shape of salt."

There were very many excises on the articles of consumption.

"You pay a tax on your shoes, soap, candles, salt, sugar, coffee, malt, beer, bricks, tiles, tobacco, drugs, spirits, and, indeed, on almost every thing you use in any way whatever."[142]

But taxation did not just have a simple, direct effect on the prices of the necessaries of life; it also had an indirect cumulative effect. Cobbett illustrated his point, by showing how the malt which he bought of the maltster was enhanced in price by the combined weight of all the taxes which the maltster had to pay.

"Recollect, the maltster has to pay for his *licence*; he has to pay taxes on the windows of his house; he has to pay taxes on all he and his family consumes; a tax on the land where his house stands; a tax on the deed or the lease of his premises; a tax on the sale or purchase of every thing, or else he is insecure for the want of a *stamp*; a thumping tax on any legacy which he may have left him; a tax on the horse which he rides to market; a tax on the iron and leather used on his carts; a tax even upon his dog that guards his malthouse…."

"The maltster has, then, eighteen pence a bushel of me, in the way of repayment to him, of my share of the taxes which he pays."

Consequently, although there was no excise directly on the most basic of necessaries – bread and meat – the prices of these were nevertheless affected by the accumulated weight of taxation.

"If I buy my bread ready baked, I must help to pay the taxes of the baker. The same with regard to the butcher; I have no objection to his meat; but I have great objection to share in the taxes which he has to pay; and, yet, he must be repaid those taxes out of the amount of his meat, or he must go to the workhouse. The thing that comes immediately from the land, pays taxes too; but the sheep the drover buys of the farmer, and that the butcher buys of the drover, come to the unfortunate eater, loaded with the taxes of the drover and the butcher, as well as the taxes of the farmer…."

"Even the loaf is taxed, because every thing is taxed from which the loaf proceeds."[143]

So Farmer Cobbett enumerated the hidden fiscal costs which inflated the price of bread.

140 Political Register. 2/11/1816 and 30/11 1816.
141 Poor Man's Friend. Part V.
142 Political Register. 30/11/1816.
143 Poor Man's Friend. Part V. Political Register. 2/11/1816.

"The tax upon bread being collected, not upon *bread*, or the *flour*, or the *wheat*, we lose sight of its march to our mouths. But, if it be collected upon the earth, in which the wheat grows; upon the house in which the grower lives; upon the horses that plough the land for the wheat; upon the iron and the leather that make up the harness for the horses that plough the land for the wheat; upon the gig that carries to church the wheat grower's wife; upon the nag that carries the wheat grower, the next day, to market to sell the wheat; upon the cloddy-heeled boy, who becomes a gentleman's servant, for looking after the nag and brushing the shoes of the wheat- grower; upon the dog whose teeth are necessary to protect the wheat grower's barns; upon the stamps of the wheat grower's lease, his receipts, and his notes of hand; upon the sugar, the coffee, the tea, the soap, the candles, the pepper, the salt, the very drugs, and a score of other things used in the house of the wheat-grower; upon the malt that makes the beer necessary to keep his nerves steady amidst the bewildering of such an accumulation; if the tax be collected upon all these, must it not be paid, at last, by those who *eat the loaf* made out of the wheat?...The tax pursues the commodity to the *mouth*, as necessarily rivers find their way to the sea. I view the wheat-grower as a collector of money to be paid over to the agents of the Government."[144]

"Now, is it not clear, then," asked Cobbett, addressing himself to the Luddites, "that you do pay taxes? And, is it not also clear, that the sum, which you pay in taxes, is just so much taken from your means of purchasing food and clothes?"[145]

Cobbett was excessively fond of quoting, in support of his assertions, a pamphlet written by a Mr. Preston, and published in 1816. What was so striking about this pamphlet was that its author was an eminent lawyer, a wealthy landowner from Devon, a member of Parliament, and, most remarkably of all, a staunch Pittite. That such a member of the enemy camp should put forward arguments that Cobbett had been propagating for years, seemed to him the ultimate confirmation of his views. The calculations of this "great praiser of Pitt" led him to the conclusion that out of the yearly earnings of a family of five, even if it was a family of the poorest class, on perhaps 7s. a week, or £18 a year, £10 of those earnings were surrendered to the government in the form of tax.

"Is it not clear," thundered Cobbett, "that, if the money, which the Labourer and Journeyman now pay in taxes, were suffered to remain in their pockets, they would not stand in need of *parish* or *subscription* relief. If this is not true, why does no one attempt to prove it false?"[146]

But the pauperising effects of excessive taxation were not just as simple as this. For the ever-increasing burden of taxes of all sorts had a disruptive, distorting, deleterious effect throughout the whole economy. The political economy of William Cobbett was complex, and detailed, and occupied an extremely large number of newspaper columns.

Excessive taxation reduced effective demand. Cobbett demonstrated this to the townsfolk of Preston in Lancashire, with the case of the malt tax.

"Take, then, I say, the two shillings off, and my malt would cost me 18l. a year instead of 70l; and here are *fifty-two pounds a year* to go from me to the tax-eaters....

"It is no laughing matter to me, to be compelled to give 70l. a year, instead of 18l. a year; and far from a laughing matter to you, to have nothing at all to be laid out in your manufactures instead of 52l..... The 52l. would get into hands, somehow or other, that would lay it out with you or some other manufacturer of some sort of thing. So that, a part of the fifty-two pounds would reach you even at Preston itself."[147]

---

144 Political Register. 21/5/1814.
145 Political Register. 30/11/1816.
146 Political Register. 14/12/1816.
147 Poor Man's Friend. Part V.

The numerous taxes which the farmer had to pay greatly reduced his and his family's ability to purchase manufactured goods.

"Now if they had not to pay these taxes, is it not clear, that they would purchase more *Stockings* and more *Lace* than they now purchase? A farmer's wife and daughters, who would lay out 10 pounds in these articles, cannot so lay it out, if it be taken away by the tax-gatherer; and so it is in the case of the Landlord and the Tradesman. I know a country town, where a couple of hundred pounds used to be expended on a *fair day*, in cottons, woollens, gloves, linen, &c. and where, at the last fair, not *fifty* pounds were expended. The country-shopkeeper not wanting the goods to the *same amount* as before, the London wholesale dealer does not want them to that amount; and as he does not want them from your employers, they do not want your labour to the same *amount* as before. So that they are compelled to *refuse you work*, or, to give you work at *low wages*, or, to give away to you their means of supporting themselves and their families, which, in reason and justice cannot be expected."[148]

Taxation also hit foreign demand for British manufactured goods, and stimulated foreign competition, by enhancing production costs.

"Thus foreign nations, which are not so much loaded with taxes, can afford to make the goods themselves as cheap, or cheaper, than you can make them. Formerly, when our taxes were light, the Americans, for instance, could not afford to make Stockings, Broad Cloth, Cutlery, Cotton Goods, Glass Wares, Linens. They now make them all, and to a vast extent! They have machinery of all sorts, manufactories upon a large scale, and, what is quite astonishing, they, who, before our wars against the French people, did not grow *wool* sufficient in quantity, for their hats and saddle-packs, grow now fine wool sufficient for their own manufactories of cloth, and to *export to Europe*!"[149]

The reduced effective demand, then, both foreign and domestic, for commodities of all types, caused inevitably by heavy taxation, had a marked unfavourable effect on employment and wages. But taxes had a similar effect also by a more direct route – by taking the money from employers which they might otherwise expend on labour. Cobbett addressed the Luddites.

"While you pay heavy taxes, the Landlord, the Farmer, the Tradesman, the Merchant, are not exempt. They pay tax upon all the articles which they use or consume, and they pay direct taxes besides, on their houses, lands, horses, servants &c. Now, if they had not to pay these taxes, is it not clear, that they would have more money to expend on labour of various kinds."[150]

A further artificial distortion of the economy caused by the excessive tax-take was the creation of monopolies. Cobbett called this process little-understood, but maintained that it was a process inseparable from heavy taxation and paper-money. The system of monopolies hurt the poor in two ways. It enabled wealthy traders to raise their prices, to an extent which could not happen where competition existed between a greater number of producers of sellers; and this process was facilitated by the ease with which a few large merchants could get together and agree on a price hike. Also, by putting a multitude of small traders out of business, it proletarianised them, creating, on the one hand, a labour surplus, and on the other, a reduction of employment opportunities.

According to Cobbett, then, it was the disruptive effects of the entire load of taxation by which the poor were oppressed; although the taxes on consumption might have an obvious effect in raising the prices which they had to pay for their necessaries, nevertheless the indirect effects of the total excessive tax-take were what constituted the main problem.

"It is the *sum total* of the taxes that ought to be kept in view, and not the details and amount of any particular tax....If 60 or 70 millions a year were raised wholly *in indirect taxes* the *effect* as to the landlord and all other classes would be precisely the same. There is no direct tax at all laid upon the

148   Political Register. 30/11/1816.
149   Ibid.
150   Ibid.

persons in the lower orders of life; yet we see, that the weight of taxation presses them down into the state of *pauperism*; and, if there were *no indirect taxes*, and all the 60 or 70 millions were raised upon the rich, in direct taxes, the effect would be precisely the same in the end. The labourer, to suppose a case, pays out of his 25l. a year, 5l. in tax upon his beer, salt, soap, candles, sugar, tea, leather &c. Take off all these taxes and lay them upon the landlord; the landlord lays them upon his tenant; and the tenant deducts them from the *wages* of the labourer, who is only just where he was before. But, if you *abolish* these taxes altogether, and cease to demand them of the *whole* of the community, the labourer will still have his 25l. a year, and will really have an additional 5l.; that is to say, 5l. more than he used to have to eat, drink and wear."[151]

In 1825, Cobbett summed up what he saw as the main cause of poverty.

"The tax-gatherer presses the landlord; the landlord the farmer; and the farmer the labourer. Here it falls at last; and this class is made so miserable, that a felon's life is better than that of a labourer."[152]

It is an interesting question how far the system of taxation was the cause of the agricultural changes which degraded and proletarianised the rural classes between the 17th century and the 19th. Cobbett certainly thought 'The Thing' had this effect; it was his constant complaint that the system concentrated property into masses.

"In the parish of Burghclere, one single farmer holds by lease, under Lord Caernarvon as one farm, the lands that men, now living, can remember to have formed *fourteen farms*, bringing up, in a respectable way, *fourteen families*. In some instances these small farmhouses and homesteads are completely gone; in others the buildings remain, but in a tumble-down state; in others, the house is gone, leaving the barn for use as a barn or as a cattle-shed; in others, the out-buildings are gone, and the house, with rotten thatch, broken windows, rotten door-sills, and all threatening to fall, remains as the dwelling of a half-starved and ragged family of labourers, the grand-children, perhaps, of the decent family of small farmers that formerly lived happily in this very house. This, with few exceptions, is the case all over England; and if we duly consider the nature and tendency of the hellish system of taxing, of funding, and of paper-money *it must be so.*"[153]

As far back as the middle of the seventeenth century, agricultural writers had been drawing the connection between taxation and what they called agricultural improvement. The Protectorate was a time of burdensome taxes, which prompted Samuel Hartlib to write.

"If the national husbandry of this commonwealth be improved, we may hope, through god's blessing, to see better days, and be able to bear necessary and public burdens to more ease to ourselves, and benefit to human society, than hitherto we could attain to."

To this end, Hartlib thought a public 'director of husbandry' should be appointed, and the Flemish system encouraged of letting farms upon improvement. A seal of official approval of his ideas was provided in the shape of a pension of £100 a year by Oliver Cromwell himself.[154]

We have already seen how the localised rural economies, where money was not much used, drew down the execrations of the writers on the subject of the national wealth, such as Steuart and Young, on the grounds that an extensive taxation could not be collected from them. Walter Harte, agricultural writer and friend of Young, emphasised the turning of produce into money in his Essays in Husbandry.

---

151   Political Register. 9/3/1816.
152   Rural Rides. Penguin ed. P.216.
153   Ibid. Pp.402-3.
154   Walter Harte. Essays in Husbandry. P. 2.

"In any country where there is full consumption at home, of commerce for exportation, the best use the land can be put to, is to cultivate THAT crop, whatever it be, which produces the greatest profit, VALUED IN MONEY."

And he unashamedly connected this with the needs of the state.

"All observing men must have remarked that our land has ever paid its grateful acknowledgements to the state, and the more its produce and profits are augmented by public encouragements and private generosities, the more cheerfully are its proprietors enabled to contribute their assistance towards the prosperity and well-being of government."[155]

When Richard Baxter wrote his last treatise in 1691, the rack-renting of estates was still being associated with taxation.

"We are kept under by taxes and publicke contributions to the King and for the warres. The maine weight lyeth on the Landlords. We have voluntarily in Parliament taken it on ourselves. And would you also deprive us of our Rents."

At the time, Baxter insisted that the burden was not an unreasonable one, but when William III introduced his system of continental warfare and Dutch finance, the case was altered. The land tax was introduced in 1693, and this seems to have been a real burden to landowners in many parts of the country.

There were two ways in which this system of taxation acted as a spur to agricultural change and the raising of rents.

The first was by putting landowners under genuine financial pressure. In many places, the land tax was normally assessed at 4s. in the pound rental, and many landowners, up until the middle of the eighteenth century at least, did in fact lose a fifth of their income in this way. It would have been particularly burdensome if assessed upon the modern rack rental, on estates where the traditional system of entry fines and low yearly payments still pertained, and would have obviously thus been a sharp spur to agricultural reorganisation. Those freeholders who farmed their own land would also have been particular sufferers, from being taxed on a rent which they were not receiving; and this may well account for the ease with which improving landlords were enabled to buy out those farmers who may have been expected to oppose their plans. In 1732, Prime Minister Sir Robert Walpole proposed to reduce the land tax. He told the House of Commons;-

"It has continued so long and lain so heavy that many a landed gentleman in this kingdom has been thereby utterly ruined and undone."[156]

Walpole doubtless had his own reasons for saying this, but it certainly seems to be true that in general the incomes of landowners in most areas failed to rise between 1690 and 1760 and in some cases actually fell. We hear lordly and even ducal complaints from the Isle of Wight, to Devon, to Lincolnshire, with the south-east, perhaps, especially badly hit. In 1708, the Earl of Bristol bemoaned his financial inability to carry out building works, having received that year less than £3,000, even though his rental was over £5,250.[157]

The second way in which taxation put pressure on the landed classes, and may have goaded them into systems of rack-renting, was by engendering social competition and disrupting the traditional hierarchies of the countryside. Warfare and excessive taxation, as we have seen, brought into being new classes of opulent, and the members of them bought estates in the country, and posed a challenge to its traditional rulers. Examples abound. Sir James Bateman was the son of a Flemish financier who settled in this country; he became deputy governor, and then governor, of the Bank of England, a

155 Ibid. Pp. 38 and 4.
156 E. Hughes. Studies in Administration and Finance. P. 194.
157 G. E. Mingay. English Landed Society in the Eighteenth Century. Pp. 54-6 and 81. R. R. Ward. The English Land Tax. P. 24.

sub-governor of the South Sea Company, Lord Mayor of London, a baronet, and his son married a Spencer. In 1705, as the established gentry of Herefordshire were struggling under the land tax, Bateman bought the impressive estate of Shobdon Court, near Leominster. The rise of Lambert Blackwell was, if anything, even more flagrant. A diplomat and a financier, Blackwell bought up estates in Norfolk to the tune of £4,000 a year rental; in 1770 alone, he laid out £10,000 in buying land.[158] In Sussex, John Holroyd-Baker, from a minor family in Yorkshire, built up a large estate on the untaxed rents of an Irish estate combined with the profits of a military career, the highlight of which was the defence of the Bank of England during the Gordon Riots of 1780. One could go on and on.

Such movements were profoundly disruptive, and engendered resentment and rivalry, as this complaint from an embittered squire to the government of Harley and Musgrave clearly demonstrates.

"You certainly ruin those that have only land to depend on to enrich Dutch, Jews, French and other foreigners, scoundrel stock-jobbers, and tally-jobbers who have been sucking our blood for many years."[159]

The fact that fortunes could be made in this way totally without the payment of direct tax, made the resentment all the more bitter, and rivalry all the more hopeless, as well as ruinously expensive. Walter Harte pointed out the unfortunate consequences of a landowner's attempt to maintain his authority and respect in his locality in the face of the arrival of opulent neighbours. He calls it "a love for shew and expence beyond their circumstances."

"A vain attempt to rival a set of people grown rich by manufactures and commerce, and opulent in treasures deposited in public reservoirs, where the payments are periodical and certain, without deduction of land-tax, poor-rates, repairs, &c."[160]

Harte's solution to this problem was to farm in such a way as to derive more profit from the land in the form of money.

By Cobbett's time, the complaint was still the same. Cobbett's allegorical landowner, squire Jolterhead, saw a new luxury disappear every time the tax-gatherer came to call, and in his reduced circumstances he saw all his neighbours prospering.

"He sees 'Squire Cracklouse, the army Taylor, and 'Squire Turpentine, the Spirit Contractor, and 'Squire Garbage, the Meat Contractor, and 'Squire Beanmeal, the Biscuit and Bread Contractor, and 'Squire Glanders[161], the Horse Contractor, and an infinite number of others all sallying out around him with gay equipages or numerous troops of hunters and followers."[162]

In their reduced circumstances, squire Jolterhead's wife took to badgering her husband to ask his friends in London to get government places for their sons.

"'Tis the land tax makes them all want places", it had been remarked, many years previously.[163]

The bitterness of this rivalry Cobbett described in his Letter to the Paper-Money Men; writing of the landowners.

"They hate you because you are keeping them poor; because their lands are upon tick to you; because you stick yourselves up along side of them, out-do them in expense, and….humble them in the

---

158   J. Carswell. The South Sea Bubble. Pp. 28, 37, 121 and 245.
159   R. R. Ward. The English Land Tax. Pp.23-24.
160   Walter Harte. Essays in Husbandry. P. 197-198 and 157.
161   Glanders is a disease of horses.
162   Political Register. 24/2/1816.
163   E. Hughes. Studies in Administration and Finance. P. 304.

eyes of each other, by your freedom and familiarity, which, were it not for the length of your purses, would earn you a beating from the hands of their groom. For these reasons, they *hate you*...."[164]

There were two possible responses to the social and financial pressure brought to bear on the landowning classes by the system of taxation; and both were disruptive of the rural economy. The first was to shift the burden of the land tax on to the tenant. Before the agricultural depression of the 1730s, some landlords succeeded in doing this; it became much easier to achieve during the times of agricultural prosperity which began in the 1760s.[165] The other response was to raise rents through a reorganisation of the estates, which, as we have seen, involved the enclosure of open fields, the consolidation of holdings, and a drastic reduction in the costs of farming, notably labour.

The farmer in the new system of agriculture was a very different man from his predecessor, as we have already seen, even when, in a minority of cases, he was sprung from the traditional peasantry. He had a social position to support in the wider world.

"When the old farm-houses are down (and down they must come in time) what a miserable things this country will be! Those that are now erected are mere painted shells, with a Mistress within, who is stuck up in a place she calls a *parlour*, with, if she have children, the 'young ladies and gentlemen' about her; some showy chairs and a sofa (a *sofa* by all means); half a dozen prints in gilt frames hanging up; some swinging book-shelves with novels and tracts upon them; a dinner brought in by a girl that is perhaps better 'educated' than she; two or three nick-nacks to eat instead of a piece of bacon and a pudding; the house too neat for a dirty-shoed carter to be allowed to come into; and, every thing proclaiming to every sensible beholder, that there is here a constant anxiety to make a *show* not warranted by the reality. The children (which is the worst part of it) are all too clever to *work*; they are all to be *gentlefolks*. Go to plough! Good God! What, 'young gentlemen go to plough!' They become *clerks*, or some skimmy-dish thing or other. They flee from the dirty *work* as cunning horses do from the bridle. What misery is all this!"[166]

Not only was a degree of luxury requisite in the modern farmer on the reorganised estate; he was loaded also with taxes, increased rent, and poor rates. These were not, in general, recoverable in the form of increased production; the money had to be got by cost-cutting; by reducing, in other words, the labour force of the farm, and the wages of those labourers who remained. Riding through Surrey in 1825, Cobbett came across a farm rented from Christ's Hospital by a man named Charrington, who, with his family before him, had leased the farm for a great many years. The farmhouse had clearly been home in former times to a large extended family, which had included farm servants, male and female. How times had changed!

"Every thing about this farm-house was formerly the scene of *plain manners* and *plentiful living*. Oak clothes-chests, oak bedsteads, oak chest of drawers, and oak tables to eat on, long, strong, and well supplied with joint stools. Some of the things were many hundreds of years old. But all appeared to be in a state of decay and nearly of *disuse*. There appeared to have been hardly any family in the house, where formerly there were, in all probability, from ten to fifteen men, boys, and maids; and, which was worst of all, there was a *parlour*! Aye, and a *carpet* and bell-pull too! One end of the front of this once plain and substantial house had been moulded into a 'parlour'; and there was the mahogany table, and the fine chairs, and the fine glass, and all as bare-faced upstart as any stock-jobber in the kingdom can boast of. And, there were the decanters, the glasses, the 'dinner set' of crockery ware, and all just in the true stock-jobber style. And I dare say it has been '*Squire* Charrington and the *Miss* Charringtons; and not plain Master Charrington, and his son Hodge, and his daughter Betty Charrington, all of whom this accursed system has, in all likelihood, transmuted into a species of

---

164 Political Register. 29/3/1817.

165 G. E. Mingay. English Landed Society in the Eighteenth Century. P. 56.

166 Rural Rides. Penguin ed. P. 185.

mock gentle-folks, while it has ground the labourers down into real slaves. Why do not farmers now *feed* and *lodge* their work-people, as they did formerly? Because they cannot keep them *upon so little* as they give them in wages. This is the real cause of the change. There needs no more to prove that the lot of the working classes has become worse than it formerly was. This fact alone is quite sufficient to settle the point. All the world knows, that a number of people, boarded in the same house, and at the same table, can, with as good food, be boarded much cheaper than those persons divided into twos, threes, or fours, can be boarded. This is a well-known truth; therefore, if the farmer now shuts his pantry against his labourers, and pays them wholly in money, is it not clear, that he does it because he thereby gives them a living *cheaper* to him; that is to say, a *worse* living than formerly? Mind, he has a *house* for them; a kitchen for them to sit in, bedrooms for them to sleep in, tables, and stools, and benches, of everlasting duration. All these he has; all these *cost him nothing*; and yet so much does he gain by pinching them in wages that he lets all these thing remain as of no use, rather than feed labourers in the house. Judge, then, of the *change* that has taken place in the condition of these labourers! And be astonished, if you can, at the *pauperism* and the *crimes* that now disgrace this once happy and moral England.

"The land produces, on an average, what it always produced; but, there is a new distribution of the produce. This 'Squire Charrington's father used, I dare say, to sit at the head of the oak table along with his men, say grace to them, and cut up the meat and the pudding. He might take a cup of *strong beer* to himself, when they had none; but, that was pretty nearly all the difference in their manner of living. So that *all* lived well. But the 'Squire had many *wine-decanters* and *wine-glasses* and '*a dinner set*', and a 'breakfast set', and 'desert knives'; and these evidently imply carryings on and a consumption that must of necessity have greatly robbed the long table if it had remained fully tenanted. That long table could not share in the work of the decanters and the dinner set. Therefore, it became almost untenanted; the labourers retreated to hovels, called cottages; and, instead of board and lodging, they got money; so little of it as to enable the employer to drink wine; but, then, that he might not reduce them to *quite starvation*, they were enabled to come to him, in the *king's name*, and demand food as *paupers*. And, now mind, that which a man receives in the *king's name*, he knows well he has *by force*; and it is not in nature that he should *thank* any body for it, and least of all the party *from which it is forced*. Then, if this sort of force be insufficient to obtain him *enough* to eat and to keep him warm is it surprising, if he think it *no great offence against God* (who created no man to starve) to use *another sort of force* more within is own controul? Is it, in short, surprising, if he resort to *theft* and *robbery*?

"This is not only the *natural* progress, but it *has been* the progress in England. The blame is not justly imputed to 'SQUIRE CHARRINGTON and his like; the blame belongs to the infernal stock-jobbing system. There was no reason to expect, that farmers would not endeavour to keep pace, in point of show and luxury, with fund-holders, and with all the tribes that *war* and *taxes* created. Farmers were not the authors of the mischief; and *now* they are compelled to shut the labourers out of their houses, and to pinch them in their wages, in order to be able to pay their own taxes...."[167]

As time went on, and the burdens of taxation became heavier, farmers were forced to diminish their luxuries, to the point where the wages of the labourers became the main fund by which this fiscal pressure could be alleviated. Clearly, what the government took could not be paid out in the operations of agriculture. Cobbett demonstrated this in 1816 in his letter to Sir Francis Burdett. In this, he compared the expences of a farm with which he was acquainted in America, under a low-taxing government, with the expences of his own farm in England, under a high-taxing government.

---

167   Rural rides. Penguin ed. Pp. 182-184.

The prices of wheat in England and America were roughly the same. The expences of the two farms were of the same order of magnitude, and therefore the profits were similar. The startling difference was in the way the expences were made up. Here is Cobbett's table of expences.[168]

	American Farm (Mr. J. Paul)	English Farm (Mr. W. Cobbett)
Wages of 5 men	£175(equivalent)	£50
Wages of two women	£26	£7
Total labour	£201	£57
Poor tax	£7	£87-5-0
Direct taxes	£15 Property	£43-17-6
		Assessed £15-10-0
		Tythes £36-0-0
TOTAL EXPENCES	£223-0-0	£239-12-6

And here we have Cobbett's comments on this table.

"His expenditure is almost wholly in *labour*; mine almost wholly in *taxes*. His expenditure goes to make little fortunes for those who till his land; mine to support armies and navies, to maintain, on the one hand, splendour and dignity, and, on the other, to preserve from actual starvation those who can labour no longer, or whose labouring parents and husbands have died without being able to leave them the means of satisfying the calls of hunger and thirst."

In America, the tax-take was around two dollars per head per year; in England, it was over forty dollars; and therein, according to Cobbett, lay the cause of the difference. In America, wages were 5s. 3d. per day, and bacon cost 8d. per pound; at Botley, in Hampshire, where Cobbett farmed, wages were 1s. 9d. per day, and bacon cost 9d. per pound. As a result of excessive taxation in England, the American labourer had three times as much to eat and drink as his English counterpart.[169]

After working for seven years, the American labourer was a man of property. But the English labourer was "still a poor labouring man, who, if he make shift with constant health, to keep from the poor-house to the age of fifty, can seldom do it beyond that period; and, if he has a family, they all become paupers even while the father is yet in his youth."[170]

The poor rates in America were given to those suffering misfortune, sickness, or accident, or were sometimes awarded to persons as an aid in escaping a state of poverty. A farmer there paid one fifth of the wages of one labourer in poor rates; Cobbett paid the whole of the wages of nine labourers.

"It would be the same as to all trades and callings, if we were to push our inquiries into them. We should everywhere find the master tradesman so hardly pressed by the tax-gatherer as to be obliged to pare down his journeymen as close as possible; and, we should trace the journeyman and his family to the poor house through the same chain of causes that impel the labourer and his family to the same miserable end."[171]

It was to the disruptive economic effects of the total tax burden that Cobbett attributed the sufferings of his countrymen

"The tendency of taxation is to create a class of persons, who do not labour; to take from those who do labour the produce of that labour, and to give it to those who do not labour....Such is the way in which taxes operate."

---

168 Political Register. 13/1/1816.
169 Political Register. 10/8/1816.
170 Political Register. 13/1/1816..
171 Ibid.

"The remedy for excessive taxation is less taxation."[172]

It was not rocket science; but still the rationale escaped the members of the establishment. In 1819, it was asserted in the House of Commons that if nineteen twentieths of the taxes were taken off, still the people would be no better off. Cobbett grew increasingly frustrated at the government's persistence in a policy of high taxation, without ever producing anything to justify it beyond gagging acts and bayonets.

"Why do not the thousands upon thousands of our learned tax and tithe-eaters draw forth their pens? Why do they not *write* at us, instead of proposing to shoot at us? We appeal to the *reason* of the people. We produce *fact* and *argument*. We make our attack on the *mind*. Why do not our opponents meet us there?"[173]

The standard of opposition which Cobbett met with is well exemplified by Lord Castlereagh's last speech in the House of Commons.

"All the existing distress might be cured by a due application of the principles of resurrection and that to expect relief from the repeal of taxes was both fallacious and injurious since the course of nature decreed that this concession could not fructify to advantage."

Meaningless political jargon is clearly not a modern invention. Lord Eldon, with his massive income, earned and unearned, from government, put the same thing much more simply. It was wrong to reduce taxes, he said, when the king was "in a bodily condition not enabling him to bear well – he has had a pretty severe gout."[174]

What can one say? Clearly Cobbett won the argument. But it made no difference....

Section six; The Paper Bubble

William Cobbett always attributed the poverty of his countrymen to a combination of two causes. Excessive taxation was the principal one; but he always took care to qualify this, by saying that it was taxation acting in concert with what he called the bubble of paper money that caused the mischief. Taxation acting on its own was perfectly capable of degrading and impoverishing a nation, he thought, but the incessant fluctuations and instability of the paper system made the thing a whole lot worse.

The paper system originated with William III's system of continental warfare, or Dutch finance, as it was called; that is, with the Bank of England and the funding system. Here is Cobbett on the paper money issues of the Bank of England.

"As to what are called *bank-notes*, the Company was not empowered to issue any such, or upon any other footing, than merely as *promissory notes*, for the amount of which, in the coin of the country, they were liable to be sued and arrested. Having, however, a greater credit than any other individuals, or company of individuals, the Bank Company issued notes to a greater amount; and, which was something new in England, they were made payable, not to any *particular person*, or his *order*, and not at any *particular time*; but to the *bearer*, and on *demand*. These characteristics, which distinguished the promissory note, gave the people greater confidence in them; and as the Bank Company were always ready to pay the notes in Gold and Silver, when presented for payment, the note became, in time, to be looked upon as being as good as gold and silver...."[175]

But the inherent weakness of this system is revealed for us in the following reflections on the nature of money.

---

172 Paper against Gold. Pp. 45-7. Political Register. 13/4/1816.
173 Political Register. 18/12/1819.
174 E. Hughes. Studies in Administration and Finance. Pp. 504-506.
175 Paper against Gold. P. 13.

"Money is the *representative*, or the *token* of property, or *things of value*. The money, while used as money, is of no other use; and, therefore, a bit of lead or of wood or of leather, would be as good as gold or silver, to be used as money. But, if these materials, which are every where found *in such abundance*, were to be used as money, there would be so much money made, that there would be no end to it; and, besides, the money made in one country would, however there enforced by law, have no value in any other country. For these reasons *Gold* and *Silver*, which are amongst the most *scarce* of things, have been, by all the nations that we know anything of, used as money.

"While the money of any country consists of nothing but these scarce metals; while it consists of nothing but gold and silver, there is no fear of its becoming *too abundant*; but if the money of a country be made of lead, tin, wood, leather, or paper; and if any one can make it, who may choose to make it, there needs no extraordinary wisdom to foresee, that there will be a great abundance of this sort of money...."[176]

The over-issue of the circulating medium was slow in coming; or so Cobbett thought, not altogether correctly.

"At first, the quantity of notes was very small indeed; and the increase of this quantity was, for the first twenty years, very slow; and, though it became more rapid in the next twenty years, the quantity does not appear to have been large till the war which took place in 1755, before which the Bank of England put out no notes under 20 pounds in amount. Then it was that they began to put out 15 pound notes, and afterwards, but during the same war, 10 pound notes. During all this time, loans, in every war, had been made by the government....The money thus borrowed was never paid off, but was suffered to remain at interest, and was, as it is now, called the NATIONAL DEBT, the interest upon which is annually paid out of the taxes raised upon the people. As this debt went on increasing, the bank-notes went on increasing, as, indeed, it is evident they must, seeing that the interest of the Debt was, as it still is and must be, *paid in bank-notes*....The cause of the increase of the bank-notes, was, the increase of the interest upon the National Debt...."[177]

Put simply, normal banking profit consists in the difference between the rate of interest a bank pays to its investors, and the rate it can itself command for its own investments. But a bank of issue, one putting out paper money, has opportunities vastly to augment those profits.

"It must be evident, that, though the Company were ready, at the time now referred to, to pay their notes in gold and silver, they had never in their money-chests a sufficiency of gold and silver to pay off *all* their notes, if they had been presented all at once. This must be evident to every man; because, if the Bank Company kept locked up as much gold and silver as their notes amounted to, they could get nothing by issuing their notes, and might full as well have sent out their gold and silver."[178]

And therein lay the weakness of the whole system. The greater the number of notes which a bank managed to put into circulation, and the smaller the amount of gold and silver it felt constrained to keep inactive in its coffers, the more profit it could make; but also the more insecure it would become. Greed was a spur impelling every bank towards insolvency, susceptibility to runs and panics, and eventual bankruptcy. It was a situation crying out for legislative interference which, in this period at least, never came.

In the case of the Bank of England, greed combined with a multitude of other factors to render its situation precarious. The ever-increasing demands of government during Pitt's war; the subsidies sent to continental allies; the operations of Boyd, Benfield and Co., and the massive imports of grain following the famine of 1795; all put enormous strain on its resources. An ill-advised invasion scare

176 Ibid. P. 6.
177 Ibid. Pp. 16-17.
178 Ibid. P. 14.

234

engineered by the government produced a run on the Bank of England, which the Bank lacked the resources to deal with. *De facto*, in 1797, the Bank of England was bankrupt.

"The Bank of England *stopped paying its notes in gold and silver*. What! Stop paying its notes? Refuse to pay its *promissory notes*? The Bank of England, when its notes were presented, *refuse to pay them*? Yes; and what is more, an Act of parliament, brought in by Pitt, was passed, to protect the Bank of England against the legal consequences of such refusal. So that, the people, who held promissory notes of the Bank, and who had, perhaps, given gold or silver for them, when they went to the Bank for payment, were told, that they could have no gold or silver, but that they might have other notes, *more paper*, if they pleased, in exchange for the paper they held in their hands and tendered for payment. From that time to this, the Act of parliament, authorising the Bank of England to refuse to pay its notes in gold and silver, has been in force. At first, it was passed for *three months*; next 'till the parliament should meet again; then it was to last to the end of *the war*; then, when the *peace* came, it was continued just for a year, 'till things should be settled; then, as things were not quite settled, it was continued 'till parliament should meet again; and as this present war had begun by that time, the act was made to continue 'till *six months after the next peace*."[179]

This was the famous Bank Restriction Act of 1797, which legalised the stoppage of the Bank, and the long-term suspension of its cash payments. What purported to be a short-term measure to save the Bank of England from collapse, turned into a semi-permanent licence to print money.

"Since that suspension took place....paper-money makers have set up all over the kingdom; and might not this well happen, when to pay paper-money nothing more than paper-money was required?"[180]

Cobbett traced the proliferation of paper-money through his time, from a gradual increase before 1797, to a rapid increase thereafter.

"There are few of you who cannot remember the time, when there was scarcely ever seen a bank note among Tradesmen and Farmers. I can remember, when this was the case; and, when farmers in my country hardly ever saw a bank-note, except when they sold their hops at Weyhill fair. People, in those days, used to carry little bags to put their money in, instead of the paste-board or leather cases that they now carry. If you look back, and take a little time to think, you will trace the gradual increase of paper-money, and the like decrease of gold and silver money....

"You have, during the last seventeen years, seen the quantity of paper-money rapidly increase; or in other words, you have, day after day, seen less and less of gold and silver appear in payments, and of course more and more of paper-money. But it was not 'till the year 1797, that the paper-money began to increase so very fast. It was then that the *two* and *one pound* notes were first made by the Bank of England. It was then, in short, that paper-money became completely predominant....

"Every part of the people, except the very poorest of them, now, occasionally at least, possessed bank-notes. Rents, salaries, yearly wages, all sums above five pounds, were now paid in bank-notes; and, the government itself was now paid its *taxes* in this sort of currency."

And now, at the time of writing, in 1810;-

"We see the country abounding with paper money; we see every man's hand full of it; we frequently talk of it as a strange thing, and a great evil; but never do we inquire into the cause of it."[181]

The proliferation of paper money continued unrestrained through the early years of the 19th century, creating, on the one hand, a superficial appearance of great prosperity, and on the other, an ever greater vulnerability of the banking system to shocks of any kind. The putting into circulation of huge amounts of currency for which there was no real need created an investment hunger.

179 Ibid. Pp. 8-9.
180 Ibid. p. 10.
181 Ibid. Pp. 7-8 and 17.

Commercial men, into whose hands most of the surplus found its way, were thereby induced to enter into speculations which prudence might have advised against. The first major cracks in the system appeared in 1810. A variety of commercial factors formed the trigger for the crisis – the sending of manufactured goods to South America in the hope of a market which failed to materialise; the importing into Britain of huge quantities of coffee and sugar for which there was insufficient demand, and which could not easily be re-exported because of Napoleon's Berlin Decrees. The embarrassments of the merchants involved in these operations exposed their bankers to danger; and as all the London banks had client banks in the country, a crisis could have a domino effect.[182]

But while the establishment press blamed the crisis on "indiscreet speculation", Cobbett insisted that such over-trading was merely the trigger; the real and underlying cause was a lack of confidence in the paper currency.

"In proportion to the magnitude of the quantity of paper in circulation men will be disposed towards alarm. They will be so disposed without being able to assign any particular reason for it. Every man knows that paper-money has no intrinsic value; that a breath destroys it…."[183]

Let Cobbett describe the consequence.

"About three or four weeks ago, a banker in London stopped payment, that is to say, he refused to pay (from want of means, I suppose) those persons who had been fools enough to put their money into his hands. – This man's breaking was followed by others; but, more especially, by some paper-money makers at Salisbury and Shaftesbury, and, they being money-grinders of the first rate and reputation, an alarm became pretty general all through the counties of Wiltshire and Dorset which, it appears, spread itself even to the lower parts of Devonshire. Two paper-money makers are said to have *cut their throats*; and, though one cannot help being sorry to hear of any such end to any human being yet, neither can one help feeling indignation against those, be they who or what they may, who have been the cause of all the suffering and all the ruin, which have now taken place in the district just named."[184]

Banking was, notoriously, an extremely easy and certain way of making large amounts of money. There was no good reason for banking insolvency; and it required an unusual combination of greed and stupidity to break a bank. But such was the nature of the system, where the closer to the wind you sailed the more profit you made; where trading insolvently was the most profitable course of all; and such the nature of the men whom banking attracted; that it would have been surprising indeed if banks did not break. And break they did, and at times by the score.

The whole situation was made worse by the suspicion that the Bank of England was jealous of the country paper-makers, and was anxious to establish its own monopoly; so that when banks were in trouble rather than baling out the less hopeless cases, as was well within its power, instead it would "lend a hand to help the lame dog over the stile", as the contemporary saying was.[185]

Such had the dependence on paper currency become that a banking collapse was a catastrophe for the localities affected. The ruined bankers deserved no sympathy, thought Cobbett, for they were the cause of the problem, "but, not so the people of Wilts and Dorset generally speaking; not so the shopkeeper, the publican, the handicraftsman, the farmer, and the labourer who, at the stoppage of the banks, had paper-money in their hands, where it instantly became as useless as a like quantity of cabbage leaves."[186]

---

182 Political Register. 28/7/1810.
183 Political Register. 21/7/1810.
184 Political Register. 28/7/1810.
185 Political Register. 18/8/1810.
186 Political Register. 28/7/1810.

The establishment press generally tried to play down the seriousness of crises such as this, but here is part of a letter from the city of Salisbury, published in the Morning Post of 15th July, and quoted by Cobbett.

"The distress in this place is extreme, it being with the *greatest difficulty provisions can be procured here*, as we have nothing apparently in circulation but the paper of the place, which is no longer current. On Saturday night *numbers of women and children were seen in a deplorable condition*, from the unfortunate pressure under which we at present labour."[187]

Cobbett elaborated a little further on the implications of a circulating medium of a sudden completely losing its value.

"In the West of England in general, you will see there the farmer, perhaps, his last sack of corn turned into paper-money, with not a pound left wherewith to get in his harvest. In many instances, rents are due, and have long been collecting in the now worthless paper-money. The shop-keepers, the public-house keepers, people in trade of every sort and size, have, in an instant, in the twinkling of an eye, been left penny-less; absolutely without a farthing of money; and, what is worse, many of them in debt, the means of discharging which, the last remaining means, thus, in an instant, swept away, never to return. In such a state of things, every man runs at once to his books to see who are his debtors; every debt is instantly demanded, and not a soul has the means of paying.

"What must be the situation of the *labourer* or the *journeyman*, in such a state of things? All need a little money put by for rent, fuel, the needs of an increasing family etc. This provision is made in the currency of the place; and, Good God! how many poor and worthy creatures must, by the blowing away of that currency, have been plunged into misery unspeakable."[188]

Sudden crises apart, the continually fluctuating value of the paper currency, put out by the Bank of England and the country banks, had a constantly disruptive influence on the economy of every part of the country; and a very harmful effect on the fortunes of its inhabitants. Up until about 1814, the banks saw it as their interest to get as many notes into circulation as they could. The result was that the value of those notes was always on the decline.

"Money, of whatever sort, is, like every thing else, lowered in its value in proportion as it becomes *abundant* or *plenty*….When apples are plenty apples are cheap….The use of money is to serve men as a sign of the amount of the value of things that pass from man to man in the way of purchase and sale. It is plenty, or scarce, in proportion as its quantity is great or small compared with the quantity of things purchased and sold in the community; and, whenever it becomes, from any cause, plenty, it *depreciates*, or sinks in value."[189]

A metallic currency has an intrinsic value of its own – the value of the metal of which it is made. A paper currency has none. And whilst for a time an over-abundant medium might consist of both paper and metal, the paper dragging down the value of the coin, sooner or later it will become apparent that the specie is worth more than the bank-notes. The paper becomes depreciated against the coin. In August 1811, Cobbett calculated this depreciation at 27½ per cent, and produced the following table.[190]

In Sterling

The Pound Note is worth 15s. 8½ d.
The Five and Sixpenny Token is worth 4s. 3½ d.
The Three Shilling Token is worth 2s. 4¼ d.

187 Political Register. 21/7/1810.
188 Political Register. 21/7/1810.
189 Paper against Gold. P. 429.
190 Political Register. 24/8/1811.

The Guinea is worth £1 1s. 0d.

The Shilling is worth 1s. 0d.

In Bank of England Paper

The Pound Note is worth £1 0s. 0d.

The Five and Sixpenny Token is worth 5s. 6d.

The Three Shilling Token is worth 3s. 0d.

The Guinea is worth £1 6s. 9d.

The Shilling is worth 1s. 3¼ d.

In an undepreciated currency, the price of an ounce of gold should have been £3 17s. 6d. But in March 1811 the price was £5. At that rate a pound weight of guinea coins, the face value of which came to £46 14s. 6d., contained gold to the value of £60. It is hardly surprising, therefore, that they disappeared. Gold and silver, according to Cobbett, were withdrawn from circulation, to fill, either "the hoards of the prudent", or "the bags of those, who have the means of sending or carrying them to those foreign countries where they are wanted, and where they will bring their value." Hoarding coin of the realm was possibly the most lucrative investment available at the time, while the depreciation lasted, and the profits were not subject to the property tax. Government attempted to discourage hoarding, but there were actual laws in existence against trading in specie – against paying more for a coin than its face value, and against taking them out of the country. And whilst an attempt was made to enforce these laws against the ordinary citizen, this illegality was practised on a massive scale, and with impunity, by such as Rothschild and Goldsmid, as Cobbett almost certainly suspected, but never openly stated.[191]

The consequence was that the whole country was drained of guineas, and of change of all sorts. In order to be able to pay the sailors of the royal navy, and the workers in the dockyards, the government stamped and put into circulation a number of Spanish dollars. Their value should have been 4s. 6d., but at that they would not circulate. The Bank raised their value to 5s. 6d., and still they disappeared. "Every three days make a change in the value of the dollar", complained Cobbett. Shopkeepers put up notices in their windows that they were prepared to take dollars at 5s. 9d., or even 6s. Even the silver shillings and sixpences, worn almost smooth and below their proper weight, were worth intrinsically more than their face value, and so were withdrawn from use.[192]

The lack of change was a major impediment to transactions of every sort, and a subject of great public complaint. In the House of Lords, Lord Folkestone mentioned a recent fair in Berkshire, at which buying and selling had been impossible for lack of change. The receivers at public offices, and the keepers of shops, were compelled either to forego the silver fractions of the sums due to them, or else to give written acknowledgements for the excess. "The business in shops and houses of public resort is become very troublesome owing to this scarcity. One of the effects produced has been the use of copper halfpence, which had sunk almost out of use before this scarcity of silver drew them forth. One of the conditions now of changing a pound note generally is, that the party receiving the change shall take 5s. or 10s. in these halfpence, five sixths of which, perhaps, are *counterfeits*, and, those not half the due weight, composed of base metal, brass for the most part, or block, or something that is very little worth."

"In the country, the distress, from want of change, is still greater than in London; and it is with extreme difficulty that people can travel from one place to another."[193]

But the biggest problem of all, of course, was the payment of wages.

191 Paper against Gold. P. 6. Political Register. 13/4/1811.

192 Political Register. 10/4/1811.

193 Political Register. 13/4/1811 and 20/4/1811.

"How is it possible for people to have silver wherein to pay workmen's wages? – For want of silver and gold for this purpose, they must take paper. They must put their men in classes and pay them three or four in one payment; or they must give them paper in *advance*, or the men must give the masters *credit*, and thus *running accounts* and all the endless trouble and vexation of them to such persons."[194]

Of course, the converting of depreciated paper into coins would have added loss to vexation.

But the principal way in which the over-issue of the circulating medium had an adverse effect on the well-being of ordinary people was in the influence which it exerted over prices.

"All of you who are forty years of age can remember when the price of the gallon loaf used to be about ten pence or a shilling instead of two shillings and six pence or two shillings and ten pence, as it now is."[195]

1810 was a year of plenty, and in November of that year Cobbett put the price of a quartern loaf at 1s. 3½d.

"This, then, is the price in a season of abundance; just after the close of an *abundant harvest*; and on the very day appointed for a General Prayer and Thanksgiving for that abundant harvest. This is the price, which the people of England have now to pay in times of *plenty*; a price at which 12 shillings, which is about the average of the country labourer's wages, will purchase about 9½ quartern loaves, rather less than 42 pounds of bread, which, supposing the labourer's family to consist of 4 persons, 2 children besides the man and his wife, will give each of them 1½ pounds of bread a day; supposing them to want neither *meat, drink, clothing*, lodging, or *fire*....What, then, would the price be, if this were a season of *scarcity*?"[196]

The depreciation of the currency, upon this reckoning, had brought the standard of living down noticeably below that represented by David Davies's budgets of the early 1790s.

Cobbett went on. In 1792, the year before war broke out, the price of the quartern loaf was 6¼d.; well under half the price of 1810. Yet in 1792 there were no prayers and no thanksgivings for an abundant harvest. "How are we to account for this?"

The modern term for this phenomenon is inflation; the use of which we have for many years been tricked into. Inflation clearly implies an upward movement, and leads us to believe that the responsibility lies with prices; or, in other words, in the increasing value of goods and services. How few of us think to attribute causative influence to the currency, and to those who issue it! Cobbett battled against that very same misapprehension. He used the example of a closed community of ten men, with a fixed amount of currency, and a horse to purchase. If the amount of currency were to be doubled, contended Cobbett, so would be the price of the horse.

"In such a state of things people would say, that the *price had risen*; that commodities had *doubled in price*, that every thing *was twice as dear* as it used to be. But, the fact would be, that *money* was become *plenty*, and like every thing else, *cheap* in proportion to its abundance. It would be, that money had *fallen* or had been depreciated, and not that things had risen; the *loaf*, for instance, having a real value in its utility in supporting man, and the money having only an *imaginary value*.

"Prices in England have been *rising*, as it is commonly called, for hundreds of years; things have been getting *dearer* and *dearer*. The cause of which, until the bank-note system began, was the increase of gold and silver in Europe, in consequence of the discovery of South America, and the subsequent working of the mines. But the increase of the quantity of gold and silver was slow. 'Nature', as Paine observes, 'gives those materials out with a sparing hand'; they came, as they still come, in regular annual quantities from the mines; and that portion of them which found its way to this country was

194 Political Register. 20/4/1811.
195 Paper against Gold. P. 8.
196 Political Register. 17/11/1810.

obtained by the sale of things of real value, being the product of our soil or of our labour, therefore, the quantity of money increased very slowly....

"But when the *funding system* began, and paper became, in many cases, a substitute for gold and silver; when the increase of the quantity of money in the country was no longer dependent upon the mines; when the check which nature provided was removed; then money, or its substitute, paper, increased at a rate much greater than before, and *prices* took a *proportionate rise*, as they naturally would. We have seen that the government, as soon as it began to make loans, was compelled to establish a Bank, or a something, in order *to get the means of paying the interest upon the loans*. The amount of the loans would naturally go on increasing in order to meet the rise in prices, and thus the increase of the paper would continue causing rise after rise in the prices, and the rise in the prices would continue causing addition upon addition to the quantity of the paper. This was the natural progress, and it was that which actually took place."[197]

The over-abundance of the circulating medium brought a great appearance of prosperity. Rapidly rising prices brought great wealth to some. The huge amount of money at large brought improvements in agriculture; caused investment hunger and enterprise of all sorts; and engendered extensive speculations, many of them, as we have seen, hazardous. It was not hard, at this point, to paint a glowing, if partial, picture, of the benefits of the funding system.

"The nation have been often told of the great effect which the paper-money system has had in advancing the *prosperity* of the country; it has been amused with glowing pictures of the *improvements* arising from the use of this species of currency; it has been by shallow-headed men, or by impostors.... by such persons every good thing now to be found in England has been attributed to the paper-money system."[198]

A writer who signed himself merely "An American", who was probably Alexander Baring, in eulogising the paper system, actually went so far as to describe the "people as being almost *too well off and too happy*; and waxed lyrical on the "*solidity of our pecuniary concerns and the happy and contented state of the people, owing to that solidity*."[199]

Leaving aside the solidity of a system which was on the point of collapse, this was still a very one-sided view. The prosperity was all a fragile veneer. All these writers, wrote Cobbett, "have carefully kept out of sight that increase of misery, which is most clearly proved by the increase of the number of paupers."

The zenith of the system, perhaps, was in 1812-3. A short harvest sent the price of wheat rocketing to 120s. per quarter, and the inevitably resulting depression in domestic demand for manufactures coincided with the disruption to trade occasioned by Napoleon's Continental System. Starving people, of course, rioted, and were subjected to the military suppression which was, as we have noted, rapidly coming to be seen as the standard establishment solution to the problem of poverty; and this with a brutality which shocked many observers, even from the ruling class. This was the paper money system at its height.

But 'The Thing' was a double-edged sword. In 1814, the war came to an end. Under the newly-established conditions of normality of trade, the inflated price of British farm produce sucked in huge quantities of continental wheat, which sent prices in England tumbling. The increasing embarrassments of their agricultural customers caused the country bankers to fear for their own safety, and consequently they started to draw in and reduce their issues of paper money. And this was the beginning of a new phase.

---

197 Paper against Gold. P. 432.
198 Political Register. 16/9/1809. See also 16/12/1815.
199 Political Register. 28/7/1810.

With the escape of Napoleon from Elba in 1815, the war was renewed for a few months. Although the prohibition on the Bank of England from paying its issues in cash was renewed until 1816, after the Battle of Waterloo there was already a need to bring the exchanges back to a rate which would prevent the sucking in of huge quantities of imports. Chancellor of the Exchequer, Nicholas Vansittart, hinted clearly that the Restriction Act would not be renewed, and that a return to cash payments was expected. To bring gold back into the Bank, the directors were compelled drastically to draw in their paper issues. The amount of currency in circulation, already diminished from other causes, took a further tumble. The result was a huge and sudden fall in prices. The distress arising from this fall was even greater than the misery and poverty caused by the constantly rising prices of the previous years.

In his Political Register, William Cobbett observed the unfolding crisis in great detail. His account is almost the only genuine source for the history of these years, as hardly anyone else had the courage to relate what was occurring.

"People do not know how it is; but they know, that they are *all in distress.*… They see *peace* and even *plenty*; and yet they are miserable. Agriculture languishes; trade follows agriculture; nobody has money to pay rent, taxes, or debts. – A *corn bill* has not protected the farmer. The cheapness of food has not lessened the misery of the poor. Nothing sells. The nation perished in the midst of the spending of the produce of successive abundant harvests.

"Nobody sees, or, at least, appears to see, that their distress arises from the *debt and the military establishment and other fixed expences*, entailed on us by the war; and from the attempt which is now making to bring us upon a *par* of exchange with other countries, by *diminishing the quantity of our paper-money.*…

"I contended,…that, if the quantity of paper were to be so *diminished* as to bring the pound note to be worth 20s. in gold, the people *who pay the taxes to support the funds must all be ruined*; and this ruin is now actually taking place in consequence of *an attempt to raise the value of the paper*. The Bank.…has plunged agriculture and trade and rents and debts and credits all into confusion.…Was it not as plain as your nose is upon your face, that the land (from which all ability to pay taxes proceeds) could never pay interest in paper worth 20s. in the pound, for money which had been borrowed for it, and salaries (including pay of soldiers and sailors) which had taken place, in a paper worth 12s. or 15s. in the pound? When wheat was 15s. a bushel, the land was able to pay; but, if wheat be, by a diminution of the quantity of paper, made worth only 7s. a bushel, can it still be able to pay?"[200]

Cobbett, of course, had his own solution to the problem.

"The remedy is, therefore, as I said before, to *disband the whole of the army*; pay the officers their just due in half-pay; reduce the navy to the state of 1788, when France and Spain, and Holland and Denmark had fleets; reduce all salaries in proportion; cut off all pensions granted during pleasure; dispose of the public property which is called crown land; curtail the expences in every department; let the fundholders see, that there are solid taxes to meet the interest due to them; then cease to raise money on account of the Sinking Fund; and we shall be able to go on without *loans* and without *corn bills*. – And why should not this remedy be adopted?"[201]

In November 1815, Cobbett published an open letter to the Chancellor of the Exchequer.

"Prices are now much about the same as they were before the Anti-Jacobin War. But, is this the case with the pay of the army, navy, judges, police-justices, clerks, &c. &c.? You know very well that it is not. You know very well, that, on the *express ground of the rise in prices*, millions have been paid to the Royal Family; that their allowances have been augmented *on that ground*. You know also, that the salaries of the Judges, that the pay of the soldiers and sailors, that the salaries of the police-justices,

200 Political Register. 28/10/1815.
201 Political Register. 18/2/1815.

that the pensions and allowances to Ambassadors; in short, that all expences have been raised, for many years past, and that some of them have had augmentation upon augmentation, *on the express ground of the rises in the prices of the necessaries of life.* Well, then; now that the necessaries of life have fallen in price *a full half*, ought not the pay, salaries &c. to fall also, at least, back to the old mark? What pretext can there be for now paying these persons at the rate of dear-corn prices?

"The average price, for years, of the quartern loaf in London, was 18 pence. The average price is now, and has been for a long while, 11d. Green bacon was 17 shillings a score. It is now 10s. Malt was 16s. a bushel. It is now 9s....Upon this comparison of prices, we have lowered the pay of our labourers, smiths, wheelwrights &c. The men to whom we used to give 30d. a day, we now give 20d. I used to pay a shilling for job work where I now pay eight-pence.

"I am sure, Sir, you will not only see the justice, but the *necessity* of my reducing the wages of my labour *one third* when the price of my produce is reduced *one half.* And, I hope you will agree with me, because I cannot well see how you can differ with me as to this point, that the pay and allowances to the king, queen, princes, princesses, clerks, police-justices, soldiers, judges, sailors, commissioners, governors, &c. &c. ought also to be reduced, at least, in all cases where they were fixed at a time of high prices, or *raised* expressly to meet those prices."[202]

Cobbett was being neither very radical nor very outlandish here, as many others, even within the political establishment, were thinking along much the same lines. At the heart of government, deliberations were taking place concerning the reducing of payments to the public creditor in line with the raised value of money.

"For some weeks past, it has been matter of doubt, amongst the best-informed men, whether the Boroughmongers would pass laws to take from the fundholders part of their property, by lowering the interest of the debt, and finally sweep all the monied race away; or whether they would still uphold the funding system. The inducements to the former were considered very great; because such a measure would, at once, have relieved the land of all its burdens, and would have brought all the farmers and the country people into a state of comfort."[203]

Francis Horner was a prominent member of the Whig opposition, and almost its appointed spokesman on all matters monetary and financial. He wrote to a friend, almost as if stating a commonplace;-

"I need not add, that the only practical measure to which I can look, as holding out any promise of easing the present suffering, would be such a reduction of establishments, as would render it practicable for the government, without violating any of its engagements to the public creditor, to remove a large proportion of the taxes that press most directly and heavily upon the capital employed in cultivation."[204]

Even the members of the government were expecting economies, apparently both in 1815 and 1816. J. C. Herries, Rothschild's man in government, wrote to a former colleague of his disappointment at the lack of any retrenchment for the second year running.

"I have been prevented from writing to you lately by a fit of business considerably beyond the ordinary course of things, in which certain meetings, calculations, and conferences, resolutions and waverings of and about the Budget have a considerable part. The crisis (behind the curtain) is now past, and I am just in that state in which you and I found ourselves upon the same occasion last year. A good, wise, and economical Budget has crumbled in our grasp, the higher powers have yielded to the subordinate departments."[205]

Two months later, he wrote to the assistant secretary of the Treasury.

202 Political Register. 11/11/1815.
203 Political Register. New York ed. 17/2/1816.
204 Leonard Horner. Memoirs and Correspondence of Francis Horner. P. 288.
205 Memoir of the Public Life of J. C. Herries. Vol. I. P. 115.

"We had much better be at war than allow so great an expenditure to continue during peace, and all our efforts here will be useless unless we check extravagance abroad."[206]

The agreed financial estimates were presented to the House of Commons by Vansittart in February 1816. Cobbett commented.

"It has been resolved, if we may judge from the estimates and intended taxation, to uphold the funding system, at least for the present, even if, to do that, it should be necessary to employ soldiers as the direct agents in the collection of taxes in England, as they have long been employed in that capacity, and with perfect success, in Ireland."[207]

Although the size of the projected expenditure astonished even Herries, it was, in the event, exceeded. Even the Prime Minister, Lord Liverpool, seemed daunted at the prospect of having to justify such an enormous expenditure.

So how was this decision arrived at, apparently in defiance of the views even of the members of the government? Cobbett, as an outsider, surmised the decision-making process to be as follows.

"Thus, at the sitting, perhaps, of one council of placemen; in the space, perhaps, of one hour; by the speaking, perhaps, of five sentences; by the mere turning, as it were, of a screw, a whole nation of tax-payers have been robbed of half their property, and that, too, by those who are paid for taking care of their concerns; but which act of robbery could not have been committed without the existence of a great Bank, closely connected with, and dependent upon the government."[208]

Those closer to the heart of government managed to point the finger more precisely. Herries's son and biographer had a more concrete idea of which department, principally, had managed to impose its will on a reluctant ministry.

"The one chiefly concerned was undoubtedly the War Office, at the head of which was, and had been for several years, Lord Palmerston, whose speeches in that year, 1816, breathe the most determined spirit of opposition to real retrenchment. He it is who must be held mainly responsible for the refusal of the then Tory Government to satisfy the reasonable demand of the nation for an immediate and sufficient relief from the immense burdens laid upon the people."

A battle was certainly going on behind the scenes (or behind the curtain, as the contemporary expression was) between the government, wanting economy, and the upper echelons of the military establishment, wishing to keep its whole structure in place in peacetime. Against the court, the Duke of York, brother to the King, and the Duke of Wellington, ministers could make little headway.[209]

But Lord Palmerston was an aristocrat with close connections not just with the military, but also with the monied interests of the City; and that should remind us that there were several powerful interests which operated "behind the curtain". The decision to keep up most of the taxes; to maintain a standing army in time of peace; to preserve salaries, pensions and sinecures at inflated levels; and to keep up the levels of interest paid on the national debt; all at a time when prices and wages were in freefall owing to the monetary policies of government and bank; this was surely one of the most glaringly disgraceful decisions ever taken by a British government. The motivations behind it were characterised by Cobbett, and published only at New York, for fear of prosecution and imprisonment.

"Many very powerful men are great fundholders, as you will easily suppose when you perceive, that the annual interest of the National Debt was equal in amount (and now surpasses) the whole of the annual rental of the kingdom. These persons naturally wished to add to their incomes by raising the value of the paper, whereby they would obtain payment in gold, or in paper nearly equal to gold,

---

206 Ibid. P. 116.
207 Political Register. New York ed. 17/2/1816.
208 Political Register. New York ed. 13/1/1816.
209 J. E. Cookson. Lord Liverpool's Administration. Pp. 30-31.

for a loan which they had made in depreciated paper. Amongst these *great fundholders* were the *King and Queen*, owning between them more, I believe, , than three millions of stock, and which stock is, by act of parliament, *exempted from the Property Tax*....The interests of these two fundholders were not the last to be taken into view by ministers. Besides, there were the interests of the Civil List, of all the Placemen, active and sinecure, all the pensioners, royal and noble....

"All had a great and immediate interest, in the *raising of the value of money*; for, in whatever degree that took place, their salaries must, of course, be augmented.

"Under the influence of such a mass of powerful motives, it was no wonder that the ministers resolved to raise the value of the paper-money, in order to wring double taxes from the people.

"The Bank of England, in concert with ministers, began to *narrow its discounts*, especially to country banks, who were forced to do the same. In less than a year the quantity of paper was so diminished that the bushel of wheat fell to 7s. after being from 15s. to 17s. for many years, while taxes of all descriptions continued the same, and were collected with daily increasing vigour."[210]

The consequences were striking.

"Never, in the history of the world, was so great a change produced, in so short a time, in any community. Paper-money is like drams, or opium. It produces an exhilaration that is quite wonderful; but the depression that follows is not less striking. It animates and sets in motion every fibre in the frame of society; but it leaves behind it a morbid melancholy, a listlessness approaching the inactivity of death."[211]

From this time, until Cobbett's flight to America at the end of March 1817, the Political Register became an increasingly gloomy catalogue of the miseries deliberately inflicted upon the English nation by its government, by means of currency manipulation combined with excessive taxation.

The extreme flow and ebb of prosperity was perhaps most clearly to be seen in the countryside.

"The whole of society here has been puffed up by the abundance of paper-money. I will give you an instance. Thirty or forty years ago, and, perhaps, twenty-five years ago, the farmers, who used to attend the market at Farnham, the town where I was born, used to walk to the market, or ride a tame old horse, to sell their corn. When they had done this in the market-place, they used to return to the place where their horses were put up, and there drink a pint of beer, price 2d., and, perhaps, add 2d. worth of bread and cheese, or get a dinner for 6d. or 8d. and then go home. The greater part of them were dressed in smock-frocks, or very plain and coarse coats. How surprised was I, when, happening to be at the head Inn in the town, on my way to London, about 15 years ago, and hearing a roaring of '*three times three*', and a thumping of tables and rattling of glasses and bottles, I learnt upon inquiry, that it was *the Farmers after their market dinner*!

"....The English farmer has, of late years, become a totally different character. A fox-hunting horse; polished boots; a spanking trot to market; a 'get out of the way, or, by G-d I'll ride over you' to every poor devil upon the road; wine at his dinner; a carpet on his floor; a bell in his parlour; a servant (and sometimes in livery) to wait at his table; a painted lady for a wife; novel-reading daughters; sons aping the young 'squires and lords; a house crammed with sofa's, piano's, and all sorts of fooleries."[212]

But in the years following 1814, the drunken fit was over, and the farmer awoke and had to face the hangover. Cobbett never tired of illustrating his changed situation in terms of the number of bushels of wheat equivalent which he was compelled to pay to the government.

---

210 Political Register. New York ed. 13/1/1816.
211 Political Register. 16/12/1815.
212 Political Register. 16/12/1815.

"The farmer, who grows 100 quarters of wheat can get on if the government demand 50 quarters towards the payment of the debt expences, and the army, and navy, and royal family and other things; but if the government demand 90 quarters of it, the farmer cannot go on."[213]

If a farmer who grew 50 quarters of wheat paid £200 in taxes, when the price was high, at, say, 120 shillings a quarter, the government relieved him of around 32 quarters of wheat. If, however, the price of wheat fell to 60 shillings, his obligation to the government rose to 64 quarters, and the farmer had to fall back on capital and stock to meet it. And this was the case all over England.

The sudden change in the quantity, and therefore the value, of the paper currency, threw all monetary dealings into total confusion.

"For instance, the Bank-note, the Pound-note, is to day worth thirteen shillings in silver. I borrow a pound of my neighbour. Next week, this same pound-note is worth twenty shillings in silver. My neighbour calls upon me to pay him the pound. Consequently I pay him a thing that is worth seven shillings more than that which I borrowed."[214]

"I will suppose a case, thousands and thousands of which exist at this moment in England. JOHN STILES is a farmer, who has saved some money; but not enough to purchase a farm which he has in his eye belonging to MR. GATES. However, he buys it for 10,000l. and borrows 4,000l. of the money on mortgage, which he is very fairly justified in doing, seeing that his *farming stock* is worth 4,000l. or, perhaps, more; and that, in a few years there is every reason to believe, that he will be able to *clear off his mortgage*. – Wheat is, upon an average of years, 15s. a bushel, and all other prices are in proportion.

"Thus stand the affairs of Stiles today. He is a man of considerable property, and his children expect to have considerable fortunes. But, the Bank begins to draw in the paper; the guinea falls in price; the wheat falls with the guinea; the receipts of Stiles diminish; his interest on the mortgage continues the same. At last, wheat comes down to 6s. He cannot get on without selling off some of his farming stock. The tax-gatherer is unrelenting. The farming goes bit by bit. It brings hardly any thing. Having so little money to lay out on labour, the land falls into decay; it produces less; the mortgagee presses; the interest is not paid; the land is sold; it scarcely brings the 4,000l. borrowed on it, and Stiles and his family are ruined.

"Now, this is an operation which has, for a year, been going on all over the country. The same effect is produced on persons in trade; for, if a man has laid in his *stock* when wheat was 15s. a bushel; if he has bought his goods or had them manufactured; if he has rented his shop, or his yards; if he has contracted debts, or has borrowed money to trade with; if he has done all, or any, of these things (and some of them *every* man in trade must have done) when the paper-money was so abundant to cause wheat to be 15s. a bushel, such a reduction in the quantity of paper-money as to bring wheat down to 6s. a bushel must be very injurious to him; and, if he trade upon borrowed money, he must be ruined."[215]

Tenant farmers who had agreed to a fixed rent could hardly produce enough income from their land to pay the rent alone. Whole parishes were unable to pay the assessed taxes, the payment of tax being quite beyond the ability of many. Those farmers who had money put by could pay taxes out of capital for the time being; otherwise resort was had to the selling off of the stock necessary for the cultivation of the land. The taxing authorities took an intolerant view of inability to pay. A wealthy landowning M.P. recited to the House of Commons in 1816 a sad set of statistics concerning writs and executions. In Norfolk, that year, 1607 sheriff's writs were issued, and executions on goods had risen from 96 to 147 in the space of a year. In Worcestershire, in the year to February 1815, there

---

213 Political Register. 18/2/1815.
214 Political Register. 16/3/1816.
215 Political Register. 20/4/1816.

were 640 writs and executions; in the year following, the number was 890. 186 parishes were being prosecuted by the Exchequer for non-payment. In Suffolk, in the same period, the number of writs and executions had risen from 450 to 870. And so on. Cobbett noticed in the newspapers many estates advertised for sale *by order of the Commissioners of the Property Tax*. He noted many sales by distress warrants for rent and taxes.[216]

"The property at these sales is really *given away*. A plough, which, only a few years ago, cost, perhaps, 5 pounds, is sold frequently for 10 or 15 shillings. A threshing machine, which cost *fifty* pounds was, the other day, not far from my house, sold for *five* pounds."[217]

In very many cases the value of the stock thus sold did not cover the arrears, and in these cases the farmer was imprisoned for debt.

"Many men in my neighbourhood, in Hampshire, supposed to be of great wealth a twelvemonth ago, are now in Winchester jail, their families in all the horrors of misery, in the midst of a community no one of whom is able to afford relief. It is computed, that there are *Five Thousand Farmers*, lately deemed opulent men, at this moment in the jails of England and Wales. The persons belonging to their families may amount to *twenty-five thousand*, exclusive of the tradesmen that they have dragged down with them."[218]

Suicides, "from pecuniary distress", were making "dreadful ravages".

"At no great distance a farmer, a fine young man, not married many years, and who had a good fortune, has just *cut his throat*. Two others, within my observation, have gone *mad*."[219]

It was hardly surprising, under such circumstances, that farmers took what steps they could to avoid the above fates. Reports reached Cobbett from all parts of the country of numerous farms being *"abandoned by the tenants in an uncultivated state."* Thousands of farms were being thrown back into the hands of the landlords. This was often done in a regular manner through notice to quit; but it became increasingly common for farming families to collect up their belongings, leave the farm by night, and flee the country. Vast swathes of the country were being abandoned to the thistles and the brambles. A member announced in parliament that "there were Parishes in Cambridgeshire which had been left as wild and desolate as any Colony which we had."[220]

Those farmers who survived were not the same as they had been.

"Farmers are drawing in their expenditure in all directions. They are lessening the number of their horses and of their labourers. Every sort of work that will admit of delay, is delayed or given up. The land is either badly tilled, or is left wholly untilled, in numerous cases….They have put a total stop to all *improvements*; to all the means of enriching land; there will be hardly any fallowing; the riches that are in the land will be drawn out of it; springs will be suffered to overflow; fences will fall out of repair; and, in two years, if things continue thus, the improvements, the sources of wealth and strength, acquired by the industry and enterprise of twenty years, will have been lost."[221]

Agriculture being fundamental to the economy, the distress of the farmers was felt throughout the whole of it, as domestic demand for commodities of all sorts melted away. Farmers could not *"suffer alone*….they cannot feel a blow, though it be ever so trifling, which is not felt by every other class of the community. If the cultivator of the land be ruined, so must the owner, so must the tradesman, so must the manufacturer, and so must every one, *who receives nothing out of the taxes*."[222]

---

216 Political Register. New York ed. 16/1/1816. London ed. 9/3/1816 and 16/3/1816.
217 Political Register. 13/4/1816.
218 Political Register. New York ed. 13/1/1816.
219 Political Register. New York ed. 2/3/1816.
220 Political Register. 4/11/1815, 11/11/1815, 13/4/1816 and 16/3/1816.
221 Political Register. 11/11/1815 and 23/3/1816.
222 Political Register. 4/11/1815.

Cobbett stopped again at that same inn at Farnham, and spent the whole day there writing his editorial.

"I found, though it was a market day, every thing as quiet as a Quaker Meeting. The retrograde movement has been more rapid than the advance. Nothing short of *wine* has, of late years, been drunk at these market dinners. That beverage has, in a twinkling, wholly disappeared. The far greater part of the farmers now go home without dining at all. At the sign of the GEORGE, in Winchester, the waiter told me, last week, that the Farmers used to spend from *ten* to *twelve* pounds of a market day, and that now they do not spend more than a pound, or thirty shillings. Thus, here at this inn alone, a diminution of the receipts, from the Farmers only, of more than £500 a year."[223]

"The tradespeople feel the effects of the want of money even more than the farmers….The market-day was, in all parts of the country, a day of gaiety and bustle in the towns. The shops were filled with customers. The villages and farm-houses sent in their money. Now they have no money to send in. All is poverty. Nobody can either make purchases or pay debts."[224]

And on the already distressed poor the weight of misery fell at last. Wages, where they could be obtained at all, plummeted. In Cambridgeshire, men were working for 8d. a day, and it was feared that worse was to come.[225]

"It is now become a common practice to *discharge* almost the whole of the labourers, send them for relief to the *parish*, and then to hire them, from the parish, at sixpence a day; thus reducing them to the lowest possible scale of bodily subsistence, and degrading them nearly to the level of beasts. Yet, what are the farmers to do? They have not the means of paying any thing worthy to be called *wages*."[226]

"Young and old, there can be little short of 2 million paupers in England, including common beggars and persons in hospitals and almshouses; and that is, upon an average, about one pauper or beggar, to every *four* who are not paupers or beggars."[227]

But poor relief could no longer be relied upon, as many parishes had been deserted, the farmers having fled before the incessant demands of the tax-gatherer and the overseer of the poor. A farmer from Kent complained that he was the only rate-payer remaining in his parish, the landlords refusing to take over deserted farms for fear of the overseer. In such parishes as this, the poor were forced to move on; the roads were crowded with paupers, as they spread themselves out across a countryside unable to support them, causing "devastation and distress wherever they proceeded."[228]

Just as it was thought that the situation could not get any worse, the government gave another turn of the screw. In April 1816, a bill was introduced into parliament to release the Bank of England from paying its note in coin for a further two years. The result was certain to be a new proliferation of paper money. Lord Castlereagh, announcing the measure in the House of Commons, assured members that banks would now "advance sufficiently to diminish the existing pressure", and that the price of wheat was likely to rise as a consequence. With a malignant triumphalism he proclaimed;-

"If it should rise to 80s. or 90s. he should be glad to know where would be the distress."[229]

By May, the effects were already being felt.

"The Paper-money begins to work….The wheat, *which two months ago*, sold at 6s. a bushel, now sells at very nearly 12s. a bushel! The moment the *Bank Bill* was proposed, the rise began; and I expect

223 Political Register. 16/12/1815.
224 Political Register. 9/12/1815.
225 Political Register. New York ed. 6/4/1816.
226 Political Register. 23/3/1816.
227 Political Register. 13/4/1816.
228 Political Register. 16/3/1816, and New York ed. 6/4/1816.
229 Political Register. 13/4/1816 and 20/4/1816.

to see wheat 15s. a bushel in a month or two more….Many of the farmers; indeed, all the small and poorer farmers feel additional suffering from this rise."[230]

Nearly the whole crop of corn had been forced off the farms and on to the market by the combined effects of the slump in prices and the incessant demands of the Treasury. Farmers were no longer in a position to benefit from a rise in prices, as most of the corn was now in the hands of the dealers. The financial establishment included many wealthy corn-dealers. It seems almost certain that some were to be found among the directors of the Bank of England. Some bankers dealt in corn. Some major loan-contractors dealt in corn. And the same applies to wealthy speculators of all sorts, the price of whose commodities was affected by constant currency manipulation. Corn had been forced cheaply into the hands of the great dealers by the reduction of paper-issues, and the price then forced up again by the subsequent monetary relaxation.

"So that here is an effect the most injurious and distressing that can be imagined; and, indeed, the most unfair and unjust; what must the state of that country be, where thousands upon thousands of industrious farmers and tradesmen, persons of property, too, without any fault of their own, without any of those accidents commonly called misfortunes, but merely by operation of a measure of the government, may, in any six months, of any year, be plunged into a state of pauperism? This is really and literally our case…."[231]

The distresses of the poor were ratcheted up once more.

"Our labourers at Botley have been, for some time, receiving about 18 or 20 pence a day. That is to say, the price of a *bushel of flour* in a week. Their wages will not now purchase much more than *half a bushel*; yet it will be some weeks, perhaps, two months, or more, before they will obtain a rise of day-wages. In the mean while, they must be half starved, or go to the parish; and thus a new batch of paupers will be created. But it is endless to describe the evils, the injustice, the cruelty, the curses, of such a system."[232]

Even before this latest rise in prices, noted Cobbett, the labourer had not enough to eat.

"Now he is wretched indeed; and, the worst of it is, that the resources of the farmers are so much exhausted, that, until long after harvest, they will not be able to add a penny to the wages of their labourers or to find employment for an additional hand. So that here we have before us five months of distress not to be described by the pen or the tongue. Here springs up new work for the Military, for the Hulks, and the Gallows!…."

"Thus THE SYSTEM goes on, continually, swagging from side to side."[233]

This swagging, this constantly engineered fluctuation of the currency, this system of boom and bust, brought down towards ruin, not just the poor, but all those classes of society who were not the beneficiaries of the system. The traditional landowning class, for instance, was disappearing fast.

"It is probable, therefore, that unless some sturdy accident should take place, the thing may drawl on, and that the fund-holders may quietly swallow up three or four fifths of the present land owners, and send ten or a dozen of loyal `Squires and their wives to inhabit snug lodgings in the outskirts of London and of the watering-places. As to their sons, the French have already knocked a good many of them in the head; the rest are Excise-men, Customs-house Officers, and the like; and their daughters will do very well for stockbrokers' wives."[234]

230 Political Register. 11/5/1816.
231 Political Register. 11/5/1816.
232 Ibid.
233 Political Register. 18/5/1816.
234 Political Register. 14/9/1816.

In society as organised along traditional lines, the presence of the landowner on his estate conferred many benefits on the poor of the locality, and increasingly, these were coming to be sorely missed.

"The people of England still remember, those who are old enough, and those who are young still hear their fathers say, how much they owed to the hospitality which formerly reigned throughout the country and particularly in the mansions of the gentlemen. These mansions they now see abandoned, literally abandoned, I mean. They see the antient inhabitants actually driven forth by the tax-gatherer, and the scenes of former plenty and mirth they see changed into a miserable solitude."[235]

The employing classes were equally badly hit.

"It is the anxiety, the heart-achings, the agonizing forebodings of the fathers and mothers in the middle classes of life, whose days have been divided between the caresses of their children and their own incessant industry to provide for their support and respectability. Let LORD HARROWBY[236] look at a father and mother of this description, when the former, after all his struggles to overcome his reluctance, has just communicated to the latter the fatal intelligence of his ruin. Let him behold the death-like gloom on their countenances. Let him hear their sighs, when their children, with inquisitive tenderness, ask the cause of that gloom….let him reflect, that such scenes are now to be beheld in a great proportion of the farmers' and tradesmen's houses in the kingdom."[237]

The middle classes, of course, were the principal employers, and their ruin had a knock-on effect throughout the community.

"How many of those employers have, of late, gone to jail for debt, and left helpless families behind them! The employer's trade falls off. His goods are reduced in price. His stock loses half of its value. He owes money. He is ruined; and how can he continue to pay *high wages*?"[238]

Many opulent families sought refuge in emigration, and the tradesmen and manufacturers followed their customers. The ending of the war in 1814 provided the opportunity; the manipulation of the currency the spur; and the cheapness of plentiful living abroad the draw. Already by early 1816, Cobbett estimated that 40,000 English families were living on the Continent.[239]

"There is now really an *alarm* felt on this account. It is not the *miserable* only that are in motion. I hear of most respectable and most valuable men, who are selling off in order to go to America…. Many hundreds of families of property, of great respectability, distinguished for their industry and knowledge of business *as farmers*, are selling off and preparing to depart."[240]

And, as Cobbett observed, they left their share of the property tax and the poor-rate to be paid by their former neighbours. Such people as these were the customers of the poor, the employers of them; their patrons, and the contributors to charity and poor-rates. Their ruin or departure was yet another major factor in the ever-increasing intensity of impoverishment and degradation.

The full extent of those sufferings we will never know. Establishment writers would not describe them; others could not. The probable reason for this was as related by Cobbett.

"Now the suffering is too dreadful to be thought of without deep mental affliction."

Lord Castlereagh had the gall to suggest in the House of Commons that "the distresses had been exaggerated".

---

235 Political Register. 10/8/1816.

236 Who proclaimed the country to be in a prosperous condition!

237 Political Register. 29/3/1817.

238 Political Register. 2/11/1816

239 Political Register. New York ed. 13/1/1816.

240 Political Register. 22/6/1816.

"By whom?", indignantly retorted Cobbett. "Not a pen, except mine, has moved on the subject of those distresses. I, indeed, have made some feeble attempts to paint them; but, it has appeared to be the chief object with the rest of the press to *disguise them*, or, at least, to palliate their nature.

"I defy any human powers, to paint the distresses of the country in their true light; I defy any pen or any tongue to do them justice, or to describe, even by partial instances, the distress, the misery, the distracted state of mind of a very large portion of the community."[241]

The most obvious manifestation of those distresses was the outbreak of disorder triggered by the sudden rise in prices in May 1816. The beginning of this phase of violence announced itself in the Political Register with a series of incidents of incendiarism in Essex and Suffolk, in which ricks, barns, outbuildings and a malthouse were set alight. That same month, there were bread riots at Bridport in Dorset. In June, rioting spread to Brandon and Halesworth in Suffolk, and to the Isle of Ely. It was put down in North Devon before it got out of hand, but, meanwhile, frame-breaking resumed at Loughborough in Leicestershire. Discontent became audible in Manchester, too.[242]

"From *Devonshire* to *Scotland*, you see, that discontents prevail, and that risings have taken place, and, every where you see *troops called out*.... We now *see* and *feel* the consequences of the war and its debt."

The most serious disturbances were at Ely and Littleport. Liberal use was made there both of cavalry and foot soldiers, and two judges were sent out with Special Commissions. "The result has been the quelling of tumults in that part of the country, and the hanging, transporting, or otherwise punishing, a considerable number of persons."[243]

A wave of subsistence criminality swept the country at the same time. In an open letter to the people of the United States, Cobbett compared their country with his own.

"There are never any riots about *prices* in your country. The market people are never attacked there. A woman, a girl, a boy, or any weak old man, sets off in the evening, and travels *all night*, with a cart or on horse back, with meat, butter, eggs, &c, from all parts of the country, to arrive at Philadelphia market at break of day. Thousands of people do this in the course of every year; and I never heard of any one being robbed on the way. Now, I will venture to say, that if a woman, so laden, was to attempt in like manner, to travel to any town in England, during the night, she would never arrive safe at the end of thirty miles; and that, if she had as many lives as a cat, she would lose them before she would, by night (and her route being previously known) carry her money home."

Of course, the United States were largely peopled by Englishmen, or their descendants.

"Am I to allow, think you, that it is in the *nature* of Englishmen to rob and murder?...It is *want*; it is *sheer hunger*; this is what fills a country with robbers, and also with murderers, seeing that murder is frequently necessary to the perfecting of robbery."[244]

Less dramatically, much of the country remained quiet under this pressure, and in many counties distress found its outlet in meetings to petition for parliamentary reform, in a campaign organised by Cobbett and his fellow radicals. Ominously, the government found these rather more disturbing than food rioting, to which the use of military force was a ready and effective response.

Such were the clearly apparent signs of distress. But behind them lay a mass of extreme misery, such as the historical sources are unable to reveal for us. Cobbett, however, described some facets for us in the Political Register.

Among these were the observations of his own eyes. At this time, Cobbett lived and farmed near Botley, in Hampshire, in an area so full of all the natural advantages that tended to the well-being

241 Political Register. 8/2/1817.
242 Political Register. 18/5/1816 and 8/6/1816.
243 Political Register. 6/7/1816.
244 Political Register. 8/6/1816.

of the poor, that distress was very tardy in arriving there. But by 1816, it was "involved in one mass of misery."

"It is useless, however, to enter into descriptions. Since my return from London, in March, more than 300 labourers have applied for work, and none have I been able to employ. I see scores of young men, formed by nature to be athletic, rosy-cheeked and bold;...I see them thin as herrings, dragging their feet after them, pale as a ceiling, and sneaking about like beggars....The paupers really swarm about our fields and hedges. Or rather, the labouring people are all become paupers."[245]

Even in the opulent and well-run neighbouring parish of Titchfield, which Cobbett thought a model for all other parishes, "decent, honest, able and well-behaved labourers, and those in great numbers, too, are compelled to become paupers."

Of course, conditions in other parts of the country were far worse. In the city of Coventry, there were 8,000 paupers, out of a total population of 20,000. And throughout the country as a whole, Cobbett estimated that there were "a million people, men and their families, supported by *subscription*, exclusive of the paupers usually so called." Indeed, the system of poor relief was breaking down, and there were extensive tracts of country where the parishes could no longer support their poor.[246]

"The Magistrates near Birmingham, at least in that part of England, have given certificates under their hands, to the poor manufacturers, declaring them to be *fit objects of charity*; and, with these, they have sent them forth in all directions to beg! This is not only not justified by the law, but it is in open defiance of the law which permits of *no begging*....The Magistrates in Warwickshire know this as well as I do, and therefore, you may easily suppose the magnitude of the distress which surrounds them....But what must be the nature of that necessity, which bears down before it all the fences of law?...The truth is, I dare say, that, the parishes to which these manufacturers belong, are utterly unable to maintain them, though to the aid of one parish other parishes may be called, if necessary. In this case whole districts of parishes appear to have been rendered incapable, and thus the Magistrates, in order to avoid riot, plunder, and murder, have sent the people forth to prowl over the kingdom in search of food."[247]

Staffordshire appears to have been in a similar situation, as some of the wandering paupers from there turned up in Cobbett's village of Botley, in Hampshire.

"The story they tell is this; that *thirteen thousand* of them, for whom no work could be found, have divided themselves into equal bodies, and marched one body into each county; that a due proportion have come into Hampshire; and we see *ten* at Southampton. They are to re-assemble, it seems, at stated times, and then agree upon new routes. Their business is to maintain themselves by *begging*; and they bring printed papers, *signed by Magistrates*, certifying who and what they are! Thus has one county sent forth thirteen thousand able men to beg! This is in direct violation of the well-known law of the land....Perhaps every fourth man that goes along the turnpike road before my door, is a 'rogue and vagabond' in the eye of the law."[248]

In his newspaper, Cobbett published reports from various other parts of the country. Two letters from the industrial West Midlands were first published in the Times. The Times, as Cobbett never tired of pointing out, was a part of the establishment press, and had therefore an interest in minimising the extent of the distress. He reprinted the letters for his readers. From Bilston, we hear;-

"If I were to transcribe all these tales of woe, or even half of them, I should fill a volume; it is sufficient to observe, that the number of poor inhabitants without employment is unprecedented.... It is a melancholy truth that there are *many families almost, if not quite, starving....*"

---

245 Political Register. 10/8/1816 and 6/7/1816.
246 Political Register. 20/3/1817.
247 Political Register. 7/9/1816.
248 Political Register. 16/11/1816.

At neighbouring Corseley, misery flooded in upon the inhabitants immediately upon the return of the peace, from which so much good was expected.

"Trade got worse, money became scarce, confidence disappeared, the bankers withheld their accustomed accommodations, the stocks of goods increased on hand, until the manufacturers were obliged to put their people to five days' work a week, then to four, to three, to two, and finally to stop them. The coal, iron-stone, and iron-masters, were in the same situation; and, therefore, pits, furnaces, foundries, forges, mills, shops, and manufactories of iron, &c, were put to stand; and it is now computed, upon a moderate calculation, that in the parishes of Bilston, Sedgley, Tipton, Dudley, and Kingswinsford, not less than 15,000 persons are thrown out of employment, some of whom have not had work for more than thirteen weeks....I would much rather leave it to your conception than attempt to describe the unutterable distress with which this sudden reverse has overwhelmed the country."[249]

The scale of the calamity completely overwhelmed the sources of charity, and stretched to breaking point, and beyond, the machinery of poor relief. Rates became insupportable, and workhouses were crammed so full that hopeful inmates were being turned away in hundreds. There were so many paupers in the poor house at Bilston that they were forced to sleep by rotation.

"These families are forced to maintain a miserable existence – some families with one shilling a week, some with less, and others with no parochial allowance at all....*I have heard of several that have actually died for want*....To tell you the truth, I have it not in my power to give what I would, and therefore I cannot bear to visit those abodes of distress which I cannot alleviate....my heart bleeds particularly for poor helpless children, *pale as death, and crawling about like walking skeletons*. To recite the sufferings of individuals would fill a volume, and tire your patience."[250]

Cobbett published the report of investigations in the parish of St. Mary's, Islington.

"They have found the cases of extreme poverty and privation SO NUMEROUS, that they must confine themselves to a general representation of facts.."

There were about 300 people "totally out of employ, almost naked, and without a bed to lie on and WITHOUT A PENNY TO PURCHASE BREAD." A further very numerous class was those partly unemployed, who lived on just a few shillings a week with large families to support. The report concludes;-

"Among these are *many people who have seen better days, and have endeavoured by every means to avoid becoming burthensome* to their Parish or their Neighbours, and who, it is to be feared, *would actually have perished* but for the investigation to which the present institution has given rise....such is the extent of the present distress, that the first object should be to meet those cases of distress, under which, without relief, *the sufferers are in danger of perishing*."[251]

A common feature of all these reports is a symptom of distress which we noticed during the famines of the 1790s – the pawning or selling of every item of clothing and every article of furniture, in order to stay alive. A report on the distresses of unemployed watchmakers in London noted huge amounts of furniture, bedding, apparel and tools of the trade pledged for money. At Corseley in the West Midlands, the people who had "*sold their furniture, their clothes and every disposable article they possessed to buy them bread with, are now left without a bed, a chair, a spoon, a knife, or cup*; to inhabit empty houses, with empty pockets and empty bellies...."[252]

At St. Mary's, Islington, goods had been pledged to the value of £1,500. In this parish, "a *poor but respectable widow*....travelled *nearly three miles*, from the extremity of the parish where she resided, TO

249 Political Register. 3/8/1816.
250 Political Register. 8/2/1817.
251 Ibid.
252 Political Register. 3/8/1816.

PROCURE THREE HALFPENCE" upon an article which she wished to pawn. Here, investigators came across families "where they have, by distress, been obliged to pawn almost every necessary, to provide in the interim a little sustenance, who are willing to work, but can find no employment; and some Families have been found, where the poor people, with hardly any thing to cover their nakedness, have not even a bed of the poorest kind, but lie upon straw or shavings, all their little earnings being unequal to the cravings of hunger."[253]

The report on the plight of the watchmakers concludes with an observation which must have been true of all these reports. The members of the committee had visited all applicants for relief, "and they have to state, that the returns made by the sufferers, far from being exaggerated, fall much short of their real distress."[254]

Another symptom of extreme distress which agitated Cobbett was the desertion of families. A placard appeared in London on behalf of the authorities of two united parishes, announcing the intention to apprehend and punish "MANY PERSONS DESERTING THEIR FAMILIES", as well as the absconding parents of illegitimate children; and also any one who should harbour them. This provoked Cobbett's indignation.

"These insolent men, while wallowing in wealth, do not reflect on the pangs which must wring the poor man's heart before he can so far subdue the feelings of the husband and the father as to make him 'desert his family'; or, if they do reflect on them, they must be more cruel than the storms and the waves. The labouring men in England, generally speaking, are the kindest and most indulgent of husbands and of parents. It has often been observed by me, that they are generally so to a fault."

And the reason for this?

"They see their children in want; they grow up in continual suffering; they are incessantly objects of compassion over and above the love which nature has implanted in the parent's breast….If I have here, as I am sure I have, given the true character of the English labourer, as a parent and a husband, what must that state of things be, which has rendered the *desertion of families* so frequent an offence as to call forth a hand-bill and *placard* such as that which I have quoted above?"[255]

Yet another report from London found its way into the Political Register – of a man dying quietly in a London street.

"The deceased is apparently *about fifty years of age*, the most *complete picture of extreme human misery*, having *no linen upon his back*, and *his bones almost through his skin*. By his dress, he appears to be a workman out of employ. He has not been OWNED."

Cobbett commented, "Hundreds must perish in this way."[256]

In March 1817, Cobbett published in the Register a letter from a *Medical Man*.

"I have, Sir, paid great attention to the subject of contagious diseases, and have read and sought for all the information I could get on the subject. It is a fact, and a well-known medical fact, too, that nothing renders the human body so liable to disease, particularly to contagious diseases, as poverty and wretchedness. Now, Sir, it is notorious that there are thousands of our countrymen in a state of starvation and living in places not fit to keep a dog in. It is only last week that I attended a starving family, affected with the putrid sore throat; they were living in a miserable cellar, with five panes of glass broken in the window, the floor was half covered with water, and they had no fire, and only one bed for six of them; the father was lying ill of the putrid fever, in the King's Bench Prison. It was with difficulty I could restrain my tears at this accumulation of misery. I find it is become a common practice, now, for the poor to sleep six in a bed; and this they are enabled to do by lying three in the

---

253 Ibid.
254 Political Register 29/3/1817.
255 Political Register. 16/11/1816.
256 Ibid.

common manner, and the other three with their feet up to the others' heads, and their heads at the bottom of the bed. To what a state of wretchedness and poverty is this country reduced to! I could give hundreds of instances of poverty equal to the above. It is only a month or two since, that a whole family was on the point of death from starvation; and had it not been that an acquaintance happened to call, they would have perished. One youth, a lad of 17 or 18, the eldest boy, was dead, and that for want of food, too; the other son, a boy of 15, was out, endeavouring to pawn his jacket for three-pence. The person who called on them was so much affected at the horrid scene, that she fainted…. Food was procured for them, and their manner of eating it was more like that of carnivorous animals than human beings, to such a state of hunger were they reduced."

This Medical Man warned of the dangers of the spread of "diseases of the most alarming and contagious nature", through a population thus impoverished and debilitated. He attributed the misery to "the weight of taxation", which was "fast destroying the health and happiness of thousands." And, like Cobbett, he traced the evil to a defective representation.

"Until a Reform takes place in the Parliament, the present system will not be abandoned, and therefore the pressure of taxation will continue – probably be increased, if possible."

Changing the subject but slightly, he continued.

"It is a fact not generally known, and one that makes a man shudder to think of, and sufficient to make an Englishman hang down his head in sorrow, that such is the condition of the poor, that the mothers of many families support their children and their husbands by the prostitution of their persons. Is this the end of the glorious war? Is this its consummation? Oh, shame! Shame!....What must be the feelings of a man who is supported, and whose children are fed by the prostitution of his wife? It is a most unnatural state of society, and speaks volumes as to the state of this unhappy country. Well might you say that crimes increase in proportion to the increase of taxation. The fact just mentioned is a most striking instance of the truth of the observation, producing the committal of a crime, which to Englishmen is odious, and which must appear horrid to every man who has either a head to think or a heart to feel. It is introducing a disease of a most loathsome kind into families, makes a brothel of the poor man's house, and subverts every moral principle."[257]

The letter from the Medical Man Cobbett inserted without comment; for what comment could he make?

"The fluctuation of price is the soul of trade." So wrote one of the corn-dealing pamphleteers from the middle of the 18th century. He was wrong. The genuine trader, with produce to sell, likes stability. It matters not to him whether prices be high or low, so long as expences are in proportion, and so long as he has, in advance, some rough idea of what those expences and those prices are going to be. It is the speculator, who produces nothing, who is benefited by the fluctuation of price, and that at the expence of the rest of the community. He profits even more if he has inside information as to when those fluctuations are to take place; and more still if he is directly in control of those fluctuations. During the debate on the Bank Restriction Bill, in April 1816, an M.P. stood up and made a plea for stability.

"If cash payments were not resumed, a great part of the paper that had been withdrawn from circulation would be gradually re-issued, increasing the price of every commodity, and proceeding in exactly the same course as that which the country had already witnessed. Something must be done to secure us from the dangers of the system. Better would it be to sit down with the loss of 20 per cent,

---

257   Political Register. 29/3/1817.

than gradually to increase the circulation of the country to an indefinite extent, and then expose the country to the dangers that might arise from a sudden panic."[258]

He was ignored. The reflation of the economy that began in April 1816 culminated in1818, when the rise in prices sucked in another massive import of corn. It was then that the powers decided that the system was too risky to be persisted in, and a genuine attempt was made to return to cash payments. The consequent diminution of the currency led once more to slump conditions like those of 1814 to 1816. A further reflation began with the Small Notes Act of 1822, combined with a generous issue of Exchequer Bills. This, in turn, led to the massive banking crash of 1825, in which even the government found itself virtually bankrupt. The system was saved from destruction then only by the bullion dealings of Nathan Rothschild. There were further serious crises in 1836, 1839 and 1847. And so on. Various legislative tinkerings went on, to try to prevent the recurrence of what were euphemistically called 'panics'; but no government and no parliament had the power or the will to put an end to the system of currency manipulation, of boom and bust; which, as we well know, persists to this day.

Summarising yet again the effects of the system, Cobbett asked his readers;-

"And is there to be no *responsibility* for all this terrible mischief? Are we to regard it as a visitation of Providence for our sins? Are we to sit down and cry, and to blame nobody on earth for it? A poor attempt has been made to make the nation believe, that all this misery has arisen from mere ordinary causes."[259]

Clearly, Cobbett reasoned, the blame lay with those who operated the system, and who were its beneficiaries; who had the power, at will, to cause prices to rise or fall; and who thus had control over the property of the entire nation, and could transfer it from one group to another.[260]

It will come as no surprise, then, that Cobbett's writings did not go down especially well with the financiers. In January 1817, a group of bankers, merchants and traders got together at the London Tavern and issued a declaration, blaming the disturbances that had been taking place in various parts of the kingdom, not on the distresses of the people, but on the writings of William Cobbett. It complained of "the endeavours which have recently been exerted with too much success, *by designing and evil-minded* men, to persuade the people that a remedy is to be found in measures which, under specious pretences, would effect the overthrow of the Constitution. To these endeavours *may be traced the criminal excesses which have lately disgraced the Metropolis and other parts of the Empire*; and the still more desperate and atrocious outrage which has recently been committed *against the sacred person of the Prince Regent.*...We cannot adequately express our abhorrence of these enormities, which, *if not repressed*, must lead to scenes of anarchy and bloodshed, too appalling to contemplate; and we feel it to be a solemn and imperious duty we owe to our country, to *pledge ourselves individually and collectively*, to support the just exercise of the *authority of Government*, to maintain the Constitution *as by law established*, and to resist every attempt, whether of craft or violence, that may be directed against our civil liberty and our social peace."

This was clearly an encouragement, possibly even an instruction, to the government, to bring in measures which would silence the vitriolic pen of William Cobbett. But still Cobbett replied in kind, issuing his own counter-declaration. In it, he asserted that the many riots had all been carried on "by persons in great want and misery", and that the objectives had been to obtain food by violent means. The fundamental cause of all the calamity was a system of fictitious money, which reduced huge numbers of people to near starvation by its sudden transitions from high to low and back again from low to high; and this was enabled to happen by the stoppage of cash payments at the Bank of

258 Thomas Frankland Lewis, quoted in Political Register, New York ed. 4/6/1816.
259 Political Register. 23/3/1816.
260 Political Register. 4/11/1815 and 16/3/1816.

England in 1797. Several of the governors and directors who had lobbied Pitt for this stoppage in 1797 were also signatories of the 1817 declaration; in fact, it was, loosely speaking, the same group. "Therefore", concluded Cobbett, "I am clearly of opinion that I have logically 'traced' the late 'criminal excesses' to those worthy gentlemen themselves."[261]

It was to no avail. In March 1817 the government brought in the repressive measures required by the financial declarers of the London Tavern, which, at best, would have consigned Cobbett to a dungeon, and, at worst, stilled his pen forever.

Incorrigible as ever, Cobbett went on the attack again.

"No civilised nation was ever in *so miserable* a state as this nation now is. This is notorious. This is denied by nobody."

And this miserable state was largely caused by the constant demands of the fundholders for interest payments on money lent to the government, in satisfaction of what they called 'national faith'.

"The talk about *national faith*, as applied to the funds, is the most foolish that ever was heard. What! Can national faith demand the payment of *double what was borrowed*? It is the same sum in *name* indeed; but as I have a hundred times proved, it is double the sum in *reality*. And this is the *real breach of faith*; and this breach of faith has been occasioned, *not by the nation*, but by you, the Men of Paper-Money, who solicited and obtained from Pitt a protection against the law of the land; who thereupon issued immense quantities of the Paper-Money; who thus debased the currency; and when you had lent *this* debased currency to the nation, then at your own arbitrary will, raised the value of the currency by diminishing its quantity, and now demand your payment in this raised currency, and by this demand the people are crushed to death. Who, then, has broken the contract? Who has been guilty of a breach of faith?...

"To alter the value of the currency of the country has always been held to be a most wicked as well as a most fatal measure. Very bad kings, before Paper-Money Men were heard of, used, sometimes, to play such tricks with the *coin*; but, it never was done, in any reign, or, in any country, without exciting great discontent and producing infinite mischief."

Cobbett then quoted at length a 17th century diatribe by Sir Robert Cotton on the evils of manipulating the value of the currency and the punishments that were due to those who attempted it.

"My good Paper-Money Men, you will perceive, that the *breach of faith* is here ascribed to *him who changes the value of money*; and, have not *you* been guilty of *this* breach of faith? It was not the nation, it was not those who borrowed, who changed the value of money. It was you....Good faith requires, that the interest of the Debt should instantly be lowered *one half* in amount; and yet we constantly hear it said, that to lower it at all would be a *breach of faith*! Sir Robert Cotton....regarded it as a *crime* in any man, or any body of men, even to *talk* of a *change in the value of the currency*; and, in speaking of the *punishment* due to this crime, he appears to have *cast his eye forward*!

"Thus, then, my good Paper-Money Fellows, we turn the Table upon you! *You*, it is, who have made all the 'disturbances in the Commonwealth'. *You* are the evil-minded and designing men. You are the seducers. You, it is, who have been working to produce an utter '*subversion* of *the laws and constitution*' of the country....

"Come, now! Say yourselves what punishment such men deserve. You are a pretty sort of people to combine and issue out *Declarations* against those who are suffering the pangs of ruin and hunger from your changes of the currency, while you are wallowing in wealth, and lending to the Bourbons the fruit of the land and the labour of England. You are a pretty sort of people to talk of your *loyalty*

---

261 Political Register. 8/2/1817.

to your King and your anxiety for the peace of your country! You, who have produced the slavery, the distress, the misery, the abject and disgraceful condition of a people once so free and so happy."[262]

Does one really need to add that, by the time this letter was published, Cobbett had fled to Liverpool, to embark on board a ship, bound for New York?

Section seven; The Politics of Exploitation

When Queen Anne came to the throne in 1702, her House of Commons presented to her an address, in the following terms.

"Many public Officers and Accountants have raised great Estates to themselves, at the expence of the Public, when it is evident they have no lawful means to attain them; and several persons, whose duty it was to hinder such Exorbitances, measuring their requests rather by their own avarice than by their merit, have obtained for themselves Grants to such a value, as in foregoing Reigns have been esteemed large Supplies towards great and public services; which has been another great cause of the Debt that lies upon the nation. This general mismanagement of the public affairs did actually spread itself over the whole kingdom, and seems to be owing to a disposition of Offices and Places, where men were rather chosen for their inclinations to serve a Party, than for their qualifications to serve the Public....We cheerfully depend upon your Majesty's wisdom, that all our Grievances, by your grace and favour, will, in due time, be redressed and removed, by punishing those, who have been the cause of them, and by entrusting none in the administration of public affairs, who, for their own private advantage, have manifestly contributed to the calamity of the country."[263]

Clearly, at the beginning of the 18th century, the Thing was already in operation. But two aspects of this address showed up in stark contrast to Cobbett's times. One was that the Queen gave it a favourable reception.

"'I shall consider the several particulars of your Address, and always have regard to the representations of the House of Commons, and to the true interests of England.' And she was as good as her word; for she, with *sincerity*, set to work to reform abuses, to punish peculators, and to set, in her own manners and conduct, an example of moral virtue, and of oeconomy without loss of dignity."

The other was that the House of Commons made such representations at all. Cobbett used this address as the motto to one of his editorials. He commented;-

"Is it possible to read the Motto to this Number, without making a comparison between the House of Commons in the reign of QUEEN ANNE and those in this Jubilee Reign? When have we, during this reign, heard such language; and, shall we ever hear it again? – This language was addressed to Queen Anne the first hour, as it were, of her coming to the throne; and the consequence of it was a reform in every department of the public expenditure....but the debt remained....But, if in the reign of William III, Peculators *bought estates* with the public money; if this was, at that time, a subject of complaint, what would the same House of Commons have said, if they had existed *at this day*, when a sum equal to the whole of the taxes raised in the reign of Queen Anne, annually, would scarcely supply the annual amount of waste?"

Clearly, between the accession of Queen Anne, and Cobbett's day, a huge transformation had taken place in the representation of the nation; in the influence of the House of Commons, and in the attitudes and objectives of those who sat there.

It is obvious that no extensive system of exploitation, such as that described by Cobbett, can exist independently of government. Government, in all its branches, must either be brought somehow to

262 Political Register. 29/3/1817.
263 Political Register. 27/1/1810.

acquiesce in such exploitation, to connive, to participate passively; or else government itself must share actively in the spoils of such exploitation, become the active accomplices of the exploiters, or, perhaps, the exploiters themselves. Whatever the case, such a system of exploitation clearly cannot co-exist with any government having a significant representative element. The laws made by a representative assembly will be incompatible with the exploitation of those whom the assembly is representing, and, if enforced, will prevent it. The Thing, therefore, could never have succeeded, without somehow eclipsing the representative part of the British government. This it did, in a gradual process that took place over many years. The desire of the powerful few to profit at the nation's expence had a profound effect on government; the gradual snuffing out of representation, in its turn, caused massive burdens to be imposed upon the people. It became a vicious circle. Causes and effects became intertwined.

Cobbett dated the process from the early part of the 18th century.

"The great protection of the people of England always had been, that they could not be taxed without their consent. This was always in Catholic times the great principle of the English government, and it is expressly and most explicitly asserted in Magna Charta. But how was it to be expected that this grand principle would be maintained, when a large part of the rich people themselves lived upon the taxes; when a man's next-door neighbour received the taxes paid by that man; when, in short, the community was completely divided, one part having a powerful interest in upholding that which was oppressive and ruinous to the other part? Taxation marched on with dreadful strides. The people did not like it. At the 'glorious revolution' it had been settled and enacted that there should be a new Parliament called every three years at least, and this had been held forth as one of the great gains of the 'glorious revolution'. Another great gain was that no pensioners and no placemen were to sit in the House of Commons. These things were enacted, they were laws of the land, they were held forth to the people as great things gained by the 'Glorious'. This last act was soon repealed, and placemen and pensioners have sat in the House of Commons ever since."[264]

Cobbett perhaps underemphasised the importance of this last act; as the ability of the government to award pensions and offices to members of the Commons constituted a massive accretion to the powers of corruption, and a counterweight to the expression of the popular will. He went on;-

"But the other act, the act securing the people a fresh choice every three years at least, that was a vital law. That law was in the new state of things, a state of taxes and debts, a state of things which demanded new taxes almost every year; in such a state of things frequent and new Parliaments, new choosings at short intervals were absolutely necessary to give the people a chance, even so much as a chance of avoiding oppressive taxation, and oppression, indeed, of every sort. It was the only means that was left to the people.

"Yet to uphold the new system it was necessary to demolish even this barrier of liberty and property; and in the year 1715….this law, this vital law, this solemn compact between the Protestant dynasty and the people, was repealed and for ever abolished, and the three years were changed for seven, and that too, observe, by the very men whom the people had chosen to sit for only three years! Yes, men chosen by the people to sit for three years enacted that they would sit for seven; and that those who had chosen them, together with their descendants for ever, should have no choice at all unless they voted for men who might at the king's pleasure sit for seven years!"[265]

"The preamble of the act laid the blame on the designs and wishes of a 'popish faction'!....The truth is these pretences were false; the people, the great body of the people, smarting under the lash of enormous taxation, became disaffected towards the new order of things; they were strongly disposed to revert to their former state; it was suspected, and indeed pretty well known, that they would at the next election have chosen almost everywhere members having the same sentiments, and therefore it

264   History of the Protestant Revolution. P. 414.
265   Ibid. P. 415.

was resolved that they should not have the power of doing it. However, the deed was done; we have felt the effects of it from that day to this."[266]

This, in itself, was, according to Cobbett, a "terrible curtailment of English liberty". But, still more significantly, it opened the way for the systematic corruption of the English House of Commons through the decades which followed, and the blocking up of any channel by which public opinion could have an influence on the measures of government. This systematic corruption was eagerly accomplished by such heroes of English political history as Sir Robert Walpole, the Pelhams, and William Pitt; until, by Cobbett's time, the representation in the House of Commons had deteriorated to the state which Cobbett dared only to describe in his New York Register in 1816.

Up until the war of 1793, or so Cobbett thought, despite the defective representation, the popular will could still make itself felt in the House of Commons because of the character of the men who sat there.

"In the gentlemen of England, who had held their estates from their ancestors; who resided always at the same place; who had a reputation to support, whose happiness consisted, in a great degree, in maintaining that reputation; who were the sons of fathers well known before them, and who, in their turn, had sons whose happiness must be affected by their father's conduct. In men of this description, so well known in their several counties and neighbourhoods; men whose interests were so closely interwoven with those of the people at large; men who had not become rich by the receipt of taxes. In this sort of natural magistracy of the country, the people had, in spite of the partial distribution of elective rights, a tolerable security for their liberties and properties. The *character* of the members supplied in a great degree the place of a fair mode of election.

"But, when Bute, and North, and Pitt, and George the Third, with their tools the Jenkinsons, and Percevals, and Addingtons, had, by their loads of taxes, swept all this race of gentry away as completely as a hurricane sweeps away the sugar canes in Jamaica, and had, by their loans, and grants, and bribes, created a new and grasping race of moneyed men, and officers, and lawyers, to supply their place, the *character* of the Members became wholly changed; and the parliament, having no longer any common interest with the people, became....a mere set of scramblers for pelf and power, falling each party in its turn upon the devoted people, as warring dens of wolves from the Pyrenees fall alternatively upon the bleating flocks in the valleys below."[267]

This process was greatly occasioned by the many years of continental warfare. The expenditure of huge sums of public money created a new class; the members of which had grown into affluence as contractors supplying goods for the armed forces; as officers in the army and navy; as the holders of posts in the tax-gathering departments; and, of course, as financiers profiting from the great increase of the national debt. This new class Cobbett labelled the mushroom gentry. The nature of government was also being changed by the proliferation of lawyers, four-fifths of whom completed their training with the sole objective of gaining employment in the public service. Equally inimical to the democratic part of the constitution was the ever-increasing influence of the great companies, and foremost among them the Bank of England and the East India Company.

"As to the *elections*, except in a very few cases, they are a mere mockery. A mockery so complete, that it is wonderful that the farce has been so long carried on. Except in the city of Westminster and about ten other places, there is not the smallest shadow of reality in the thing."

Mockery was a mild word to describe the elections of Cobbett's day. At every general election, complained Cobbett, the country was covered with "drunkenness, breaches of the peace, black-eyes, bloody-noses, fraud, bribery, corruption, perjury, and subornation of perjury."[268]

266 Ibid. P. 419.
267 Political Register. New York. 3/2/1816.
268 Political Register. 2/11/1816.

At best, the whole system was riddled with absurdities. Decayed boroughs, like Gatton in Surrey or Old Sarum in Wiltshire, where the electorate had virtually disappeared, still sent two members to parliament. Westminster and Liverpool sent no more; whilst the newly populous cities of Birmingham, Sheffield and Manchester sent none at all. In hardly any case was there any representation whatever.

"The truth is, that the seats in Parliament are the *property*, in most cases, of particular persons. That they are bought and sold as other property is. That they are sometimes sold in the *fee simple*; sometimes let on *lease* for the duration of a certain Parliament; sometimes they are let for one, two, three, or more sessions, according to the wants of the tenant and the owner. These contracts are made, and the deeds executed, in just the same form, and with just as little reserve, as are the contracts for the sale and the letting of land or houses.

"This property is not in a great number of hands. It is chiefly owned by the Peers, though there is, amongst the laws which help and make up the prodigious mass of frauds of the system, a law strictly forbidding Peers to interfere at all in Elections, while they not only interfere, but actually sell and rent the seats in the House of Commons."

According to Cobbett, 300 of the seats in the House of Commons were owned by 216 peers, whilst a further 171 were owned by 156 commoners and 16 by the Treasury. This left 171 county and independent seats. County seats, however, were not independent. In Hampshire, for example, the Treasury had the nomination of M.P.s, as the electorate was inundated with government employees from the barracks and the dockyards; in other counties a few great families would take the seats in rotation, "the number of freeholders being small compared with the means of overawing them." Cobbett thought that it would be an improvement on this mass of fraud if members were directly nominated by the peers or the ministers. "There would be none of that *deception* which has so long kept this rotten thing in existence, and enabled it to do so much damage to the world.

"The seats are made use of by the owners in various ways. The late Duke of Norfolk, who owned *eleven*, and whom our death-recorders hold up as a staunch *friend of freedom*, used to let all his for longer or shorter periods of time. The owners sometimes fill them with *relations*, in order that those relations may buy good places with their votes. Sometimes the owners fill them with persons who are to vote just as the owners shall order them upon every question; and thus they have all their votes constantly at hand to back any demand that they have to make for emoluments or honours, for themselves or families. Sometimes the owner lets the seat *conditionally*; as, for instance, on condition that the member always votes as the owner shall direct, except in certain cases; or, that he shall always vote with the Minister; or with the opposition. At other times the owner lets the seat *clear of all restrictions*, in which case the rent is *much higher*, because the Member may, of course, vote just as it suits his own advantage; and such a man is called an INDEPENDENT Member!"

During the French wars, when contracts and posts and loans were constantly up for grabs, and were being freely bestowed on members who voted as required, a so-called independent seat might let for £5,000 for a whole parliament or £1,500 for a single session. But with the war now being over, the value had sadly fallen away to between £400 and £500.

"Does not all the world see, that the House of Commons is composed of a set of corrupt men, battling either to gain place, or to keep place, and that the House of Lords, owning a great part of the seats in the other House, both Houses are, in fact, one body, the members of which occasionally divide into parties in contending for power and profit, but all of whom have one common interest, which never fails to make them *unite against the people*.

"It is hardly necessary to trace in their effects the deeds of such an assembly; for, having the whole property of the country at its mercy; being under no check or control, it is manifest, that the effect of its power must be universal corruption and oppression, going forth like pestilence and famine to savage the land. It is notorious, that, in exchange for *seats* and *votes*, all sorts of employments , and all degrees of profit are given. Peerages, the Governorships of Colonies, Commissaryships, Contracts, Loans, Commissions in the Army and Navy, Commands on profitable Stations, Grants or Leases of Crown Lands, Judgeships, Chancellorships, Ambassadorships, Bishopricks, Deaneries, and other Dignities and Livings in the Church; it is notorious, that in *all* cases, what is called *parliamentary interest* decides the choice of persons to be employed….In some cases a post, or a living, or a commission, is given for a *single vote*; or for two votes at different times. Then again for a year's voting, or for a month's voting. And so on, according to the *character* and *estate* of the person voting. A man of ancient family, who is generally represented in the country will get a good living for his *son* by one vote, whereas a mere upstart must vote for a year or two to obtain the same thing; and yet both their sons go very coolly, and solemnly declare `before Almighty God, the searcher of hearts'*, that they 'take upon them the care of souls, being thereunto moved and called, as they verily believe, by the *Holy Ghost*'; when they well know, all the while, that they are really called to the office by the base corruption of their fathers! These seats and votes are applicable to all purposes. Sometimes they are used to provide for a mistress, a bastard, a pimp, or a valet, or chambermaid who possesses a valuable secret. Sometimes innocent men are persecuted and utterly ruined at the instigation of those who have seats and votes to give as the price; and, at others, guilty villains are saved by the same all-powerful means.

"….In such a state of things, there can be nothing worthy of the sacred name of *liberty* and *law*;….amongst all the other barriers against despotism, the press must of necessity become nothing, or be….converted into an instrument of that very despotism. This is, indeed, one of the principal of its instruments. Without a press at its command such a government never could have stood to this day. If its *sham* proceedings had not been constantly sent forth under all the appearances and the ancient and settled forms of law and justice, and freedom; if its exactions and cruelties had not been constantly glossed over; if the people had not been amused and cajoled by the mummery, the impudent professions of the parliament and the courts; or, if any man had dared to expose these in their true colours, this mass of fraud and violence never could have endured so long.

"Nay, even *with* this corrupt press, and with all the appearance of regular legal proceeding, the thing could not have remained to this time without the actual support of the *bayonet*. This is so well known to the usurpers of our rights and our property, that they have erected Barracks, as strong as tolerable forts, all around them. One at Knightsbridge, one at Marylebone, one at St. James's Park, which, with that of the Tower, completely surrounds the scene of their iniquities. Then, in case of emergency, there are Barracks at Hounslow Heath;….at Guildford;….at Croydon….; then, coming up the Thames, at Worley;….coming still round, at Chelmsford….Thus surrounded by a double line of forts, from which it could bring, at three hours' notice, more than fifty thousand swords and muskets to their support, what need they fear? They have one Barracks close to the House; or, at least, not more than four hundred yards from it, where the soldiers, some of whom are always in readiness, can be brought to their avenues in five minutes. When the people of Westminster assembled against the Corn Bill last year, the House was surrounded with guards in an hour. The third day saw fifty thousand regular soldiers in London, and fifty thousand more moving out of distant Barracks to make their approaches, and to come, in case of need. And, it is notorious, that this law was passed while the regular soldiers surrounded the House, as regular soldiers are now employed in Cardiganshire, to enforce the collection of taxes."

So this was Cobbett's borough tyranny, as he called it. "Behind the curtain", it was the owners of the seats in the House of Commons who controlled the outcome of debates and divisions, and who therefore wielded the absolute power. Or so Cobbett thought. The King had no power. The Prince Regent was equally under the thumb, and was allowed no say at all in appointing ministers or officials, granting pensions or sinecures, or distributing the patronage of the Church. Ministers were mere tools. Both the political parties were similarly under the thumb of the boroughmongers, as Cobbett called them; so was the group known as the Saints, which affected to maintain an independent stance between the parties.

"As to the *deciding* of *any question*, affecting the honour, liberty, or happiness of the country, the Duke of Newcastle, who was, only a few years ago, a baby in his cradle, had, even while he was living upon pap, more power than this whole rabble of great senators all put together; and, I dare say, now that he is grown to be a man, he pays much more attention to the voice of his fox-hounds than to the harangues of these bawlers, and that he has more respect for the persons and motives of the former than for those of the latter.

"After this view of the situation….how we must laugh at De Lolaie's pretty account of the *English Constitution*. After seeing that about three or four hundred Boroughmongers actually possess all the legislative power, divide the ecclesiastical, judicial, military, and naval departments amongst their own dependents, what a fine picture we find of that wise system of *checks* and *balances*, of which so much has been said by so many great writers! What name to give to such a government it is difficult to say. It is like nothing that ever was heard of before. It is neither a monarchy, an aristocracy, nor a democracy; it is a band of great nobles, who, by sham elections, and by the means of all sorts of bribery and corruption, have obtained an absolute sway in the country, having under them, for the purposes of show and of execution, a thing they call a King, sharp and unprincipled fellows whom they call Ministers, a mummery which they call a Church, experienced and well-tried and steel hearted men whom they call Judges, a company of false money-makers whom they call a Bank, numerous bands of brave and needy persons, whom they call *soldiers* and *sailors*; a talking, corrupt and impudent set, whom they call a House of Commons. Such is the government of England; such is the *thing* which has been able to bribe one half of Europe to oppress the other half, such is the famous 'Bulwark of *religion* and *social order*', which has surrounded itself with a *permanent standing army* of more than a hundred thousand men, and very wisely, for without such an army it could not stand a month."

This was a state of affairs, then, in which those who benefited from the taxes, raised the taxes. The consequence was as may be expected.

"After the passing of the Septennial Act the people would, of course, lose nearly all the control that they had ever had with regard to the laying on of taxes and to the expending of the public money. Accordingly taxes went on increasing prodigiously. The excise system, which had a little beginning in former Protestant reigns, and the very name of which had never been heard of in Catholic times, now assumed somewhat in its present form, and the 'castles' of Englishmen became thenceforth things to be visited by excisemen."[269]

It is hardly surprising, therefore, that the total sum of taxes in 1760 was eight times that in the reign of James II. One despotism was exchanged for a worse. The historians of the struggles of the seventeenth century seem to eulogise the right of the House of Commons to refuse supplies to the government as a fundamental constitutional freedom. The refusal of the American colonists to submit to taxation without representation is generally portrayed as heroic in the histories. But is any historian to be found to censure the supineness in this respect of the British House of Commons in the 18th and 19th centuries?

"Here the parliament never refuses to grant what the government calls for; and no man would think of refusing to pay the tax-gatherer any more than he would think of refusing to submit to rain or thunder."[270]

In 1816, the House of Commons finally roused itself to block the continuance of the income tax, and Cobbett commented;-

---

269   History of the Protestant Reformation. P. 420.
270   Political Register. 6/1/1816.

"I do not recall any very serious opposition ever having been made before to a tax of any sort."[271]

Even when Chancellor of the Exchequer Vansittart, in February 1816, announced the outrageous decision to continue the war taxes into the peace, in order to keep up the standing army in defiance of every principle of law and government, and to pay the interest on the national debt at inflated levels, no member stood up to oppose him. The national debt had acquired a sacred quality; national faith became, as its name implies, a kind of religious orthodoxy in which all who aspired to respectability were compelled to believe.

"When a demand is made for money, the *mode of raising* it is the only subject of censure or criticism; and, when the minister is driven hard upon that head; 'Well', says he, 'shew me a better way; if not you cannot find fault that I pursue this, for I tell you that so much must be got, or I cannot pay the interest of the national debt'. To put an end to the payment of that interest; to suspend the payment during war; even to reduce it in amount; never seems to come athwart the mind of any man. To hear people talk upon this subject, a total stranger to our situation and circumstances, would think the national debt to be something belonging to the soil or the atmosphere of the country."[272]

The purpose of government had been completely altered. Those functions which are usually considered the primary duties of government – the defence of the realm, and the maintenance of law and order and administration of justice – had become subordinate and subsidiary functions – side-issues, perhaps. The primary purpose of government had now become the gathering up and redistribution of the wealth produced by the nation. And this, as we know, remains the case to this day.

"The government is a great partner, that is, *part-owner*, in every man's goods and estate; it has its eye upon all that he does; it has its hand continually in his pocket....When a man in this country, or in Ireland, receive a hundred pounds in income, the *law*, that is to say the government, steps forward and disposes of the greater part of it, in one way or another."[273]

The taxing system had become a monster of despotism.

"A hundred thousand tax-gatherers and of troops employed to assist them; revenue cutters and custom-house dragoons in such abundance; custom-house officers with power to rummage our trunks and pockets, and in certain cases, to search us even between our shirts and our skin; excise officers, without whose permission we cannot remove our drink from one house to another; who have authority to enter our house in innumerable cases, at any hour of the day or night, and in some cases, to lock certain doors of our premises and to keep the keys of them in their pockets; all these, together with a code of custom-house, excise, and tax-laws, forming altogether several thick volumes, in quarto, and embracing penalties of every description, not excepting that of death...."[274]

"A government which rests upon a system of funding cannot be carried on by any body but lawyers. It is a system of exactions, impositions, restraints, and prohibitions; and, of course, of informations, rewards, forfeitures, fines, seizures, pains and penalties. It marches forth upon a people, the whip in one hand and the cord in the other. The bulk of the enactments of *penalties*, only, which have been caused by this system, surpass *three-fold* the bulk of all the laws taken together, which were passed previous to the existence of that system; and the Bank of England alone has of late years prosecuted more men for capital crimes, and has caused more to be hanged and transported, than

---

271 Political Register. 9/3/1816.
272 Political Register. 23/3/1811.
273 Political Register. New York ed. 4/ 5/1816.
274 Political Register. 16/3/1816. For a list of the fiscal inconveniences and absurdities by which Cob-bett was personally afflicted during a period of just nine months, see Political Register 13/12/1806.

used formerly to be hanged and transported in a like space of time, for all the crimes committed in the kingdom.

"Against the counsels of a Stock-broker grafted upon a lawyer, good Lord protect every people on earth!"[275]

❋

The defective state of the representation had come about as the necessary consequence of the desire of a powerful few to profit personally at the nation's expence. It became, in its turn, what enabled them to do so. It was both an effect and a cause. William Cobbett saw a restoration of that representation as the grand remedy for the poverty and degradation in which the English people were being held. All the acts of tyranny were "effects, and natural effects too, of one cause; that is to say, the withholding from us of our rights; and especially our right of choosing our own representatives.... Can I believe, that what has been done against the people would have been done, if the parliament had been chosen by the people?"[276]

In 1813, a petition was presented by the city of Liverpool by its M.P., George Canning, who nevertheless disowned its contents. It lamented "the grievances of the country, the protraction of the war, the decay and ruin of our manufactures, and ascribing these evils to the defective state of Parliamentary Representation", it proposed, "as the most effectual remedy, the shortening of the duration of Parliaments, the extension of the elective franchise, and the exclusion of placemen and pensioners from the seats in that House."

Cobbett commented;-

"It is in vain for the people to complain of taxes, of war, or of any grievance, unless they call for a reform of the parliament. To the want of this, and not to any other cause, we owe *all* that we have to complain of and to lament. Every evil may be traced to this source, and while it continues to flow, every evil will exist.

"The old cheat of a change of ministry is, however, now become too stale to deceive any body. There is no man will now say, that he wishes for such a thing, unless he is to have a place or profit of some sort in consequence of it. The Whigs....are now by far the worst set of the two. They first betrayed the people, and then became their most bitter enemies. They dread a reform of parliament much more, I believe, than their opponents."[277]

The party system was part of the anti-democratic machinery of government.

"It is one of the tricks of faction to amuse the people with the squabblings between themselves. Just as if the thing was right, or ought to be borne a moment, because both the factions were equally guilty of doing it.

"There are other men in the country besides these two factions...."[278]

The Liverpool petition asked for the shortening of the duration of parliaments. As we have seen, the seven-year parliament, brought in by the Septennial Act of 1715, Cobbett considered one of the major ways of excluding the people from decision-making. But even the three-year parliamentary life brought in at the Revolution of 1688 Cobbett thought too long to ensure a proper representation, and annual parliaments became one of his demands.

The Liverpool petition also asked for the exclusion of placemen and pensioners from the House of Commons. Cobbett attached great importance to this.

---

275 Political Register. 16/11/1816.
276 Political Register. 18/1/1817.
277 Political Register. 22/5/1813.
278 Political Register. 7/9/1816.

264

"All that I wished to accomplish was this, that persons, once chosen to be the *guardians of the people's money*, never should, during their whole lives, pocket either by themselves or their relations and dependents any part of that money....I confess that my wish would be, that men who are chosen members of parliament, should *never* become servants of the king. A man cannot serve two masters."[279]

It is surely obvious that a member of parliament who is, in any way, in the pay of the government, as soon as any conflict arises between the interests of the executive and the interests of the people – and such conflicts arise every day – will not be a conscientious representative of his constituents.

In Cobbett's day, the great inflation of the navy and the military meant that many officers sat in the Commons, who were "holding offices and emoluments at the mere will of the crown, and can at any moment be deprived, at the sole pleasure of the crown, and no cause assigned."[280]

There was a huge number of naval and military M.P.s. Government contractors sat in the Commons under certain circumstances; loan-contractors sat there; so did the directors of the Bank of England.

"The Act of Settlement declares persons holding offices of profit under the Crown to be incapable of serving as members of parliament. This act, till base and corrupt ministers found it troublesome, remained in force, and no inconvenience was experienced from it."

The absence of members of the executive from the House of Commons would render the debates there far more interesting, because their outcomes would not be determined in advance, and speeches would proceed from unbiased minds.

"As for the advantage of 'questioning the minsters face to face', they were so questioned when they were excluded from parliament. They were sent to the House by the king, to bear his Messages; to ask for Money in his name; and to give such explanations as the representatives of the people required at his hands. There is, surely, nothing difficult in this. It is the regular and natural course of proceeding; but can any one pretend, that it is not a monstrous absurdity, that ministers, that the servants of the king, or, indeed, that any body else in this world, should be *called to account by themselves*; that they should sit in judgment, and vote, and assist in the deciding upon the merits, or demerits, of their own conduct; and especially when it is known beforehand, when it is acknowledged to be essential to the system, that they have, and must have, a majority in their favour, it being, according to that system, impossible for them to hold their places any longer than they have that majority?"

A House of Commons without placemen or pensioners "would busy themselves in doing that which belonged to their office, as guardians of the public treasure and the public liberty. – If the House of Commons contained no placemen; if it were unmixed with the servants of the king; if it were composed of men who never could touch the public money, can it be believed, that the public money would not be better taken care of?

"The old constitutional course of *refusing money*....is now, all the world knows, a power that is never exercised, nor is it ever thought of being exercised. – Is there an evil we complain of, or feel, which cannot be traced to this source?"[281]

"A House of Commons, having in it neither place men nor pensioners; a House, none of the members of which touched the public money, would naturally become the scrupulous managers of that money, because every man of them would feel, that he was managing his own money as well as that of his constituents, and that wherever he could save in the public expenditure, he would really be saving for his neighbours and himself...."[282]

---

279   Political Register. 14/1/1809.
280   Political Register. 13/12/1806.
281   Political Register. 14/1/1809.
282   Political Register. 13/12/1806.

The Thing had two branches. The political wing was the Boroughmongering system, which corrupted politics and government, in order to exclude the influence of popular representation. The other branch, the financial system, was thus enabled to draw up the wealth of the country and distribute it among its adherents. Each branch was dependent upon the other, and therein, or so Cobbett thought, lay the weakness. For, in his opinion, the financial system was unsustainable.

No one is right all the time. In his analysis of the trends, the institutions and the attitudes of his time, Cobbett displayed massive perspicacity as well as great courage. But he insisted upon making predictions, and sometimes with a smugness which with hindsight appears ridiculous. By nature, Cobbett was of a supremely confident, positive frame of mind, and it is not therefore surprising if his predictions turned out to be over-sanguine. He was convinced that the funding-system contained within itself the seeds of its own imminent destruction. This was to happen in one of two ways. Either the uncontrollable greed of the bankers would cause ever-increasing amounts of paper-currency to be forced into circulation, creating a type of hyper-inflation, and a system of "two prices", where much higher prices would be asked for paper transactions than for payment in coin. Or else, in order to prevent destruction by this means, the issues of paper-money would be so far reduced as to produce ruin and starvation on a massive scale, and finally a total inability to pay taxes, and mutinies among the soldiers who were retained for purposes of enforcing payment. Deprived of the support of the financiers, the borough-mongers would have no alternative but to turn to the people in order to maintain their position; and to concede a reform of the parliament along the lines suggested by Cobbett. But, with the benefit of hindsight, we know that the funding system has remained in existence from Cobbett's day to our own; and that the reform of the House of Commons, as he envisaged it, has never taken place.

Predicting the future is, of course, impossible; but the scenarios put forward by Cobbett were not, in fact, particularly far-fetched. Even in his day, history provided examples of currencies being destroyed by over-issue, the assignats of Revolutionary France being the most notable. And in 1825, if at no other time, the whole system was within a hair's breadth of collapse. It is instructive to analyse the slight miscalculations which Cobbett made, which led to his over-optimistic assessment of the prospects for the British tax-paying public.

Cobbett's feeling was that the boom would break the system rather than the bust.

"In no way that the craft of Satan can devise, is it possible to prevent the quantity of paper-money from *increasing*, unless the tyrants return again to the *ruining* and *starving* experiment; an experiment which, I imagine, they will not be in a hurry to repeat."

Cobbett was wrong, for repeat it they did.

"I thought that the fools, fools as they were, would either let the thing go on to two prices, or reduce the interest of their Debt; I thought they would leave the fund-holders with their eyes to cry with and *give us our Reform*....But, instead of this, the Borough-tyrants, chose to *break for ever* with the people rather than separate from the fund-holders, with whom they made common cause, and with whom they must now *stand or fall*."[283]

There were two things here which Cobbett had failed to take into account. The first was the extent of the savagery and ruthlessness which the ruling classes were prepared to use against the people.

"Never did I dream, that the Boroughmen would be fools enough to ruin and starve their tenants and labourers in order to make an effort to save the fund-holders by the resumption of cash payments! I ought, long before, to have known that they were fools enough for any thing; but, it never entered my head, that they would attempt to do this. They did, however...."

---

283 Political Register. 26/9/1818.

The second was that the system could be kept afloat bt "swagging from side to side". Paper issues could be reduced just before the state of two prices was arrived at; and inflated again when depression was so severe as to threaten tax revenues. Thus, the system was prevented from breaking on either rock, if, perhaps, only narrowly. Swagging from side to side created the perfect environment for the great speculators, who were thus presented with a further opportunity for drawing the wealth of the nation away from the productive classes. Cobbett was well advanced in years, before he fully understood the role which speculation played in causing the distresses of the nation.

Underlying these two misapprehensions was a more fundamental one, concerning the balance of power within the establishment, between the seat-owners and the financial interest. Cobbett himself tended to be a little ambivalent about this; but on balance his opinion seemed to be that the Thing had been put in place by and for the benefit of the Boroughmongers.

"I think that I, long ago, clearly proved, that the Borough tyranny is the sole cause of the nation's misery and disgrace. I have also proved, I think, that this tyranny depends for its existence solely on the Bank paper continuing to pass current."

"The Bank is now proved to have acted merely as their tool."[284]

What went on in the inner recesses of government, "behind the curtain" as the expression was, is difficult enough for the historian to make out. For a journalist who was both habitually and dynamically hostile to that government, a long-term thorn in its side, whose vitriolic pen was perhaps what it feared most, to peep "behind the curtain" was an impossibility. The signs are that Cobbett got it wrong.

The financial branch of the Thing, as we have seen, was set up by the government of William III. One of its objectives was to provide a basis of support for the new dynasty in the face of the widespread popular discontent cause by excessive taxation.

"If all, or a great part of those who had money to lend, could by the temptation of great gain be induced to lend their money on interest to the government….it was easy to see that all this description of persons would then be embarked in the same boat too; and that they, who must necessarily be a class having great influence in the community would be amongst the most zealous supporters."

The purpose was to bind "to the government all those persons who wished to lend money at high interest, and these were, as is always the case, the most greedy, most selfish, least public-spirited, and most base and slavish and unjust part of the people."[285]

For sure, there was a time when, as Cobbett said, the financial system was the tool of the boroughmongers. But already when Edmund Burke was writing his Reflections in 1790, the balance of power was shifting.

The French Revolution originated in a financial crisis. Here is William Cobbett on the causes of the Revolution of 1789.

"The people of France, were *unable* any longer to pay the full amount of the annual interest of the debt, without submitting to such vexation and oppression as were beyond mortal endurance…. The deficit in the finances was the grand cause; and, the deficit arose, not out of the want of will, but out of the inability to pay, without a submission to that which would have rendered life not worth preserving. The fund-holders, the 'blood-suckers', hung on like leeches; the government had not the courage to tear them off; an outcry….prevailed; the state went reeling on, buffeted on one side by the people, and on the other by the fund-holders; and, at last, down it came, never to rise again, an awful warning to all those nations who have been so unwise as to contract great public debts, and who have thereunto added the folly of acting upon the maxim, that, let come what will, the interest upon those debts is to be paid. The question in France was, 'shall the nation destroy the debt, or the

---

284   Political Register. 28/8/1819 and 30/10/1819.
285   History of the Protestant Reformation. P. 409.

debt destroy the nation?' that is to say, the government and constitution; and such is, at this moment the question in England…."[286]

Edmund Burke wrote his Reflections on the Revolution in France largely as a warning to England.

"Nations are wading deeper and deeper into an ocean of boundless debt. Public debts, which at first were a security to governments, by interesting many in the public tranquillity, are likely in their excess to become the means of their subversion. If governments provide for these debts by heavy impositions, they perish by becoming odious to the people. If they do not provide for them they will be undone by the efforts of the most dangerous of all parties; I mean an extensive, discontented monied interest, injured and not destroyed. The men who comprise this interest look for their security, in the first instance, to the fidelity of government; in the second to its power. If they find the old governments effete, worn out, and with their springs relaxed, so as not to be of sufficient vigour for their purposes, they may seek new ones that shall be possessed of more energy; and this energy will be derived not from an acquisition of resources, but from a contempt of justice."[287]

It was this "most dangerous of all parties" which put the fear of God into the English ruling class. The boroughmongers had reared up a monster which threatened to consume them. The fear was of a French-style revolution, initiated by the financiers, because of a perceived lack of will on the part of the governors to continue paying the interest on the national debt; or a perceived lack of ability to collect sufficient taxes to do so. A vigorous attitude towards the tax-paying classes had to be manifested. As Burke put it, the "innocent, innoxious indolence of proprietors" was not enough, as it "may be argued into inutility, and inutility into an unfitness for their estates." And this was the fear of the English ruling class well into the 19th century.

Burke must very soon have felt the power of the monied men. The sequel to the Reflections, as we have seen, was called An Appeal from the New to the Old Whigs. In tone and content, this was a completely different work. In it, the financiers are not only no longer cited as the greatest danger to the state; they are barely mentioned at all. And Burke's attitude toward the common people had swung dramatically round, from the grudging sympathy displayed in the Reflections, to the violent aggression of the Appeal. What, in the meantime, had induced Burke to change his tune, we may never know. Burke's opponent, Thomas Paine, must also have been aware of the power of the financiers, for his attitude also changed dramatically. Up until the first part of the Rights of Man, wars, taxes and funding were the principal cause of the degradation of ordinary folk in England. All of a sudden, in the second part, most of the taxes were to remain; the fundholders were to retain their debt and their interest; and it was only the sinecurists and the pensioners who were to lose their income, which was to be redistributed back to tax-payers in the form of a national poor-relief system. Cobbett himself knew very well what financial power was capable of. When, in 1810, Cobbett was sentenced to two years in Newgate Prison, it was ostensibly for libel; but in reality it was his financial writings that had landed him there. It was by way of revenge that Cobbett wrote Paper Against Gold from his prison cell; and a robust resentment at such treatment clearly rankled with him for the rest of his life. Early in 1817, as we have seen, it was the financial interest which put pressure on the government for stern measures against "evil-minded and designing men", meaning, principally, Cobbett, and which forced him into exile. Cobbett later commented;-

"I have no doubt that the dungeon, the poison, the dagger, were all prepared. I have no doubt, that I should, long ago, have been buried with a stake driven down through my body."[288]

---

286 Political Register. 22/2/1806.
287 Edmund Burke. Reflections on the Revolution in France. P. 151.
288 Political Register. 21/7/1810, 8/2/1817 and 1/5/1819.

In fact, Cobbett's newspaper abounds in articles on the power of the financiers. This is from 1819.

"If the old Lord Chatham were now alive, he would speak with respect of the MUCKWORM, as he called the 'Change-Alley- people. Faith! They are now become *every thing*. *Baring* assists at the Congress of sovereigns, and *Ricardo* regulates things at home. The Muckworm is no longer a creeping thing, it rears its head aloft, and makes the haughty Borough Lords sneak about in holes and corners."[289]

Already by 1804, Cobbett was complaining of the power of the "paper aristocracy".

"I mean an interest hostile alike to the land-holder and the stock-holder, to the real merchant, and to the manufacturer, to the clergy, to the nobility and to the throne; I mean the numerous and powerful body of loan-jobbers, directors, brokers, contractors and farmers-general, which has been engendered by the excessive amount of the public debt, and the almost boundless extension of the issues of paper-money."[290]

It was the paper aristocracy of France who produced the revolution there, and initiated the destruction of the monarchy. In England, all their suggested oppressive projects were eagerly put into operation by William Pitt, including the commutation of tithes, the redemption of the land tax, a bevy of laws favouring the great dealers and speculators, and a "law compelling men to take their paper in payment of just debts, while they themselves were exempted by the same law, from paying any part of the enormous debts which they had contracted, though they had given promissory notes for the amount."

"The influence which the paper-aristocracy has had, and has now more than ever, in politics, may easily be seen by reference to a list of the present House of Commons. Indeed, for them and them alone, war appears to be made and peace concluded. The disasters of the last war, and, finally, the total failure of its avowed objects....were all to be ascribed to the interests of the 'Change having been consulted, in preference to the interests of the nation."

By 1806, the departments of the government were in the habit of making official reports to the Lord Mayor of London and to Lloyd's Coffee House, both of measures passed and measures anticipated; and day by day, according to Cobbett, influence was draining away from every part of the country, and accumulating in the hands of the monied men.

The men at Lloyd's, "that is to say, the stock-jobbers of London", set up a committee for awarding cash prizes to those who, on their reckoning, had distinguished themselves in the armed services. The "little government at Lloyd's" Cobbett denominated "this dangerous and hateful combination of illegal taxers and rulers....They are ignorant of every thing except the art of working the taxes into their pockets."[291]

The Lloyd's scheme for rewarding soldiers and sailors was a deliberate attempt by the men of money to eclipse the crown and the government in the loyalties of the armed forces. Cobbett commented;-

"Of all the means of creating confusion, of all the combinations that ever were formed for the oversetting of a government, the confederation at Lloyd's is the most likely to succeed. It possesses the means of making a formidable opposition to the government, *money*; and it addresses itself to those who, in all commotions, must give the turn to the tide, the *army and the navy*. Its funds now amount to more than a quarter of a million of money; it has upon its *pension list* great numbers of officers, soldiers, and sailors."[292]

---

289 Political Register. 4/9/1819.
290 Political Register. 8/9/1804.
291 Political Register. 11/1/1806.
292 Political Register. 24/1/1807.

The sums awarded were greater than those granted by the crown, and came free of duty and obligation. The whole represented an unconstitutional invasion of the royal prerogative; its mode of collecting money was illegal.

Most importantly of all, the intentions behind the scheme were sinister, and boded great ill for the future, as we shall see.

"There was something audaciously unreasonable and bold in this attempt; something that argued a consciousness of strength too great to be overcome, if not too great to be thwarted by any power in the state."[293]

For a variety of reasons the influence of the financiers was fundamentally and inevitably inimical to public liberty and to representative government.

"Commerce *must* have a corrupting tendency. It forms men together in large companies, or bodies. They soon acquire great pecuniary powers; and they soon perceive, that the minister of the day, be he who or what he will, has great control over their interests. Hence they become his own faithful adherents upon all occasions; and, when the government becomes interwoven with a funding system, the commerce and the minister can, at any time, set the country at defiance."[294]

Here Cobbett was dwelling on the role of the monied interest as the tool of the minister, who, in turn, was the tool of the borough-monger.

"It is to the minister of *the day*; not to this or that minister, but to the minister of the day; the minister who makes loans and lotteries, and who gives bonuses; the minister who makes contracts for hemp and timber and tents and baggage and ships and corn and wine and brandy, and who expects, perhaps, to be *treated civilly in return*."[295]

Only rarely does Cobbett suggest that the financial interest may have had an anti-democratic agenda of its own.

"Amongst the great and numerous dangers to which this country, and particularly the monarchy, is exposed in consequence of the enormous public debt, the influence, the powerful and widely-extended influence, of the monied interest is, perhaps, the most to be dreaded, because it necessarily aims at measures which directly tend to the subversion of the present order of things."[296]

It was the financiers who put pressure on the government for a suspension of Habeas Corpus in1817. Ministers yielded with a degree of openly-avowed shame, and when it was done Prime Minister Liverpool announced that the price of government stock had risen as a consequence.

"The late Lord Chatham said, more than forty years ago, that the spirits of the Fund-holders and Money Dealers always rose in the same proportion as the liberty of their country fell."[297]

Cobbett seldom hints that, "behind the curtain", it was the financiers who were actually in the driving seat. Whilst the ministers may have been more or less directly appointed by the seat-owners, we have already seen that most or many of the officials of government were indebted to, or were otherwise connected with, the great financiers. Pitt was close to Benfield and Huskisson to Boyd. Rothschild had an extensive sphere of influence, which included Castlereagh, Liverpool, Vansittart, Wellington, and many lesser officials. And so on. Cobbett seldom hints that the boroughmongers had actually become the tools of the financiers, held in check and in awe by this "most dangerous of all parties", as Burke called them, and by the threat of a French-style revolution if their demands were not met. In 1821, Cobbett wrote of "a sort of indefinable something which tells the landowners,

---

293 Political Register. 8/9/1804.
294 Political Register. 12/12/1807.
295 Political Register. 11/1/1806.
296 Political Register. 8/9/1804.
297 Political Register. 8/2/1817 and 29/3/1817.

that if they were to meddle with the funds, their property would not be safe."[298] Nor, perhaps, would their lives. The something may not have been quite as indefinable as Cobbett thought. Cobbett emphatically and repeatedly labelled the boroughmongers "fools"; but maybe cowards might have been a better epithet. And perhaps it was to stave off this revolutionary threat that many of the great magnates exhibited an exaggerated anxiety to display their anti-democratic credentials, by their great and unnecessary severity towards the tax-paying public. It was as Burke had observed back in 1770. If it was felt, by those with the real power "behind the curtain", that too much indulgence was being shown to the people, the executive would be driven "to some act of atrocious violence, which renders them completely abhorred by the people."

❋

The twin pillars of despotic government are physical force and mental force.

With regard to revolutionary France, Edmund Burke prophesied that the financiers who set up the new government would be compelled to rely upon military force to maintain their position. "Everything depends upon the army in your government." The National Assembly had voted for a very large army, and it was distributed about the country "with a view of internal coercion."[299]

"You have got the wolf by the ears, and I wish you joy of the happy position in which you have chosen to place yourselves....There must be blood!"[300]

Of course, Burke was writing primarily about England. Here, the military despotism, tentative moves towards which were already being made in the 1760s, was greatly developed by the government of William Pitt. But it was during the years following the end of the Napoleonic Wars that it reached its climax. Cobbett commented;-

"This *Standing Army* is the thing by far the most hideous amongst all the hideous features of despotism....freedom *cannot exist* in society with a standing army in time of peace!....We might talk about liberty, but....we never could have it, *while there was such an army*! How often have many of us taken pains to prove, that, in fact, this army was kept up for the sole *purpose of preventing a Reform*!"[301]

In fact, the respected legal authority Blackstone, writing in 1768, maintained that a standing army in peacetime was actually illegal and unconstitutional. But it was under cover of warfare that the Barrack system was set up in England. Cobbett complained of those who, during the 1790s, "in order to defend the country against France, thought barracks were necessary at Sheffield, York, Birmingham, Northampton, Nottingham and Manchester." By 1812, the government was being pressed to set up camps and fortresses all over England and Ireland, "for the avowed purpose of keeping the people in subjection". Three new barracks were actually proposed, at Bristol, Liverpool and Marybone Park. This last was to cover twenty-seven acres, an area capable of holding 10,000 to 15,000 troops, which was to be surrounded with a high, thick wall, at enormous expence.

Samuel Whitbread and others complained in parliament that there were already barracks at King-Street, Knight's Bridge, Kensington and Hounslow.

Inland fortresses could only be intended for use against the people, and Blackstone had maintained that all camps and barracks of this sort were illegal and a danger to liberty.

---

298 Political Register. 17/3/1821.
299 Edmund Burke. Reflections on the Revolution in France. Pp.217 and 206.
300 Ibid. P. 213.
301 Political Register. 14/3/1818.

During the widespread rioting of 1812, the barrack system was put to its intended use, and rioters in the industrial areas were confronted with armed troops who were not afraid to use their weapons. Complaints were made in parliament about the illegal killing of civilians by the army.

"Were not soldiers daily committing murders on the people?"

Cobbett commented;-

"The use of soldiers, upon such occasions, has, of late, been so frequent, that most people have imagined, that the *law* has prescribed such use, and, in fact, that the law says, that if rioters do not disperse in an hour after the proclamation has been read, the magistrate may order the troops to shoot them or otherwise kill them."

The truth was that the Riot Act allowed the constitutional civil officers to disperse crowds by force if they did not disperse voluntarily – officers such as J.P.s, Sheriffs, Constables and Mayors – and these were entitled to call for assistance on local people in general. But it said nothing about soldiers, nor did it "authorise a starving population to be given up to military execution."

"It says not a word about shooting at rioters, nor even about using any deadly weapon against them; much less did it speak of, or even hint at, the employment of any military force."[302]

During the long war years, the internal military system of the British government was not readily apparent.

"They wished to disguise the fact, that they *were ruling by the force of an army*. While the war lasted, this horrid fact was easily disguised. The troops were wanted *to defend the country*; they were *going abroad*; they were *just come home*. There was always some pretext or other….It was clear to us, long ago, that there must be a Reform of the Parliament, or, that a military despotism, perfectly naked, must be exhibited."[303]

When the war ended, it was exhibited in all its nakedness. Given the extent and the intensity of the suffering inevitably consequent upon the currency manipulation of these years, an army was clearly going to be necessary for "internal coercion".

"The distress which the taxes will occasion at home will be very great; but, bitter as the pill may prove, it will go down with the aid of the bayonet."

In the Commons, Lord Castlereagh announced that large numbers of troops were to be retained for use in England and Ireland. He attempted, rather feebly, to justify this by the need to be prepared for war. "We affect to fear for our safety" There were further large numbers of British troops ostensibly involved in the occupation of France, but these could quickly and easily be brought home in case of need.

But Castlereagh also said that these troops would pay for themselves, by enforcing the payment of taxes in cases of default, and by assisting the civil officers in seizures of crops and livestock. "If we were to take a map of England, we should see, that there is not any one spot, to which troops cannot be brought within the space of 24 hours."[304]

The whole internal military system acquired during these years an almost incredible sophistication. During the 18th century, the officers in the army were, many of them, men risen from the ranks. Blackstone, in fact, asserted that choosing the officers of the army from among the mass of the people was what prevented the army from becoming an instrument of despotism. However, from the time of Melville and the Duke of York, commissioned officers were being specially reared in academies, and these tended to be the sons of the aristocracy and the elite. The Royal Military Academy at Sandhurst was a huge complex of buildings, lavishly planned and elegantly fitted out. There was another at Woolwich; the Royal Naval College at Portsmouth; and another academy for the engineers. Here,

---

302 Political Register. 9/5/1812.

303 Political Register. 11/4/1818.

304 Political Register. New York ed. 17/2/1816.

boys, future officers, were trained from infancy. They were kept isolated from normal society – no one could enter the academies without permission; their reading matter was prescribed to them by the authorities; and an unquestioning obedience was inculcated to the sovereign and the ministers. The result was the creation of an insular officer class with nothing in common with ordinary people, and entirely dependent upon the army, having no skills or abilities other than that of being an officer. Similar considerations underlay the Barrack System. The goal was to produce a "soldiery with feelings wholly distinct from those of the people". Astonishingly, given the unconstitutional nature of the proceeding, Lord Palmerston quite openly announced to parliament that barracks were necessary for "keeping the soldiers from having any communication with the people". In 1817, a law was passed which made it a capital offence to attempt to seduce a soldier from his duty, with the punishment enforceable merely upon the oath of that soldier. Henceforth, for a civilian even to talk to a soldier was dangerous. The military had been turned into a distinct caste, along the lines of German militarism. Austrian modes were adopted in names, uniforms and manners, and soldiers ordered to grow whiskers in order to make them look foreign. The ideas behind the whole system, Cobbett thought, had been brought back from the European congresses by Lord Castlereagh.[305]

❋

"You may be well assured that there is no body of men, down to the very chimney-sweepers and gipsies, in this kingdom, upon which this watchful and crafty government has not its eye, and over which it does not endeavour to maintain a powerful and constant influence. It is no matter of what description any part of society may be. It has it's eye upon all. All the sects of religion; all the divisions of trade, commerce, agriculture. All the sports. Every thing and every body high and low it endeavours to wheedle and get within it's grasp. It proceeds in the way of blandishment and seduction till these be found unavailing; and then it proceeds by force."[306]

The mental force necessary for the continuance of elitist, unrepresentative government, can be divided into two categories; the restraining of the expression of opinions unfavourable to itself; and the influencing of the thought processes of the people under its sway.

With regard to the first category, a variety of unpleasant experiences awaited those who expressed opinions unfavourable to the establishment. The country was covered with spies and informers. Already by 1806, Cobbett was asking;-

"What can be the reason that the country is charged with nearly 200,000pounds a year for *secret services*, a great part of which is said to be for secret services *at home*? Yes, certainly we will ask, what occasion can there be for *secret* services *at home*, and of what description, for our good, these *services* can possibly be?"[307]

By 1816, the amount voted for secret services had accumulated to a total of £4 millions, and Cobbett seems to have been unaware that much of the secret service was actually paid for out of the civil list.[308]

Apart from the official secret service, the government had a spy in every parish, and he was called a clergyman. Then there were the 100,000 officials of the tax-gathering departments. Then there were the country bankers, all heavily dependent upon the Bank of England.[309]

Thus, the incautious expression of unsound opinions would set in motion what Cobbett called <u>the calumniating</u> system, or what we would call a smear campaign.

305 Political Register. 23/9/1820 and 7/10/1820.
306 Political Register. 14/9/1816.
307 Political Register. 13/12/1806.
308 Political Register. 9/11/1816.
309 Political Register. New York ed. 13/1/1816.

"Public robbers have always calumniated those who endeavour to detect them....This terrible system never could have got to any head, had not the people been credulous enough to listen to the calumnies, which the peculators propagated against the enemies of peculation."

Cobbett cited the moderate reformer Mr. Waithman, who having been labelled a Jacobin and a leveller by the establishment press, was reviled as such around the city. In later years, Cobbett singled out Walter of the Times, and Stewart of the Courier, "and other miscreants of the hired press", who blackened the character and disturbed the peace of the families of public-spirited men.

"You have often traced a *whisper*, begun at Whitehall, to the utter ruin of men of character and of talent.

Henry Hunt, the prominent radical public speaker, was a notable victim of the system.

"MR. HUNT's politics have risen up in judgment against him in all the pursuits and capacities and functions of his life....A man so perfectly *gentle* in all his manners, I never have seen. To all his people he is indulgence personified. Yet he has been designated as *a cruel Landlord and Master!*"[310]

Cobbett himself was frequently on the receiving end of the calumniating system; and although a stronger or more resilient psyche it is difficult to imagine, and although he declared himself unconcerned by such treatment, it is clear that continual abuse over time made inroads upon his internal tranquillity. The object of the exercise was to deter others from voicing inconvenient views; and it is surely obvious that with many men of talent, but of less courage than Cobbett or Hunt, it must have succeeded.

But it went further than this. Financial ruin also awaited the unwary voicer of opposition to government. There were few men, of any substance, whose businesses were not dependent upon loans from the banks – on the discounting system as it was known. In particular, the Bank of England discounted around £36 million a year, and had the power of making or breaking its customers. The directors of the Bank, according to Cobbett, were "actuated by the strongest political prejudices", and had become "one of the most potent instruments of political corruption and political vengeance. I could name 20, who stood high in trade and credit, who have been totally ruined, reduced almost to mere beggary, by stoppage of discounts for having taken part in opposition to acts of government."[311]

Much the same was true of the country banks. These were financially dependent upon the Bank of England; but were also obligated to, and under the surveillance of tax officials. As a result, the country banks were, politically speaking, mere tools of the Treasury, and would not lend money to opponents of the government.

Few were beyond the reach of the authorities.

"If a man is to be come at by none of the *open* means; under no shape that the catalogue of public crimes, or pretended crimes, afford; there is the *Bank* to work him, if he be in trade; if a farmer, there is the *Landlord* and the *Parson*; and, if he have any thing of visible property beyond the shirt on his back, there is the *Taxgatherer*. If all these fail, a man has *friends*, he may have a *mortgagee* or a *creditor* of some sort. He has a wife, a mistress, a child, or a servant to be stirred up against him."[312]

Fearful of such fates as these, and of the vengeance of the Bank of England, the country banks, and the tax officials, few men were prepared to speak up in public, or to sign petitions, no matter how flagrant were the abuses of government; and this, said Cobbett, was universally understood.

The law was a blunter instrument still. In March 1817, under pressure from the financiers to silence Cobbett and other evil-minded and designing men, ministers suspended the Act of Habeas Corpus. Other repressive laws followed. Henceforth, no public meetings could take place unless

---

310 Political Register. 27/1/1810 and 25/10/1817.
311 Political Register. New York ed. 13/1/1816.
312 Political Register. 25/10/1817.

approved by the local officials and magistrates; and any one resisting their authority was liable to be hanged. Political clubs and societies were no longer legal. Reading rooms and lecture rooms all had to be licensed by a magistrate, and the licence could be revoked at any time. Obstacles were placed in the way of the free circulation of pamphlets. Further such laws were passed in 1819.

Suspending Habeas Corpus removed the machinery for getting prisoners released from illegal custody, and although arbitrary imprisonment remained illegal under the common law, acts of indemnity could be passed to protect ministers from the consequences of their own criminality. The power was used liberally.

"Those who press for the representation of Birmingham etc. are put in dungeons....No man, in lying down on his bed, could be sure that he would not wake up with the pistol of a king's messenger at his throat. Many were seized, *loaded with irons*, shut up in dungeons, kept there for nearly a year, without being furnished with any charge, without being confronted with any accuser; and, at last, when turned out of their dungeons, to return to their ruined families, they found, that a law had been passed to *prevent them from obtaining redress*, and for *screening for ever those who had thus treated them*."[313]

Cobbett himself, of course, narrowly escaped such a fate. But an acquaintance of his, Mr. Benbow, a shoemaker, was held in prison by Home Secretary Sidmouth. Benbow had attended a meeting of deputies called late in 1816 to discuss parliamentary reform, and all had been imprisoned without trial.[314] Cobbett addressed one of his open letters to some of the victims.

"To Messrs. Benbow, Evans senior, Evans junior, John Roberts, John Smith, Francis Ward, John Jonson, John Knight, Samuel Brown, John Baguelly, and the rest of those, who have acted the same noble part."

"There had been about fifty innocent men shut up in dungeons for many months, cut off from the use of pen, ink and paper, and allowed to have no newspaper to read."[315]

Their families were not permitted to know where they were imprisoned, and had no idea when, or if, they would ever see them again. One man committed suicide in prison.

"Alas! Where is the county of our country, which has not now its Bastille!"[316]

But a worse fate still could befall those who were unguarded in the expression of their opinions. Francis Raynes was a captain in the Stirlingshire militia, who was employed as a spy by two senior officers in the army. It was his job to collect information about the acts and opinions of "the disaffected". The method was to participate in mutual oaths of fidelity to gain the confidence of the victims, and then to break the oath and betray the accomplices. For this, he was paid by the taxpayer. Various magistrates cooperated with Raynes; one of them was Colonel Fletcher of Bolton in Lancashire, who was himself a spy, and who had "long been the chief agent of Corruption in her Spy-works in the North, and who is said to have brought more men to the gallows than....any other of the profession."[317]

Free speech no longer existed. Already by 1816, Cobbett was commenting;-

"It is a lamentable fact that thousands of men, who, sitting amongst private friends, execrate the oppressions under which the country groans, come forth in public and range themselves on the side of the oppressors."[318]

After the passing of the acts of 1817, the situation became worse.

---

313 Political Register. 6/11/1819.
314 Political Register. 11/4/1818.
315 Political Register. 23/5/1818.
316 Political Register. 9/5/1818.
317 Political Register. 10/1/1818.
318 Political Register. New York ed. 13/1/1816.

"In a time of profound peace, and without any insurrection or any commotion in the country, laws have been passed to take away the personal safety of every man, to expose free conversation to the malignant construction of spies and informers, to render the intercourse between man and man dangerous, and even perilous...."[319]

All political discussion, except it was wholly on one side, was at an end. Cobbett complained of "ministers who, as the only answer to our repeated and humble supplications for the lightening of our burdens, and for the restoration of our undoubted and unalienable rights, have shaken the halter in our faces, and have rattled in our ears the keys of the dungeon."[320]

"The laws, which have now been passed, especially if we take into view the real objects of those laws, forbid us to entertain the idea, that it would be possible to write on political subjects according to the dictates of truth and reason, without drawing down upon our heads certain and swift destruction. It was well observed by MR. BROUGHAM, in a late debate, that every writer, who opposes the present measures 'must now feel that he sits down to write with a halter about his neck'."[321]

The last remaining channel through which public opinion could be represented to the government had been enshrined in the revolution settlement of 1688. This was the right of petition. But even this channel the authorities were attempting to block up. Early in 1817, the people of Lancashire met in order to form a petition, but were attacked by an armed force. Cobbett complained of "the beating and wounding of many of these people; the driving of great numbers of them at the point of a bayonet, into jails and jail-yards; the keeping of them night and day in the open air under rain and in the dirt and without food; and, finally, the compelling of many of them to give bail to be of the peace and good behaviour for a great length of time; though....these people had committed no crime, but, on the contrary, were assembled, in a peaceable and orderly manner, in order to consult and agree upon petitions to your Honourable House, in pursuance of one of those well known rights, which the law expressly and emphatically declares to be the 'birthright' of the people of England."

The meeting of the Blanketeers was entirely legal; the method of its dispersal entirely illegal.

"It is notorious that the right of petition, where alone it is calculated to be of real use, is now taken wholly from the people;.... That they cannot, without the utmost peril to their own lives, meet for the purpose of petitioning against any act of oppression however grievous and however extensive in its effects;....that, if assembled for the purpose of petitioning, they are liable to be dispersed by force of arms, at the sole will of persons appointed by the advice of Ministers of the Crown; that if they utter any words, though in the reading of a proposed petition, of which words those persons disapprove, they are liable to be so seized by those persons, or by armed men at their command, and, in case of resistance, *to suffer death*."[322]

Even if the petition could be framed, it could not be presented.

"We have a right *to write petitions*; but, by no means to present them. There are soldiers and policemen to hinder us from *presenting* our petitions in person. We may give them to a fellow, called a Secretary of State, or a member of parliament; but he may fling them into the fire if he choose, or he may fling them in our faces, saying that they are too long, or too short; too black, or too white, or he may curl up his lip and say nothing at all....

"And thus I am as completely deprived of the right of petition as if I lived in Algiers; and even more completely; for there a man may approach the Dey, and give him his petition, without being seized and treated as a malefactor...."[323]

---

319 Political Register. 5/4/1817.
320 Political Register. 29/3/1817.
321 Political Register. 5/4/1817.
322 Political Register. 6/6/1818.
323 Political Register. 1/5/1819.

"I know of no ruler, however despotic, that may not be approached with a *petition*. To the autocrat of Russia, any man may, in person, deliver a paper. Napoleon received petitions in the streets. In short, England is the only country in the world, where writing is practised, where any man, be he who he may, cannot present a petition to the Chief Magistrate."[324]

To this it had come.

Of course, restrictions on the expression of opinion are rendered completely unnecessary if the views of a large proportion of the population can be moulded along the lines of establishment thinking; and it is an interesting question how far all the measures outlined above were merely cosmetic, and put into operation merely for the purpose of placating the wild men of the City. For the measures existed alongside an extremely effective system of propaganda; and Cobbett had always maintained that the great and overriding failing of the English people was credulity.

The press Cobbett always considered as one of the most potent weapons of the establishment.

"The state of the case is this; that about seven hundred newspapers, magazines, reviews, and other periodical works, together with tracts, pamphlets, and other publications without number, supported by those who live and fatten upon the taxes, and left unchecked by any law, to abuse whomsoever they please, who do not live and fatten on the taxes; all these are constantly at work *against Reform*, and only about fifty publications *for it*; and those fifty continually supervised and harrassed by the myrmidons of the law, who, in all manner of ways, suppress and destroy them. Add to this that the tax-eaters have about *twenty thousand preachers* on their side, while the Reformers have but the solitary Mr. Harrison of Stockport."[325]

Because of this wicked and powerful press, poor gullible John Bull had been induced to act in ways in which he never would otherwise have acted.

"His press consists, nineteen twentieths of it, of what is, in one way or another, hired to deceive him; and the other twentieth dares not speak out for fear of punishment. This poor animal, therefore, is kept *in hand*, as they call it, and *noodled* along from one embarrassment, from one state of suffering, to another, without ever knowing the real cause of any of them."[326]

And, as we might by now suspect, it was indeed the causes of that suffering that formed the substance of this propaganda. We can trace the evolution of it from the time of the great slump that began in 1814.

Early in 1816, the first instinct of the propagandist was still the same as it was during the 1790s – to attempt to deny that poverty existed at all. At the opening of the parliamentary session of that year, the Prince Regent failed altogether to mention poverty and distress, and painted a picture instead of prosperity both in trade and in national revenue. This impression was preserved in the answering addresses of both Houses of Parliament.[327] When the subsistence riots of that year, which took place at Ely and Littleport, had been put down, the judges at the trial of the rioters attempted to make out that material deprivation formed no part of the motives of the rioters. Here is the Chief Justice of the Isle of Ely.

"The conduct of the rioters cannot be attributed to want or poverty; the prisoners were all robust men, in full health, strength and vigour, who were receiving great wages; and any change in the price of provisions, could only lessen that superfluity which, I fear, they too frequently wasted in drunkenness."[328]

---

324 Political Register. 27/2/1819.
325 Political Register. 6/11/1819.
326 Political Register. 20/4/1816.
327 Political Register. 6/7/1816.
328 Political Register. 13/7/1816.

Later that year, the courier newspaper claimed that there was no poverty in or around London. Cobbett wrote;-

"They hate every one, who dwells upon the *miseries* of the country; for, *to them*, it is confusion to acknowledge that misery exists. The Courier asserted, only the other day, that there was *no suffering* in or near London, and *abused* the people for *complaining*! Such men would kill you or me or any man who talks of the people's sufferings. They call the complaints of hunger *sedition*...."[329]

Such a line of reasoning, it was found, could not be maintained in the face of an obvious reality, and by the end of the parliamentary session the Prince Regent was deeply regretting "the continuance of that pressure and distress which the circumstances of the country at the close of so long a war, have unavoidably entailed on many of his Majesty's subjects."[330] Distress was now said to be the consequence of "a sudden transition from war to peace." Attempts were made to make out that it would be short-lived; that all other countries were suffering equally. Cobbett quoted from one of the ministerial newspapers.

"Do not let them be told that they are suffering, without being told also that those sufferings will only *be temporary*, and have not been occasioned by their Government; that what they have already endured has been to preserve all that makes life and country dear and honourable; for their freedom and their independence, the homes of their families, the graves of their fathers, the altars of their *GOD*. All were in peril and all have been preserved; and the people of the British Empire may safely stand up and claim the praise and the part of being the freest, the happiest, and the greatest people upon earth."[331]

The glories of war were liberally used as a smokescreen to divert attention from ruin and starvation. The Prince Regent spoke of "the ultimate success which has attended our glorious and persevering exertions." The Chancellor of the Exchequer declared it "a proof of baseness in an Englishman not to be proud of the state of his country."[332]

The sudden transition from war to peace served the turn of the propagandists for an amazing number of years, but as distress and poverty stubbornly refused to abate – as, on the contrary, they became steadily worse – even that began to wear thin. The emphasis had to shift towards demonstrating the lack of responsibility of the government for producing such suffering.[333]

"The supporters of the system would fain persuade us, that this *could not be helped by the government*; that it is *no fault* of any persons in power; that it is a thing *come upon us* some how or another; that we must submit *with resignation*...."

"What?", exclaimed Cobbett, on the widespread belief that the government caused the distress. "What sad rogues the discontented must be! To pretend to believe that the Regent and the Ministers had contributed towards the distress; what sad fellows!"[334]

The by now well-worn theme of the wickedness of the poor was wheeled out yet again.

"It has been the constant endeavour of the enemies of freedom in England to persuade the people, that the taxes have nothing to do, in making them poor and miserable. These writers attribute the poverty and misery of the lower classes to their *vices*, and to their ignorance; to any thing, in short, but the true cause.

"Hence all the projects for *educating*, as it is called, the poor. It has been pretended, that, if all the people were educated, that is to say, taught to read and write, that they would none of them be

---

329 Political Register. 14/12/1816.
330 Political Register. 6/7/1816.
331 Political Register. 13/7/1816 and 9/11/1816.
332 Political Register. 6/7/1816 and 14/12/1816.
333 Political Register. 14/9/1816.
334 Political Register. 6/7/1816.

miserable; that there would be no crimes committed by them, and, in short, that they would all be happy as princes.

"These pretended causes of misery and of crimes are put forward by some persons from ignorance, but, by the chief movers, they are put forward for the purpose of disguising the *real* cause, which cause it would be very inconvenient to these movers to have clearly understood. It is manifest to them, I mean the persons who fatten upon the taxes; it must be manifest to them, that a people cannot long remain quiet under great suffering. They must see clearly, that if the people are left alone to reflect, they will, sooner or later, perceive that their sufferings arise from the circumstance, that their earnings are carried away by those who roll in riches out of the taxes. Hence the necessity of putting them on a wrong scent. Hence all the innumerable projects for amusing and misleading them; for exciting false hopes in their bosoms; for lulling them and keeping them tranquil."[335]

Propaganda such as this, as we have already seen, became a part of the problem – a cause of poverty in itself. The "terrible and unexampled distress....can never be mitigated, but must be augmented, by every attempt, whether arising from folly or knavery, to disguise its real and all-powerful cause."[336]

From time to time, and increasingly, a member of the establishment would come out and attribute the mass of suffering to man-made causes very much along the lines of Cobbettian theory. In such cases, attention turned to remedies. And, of course, remedies were carefully formulated to avoid reducing the taxes or affecting the interests of the monied men. It was widely asserted that neither government nor parliament could do anything to alleviate the distress. It was claimed in debate "that if nineteen twentieths of the taxes were taken off, the people would not be thereby benefited."[337]

"Alas! my Lord", Cobbett wrote to Prime Minister Liverpool, "this is an evil not to be stayed by minimums with regard to wages; by pitiful attempts to relieve the starving people by raising money upon those not quite starving; by making little shillings and sixpences; nor by any such devices."[338]

The gross absurdity of the whole campaign was shown up in a gently mocking open letter to Judge Garrow.

"All the alledged causes of the misery appear now to be exploded. At first, it was a *sudden transition from war to peace*, that had done the mischief. Then it was a *super-abundant produce*; too much food and too few mouths. Next it was a *surplus population*; too many mouths and too little food. Next it was the *use of machinery and of draught horses*. And, all along, a *want of employment* has been a symptom of the malady. The remedies have been an *expedition to the North Pole*; a *Corn Bill* to lessen the quantity of food, and *a promotion of emigration* to lessen the number of mouths. And, to remedy the want of employment, projects of *spinning-wheels* and *spade-husbandry*, and *for digging holes one day and filling them up the next*."[339]

Much of the propaganda of these years was actually aimed at the middle classes, it being the great fear of the elite that these would be won over to the cause of the poor. In 1819, Cobbett addressed a letter to the middle classes, on their attitude to the poor.

"You stand aloof, and, at best, content yourselves with *wishing them success*; when, by one single movement of *yours*, in only one great town, that success would be assured.

"We are called *wild* and *visionary*....the tendency of the accusation, if believed, is *to make the Middle Classes keep aloof* from *the Labouring Class*; in order that the latter may be an *easy prey*. You see the Boroughmonger prints continually comforting themselves with saying, that such or such a meeting was composed of '*nothing* but the *labouring classes*'. These classes are not *direct* tax-payers;

335 Political Register. 7/9/1816.
336 Political Register. 8/2/1817.
337 Political Register. 11/12/1819.
338 Political Register. 18/12/1819.
339 Political Register. 27/5/1820.

they have no magistrates to depend on for *licences*; they have no *customers* to be afraid of; the sheriff cannot come to take away their *bundle of straw*; they are afraid of no *creditors*; they are free from all those ties which keep *you* in check. If you, in any one great town, such as Manchester, Birmingham, Bristol, Nottingham, or the like, were to join heartily and cordially with the Labouring Classes, for one week, we should have a reform in one month from that day."[340]

Anti-poor propaganda was a prominent feature of these years. Joseph Townsend's Dissertation on the Poor Laws was reprinted in1817. Hannah More published selections of her old works, together with new ones. And a new edition of Malthus was brought out; we have already remarked how socially divisive this work was intended to be, and how it set out to prejudice one part of society against another.

The engendering of fear has always been a primary objective of the propaganda of despotic regimes. By attributing sinister and revolutionary motives to those who advocated the rights, and agitated the distresses, of the populace, the establishment hoped to frighten the middling sort away from supporting them. Those who wished for change were constantly charged "with a design to subvert the constitution". This charge, said Cobbett, was "always preferred against those, who are opposed to Corruption and Peculation and Tyranny. Here is a man who does not like to be shut up in a dungeon. Oh the villain! Not like a dungeon? He wants to *subvert the constitution*! Here is another; who dislikes to see a punk's foot-boy made a military commander. Oh! Wretch! He certainly wants to subvert the constitution! In short, any man, that does not like any thing that it suits any boroughmonger to do, or to say, is accused of wanting to subvert the constitution."[341]

Here is another example, from 1812. The Courier newspaper denied that distress was the cause of the riots of that year, and blamed, instead, treasonable intentions. Cobbett responded with the following. Read between the lines.

"Far be it from me to attempt to justify people in the commission of unlawful acts. I do not wish to justify the woman, who, according to the newspapers, committed *highway robbery* in taking *some potatoes out of a cart at Manchester*, and who, according to the newspapers, was HANGED FOR IT. I do not pretend to justify her conduct. But there is, I hope, no harm in expressing my *compassion* for her; and, I further hope, that my readers would think me a most unfeeling brute, if I were to endeavour to deprive her and her fellow-sufferers of the compassion of the public, by asserting that she was actuated by a *treasonable* motive, and that she hated the whole form of our government and wished to destroy it. No, reader, I will not lend my aid to this. I allow her to have been guilty of *highway robbery* in forcibly *taking some potatoes out of a cart at Manchester*. I allow this; and I allow that, the law makes *highway robbery* a crime punishable with *death*, if the judges think proper; but, I cannot and I will not allow, that her forcibly taking some potatoes out of a cart at Manchester, was any proof of a *treasonable* design and of hatred against the whole form of our government."[342]

It was the continual endeavour of the ministerial press to pin violent motives upon the leaders of the radical movement. Men such as Cobbett and Hunt were constantly labelled as evil-minded and designing men, whose greatest wish was to stir up violent disturbances. And this was a ploy to deter people from supporting them. The reality was that Cobbett, Hunt and others were scrupulous about recommending only peaceful methods. This was an inconvenient truth. The Spa Fields Meeting of 1816, for example, was "conducted with propriety in all respects with anxious desire to preserve public peace."

"But, the truth is, that it is *this manner* of conducting popular discussions, which stings the authors and abettors of these corrupt publications to the soul. They wish to see the friends of *Reform*

340 Political Register. 13/11/1819.
341 Political Register. 30/10/1819.
342 Political Register. 4/7/1812.

guilty of folly and violence. This would answer *their* purpose; and the writers in the Courier expressly said, a few weeks ago, that it was this *peaceable* conduct which was the greatest cause of *suspicion* and *alarm!*"[343]

"What! Was the country *too quiet* for them? Yes, and you will remember with what *peculiar malignity* they spoke of those essays of mine, the main object of which was to prevent disorder and riot. Amongst the endless abuse, heaped upon me by those choice tools of corruption, *Walter* and *Stewart*,[344] there was none equal to that which was drawn forth by my endeavours, to put an end to the destruction of machines and to the attacks on bakers and butchers. These were the things, which these ruffians wanted to see continued; because, against acts like these all good men would naturally say that *force* must be employed."[345]

The establishment press stood accused of deliberately attempting to stir up violence, and not just by Cobbett. Those who took part in public meetings were provocatively called miscreants, robbers, assassins, and contemptible rabble; they were jeered, flouted, reproached and despised….[346]

There were attempts made to turn peaceful public meetings into violent disturbances; a tactic not unknown in modern times. At one of the Spa Fields Meetings, a bill was posted up, *"exciting the people to riot"*; and this, according to the Lord Mayor of London, emanated from Lord Sidmouth's Home Office. At another, a handbill was passed around the crowd, saying;-

"A pot of beer for a penny and bread for two pence; HUNT REGENT and COBBETT KING; Go it my Boys!"

This was circulated by the Post Office.[347]

But the greatest propaganda coup of all was the discovery of a treasonable conspiracy.

"They sigh for a PLOT", Cobbett wrote to Hunt. "Oh, how they sigh! They are working and slaving and fretting and stewing; they are sweating all over; they are absolutely pining and dying for a Plot!"[348]

In the absence of any such plots, they had to be created. A friend of Cobbett's observed to him that, "as there *were no treasons*, treasons would be *made*, and traitors would be hired."

"The fabrication of treasonable plots by hirelings of the Government, for the purpose of alarming '*the Loyal*', of justifying the misrepresentations which corruption has been driven to, as to the views of the Reformers; and in support of their despotic measures, to which the ponderous system of fraud and extravagance has had recourse for the prolongation of its existence."[349]

The hirelings of the government described here were spies. Spies were not just informers – they were paid to be *agents provocateurs.*

"By a spy something is meant more than *a watcher*; mind *that*." Spies were guilty "of *aiding*, of *abetting*, of *incitement*, of *instigation*, of *shewing how*, of *furnishing the means*, and, indeed, of paying men to be conspirators."[350]

The system was not new. "The System of Spies and Informers….the *sham plots*, the *hired spies*, the *dealing in human blood*", these all originated with the changed nature of government at the

---

343 Political Register. 7/12/1816.
344 The editors of the Times and the Courier respectively.
345 Political Register. 25/10/1817.
346 Political Register. 7/12/1816.
347 Political Register. 25/10/1817.
348 Political Register. 14/12/1816.
349 Political Register. 25/10/1817 and 10/1 1818.
350 Political Register. 13/5/1820.

time of Pitt's war against France. But it rose to new heights during these years; and its purpose was propaganda.[351]

The Derbyshire Rising of 1817 was notorious. Instigated and organised by the government spy Oliver, it ended with the men whom Oliver had entrapped being hanged and beheaded. On the scaffold, the condemned men placed the responsibility firmly on the government.

"Brandreth was beginning to address the people, and had got so far as to say something about CASTLEREAGH, when the chaplain *got between him and the people;....*Turner had said '*this is the work* of OLIVER and the GOVERNMENT, and....' when he was, in like manner, interrupted; and then their voices *were silenced for ever!*"[352]

At the trial of the so-called conspirators, a lawyer was nominated for the defence by the government. Cobbett commented;-

"The assigned counsel, Cross, bent his efforts, not to obtain a verdict for the prisoners, but to cause it to be believed, that they had been instigated to act, not by the hired instigators, but by *me*, against whose writings, as is very notorious, the infernal measures had been levelled....Cross studiously kept the hired spies out of sight partly to afford a justification for the Bourbon System, and partly to *pave the way* FOR FURTHER MEASURES AGAINST THE PRESS."[353]

Much the same can be said of the Cato Street Conspiracy of 1820. Upon its being made public, the ministerial press launched yet another campaign against "*seditious and blasphemous publications*", with a view to pressing for further censorship. This plot was entirely the creation of the government spy Edwards, and the unfortunates whom he ensnared met a similar fate to that of their Derbyshire predecessors. At their trial, the Lord Chief Justice asserted;-

"It was plain to see, that they did not embark in their wicked designs until they had first suffered their minds to be corrupted and inflamed by those seditious and irreligious publications, with which, unhappily for this country, the press had but too long teemed."[354]

Various other methods were used to propagate fear of those who agitated on the subject of the distresses of the people. The French Revolution was still serving this purpose, thirty years on.

"We want to have our earnings to purchase us food and raiment instead of giving them up to deck out pensioned ladies and gentlemen....we *pray* most humbly for this; and immediately we are told that we want a *French Revolution*....We do not like to be put into dungeons at the sole will and pleasure of the Boroughmongers. Ah! That is a sure sign that we want a French Revolution....It is a *crotchet* indeed to suppose, that the moment the bank-paper is destroyed and the Boroughmongers are deprived of their means longer to oppress and insult king and people, we shall *begin to kill one another!*"[355]

Ministerial propagandists were keen to inculcate the fear that political reform would deprive all classes of their property. Cobbett taunted George Canning with this.

"Your main object is to instill the notion, that the Reform, contemplated by the Radical Reformers, that is to say, *real personal representation*, a representation of the *people's will*, would *destroy all property*, that is, all the *laws of property*. The *destruction of property* is the bugbear, on which you place your chief reliance for terrifying."

The use and abuse of religion, was, if anything, an even more powerful ploy. The idea that political reform would deprive the people of their cherished religion was, of course, absurd. But it was widely spread around, and George Canning tried to make out that, before the repressive measures of

351   Political Register. 10/1 1818.
352   Political Register. 25/4/1818.
353   Ibid.
354   Political Register. 6/5/1820.
355   Political Register 1/5/1819.

1819, there was "not a man of moral and religious principles, who did not fear, that those principles *were about to be cut from under the feet of succeeding generations.*" This was "insufferable nonsense", according to Cobbett.[356]

"The grand battery of Corruption has been the charge, against the Reformers, that they were irreligious men; that they were blasphemers; and that it was principally to their *want of religion* that their complaints were to be ascribed. Shocking hypocrisy was this, to be sure; but still it *took*; it had its *effect*; it assisted Corruption; for there are hundreds of thousands of persons, who will almost cut one's throat, if one dares to hint, that they are wrong on the score of *religion*, upon which subject the most foolish of mankind generally think themselves the most wise….

"A *love of religion* has been the pretext for committing the most wicked acts that the world has ever witnessed….What has there ever been done to harrow up the very souls of men, which has not been done under the pretext of a *love of religion*? It has been the great stalking horse of tyranny in all ages…."[357]

By 1819, the system of exploitation which Cobbett denominated THE THING had been in existence for around 130 years. In that time, it had profoundly altered the system of government in this country. The desire to exploit had been the underlying cause of changes in government; those changes, in their turn were what enabled that exploitation to take place.

The material well-being of a people can, to a large extent, be defined in terms of the relationship between the leaders of society, and the rest. Before the arrival of William III, England was, generally speaking, possessed of a paternalistic localised economy, in which the leaders of society had strong provincial connections, and represented the interests of the localities to the central government. Such a society may be expected to display a gradual hierarchy of wealth, in which the rich were not excessively rich, and the poorest able to maintain themselves in some degree of comfort.

But from the 1690s, the leaders of English society became ever more closely connected with a class of men who had no local ties of loyalties, and whose sole objective in life was financial gain. The traditional aristocracy and the new monied interest merged to form a small, centralised, metropolitan elite. Indeed, this elite was far more cosmopolitan than national. And the rest of society became nothing more than the source from which this elite competitively drew its wealth.

Such a society may be expected to display a tendency towards the polarisation of classes, with an increasingly yawning gulf dividing them. The rich might possess a massive superfluity, and live in a magnificent and indolent luxury. The poor might face a constant struggle merely to survive, with those at the bottom of the scale starving. These two classes Cobbett defined as the tax-eaters and the tax-payers.

The elite regarded the poor with an affected contempt and disgust; the poor were seen as less than just another class of society, but almost as a different race, alien, unworthy, wicked, barely human. Many members of the elite harboured powerful feelings of aggression and violence towards them; those aspiring to respectability affected to do so.

The hunter has a healthy respect for his prey; but the parasite has not.

The political consequences of this state of society were such as were described by William Cobbett.

"So far from having *property* and *political liberty*, we have no safety, not one moment's safety, for our persons. We are as much the property of the Boroughmongers as negro slaves are the property

356 Political Register. 8/4/1820.
357 Political Register. 13/5/1820 and 8/4/1820.

of their masters. They can, and do, take from us what they please. They shut us up when they please, and they let us out when they please. They compel us to serve as sailors and soldiers. They treat us as they treat all those animals that they openly call their property, only they treat us with less gentleness. There is no mode left us of obtaining *redress*. They compel us to refrain from seeking to recover the money that the Bank has got from us for its notes. They make laws to protect those who have committed violences against us. If we meet to petition in numbers, they cause us to be attacked by armed men and treated as open rebels. And, if we wish to petition singly, they will not suffer our petitions to be presented. It is against this monstrous tyranny that we, the people of England, are now struggling...."[358]

Section eight; Potatoes, National Wealth, and "The Improvement of the Age"

In 1834, the Whig ministry introduced its bill for altering the Poor Laws. Cobbett thought this the most important question ever to have been discussed in his lifetime.[359]

Cobbett had it on reliable authority that the government's instructions to the barrister who drew up the bill stated that;-

"IT IS DESIRABLE TO BRING THE WORKING PEOPLE OF ENGLAND, BY DEGREES, TO LIVE UPON COARSER FOOD THAN THEY NOW LIVE UPON."[360]

Cobbett addressed Lord Radnor on the subject.

"There is not a man in his senses who does not believe that the main object"....is "to bring the English labourers down to live upon the base food, and to be clad in the miserable rags, which are the lot of the wretched people of Ireland, where a good and honest labourer, as good and as true as any in the world, works for sixpence a day, and sometimes for two-pence. This is the object; if not of yourself, it must be the object of the inventors of the scheme."[361]

The idea that parliament could be induced to pass an act, the deliberate intention of which was to reduce the standard of living of an already chronically under-nourished population, was profoundly shocking to William Cobbett. Perhaps, even, it may seem shocking to us today. But to those of the establishment way of thinking, the ideas behind the act were a commonplace, and by the 1830s had already been entertained for many years. All that had changed was that the entertainers of those ideas had acquired the audacity openly to enshrine them in an act of parliament.

We previously encountered the doctrine of the national wealth. We saw how writers such as Sir James Steuart, Arthur Young and the Earl of Selkirk justified the agricultural changes which were taking place on the grounds of the wealth which, as a result, accrued to "the nation". The localised agricultural and economic systems of traditional cultivators were denominated subsistence farming, which was supposed to contribute nothing to "the nation", and the practisers of which were vilified as indolent and parasitic. The reorganisation of agriculture was advocated; the amalgamation of farms and the conversion of large acreages to grazing land; so that these useless mouths could be cleared from the land; so that they would no longer be able to intercept the food before it reached the market; so that a greater proportion of produce could be turned into money, collected as rent, taxed, and drawn up to the metropolis; where "the nation" was eagerly waiting to receive it.

Even Steuart conceded the risk of starvation which was the result of such changes. But, in general, the useless workers cleared form the land were to be turned into "free hands" – soldiers, sailors, manufacturers, who were said to be of service to the state, as traditional cultivators were not.

---

358 Political Register. 1/5/1819.
359 Political Register. 12/7/1834.
360 Political Register. 18/10/1834.
361 Political Register. 25/10/1834.

Thus, as a result of the vast suction of resources from the productive, provincial parts of England, to the unproductive metropolitan part, there occurred a massive proletarianisation of the population. Thousands of families who had lived independently, or semi-independently, from their own resources, perhaps augmented by wage-earning at times, were forced to become completely dependent upon paid employment. In this way, an aspect of the national economy which traditionally had been of only marginal importance, within a relatively short space of time became of monumental importance – and that aspect was wages.[362]

Those who promoted the doctrine of the national wealth may have wrested the property and the means of production from these families; but the families still, for the most part, existed; they still had to eat; and the poor laws did not permit them to be starved. The subject of wages became the more important because, in defiance of the theories of Malthus, those who were displaced from their traditional societies, and deprived of their property, married much younger and produced more children than their parents and grandparents had done. Wages, however scanty, became the next great cause of wealth being retained in the localities, consumed on the spot, and kept out of the hands of the landlord, the tax-collector, and the political classes generally. Those wages became an important economic and political issue; a point of great sensitivity with the establishment class; and the national wealthers cast their eyes upon them.

The subject of wages exercised scores of economic writers from the 17th century onwards; and the burden of their wisdom generally was that real wages should be kept as low as possible. Various reasons were put forward for this. An article which appeared in the Gentleman's Magazine in 1739 provides a good sample of the arguments that were used.

"It is an incontestable truth that the poor in the manufacturing countries will never work any more time in general than is necessary just to live and support their weekly debauches....We may justly infer that the reduction of wages in the wool manufactures would be a blessing and advantage, and no real injury to the poor. By this means we should be capable of extending our foreign trade further, to find out sufficient employment for all our manufacturing hands at home; and should thereby reduce idleness and debauchery only, of which high wages and spare time are the nurses and supporters."[363]

These, in general, were the orthodoxies. The proposition that men will work harder for a subsistence than for a competence is, of course, open to serious question. But the accompanying concept that by forcing them to do so, the nation will be benefited by the expansion of cheap exports and the consequent inflow of specie, represented an absurd over-estimation of the importance of foreign trade in the economy of the time.

Nevertheless, the Rev. Josiah Tucker was stating conventional opinion when he wrote that "if the price of labour is continually beat down, it is greatly for the public good", and various methods of doing this were recommended. In 1736, William Allen thought that wages ought to be reduced by law, and that workers could be compelled to work for specific rates. Increasing competition between workers was a more popular ploy. Agricultural change, of course, was doing this all the time. Tucker was a keen advocate of unrestricted immigration, whilst others suggested methods of stimulating the increase of population. Raising the cost of living had the same effect – that of reducing real wage-rates. This might be done, William Petty thought, with public granaries to restrict supply; others supported the introduction of excises on the necessaries of life.

---

362 Sir James Steuart. Principles of Political Oeconomy. Pp. 135 and 55.

363 E.S. Furniss. The Position of the Labourer in a System of Nationalism. P. 132. Gentleman's Magazine. IV. 1739. P. 235.

"Living must be rendered dear", wrote Arthur Young, "before that general industry which alone can support a manufacturing people will be rooted among them."[364]

Almost the whole of this literature was interlaced with liberal dosings of anti-poor propaganda. One writer described wage-earners as "the vile and brutish part of mankind"; whilst another professed to think them "as bad as can be described; who become more vicious, more indigent and idle in proportion to the advance of wages and the cheapness of provisions". This defamation of the poor, *en masse,* might lead us to suspect that much of this literature was, in fact, special pleading; that the national interest was being invoked merely as a justification for the exploitation of one class by another. Against this long-standing background, perhaps the first writer openly to suggest that the standard of living of the poor could be reduced merely to increase the wealth of the rich was Adam Smith. By his time, the idea had acquired respectability. Significantly and ominously, the method to be adopted involved the use of potatoes.

"The food produced by a field of potatoes is not inferior in quantity to that produced by a field of rice, and much superior to what is produced by a field of wheat....An acre of potatoes will.... produce....three times the quantity produced by the acre of wheat. An acre of potatoes is cultivated with less expense than an acre of wheat; the fallow, which generally precedes the sowing of wheat, more than compensating the hoeing and other extraordinary culture which is always given to potatoes.[365] Should this root ever become in any part of Europe, like rice in some countries, the common and favourite vegetable food of the people, so as to occupy the same proportion of the lands in tillage which wheat and other sorts of grain for human food do at present, the same quantity of cultivated land would maintain a much greater number of people, and the labourers being generally fed with potatoes, a greater surplus would remain after replacing all the stock and maintaining all the labour employed in cultivation. A greater share of this surplus, too, would belong to the landlord. Population would increase, and rents would rise much beyond what they are at present."

Here is how the great man justified converting the English people into potato-eaters.

"The chairmen, porters, and coalheavers in London, and those unfortunate women who live by prostitution, the strongest men and the most beautiful women perhaps in the British dominions, are said to be the greater part of them from the lowest rank of the people or Ireland, who are generally fed with this root. No food can afford a more decisive proof of its nourishing quality, or of its being peculiarly suitable to the health of the human constitution."[366]

However flimsy, absurd and amoral the pretexts put forward by the current occupant of our £20 notes, it was around this time that the potato started the gradual process of becoming the staple of the English diet.

We can assume with confidence that the opinions of Adam Smith reflected more or less accurately those of the ruling class. Forcing the people on to a cheap potato diet would enable wages to be reduced and national wealth increased. But, in general, it was only economic hardship which could overcome their resistance. Here is William Cobbett again, writing of Smith's time.

"This American War caused a great mass of new taxes to be laid on, and the people of England became a great deal poorer than they had ever been before. During that war, they BEGAN TO EAT POTATOES, as something to 'save bread'. The poorest of the people, the very poorest of them, refused, for a long while, to use them in this way, and even when I was ten years old, which was just about *fifty years ago*; the poor people would not eat potatoes, except with *meat,* as they would cabbage, or carrots, or any other moist vegetable. But, by the end of the American War, their stomachs had come to! By slow degrees, they had been reduced to swallow this pig-meat (and bad pig-meat too),

364 E. S. Furniss. The Position of the Labourer in a System of Nationalism. Pp. 132-138.
365 Agriculture never was Adam Smith's strongest subject!
366 Adam Smith. The Wealth of Nations. Penguin ed. Bk. I. Pp. 264-5.

not, indeed, without grumbling, but, to swallow it; to be reduced, thus, many degrees in the scale of animals."[367]

Here Cobbett demonstrates well the ambivalent role played by potatoes in the deteriorating dietary standards of the people. They could be used as a supplement, or a substitute. In the north of England, in the south-west, and in Wales, they had long been used as part of a traditional diet based on bread of the inferior grains, which, however, still contained some meat and dairy produce. In other areas, during the famines, working families increased their consumption of potatoes, as the prices of bread and flour soared ever higher. Many of the correspondents to Arthur Young's Annals of Agriculture write of the increasing use of potatoes, but seemed unsure whether to class this as substitution or not. The Earl of Egremont was fairly typical, when he reported from Sussex that no attempts were being made to substitute other foods for bread, "but the consumption of potatoes is considered increasing". Many more simply state, with John Wickens of Dorset, that no article of food was being used as a substitute for bread.[368]

But within that tiny minority of the population which constituted the political establishment, the idea, that had surfaced in Adam Smith's Wealth of Nations, that potatoes could be used to lower the standard of living of the labourer, in order to increase rent, and, by implication, taxes; in other words, that national wealth could be increased in this way; had taken root. "Retrenching" the diet of the labourer, and depressing his wages, became the twin concerns of William Pitt's government.

Out in the real world, labourers and local authorities of all sorts tended to see potatoes as a useful resource; a kind of insurance; a last resort, perhaps, in times of scarcity. The characteristic of the retrencher, and the oppressor, was the advocacy of reducing the poor to a total dependence on substitute foods, of which potatoes were the foremost; and that on a permanent basis. None of those who displayed this characteristic were far removed from government.

F. M. Eden was one. In his State of the Poor, published in 1797, he several times clearly implied that the poverty of the people was to be attributed to their stubborn and extravagant adherence to a diet of wheaten bread. He had other plans for them.

"The Naturalists of Queen Anne's time would probably have been astonished to hear, what the Board of Agriculture mentions as a fact of the greatest importance, 'that potatoes and water alone, with common salt can nourish men completely'.....Potatoes are perhaps as strong an instance of the extension of human enjoyment as can be mentioned; and progress which various districts have made in the cultivation of the valuable root....(suggests) that in the course of a very few years, the consumption of potatoes in this Kingdom will be almost as general and universal as that of corn."[369]

Early in 1796, Samuel Whitbread's Minimum Wage Bill was under discussion in the House of Commons. It was Whitbread's idea that the wages of labour should be made to fluctuate with the price of wheaten bread. Prime Minister Pitt had been well briefed by Edmund Burke, the mouthpiece of Earl Fitzwilliam and the Portland Whigs, that the price of labour should be determined solely by what it was worth to the buyer. Pitt opposed Whitbread's Bill, as we have seen. He denied that Whitbread's comparison of the labourer's present state with his former one was valid because "it did not embrace a comprehensive view of the relative situations."

"Corn which was then almost the only food of the labourer was now supplied by cheaper substitutes, and it was unfair to conclude that the wages of labour were so far from keeping pace with the price of provisions, because they could no longer purchase the same quantity of an article for which the labourer no longer had the same demand."[370]

---

367 Poor Man's Friend. IV. P. 94.
368 Arthur Young ed. Annals of Agriculture. Vol. 24. P. 74.
369 R. N. Salaman. The History and Social Influence of the Potato. P. 504.
370 Edmund Burke. Thoughts and Details on Scarcity. P. ?. Parliamentary History. 1796. P. 705.

What Pitt told the House of Commons was a glaring falsehood; the labourer still demanded wheaten bread whenever he could afford it. He was telling the House, not what was, but what he wished to bring about. The sub-text of Pitt's speech was that there would be no need to raise wages to a subsistence level if the poor could be induced to live off inferior articles of provision. There is even a suspicion that he thought it politic to keep wages low in order forcibly to bring about that desirable end. Whitbread's Bill was defeated. And employers the country over took their lead from parliament and kept wages below subsistence level. The Gagging Acts, passed in the autumn of 1795, made it treasonable to agitate on the subject of the distresses of the poor, and nipped in the bud what was probably an incipient petitioning movement in support of Whitbread's Bill. [371]

As the second famine began to tighten its grip in 1799, Pitt and Wilberforce launched a further attack on the living-standards of the wage-earner. The Combination Act was rushed through parliament without any time being allowed to hear petitions against. Any concerted action by workers became subject to the severity of the law. This not only outlawed any attempts to gain better wages and conditions; it also gave employers perfect freedom to reduce wages at will; and it forced the children into the mills and the mines, without whose earnings working families could no longer survive. The greater exploitation of child labour had already been held up in the House of Commons as a desirable objective by William Pitt.[372]

The unavailability of living wages forced many thousands of working families on to the parish poor rate; and government attempted to induce local authorities to use the poor laws as a lever by which the poor could be brought to change their eating habits. When the Board of Agriculture suggested that the proceeds of charity and the rates should be used to supply the poor with flour and bread at a reduced cost, the idea had to be withdrawn at the insistence of government. Instead, recipes were sent out to correspondents for making soups with meat, turnips, potatoes and carrots. In July 1795, the government tried to increase the supply of rice by imposing an embargo on its re-export. In 1800, an act allowed fish to be imported from Newfoundland free of duty; the salt used in the curing of fish was exempted from tax; and systems of distribution and publicity aimed to get large quantities of cheap fish supplied to the poor mainly through the parish authorities. Soups using these ingredients were great favourites with propagandists, if not with the poor themselves. In 1800, reports were published by committees of both Houses of Parliament recommending the use of potatoes, peas, rice and maize, as well as "a good pottage for labourers", which contained mixtures of rice with cheap cuts of meat. The Blackburn Mail, the Bath Chronicle and the Norfolk Chronicle all joined in the chorus, whilst Lord Sheffield conducted his own campaign through the Sussex newspapers. Much nonsense was written on the great nutritive and epicurean qualities of these new foods. The soup kitchen became an increasingly popular method of relieving the poor; the one at Leeds handed out 33,572 quarters of rice, 270 barrels of herrings, and 20,000 quarts of soup. In January 1800, the magistrates of Berkshire recommended that parish relief should be given in soup, potatoes, pease, meat, herrings and rice, rather than in bread or money.[373]

It is not always easy to distinguish laudable and well-meaning efforts to sustain a dependent populace through a time of hunger and hardship, from the rather less laudable attempts to use the famines to reduce the standard of living on a permanent basis. But behind some of the schemes and suggestions lay transparently sinister intentions; and these generally originated with those closely connected with government. A report issued by a committee of the House of Commons in 1800 pointed the way.

---

371 R. Wells. Wretched Faces. P. 6. J. L. and B. Hammond. The Village Labourer. P. 113-115.
372 J. L. and B. Hammond. The Town Labourer. Pp. 115-142.
373 R. Wells. Wretched Faces. Pp. 215-224.

"Your committee have heard, with very great concern, that from the mistaken application of the charity of individuals, in some parts of the country, flour and bread have been delivered to the poor at a reduced price; a practice which may contribute very considerably to increase the inconveniences arising from the deficiency of the last crop; and they recommend that all charity and parochial relief should be given, as far as is practicable, in any other article except bread, flour, and money, and that part of it which is necessary for the sustenance of the poor, should be distributed in soups, rice, potatoes, or other substitutes. Your committee are of opinion, that if this regulation was generally adopted, it would not only, in a very great degree, contribute to economise at this time the consumption of flour, but that it might have the effect of gradually introducing into use, a more wholesome and nutritious species of food than that to which the poor are at present accustomed."

For wholesome and nutritious, read cheap. This committee took detailed expert evidence on the nutritive value of all the different sorts of bread, but, of potatoes, rice, or soup, none.[374]

The grandees themselves were not slow to follow the advice of the committee. In Yorkshire, at Malton and at Wentworth Woodhouse, Earl Fitzwilliam insisted on having the poor relieved in soup and herrings, but the charitable of those boroughs refused to subscribe, not relishing the resulting ill-will of the people. Fitzwilliam got his way, but had to pay himself.[375]

A much subtler, and consequently more sinister scheme was on foot at Gosfield, in Essex. It was financed by the Marquis of Buckingham, frequently complained of by Cobbett as one of the greater sinecurists. The scheme is described by the Rev. Mr. Thurlow.

"Potatoes are in great use here, which necessarily lessens the consumption of bread....A school of industry, open every day in the week, is supported here by the liberality of the Marquis of Buckingham; a breakfast and dinner are given to the children every Sunday; the breakfast is milk gruel with bread; the dinner, meat soup thickened with potatoes and bread; besides a large quantity of potatoes boiled by themselves; so that each child has his trencher well supplied with potatoes, and his dish with soup; the children are thus habituated to the use of, and acquire a taste for potatoes...."[376]

This scheme had an obvious eye on the future well-being of the Marquis's rent-roll. But in general it can be assumed that most relief schemes were conducted with good motives. The poor stoutly resisted dietary change imposed from above, and when the pressure of the times abated in 1801, they reverted to their accustomed foods. This was lamented by Lord Sheffield, who was a tireless campaigner for permanently reducing the expences of the poor.

"When the difficulty has been in any degree superseded, we neglect all those measures which might prevent the recurrence of the calamity.

"We have learned from experience that neither law, regulation nor recommendation will effectively turn the people from the Use of Wheaten Bread, and that the high price of Wheat alone will introduce substitutes, economy and good management."[377]

Sheffield was correct in his assumption that only economic hardship could force the poor on to potatoes. It was more or less accomplished, but gradually, and in the face of stubborn resistance, and over a period of many years. By the "hungry forties", potatoes were in use in every family, and had become almost essential to the survival of most.[378]

Economic hardship, however, can take many forms. The high price of wheat was the form complained of at the time when Sheffield was writing. The suspension of payments in specie at the Bank of England in 1797, and the resulting uncontrolled issue of paper money, insured high wheat

---

374 Arthur Young ed. Annals of Agriculture. Vol. 34. P. 456.

375 R. Wells. Wretched Faces. Pp. 220 and 227.

376 Arthur Young ed. Annals of Agriculture. Vol.24. P. 150.

377 R. Wells. Wretched Faces. P. 335.

378 R. N. Salaman. The History and Social Influence of the Potato. P. 532.

prices for most of the war years, up to around 1814. But the system was far too dangerous to be persisted in. It distorted the exchanges, and gave an artificial direction to foreign trade. It could not be disconnected from the competitive cupidity of the financial interest, and ever increasing issues of currency were seen as inevitable. This led to the danger of hyper-inflation, and a system of two prices, which William Cobbett saw as the virtual overthrow of the state. It also rendered the system vulnerable to destruction by forgery; by a foreign enemy, in the case of war; or by internal opponents of the system; and this Cobbett termed the puff-out.

A return to cash payments was thus seen as essential. This involved drastically reducing the amount of paper currency in circulation, in order to increase its value, and to attract the precious metals back into the country. This entailed a whole new set of economic circumstances, the most notable of which was a plummeting price of wheat and of produce of all types. The resumption of payment in coin Cobbett persistently maintained could not be done, without an "equitable adjustment"; by which he meant a reduction of government expences of all types in line with the increased value of money; a proportional adjustment of the interest payable on the national debt; and a consequent proportional reduction of taxation. This the government persistently refused; and as a result the political classes were all of a sudden draining twice as much out of the nation as previously; and at times almost treble.

This Cobbett denominated the ruining and starving system, and we have already heard his descriptions, only partial by his own assertion, of the distresses which afflicted the nation as a result of the aborted attempt to return to cash payments, which took place around 1816.

I used this period merely as an example of what happened when the government pursued this policy. Cobbett was repeatedly proved right in his assessment of the difficulty of the thing. The ruining and starving system put massive strains on agricultural rents and the yields of taxes, and the government was repeatedly forced to retreat from it, and to pump paper currency into circulation once more. This happened between 1816 and 1818. In 1819, a determined effort was made to return to cash payments, with the passing of Peel's Bill, and a new period of ruining and starving followed, which lasted until 1822. In this latter year, it was abandoned again, with the passing of the Small Note Bill, which allowed excessive issues of paper money to circulate until 1833. The over-speculation consequent upon this measure led, in turn, to the great banking crash of 1825, which came to within an inch of destroying the government. To avoid further crises, the "Panic Act" was passed in 1826, which stipulated that no new notes under the value of five pounds were to be issued, and that those already out should cease to circulate on 5th April 1829. This produced yet another period of ruining and starving, which intensified as the month of April 1829 approached and passed.

Each of these periods of monetary tightening brought forth schemes for reducing the amount of national wealth intercepted by the labouring classes, in order to facilitate the continued collection of rents and taxes, and to bolster the financial system in its time of crisis.

"Committee after committee, bill after bill, report after report, scheme after scheme have been witnessed, all having for their object the discovery of the means of making the quantity of their food *as small as possible consistent with strength sufficient to do your labour for you.*"[379]

What these periods brought forth, first and foremost, was controversy over the poor laws. The year 1817 saw new editions published both of Malthus and of Townsend; and bills passed through parliament, enabling parishes, if they wished, to change the basis upon which poor relief was managed. These bills were sponsored by Hampshire lawyer, Sturges Bourne, who, as his reward, acquired a huge and deserved infamy through the pages of the Political Register.

"Billy Sturges, as the people of Winchester call him, made the vestries somewhat like the Honourable House, by diminishing the right of voting in those vestries….Sturges Bourne's Bill took

379 Political Register. 14/11/1829.

the management of the poor out of the parish in general, and gave it to the rich. It authorised those rich to employ what are called assistant overseers; that is to say, men hired with a salary to be paid out of the rates; and in most cases they have been hired to receive a salary that becomes *great in proportion as the rates are small*, which is, in fact, a bargain with them to grind the poor down as much as they possibly can. This bill has certainly lowered the amount of the poor-rates; but it has prodigiously augmented the number and magnitude of thefts."[380]

Many other such schemes were mooted at times of financial stringency.

"We had the LAWYER SCALETT project, and, before that, the STURGES BOURNE project; we have since had the LAWYER NOLAN project, and that poor man went off to heaven, (at least, we ought to hope so,) before he could bring his project to perfection; we had then the LORD JOHN RUSSEL project; next in order came the HORTON WILMOT or WILMOT HORTON project. All these treading in the steps of the great PARSON MALTHUS himself, have had, as a principal object, *a lessening of the amount of the poor-rates*.…Lawyer Scarlett was for acting upon MALTHUS' principle, and for refusing relief to all able- bodied married men and their families; LAWYER NOLAN (God rest his soul!) was for compelling those who had ever received parish relief, to serve as soldiers in the militia, and to excuse all others from such service, as long as there should be enough of that description; WILMOT HORTON, or HORTON WILMOT, who has two townships dedicated to his two names, in that *fertile* country, NOVA SCOTIA, was for sending the surplus population away bodily out of the country; LORD JOHN RUSSEL was for doing a something (exactly what I could never understand), for the checking of breeding amongst the labourers, and thereby diminishing or preventing the increase of the poor-rates; lastly came, or is come, ROBERT SLANEY, ESQ., a Member for SHREWSBURY, whose project has undergone, since its first appearance, very great transformations."[381]

And then, there was the Winchester Manifesto. 1822 was a year of the most appalling agricultural distress. Cobbett commented upon the deplorable state of the farmers whom he met passing through Uphusband.

"I proved years ago that if we returned to cash payments without a reduction of the Debt, and rectifying of contracts, the present race of farmers must be ruined."

And so it was turning out.

"In all parts of the country, I hear of landlords that begin to *squeak*, which is a certain proof that they begin to feel the bottom of their tenants' pockets. No man can pay rent; I mean any rent at all, except out of capital; or except under some peculiar circumstances, such as having a farm near a spot where the fundholders are building houses."[382]

It was the inflated value of the tax burden that was obliterating both the landlord's rent and the farmer's capital. Those in power wished "the *taxes to be kept up* and *rents to be paid too*. Both cannot be, unless some means or other be found out of putting into, or keeping in, the farmer's pocket, money that is not now there.

"The scheme that appears to have been fallen upon for this purpose is the strangest in the world.…; namely, that of reducing the wages of labour so low as to make the labourer a walking skeleton."[383]

Cobbett was referring to a meeting of magistrates which took place at Winchester in September 1822; foremost among whom was Sir Thomas Baring, the great financier. These dignitaries proposed to regulate the rewards of labour, in the shape both of wages and relief, limiting them to new, absurdly low levels; and making even those rates dependent upon labourers not going out of their parishes at

---

380 Political Register. 1/8/1829.
381 Ibid.
382 Rural Rides. Penguin ed. P. 32.
383 Ibid. P. 17.

harvest-time to seek better-paid employment. The magistrates invited some of the greater farmers to attend this meeting, and attempted to attach their names to the resulting Manifesto; but the names were erased at the insistence of the farmers themselves, who had no relish for the prospect of living in the same village with labourers who were paid from 3s. to 5s. per week.[384]

The Winchester Manifesto, perhaps, did not succeed to its full extent, but it was a sign of the direction in which, despite Cobbett's best efforts, events were moving. The following month, Cobbett noted that wages in Hampshire had been brought down to 6s. a week, and he had heard that the situation in Wiltshire was even worse.[385]

It was during this agricultural depression that a House of Commons committee investigating agricultural distress heard evidence "that the general drink of the labourers was *water*; and that their general food was *potatoes*, and this so entirely and exclusively, that the ploughmen were in the constant habit of carrying these roots to *eat cold in the field*".[386] It was thus during periods of low prices, rather than high ones, that the people were reduced to the potato standard; because low prices had, as concomitant circumstances, unemployment, underemployment, and the deliberate efforts of the ruling classes to bolster the financial system out of the wage economy.

As the effects of the withdrawal of the small notes bit deeper and deeper in 1829; as the currency became ever more inadequate; Cobbett, in an open letter to the Prime Minister, the Duke of Wellington, attempted to describe the symptoms.

"The state of the country is this; the labouring people, whether in agriculture, handicraft, or manufactures, are in a state of half-starvation, from one end of England to the other; farmers cannot pay, have not paid, and will not pay, more than sixty per cent, on an average, of their Lady-day rents; corn (taking the six sorts together) is now, notwithstanding the last short crop and bad harvest, *seven per cent cheaper than it was last year at this time*, after a good crop and a good harvest; foreign commerce is in so wretched a state, that freights are at about a *fourth* of what they have been on an average of the last ten years; master manufacturers are every where ruined, or doing nothing; tradesmen do not take on an average, whether in shops or for work done, half the money that they have for many years been accustomed to take; confidence in dealings is almost wholly destroyed, punctuality in payments is now laughed at; insolvency is general, and compositions with creditors have, in a great measure, set aside the laws for the making of bankrupts and insolvents. While this is the case in all parts of the country, *the taxes are undiminished*, and those who receive them become richer in the exact proportion in which those who pay them become poorer. Such is the real state of this now miserable country."[387]

In the midst of starvation, the concern of the authorities was to enforce tranquillity. In the north, the newspapers "give account of *great bodies of troops* marching into the 'distressed *districts*'. To *carry victuals*, I presume! Good God! These vagabond newspaper cheats *congratulate* their readers on the arrival of troops, when *one cavalry horse* eats every week as much of the same sort of food as is now eaten (according to these fellows own account) by *four families* of that people whom these troops are sent to keep in order."[388]

---

384 Ibid. And Political Register 5/10/1822.
385 Rural Rides. Penguin ed. P. 28.
386 Political Register. 14/11/1829.
387 Political Register. 23/5/1829.
388 Ibid.

It was in the countryside that the symptoms of the financial stringency seem to have been felt most keenly; or, at least, the countryside was Cobbett's primary concern. He wrote to the 'Farmers of England' on the causes of their distress.

"The *immediate* cause is the withdrawing of the one pound notes....you see no ones circulating, except by stealth or in violence of law."

The small notes, Cobbett thought, would disappear, and the five pound notes would follow, bringing prices down to the level of 1793.

"Long before this, however, you will all, as *farmers*, be ruined....All your corn stacks are gone; your barns are empty; your fields in bad culture; your stock insufficient, and scarcely any part of it of sufficient age; your wool on your hands is worth next to nothing; or if sold, sold for a song; you have no stores of any thing; your Lady-day rent is half unpaid; your crop bespoken by the banker, or due to the landlord and parson, before it be cut; you must thrash it instantly out, and force it into the market, to give profit to the monopolising jobbers; to pay for your harvest work you must drive your hogs to market, or make your crops over, standing, or in the straw, to the landlord or banker; and a third part of you will be unable to fallow, and manure, and sow your fields for the next year.

"This, with very little exaggeration, with very little high colouring, is the real state of more than one-half of you."[389]

Farmers could not afford to pay wages; much land was left uncultivated; much more half-cultivated; tradesmen and their employees were in much the same plight; and those who should have been doing the work were set to work by the overseers on cracking stones on the roads.

"It is notorious, that, from one end of England to the other, the working people are in a state of misery hardly to be described; that they are generally accused of what is called *thieving*; that poultry, sheep, and even pigs are hardly looked upon as property, on account of this general *thieving*, as it is called; that barns and stacks are no where regarded as being secure against *fire*; that, in short, the gentlemen and farmers live amidst a labouring people who hate them, whose enmity they dread, and who have defeated or set at nought all the laws made to restrain them; and finally, the jails, though tripled in size, are still too small, and that the culprits make a jest of *imprisonment*, and even of *transportation*, either being a relief from the starving and perishing life that they lead...."

"Hundreds of country-labourers come to my farm, ready to drop down for want of food. Many of them tell me, that they have not had anything to eat for two or three days; and their looks corroborate what they say."[390]

It may seem a paradox, but was nevertheless the case, that on top of all this, and in spite of the greatly increased proportion of the national produce being collected in taxes, the diminution of the circulating medium put great pressure even on the financial system itself. In May 1829, Cobbett reported that six banks had collapsed in the space of two weeks. The remaining bankers were drawing in their issues as quickly as they could; many others had ceased trading. In November, two substantial banks at Bury St. Edmunds merged. They were in no danger of breaking, but Cobbett saw it as a sign that their business had dropped by over a half; and he thought their best option was to stop trading altogether.

"They could pay their notes; but can those who have borrowed their notes *pay them*? If they cannot, the banker is in a perilous state. In short, there are many he must continue to lend to, until they can pay him."[391]

And if a farmer could not pay now, he was hardly likely to be able to pay later.

---

389 Political Register. 15/8/1829.
390 Political Register. 14/11/1829 and 20/6 1829.
391 Political Register. 30/5/1829 and 14/11/1829.

By October of 1830, Cobbett was even writing, with affected concern, and inner rejoicing, of the sickness of the Old Lady of Threadneedle Street![392]

Even the revenue of the state was under pressure. Cobbett thought it impossible for the country to pay even £30 millions in an over-valued currency for any length of time. The tax-take was actually £56.5 millions; how could that be paid, with wheat at 4s. 6d. a bushel, and only at that price because of poor harvests; the prices of other produce having fallen even more?[393]

"During the last session of parliament incessant petitions were presented for the DIMINUTION OF TAXES, at the same time that the REVENUE WAS FALLING OFF, in consequence of the extreme poverty of the people. The government, in order to appease this loud and general cry, took off some imposts, but laid on others at the same time....Notwithstanding the enormous amount of taxes, the government is now RAISING MONEY ON ANNUITIES; and in this manner is ADDING TO THE DEBT OF THE STATE, in order to CARRY ON THE PEACE."[394]

Neither the monumental avarice, nor the monumental incompetence, of the governments of these years seems much to have engaged the attention of modern historians.

This, however, was the state of affairs which confronted the Duke of Wellington as Prime Minister; and this, for which, according to Cobbett, it was his duty to find a remedy.

In Cobbett's opinion, Wellington had but two options.

"The poor in England *will not lie down and starve quietly*, as long as the country abounds in food. And what has produced this state of things? Not an overstock of labourers; not an overstock of manufacturers; not a want of employment; but a want of money to pay for the employment. And what has produced this latter want? Why the demands of the tax-gatherer, direct and indirect, co-operating with measures which have, since the peace, augmented the value of money three-fold, and which have, therefore, augmented the value of the taxes in the same degree. Continue these measures, will you? Continue them you cannot; you must do one thing or the other, lower the value of money, or lessen the nominal amount of the taxes."[395]

Lowering the value of money involved pumping into circulation, once more, large quantities of paper currency. This was the solution being urged by weighty sections of public opinion. Traders and manufacturers were against a return to paper issues, because they still had vivid and unpleasant memories of the crash of 1825. But, in general, the landowners and the clergy were in favour, as they valued their sinecures, and pensions, and tithes, and dividends, more than they valued their rents. And in parliament, majorities of both Houses were hoping for a return to artificial prosperity.[396]

But it could not be done; as Cobbett wrote to the Duke of Wellington.

"Every man of sense perceives that there is now no return to the base paper-money, without protecting the Bank in London, and all other banks, against demands of payment in gold. It has not required me to tell them, that, with the present quantity of gold in the country, such a protection of the bankers must lead to two prices in the market; and that, when it comes, it will go on, and would go on in spite of laws like those of ROBESPIERRE, until the whole amount of a year's taxes would not pay for the ornaments of a single gateway in St. James's Park.

"Therefore, the general impression is, that you will not recoil....Besides the monstrous injustice of such a measure, and the evident peril of it to the state itself; besides these, there is your own character. For, what defence would you have to offer? Having inflicted all this suffering to enforce a gold payment, in order to prevent the greatest dangers to the state, where are you to look to for a defence

392 Political Register. 23/10/1830.
393 Political Register. 27/3/1830.
394 Political Register. 14/8/1830.
395 Political Register. 19/9/1829.
396 Political Register. 13/2/1830.

of your conduct if you now go back? You must confess yourself to have inflicted all this suffering; to have brought to ruin so many hundreds of thousands of happy families; you must confess that you have done this in mere sport, in the mere wantonness of cruelty; or, that you have done it through the most profound ignorance."[397]

Cobbett mercilessly satirised the absurd waverings of parliament over this whole subject.

"Now, the putting out of the paper again, and thus debasing the money, would, in effect, reduce the interest of the debt as completely as if reduced by act of Parliament; but then, the *'wisdom of Parliament'*; the *'collective wisdom of the nation'*; for this sublime and omnipotent body, who have resolved, as many times as they have fingers and toes, that they would never be guilty of a *'breach of national faith'*; for this immaculate body; those senators of the British Empire, whose all-searching eyes sweep over the surface of the country, and descry the means of imposing a tax where no one of mortal mould ever supposed those means to exist; that this illustrious and almost supernatural body....who are the rulers of the destinies of that which is the 'envy of surrounding nations, and the admiration of the world'; that this stupendous set of seat-fillers[398] should, after resolving, unresolving, re-resolving, enacting, repealing, re-enacting, RE-ENACT AGAIN, and all upon a subject which they had *'set at rest forever'*, when they passed their first act;....that this body, this renowned assembly, should at last pass another act, to annul its former acts and resolutions....is quite terrific to think of, especially by those who are interested in keeping up this dreadful concern."[399]

Clearly, the idea of once again inflating the amount of the currency, and depreciating its value, had become a non-starter, and by February 1830 nobody really entertained it any more. The Duke did not recoil; he stood firm.[400]

Indeed, standing firm, and insisting upon a return to payments in gold and silver at the bank, was the second option which Cobbett offered to the Prime Minister.

"If you persevere, you are consistent, and I say you are just and wise, provided you bring back the taxes to bear a due proportion to the increased value of money; and this, I hope, is what you intend to do".

What Cobbett was driving at here was what he called the 'equitable adjustment'. If cash payments returned, prices would fall to below 1791 levels; and if those prices were to prevail, without starving one section of the population and bankrupting another section, a massive reduction of taxation was necessary; the interest payable on the national debt had to be diminished in proportion; sinecures and unmerited pensions had to be abolished, and salaries put back to pre-war levels; tithes had to be reduced or abolished, and the surplus property of the Church of England appropriated to the use of the state; and a general rectifying of debts and contracts of all sorts had to take place. None of this would be possible without a reform of parliament. And this, Cobbett maintained, was what the Duke ought to do.[401]

In March 1830, Cobbett received his answer. The Duke of Wellington announced, in effect, in parliament, that there was to be no reduction of taxation, and on the flimsiest of pretexts. If the country wished to retain the foreign conquests made during the Napoleonic Wars, he asserted, then government expenditure would have to be maintained. The return to cash payments was to be achieved without any equitable adjustment.

---

397 Political Register. 16/1/1830.
398 Do not miss the pun here!
399 Political Register. 12/12 1829.
400 Political Register. 27/2/1830.
401 Political Register. 16/1/1830.

When Cobbett wrote to the Duke of Wellington that there were only two courses of action open to him – the debasing of the currency or the equitable adjustment – he was wrong. There was a third option....

❋

Millions of working people in this country were being forced to exist on the scantiest amounts of wages and relief. But because of the very large numbers of people in receipt of these pittances, the total of the wages and the relief actually came to a very large sum of money. If that sum could be significantly reduced, a large proportion of it could remain with employers, both agricultural and manufacturing, and could then be drawn, in the form of rents and taxes, towards the governing classes. In this way, the return to cash payments could be accomplished; whilst at the same time fundholders, sinecurists, pensioners and employees of the state could remain in tranquil possession of their inflated dividends and emoluments. No necessity would exist for reducing taxation. We are, perhaps, unlikely ever to be able to look "behind the curtain" to see this decision-making process taking place. But the processes out in the real world are clear enough.

With the huge proportion of the population now dependent upon parish relief, the operation of the poor law had become a lever whereby the fortunes of the labouring classes could be altered and manipulated.

"The *poor-law*, that famous law of Elizabeth, which was the greatest glory of England for ages, has by degrees been so much mutilated and nullified, that, at last, it is so far from being a protection to the working people, that it has, by its perversions, been made the means of reducing them to a state of wretchedness not to be described."[402]

The acts brought in by William Sturges Bourne, noted earlier, changed the whole complexion of the poor law.

"*This law* is not in force; relief is not always at hand; the real overseer's power is annulled; the *hireling* has supplied his place....Is it not notorious that many hundreds have been starved to death!

"And is not the parish allowance *slow starvation*?"[403]

In many places, labourers were set to work by the parish at absurdly low rates. In the House of Lords, the Duke of Richmond complained that not only in Sussex, but also in Wiltshire and Dorset, labourers were set to work on the roads at 3d. or 4d. per day. But it was not just through lowering the amounts of relief that money was to be saved. In many places, the ways in which relief was administered had become deterrent, in the hope that the poor would simply not apply. The idea, as it was expressed at the time, was to throw the labourers back "upon their own resources"; but, of course, they had been deprived of their own resources long before. In his evidence to a committee of the House of Commons in 1828, Mr. Lister Ellis asserted that in the workhouse in Liverpool, they made "the labour as irksome and disagreeable as they can, in order to induce the labourers to *resort to their own resources*"; and that he actually thought that able-bodied labourers were made too comfortable. Henry Boyce, a great farmer from Waldershare in Kent, told the same committee that he had "seen 30 or 40 young men, in the prime of life, degraded by being hooked on to carts and wheelbarrows, dragging stones to the highways." Indeed, the humiliating of paupers by harnessing them up to carts and wagons, in the manner of horses, oxen or asses, was a frequent complaint.[404]

"They have been shut up in the pounds made to hold stray cattle; they have been made to work with bells round their necks, like cows put out to graze; they have been made to carry heavy stones

402 Political Register. 4/12/1830.
403 Political Register. 11/12/1830.
404 Political Register. 14/11/1829.

backward and forward in fields, or on the roads; and they have, in these cases, had drivers set over them, just as if they had been galley-slaves; they have been *sold by auction* for certain times, as the Negroes are sold in the West Indies."[405]

Here is what Cobbett gleaned from the Nottingham Review, concerning the treatment of paupers in the parish of Stapleton.

"The people are treated, not as slaves; not as negro slaves; but actually as beasts, whose *sexual connexion* is superintended by their masters, after the same manner that farmers and breeders superintend, for similar purposes, the connexions amongst their cattle, sheep and pigs; or as a dog-breeder superintends the connexion between canine animals of different sexes. In short (for I must come to it at last), the plain and humble tale is this; that, in some places, those who have the command over the poor, keep the married women separate from their husbands; do not suffer them to see each other but once in so long a time; then, only for so many minutes, and never out of the presence of the overseer or person appointed by him; and all this for the odious, the shameless, the beastly purpose of preventing that increase of family which the parson at the marriage has joined with the parties in praying God may take place…."[406]

According to Cobbett, the treatment of the English poor was characterised by "*wanton cruelty*" and "*base insolence*".

"No human beings were ever before treated so unjustly, with so much insolence, and with such damnable barbarity."

Yet, in spite of this state of affairs, and in spite of the notoriety of it, there was actually a committee of the House of Commons sitting in 1828, "the object of which Committee was to devise the means of lessening the poor-rates."[407]

The various methods of reducing poor relief constituted just one of the ways by which the working people could be prevented from intercepting the national wealth, before it could be turned into rent or tax. For some years, schemes had been suggested for lessening their numbers by subsidised emigration. The reasoning behind this was explained by William Cobbett, in an open letter to the labourers of England.

"Let me explain to you why it is that it (the government) now wishes to get rid of you. It wants to get you away because you make so large a demand on the poor-rates; because you are all become what they call *paupers*; because, in that character, you take away so much from the farmers, the gentlemen and others, who own and occupy the land; and they think that if they can make you smaller in number, they shall have less to give you."[408]

It was not as simple as that. In parliament, select committees had deliberated upon this subject in 1826 and 1827, and had decided against the introduction of any scheme. For this topic could not be separated from the issue of Irish immigration. According to the writers of the Edinburgh Review, there were, in Ireland, six million peasants who lived in huts without chimneys or furniture; who wore rags or went naked; and who lived entirely upon potatoes, which crop was prone to failure every five or six years.[409]

"The condition of the people is the very worst that can possibly be; nothing can be worse than the lower classes of labourers, and the farmers are not much better."[410]

---

405 Political Register. 4/12/1830.
406 Political Register. 26/12/1829.
407 Political Register. 6/3/1830, 4/12/1830 and 14/ 11/ 1829.
408 Political Register. 12/3/1831.
409 S. C. Johnson. The History of Emigration. P. 18.
410 Edinburgh Review. Vol. 45. Pp. 49-50.

This mass of misery overflowed into England and Scotland, where conditions were already far from idyllic. The Edinburgh Review estimated that between a quarter and a third of the labourers in the western areas of England and Scotland were Irish immigrants. The labour markets of the new industries became flooded with Irish; the wages at Lanark, for example, undergoing a decline from 21s. in 1805, to 9s. 6d. in 1838. But perhaps most significant was the annual influx into all parts of Irish harvest workers. Traditionally, harvest was a time when the agricultural labourers could earn a small cash surplus, through working longer hours at higher rates. Cobbett reckoned that it provided the means of paying house-rent, of getting a pig, and of buying fuel and clothing against the winter. Increasingly, the labourers were losing all this to the Irish, who worked for half wages.[411]

The Select Committees observed;-

"Two different rates of wages and two different conditions of the labouring classes cannot permanently co-exist....The question whether an extensive plan of emigration shall or shall not be adopted appears....to resolve itself into the simple point whether the wheat-fed population of Great Britain shall or shall not be supplanted by the potato fed population of Ireland?"

The emigration of the English labourer would merely create a vacuum which would be filled by the Irish. From the point of view of the well-being of the English labourer, what was needed was to redirect the migration of the Irish.

"The question of emigration from Ireland is decided by the population itself, and that which remains for the legislature to decide is, whether it shall be turned to the improvement of the British North American colonies, or whether it shall be suffered and encouraged to take that which will be its inevitable course, to deluge Great Britain with poverty and wretchedness and gradually but certainly to equalise the state of the English and Irish peasantry."[412]

This was a reasonable conclusion. It was well-known and acknowledged fact. But the question was not being agitated from the point of view of the well-being of the English labourer. Already by 1829, many parishes, "in order to get rid of their workers", were paying large sums to *American ship-owners to take the labourers away to America...."* And in 1829, a committee of the House of Commons, notwithstanding the well-known Irish problem, "reported in favour of a scheme for *mortgaging the poor-rates* for the purpose of raising money to pay for *sending the labouring people out of the country.*" This recommendation was embodied in a bill brought forward by Lord Howick, the son of Prime Minister Grey, and although the bill was dropped, a board was nevertheless established for promoting the emigration of the English.[413]

The pretext for doing this was the Malthusian doctrine that there existed in England a "surplus" and a "redundant" population; too many labourers and not enough work. Cobbett fulminated against the whole idea.

"Many great agriculturalists assert that there are not enough hands in England to get the harvest in."

These included Mr. Bennett from Wiltshire, the Marquis of Salisbury, Mr. Western and Earl Stanhope. Many other men of great experience said the same; it accorded with Cobbett's own experience.

"While this project is on foot for sending away the native labourers of England, there is no project on foot for keeping out the Irish and the Scotch labourers. There is, indeed, complaint that the Irish come and sweep away the best part of the employment of many of the English labourers; but no law is proposed to prevent this."

---

411 Ibid. Pp. 53-54. Political Register. 11/6/1831.
412 S. C. Johnson. The History of Emigration. P. 18.
413 Political Register. 14/11/1829 and 2/7/1831.

"Here are two facts; the first, that the ministry are using all the means in their power; that they have even the desperate project of mortgaging the land and the houses of the whole country; in order to raise money to get the labourers away from it; and we have the other fact, that the English labourers are so scarce that the English harvests cannot be got in, in good time and in good order, without the assistance of labourers from Ireland."[414]

The plan was to depopulate the rural parishes as far as was consistent with their continued cultivation; to bring in Irish workers for the peak periods of the farming year at half wages; and, by exposing the remaining English labourers to Irish competition, to force them down to the potato diet. The Irish labourers had the further advantage that they were sent over by Irish landlords, many of whom were actually English, in order to earn the money to pay for their cabins and their potato plots back in Ireland. Consequently, while they lived on potatoes and slept in barns, their money wages were paid straight into the London bank accounts of the great landlords; making, thereby, a great addition to the national wealth.

Cobbett observed the whole process in action.

"Now, mind, while our wise Government has been proclaiming, in all sorts of ways, that the misery of the working people arose from their *excessive numbers*;....while this has been dinned in the ears of the working people, they have seen, every year, thousands upon thousands of Irishmen, sent over by the base and cruel SQUIREARCHY of Ireland, to come here and wipe away *the cream* of the English labourers' year, by doing the harvest work at *half price*; and by sleeping and feeding like hogs. In the month of July, 1830, just after the harvest had begun in the *Isle of Thanet*, several scores of these wretched slaves poured into the Island, and agreed to work at less than half-price, were lodged in barns by the farmers who agreed with them, and fed them potatoes. Instantly the English labourers received notice that they must work *at the price of the Irish*."[415]

Similar thinking underlay the widespread introduction of threshing-machines. These had much the same effect on wages and conditions as the annual Irish invasion. But whilst the plan was that the peak-time work of the English labourers should be done by the Irish, the threshing-machine was to take over the winter work. Cobbett commented;-

"Please to observe, one effect of *heavy taxation* is to cause the invention of *machinery*. The farmer or manufacturer is so pressed for money by the Government, that he resorts to all possible means of *saving the expense of labour*; as machines will work cheaper than men....Suppose that the land could be ploughed, and the corn cut and carted as well as thrashed by machinery, there would be a country *with crops*, but *without people*.

"The labourers of England see, at any rate, that the thrashing machines rob them of the wages that they ought to receive."[416]

Farmers in general seem to have been reluctant users of threshing machines, and there is some reason to suspect that mechanisation was forced upon many from above; by their landlords, with a view to protecting, not farm profits, but rents, at the expence of the labour force.

In all these ways, the labourer was being forced down to the potato standard. In addition to the economic pressure, the authorities conducted a vigorous propaganda campaign on behalf of the potato. Potatoes were good for the body, and good for the soul.

Cobbett's Two-penny Trash, or so he complained in 1831, was the only cheap publication that went out to the people on his side of the question, "while the '*Society for promoting Useful Knowledge*'; while the parsons, with their pamphlet societies; and while the nasty, canting, lousy Methodists, who inveigle the pennies even from the servant-girls; while all these are pouring out their pamphlets by

414 Political Register. 11/6/1831 and 9/4/1831.
415 Political Register. 24/3/1832.
416 Political Register. 4/12/1830.

millions, and all of them preaching up the doctrine that bacon, bread and beer corrupt the soul of man, and that potatoes, salt, and water are sure to lead to eternal salvation."[417]

The Society for the Diffusion of Useful Knowledge was presided over by Lord Brougham, the Lord Chancellor in the Whig government of the 1830s, and contained many establishment figures. A pretended "*education*" scheme, Cobbett labelled it "a combination for the purpose of *amusing* the working classes, and *diverting their attention from the cause of their poverty and misery*." It became little more than a government propaganda machine, and its main organ was the Penny Magazine. One of the publications that was serialised in the Penny Magazine was particularly noted by Cobbett. It was called "Journal of a Naturalist", and it used observations on the natural world, mostly plagiarised, as a vehicle for a section called "A Worthy Peasant". The author asserted that good wages were not necessary to the well-being of the labourer, and eulogised a worker of his who made good on 10s. a week. This idyllic account of prosperity, savings, and increasing livestock numbers was ridiculed by Cobbett, who demonstrated the absurdity and impossibility of the whole story. Anti-poor sentiments were characteristic of this sort of writing.

"And every village boy with his cur detects the haunt of the poor hedgehog, and assuredly worries and kills him. Killing everything and cruelty are the common vices of the ignorant.

"The ass, probably and happily, is not a sensitive animal, but the poor horse no sooner becomes the property of man in the lower walks of life, than he commonly has his ears shorn off; his knees are broken, his wind is broken, his body is starved, his eyes ___!! I fear, in these grades of society, mercy is only known by the name of cowardice, and compassion designated simplicity and effeminacy."[418]

Here is what the author had to say about the potato. It was;-

"….a root which must be considered, after bread-corn and rice, the kindest vegetable gift of Providence to mankind. This root forms the chief support of our population as their food and affords them a healthful employment for three months in a year, during the various stages of planting, hacking, hoeing, harvesting….the profits enable him frequently to build a cottage, and, with the aid of a little bread, furnishes a regular, plentiful, nutritious food for himself, his wife and children within, and his pig without doors; and they all grow fat and healthy on this diet, and use has rendered it essential to their being….

"It gives infinite comfort to the poor man, which no other article can equally do, and a plentiful subsistence, when grain would be poverty and want.

"We have very few instances, where a potato-land renter to any extent is supported by the parish. In this village a very large proportion of our peasantry inhabit their own cottages, the greater number of which have been obtained by their industry, and the successful culture of this root.

"If we consider it merely as an article of food, though subject to partial failures, yet exempted from the blights, the mildews, the wireworms, the germinatings of corn, which have often filled our land with wailings and with death, we will hail the individual, whoever he may be, who brought it to us, as one of the greatest benefactors of the human race, and with grateful hearts thank the bountiful giver of all good things for this most extensive blessing."[419]

Many of the clergy were labourers in the same vineyard.

"One of these fat and malignant fellows, who calls himself 'the *Reverend* Charles Day, LL.B., Vicar of Rushmere and Playford, Suffolk', has just published a pamphlet, price *one penny*, the object of which is to wheedle the labourers of his parishes and neighbourhood to be content *to eat potatoes*, while he greases his rosy gills with roast beef and turkeys."[420]

---

417 Political Register. 22/1/1831.
418 Political Register. 29/1/1831 and 2/3/1832.
419 Journal of a Naturalist. Pp. 32-42.
420 Political Register. 11/12/1830.

This pamphlet was sent to Cobbett by one of Day's parishioners. Day denied writing these things.

In spite of Cobbett's advice to the labourers of Wiltshire to "fling away the nonsensical little books which are given you to read, and to make you believe that it is necessary for you to be starved to death in order to ensure you a place in heaven after you are dead", the campaign, in combination with the economic pressure of the times, seems largely to have succeeded.

"Nobody, fifty years ago, would have believed, that English labourers could be brought to live on *potatoes*. They have been, however."[421]

Both in town and country, large masses of the population hardly consumed anything but potatoes. In Manchester, a Mr. Potter was investigating the miniscule sums doled out as poor relief.

"He made his visits generally about the time the people were preparing dinner; and among the 105 families which he visited, he found only four cooking any portion of butcher's meat; and these four were only preparing a few pieces of bacon. The remaining 101 families were unable to afford even that humble luxury, and had to subsist only on potatoes and salt."[422]

Cobbett commented, on the Wiltshire labourers, that amongst a hundred of them "there is not to be found, perhaps, one whole linen shirt; and not one man that has tasted anything but damned potatoes and salt for months...."[423]

From these years, there is the first evidence that some sort of existence was possible even below the potato standard. Amongst the operatives of Nottinghamshire and Leicestershire, "potatoes appear to be the best of their diet. Some live upon boiled cabbage and salt, and others are said to live on scalded bran, which, as most readers know, is what is called a mash, given to horses when they have colds. As to the potatoes, the cabbage, and the bran, they are not sufficiently good food for even a lean hog, in the winter season."[424]

The degradation of the English people can perhaps best be gauged by their diet.

"The *sole* food of the greater part of them has been, for many years, *bread*, or *potatoes*, and not half enough of that. They have eaten sheep or cattle that have *died from illness*; they have eaten garbage such as a lord or a loan-jobber would not give to his dogs; children have been seen *stealing* the food out of the hog-troughs; thousands of them have died for want of food."[425]

What was being aimed at by the ruling elite was the establishment of a rural economy such as was to be found in the extreme north of England and in Scotland. Cobbett visited these areas in the autumn of 1832. These are his observations on the farms on the English side of the border.

"Here the farms are enormous; the stack-yards containing from fifty to a hundred stacks each, and each stack containing from five to ten large southern wagon-loads of sheaves. Here the thrashing-machines are turned by STEAM-ENGINES; here the labourers live in a sort of *barracks*; that is to say, long sheds with stone walls, and covered with what are called pantiles. They have neither gardens nor privies nor back-doors, and seem altogether to be kept in the same way as if they were under military discipline. There are no villages; no scattered cottages; no upstairs; one little window, and one door-way to each dwelling in the shed or barrack. A large farmhouse and large buildings for the cattle and implements; one farmer drawing to one spot the produce of the whole country all around; a sort of manufactory of corn and of meat, the proceeds of which go, with very little deduction, into the pocket of the landlord, there being no such thing as a small proprietor to be seen, though the land is exceedingly fine and produces the most abundant crops; the good part of the produce all sent

421 Political Register. 12/2/1831 and 14/11/1829.
422 Political Register. 20/2/1830.
423 Political Register. 12/2/1831.
424 Political Register. 26/12/1829.
425 Political Register. 4/12/1830.

away; and those who make it all, compelled to feed upon those things which we in the South give to horses and to hogs."[426]

Travelling north, over the border, Cobbett was struck with the great productiveness of Scottish farms.

"But, say you, what do they do with all the wheat and all the beef and all the mutton; and what becomes of the money that they are sold for? Why the cattle and sheep walk into England upon their legs; the wheat is put into ships, to be sent to London or elsewhere; and as to the money that these are sold for, the farmer is allowed to have a little of it; but almost the whole of it is sent away to the landlord, to be gambled or otherwise squandered away at LONDON, at PARIS, or at ROME. The rent of the land is enormous; four, five, six, or seven pounds for an English acre; the farmer is not allowed much; almost the whole of the produce of these fine lands goes into the pockets of the lords; the labourers are their slaves, and the farmers are their slave-drivers. The farm-yards are, in fact, factories for making corn and meat, carried on principally by the means of horses and machinery. There are no people; and these men seem to think that people are unnecessary to a state. I came over a tract of country a great deal bigger than Suffolk, with only three towns in it, and a couple of villages; while the county of Suffolk has twenty-nine market towns and 491 villages. Yet our precious Government seem to wish to reduce England to the state of Scotland."[427]

This was the state of affairs to which the poor-law schemes; the emigration project; the threshing-machines; and the potato propaganda were all tending. And it was in this way that the extra wealth was to be drained off, in order to resume payments in cash at the Bank of England, without a curtailing of government expences, without a proportionate lessening of the interest on the debt, and without a reduction of taxation.

So when, in March 1830, Cobbett heard the Duke of Wellington announce that the resumption of cash payments was to be accomplished without any taking off of taxes, and on the obviously false pretence of the need to retain Britain's foreign conquests, he knew precisely what to expect. He had always prophesied that the funding-system would end in convulsion, and that that convulsion would begin in Kent or Sussex. Haymaking and harvest would give a little extra employment to the labourers; the warm weather would make their sufferings less. "They will go on in a grumbling sort of state until *November* or *December*." But then the war would begin. About the middle of next winter, the nation would be roused from its half-dreaming state by "the fellows with hob-nails in their shoes."[428]

It seems safe to assume that throughout 1830 the financial distress was intensifying. For, in the absence of any retrenchment of government expences, the return to cash payments was being attempted without any adequate supply of specie with which to replace the small notes.

"My opinion is, that if we persevere with this law for two years, prices will be lower than they were in 1791, because there are less gold and silver in Europe than there were in 1791. There having been scarcely any brought from the mines for the last twenty years; and the drain from Europe to China having been so great during that time. By the perverseness of the English Parliament, North America has been created a commercial country since 1791, and she wants, and will have, a share of the gold and silver which was before confined to Europe."[429]

426 Political Register. 13/10/1832.
427 Political Register. 20/10/1832.
428 Political Register. 6/3/1830 and 13/ 3 1830.
429 Political Register. 16/1/1830.

The situation deteriorated further. The revolution which took place in Paris in 1830 created a further drain of bullion.

"The newspapers say, that *two millions of ounces* of gold and silver have been sent out of the country within about ten days. They do not particularly say how much gold and how much silver. One million of ounces of gold is about a fifth part of the quantity that was ever in the country for many years past."

Cobbett believed that this was being sent out to prop up the Bank of Paris. Much of it, in fact, was being sent to the Paris House of Rothschild; Nathan's brother James having endangered the security of his bank by unwisely speculating on the survival of the old regime in France. The Rothschilds no doubt made a handsome profit on this operation, as an English sovereign at Dieppe was worth eleven pence more than its face value. The British government was in the amazing and anomalous position of having too little currency in circulation for the routine transactions of the country, but still so much as to be driving the precious metals out. The Bank of England was already in a perilous position; any increase in paper currency would render it vulnerable to a certain and destructive run.[430]

In this situation of worsening financial stringency, it seems likely that the degree of distress and deprivation being experienced in the country increased still further after Cobbett made his prediction of convulsion in March 1830.

The first signs of the gathering storm appeared in Kent in the summer of 1830. The labourers on the Isle of Thanet drove out the Irish harvest workers.

"They armed themselves with what they called BATS; they went to the several barns, where the poor Irish fellows were *snoozled* in among the litter and rubbish, roused them up, and told them, that they must *march out of the Island*....The invaders were thus marched in bands to a bridge at one corner of the Island, on the Canterbury road, and were compelled to cross the bridge, with an injunction not to return into the Island on pain of the *bat*, of which several of them had just had a taste by way of warning."

The Thanet labourers "reared *a banner* or standard, on which was inscribed; 'WE WILL NOT LIVE UPON POTATOES'."

Through the autumn of 1830, the disturbances spread.

"The same principle which pointed out the necessity of driving out the Irish invaders, pointed out the necessity of putting down *thrashing-machines*."

And the putting into practice of that principle led to numerous outbreaks of machine-breaking in east Kent in October and November. Most of the farmers, who were in any case not entirely convinced of the wisdom or benefits of using these machines, consented to this destruction or even colluded. Those who called in military assistance subsequently saw their barns burnt down, according to Cobbett, without a single exception.[431]

Rioting spread steadily westwards. In many of the villages of East Sussex, the poor had been subjected to the rigours of the assistant overseers under the Sturges Bourne Acts; and here demands for higher wages were combined with moves against these unpopular officials. Notoriously, a Mr. Abell, who had made himself obnoxious in the village of Brede, was himself put in the parish cart, and forcibly removed form the parish.[432]

From Sussex, the movement spread rapidly – from Kent to Cornwall and from Sussex to Lincolnshire. Fires raged in twenty-six counties. Machinery was destroyed, both agricultural and industrial. But perhaps the typical manifestation of discontent was the wage-meeting.

---

430 Political Register. 28/8/1830 and 2/10/1830.
431 Political Register. 24/3/1832.
432 E. J. Hobsbawm and G. Rude. Captain Swing. Pp.104-106.

"They go in bands of from 100 to 1,000 men, and summon the farmers to come forth, and they demand that they shall agree to pay them such wages as they think right; and you will please to observe that even the wages that they demand are not so high by one-third as their grandfathers received, taking into consideration *the taxes* that they have to pay."

Where troops were called out, against whom the labourers could do nothing, or where farmers proved uncooperative, there were fires, against which the forces of law and order were generally powerless. Barns, farm buildings, and stacks or ricks of wheat, barley, oats, beans, peas and hay were all destroyed, the property of those farmers who refused to give up the use of their threshing-machines, or whom the labourers thought the cause of their poverty and misery.[433]

For two or three years previous to the riots, there had been a small upsurge of sympathy in the country for the working people. The subject of their distresses was raised in the House of Lords; the newspapers began to display a much more positive attitude; and people were starting to say some of the things that Cobbett had been saying for decades. The demands of the rioters fell on generally sympathetic ears, and most farmers raised wages to the levels demanded; and though some no doubt did this from fear alone, many more seem to have been convinced that the demands were just.

"It is universally acknowledged that the labourers *ought to have that which they demand.* The LORDS have, indeed, not said this, nor has it been said in the INCOMPARABLE HOUSE; nor do the FAT CLERGY say it; nor do the LOAN-MONGERS and JEWS say it; but every-body else says it; it is said by all the *middle class,* in town as well as in country."[434]

The momentous events of these years bring into sharp relief the fact that what was being contended about was the distribution of the wealth produced by the country.

"It is beastly nonsense to suppose, that the increase of wages *can be squeezed out of the farmers and traders.* The truth is, that, for many years past, about *forty-five millions a year* have been *withheld from the working people of England*; about five or six millions have been doled back to them in *poor-rates*; and the forty millions have gone to keep up *military academies, dead-weight, standing army, military asylums, pensions, sinecures,* and to give to parsons, and to build new palaces and pull down others, and to pay loan-mongers and all that enormous tribe; and to be expended in various other ways not at all necessary to the well-being of the nation.

"These *forty millions a year* must now *remain with the working people....*"[435]

Rioting labourers were perfectly well aware that, in the economic circumstances of the time, it was completely out of the power of their employers to pay the wages which they deserved. When the farmers of East Sussex told their labourers that the low price of corn combined with the great burden of the rates prevented them from offering increases, the labourers asserted that "the great ones must do it."

"Comply (they added) with our demand, and we will stand by you; refuse, and there are one hundred men ready to join us at a moment's notice."

"Mark", said Cobbett, *"the great ones must do it."*[436]

It was perfectly clear that any wage rise would have to come out of rents, tithes and taxes. An account of perhaps a typical proceeding found its way into the Political Register from Kent.

"The labourers of Appledore and Woodchurch, about 500 in number, summoned the farmers to meet them on Woodchurch Green, and made them agree to a rise of wages; and then they dispersed, telling the farmers that they might *compensate themselves by withholding the rectorial tithes,* by *making the landlords reduce the rents,* and by *refusing to pay taxes*; and they *offered their services* to effect these

---

433 Political Register. 4/12/1830.
434 Political Register. 27/11/1830.
435 Political Register. 27/11/1830.
436 Political Register. 20/11/1830.

purposes for the farmers. Next Saturday is appointed for these farmers and the men to meet to petition for *parliamentary reform, reduction of taxes*, and a *revision of the tithe-laws*."[437]

Such a petition was sent into parliament from Staplehurst, also in Kent. It set out the consequences of the failure to reduce tithes and taxes.

"It was then that we found ourselves compelled to reduce the price of labour, and we have seen our peasantry deprived of the comforts and, in part, the necessaries of life, without the means of alleviating their condition. Nevertheless, until now, the oppressed labourer has borne his load, complaining but not resisting. But the time has arrived when he will bear it no longer. Desperation has urged the labourers of this and the neighbouring parishes to rise and congregate. They have surrounded the houses of your petitioners in fearful numbers, claiming at our hands that which we believe to be their right, and which we have felt it our duty and interest to give. We have increased their wages, and now, with our augmented burdens (insupportable before), we approach your Honourable House; we tell you in language respectful yet plain that our burdens are such that we can bear them no longer." And the Kentish farmers went on to ask for a practical reform of parliament, and the appropriation of all that church property not absolutely necessary for a liberal support of the clergy.[438]

It was in all these ways, then, that the oppressed and starving agricultural labourers of England finally succeeded in bettering their lot, and raising their wages. We have seen repeatedly that the instinct of the local rulers of society was often to deal with hungry rioters with measures of conciliation; but that central government, from the 1760s onwards, pressurised them into using military force whenever they could; and highly dubiously, from a legal point of view. In 1830, in spite of the sympathetic attitude of many farmers and landowners, the troops were sent out again. The use of military force, according to Cobbett, was supported by all the greater farmers and landlords, especially the clergy; and by the "innumerable swarms of Jews and fund-jobbers and pensioners and state dependents." Harsh justice was meted out to rioters, especially in the counties of Hampshire and Wiltshire, to which the government sent Special Commissions, to ensure that measures of "severity", "vigour", and "determination" were put into force. Hundreds were imprisoned, transported, or hanged, and often for the most trivial offences.[439]

With the forcible suppression of the riots, wages were lowered once again. But there was little the authorities could do about the fires.

"The fires of which you have read, as having taken place in the last fall and this winter, are from the *lowering of wages*. The formidable attitude of the chopsticks, and the numerous fires blazing at the same time, induced *the farmers to promise to keep up the wages in future*, so that the working people might have meat and bread. In many instances the parsons agreed to lower their tithes in proportion to the rise in the wages of the chopsticks. But imagining, I suppose, that the terrible hangings and transportings had so terrified the labourers as to make them again submit to a potato-diet, the farmers in many instances reduced the wages to a potato standard; and wherever new fires have blazed, this appears to have been the case...."[440]

So although wages were brought down again from their Captain Swing levels of the winter of 1830-1, nevertheless an improvement had taken place, which, to Cobbett, appeared permanent. A Norfolk farmer, giving evidence to a parliamentary committee in 1833, related that the wages of the labourers in his area were 11s. per week; whereas, had no disturbances taken place, they would only have been 10s.[441]

---

437 Political Register. 27/11/1830.
438 Political Register. 20/11/1830.
439 Political Register. 4/12/1830.
440 Political Register. 24/3/1832.
441 Political Register. 23/11/1833.

"The country labourers, including the smiths and wheelwrights and collar-makers and all the village shoemakers, and tailors, and the like, are much better off than they were two years ago. In the north of HAMPSHIRE, in WILTSHIRE, perhaps in some other parts of the country, the cruel monsters have endeavoured to get them back to the bag of cold potatoes at plough; but they have not succeeded….Many means are used to prevent *the positive rise of wages*; but there are various ways in which more food and drink find their way to the mouths, and in which more clothing finds its way to the backs of the working people…."[442]

Something, at least, had been achieved.

"The wages and parochial allowances that *now* exist are by no means sufficient. Though I was prosecuted for saying that the works of the Southern labourers had *done good*, they certainly put an end to *cart-drawing* by old men and women. *That* has not been attempted since, at any rate. The wages were raised too; some *bacon* came instead of the infernal soul-degrading potatoes; some beer came instead of the water and the tea-slops; I at this moment hear two flails going merrily 'rap-rap-rap-rap', where a machine used to be rumbling. But still the wages, on an average through the country, are not what they ought to be…."[443]

Although all this represented but a very modest amelioration in the condition of the labourer, it nevertheless involved a sizeable alteration in the balance of wealth distribution between the local producing economies and the central metropolitan one. Cobbett demonstrated the overriding importance of the wage economy, and of the people who made it up.

"And, now look at their numbers. Why, it is, in fact, all the people except about three or four millions. Consider, then, what it is to add seven or eight pounds a year per man, to the wages of millions of men. Suppose it to be only four pounds; and you will find, taking in the wages of women and boys, that here is quite a sufficient cause for the penury that now reigns amongst landlords and parsons and all who are dependent upon them".[444]

The wage rises obtained by the labourers sent shock waves through the whole financial system.

"You will please to observe, that it is *impossible* for the farmers to pay the wages which they are every-where agreeing to pay; it is impossible for them to do this and to pay the present rents, tithes and taxes; and, as they would be out of danger if the labourers were well paid, they wish to obtain a diminution of those burdens, and thus to be able to pay the labourers well. The tradesmen, in the country-towns, have the same interest in this matter as the farmers."

Landlords were expected to play their part in helping their tenants to meet an increased wage bill, but they were also under pressure.

"Why, the landlords, to keep rents, must *get the taxes taken off the malt, soap, sugar, candles, tobacco, tea and other things of the labourer, and the assessed taxes of the farmer and shop-keeper.*"

There was widespread pressure for the abolition of tithes, and the appropriation of a portion of the property of the church to the exigencies of the state.[445]

Even the precious tax revenues were on the decline, as a result of the improved condition of the working people. Cobbett wrote to Sir Robert Peel on the reduced circumstances of the Chancellor of the Exchequer.

"Here is….the cause of honest Lord Althorp's straightened means; here is the true cause of the falling off of his taxes; for though the additional millions, received by the labourers, are in part laid out in beer, they are, in much greater part, in ten thousand times greater proportion, laid out in bread and meat and shoes and smockfrocks and hats and other necessary things upon which my

442 Political Register. 4/8/1832.
443 Political Register. 10/9/1831.
444 Political Register. 13/7/1833.
445 Political Register. 4/12/1830.

Lord ALTHORP has not so direct a lien. This is the true cause of the falling off of the taxes. The labourers have taken from the big farmers, the parsons, and the landlords, a part of that which they had to spend in taxable commodities. The Government is compelled to pinch as much as it can. Its squanderings are rather restricted compared to what they were...."

It all had amazing repercussions on the metropolitan economy. Building works ground to a halt.

"Cry as much as they will about it, the 'vast improvements' of REGENT-STREET, 'PALL MALL EAST', and 'WEST STRAND' are destined to see the grass grow before them."

The tables had finally been turned.

"You will find no difficulty to account for the distress and beggary that are now creeping over the West-end of London, and over BATH, BRIGHTON, CHELTENHAM, and all the other places of fashionable resort; you will see a reason for there being a hundred shops shut up in FLEET-STREET, and the STRAND. The short view of this matter is this; as long as these millions of labourers (including all the working people in the country) could be made to live upon potatoes, so long luxury could reign in these fashionable places; but when the working people obtained something like their share of bread and of meat, this luxury could be supported no longer."[446]

Cobbett reported "monstrous suffering amongst the manufacturers and artisans in great towns, especially, amongst such as are employed in the making of articles of luxury. Jewellers, watch-makers, bracelet-makers, bell-pull makers, carvers and gilders, engravers and painters, polished-steel workers, people employed in making iron-fences, and the like; fine furniture makers; in short, all those who are employed in making things not of real solid use and necessity. For frying-pans, porridge-pots, brass-kettles, iron candlesticks, strong knives and forks, there is a greater demand than ever.... Amongst other sufferers from this change are the makers of high-priced fowling pieces....a gun-maker in London, who used to have about *three hundred* orders for guns at the approach of the shooting season, has this year received *three* orders."[447]

Retrenchment among the upper classes, noted one of the newspapers, had never been so great. Many aristocratic families had moved out of London to save expence. Among the leading retailers of Regent Street, Oxford Street and Bond Street, receipts in 1830-1 were down a third on 1828-9. In Fleet Street, thirty-five shops had closed down, even though rents there had halved in not much more than a decade. Even the best tradesmen there were only just keeping their heads above water; of the total, a third were overtly bankrupt, while most of the rest disguised their insolvency by compositions with creditors. The theatres were deserted. There were fears for the futures of Drury Lane and Covent Garden; a merger was proposed, with reduced prices of admission, and one company of actors to play both theatres. Cobbett made good sport with the idea of pastoral maidens compelled to become real-life shepherdesses. At the Opera House, many of the wealthy aristocrats were seriously in arrears with their payments for boxes; even the Queen was demanding a discount![448]

"And what is the cause of this melancholy change?" asked Cobbett. "Simply this; that the chopsticks will no longer live upon potatoes."[449]

"In short, the thing had gone on, till it became a question, whether the labourers of England would or would not live upon potatoes, and occasionally die by scores from starvation. This became a question; and this question having been answered in the negative, some one or more of the other great heads of expenditure *must give way*."[450]

---

446 Political Register. 4/8/1832.
447 Political Register. 13/7/1833.
448 Political Register. 24/3/1832, 23/3/1833 and 7/4/1832.
449 Political Register. 7/4/1832.
450 Political Register. 24/3/1832.

"Something must give way" was a phrase which constantly recurred in the Political Register during these years. The expansion of the wage economy put in danger the estates of the landlords, the property of the church, the revenue of the government, and the dividends on the national debt. Some retrenchment had to be found in one or more of these if the people were to escape ever-increasing misery and degradation. "Something must give way." But the establishment did not share this view.

"We are now in a struggle for preserving the whole; the Government seems to have no notion of giving way. God send, that they may be convinced, *in time*, of the utter impossibility of upholding the whole system, and that, by yielding to that which common sense and necessity dictate, they may preserve the country in peace, (and) restore to it its liberties and its prosperity."[451]

God did not send; Cobbett was destined to be disappointed....

The Great Reform Act of 1832 arose directly out of the agricultural riots of 1830-1. The wage increases which resulted were far short of what was needed; but were nevertheless, as they stood, beyond the means of the employers to pay. If these were to avoid ruin, considerable reductions had to be made in tithes and taxes, and the corrupt parliament was most unlikely to agree to them. Suddenly, everyone was a reformer.[452]

"The *ruin* has come; the *misery* has come; the *fires* have come; and the REFORM has, at last, peeped out, and is struggling for vent! And do you imagine, that the great manufacturers and merchants and bankers are crying for REFORM, because they have been converted to a love of *popular rights*! Bah! As the French say; you are not quite stupid enough for that, I think. Do you imagine, that the *yeomanry cavalry* have, all of a sudden, become enamoured of the Goddess of Liberty! They would kick the Goddess to the devil; or, at least, chop her down, if she had nothing in store for the *relief of their pockets*. Oh no! the Chopsticks have made them raise their wages; these they cannot pay and *pay tithes and taxes* also; they see that they cannot again get down the wages, and that *reform* is *necessary to relieve them from the tithes and taxes*. Therefore are they *reformers*; therefore they throw their lusty arms round the waist of the Goddess, and you will have 'a job of it', if you get her from their ardent embraces."[453]

The government resisted parliamentary reform as stoutly as it could. But with the new pressure for it from all sections of the nation; with renewed rioting in such centres as Bristol, Birmingham and Nottingham; and with a financial crisis appearing as the likely result of these; the reform became law. But the question then became; - was this to be a genuine attempt at improving the condition of the nation, or a sham and a sop to popular opinion, to see the government through the exigencies of the moment?

"If the *Reform Bill* be to leave the system of sway that which it now is; if the same sort of management of our affairs be to go on after that bill shall have passed, as is going on now; and really, to judge from the language of the Ministers, one would say that *they contemplate no change*; if the *tithes* and *taxes* be still to remain such as they now are; if a Bourbon gendarmerie be still to dog out our steps, and stop us when they like at any hour of the day or night; if the Englishmen, who do all the work, be still doomed to live on potatoes and water, while those who take from them the fruit of their labour are living on all the choice products of the earth; if Englishmen and women be still harnessed and made to draw like beasts of burden; if a reformed parliament cannot find the means

451 Political Register. 24/3/1832.
452 Political Register 19/11/1831.
453 Political Register. 22/10/1831.

of protecting the *dead bodies* of the working poor….then….a greater delusion, a greater fraud, never was attempted to be practised on any part of mankind."

"We all agree….that unless the Reform Bill lead to measures of *relief*; unless it lead to a great taking off of taxes, it will be a mere mockery of the people; and that….it will make things worse than they were before….The labourer, who is discontented at having nothing but potatoes, when he ought to have bacon and bread, will not feel satisfied with those potatoes, upon merely being told that he has now got *reform*."[454]

Cobbett never had very great faith in the reform of parliament in the form in which it was finally passed; but he waited to see which way the wind was blowing. He was actually a member for Oldham in the new parliament, and was hoping for the election of a hundred members of his persuasion. In the event, there were around ten. The signs were not good. Cobbett himself was often roughly treated by the members when he was speaking. His fellow member for Oldham was John Fielden, a wealthy factory owner and radical. When he delivered a statement on the distresses of the factory operatives brought about by continually falling prices, with payments per piece having declined from 8s. in 1814, to 1s. 3d. in 1833, he was greeted with laughter from the members. The reformed House clearly had no concern with the condition of the poor. In April 1833, a proposal to set up a committee to inquire into the distresses of the country was rejected by 271 votes to 154; "that is to say, by a majority of 117!"

"Well done, 'reformed Parliament'!"[455]

It was not that the Prime Minister was lacking in good intentions. Before the election of the reformed parliament, Lord Grey had it genuinely in mind to bring about great improvements, with regard to taxation and the expences of government, the Church, pensions, sinecures and unmerited pay.

"But when he came to look at the matter more closely; when he came to look into the enormous difficulties which he had to encounter; and particularly when he came to hear assailing him from all quarters, the clamours of the parties who would have been affected by the changes, he wanted the resolution to proceed. He thought it a matter of less difficulty to get along with the old system, such as it was, than to set in earnest about this extensive change….There was the ruin which the making of the change would have brought upon so many thousands upon thousands of persons who were living at their ease and splendour upon the fruits of the industry of the people. To have popularity; to enjoy the remainder of a life of popularity, was a thing which he must naturally have desired; but, to see the ring in Hyde Park divested of its brilliancy; to see 'Pall Mall East' and 'Strand West' smashed before they were hardly finished; to see the glittering gorgets all disappear from Horse-Guards; never again to hear the troop beaten from the scores of drums and played from the two score of musical instruments under his window at Downing-street; to contemplate this change appears to have been too much for him, especially as he could not have under his immediate view that side of the picture which would have been more than a balance for this. To behold the change which would have been produced in the house of the tradesman in every town in England but London, and in the resorts of the idlers; to behold the mended lot and more moderate labour of the artisan and the labourer; to behold the renewed happiness of the hedger and the ploughman; to see the beer-barrel, the clock, the Sunday coat, the brass-kettle, the good bedding; to see these return to the dwellings of the agricultural labourers, was a thing too distant and not sufficiently captivating to weigh for a moment against the melancholy state of the ring in Hyde Park and the smashing of the brilliant clubhouses….He appears to have resolved to make no change at all; to keep on all burdens; and to rely upon force; upon a

---

454   Political Register. 31/12/1831 and 4/2/1832.
455   Political Register. 16/3/1833 and 27/4/1833.

forcible exercise of the law, rather than make any appeal whatsoever to the good will of the people in order to obtain their cheerful submission."

In addition to all these circumstances, there was, no doubt, the usual irresistible pressure "behind the curtain" from the wild men of the City.

"He is carrying on the same system; the taxes are all to be kept up; we are still to pay in gold, debts contracted in depreciated paper; and in every direction *force* seems to be intended to supply the place of obedience proceeding from good-will."

"The government had made a little reform to prevent the people from making a great one."[456]

And yet, as Cobbett repeatedly said, it was impossible to go on in the same way. Something, indeed, had to give way; and everybody realised this. But, according to the intention of the establishment, that something was not to be the taxes, nor the bloated establishments of government; it was not to be the tithes nor the property of the church; and it was most certainly not to be the inflated interest on the national debt. It was to be the wage economy. As Cobbett was writing, plans were already formulating for bringing this about. Cobbett, for a while, took his eye off the ball; never imagining, that what was intended, could possibly be put into practice. To his horror, he was wrong.

Partly as a result of the upsurge of sympathy for the working people among the landowning and employing classes, which we can date from some time in the later 1820s; and partly as a result of the riots of 1830, and the incendiarism which continued after their suppression; conditions in the country were a little improved.

"Though there are some hard-hearted landowners and parsons, and more hard-hearted farmers, I believe, that, take all the classes together, nine out of every ten men of them, are now convinced, that the lot of the working man is still too hard; and that justice, as well as sound policy; that justice as well as their own interest dictate to them to conciliate the working people by better treatment, and not to suffer the breach to become wider than it is."

"The working people are better off; they do get a greater portion of relief; the magistrates and the gentlemen are satisfied that they ought to have it, and they say so…."[457]

And as a result of the improved condition of the working people, the amount collected in poor-rates actually showed a small but significant decline of around 3½ per cent.

According to establishment doctrine, consumption upon the spot, in the provinces, in the producing areas, was inimical to national wealth. It was seen as an interception of the produce which ought to have been turned into money, and transferred to the metropolis in the form of rents and taxes. We have seen all the melancholy consequences which improvement in the country held for the metropolitan elite; above all, the creaking financial system was strained to breaking-point. Something had to be done to turn the balance back in favour of the elite.

Ever since the closing years of the 18th century, the poor laws had been a useful tool in the hands of the government for manipulating downwards the standard of living of the English people; they had served, also, as a weapon of propaganda; a socially divisive stick with which to beat the poor, and to alienate from them the sympathies of the rest of the community; and thus were they used by writers such as Townsend, Malthus and Harriet Martineau. So it was to the poor laws that the government now turned to redress the balance between provincial consumption and metropolitan luxury.

Already in 1831, a Commission was set up, on the pretext of looking into the workings of the poor laws. Ominously, among its members were the Malthusian economist, Nassau Senior, and one of Cobbett's favourite bugbears, the lawyer William Sturges Bourne.

"Amidst all the talk about abuses of the poor-laws; about mischiefs of the poor-laws, the projectors seem to think that the public, and particularly the poor, never perceive what it is that they mean, never

---

456   Political Register. 1/6/1833 and 3/5/1834.
457   Political Register. 13/7/1833 and 6/7/1833.

perceive what it is that they are driving at; and what is it that they are driving at?...Why, it is this; *to cause less to be given in relief than is now given*! To cause the same pensions, sinecures, grants, and dead-weight to be paid; to cause the same tithes to be gathered; to cause the same immense masses of income to be received by the deans and chapters, by the bishops, by the colleges; to cause the same standing army, the same military and naval academies; to cause the same mass of fundholders; to cause all these to be kept up, and to be paid in full tale, and in gold of full weight and fineness; and to cause, at the same time, the working people who are taxed to contribute to all these, to die in ditches with hunger, when they can no longer labour and when they have been beggared by these contributions. This and this alone is what all the Malthusians are driving at."[458]

The Poor Law Commission sent its assistant commissioners into the provinces to collect information about the workings of the poor laws. Upon the returns of these roving commissioners, or runners, a report was founded. Much of the information collected constitutes a useful body of evidence for the social historian. Much more was simply propaganda; and it is telling that when the material required for the final report had been extracted, the original documents were destroyed. Perhaps the greatest criticism that can be levelled at this report, is that the conclusions drawn were not supported by the evidence presented; and this criticism Cobbett made.

The basic premise of the whole project was expressed by the roving commissioner for Sussex, Lewis Majendie, who voiced the opinion that the working people in his area "lived too high".

Cobbett commented upon the new-found good relations which existed between the rich and the poor, especially in the counties of Kent, Sussex and Surrey, as a result of the more comfortable lives of the agricultural labourers. Landowners and magistrates were doing what they could to make the working people more contented, and "to rule by securing willing submission to the law, instead of seeking to rule by coercion." And this was the situation which the Poor Law Commission was seeking to reverse.[459]

The "merciless miscreants perceive that the working people in the country are now better off than they were before the riots; one of the *rovers* says, *that the working people of Sussex have been used to live too high*. The general tone of the book is, that the working people now get *too much*, and that they get it by INTIMIDATION."[460]

This intimidation was a major propaganda ploy. The attempt was being made to show that the improvement in the condition of the people was merely the result of their violence and illegality.

"That is to say, that the gentlemen and farmers would adopt the *Malthusian* system, only they are afraid of the labourers; afraid of their resentment; afraid of their vengeance; afraid of their firing of their ricks and their barns and their fields; afraid of the poisoning of their cattle, horses, sheep, pigs, and poultry. The word 'intimidation' means all this, and I hope, and believe, that it means an atrocious falsehood....

"The *feelosophers*....ascribe the giving of relief to the poor; this better treatment of them; this conciliatory disposition in the gentlemen, the clergy, and the farmers; they ascribe these solely to the *fears* of the parties; and thus deprive those parties, as far as they are able, of every particle of praise which is their due on this account."

One of the poor law runners, a Mr. Maclean, sent in a report about Horsham in Sussex, in which he attributed the rise in the rates to "the disaffected and malicious conduct of the lower class. The more respectable inhabitants live in a continual dread of the destruction of their property."

The anger which this report aroused in those more respectable inhabitants found expression in a petition to parliament. The allegation, it said, was an uncalled-for, unmerited and unjust stigma. The

458 Political Register. 11/2/1832.
459 Political Register. 22/6/1833.
460 Political Register. 6/7/1833.

conduct of the Horsham poor had been good since 1830, and the trifling rise in the rates had been caused by a lack of employment.

"To denounce the conduct of the poor of this parish as disaffected and malicious, is equally as base a denouncement, as that your petitioners live in continual dread of the destruction of their property, is false and unfounded."

And the petition went on to accuse the author of the report of a deliberate attempt to irritate the feelings of the poor and to stir them up to acts of insubordination.

Another of the roving commissioners was D. O. P. Okeden. He produced a report on the Sturminster Newton area of Dorset, which attempted to cast aspersions on the abilities and efficiency of the local magistrates. This provoked two lengthy and detailed replies from one of the magistrates, the Rev. Harry Farr Yeatman, who refuted the charges, and accused Okeden of presenting selective evidence and multiple inaccuracies, in a predetermined attempt to demonstrate the unfitness of the local magistrates to administer the poor laws.[461]

False as the premises were, plans of action were to be based upon them; and these plans amounted to a "project for reducing the country to a species of Austrian government"; to destroy, in fact, all the local traditions and institutions of government.[462]

"Having laid it down as an indubitable truth, that the more comfortable living obtained by the labourers has been obtained only by the means of 'intimidation', they proceed to suggest the means of putting an end to the '*intimidation*'. And what are those *means*?....Why, the means are, to introduce and establish what they call A RURAL POLICE. That is to say....to have a half-military police and a *gendarmerie* throughout all the villages of England and Wales; this to make England just what France was under the old blackguard Bourbon government!"[463]

And a plan was floated for taking the administration of the poor law out of the hands of those who had so recently discovered a sympathy for those poor; and to place it in the hands of those who were unlikely to display such a weakness; all on the pretext of placing the administration beyond the reach of intimidation.

"They let out, that the present sort of justices of the peace *would not do to have the command of this rural police*; and, that, therefore, they must be supplanted by *hired magistrates*, appointed by the Government, and stationed all over the country, uniting in their persons, justice of the peace and commandant of police!

"You must perceive from this mere fact; from the mere fact of such a thing having been laid before Parliament; you must perceive, that a *revolution* is, in fact, going on."[464]

The report of the Poor Law Commission reproduced over again all the establishment mantras about the causes of poverty that, by now, we have come to expect. There was, in fact, no real poverty.

"We can state, as the result of the extensive inquiries made under this commission into the circumstances of the labouring classes, that the agricultural labourers, when in employment, in common with the other classes of labourer throughout the country, have greatly advanced in condition; that their wages will now produce to them more of the necessaries and comforts of life than at any former period.... A condition worse than that of the independent agricultural labourer, may nevertheless be a condition above that in which the great body of English labourers have lived in times that have always been considered prosperous. Even if the condition of the independent labourer

---

461 Political Register. 13/7/1833.
462 Political Register. 22/6/1833.
463 Political Register. 13/7/1833.
464 Political Register. 13/7/1833.

were to remain as it now is, and the pauper were to be reduced avowedly below that condition, he might still be adequately supplied with the necessaries of life."[465]

Where hardship occurred, it was almost always, if not invariably, the fault of the poor themselves.

"Wherever inquiries have been made as to the previous condition of the able-bodied individuals who live in such numbers on the town parishes, it has been found that the pauperism of the greater number has originated in indolence, improvidence, or vice, and might have been averted by ordinary care and industry. The smaller number consisted of cases where the cause of pauperism could not be ascertained rather than of cases where it was apparent that destitution had arisen from blameless want."[466]

The poor, it was asserted, feigned distress in order to obtain their relief payments.

"You will remember when ragged clothes were kept by the poor for the express purpose of coming to the vestry in them."

Labourers were "afraid of having a good garden with vegetables and fruit in it"; they were "afraid of having a pig"; "afraid of being tidy"; and all for fear of losing their parish pittance as a result![467]

A large part of the problem was the poor law itself. The problem, supposedly, was that the pauper was raised in condition by the giving of relief, above the lowest class of independent labourers. Quite where this lowest class of independent labourers was to be found, it is difficult to say, but the description seems best to fit the Irish potato-eaters.

"Every penny bestowed that tends to render the condition of the pauper more eligible than that of the independent labourer, is a bounty on indolence and vice. We have found that as the poor's rates are at present administered, they operate as bounties of this description, to the amount of several millions annually."[468]

According to this reasoning, then, it was in the amendment or abolition of the poor laws that the solution to the problem of poverty was to be found. The key to solving the problem of poverty was deterrence – the same principle which underlay that notorious act of 1723.

"The restoration of the pauper to a position below that of the independent labourer always leads to the dispauperisation of parishes."

There was a handful of parishes in England and Wales which had become what the report called dispauperised; where, by a strict enforcement of the principle of "less eligibility", the rates had been reduced by discouraging the poor form applying. These parishes were held up by the report as models to be copied the country over. One of them was Cookham in Berkshire, where this was the principle followed.

"As regards the able-bodied labourers who apply for relief, giving them hard work at low wages by the piece, and exacting more work at a lower price than is paid for any other labour in the parish. In short….to let the labourer find that the parish is the hardest taskmaster and the worst paymaster he can find, and thus induce him to make his application to the parish his last and not his first resource."[469]

If dispauperisation sounds like the abolition of poverty, that is because it was meant to, and an invariably rosy picture was painted of those parishes where the poor laws were administered along these lines. Here is Mr. Chadwick.

---

465   S. G. Checkland. The Poor Law Report of 1834. P. 336.
466   Ibid. P. 378.
467   Ibid. Pp. 354-355.
468   Ibid. P. 335.
469   Ibid. P. 337.

"I visited a large proportion of the cottages in the village of Cookham and some in Cookham Dean. Their internal cleanliness and comfort certainly corresponded with the condition of the exteriors….in company with Mr. Whately (the overseer) I visited several of the residences of the labourers at their dinner-time, and I observed that in every instance meat formed part of the meal, which appeared to be ample, and was set forth in a very cleanly manner….I noticed some very trim hedges and ornaments in the gardens of the labourers, and it was stated to me that nothing of that sort had been seen in those places before the parishes had been dispauperised."[470]

Mr. Whately, the overseer, confirmed this depiction of serene well-being.

"Nothing can be more prosperous than we are here. I am at this moment returned from the vestry, which meets every fortnight, and where we talk of the state of Portugal, having nothing else to do there."[471]

However, when Alexander Somerville travelled through the village of Cookham a few years later, he saw things rather differently.

"I was within a few miles of the Great Marlow Union Workhouse, crowded with the unemployed poor; within a mile of Cookham and Maidenhead, in which the half-employed, and less than half-fed labourers were crawling about, asking, in return to every question asked of them, for 'something to get a drop of beer', adding that 'times be so terrible bad that they couldn't get half enough of work to do', that they couldn't get 'bread enough no how'."[472]

But the parishes which the Poor Law Commission held up for even greater admiration were those where relief was confined to the inmates of a workhouse. One such was Llangaddock, in Brecon.

"We placed the parish under Mr. Sturges Bourne's Act; we made a small poor-house out of some houses adjoining one another, borrowing £300 upon the security of the rates. All persons applying for relief were compelled to move into the poor-house or go without."[473]

The Commission thought the examples of the Nottinghamshire parishes of Bingham and Southwell worthy of imitation by every parish in the country. Here, the conditions inside the workhouse were what acted as the deterrent to dependent poverty. The Rev. Lowe at Bingham worked on the principle of "rendering it more irksome to gain a livelihood by parish relief than by industry." This irksomeness, asserted the report, was not to consist of rags and starvation, but in hard work, strict discipline, and a ban on luxuries of any sort. In George Nicholls's parish of Southwell, the workhouse regime was as follows.

"1. To separate men and women. 2. To prevent any from going out or seeing visitors and to make them keep regular hours. 3. To prevent smoking. 4. To disallow beer. 5. To find them work. 6. To treat and feed them well."[474]

It was the breaking up of families which angered the poor more than any other aspect of the whole system.

When this system was put into practice in Mr. Lowe's parish of Bingham, it was stated by roving commissioner Cowell that the poor all went out and found themselves work at 12s. a week. The poor of Bingham, he reported, were all contented and happy, and even found fault with those who applied for relief. The workhouse system produced "harmony, peaceable demeanour, plenty, happiness and content." Cobbett ridiculed the absurd idea of the farmers of Nottinghamshire being able to provide unlimited work at 12s. a week. He had no need to, for the idea ridiculed itself; Parson Lowe's corn-

---

470 Ibid. P. 355.
471 Ibid. P 359.
472 Alexander Somerville. The Whistler at the Plough. P. 23.
473 S. G. Checkland. The Poor Law Report of 1834. P. 339.
474 Ibid. Pp. 338-339.

stacks were set alight by two of his unemployed and discontented parishioners, one of whom, even according to Lowe himself, had been of good character up to that point.[475]

While the report of the Poor Law Commission was being compiled and published, and the resulting bill making its way through parliament, a wider campaign of propaganda was being put into circulation. Lord Chancellor Brougham was the public face of the originators of the bill, and it was his Society for the Diffusion of Useful Knowledge which published the propaganda which was to win over the public. The campaign was spearheaded by Harriet Martineau, who had come to Brougham's attention through her allegorical tales defending capital accumulation, taxes and rents, and vilifying the mass of the people, and in particular the traditional rural classes. Working in a room adjoining Lord Brougham's office, and backing on to Downing Street, Martineau received the reports of the Poor Law Runners, and selectively cobbled them into four stories, which, collectively, she entitled Poor Laws and Paupers Illustrated. She vouchsafed for the truth of her illustrations by invoking the "unquestionable authority in the Reports of the Poor-Law Commissioners"!

Just about every establishment orthodoxy concerning the poor that had appeared in print during the previous seventy or eighty years found its way into Martineau's stories, with a few new ones. The principle story of the set was called The Parish, and was intended to represent the appalling state of a village under a maladministered poor law.

There was, as we might by now have come to expect, very little real poverty in this Parish. Most pretended paupers had plentiful resources. A liveried servant on high wages, exclusive of board and lodging, comes to the vestry to claim relief payments for his wife and children. A widow pauper turns out to have enough capital stashed away to open a beer-shop. And three labourers claim relief on the ground that they only had three days' work in the week, when their wages for those three days amounted to 15s! Such payments as these were enforced through a combination of intimidation – it required the overseer, the squire, and a farmer all together to stand up to the paupers on pay-day – and the over-indulgence of the local magistrate. The abuse of the local magistracy in the reports of the runners found its way into Martineau's stories. One magistrate is represented as despotic and as routinely exceeding his legal powers; and another as of unsound mind and ready to acquiesce in anything.[476]

The paupers lived well on their extorted allowances. The village shop did particularly well on parish pay-days, paupers spending liberally on candles, tea, sugar, bacon and "things in general". The beer-shop benefited similarly, of course. Paupers were using an increasing number of candles, as they must have a candle to gossip by. One female applicant demanded an increased allowance with which to buy shoes. "I wear a good many shoes", she said. In the workhouse, paupers luxuriated on boiled mutton, turnips and beer.[477]

Conditions were so good, that there was no need for discontent. Discontent, however, was assiduously stirred up by evil people for their own selfish ends, and Martineau followed the tradition of earlier writers by abusing those who wrote in defence of the poor. The village apothecary was a radical, and an obvious parody of William Cobbett. He spouted nonsense about the consolidated wealth of landlords, and was an inciter of incendiaries. He fathered an illegitimate child in the parish, but used dishonest means to shift the financial burden on to the rate-payers, and the odium on to an innocent party. In the beer-shop, people congregated and stirred each other up to acts of violence. The apothecary preached treason, and plans were laid for firing the stacks and barns of the farmers.[478]

---

475 Political Register. 9/8/1834 and 23/8/1834.
476 Harriet Martineau. The Parish. Pp. 14, 1-2 and 106-107.
477 Ibid. Pp. 17, 124, 68 and 167.
478 Ibid. Pp. 42, 157 and 80.

Martineau's radical, however, did not put forward a detailed analysis of how the sucking up of the national wealth caused poverty and misery on a scale unprecedented. The Parish was a place where taxes and tithes were never heard of; where the constant depressing of the prices of farm produce and the concurrent inflating of farm expences caused no problems at all. All the disorders of The Parish were caused by the poor laws.

The depression of agriculture, the acres of land being forced out of cultivation, and the ruin of the farmers, were all to be attributed to the burden of the poor. As a result of high parish rates, employment had become scarce, and wages lowered. The "independent" labourers, cited by the Poor Law Report, became transmuted in Martineau's stories into the "honest" labourers – the largely fictitious class who lived on their wages alone – these were the ones who had been reduced to living on potatoes, and that because of the abuses of their "dishonest" neighbours.[479]

Blaming every evil of society on the poor laws served a turn when the objective was the abolition or amendment of those laws. But identifying the poor laws as a cause, to Martineau, was merely a pretence to which she paid lip service. Her real target was the poor themselves, and, following Townsend and Malthus, the poor laws became just a stick with which to beat them. Martineau prefers such a catalogue of accusations against the poor of her Parish that one scarcely knows where to begin. With very few exceptions indeed, they were a worthless crew. They were workshy – "hardly a man in the parish knew the pleasure of a good day's task of work". They were noisy, dirty and quarrelsome. They were, almost uniformly, drunkards, and prone to violence when in their cups. They were incompetent at their work, and none of the womenfolk knew how to spin, knit, bake or brew. They were sexually promiscuous, and lacked all notion of familial affection; routinely, they turned their aged parents out of their houses and deserted their children. The farm servants were careless, idle and ungrateful. The villagers were habitually dishonest, and Martineau recycles the mantra of the corn-dealers of the 1750s, that high food prices were caused by the poor running up debts and refusing to pay. Thieving was endemic, and poaching the normal alternative to parish pay.[480]

Malthus, in the second edition of his Essay, attempted to dispel any sympathy for the poor that may have arisen as a result of the famine of 1800, by prejudicing the other sections of the community against them. Martineau followed Malthus; now in a time of permanent famine, she wrote against the poor to counter the growing feeling that their lot ought to be improved. On the contrary, a harsher treatment of the poor was necessary if the return to cash payments was to be made without any retrenchment of government expences, and without any reduction in the interest on the national debt. Martineau wrote to justify that harsher treatment. And the Poor Law Amendment Bill was the means by which that harsher treatment was to be brought about.

"Give a dog a bad name, and you may hang him if you will. The writer endeavours to extinguish sympathy for the poor by representing them as already the most wretched, vile, loathsome and noxious to society – death to such vermin would be a blessing to every one."[481]

The House of Commons was somewhat taken by surprise with this bill. It was, Cobbett said, deceived all the way through. For the government, Lord Althorp attempted to maintain that the bill was for the benefit of the poor themselves; that the poor were "to be *bettered* by the system of Parson Lowe".

479   Ibid. Pp. 33-34 and 66.
480   Ibid. Pp. 159, 12, 165, 29, 124, 3-4, 41, 155, 175, 127, 15, 28, 16, 135-136 and 96!
481   Political Register. 19/ 4/ 1834.

"This is the most shameful pretence of all; the most unblushing of all the instances of impudence on the part of the supporters of this bill….the impudence of all impudence…."[482]

Althorp also based his argument on the need to relieve farmers and traders from the burden of the poor-rates; "to relieve the *industrious farmer and tradesman* from the burden of maintaining the idle and profligate poor."[483]

Cobbett railed against the idea. Even according to the evidence of the Poor Law Commission, most rate-payers recognised that the poor had to be maintained somehow, and that the rates actually afforded a security for their property. And most farmers saw the rates as a portion of rent paid to the poor instead of to the landlord.

"Clear as day-light it is, that whatever is squeezed out of the belly or bones of the labourer, whether in rates, or in wages, must go into the pocket of the landlord, and not one farthing of it into the pocket of the farmer."[484]

Upon these pretexts, the bill was bounced through the House of Commons.

"The bill was hurried along; there was too much of it for men to understand in so short a space of time; the House of Commons is less to blame than people generally think; the members had no time to read the reports, and no time at all to reflect on them. Not one member out of ten saw the drift of the scheme. Now every one sees it."[485]

When the bill reached the House of Lords, however, the story had changed again. Lord Chancellor Brougham, the ostensible originator of the bill, made a long speech exhorting the peers to pass it.

"His Lordship was pleased to tell the Peers, that in determining whether they would or would not pass the Poor-Law Amendment Bill, the question was, whether they would or would not take the measures necessary for preserving their estates."[486]

However you interpret this threat, with which Brougham confronted their Lordships, of the loss of their estates, and from whatever quarter the danger to those estates may have emanated, the threat served its turn, and the bill became law.

Most of the provisions of the Act were taken up with establishing the administrative machinery by which the bill's objectives were to be achieved.

"It takes away wholly from the gentlemen magistrates of the county; it takes away from the native overseers, and guides and rulers of the parish, who alone can know the parties, and who alone can feel for them as they ought to do; it takes away from all these all power whatsoever. It provides for the erection of immense workhouses by the uniting of so many parishes into one for this purpose; it provides for the bringing in of utter strangers to be the masters, the managers, and rulers of the poor; it provides for the putting of all these powers into the hands of three persons in London, to be appointed by the Ministers of the day, and renewable at their pleasure. Its main object is, that the poor may receive less than they now receive."[487]

Cobbett was convinced that a great deal more was intended by this act than was openly avowed. In spite of the pretended belief that the poor laws depressed wages, and that therefore their amendment would raise them, it seems clear that the principle of deterrence which it was intended to put into operation, by raising the threshold of suffering at which the poor would apply for relief, was always going to intensify competition among labourers, and thus reduce wages. Every worsening in the condition of the pauper in pursuit of the principle of "less eligibility" was likely to drag down also

482 Political Register. 16/8/1834 and 18/10/1834.
483 Political Register. 25/10/1834.
484 Political Register. 25/10/1834 and 18/10/1834.
485 Political Register. 18/10/1834.
486 Political Register. 12/7/1834.
487 Political Register. 21/6/1834.

the condition of the employed poor. This point was not lost on Cobbett, as he angrily wrote to the Earl of Radnor.

It is "evident to the farmers and tradesmen that is not all that is intended....They think they see in it a project for drawing the poor-rates into the pockets of the landowners; and what is worse, *to draw the wages of the poor into their pockets also*....This is the general opinion amongst all persons in the middle class of life, who think, and who say, that this bill is a first step towards reducing the working people in England to the state of the working people in Ireland....They know that, if the whole of this sum given as relief to the poor could be put into the pockets of the landlords, it would be but a mere pittance, to gain which it would not be worth while to set the middle and working classes at defiance; but they know that the WAGES amount to fifty or sixty millions a year, and that if the wages of labour could be reduced to the Irish scale, two-thirds of all these millions would go into the pockets of the landlords; and while these things are well known to every intelligent man in the middle ranks of life, they have all heard, and I vouch for the fact, that one of the poor-law runners complained that the labourers of Sussex were accustomed to *too high living*; and they have heard, and I vouch for the truth of this fact also, that the instructions to the barrister who drew the bill state, that IT IS DESIRABLE TO ACCUSTOM THE WORKING PEOPLE TO A COARSER KIND OF FOOD!

"....It is impossible not to perceive that whatever may be intended, the effect of this bill must be, to reduce wages to the Irish standard; to reduce the working people to the state of the Irish working people, and to put three-fourths of the present wages into the pockets of the landlords. The first effect in the country will be, to raise the rents of farms, upon the ground, that the poor-rates were diminished, or abolished; and the augmentation would be so great, that the farmer would be compelled to lower the wages. Men would, at first, refuse to work for reduced wages; there would be the great workhouse for them, and the COARSER SORT OF FOOD. They must then submit, and come down to the potatoes and sea-weed, and the rags and nakedness. The farmer would not gain a straw, but would be poorer than he is now; for the landlord would demand high rent in proportion to the low wages."[488]

It was obvious to William Cobbett that such a system could never be put into execution without a degree of physical force. He accused the authorities of the intention to introduce a sort of Bourbon police into all the country towns and villages, under the pretence of protecting property, "a police in uniform, carrying daggers and pistols, like those in London....thus, the potato-diet....would be.... completely enforced. The fact is this; the country labourers insist on not being starved. They have the means of preventing their starvation, and the police force is to deprive them of those means."[489]

It was no less obvious to the authorities. There was no mention of the subject in the Act itself, but discussions took place behind the scenes; and, sure enough, in the autumn of 1834, Lord Melbourne, "the head of the coarser-food Ministry", announced in the House of Lords that a rural police was to be established across the country. Cobbett recalled that when Lord Melbourne had been Home Secretary, the Home Office had routinely employed police spies, and Melbourne himself had received written reports from spies, not only about public and political meetings, but even on what occurred in private families.[490]

Reducing wages and lowering standards of nutrition were only a part of the project for bolstering the metropolitan economy. Clearing away the people from the villages would allow even more of the subsistence of the poor to be sucked up to London. Emigration was an essential part of the scheme. The act contained a clause enabling, encouraging even, the parishes to mortgage the poor-rates in

488 Political Register. 9/8/1834.
489 Political Register. 6/4/1833.
490 Political Register. 29/4/1834.

order to send the villagers out of the country; so that, at last, all the emigration schemes of the previous decade finally found legal expression in the Poor Law Amendment Act. The reduced standard of living was intended, in part, to act as a spur to emigration; as was noted by a country magistrate in a letter to the Times, which Cobbett inserted in the Register. Compulsory emigration, he wrote, was the soul and object of the new or revolutionary Poor-Law Bill.

"For what does the bill say? That able-bodied men, for whom work cannot be found in their several parishes, and who cannot in consequence maintain themselves and their families, are not to be relieved but with the consent of the commissioners, except in the new district workhouses. View such men, therefore, immured in these workhouses. The human mind would despair, the human frame would sink, under such confinement, in healthy subjects, if there were no hope of liberation. But there is hope of liberation; the prisoners need not stop a day longer than they please; Australia offers them its hospitable shores and boundless plains; they will be conveyed thither free of expence. Is it not clearly therefore the object of the bill, - is it not the avowed opinion of all those on whose recommendation the bill has been framed – that the British labourers, of whom these political economists say there is a redundance, should be forced to seek an escape from prison by for ever quitting their native land.... Extreme pressure is to be created on the poor, and emigration is the safety-valve."[491]

Emigration, as we have seen, and as was well known at the time, had certain implications concerning the sucking in of Irish labour, and the exposure of the English workforce to competition from those who lived on potatoes, slept in barns, and whose scanty wages were paid directly into the London bank accounts of their Irish landlords.

Periodic starvation was to be a settled part of the whole system. The idea was not new. We have already seen that, in 1766, Sir James Steuart came very close to saying that the starvation of 250 farmers was an acceptable price to pay for the increase of national wealth. It was such a shameful point of view, that it seems safe to assume that it was held far more commonly than it actually appeared in print. Nevertheless, it crops up again and again.

"Some indeed, say, 'Let the farmers starve'", noted Stephen Addington in 1772. Famously, it appeared more than once in the writings of Malthus, to whom Cobbett attributed the philosophy behind the New Poor Law. Malthus's metaphor about the limited number of places available at nature's feast is notorious. So is his assertion that the children of those who marry without sufficient means to support themselves should be left to the punishment of nature. Martineau, of course, followed Malthus. The only virtuous poor man in her Parish "was not fond of blistering his tongue.... He would rather struggle on as long as he could, without losing heart or temper, and submit with as good grace as he could if the worst came to the worst."[492]

In Cobbett's day, it was well known from Irish experience, if from no other, that dependence upon a potato diet involved the near-certainty of famine every five or six years. And, indeed, it was the example of the Irish who starved with a quiet resignation that was held up for imitation by the working people of England. But the English, Cobbett thought, had far too much spirit for that.

"I knew that they would never receive the *extreme unction* and die of hunger, as the poor Irish did, and be praised for their *resignation* by Bingham-Baring or Baring-Bingham, or whatever else he is....O God! with what indignation did I hear the unfortunate Irish *praised* because *they died of want*, while their country abounded in the means of subsistence."[493]

---

491 Political Register. 12/7/1834.

492 Stephen Addington. An Inquiry into the Reasons for and against Inclosing Open-Fields. P. 32. T. R. Malthus. An Essay on the Principle of Population. 2nd. Ed. Ed. P. James. Vol. II. P. 140. Harriet Martineau. The Parish. P. 163.

493 Political Register. 13/11/1830.

It may not be a coincidence that Bingham Baring was a member of the great banking dynasty, of that name.

The consequence of starvation was the same as that of emigration – it cleared the parishes of people. But, of course, it did it much more cheaply. Starvation could also play another role – as an example, and a threat which would increase the numbers willing to go abroad. With a poor law which now acted deterrently, it seems likely that starvation was now a settled, if not a proclaimed, part of official policy.

D. O. P. Okeden was one of the roving poor law commissioners. He called a meeting of the magistrates of Dorset at Blandford Forum, where he "broached for the first time, in a formal manner, the doctrine which he has since promulgated and maintained." It was rather an unguarded statement of doctrine, as it found its way into a pamphlet by the Rev. Harry Farr Yeatman, and from thence into the Political Register. The doctrine was "that no relief whatever ought to be offered to the able-bodied man, and that if he and his family could not subsist upon their wages, they might lie down and die by the roadside, (these were the words of Mr. Okeden) whether the wages, so received, were or were not per head, sufficient for the support of the able-bodied father and his family."[494]

The object of the Poor Law Amendment Act was to bring into England the rural economy of Scotland, as previously described by Cobbett. There, vast areas contained very few inhabitants; the few farm servants that could not be dispensed with were lodged and fed at the lowest possible level, and as much work as possible done by horse and by machine. As the Poor Law Bill was under discussion, news reached London of the clearances in the Scottish county of Sutherland, "which is said now not to contain one single soul WHOSE GRANDFATHER LIVED IN THAT COUNTY." With so few mouths to feed, the plentiful produce of the farms was turned into money. The tenants were kept poor, and the bulk of the produce added to the rent-roll. A correspondent to the Register noted that of three acres of tithe-free land of equal quality, one each in England, Scotland and Ireland, a typical English rent might be 20s., whereas in Scotland it was more likely to be 40s.; in Ireland, the rent might be "not less, perhaps, to the immediate cultivator than 4l. sterling." This is what the legislators had in view.[495]

Cobbett estimated the typical expences of a typical English farm of 100 acres.

Rent £100

Poor-rates £27

Tithes £25

Tradesmen's bills £37

Labourers £180

The total wage bill, therefore, came to £217, out of a total expence of £369.

"It is the wages which the advocates of coarser food have all along had in view; envying the happy state of the *landlords of Ireland* and the *heritors of Scotland*….The English farmer would not be benefited by the change; but, on the contrary, greatly injured by it. It is notorious that the Scotch farmers are in a great deal worse state than the farmers in England. This is very well worthy the attention of the farmers; no lightening of their share of the burden is intended by this bill….The greedy English heritors want to get the wages and the amount of the relief into their own pockets, as they do in Scotland and Ireland. If they could rob the poor, make them work for next to nothing, and make them live upon the meanest of food, they would make the farmers pay them *double* rent, and the parson would get from them double tithes".[496]

---

494 Political Register. 6/7/1833.

495 Political Register. 25/1/1834 and 21/6/1834.

496 Political Register. 18/10/1834 and 21/6/1834.

The Poor Law Amendment Act was a measure of the most amazing complexity, involving within itself layer upon succeeding layer of pretext, motivation, objective and pretence. And we have not penetrated to the heart of it yet. Lord Brougham forced the bill through the House of Lords with the threat that if it were not passed, their Lordships would lose their estates. The idea that five or six millions a year collected in poor-rates endangered the solvency of the landowners was clearly absurd. So while the Lord Chancellor's menacing was a clever propaganda ploy, for attaching the popular odium of the measure to the peers, the danger to their estates must have come from elsewhere. The amount of the rates and a large proportion of the amount of the wages may have been intended to go into the pockets of the landlords; but they were not intended to remain there for long.

The great point at issue during these years was the improvement in the condition of the people pitted against the continued financial accumulation of the men of the City.

"The next thing to be considered is, how this lightening of the burdens of the people is to take place; and every one must answer, that it cannot take place at all, and that it is an abuse of words to talk of it, unless there be an alienation of the debt. When you hear men talk of retrenchment and economy, as you will hear Babington Macaulay, and others, and all the school of Brougham, and all the Whigs themselves, who are in power, and hear them at the same time declare their firm resolution not to touch the interest of the debt; declare that *national faith*, as they call it, must be kept sacred, though, by-the-by, their *national faith* means a most infamous plundering of the nation; when you hear men talk thus, set them down as hypocrites or madmen; for how is relief to come, except by ceasing to pay interest on the debt?"[497]

What this country witnessed in the early 1830s was a vigorous fightback by the financial interest against the short-lived upturn in the fortunes of ordinary people, brought about by the softening attitudes of the ruling class in the later 1820s, and the riots and fires of 1830-1. The Poor Law Amendment Act was the instrument of that fightback; and was, first and last, a measure of finance. As Cobbett pointed out to the President of the United States in 1835, it was the Money Monster that was behind the act, looking around him in all directions, "*in order to insure the payment of his interest*".

"You have seen, sir, an account; or you will see it, in the little book which I do myself the honour to send you, of what is called the Poor-law Amendment Bill; you will see that its avowed object was to save the estates of the landlord from being swallowed up. You will see that it has been avowed and professed distinctly, that in order to effect this, the working people must be reduced to a coarser sort of food. It is the same money-monster that is at work here; he is grasping hold of the land by mortgages innumerable, and almost as general as the land itself; the falling off of rents endangers the mortgagees. To restore rents, *the wages of labour must be taken, and put into the pocket of the landlord*; and this bill, sir, so very dangerous as it is; so hated as it is, is really and truly, at the bottom, the work of the....small number of concentrated and combined men-mountains of gold."[498]

So many of the circumstances surrounding the passing of this law proclaim its financial origins. The first person publicly to suggest the withholding of relief from the able-bodied man, in order to present him with the alternatives of starvation or emigration, was Alexander Baring, the great loan-monger. The most senior of the three Poor Law Commissioners, "stuck up in London" under the new act, had worked for the Bank of England. Harriet Martineau was from a family of bankers; and in The Parish, all the good people, that is to say the rich people, had banking names – Manning, Goldby, Bingham and Morgan. Indeed, much of the propaganda that was put out to facilitate the passing of the bill concerned, not landlords and rents at all, but the benefits bestowed on society by

497 Political Register. 4/2/1832.
498 Political Register. 14/2/1835.

the wealthy capitalist. Cobbett complained about laudatory writings "on the system of accumulation, concentration, and centralization."[499] Martineau herself churned out tales on this theme.[500] More material was published by Brougham's Society for the Diffusion of Useful Knowledge – much of it written by Charles Knight, publisher of the Penny Magazine[501] - some, it is suspected, written by the eccentric Brougham himself. Perhaps most startling of all, because most bare-faced, was a pamphlet written by Stuart Wortley, the son of a wealthy Yorkshire landowner, which was comprehensively demolished by Cobbett in the Political Register.

"The object of your pamphlet is to show, that it is a gross mistake to suppose that the nation is now paying the fundholders too much in the way of interest; or that the nation has paid them too little hitherto, and, that it ought to continue to pay them, at least as much as it now does."

Wortley was clearly acting the part of the uncomprehending puppet, with his strings being pulled from elsewhere.

"What might be your *motive*, it is impossible for me to say….I could show you….how low, how very vulgar, how much resembling the ideas of Capel-court, are your calculations and your reasonings; how much like a stock-jobber, or a bill-broker, is your phraseology."

"Is there any just man", thundered Cobbett, "who will say that '*good faith*' requires the nation now to pay the interest of this Debt in full tale, and in gold of full weight and fineness; that is to say, in money of the same value of 1792; is there another man besides you on the face of this earth, who will say, that this toiling nation ought to be compelled to pay two bushels of wheat for the one bushel that was borrowed?"[502]

The emigration scheme was also capitalist in origin. William Whitmore was a former governor of the Bank of England, who spoke strongly in favour of the emigration clause of the New Poor Law in the House of Commons. It turned out subsequently that Whitmore had been appointed chairman of a joint-stock venture formed for the purpose of establishing a new colony in South Australia; which was to receive the working people cleared from the parishes of England. Of his fellow-directors, Mr. Grote was a banker, and Mr. Clay a shipowner. The nature of the enterprise dawned slowly on William Cobbett.

"Oh, oh! Now who will bet me two to one, that the money taken from the parishes to be paid for the emigration of the working people will not be paid over to this company? Who will bet me two to one of that; and who will tell me, or can tell, how far the poor-law project was originally connected with this project? When I heard Mr. WHITMORE detailing the wondrous gains of new settlements all over the world, and saying, (according to his explanation), that the present system of poor-laws had the malignity of a fiend; and especially when I heard him go into details of the vast gains of the new settlements, I could not help wondering what all this had to do with the Poor-law Bill. I now understand it all. It all had a great deal to do with the Poor-law Bill; and, as I said before, it would be curious to know what each of these projects had to do in giving rise to the other."[503]

One is led strongly to suspect that other, similar capitalist concerns were in existence in connection with different parts of the world, notably Canada, but drawing their profits also from the rates collected for the relief of the poor.

The parish rates, in this way, were to be not so much reduced by this Act as redirected. Before 1834, the rates formed part of the localised, provincial economy, being expended, for the most part,

---

499   Political Register. 25/10/1834.
500   E. g. The Hill and the Valley.
501   E. g. The Working Man's Companion 1831 and The Rights of Industry 1831.
502   Political Register. 7/9/1833.
503   Political Register. 5/7/1834.

within the parish in which they were collected. This was pointed out in evidence to the Poor Law Commissioners by the gentlemen of Broadway in Worcestershire.

"Agricultural capital is diminishing; but not on account of the poor-laws, which rather tend to keep capital in the parish; but because great landowners spend less in their parish, by carrying the great bulk of their income annually to London, where it accumulates in the hands of usurers and stock-jobbers, and consequently does not return to the parish with the same rapidity nor in the same proportion as it is drawn out of it."[504]

Clearly, this was the wrong answer. Attempts were to be made to bring the parishes into debt, both to the joint-stock emigration concern, and the Treasury. A correspondent to the Register noted that "the emigration clause facilitates and tempts parishes to borrow by furnishing them a lender, and asking for no valid and satisfactory security." The rates collected for the relief of the poor were also to be directed to "commissioners, sub-commissioners, perhaps also travelling architects and surveyors, for the construction of the new workhouses". Henceforth, a proportion of the parish rate was to be considered part of the national wealth, and sucked out of the locality.[505]

And then there was the curious and little noticed affair of the Slaves' Emancipation project. In 1833, provisions passed into law for abolishing slavery throughout the British Empire. But what shocked William Cobbett was that the slaves were to be bought from their owners, thus recognising a legal right hitherto existing for one human being to claim another as his property. "Those who keep the blacks in slavery", opined Cobbett, "should not get a single farthing". Instead of that, the House of Commons voted the slave-owners £20 millions, and by a large majority.

"The *interest* of this money is equal to *good farm-wages* for 33,000 labourers' families; that is to say, more labourers' families than there are in the two counties of *Bedford* and *Berks*. If paid, it must come out of the sweat of those *who work*; and will not be paid by those who have been petitioning on the subject."[506]

What was worse, the bulk of the slaves belonged to wealthy English landowners.

"It now appears, that, in fact, these slaves are, in general, *the property of the English borough-mongers*; that they are so in great part at least; and that the fruit of the labour of these slaves abroad, has long been converted into the means of making us slaves at home. Travelling in WILTSHIRE some years ago, I found a whole village the property of one man, and I found the *neighbouring borough* half his property also. His establishments were those of a prince, both in town and country; and I *now* find, that the source of all this, was the labour of slaves in *Jamaica*....I find the Marquis of CHANDOS, the Earl of HAREWOOD, and great numbers of the deadly *enemies of reform*, to be great holders of slaves."[507]

This £20 million was to be raised by way of a loan; it was to be added to the national debt, and £800,000 a year was to be added to the tax burden in order to pay the interest. The question that remains unasked by historians is; - how was this possible with the nation's finances in such a parlous state as they were in the early 1830s? The loan was awarded to Nathan Rothschild and J. C. Herries, both experienced and capable operators. But how could they possibly anticipate a profit, with money so scarce and credit so tight?

The answer can only be that the whole operation was undertaken in anticipation of the great freeing up of capital that was to be the consequence of the Poor Law Amendment Act. Christmas came early for all the classes of the metropolitan elite. Nathan Rothschild, however, was a subject which Cobbett took care never to tangle with.

---

504 Political Register. 25/10/1834.
505 Political Register. 12/7/1834.
506 Political Register. 15/6/1833 and 3/8/1833.
507 Political Register. 4/8/1832.

How many English aristocrats contributed to this loan, thereby gaining interest from the English taxpayer, on money which the English taxpayer paid to that aristocrat, by virtue of his ownership of black slaves?

The Poor Law Amendment Act, therefore, represented a complete reversal in the fortunes of all the productive classes of England, after the very modest improvement of the previous few years. It facilitated the sucking up of a much greater proportion of the wealth produced in the country into the hands of a relatively small metropolitan and cosmopolitan class. It was also a massive dashing of the hopes of one William Cobbett; both for the well-being of his "oppressed and insulted countrymen", and for his own personal victory over his long-standing enemies in the political establishment. After thirty years of positive thinking, and of confident predictions that The Thing was on the point of expiring, and that all would soon be well, it slowly began to dawn on him that all his laudable efforts had been in vain. Increasingly, in the articles of his later years, it is possible to detect a kind of impotent fury; a dawning consciousness that for all his half a lifetime of endeavours; for all the tirelessness, and selflessness, and courage, and brilliance, and dogged determination of his one-man campaign on behalf of the English people; he was about to leave them in a worse state even than that in which he found them. This manifested itself, in his final years, in a bout of frenetic activity not normally associated with old age. In addition to his burdensome duties as an M.P., he conducted vigorous campaigns on a number of subjects, such as church reform and the malt tax; toured the north of England and Scotland; even visited Ireland; and undertook punishing schedules of lecturing all over the country. The whole, inevitably, took a toll on his health; and he died at his farm near Farnham in June 1835, just as the provisions of the New Poor Law were being put into effect. He died, beaten and broken, but still fulminating. His last article, dictated from his bed, concerned the implementation of a much harsher workhouse regime in the Chichester area of Sussex. For sure, the best man does not always win.

Here is William Cobbett's own description of the force which rendered his life's work so completely unavailing, and which he denominated the "Money Monster".

"We do not perceive the great cause that is at work, devouring up the church, straining at the Poor-rates, endeavouring to make the working classes live upon garbage, ruining the landlords and the farmers. It is this monster that is at work; and it seems destined to pull down, in one way or another, every ancient establishment of this realm. *Nothing can stand before it*; and, it is so interwoven with all the classes of society; that there will never be any body found to endeavour to check its progress."

"Perhaps more than half the members of both Houses of Parliament are fundholders as well as landowners. No small part of them have children, whose fortunes are locked up in the funds. Then the dead-weight (amounting to little short of 5 millions a year); the pensioners; the grantees; the sinecure placemen and women; all feel that they are in the same boat with the fundholders. Then come those who have annuities paid for, and receivable, or to become receivable, in insurance-offices. Touch the funds and you touch these, too. The beneficed clergy are all fundholders to a greater or less extent. A large part of the dead-weight people are fundholders, or have annuities dependent on the funds. In this state of things, who is to expect that anything will be done with the debt?"[508]

At the head of this list of fundholders, and forming rather a class on their own, were 152 great men, who each received, on average, over £50,000 a year in interest, paid by the English taxpayer.

"It is utterly impossible that any ancient institution; that any set of laws, securing liberty and securing people's earnings; it is utterly impossible that either of these can exist, in a country where a hundred and fifty-two men have this hold upon the resources of that country. These men are not *seen*; nor are they heard, except in the strange sounds about 'national faith' and 'public credit', in the uttering of which, Ministers, Parliaments, and Kings are their mouth-pieces. But, sir, look at the

508   Political Register. 26/4/1834 and 3/5/1834.

natural consequence which must arise, if any one or more of these hundred and fifty-two men were to be INVESTED WITH POLITICAL POWER! Think, I beseech you, of the consequence of this; for you do not want to be assured by me, that when once love of interest of money has taken possession of the soul of man, it swallows up every other consideration, whether as to this world or the next."[509]

509   Political Register. 14/2/1835.

The Sentimental Mercenary
The Psychology of Exploitation[1]

> You were a sentimental mercenary in a free-fire zone,
> Parading a Hollywood conscience;
> You were a fashionable objector with a uniform fetish,
> Pavlovian slaver at the cash-till ring of success. <u>Marillion. The Assassin.</u>

The reader of this book might be tempted towards the conclusion that wherever one human being has the power to oppress and exploit another, then that oppression and exploitation will certainly take place; that the parasitic mindset is inherent and fundamental to the human psyche. But that is not the conclusion of this study. We have seen William Cobbett attribute the suffering of the English people to its government's system of fiscal exploitation, combined with the currency fluctuations caused by an even more exploitative financial system. We have followed him through his descriptions of the political institutions which allowed all this oppression to take place. And we have seen him conclude from this that poverty and degradation sprang from the want of a reform of parliament. But we can go back further than that. The alteration, corruption and setting aside of the British constitution was brought about by those who had the will to exploit, in order to facilitate that exploitation. The will preceded the power; and went on to create it. This chapter is a speculation upon the circumstances and influences which brought that will into being; upon their consequences and psychological effects.

From some point during the second half of the 17th century, there began to be apparent among the landed classes a growing feeling of insecurity and status-anxiety.[2] This originated, perhaps, in the troubled times of mid-century, engendered by heavy taxation on the one hand, and violent disorder, destruction and sequestration on the other. Straitened financial circumstances became the norm, with many estate incomes tending to fall during the 1670s and 1680s; until William III's war against the French king in the 1690s brought severer pressure still, in the form of the land tax. In time, other taxes followed and augmented the burden; on houses, for example, and servants and even windows. All the while the rents of the landed estates which had to support all this extra expenditure were in a state far from flourishing. The 1690s saw a run of difficult years; whilst the first half of the 18th century was notable for periods of unusual weather conditions; epidemics among domestic livestock; and lengthy spells of low agricultural prices. With tenants struggling amidst all these difficulties, and trapped between high taxes and low prices, rents fell or were paid chronically in arrears; some farmers went bankrupt. Consequently, the income of the landed estates, after all the necessary outgoings, tended at best to remain static, or in some cases even to fall. Indebtedness among landowners became common. Many smaller estates became absorbed into the larger; or else were swallowed up by wealthy outsiders from the worlds of law, commerce and banking. Walter Harte, the agricultural writer, commented in 1764.

---

1 I should like to thank Katy Baboulene for pointing me in this direction.
2 Much of this section is based on James M. Rosenheim. The Emergence of a Ruling Order, and G. E. Mingay. English Landed Society in the Eighteenth Century.

"Happy are those whose annual income is not liable to be affected with inclemency of seasons, losses, or frauds from tenants, or a circumstance equally mortifying, which is sometimes having no tenants at all!"[3]

Indeed, there were such. For while landed proprietors, great and small, groaned under the burdens of war taxation and increasing official profligacy, there were those, as we know, who fared very prosperously under the new system. These were the numerous contractors who grew rich from providing the supplies necessary for warfare; the appointees to the proliferation of offices that occurred during times of conflict; and, most glaringly of all, the financiers; all, in fact, for whom, as Paine put it, war was the harvest. The landed aristocracy had always been partly recruited from those who had made good in trade and commerce; who had aspired to nobility and had assimilated themselves into it. But what was happening now was different. A new opulent class was being created by connections with government; it was growing rich on the taxes paid by the landowning class; and it was causing wars to be fought by means of those taxes, to which its members did not contribute, which brought great financial gain to the mercantile, banking and official classes, but none to the landed. Much resentment was thus engendered.

"You certainly ruin those that have only land to depend on to enrich Dutch, Jews, French and other foreigners, scoundrel stock-jobbers, and tally-jobbers who have been sucking our blood for many years."[4]

Many members of this new financial elite were rootless individuals, outsiders or foreigners. Non-conformists were numerous in the business community, seen as outsiders by the majority because of their religious opinions. Many more were Dutch who had arrived with William of Orange, or who, like the Barings settled later. Many of the financiers were French Huguenots, driven from their homeland by religious persecution. Jews of Portuguese origin, who had previously settled at Amsterdam, and who were drawn to this country by the rich pickings presented by its government, figured largely among the monied interest. The Goldsmids were German Jews, who arrived also via Amsterdam. Walter Boyd was a Scotsman, who was driven from his Parisian banking business by the Revolution. This rootlessness, this absence of any patriotic or community mentality, led to an aggressive, competitive and thrusting attitude towards status, power and influence, and, above all, the acquisition of material wealth. It is not difficult to see how Nathan Rothschild's lowly origins in the despised ghetto of Frankfurt led to his single-minded and all-consuming devotion to the pursuit of wealth and power.

The ambitions of this class represented a very direct and a very serious threat to the landed classes; to their influence both locally and centrally; to their financial well-being; to their very existence. Daniel Defoe, in 1722, noticed the beginnings of this process, whilst he was travelling in Essex.

"It is observable, that in this part of the country, there are several very considerable estates purchased, and now enjoyed by citizens of London, merchants and tradesmen, as Mr. Western an iron merchant, near Kelvedon, Mr. Cresnor, a wholesale grocer, who was, before he died, named sheriff at Earls Coln; Mr. Olemus, a merchant at Braintree, Mr. Westcomb, near Malden, Sir Thomas Webster, at Copthall, near Waltham, and several others. I mention this, to observe how the present increase of wealth in the city of London, spreads itself into the country, and plants families and fortunes, who in another age will equal the families of the ancient gentry, who perhaps were bought out."[5]

Numerous families of declining gentry were thus forced to sell up and move away. Cobbett, who wrote frequently on this subject, often noted the mansions of the old families, empty and derelict.

---

3 Quoted in G. E. Mingay. English Landed Society in the Eighteenth Century. P. 55.
4 R. R. Ward. The English Land Tax. Pp.23-24.
5 Daniel Defoe. A Tour through the Whole Island of Great Britain. Penguin ed. Pp.56-57.

In the Valley of the Wiltshire Avon, there were forty, either falling down, or else wholly gone.[6] In many cases, the old families were supplanted by the newly-rich. The family of Arcedeknes, who took over Glevening Hall in Suffolk, had made their fortune in Jamaica; the Beckfords of Basing Park in Hampshire were West India planters, and presumably slave-owners. At Brightling, in Sussex, the Fuller family made fortunes as trustees and executors, as iron-founders and cannon-makers, and as West Indian slave-owners.[7] The purchases of the greater financiers displayed even more glaring effrontery. In Hampshire, in 1822, Cobbett passed between the two constantly expanding estates of the Baring brothers. Sir Thomas Baring replaced the Duke of Bedford, and was a ruthless financial exploiter of his estate. His brother, Alexander, had supplanted Lord Northington. He had no talent for the job of landowning.

"Every thing that has been done here is to the injury of the estate, and discovers a most shocking want of taste in the projector."[8]

In Worcestershire, Cobbett chanced upon Gatcombe Park, the property of David Ricardo, the renowned Stock Exchange speculator.

"This estate of GATCOMB belonged, I am told, to a Mr. SHEPPERD, and to his fathers before him. I asked, where this Shepperd was NOW? A tradesman-looking man told me, that he did not know where he was; but, that he had *heard*, that he was living *somewhere* neat to *Bath*! Thus they go! Thus they are squeezed out of existence. The little ones are gone; and the *big ones* have nothing left for it, but to resort to the bands of *holy matrimony* with the *turn of the market watchers* and their breed."[9]

Ricardo's fortune actually stretched to two estates; for a little further on was the estate of his son.

"On our road we passed by the estate and park of *another Ricardo*! This is OSMOND; the other is DAVID. This one has ousted two families of Normans, the HONEYWOOD YATES, and the SCUDAMORES. They suppose him to have *ten thousand pounds a year in rent here*! Famous 'watching the turn of the market'! The BARINGS are at work down in this country too. They are every where, indeed, depositing their eggs about, like cunning old guinea-hens, in sly places, besides the great, open, showy nests that they have."[10]

The arrival in the country of some wealthy outsider from London could have a profoundly disruptive effect on the traditional social hierarchy. The landowning gentry could never hope to compete in terms of wealth and display – of cutting a figure in the neighbourhood – and they felt, with much bitterness, and some justice, that those fortunes had been made at their expence. Some newcomers attempted to eclipse their neighbours in local government – Sir Thomas Baring, for example, was prominent in the Commission of the Peace for Hampshire. The traditional role of the great landowner in representing the interests of the locality to central government also came under threat – it was the close contacts with government that had earned these *nouveaux riches* their fortunes. Sir Thomas Baring became M. P. for the county of Hampshire, whilst one member of the Fuller family of East Sussex was kept in the Commons to look after the family interests, who was well known to all the great politicians of the day.

The resulting rivalry between the monied and the landed families was well described by William Cobbett, in his letter to the Paper-Money Men.

---

6 William Cobbett. Rural Rides. Penguin ed. P. 291.

7 G. E. Mingay. English Landed Society in the Eighteenth Century. Pp. 102 and 106.

8 William Cobbett. Rural Rides. Penguin ed. P. 15.

9 Ibid. Pp. 346-347.

10 Ibid. Pp. 354-355.

"You hate one another most cordially. They hate you, because you are keeping them poor; because their lands are upon tick to you; because you stick yourselves up along side of them, out-do them in expense, thrust your noses in their face, and….humble them in the eyes of each other, by your freedom and familiarity, which, were it not for the length of your purses, would earn you a beating from the hands of their groom. For these reasons, they *hate you*; and you hate them, because they have titles, and particularly *family* pretensions, which the possession of millions of '*Consols*' (what a word!) will never give you. You do get, and have got, a good many of their manors and mansions and parks; but you cannot get the *family names* of the owners, and the family pretensions. Your wives and daughters may twist up their mouths and talk about 'the *peasantry* and the *population*,' in speaking of the *people*; they may put on all the airs of the Gentry, and, if they do not find an old *Gothic Mansion* to their hands, they may make you *build one* out of the gains of your Scrip; but, still, they know, that the old gentry soon *smoke* you. Country people are very inquisitive. You may have a thousand fine things about you; your wives may dress as fine as the cream-coloured horses; but, the old gentry will trace you back to Mincing Lane in a twinkling. This they do; and, in revenge for your display of wines and plates and fineries, they now and then, as if by accident, kindly invite you to talk a little about *your fathers* and *mothers*. For this, you hate them and all the Boroughmongering tribe,"[11]

The aggressive competitive mindset of a thrusting new class of opulent – a mindset which itself grew out of insecurity and rootlessness – brought a not altogether dissimilar mindset of insecurity and status-anxiety to the traditional rulers of the nation. In general, the landowning classes had no answer to this challenge. They were the losers. Over very many decades, reaching even into quite recent times, they declined and they disappeared. Nevertheless, there was a minority of the landowning class which did find the means of competing; and that minority consisted of the very richest of them – about 400 families. They survived and they prospered.

The challenge by which the landed class was now confronted led, in the members of that class, to a greatly increased pre-occupation with wealth, power, and status. And this pre-occupation manifested itself in a number of ways.

The re-organisation of the agricultural estates, as we have seen, was a principal feature of the age. Landlords sought to increase their rental incomes, by very large proportions. Enclosure was, perhaps, the most profitable investment available at the time, yielding a return of between fifteen and thirty per cent. In areas where enclosing was not practised, as well as on enclosed land, holdings were consolidated, and let out to highly capitalised farmers. Farms were mostly rented out at will, without leases, and from year to year, to enable the landlord to tap into any increase in agricultural prosperity with a minimum of delay. Arable land was converted to pasture where possible, in order to reduce the expences of cultivation. The old system of entry fines and nominal yearly payments was replaced by rack-rents; and this regular and large income enabled landlords to mortgage their lands in order to finance their outgoings. In many cases, professional stewards were put in charge of administering the estates, whose expertise tended often to be financial or legal rather than agricultural. In time, the burden of the land tax came to be shifted largely on to the shoulders of the tenant. The new arrangement of farms reduced the expences of repairs and maintenance, and, in some cases, these too came to be added to the responsibilities of the farmer. By the latter half of the 18th century, the incomes of the larger estates were in an extremely flourishing condition, and the greater landowners were buying up the estates and holdings of those for whom the times were less propitious.

But this was only a part of the process. The great landlords found many other opportunities of adding to their fortunes. The Lambton Earls of Durham, the Duke of Portland, and Earl Fitzwilliam, for example, were all coal-owners. Lord Grosvenor derived a good income from his lead-mines; and Lord Ashburnham from his timber sales and mortgage investments. Others took to financing

---

11   William Cobbett. Political Register. 29/3/1817.

turnpike roads or canals. At Leeds, the Stanhope family had interests in coal, iron, brick-making, woollen manufacture, canals, turnpikes and docks. More lucrative still were building developments in London, the evidence for which still remains in the names of the streets and the squares; the occupiers of Woburn Abbey, for instance, are still commemorated under the names of Russell, Tavistock and Bedford. But for sheer ease and magnitude of profit, few could compete with the beneficiaries of that grossest and most brazen oppression of all – that of the people of Ireland – the rents from which were not subject to taxation of any sort.

Links with the monied interest could be lucrative, and were therefore not to be eschewed merely on account of a dislike of its members. Landowners invested money in the funds; they borrowed on loan and on mortgage to finance agricultural schemes or their lavish lifestyle. Most significantly of all, they married into the monied families, and acquired a portion of their wealth by dowry, in exchange for an association with true nobility. Marriage became a commercial operation.

"The big, in order to save themselves from being *'swallowed up quick'*....*fall in love* with the *daughters* and *widows* of paper-money people, big brewers, and the like; and sometimes their daughters *fall in love* with the paper-money people's sons, or the fathers of those sons; and, whether they be *Jews*, or not, seems to be of little matter with this all-subduing passion of love."[12]

Power and wealth became intertwined. The Septennial Act, and the progressive corruption of Parliament, put growing power into the hands of the owners of the parliamentary constituencies – Cobbett's reviled 'boroughmongers' – and this power was assiduously cultivated by the greater landlords. The control of boroughs could be translated into votes in the House of Commons, and those votes, in turn, traded for offices of all sorts, pensions and sinecures. The wealth thus siphoned off could be channelled into estate expansion or conspicuous consumption. Many stately homes were built, or rebuilt, at the expence of the taxpayer. The notoriously corrupt Walpole remodelled Houghton in Norfolk; whilst the Earl of Chandos bought and rebuilt the ancestral home of his wife from the profits of office. The costs of providing for younger sons could be saved by "quartering them on the public", and dependents could be patronised at the taxpayer's expence. In sum, the greater landowners came to see the British state as "a usable resource", and herein, principally, lay their ability to compete with the new monied class.

This insecure, competitive mindset had a number of other consequences. William Godwin understood what was going on as well as any man living.

"There is a numerous class of individuals who, though rich, have neither brilliant talents nor sublime virtues; and, however highly they may value their education, their affability, their superior polish and the elegance of their manners, have a secret consciousness that they possess nothing by which they can so securely assert their pre-eminence and keep their inferiors at a distance, as the splendour of their equipage, the magnificence of their retinue and the sumptuousness of their entertainments....An embroidered garment may frequently cover an aching heart."[13]

The competition between the landed and the monied classes brought into being an entirely new culture, as it were; and this culture was metropolitan, cosmopolitan, and implacably hostile to, and separated from, the ordinary people of the country. The characteristics of that culture, which were competitively exhibited by the members of the elite, consisted of those distinctions which placed a distance, or pointed out a contrast, between them and the working people.

The magnate of the 16th and 17th centuries was generally the leader of his locality. He was active in administration, busied himself with estate affairs, and took care to represent the interests of his country to the central government. He was at the top of a hierarchy, consisting of all classes. But his descendant or successor of the 18th century was of a separate class altogether. He spent most of his

12 William Cobbett. Rural Rides. Penguin ed. Pp. 223-224.
13 William Godwin. An Enquiry Concerning Political Justice. P. 36.

time in London, or one of the fashionable resorts. He entrusted the affairs of his estate to his steward; and if he visited he remained hidden from the view of his neighbours and tenants. He abandoned the arduous and unpaid duties of local administration, and swapped them for the lucrative sinecurism of central government. Indeed, it was his ability to live idly that was, perhaps, the foremost point of separation from the working populace.

Ostentatious luxury was a principal part of the whole culture. Huge amounts of money were spent on the reconstruction, enlargement and repair of the great country houses. The Duke of Devonshire, for example, spent over £40,000 on the rebuilding of Chatsworth House; whilst the Earl of Rockingham spent £83,000 over a period of twenty years on Wentworth Woodhouse. Much of this was unnecessary, but the resulting house had to symbolise the status and political influence of the family that lived there. The country seat was a centre of entertainment and conspicuous consumption. Inside, it was filled with fine furniture, valuable paintings and *objets d'art*, much of it collected from abroad. The number of servants catering to the needs of the family was constantly on the rise through the 18th century. The clothes of the inhabitants were made by the London tailors, from the finest imported cloth – linen and lace from the Low Countries, silks and satins from Italy. The standard of fare was sumptuous. Dinner might last for two hours, and consist of meats, poultry and fish, puddings and pies, and would be followed by desserts of fruit pies, tarts, jellies, fruit and nuts, tea and coffee. This was followed by supper. Increasingly, delicacies brought in from a distance came to replace the more homely local fare. Artistic depictions of aristocratic consumers provide evidence of their comfortable lifestyle, and complaints about the ailments connected with over-indulgence, especially gout, were common.

Outside the house, and surrounding it, the parks and gardens could swallow up sums of money almost as great. Artificial landscapes were created. Gardens were re-arranged and trees planted. Water features were *de rigueur*. The Duke of Kingston, whilst extending his park at Thoresby, made a lake of 65 acres by damming a small river! Fripperies were installed which astonished by their superfluity as well as by their expence – menageries of animals, gothic ruins, follies of divers sorts.

Expensive leisure activities, replacing the traditional administrative duties of landowners, became a hallmark of gentility. Hunting, of course, was ubiquitously the pastime of the elite, involving horses only of the highest quality, and kennels full of hounds. Horse-racing was also indulged in – the Duke of Kingston in 1770 spent £506 on stables and horses at Holme-Pierrepoint, in addition to his stables at Thoresby, where he kept a staff of eleven. Those numerous noblemen who kept permanent establishments at Newmarket laid out much more.

More sedately, social life centred on the London season, the fashionable resorts, such as Bath and Cheltenham, and mutual visits to country houses. A social season in London could cost a nobleman a small fortune, with the need to keep up a lavish and fashionable establishment, and the arduous round of balls, assemblies, trips to the theatre and the opera, constant card-playing and gambling.

"And what shall the rich man do with his wealth?" William Godwin was of the opinion that by far the greater part of the outlay of the great families consisted in the expences of ostentation. "No man, but the most sordid epicure, would long continue to maintain even a plentiful table, if he had no spectators, visitors or servants, to behold his establishment."[14]

Conspicuous consumption bound the elite together into a single class, and distinguished it from those whom it saw as its inferiors. It was all part of a code of conduct, put into place to act as a barrier between the elite and the rest of society. The truly genteel were wealthy enough to live without work, which was held in contempt; indeed, to spend their lives in the pursuit of expensive pleasures. Refinement and cultivation were crucial facets of this code. Consumption displayed a man's taste – in architecture, landscaping, furniture, interior décor – as well as in cultural and intellectual pursuits.

---

14 William Godwin. An Enquiry Concerning Political Justice. P. 792.

The ideal of the gentleman was something to be aspired to by all those wishing to be part of this privileged class, with growing emphasis being placed upon the virtues of sociability, politeness and manners. Even in language, the 'polite' tongue of the elite began to supersede the regional accents and dialects from the later 17th century.

But the purpose of the whole code was display; it was a superficial mode of behaving designed to be seen; a mode adopted by rootless, insecure people, concerned with their social status, with a view to being accepted and respected by those seen as powerful and fashionable. Modes of behaviour were adopted, and companions chosen, because they were 'suitable'; because they attuned with convention; because they conformed with ideals pre-existing in the minds of those whom they wished to impress and emulate. These conventions and ideals were external to the individual ego; they were imposed from without. And, for that reason, they were bound to have important psychological consequences. Over the course of many decades, these psychological tendencies became reinforced, and more widespread, and more entrenched. And, as the most important part of a person's psychological development takes place during the early and adolescent years, the years we call formative, it is necessary to look at the upbringing and education of the young gentlefolks who aspired, or rather whose parents aspired for them, to membership of the respectable elite.

The social changes outlined above were accompanied by changes in the attitudes of parents towards their children, and consequently in their methods of upbringing and education. It is impossible to lay down any hard and fast rules here, because people are infinitely various. But a trend is definitely discernible over the course of many decades.

During the 16th and early 17th centuries, if the diary of Lady Grace Mildmay is taken as typical, parents were concerned with the fitness of the environment in which their children were to be reared; their best efforts were directed towards making their children 'good'; and education consisted of a mixture of academic and religious subjects.[15]

With the emergence of the metropolitan elite, however, all this began to change, and education became merely yet another aspect of social status. From the later 17th century, academic subjects, appearing no longer essential for the lifestyle of the leisured gentleman, declined in importance. They were replaced by the inculcation of the attitudes and the behaviour patterns, the refinements and the civility, of gentility.[16]

The idea of moulding a child into shape had not been a prevalent one in the 16th century. But, increasingly through the 18th, 'training' children came to occupy the concerns of parents. The character of a child was seen as malleable; it could be formed into a shape which would render the child acceptable to those who were seen as the leaders of society. The politest modes of behaviour would be imbued; the most refined tastes; and the correct, necessary and orthodox beliefs, views and values. Boys learnt "to conduct themselves in the manner of gentlemen and their sisters learned the conduct of a lady." Thus, whereas 16th century parents worried about the suitability of the environment in which their children grew up, their successors and descendants were hammered into shape in order to fit them for their environment.[17]

William Godwin put it like this.

"Public education has always expended its energies in the support of prejudices; it teaches its pupils, not the fortitude that shall lay every proposition to the test of examination, but the art of

15 L. Pollock. Forgotten Children. P. 113.
16 James M. Rosenheim. The Emergence of a Ruling Order. P. 196.
17 L. Pollock. Forgotten Children. Pp. 111 and 116-120. James M. Rosenheim. P. 269 and 256.

inculcating such tenets as may chance to be previously established; even in Sunday schools, the chief lessons that are taught are a superstitious veneration for the Church of England, and how to bow to every man in a handsome coat."[18]

It was a highly artificial and externalised set of values and modes of behaviour that was increasingly being imposed upon the children of the elite and the aspiring elite throughout the 18th and early 19th centuries. This, we may surmise, was a far more difficult educational objective to achieve than merely aiming to channel and develop the natural abilities and inclinations of the child. A much harsher and more radical regime must perforce be implemented in order to achieve it. And such there was.

In the 16th century, such little evidence as we have suggests that many parents preferred advice to commands, and that children in general were not held to unquestioning obedience. But the tendency for parents to require 'implicit compliance' seems to have increased alongside the tendency to implant received beliefs and behaviour patterns. The two tendencies are psychologically similar, involving the acceptance by the child of the ideas and wishes of others, which may have no connection at all to the true nature of the child himself, and, indeed, may require him to suspend his powers of reasoning. The implementing of unquestioning obedience almost seems a necessary prerequisite if a child is to be forced into an externalised set of beliefs and social *mores*. The connection between demands for unquestioning obedience and the desire for social advancement is well demonstrated by the diary of a fifteen year old American girl, Nancy Shippen, who, understandably enough, frequently quarrelled with her mother. Her father wrote;-

"Have you persuaded yourself that your dear Mamma knows better than you & that it is your duty to obey her cheerfully always, altho it may sometimes seem hard. She loves you & wishes to make you one of the finest women in Philadelphia this should excite your love & gratitude & I flatter myself does."[19]

Back in England, John Stedman recalled his childhood; who, perhaps not insignificantly, ended up a soldier.

"I was teached blindly to obey, without consulting either my feelings, or my senses….All this may be intended for the best and term'd, good education, but I shall ever insist, that nothing can be worse than never to consult a child's motives or desires which not only makes them miserable, but ten to one must end in making them bad men."[20]

Although it was by no means a ubiquitous trend, as the 18th century turned into the 19th, there seems to have been a definite increase in the number of parents willing to use harsh methods to enforce this discipline; and an increase in the harshness of those methods. Already by the second half of the 17th century, the use of physical punishments was becoming more common. Through the 18th, whilst most parents seem to have wished to pursue a middle course between severity and indulgence, there was nevertheless a significant and growing number aiming to maintain an absolute control over their children by the use of rigorous methods, which included corporal punishments. By the early 19th century, a further increase in severity is discernible, with more repressive methods being used, and a greater proportion of parents using physical punishments and demanding total obedience. Some children there were who were subjected to "intense brutality".[21]

Routine corporal punishment, however, was generally only to be found in the public schools. Only the upper echelons of English society could afford to send their children to these, and so it is in the autobiographies of the upper class that we find accounts of the ill-treatment and harshness

---

18   William Godwin. An Enquiry Concerning Political Justice. P. 357.

19   L. Pollock. Forgotten Children. Pp. 148 and 167.

20   L. Pollock. Forgotten Children. P. 160.

21   Ibid. Pp. 154, 160 and 184.

that were associated with school discipline. A "regime of inhumane cruelty" was enforced by teachers believing in the necessity for brutal enforcement.

"Every body says it is the only way to bring up boys."[22]

Note that; "every body says."

Accompanying these changes was a growing tendency among parents to regard their children as a burden rather than a blessing. Whilst in the 18th century, parents who have left us written accounts still use positive epithets for describing their children, these are already intermixed with such terms as 'cares' and 'incumbrances', and increasing emphasis is placed on the amount of time, trouble and money which children take up. By the 19th century, they come to be described as 'frog-like', 'a plague', and 'trying'. Many parents affected an exaggerated fear of spoiling their children, and displayed an inflated idea of the educational usefulness of punishment. The parental projection of their own unacceptable feelings on to the child led to unrealistic estimations of the child's character, and excessive demands for unquestioning obedience; possibly also role-reversal, where parents expect their own needs to be fulfilled by the child, rather than the other way around. All these are the characteristics of the child-neglecter, and the child-abuser, then as now. The unnecessarily harsh treatment of ones offspring, and especially the use of physical correction, tends to be characteristic of parents who see the relationship with their children as a power struggle or a battle of wills; in short, of parents who are psychologically insecure. And in this way they must necessarily produce insecurity in their children.[23]

The damaging psychological effects of corporal punishment might vary with the reasons for which it is inflicted. That a salutary lesson ought to be taught to the child caught lying or stealing, nobody can argue with, even if one might disagree with the method. But to punish a child for 'obstinacy', or 'disobedience', is like administering a punishment for daring to think for himself; and the same applies even if that punishment is not physical. The influential John Locke strongly recommended the use of 'shame' as a punishment in preference to a beating, which was a last resort. William Cobbett once wrote that a mother was a person who could pass all her bad habits on to her offspring without the use of any force at all.[24]

Whatever the method, it is the enforcement of blind submission to authority that concerns us here; and the inculcation of the unquestioning, unthinking and unreasoning mindset. All of which was becoming increasingly common as a result of the social and economic changes of the 18th and 19th centuries.

In the aftermath of the Second World War, a team of American psychologists, shocked at the ease with which the extermination of the Jewish race became an acceptable political objective in Germany, and fearing for the fate of their own country, undertook a study of the anti-democratic mindset. The study based its conclusions on a sample of American subjects who exhibited fascist tendencies; which sample it compared with other subjects, exhibiting different ideologies. Hard and fast rules are impossible to state, because individuals display great variation in all the psychological tendencies involved. But the psychologists identified a number of common denominators in the anti-democratic subjects, which could justifiably be considered as forming a syndrome. The study was

---

22 Ibid. Pp. 200 and 197.

23 Ibid. Pp. 110, 41-42, 57 and 269.

24 John Locke. Thoughts Concerning Education. Pp. 70-82. William Cobbett. Political Register. 14/9/1816.

called The Authoritarian Personality. It was published in New York in 1950. And the leader of the team was T. W. Adorno

The Adorno team thought the anti-democratic syndrome had probably been established during the previous four centuries; and the conclusions which the team drew, though based on twentieth century Americans, seem to apply with remarkable closeness to the situation of the English ruling classes in the 18th and 19th centuries. Psychology as a science, of course, was unknown then; but the issues involved were quite familiar to contemporaries, and were discussed in the literature of the day, and from both points of view, far more frequently than they seem to be in out own time.[25] Today, the whole subject seems to have become yet another elephant on the sofa; outside, that is, of the music of the rock group Marillion.

Personality, and the political ideology which results from the needs of personality, are greatly affected by the circumstances of the child during the formative years; by the 'training' which the child receives in his family life and his education. Economic and social considerations can exert great influence over the ways in which parents bring up their children. Although the Adorno team did not consider it a part of their remit to elaborate on the social and economic processes that played their part in the formation of personality and ideology, they conceded, what we have observed already, that social change could bring about changes in the way children were reared, and could therefore contribute to widespread changes in personality and ideology formation.[26]

The anti-democratic subjects studied by the Adorno team seem to have had one factor very noticeably in common – a strict upbringing. Their fathers tended to be either aggressive, or else silent and distant, and expected their commands to be obeyed without question. One subject complained of victimisation and childish treatment; another of frequent beatings for disobedience and of being broken by his father; a third of severe physical punishments which were seen as unjust, arbitrary, and often for petty offences.[27]

Almost uncannily, the Adorno team identified those parents who were most pre-occupied with social status as the most rigid disciplinarians; they were the parents with issues about personal security, and were often themselves the children of foreign-born parents. It was the pressing social needs of the parent – his insecurity and his status-anxiety – that turned him into the abuser of his children. His precepts were obeyed because they were implemented with superior force; out of a respect based on fear rather than on reason. Such a parent would not attempt to carry his child with him; he would not discuss or explain or get the child to understand why one course of action was preferable to another. He would expect the child merely to obey.[28]

A further potent factor in the formation and development of the anti-democratic personality was the inculcation of religion. In twentieth century America, religion, of course, did not exert anything like the influence which previously it had done. But the Adorno team noted that an adherence to established religion tended to be associated with the anti-democratic tendency; whilst a belief in a more personalised, individual religion, or else the rejection of religion altogether, was a feature of the more open mindset. It was not religion itself which posed the danger, but the unquestioning acceptance of its established tenets.[29]

In the 18th century, of course, religion played a much greater role. William Godwin noted the tendency of it.

---

25 See the motto to this book.
26 T. W. Adorno. The Authoritarian Personality. Pp. 6 and 972.
27 Ibid. Pp. 792, 348 and 761.
28 Ibid. Pp. 483, 338, 384-5, and 371.
29 Ibid. Pp. 727, 731, and 209-15.

"There is nothing perhaps that has contributed more to the introduction and perpetuating of bigotry in the world, than the doctrines of the Christian religion….It is the characteristic of this religion, to lay the utmost stress upon faith. Its central doctrine is contained in this short maxim, He that believeth, shall be saved; and he that believeth not, shall be damned. What it is, the belief of which is saving, the records of our religion have left open to controversy; but the fundamental nature of faith, is one of its most unquestionable lessons. Faith is not only necessary to preserve us from the pains of hell; it is also requisite for temporal blessings."

"The system of religious conformity is a system of blind submission."[30]

What was thus imposed upon the child was a set of rigid conventional rules and received orthodoxies quite beyond his comprehension. And the object of all such rules and orthodoxies was social climbing. The whole system came to colour a child's perception of right and wrong. What was socially acceptable and contributed towards social advancement came to be seen as good; what was generally frowned upon, and therefore hindered that advancement, was seen as bad.[31]

Thus, the Adorno team identified three factors common to the upbringings of those subjects displaying strong anti-democratic tendencies – the inculcation of social values and customs foreign to the ego of the child; the lack of any discussion of those values and customs, or of any encouragement to the child to reason about them; and the use of strictness and rigour, possibly extending to physical force.

This type of upbringing had a number of rather alarming psychological implications. Here is the perceptive Godwin again.

"Man, while he consults his own understanding, is the ornament of the universe. Man, when he surrenders his reason, and becomes the partisan of implicit faith and passive obedience, is the most mischievous of all animals. Ceasing to examine every proposition that comes before him for the direction of his conduct, he is no longer the capable subject of moral instruction. He is, in the instant of submission, the blind instrument of every nefarious purpose of his principal; and, when left to himself, is open to the seduction of injustice, cruelty and profligacy."[32]

The child of socially insecure, and consequently socially ambitious parents, brought up in blind submission to a set of social conventions and orthodox beliefs, was thus the victim of a dichotomy which would colour his whole life, and his whole way of thinking. Faced with the overwhelming power of his parents, he became acutely conscious of his own weakness. The underlying craving for affection and approval from the source from which he received only commands produced a deep psychological need to be associated with that power; and an equally profound revulsion at his own weakness. It was a profoundly competitive mindset; the holder of which saw himself as pitted against all his fellows in a struggle for domination, material wealth and social success. During the years of adolescence, one guesses, this dichotomy would take over his whole personality, burying, without trace and forever, his real ego, and playing the crucial determining role in all his social relationships and political views. As Adorno put it, the lack of an internalised approach to the child and the transmission of conventional rules and customs led to a lack of development of any clear-cut personal identity.[33] Here is the concept of the "Misplaced Childhood" as found in the music of Marillion. William Godwin called this mindset "a sort of non-ductor to all the sympathies of the human heart." Its exhibitor was "not subject to the fervours and the shocks of humanity." He was "no longer a man; he is the ghost of departed man."[34]

---

30 William Godwin. The Enquirer. Pp. 322-3. An Enquiry Concerning Political Justice. P. 604.

31 T. W. Adorno. The Authoritarian Personality. Pp. 483, 338, 384-5, and 371.

32 William Godwin. An Enquiry Concerning Political Justice. P. 174.

33 T. W. Adorno. The Authoritarian Personality. P. 385 et passim.

34 William Godwin. The Enquirer. P. 256. An Enquiry Concerning Political Justice. P. 668.

Power is of the essence. The anti-democratic subject sees society as organised along the same lines as his family was when he was a child; as a hierarchy of power, in which commands were handed down from the father and the senior members, and an unquestioning obedience required of the child. The child's consciousness of his own weakness, combined with his unfulfilled need for affection from his parents, lead to a deep-seated need to be associated with the source of power in society. The groups whom he sees as possessed of the greatest concentrations of wealth and influence, he idealises irrationally. His profound sense of insecurity produces a need to be closely associated with them; to be on the inside and in the know. He strives to be like them; to be with them.[35]

"What base and degenerate dogs those must be, who, while the world is looking at them with scorn, can crawl upon their bellies to obtain marks of approbation from ministers and kings."[36]

The overriding need is for social advancement. The anti-democratic subject attempts to emulate all the external and superficial qualities which distinguish the dominant group from the rest of society. Obedience and loyalty, of course, are prime requisites; then, self-control, honesty of a certain sort, good manners and politeness; and above all, perhaps, a healthy contempt for all those he sees as below him in the social scale.[37]

It very often happens that the researches of the Adorno team merely confirm the observations upon his own times of William Godwin. Towards the end of the 18th century, Godwin wrote in great detail on the characteristics of that honesty, as it was called, which brought reputation and social success to the possessor of it. Honesty, in Godwin's day, was not a moral quality of straightforwardness and openness, as we might think; it was a policy – a means to an end – commonly denominated "the best".

"The cheapest plan for acquiring reputation will be found to consist in the conforming ourselves to the prejudices of others. He that acts in unison with other men's sentiments and expectations, will be easily understood."

The man intent on courting success and popularity must never think for himself. If he did, he would run the risk of espousing "some opinions that are not embraced by the multitude. This is an obvious disqualification in a candidate for common fame."

He therefore has to take over morality as commonly accepted. Common honesty "readily indulges in all those things which, the world has agreed, constitute no impeachment upon the character of an honest man....What the majority of mankind has determined to be essential to a moral character, it submits to with the most edifying resignation; those things, which a severe and inflexible examination might pronounce to be dishonest, but which the world has agreed to tolerate, it can practise in all instances without the visitings of compunction."

And he must adhere to these views even when they are "the most ridiculously absurd, or flagrantly indefensible."

To achieve this "superficial plausibility", moderation and mediocrity will never fail; the world is taken aback by those who are great, magnanimous or ardent. "A certain regularity of conduct" is required; and following the rules is carried so far, as to preclude any concern for the feelings or misfortunes of others. It is not necessary to practise benevolence or charity.

"A certain coldness of character seems indeed to be essential to that species of honesty which is most applauded in the world."

The motive that propels men to this line of conduct is generally a selfish one.

"It may be vanity....unmixed with almost any discernible portion of sympathy or kindness.

---

35 T. W. Adorno. The Authoritarian Personality. P. 150, 8, 48, 54-55 and 414.
36 William Cobbett. Political Register. 29/9/1832.
37 T. W. Adorno. The Authoritarian Personality. Pp. 55 and 414.

"The motive may be ambition….confused and doubtful in its judgment of itself, it seeks the suffrage of the world, to confirm it in its propensity to inordinate self-admiration.

"The motive may be mere desire of wealth….In the majority of cases at least, a fair character seems essential to eminent success in the world."

"It is certainly to be regretted, that the applause of the world, and all general moral reputation, should be confined to characters of this description."[38]

Here is Godwin on the renowned politeness and elegance of manners which distinguished the rulers of society from their more earthy inferiors.

"By politeness many persons understand artificial manners, the very purpose of which is to stand between the feelings of the heart and the external behaviour. The word immediately conjures up to their mind a corrupt and vicious mode of society, and they conceive it to mean a set of rules, founded in no just reason, and ostentatiously practised by those who are familiar with them, for no purpose more expressly, than to confound and keep at a distance those who, by the accident of birth or fortune, are ignorant of them….Politeness is not precisely that scheme and system of behaviour which can only be learned in the fashionable world. There are many things in the system of the fashionable world, that are practised, not to encourage but depress, not to produce happiness but mortification. These, by whatever name they are called, are the reverse of politeness; and are accordingly commonly known by the denomination of rudeness, a word of exactly opposite application…."[39]

This type of personality rises through society, not by means of hard work, which is beneath him, nor by merit, nor professional competence; but through pull and influence.[40]

"He that from beggary ascends to opulence, is usually known not to have effected this transition by methods very creditable to his honesty or usefulness."[41]

He chooses his friends not for any human characteristics, which he does not understand, but because they can be of use to him; because they are in a position to help in his career or social advancement, or because, on a superficial examination, they are the right sort of people to be seen associating with.[42]

His obsessive preoccupation with status leads him to exaggerate the social position of his own family; he has a burning desire to make it appear that his family was possessed of great prestige and reputation.[43] Here is William Cobbett, writing to Baron Garrow, of recent television fame.

"It is very strange, that, while, in every other part of the world, this attachment to antiquity of birth is becoming an object of contempt and ridicule, it is cherished in England with a sort of revived infatuation….The sickly taste of affecting a *descent* from the *Conquest* is daily gaining ground. We have *Hutton of Hutton*; *Trafford of Trafford*; *Antrobus of Antrobus*; *Brougham of Brougham*; and we shall, I dare say, have, by-and-by, *Canning of Canning, Baring of Baring, Ricardo of Ricardo*. Next there will be a change of the of into a *de*; and then we shall be told, that they all 'came in with the *Conqueror*.'

"The fundholders will have families, I'll warrant them. They have a great taste, in general, for family memorials. They soon get *coats of arms*; and they seem to have an instinct that leads them to the possession of ancient seats.

---

38 William Godwin. The Enquirer. Pp. 253-263.

39 William Godwin. The Enquirer. Pp. 326 and 335.

40 T. W. Adorno. The Authoritarian Personality. P. 684.

41 William Godwin. An Enquiry Concerning Political Justice. P. 794. Here we have honesty being used in the sense in which we might understand it.

42 T. W. Adorno. The Authoritarian Personality. Pp. 416-418.

43 Ibid. P. 357.

"....However, as I said before, the Fundholders and Army Taylors and Contractors and Commissaries will soon have families, and *ancient families* too. So that there will be no deficiency in that respect."[44]

It was money, however, that played the crucial role in the whole syndrome. The insecurity inherent in the anti-democratic personality created an insatiable desire for the accumulation of money and property; to this, all other considerations were subsidiary. Money was the standard by which success was judged; money gained the respect of the members of the elite, and was the key to entry into their counsels and their confidence.[45] William Godwin noted the undue reverence and importance accorded to wealth.

"The matters prevailing in many countries are accurately calculated to impress a conviction, that integrity, virtue, understanding and industry are nothing and that opulence is everything....Money is the great requisite for the want of which nothing can atone. Distinction, the homage and esteem of mankind, are to be bought, not earned. The rich man need not trouble himself to invite them, they come unbidden to his surly door. Rarely indeed does it happen, that there is any crime that gold cannot expiate, any baseness and meanness of character that gold cannot cover with oblivion. Money therefore is the only object worthy of your pursuit, and it is of little importance by what sinister and unmanly means, so it be but obtained."[46]

When Alexis de Tocqueville toured England in the 1830s, he saw a great difference in attitude between this country and his native France. In France, he noted, a man might be said to have an annual income of 100,000 francs; but in England, a man might be said to be *worth* £5,000 per annum. The sum of an Englishman was no more than his money. De Tocqueville wrote to his fiancée.

"The respect paid to wealth in England is enough to make one despair."

"Money is the real power. So in England wealth has become not only an element in reputation, enjoyment and happiness; it is also an element, and one might almost say the only element, in power....In England it is a terrible misfortune to be poor."[47]

The compulsive attraction to power, then, was one half of the psychological dichotomy of the anti-democratic personality; and because power was intertwined with the memory of an almighty father, so power came to be associated unreasoningly with good. The other side of the coin was weakness; and because weakness was intertwined with the contempt felt by the subject for his own submissiveness to his parents, so weakness was associated with evil.

Thus, the other half of the dichotomy consisted in the attitude of the anti-democratic personality to those he saw as weaker than himself, and below him in the social scale.

Because of the conditioning which he had received in his youth, Adorno's anti-democratic subject of 1950 had come to see society in terms of a dichotomy between a rich and powerful in-group, and one or a number of out-groups.

"What principle in human nature is more universally confessed than self love, that is, than a propensity to think individually of a private interest, to discriminate and divide objects which the laws of the universe have indissolubly united? None, unless it be *esprit de corps*, the tendency of bodies of men to aggrandize themselves, a spirit, which, though less ardent than self love, is still more vigilant, and not exposed to the accidents of sleep, indisposition and mortality."[48]

Just as the idealisation of the in-group had no basis in rationality or reality, so the vilification of the out-group was equally devoid of observation and objectivity. The Adorno study was primarily

---

44 William Cobbett. Political Register. 27/5/1820.
45 T. W. Adorno. The Authoritarian Personality. Pp. 155 and 433.
46 William Godwin. An Enquiry Concerning Political Justice. Pp. 38 and 433.
47 Alexis de Tocqueville. Journeys to England and Ireland. Ed. J. P. Mayer. Pp. 91, 17 and 15.
48 William Godwin. An Enquiry Concerning Political Justice. P. 459.

concerned with anti-Semitism, and so it was the Jews who made up the out-group principally considered. Jews might increase competition for employment, thereby causing reductions in living standards, and arousing a hostility, which, however unfair, was at least rational.

"But….to go on, as do most people who oppose Jews on occupational grounds, and accept a wide variety of opinions, many of which are contradictory, about Jews in general, and to attribute various ills of the world to them, is plainly illogical."[49]

What we are talking about here, of course, is prejudice. Prejudice is a way of seeing the world in conformity, not to experience or objectivity, but to the psychological needs of the person seeing. Largely, it is a manifestation of repressed aggression. The hostility which the subject naturally feels against his domineering parents, and, by transference, against authority in general, but which he can never allow himself to express, is displaced against those whom he sees as weak and inferior. It is the "kick the dog" syndrome. A man may hate Jews with a passion, even though he has no knowledge or experience of them; even though the limited experience which he may have of them contradicts his views.[50]

Prejudice against Jews, then, is a state of mind, which has nothing to do with the characteristics of the Jewish people, and everything to do with the psychological dispositions of the exhibitor of that prejudice. It therefore follows, as Adorno puts it, that "a man who is hostile toward one minority group is very likely to be hostile against a wide variety of others". This is demonstrated by the ease with which a prejudice can transfer itself from one object to another. In Cobbett's day, of course, the prevailing prejudice was not against Jews, but against the English poor in general, and more particularly against the traditional rural class; but the principle appears to have been the same. Prejudice was a way of thinking.[51]

Stereotypy is a comfortable way of seeing the world characteristic of the prejudiced person. It attributes generalised traits to the out-groups in question. The anti-democratic subject will subscribe unquestioningly to any established and commonly accepted accusation that happens to come from an authoritative source. His "ideological receptivity", as Adorno puts it, will be determined by his membership of a social group. "Individuals, out of their needs to conform and to belong and to believe, and through such devices as imitation and conditioning, often take over more or less ready-made the opinions, attitudes and values that are characteristic of the groups in which they have membership." There might be an obvious reality gap between the actual diversity of the members of the vilified group, and the uniformity assumed by the prejudiced person. But it is nevertheless asserted that the members of the group are "all alike"; and the group condemned *en masse*. The experience of acquaintance with some member of the group who does not display the assumed characteristics will not necessarily change the perception. If the individual is not seen, as he probably will be, as inevitably a specimen of the group as a whole, the doctrine of "good Jews" and "bad Jews" will be brought into play, in order to bridge that reality gap; the equivalent from Cobbett's time being "the deserving poor" and "the idle poor".[52]

Thus, the repressed aggressive tendencies of the anti-democratic subject manifest themselves as a hostility against those social groups whom he sees as weak and inferior, and express themselves as a moral condemnation; a stricture upon the group's supposed failure to adhere to his in-group's conventional modes of behaviour and orthodox beliefs.[53]

---

49 T. W. Adorno. The Authoritarian Personality. Pp. 8-9.

50 T. W. Adorno. The Authoritarian Personality. Pp. 51, 96, 607, et passim.

51 Ibid. Pp. 9, 612, 607 and 617.

52 Ibid. Pp. 9, 57 and 621-623.

53 Ibid. P. 406.

It is the mechanism of projectivity that largely determines the faults by which an out-group is collectively condemned. According to Adorno, anti-Semites struggle "to inhibit in themselves the very tendencies which they find so unbearable in Jews". They accuse "Jews of wishing to establish a closely cohesive and selfishly exploitative in-group", because that is precisely what they want themselves, and so they see the world in those terms.[54]

The prejudiced character's contempt for himself; his inability to face up to his own weakness; leads him to feel projective contempt for mankind in general. He believes human nature to be intrinsically and irremediably evil; and this Adorno calls the doctrine of cynicism.[55] In the 18th and 19th centuries this very idea was encompassed in the religious doctrine of original sin. This traditional Catholic doctrine was brought to the fore by establishment writers, in order to justify "restraints" on the common people, and government as at the time existing; and adherence to it, or its rejection, therefore can be taken as a valid litmus test distinguishing establishment writers from radical ones.

William Wilberforce, for example, thought that men generally underestimated human corruption. From Christianity, he drew the lesson "that man is an apostate creature, fallen from his high original, degraded in his nature, and depraved in his faculties; indisposed to good, and disposed to evil; prone to vice, it is natural and easy to him; disinclined to virtue, it is difficult and laborious; that he is tainted with sin, not slightly and superficially, but radically and to the very core."

On the other side of the argument, Thomas Paine believed man to be essentially good. Godwin went not quite that far.

"We bring into the world with us no innate principles; consequently we are neither virtuous nor vicious as we first come into existence."

When a correspondent to the Political Register begged Cobbett to think better of the Germans, he replied;-

"I do not think ill of the people of Germany. There are no bad people naturally. When they are bad, they are made bad by their governments."[56]

Dependency is an important trait of the anti-democratic personality which resulted from his upbringing. His total dependence on his parents prevented the formation of the qualities of self-reliance. He developed an exploitative need to be taken care of by other people, and to be supplied by them with his material needs. Unable to face up to this aspect of his own weakness, he projects the faults of dependency on to the vilified out-group.[57] The anti-poor propaganda of the 18th and 19th centuries, as we have seen, abounds in accusations of this sort. The renowned idleness of the poor was standard fare, exercising establishment writers from Defoe to Martineau. Their extravagance and improvidence were scarcely less enlarged upon; the abandonment of their children and elderly relatives to be taken care of by the parish. All these faults were emphasised in connection with a critique of the Poor Laws, and were meant to imply a parasitic dependence upon the rate-payer. This was intended for the consumption of an elite whose principle line of demarcation from the masses lay in their ability to live idly; for whom luxury, ostentation and waste were the hallmarks of a cultured existence; and all of whose children but the eldest were supported by the taxpayer. The psychological mechanisms at work here are obvious enough.

"The potentially fascist character blames the poor who need assistance for the very same passivity and greediness which he has learnt not to admit to his own consciousness."[58]

54 Ibid. P. 96.

55 Ibid. Pp. 148 and 806.

56 Robert Hole. Pulpits, Politics and Public Order. Pp. 132-143. William Wilberforce. Practical View. Pp. 24-30. William Godwin. An Enquiry Concerning Political Justice. P. 12. William Cobbett. Political Register. 15/5/1813.

57 T. W. Adorno. The Authoritarian Personality. Pp. 353, 386, 400 and 414.

58 Ibid. P. 699.

And whilst Malthus, Townsend and their like were calling aloud for the abolition of the Poor Laws in order to "throw the poor upon their own resources"; to expose them to the danger of starvation in order to force them to work harder; so, 150 years later, in Adorno's America, anti-democratic subjects were still advocating the abolition of the dole; the freeing up of the labour market, which meant, in effect, the engendering of an artificial competition between workers; and dwelling on such themes as the biblical adage of "he who works not, neither shall he eat", and the cynical idea that people are inherently too idle to work unless put under pressure. Nothing changes. Such statements, the Adorno team believed, were expressions of punitiveness and authoritarian aggression, and were "ideal receptacles of some typical psychological urges of the prejudiced character."[59]

The fascist personality's overwhelming but repressed fear of his own weakness promotes an aggressive attitude towards the poor and oppressed, and prevents any feeling of sympathy.

"It is indeed but too common to see anger against the sufferer supply the place of that compassion which ought to fly to his relief. He who wants the disposition to relieve seeks a justification of himself in some charge or other against the sufferer. This is but too common a thing all over the world; and, therefore, I am by no means surprised to hear reproaches cast upon the poor."

"To hear them, one would think, that *you* had been the guilty cause of the misery you suffer; and that you, and you alone, ought to be made answerable for what has taken place."[60]

Victim-blaming was a distinctive characteristic of Adorno's anti-democratic interviewees. One of them laid the responsibility for all the persecutions suffered by the Jews, including the Nazi extermination, squarely upon the victims themselves; they must have done something to deserve it; they need to change and to adhere to the cultural conventions of the mainstream, or else they deserve all they get. Another asserted that negroes bring their problems upon themselves, by aspiring to equality with whites. It was the same in Cobbett's day.

"These fellows always proceed upon the ground, that the poor are *to blame*, somehow or other for their poverty; and that the measure to be adopted ought to be of a *corrective* kind. They ascribe the increase of the poor-rates to the *idleness*, the *drunkenness*, the some fault or other of the poor. They, therefore, set to work to *match them*; to be *up with them*; to *out-wit them*."

In Adorno's America, the prevailing opinion concerning the poor seemed to be that "most people get pretty much what they deserve". God helps those who help themselves, and the able will always succeed in life; those who fall by the wayside are not worthy of sympathy, as they clearly do not possess the attributes requisite for success.[61] It was an obsessively competitive point of view; but not an original one. Here is Joseph Townsend, writing 164 years earlier.

"If a new and equal division of property were made in England, we cannot doubt that the same inequality which we now observe would soon take place again; the improvident, the lazy, and the vicious, would dissipate their substance; the prudent, the active, and the virtuous, would again increase their wealth."[62]

Here is a good example of the cynical view of human nature being used to account for poverty; here also is the "pseudoscientific, hereditarian" explanation of the hardships suffered by the down-trodden, which the Adorno team judged typical of the prejudiced personality.

By 1830, the genetic explanation of poverty had become "the fashion", as working people in general, and the agricultural labourers in particular, came to be regarded as an "inferior race", and treated as such.[63]

59 Ibid. P. 699.
60 William Cobbett. Political Register. 24/2/1821 and 2/ 11/ 1816.
61 T. W. Adorno. The Authoritarian Personality. Pp. 630, 621, 626 and 155. William Cobbett. Political Register. 11/9/1819.
62 Joseph Townsend. A Dissertation on the Poor Laws. California ed. 1971. P. 40.
63 William Cobbett. Political Register. 25/12/1830.

"It is curious, too, that this contumely towards the great mass of the people should have grown into vogue amongst the Country Gentlemen and their families, at a time when they are daily and hourly losing the estates descended to them from their forefathers. They see themselves stript of the means of keeping the hospitality for which England was once so famed, and of which there remains nothing now but the *word* in the dictionary; they see themselves reduced to close up their windows, live in a corner of their houses, sneak away to London, crib their servants in their wages, and hardly able to keep up a little tawdry show; and it would seem, that, for the contempt which they feel their meanness must necessarily excite in the common people, they endeavour to avenge themselves, and at the same time to disguise their own humiliation, by their haughty and insolent deportment towards the latter....They have been blinded by their foolish pride; that pride, which has nothing of mind belonging to it, and which, accompanied with a consciousness of a want of any natural superiority over the Labouring Classes, seeks to indulge itself in a species of vindictive exercise of power. There has come into the heads of these people, I cannot very well tell how, a notion that it is proper to consider the Labouring Classes as a *distinct cast*...."

"With what indignation must you hear yourselves called the Populace, the Rabble, the Mob, the Swinish Multitude....You have been represented by the *Times* newspaper....and others, as the *Scum* of society."[64]

We have seen time and again in this study the labouring poor stereotyped, and their poverty accounted for in terms of the stereotype, as idle, drunken, vice-ridden, worthless, abandoned, depraved, debauched, profligate, improvident, criminal. Of such contemptible people as these the anti-democratic personality had a profound fear, which on the face of it appears paradoxical. His own weakness produces feelings of vulnerability and victimisation, which in turn provoke extremely violent impulses. He therefore imagines that groups who are weak and down-trodden feel the same way. Here is Cobbett on the fear produced in the ruling classes of his day by the passing of the repressive measures of 1817.

"They are very great fools; but, they see, that *something is wrong*....They have triggered themselves up, perhaps, with the help of the bottle, and have, from time to time, said in their foolish hearts; 'We will stick to it! We will subdue them, d—n them, or we will kill them!' But, ever and anon, the misgiving fit would return. They could not help, now and then, looking at their mansions, their gardens, their parks, their woods and lakes and lawns, with a little less confidence of secure possession than formerly....They must have *felt*, that there was something to be decided between them and the people."

The boroughmongers, wrote Cobbett, appeared never to sleep. They looked as if they saw curses in all the features of the people. And their actions plainly indicated a desire "to rip out our hearts to get at our thoughts.

"What a life to lead! To walk about, conscious that the air which encircles them, and that which they breathe, is charged with the execrations of the people!"

To the prejudiced personality, therefore, weakness constitutes a danger; and he is thus led to advocate discriminatory measures against such groups, in order to isolate them in society and prevent contacts with other groups; and in order to maintain the dominant political and social position of the in-group of which he aspires to be a member. Such discriminatory measures, says Adorno, might include segregation and cultural suppression.[65]

Indeed, in 18th century England, they did. Bit by bit, the landed classes, and those who would emulate them, withdrew from all contacts with tenants, neighbours, and social inferiors in general;

---

64 William Cobbett. Political Register. 5/4/1817 and 2/11/1816.
65 T. W. Adorno. The Authoritarian Personality. Pp. 803 and 100. William Cobbett. Political Register 23/5/1818 and 11/ 4/ 1818.

and increasingly tried to enforce a social separation. In earlier times, landowners had taken a close interest in the affairs of their estates and their localities. Some still did in the 18th century. The Duke of Grafton dealt personally with his tenants, and on occasion visited every house on his estate. Coke of Norfolk, Robert Bakewell wrote, "receives his own rents and himself hears the complaint of all his tenants; in short, he is like a prince of the best kind amongst them, being loved by many and feared by few." These were now the relics of a bygone age.[66] Cobbett addressed the Nobility of England, on the new circumstances in which they found themselves.

"You are great men....But, you have, at last, found something to shake you. You are not the men that even your grandfathers were, and nothing at all like the men that your ancestors were four hundred years ago. In your carriage towards the common people, you are loftier than your ancestors. You are not insolent and rude like the upstart jobbers and loanmongers; but, those *halls* in which your forefathers used to sit at the head of their tenantry, are now objects of wonder at what they were used for. The communication between you (even the most gracious and condescending of you) and those who till your lands has been growing more and more slender; until, at last, it has been completely cut off by the intervention of attorneys, stewards, land-agents and surveyors. It is, I confess it with pleasure, a compliment to your minds, that the hard things which have to be done to those beneath you, are such that you cannot bring yourselves to do in person. *You know nothing of the matter*, when a hard thing is to be done; you leave it all to your steward or whatever other name he may bear; but, the thing is not less hard for that; and the sufferer fails not to trace the hardship to its source."[67]

Landlords now spent most of their time away from their estates, and abandoned their traditional duties of charity and local government. On the rare occasions when they were at home, they remained hidden away in splendid isolation, and shunned the local events at which their forebears had presided. Houses were re-organised to keep the families segregated from their servants, tenants and neighbours. Those who came on business were received in the steward's rooms and tenants' halls, instead of by the owner himself. What hospitality was still provided took place in the servants' quarters instead of the great hall. Back stairways were installed for the lower orders, and kitchens and offices removed to out-of-the-way locations. The fashion for forbidding the children to mix with the servants, complained William Godwin, taught "a lesson of the most insufferable insolence and magisterial aristocracy." Outside the house, parks provided a landscape entirely free from domestic or agricultural activity of any sort; and to achieve this, on occasion, whole villages were moved, or, one suspects, simply destroyed. The Earl of Orford relocated a village near Chippenham; Sir Robert Walpole did the same at Houghton in Norfolk.[68] In Dorset, the whole village of Milton Abbas was flattened and re-sited; and all to free the mansion from the taint of proximity to agricultural people!

When members of the elite were in London, or at their various pleasures elsewhere, an even stricter regime of separation was enforced. In London, continuous development resulted in residential segregation, as landed families were isolated form the general population in exclusive areas. Even in public places, there was no mingling. Gentle families would travel in curtained coaches; at the theatre or the opera, they would hire their own personal boxes; in church, they had private pews; and at the races, grandstands were erected in order to keep the upper orders out of the sight of the lower ones.[69] The Duke of Somerset actually employed retainers to clear the roads before he passed along them, in order that he should not be seen by the common people. The Earl of Lincoln went further still;

---

66 James M. Rosenheim. The Emergence of a Ruling Order. Passim. G. E. Mingay. English Landed Society in the Eighteenth Century. P. 188.

67 William Cobbett. Political Register. 13/1/1827.

68 James M. Rosenheim. The Emergence of a Ruling Order. Pp. 12, 96, 187 and 192. William Godwin. The Enquirer. P. 203.

69 James M. Rosenheim. The Emergence of a Ruling Order. Pp. 216, 247 and 184.

he had a servant beat an apprentice to death, for staring at him as he went by.[70] These being two of a number of scattered pieces of evidence suggesting a culture of vicarious violence existing among the ruling classes.

In 20th century America, the Adorno team interviewed subjects who held the view that Jews ought to assimilate themselves into mainstream society, and drop their "foreign" ways. Unless they abandoned their cultural identity, it was perfectly natural that they should suffer exclusion and restriction. In the England of the 18th and 19th centuries, determined and successful efforts were made by the ruling classes to stamp out the culture of the English agricultural communities.

The prejudice of the ruling elite, and those who thought like them, extended from the agricultural poor to the English nation as a whole. In post-war America, Adorno observed that those who displayed a patriotic attitude towards their own country in relation to others, actually saw the majority of Americans as belonging to one of a number of out-groups; members of religious and racial minorities, criminals, radical thinkers, and the mass of the people in general, were all stereotyped and vilified.[71] This whole issue of pseudo-patriotism was well discussed by Dr. Richard Price, in his Discourse of the Love of our Country, published in 1789. Cobbett himself noticed this anti-English feeling among the ruling classes.

"Here are two facts; the first, that the ministry are using all the means in their power; that they even have the desperate project of mortgaging the land and houses of the whole country, in order to raise money to get the labourers away from it; and we have the other fact, that the English labourers are so scarce that the English harvests cannot be got in, in good time and in good order, without the assistance of labourers from Ireland.....All manner of creatures that are wasters of the public money are received, encouraged, fostered and caressed, come from what country they will. The Flemish women swarm over England. I have seen them in Lincolnshire, in Somersetshire, in Kent; and not only in the great towns, but even in the villages and hamlets, straddling about in a sort of half-masculine dress, fat as hogs. To these, we may add an enormous number of Italians and Jews, who are also to be seen in the very villages. In every nobleman's and gentleman's house there is some one or more Swiss or outlandish devil. The nobility themselves, the far greater part of them make it their boast that they are descended from the Normans. Even the bloated up loan-mongers, the BARINGS, *boast*, in their pedigree, that their origin is Dutch. So the country people in England really appear to be the only natives that are in it, and according to the notions that are afloat amongst those who rule us, they appear to be the only people that have no right to be in it."[72]

This anti-English prejudice permeated right up to the very seat of power. Here are the observations of Sir Francis Burdett, M. P.

"So far from the House of Commons representing the sense of the people of England, I have ever found, since I have been a member of the House of Commons, that the most popular sentiment which can be expressed in that place, is a sentiment of contempt for the people of England, whose representatives they still profess to be.....There they are calumniated, there the characters of Englishmen are lightly spoken of, and their feelings and opinions set at nought."[73]

The members of the new elite, therefore, branded the ancient vernacular customs and the notions of community of the traditional English as the leftovers of barbarism. Rural sports and entertainments were proceeded against by the authorities as public nuisances. Dancing on the village green was suppressed. "The sound of the fiddle calls forth the magistrate to dissolve the meeting", as William Windham uncharacteristically observed in Parliament; and the success of this campaign is evidenced

---

70 G. E. Mingay. English Landed Society in the Eighteenth Century. P. 286.
71 T. W. Adorno. The Authoritarian Personality. P. 148.
72 William Cobbett. Political Register. 11/6/1831.
73 Sir Francis Burdett's speech at Westminster 30/3/1809 quoted in Political Register 30/5/1829.

by the almost complete disappearance of traditional English music, and its replacement by music based on imported influences. Throughout the 18th century, and into the 19th, magistrates the country over waged a campaign against the holding of village wakes. Traditional popular knowledge, beliefs and customs all came to be ridiculed as superstition and "vulgar errors".[74]

By contrast, the landed classes cultivated continental tastes; in *cuisine*, apparel, art, architecture, *décor*, etc. etc., and rejected everything native, or vulgar, as they chose to style it. The historian of these changes puts a positive spin upon the process, by saying that rusticity gave way to cosmopolitan urbanity. But one might equally well say that the accumulated and hereditary wisdom of countless centuries was suppressed in favour of the orthodoxies and prejudices of the new elite.

But segregation and cultural liquidation were not enough. At base, prejudice is a manifestation of repressed aggression, so it would be surprising if some holders of prejudiced opinions did not go on to advocate sterner measures still. The Adorno team found that the more extreme anti-democratic subjects quite openly wished for violence against Jews, with a view to their "total liquidation or permanent suppression or restriction".[75] The anti-democratic bible of the later 18th century was Edmund Burke's Appeal from the New to the Old Whigs. Underlying much of this defence of what was misleadingly portrayed as the existing order lay a sinister tone of menace towards the common people.

"When you separate the common sort of men from their proper chieftains, so as to form them into an adverse army – I no longer know that venerable object called the 'people' in such a disbanded race of deserters and vagabonds. For a while they may be terrible, indeed – but in such a manner as wild beasts are terrible. The mind owes to them no sort of submission. They are, as they have always been reputed, rebels. They may lawfully be fought with, and brought under, whenever an advantage offers. Those who attempt by outrage and violence to deprive men of any advantage which they hold under the laws, and to destroy the natural order of life, proclaim war against them."

Burke went on to justify the cruel vengeance inflicted upon participants in the insurrection of the French people called the *Jacquerie*.

"The people are not to be taught to think lightly of their engagements to their governors, else they teach governors to think lightly of their engagements toward them. In that kind of game, in the end, the people are sure to be the losers."[76]

This was written in an age of increasing official violence against the populace. The use of the military against food rioters was illegal and unconstitutional; but we have noticed the intensifying pressure placed upon the local authorities from the 1760s onwards to use military force as a preferred option in case of disturbances; until by the 1790s, we find a Home Secretary with an almost manic and obsessive wish to make war on the people.

In America, the Adorno team alluded to a "fantastic disproportion between Jewish guilt – even as conceived by the anti-Semite himself – and the judgment pronounced." No matter how trivial, or unfounded, the accusations made against the out-group, the extreme anti-democrat has no difficulty in passing the severest sentence.[77] Many years previously, this tendency did not escape William Cobbett.

"Even a lazy man….is not to be punished in a degree beyond that of the nature of the crime. To be deemed a pauper, to be put into a poor-house, to have his pittance doled out to him reluctantly;

74 James M. Rosenheim. The Emergence of a Ruling Order. Pp. 198-211. J. L. and B. Hammond. The Village Labourer. Pp. 199-200.
75 T. W. Adorno. The Authoritarian Personality. P. 97.
76 Edmund Burke. An Appeal from the New to the Old Whigs. Pp. 105-106 and 93.
77 T. W. Adorno. The Authoritarian Personality. P. 632.

these constitute a pretty heavy punishment; a man is not to be *starved*; that is to say, he is not to be *put to death* for being lazy or drunken.[78]

According to the Adorno team, nobody in their right mind would suggest that "somebody who is bad-mannered or even a cheat should be punished by death". But the more extreme of Adorno's subjects simply could not help themselves.[79]

In 1772, Stephen Addington noted a similar tendency.

"Some indeed say, 'Let the farmers starve, they are a selfish set of people that would starve the country'. But outcries against whole bodies of people, are generally rash and unreasonable; they frequently betray want of judgment, or want of candour, and, very often, apparently both….If they do not part with their money in general as freely as many principal tradesmen and manufacturers do….it is far from being a proper method of teaching these people generosity, to deprive them of the means of subsistence."[80]

In Addington's time, the starvation of the poor was still not a respectable political objective to express openly. But, according to Adorno, over a period of time, such views can acquire a respectability. If extreme anti-poor sentiments are presented as no longer beyond the pale, but as a reasonable and legitimate subject for discussion, then the conscience can be by-passed. If such statements emanate from a respected and authoritative source, the anti-democratic subject will take them over without question.[81] This function was performed largely by Malthus.

Here is what Malthus had to say about the man who married, with no prospect, other than that of parish relief, of supporting the resulting family; that is to say, the great majority of the labouring poor.

"When nature will govern and punish for us, it is a very miserable ambition to wish to snatch the rod from her hands, and draw upon ourselves the odium of executioner. To the punishment, therefore, of nature he should be left, the punishment of severe want. He has erred in the face of a most clear and precise warning, and can have no just reason to complain of any person but himself when he feels the consequences of his error. All parish assistance should be most rigidly denied him; and if the hand of private charity be stretched forth in his relief, the interests of humanity imperiously require that it should be administered very sparingly. He should be taught to know that the laws of nature, which are the laws of God, had doomed him and his family to starve for disobeying their repeated admonitions; that he had no claim of right on society for the smallest portion of food, beyond that which his labour would fairly purchase….

"If this system were pursued, we need be under no apprehensions whatever that the number of persons in extreme want would be beyond the power and the will of the benevolent to supply. The sphere for the exercise of private charity would, I am confident, be less than it is at present." (!!)[82]

With Malthus, starvation became acceptable. Indeed, with the passing of the new Poor Law in 1834, it became an official instrument of economic policy, supported by many of the officials of government, and presented to the poor as the alternative to emigration or the workhouse.

If Adorno's conclusions are applicable to the England of the 1830s, one must assume that many people were prepared to acquiesce in the policy of starving the poor.

"Those who humiliate mentally those who are down-trodden anyway, are more than likely to react the same way when an out-group is being 'liquidated'."

---

78 William Cobbett. The Political Register. 14/7/1832.
79 T. W. Adorno. The Authoritarian Personality. P. 633.
80 Stephen Addington. An Inquiry into the Reasons for and against Inclosing Open-Fields. P.32.
81 T. W. Adorno. The Authoritarian Personality. P. 607.
82 T. R. Malthus. An Essay on the Principle of Population. 1803 ed. P. James ed. Vol. II. Pp.140-141.

And Adorno associates this accepting mentality with the sociological determinants of upward social mobility, an identification with, and aspiration to belong to, a higher social class, a competitive mindset, and a fear of the impoverished masses.[83]

Back in 1770, Arthur Young had suggested that the best solution to the problem of the poor lay in lining them up in front of the guns of an enemy.[84] Ultimately, of course, it was done.

❊

The political views of Adorno's anti-democratic subject amounted to no more than a system of thought, which arose out of his upbringing. The social dichotomy presented to him by the power structure of his family life spilled over into his political thinking, which consisted of a rigid categorisation into strong and weak, or, what to him was the same thing, good and evil. Politics is a struggle for power between the rich and powerful in-group of which he aspires to be a member, and one or a number of out-groups. He assumes competition and conflict. He assumes that the out-group has a self-seeking exploitative and materialistic agenda of its own, which it intends to enforce by taking over the reins of government. He assumes this projectively; because those are precisely the characteristics of his own in-group.[85]

The anti-democrat wishes to preserve the existing distribution of wealth. In that sense, he might be seen as a conservative. To that end, power must be confined and concentrated in the wealthy in-group with which he identifies. It must reside "in the right hands".[86] Here is Edmund Burke's largely fictional description of the aristocratic in-group which, in his opinion, ought to hold sway in England.

"A true natural aristocracy is not a separate interest in the state, or separable from it. It is an essential integrant part of any large body rightly constituted. It is formed out of a class of legitimate presumptions, which, taken as generalities, must be admitted for actual truths. To be bred in a place of estimation; to see nothing low and sordid from one's infancy; to be taught to respect one's self; to be habituated to the censorial inspection of the public eye; to look early to public opinion; to stand upon such elevated ground as to be enabled to take a large view of the widespread and infinitely diversified combinations of men and affairs in a large society; to have leisure to read, to reflect, to converse: to be enabled to draw the court and attention of the wise and learned, wherever they are to be found…. these are the circumstances of men that form what I should call a 'natural' aristocracy, without which there is no nation….Men, qualified in the manner I have just described, form in Nature….the leading, guiding and governing part. It is the soul to the body, without which the man does not exist. To give, therefore, no more importance, in the social order, to such descriptions of men than that of so many units is a horrible usurpation."[87]

In America, Adorno's anti-democratic subject also wished to maintain the existing power-structures. He professed agreement with the many conservative American political slogans, and voted for candidates who spoke up for traditional democratic values in government. But the methods which he advocated for confining power to the dominant in-group actually involved massive political change; and would actually have destroyed many of the institutions which he professed to value. Such a mentality Adorno labelled pseudoconservative; and he thus drew a distinction between the pseudoconservative and the genuine conservative.

---

83 T. W. Adorno. The Authoritarian Personality. P. 700.

84 Quoted in K. D. M. Snell. Annals of the Labouring Poor. P. 111.

85 T. W. Adorno. The Authoritarian Personality. Pp. 51, 46-47 and 149.

86 Ibid. P. 47.

87 Edmund Burke. An Appeal from the New to the Old Whigs. Pp. 104-105.

The aim of the pseudoconservative was to establish a dictatorship of the economically strongest group. He favoured an ever greater concentration of power into fewer and fewer hands. He wished for a strong leader, with absolute authority, with a small and select council of ministers and advisers.

The dependence implicit in the pseudoconservative's mindset enabled him, on the surface at least, to look up and submit to an authority of this type. His repressed hostility to such authority he displaced against excluded groups. These, he thought, should be segregated and suppressed, and their traditional legal and constitutional rights suspended by the dominant power. The ideal aimed at was a hierarchy of power in a rigidly stratified society, in which numerous forms of discrimination would prevent social mobility. In the last resort, power should reside in a combination of politicians and the greater capitalists. All this he clearly wished for, whilst at the same time paying lip-service to free enterprise, social mobility and traditional democratic values.[88]

The genuine conservative and patriot was the man who displayed a serious wish to preserve all that was best in the American tradition. Here is what Adorno had to say about him.

"'Genuine' conservatives….may develop an increasingly bad conscience because they become aware of the rapid development of important conservative layers of American society into the direction of labor baiting and race hatred. The more this tendency increases the more the 'genuine' conservative seems to feel compelled to profess democratic ideals, even if they are somewhat incompatible with his own upbringing and psychological patterns."[89]

This, of course, was an uncannily accurate description of William Cobbett; who, himself, was only too well aware of the distinction between the genuine conservative and the pseudoconservative.

"The things we pray for are called *innovations*….But….we propose *no innovations*. We propose *annual parliaments*, and that every man *who pays taxes* shall have a vote choosing those *who lay the taxes on us*; and we are ready to prove that these are not *new*, but very old indeed.

"But, for argument's sake, if we did propose an innovation, I should be glad to know what objection that would be to us, supposing the proposition to be *good in itself*? Is every thing to go on undergoing changes except such changes as may favour the people of England? To hear this objection, especially in the House of Commons, one would imagine, that our laws had never been changed since the island was first settled by a civilized people. Far different however is the fact….."[90]

During the time that power was held in England by men who claimed to be upholding the laws and defending the constitution, and whom historians in general have labelled reactionary, the nature of those laws and the complexion of that constitution were altered almost beyond recognition. Cobbett mentioned the numerous regulations relating to printers, printing-presses, newspapers and pamphlets; Special Juries nominated by the master of the Crown Office: the novel powers recently granted to the Attorney-General; the prosecution of libels that were true; the Game Laws; the Excise Laws; all the laws necessitated by the paper currency, the national debt and the funds; Police Justices; and the stoppage of cash payments at the Bank of England.

"Are not the absolute-power-of imprisonment Act, the gagging Act, the Soldier's Act, the New Treason Act, *something new in England*?...Is it not *something new in England* to see judges guarded by dragoons? To see the prisoners brought to court by a standing army in time of Peace? Is not the employment of hired Spies and informers, to bring men to the block, *something new in England*?"[91]

Cobbett addressed George Canning in 1820.

"You talk about '*the constitution*' as if nothing had been done to it during the last thirty years. You know, that we may now be ruined and banished, and even hanged, for doing things which we

88 T. W. Adorno. The Authoritarian Personality. Pp. 44-50, 100, 182-185, 600and 676-686.
89 Ibid. Pp. 182 and 684.
90 William Cobbett. Political Register. 15/12/1817.
91 William Cobbett. Political Register. 30/5/1818.

might *lawfully* have done only a very few years ago; and yet you will have 'no *innovation*'. Whatever has been done in this way you do not call '*innovation*'. According to you, nothing is innovation, except what it is wished to have done for the relief and protection of the people."

Even where laws were not altered to favour the governing classes at the expence of the people, existing laws could nevertheless be serially ignored, and the constitution by-passed with impunity, by those who claimed to be their defenders.

"Were spies appointed by law? Was Napoleon, a prisoner of war, transported for life according to *law*? Was it law that authorised Lord Castlereagh and his associates to *sell seats* in the House of Commons?"[92]

Back in the twentieth century, the Adorno team made the observation that fascist movements, in general, employ traditional ideas and values, but for public consumption only. Ideas of conservatism, as well as of liberalism, can be turned on their head, and used as a smokescreen to hide much more sinister intentions. The violently aggressive and destructive traits in the fascist personality manifest themselves politically as a demand for repressive measures against the people.

"The pseudoconservative is a man who, in the name of upholding traditional American values and institutions and defending them against more or less fictional dangers, consciously or unconsciously aims at their abolition."[93]

William Henry Cavendish Bentinck, third Duke of Portland, was a classic exhibitor of the anti-democratic mindset. He was descended from the William Bentinck who was a close associate of William of Orange, with whom he came over to England in 1688. Bentinck became the new king's most favoured counsellor, receiving massive grants of land, as well as the earldom of Portland. This did not earn him the favour of the English aristocracy. It was not just the confidence which the Dutch king placed in his compatriot that aroused their hatred; Bentinck displayed a great and unsavoury acquisitiveness.

"In England, Portland was, during the whole of William's reign, probably the most unpopular man in the country."[94]

His descendant, the third Duke, attended Westminster public school, Christ Church Oxford, and went on the grand tour. Still, he was not entirely integrated with the English aristocracy. He kept in touch with his Dutch relatives; but made enemies of some of the leading English politicians of the day, such as the Earl of Bute and the Duke of Grafton; as well as traditional gentry families such as the Lowthers. Financially, there was a yawning chasm between him and some of the greater aristocrats. The Duke of Devonshire and the Marquis of Rockingham each had an income over £40,000 a year. Portland's income was a mere £17,000 in 1785. He possessed the title of a duke, but not the means to live up to it. He received but a modest income from the estates inherited from his father, and was not allowed into his full inheritance until the death of his mother. A poor manager of his finances, he lent unadvisedly, and lived in a state of constant financial crisis.[95]

In spite of all this, or perhaps, rather, because of it, he aimed to cement his place in society through conspicuous consumption. The idea that circumstances were compelling him to economise was one which he would not have wished his fellow aristocrats to entertain; so he spent lavishly. Between 1775

---

92 Ibid. 8/4/1820.

93 T. W. Adorno. The Authoritarian Personality. Pp. 682 and 676.

94 Dictionary of National Biography. William Bentinck.

95 D. Wilkinson. The Duke of Portland. Pp. 1 and 60-61. Dictionary of National Biography. William Bentinck, third Duke of Portland.

and 1779 he laid out £2,000 on pleasure grounds, £10,000 on repairs and alterations to houses, and £12,900 on stables and kennels; he created parkland and planted trees around Welbeck Abbey; and attempted to establish a reputation for fine tastes through his expertise in art.

In an attempt to cover all this expence, he resorted to the usual twin expedients of ambitious aristocrats – agricultural reorganisation and government office. He enclosed 1,800 acres around Welbeck, and 2,400 more in Sherwood Forest. As Home Secretary up until 1801, he received a salary of £6,000 a year, which allowed him to increase his expenditure again. Despite all, in 1809, the year of his death, he was in debt to the tune of £520,000![96]

The respect paid to Portland by the Whig aristocracy he owed to his ability to get chosen men nominated to Parliament. He was at the head, in other words, of an extensive network of corruption. At the same time, he harped upon the virtues of the aristocratic Whigs.

"Our character is essential to, and is even the soul of our existence as a party, and is inseparable from us, as well in a private as in a public view."[97]

And yet, while in the political wilderness during the 1780s, he complained of the corruption of Pitt and his financier backers, which kept him and his associates out of power. The dichotomy of power between in-group and out-group, the projective vilification, and the feelings of victimisation and persecution inherent in the anti-democratic personality are all here.

"The characteristic feature of the present reign has been its uniform and almost unremitting attention and study to debase and vilify the natural aristocracy of the country, and under the proper pretence of abolishing all party distinctions, to annihilate if possible, the Whig party. For these express purposes the present ministry was formed....they have most religiously adhered to and exemplarily fulfilled the purpose of their creation."[98]

But when, in the 1790s, Pitt needed the support of Portland's Whigs in the face of the upsurge of agitation about the poverty of the people and the abuses of government, Portland showed little compunction about uniting with the wealthy and powerful financial interest, and against the people. Portland was a violent anti-populist. In earlier years, he had condemned the radical politicians for lack of character, lack of breeding, and lack of any reputation which they might be ashamed of losing. By 1792, on the brink of government office, his tone had become loftier still.[99]

"The idea of *courting* popularity by any means I have always reprobated; the possession or enjoyment of it has always something in it very suspicious, and I hardly know any act or measure *vulgarly or commonly called* popular which has not originated in a bad cause, and been productive of pernicious effects."[100]

The main principle of Whiggism, he asserted, was "attachment to the present form of our government to all its establishments and orders, religious and civil." He absurdly supposed some danger to exist to the constitution, which could be removed by the war against France. In 1793, he declared that he "should give his firm support to a war, the object of which was to resist doctrines that....went to the overthrow, not merely of all legitimate government, of the security of nations, of peace and order, but even of religion itself, and of every thing for which society was instituted."[101]

But as Home Secretary, as we have seen, he supported, pressed for, and implemented various repressive measures suspending both liberty and constitution; and was the perpetrator of the grossest illegalities. He allowed the illegal deployment of Hessian mercenaries in England. He obtained, under

96 D. Wilkinson. The Duke of Portland. Pp. 60-64.
97 Ibid. Pp. 22-26.
98 Ibid. P. 102.
99 Ibid. P. 31.
100 Ibid. Introduction P. ix.
101 Ibid. Pp. 102 and 99.

false pretences, money from the Treasury for the purpose of corrupting the Irish Parliament in 1799, in defiance of the law. He supported the illegal monopolisation of grain in the hands of the great corn-dealers, and condemned traditional open marketing for "locking up or diverting into another channel that capital which is….beneficially employed in the improvement of land." By which he meant that the popular opposition to the price-fixing mechanisms of the corn trade posed a threat to the increasing of rents through consolidating and enclosing, which were necessary to support the ducal lifestyle, which Portland could not afford. And to counter this popular opposition, he not only sent the army out against the starving, but also put massive pressure on local authorities to do the same, in contravention both of custom and law. He encouraged his commanders to by-pass the Riot Act; and promised them indemnity for their illegal acts, without consulting Parliament.[102]

Here was Adorno's pseudoconservative.

There was one massive and glaring difference between Adorno's anti-Semites and the promoters of and subscribers to anti-poor and anti-English sentiment in England in the 18th and 19th centuries. However unfair the treatment of Jews may have been in post-war America, they were not systematically deprived of their substance and their subsistence in order to support the ever-increasing material wants of a competitive governing elite. In England, the worsening poverty of the masses, as we have seen, was what formed the basis of the great prosperity of the financial system, the massive extravagances of crown and state, the patronage that bought influence, the wealth of the great speculators, the profits of commerce and of large-scale industry, and the luxurious lifestyle of the governing classes of all types. In England, the in-group lived upon the out-group; and vilified its members in order to justify this parasitism not only to the world, but to themselves; and to facilitate the placing of ever-increasing pressure upon them. In the age of the enclosing and consolidating of farms, it was the traditional farmers, the dispossessed victims of the new agriculture, who formed the object of such vilification. Here is Arthur Young, attempting "to obviate the torrent of ridicule the new improvements in husbandry let loose against them."

"The conversation in any company seldom turns on country business, but the common farmers are stigmatised with the appellations of *stupid fellows, prejudiced clowns, senseless men*, who tread in the steps of their forefathers without the idea of improvement, who drudge on in the old road, rather like machines than rational animals. Much declamation have I heard of this sort….not always so justly founded as peremptorily asserted."[103]

Young was very far from guiltless of what he himself was complaining about; and this passage was omitted from subsequent editions.

In later years, William Cobbett at one time equated the out-group with all those who laboured. He noted the derogatory use made of the word 'populace'.

"It means, then, as far as I can gather from the use I see made of it, all that part of the people who are obliged to work for their bread; who, in the words of the Bible, live by the sweat of their brow."[104]

At another time, he identified the out-group as all those who paid taxes. The "Lower Orders", he asserted, was an insulting epithet used by the tyrants to describe "all those who pay the taxes out of the fruit of their labour."[105]

---

102 Ibid. Pp. 151 and 123.
103 Arthur Young. Farmers' Letters. 1767 ed. Pp. 256-257.
104 William Cobbett. Political Register. 23/5/1812.
105 Ibid. 26/9/1818.

In America, anti-Semitism never became government policy. In England, the anti-democratic mindset seeped into government, slowly but inexorably, as the financial demands of the competitive elite increased, over a period of a century.

To begin with, the representative elements of the constitution were diluted, by-passed, or abolished. Government officials were placed in the House of Commons; the Septennial Act was passed; and the Commons controlled through a policy of wholesale corruption.

This facilitated the promotion in Parliament of sectional financial interests. The paternalistic governments of previous years had passed measures to prevent enclosure; had vigorously protected the legal rights of small farmers of all types; and had been the doughty defenders of open marketing, with laws against engrossing, regrating and forestalling. The 18ᵗʰ century, however, saw a fast-flowing stream of measures that favoured the financial prosperity of commerce, banking and aristocracy, at the expence of the well-being of the ordinary people. Bit by bit, the tax burden was taken from the landed aristocracy and placed upon the consumer. Hundreds of enclosure acts were passed without any consideration of their justice or their consequences. The marketing laws were repealed in 1772. Food rioters were confronted by the military. Numerous wars were fought, pointlessly and unjustifiably, but to the enormous profit of those connected with government. Taxes rose inexorably, and enriched financiers, and sinecurists, and pensioners, at the expence of the people. All of these measures were accompanied, as we have seen, by a large body of justificatory literature, generally written by people either connected with government, or else hoping to curry favour with the governing classes; but written, nevertheless, largely spontaneously. There was also a smaller but significant body of literature written against all such partial measures.

The anti-populist mindset first becomes obvious in government during the 1760s, with the government of the King's Friends. It is eclipsed for a while, and resurfaces with the anti-reform ministry of Lord North. North's government was the first to engage in directly sponsored campaigns of propaganda, but on a very modest scale compared with what came later. During the 1780s, anti-populism was in remission again, but resided in the Church of England, particularly the High Church circle based on Bishop Horne of Norwich; in the legal profession; and in the network of friendship and influence connected with the Earl of Bute and Lord Mansfield. The anti-democratic, pseudoconservative mindset then exploded on to the government scene, with the establishment of the "Pitt system" during the 1790s – "the Thing", as elaborated by William Cobbett.

According to the Adorno team, the use made by governments of anti-democratic propaganda, and the suppression of opposing ideologies, depend "primarily upon the situation of the most powerful economic interests, upon whether they, by conscious design or not, make use of this device for maintaining their dominant status."[106]

All the dominant financial interests in England had reason to feel insecure at the start of the 1790s. A huge amount of popular agitation was taking place, having, as its underlying cause, the worsening poverty of the people, and the very many ways in which this was seen as connected with the abuses of government. This was triggered by the French Revolution, and more directly by the writings of Thomas Paine. Edmund Burke, writing his Reflections in 1790, warned of the dangers posed to established government by a powerful and discontented monied interest.

The consequence was a re-alignment of the powerful forces of the state. The entry into government of the Portland Whigs, which took place between 1792 and 1794, represented the union of Pitt's financial backers with the traditional aristocracy, in a coalition formed against the people. As a signal of the change, Burke was prevailed upon to alter his position yet again. The Appeal from the New to the Old Whigs contained not a single reference to the monied men; merely maintained the rights and privileges of a leisured aristocracy in contradistinction to the toiling multitude.

---

106 T. W. Adorno. The Authoritarian Personality. P. 7.

"Very curious, too; but, quite natural, when one reflects, in proportion as the nobility and gentry have thus debased themselves before the money-monster, they have become haughty and severe towards the common people; and have treated them with a degree of scorn and of insolence which they never experienced from their forefathers."[107]

The resulting government held out no prospect whatever of any improvement in the conditions of life for the population at large. On the contrary, a new war had already begun; the financiers were allowed a free rein; taxes were on the rise again; patronage, corruption and sinecurism were running rampant; and wealthy speculators in corn were become the cherished favourites of the state. A feeding frenzy was in prospect for all those connected with government; the wealthy and powerful in-group was poised to prosper at the expence of the despised and the outcast. To enforce all this, the political liberties of the citizen were progressively suspended on the pretext of fictional dangers; and a military system put into place the country over.

The problem facing an anti-democratic government such as this was well described by Adorno, many years later.

"Fascism, in order to be successful as a political movement, must have a mass basis. It must secure not only the frightened submission but the active cooperation of the great majority of the people. Since by its very nature it favours the few at the expense of the many, it cannot possibly demonstrate that it will so improve the situation of most people that their real interests will be served. It must therefore make its major appeal, not to rational self-interest, but to emotional needs – often to the most primitive and irrational wishes and fears."[108]

Propaganda, or spin, is a necessary concomitant of all anti-democratic governments – of all those which intend to rule in the interest of a confined in-group at the expence of the population at large; almost, indeed, a defining characteristic. The union of Boyd and Benfield with Portland and Burke triggered a massive pumping into circulation of literature sponsored directly by the state, on a scale vastly greater than anything before experienced. Adorno identified some of the arguments used by his anti-democratic interviewees to justify the most glaring injustices in society.

In the course of his researches, Adorno encountered the "everything is fine" mentality – the "keep smiling" attitude which he connects with an underlying cynicism about human nature. The American system "works well", and the way to deal with social injustice is simply to ignore it.[109]

Then, he came across subjects who rationalised social problems by attempting to depict them as "natural" phenomena – unavoidable and irremediable. Economic depressions, for example, "are like occasional headaches and stomach aches; it's natural for even the healthiest society to have them once in a while." "This both exonerates society and helps to establish the idea of unchangeability on which the denunciation of utopia feeds."[110]

The next stage is victim-blaming; and we have already seen how Adorno's interviewees held Jews responsible for their own misfortunes by refusing to conform to mainstream culture; how negroes brought their troubles upon themselves by demanding equal rights; and how the poor were seen as genetically lacking in the talents necessary for success in the world.[111]

Finally, there was the "shoot the messenger" syndrome. All the faults of society are laid at the door of those who criticise. Adorno interviewed a man who thought as follows.

---

107 William Cobbett. Political Register. 14/2/1835.

108 T. W. Adorno. The Authoritarian Personality. P. 10. One might take issue here with the use of the word primitive, since the syndrome is the result of complex changes in a highly artificial society.

109 Ibid. Pp. 696 and 153.

110 Ibid. Pp. 696 and 154.

111 Ibid. Pp. 630 and 621.

"There is nothing wrong with our American system. It is as good as it ever was, but we must do all we can....to get rid of the charlatans, fakers and agitators who are responsible for so many problems." By these, he meant liberal politicians and those who spoke up for labour.[112]

All of these lines of reasoning the reader will no doubt recognise from the masses of propaganda pumped out during the 1790s and afterwards. Adorno has given us here, for example, an accurate *resume* of the works of Malthus. And the charlatans, fakers and agitators are surely recognisable as the 20th century representations of the Jacobins, levellers and republicans of Cobbett's day; of the evil-minded and designing men who would inflame the groundless discontents of the poor for their own sinister and selfish ends. It should be noted, also, that from around the end of 1794, while this campaign of information was under way, scarcely anyone dared, in public at least, to give voice to a contrary opinion; Godwin excepted. This absence of open opposition lasted right up until the radicalisation of William Cobbett, a decade later. And Cobbett was a quirky combination of courage and ability, such as is seldom thrown up in any age.

But to circulate huge amounts of propaganda does not necessarily reconcile a nation to an exploitative government. There must be receptivity in the target audience.

"If it be argued that fascist propaganda fools people into believing that their lot will be improved, then the question arises; Why are they so easily fooled? Because, it may be supposed, of their personality structure; because of long-established patterns of hopes and aspirations, fears and anxieties that dispose them to certain beliefs and make them resistant to others. The task of fascist propaganda, in other words, is rendered easier to the degree that antidemocratic potentials already exist in the great mass of the people."[113]

Individuals display an infinitely varying degree of readiness to subscribe to the tenets of anti-democratic ideology, and therefore of susceptibility to propaganda. But the unquestioning mindset of the authoritarian personality, instilled into him by his upbringing, makes him peculiarly easy to manipulate. His dependency, and readiness to submit to authority, preclude independent thought and objective, critical analysis; and render him susceptible to any opinion that can be seen as conventional and orthodox, which may come from a commonly respected figure or an authoritative source.

In spite of all the good qualities possessed by the English people, Cobbett identified their great failing as credulity – "that facility to be deceived which exposes them to the designs of craft and cunning". In part, he ascribed the misfortunes of the English nation to "the stupid, the brutal credulity" with which they received establishment publications. On the other hand, he excused them on the same ground – that of having been "infamously treated" by a press that was as wicked as it was powerful.

"Without the aid of the press, Pitt never would have been able to do half what he did during his terrible administration."[114]

Credulity had become ingrained in the English psyche.

"We have been brought up to hear these corrupt men, this mass of wickedness and folly, spoken of with respect and deference. It is a notion that has descended from father to son; and a notion, too, sedulously inculcated in romances, novels, in all school-books, story books, children's books of every size. Look at the 'Religious Tracts', - you will find every one of them contains something to impress this notion of superior wisdom in these men....

"Then, for the merry and thoughtless, they have songs, to delude and deceive and intoxicate them. The play-house is a grand instrument for inculcating a base subserviency to the stupid tyrants; and

---

112 Ibid. Pp. 735 and 154.
113 Ibid. P. 10.
114 William Cobbett. Political Register. 30/3/1816, 13/4/1816 and 29/8/1807.

of that they have the absolute management and direction. Even the Puppet and Juggling exhibitions carry the same notions at the fairs and wakes....

"*Judge not a man by his clothes*' is a maxim that we are always repeating. But we are apt to forget it, when we see big wigs, long gowns, purple, red, white, black and ermined....What are you to do? You must pluck a child's eyes out before you can prevent it from receiving in at those eyes an impression of respect for a villain or fool distinguished from other men by a grand costume; and when once the impression is in, get it out if you can."[115]

Cobbett foreshadowed Adorno in his understanding of receptiveness to authoritarian propaganda.

"I am aware, that, the assertion of one of those who have the distribution of fifty millions of taxes annually, will, by the hirelings and sycophants of the day, be regarded as superior in point of proof, to all the conclusions drawn from experience or from reasoning."[116]

There can be no doubt that William Pitt's campaign of propaganda was an outstanding success. This can be seen in the fervour of the Church and King riots; in the widespread attacks on the holders of radical opinions; the founding of constitutional clubs all over the kingdom; and the loyal addresses which came flooding in from all parts. We might conclude from this that a large proportion of the population by this time had come to exhibit anti-democratic potentials. In later years, the power of propaganda waned somewhat, and the British state was thrown back on to a growing reliance upon military force for its support. But the fact remains that the exploitative and totalitarian regime of William Pitt's later years was brought into being through the agency of the journalist and the pamphleteer. This might lead us to ask what the circumstances in society may be that can raise the proportion of prejudiced and anti-democratic individuals, to a point where an exploitative and repressive regime can be brought into existence.

The widening dichotomy between the in-group and the out-group, between the respectable and the lower orders, is a fundamental aspect of the social history of the years covered by this book. Adorno maintained that those of his subjects who did not exhibit anti-democratic potentials were far too diverse to form a group; there was no pro-democratic syndrome. Nevertheless, Cobbett and Godwin both recognised traits which distinguished the so-called respectable from the rest of society.[117]

The distinction largely concerned the mindset of dependency instilled into the anti-democrat by his upbringing – the need for a luxurious lifestyle to be provided for him by others.

"The greatest of all human benefits, that at least without which no other benefit can be truly enjoyed, is independence.

"He who lives upon the kindness of another, must always have a greater or less portion of a servile spirit....

"The question relative to the establishment and maintenance of independence, is intimately connected with the question relative to our taste for, and indulgence in, the luxuries of human life....

"The man who is anxious to maintain his independence, ought steadily to bear in mind how few are the wants of a human being. It is by our wants that we are held down, and linked in a thousand ways to human society. They render the man who is devoted to them, the slave of every creature that

115 William Cobbett. Political Register. 26/9/1818.
116 William Cobbett. Political Register. 18/12/1819.
117 T. W. Adorno. The Authoritarian Personality. P. 1.

breathes….Any man possessing the command of a certain portion of the goods of life, may order him this way or that at his pleasure."[118]

Godwin was pointing out here the huge difference in values, priorities and outlook between the possessors of the two differing mindsets.

Cobbett drew the distinction between the "producer" and the "accumulator"; between the man who worked, and the man who was too proud to work. He complained of the scoundrels who desired "to live in idleness upon the labour of other people."

"These vagabonds are a RACE, and some of them are found in all countries, like rats….This race pretend that they are '*gentlemen*', and the name of gentleman they interpret to mean, one who has a right to stuff his maw, to cover his back, and to stretch his lazy limbs, with the aid and assistance of the best food, drink, clothing and bedding, that are to be found in the country; no matter at whose cost; no matter who toils, who sweats, or who starves, on account of their being thus kept and entertained. This race regard every man of real industry, as having been created for the express purpose of causing them to live in idleness and luxury."[119]

In essence, it was the distinction between the host and the parasite.

But we can go back further than that. Surely what we are really comparing here is the settled, cooperative, community mindset of the villagers of Wigston Magna; with the socially insecure, competitive mindset of Cobbett's 'gentleman' and Adorno's anti-democratic personality. The community mindset is connected with production, subsistence, and ultimately with survival; and must already have been ancient in the era of communal agriculture, permeating, perhaps, tribal and pastoral peoples, nomadic peoples, hunters and gatherers. The competitive mindset, presumably of much more recent origin, is connected with social status and advancement, and brings with it, as we have seen, large amounts of extraneous issues concerning wealth, power and political ideology. The holder of the competitive mindset will always hold the advantage over the other, because, projectively, he assumes hostility in the environment around him, and sees life as a battle which needs to be won. If, as we have maintained, the competitive mindset is the result of social insecurity – a symptom of the absence of any community feeling with which to underpin the ego and engender self-respect – then the continual destruction of rural communities which took place during the 18th and 19th centuries would have created an ever-increasing class of anti-democrats.

"Crude economic factors affect directly the parents' behavior toward the child. This means that broad changes in social conditions and institutions will have a direct bearing upon the kinds of personality that develop within a society."[120]

The results of the 1801 census revealed a growing disproportion in English society between those who worked and those who merely thought. The dispersal of the English peasantry brought about over time the continual augmentation of the classes of the rootless and the socially insecure, many of whom, it might be surmised, would eventually have developed into the anti-democratic respectable. We are pushed, in our speculations upon this subject, towards the tentative conclusion that the progressive impoverishment of the English people, once got beyond a certain tipping-point – which point occurred almost certainly during the 1760s – became a self-perpetuating process; a vicious circle; and that this process was driven by the psychological propensities and personality needs of the sentimental mercenary.

---

118   William Godwin. The Enquirer. P. 240.
119   William Cobbett. Political Register. 13/7/1833.
120   T. W. Adorno. The Authoritarian Personality. P. 6.

Nadir?

Comparisons, speculations, and suggestions for further study.

Is there *never* to be an end to these things? Are they to be endured *for ever*?
<u>William Cobbett</u>[1]

The Poor Law Amendment Act of 1834 was, perhaps, never implemented with quite the consistency of rigour that its projectors intended, or would have liked. Nevertheless, for the economic well-being of the mass of the people in England, it was the ultimate catastrophe, and led on to the period of the greatest poverty, hardship and starvation that the historical sources allow us to identify in the history of our ancestors – the "hungry forties" of the 19th century.

The principle underlying the new law was deterrence – the making of relief so unpalatable to its pauper recipient that he would undergo the extremities of privation rather than apply. Paid relieving officers were recruited from outside the parishes, and selected for their ability to intimidate. Former army officers were often chosen. "Brutality and insolence" were the requisite qualifications. In many areas, the giving of "outdoor relief" was suspended, and claimants forced to enter one of the new, larger workhouses which parishes were compelled to combine into unions in order to build. These workhouses were run on the principle of what was euphemistically termed "less eligibility". In other words, conditions inside were made so bad that the poor simply would not apply. The poor thought of these places as prisons, and called them by that name.[2] Alexander Somerville, in the course of his travels during the 1840s, saw many of them.

"It has always seemed to me a grievous error in the national economy to shut people up within workhouse walls because they sought employment and could not get it, and that in a country whose soil has treasures buried and wasted in it for the want of labour – a grievous error in moral economy to think of making the idle industrious by shutting them up where they have no useful thing to do, and where they can learn, and feel, and understand nothing but how to hate their fellow-men. It has always seemed to me a grievous error to deny outdoor relief to families in temporary distress, whereby they are compelled to undergo the most cruel privations, or submit to break up their little homes, sell off their furniture (their homes and gardens it may be, as in the parish of Heyshot, in Sussex, and in numerous other parishes) and become thorough, confirmed, irredeemable paupers. To me, it has seemed cruel, terribly cruel, to take the aged and infirm from the cottages they have laboured to keep above their heads, and which they have sanctified with their affections, and shut them up in the workhouses, drilling them in their old days under the discipline of a barrack-yard, conducted by some non-commissioned officer of the army, whose fitness for keeping the workhouse in order is estimated by his success on the drill-ground and in the barrack-yard over a long period of years....

"The impolicy of shutting up the able-bodied who cannot get work outside, compelling them to do worthless, profitless, filthy work inside, merely to punish them, is only surpassed in enormity, by this cruel treatment of the aged and infirm...."

---

1 A History of the Last Hundred Days of English Freedom. P. 14.
2 K. D. M. Snell. Annals of the Labouring Poor. Pp. 120-122.

Somerville found it strange that it was the moral reformers who were "foremost in making industry compulsive, not by leading the idle to work, but by driving them in one common herd, idle, unfortunate, aged, infirm, and sick, as the worst-used of brute-beasts are driven, to compel them to work or die quickly at little expence"; who recommended the use of "cruelty and coercion in the rear of their moral army, upon the aged, the infirm, and unfortunate – upon the *helpless*, who in all ages and countries the most ignorant and barbarous, have been spared and protected….This is….a feeble expression of what I have found during the last three years in my travels through almost every parish (two or three unions excepted) in the south and south-west of England."[3]

Of course, providing the inmates of workhouses with a dietary standard inferior to that endured by those on the outside was an impossibility; so other ways had to be found of making life intolerable; as the relieving officer of the Wilton workhouse told Somerville.

"We would have many more (demands for admission) were we not to make the diet as low as will possibly sustain life….It is low, but low as it is, one-half the working population of Wilton and neighbourhood don't live better in their own houses – many of them not so well. How can they, with wages so low, and many of them without work? In short, we are obliged to feed them meagrely, and give them hard task-work at breaking bones, or some such thing, lest they find the house too comfortable."[4]

But the aspect of workhouse life which most aroused the bitterness and enmity of the working people was the splitting up of families.

"They won't give us anything", exclaimed a poor man, "except we goes into the house, and as long as I can arne a sixpence anyhows, they sharn't part me from my wife."

The Select Committee of 1837 thought that families from time to time should be given some time to converse together; but in 1846 a man claimed that in ten weeks inside the house, he had only seen his children by chance, as they happened to pass on the way to chapel.[5]

It was well known to the poor that the life of the convicted criminal was far better than that inside the workhouse.

"They escape to kill game, steal sheep, rob hen-roosts – to do anything, to take any chance, rather than be punished in the workhouse for seeking parish relief; they escape from the dietary of the unions to the better fare of the prisons and the hulks, and the better fed convict gangs of the Bermudas, Gibraltar and New South Wales…."[6]

But as Cobbett had foreseen, this new Poor Law did not have as its objective, merely the limited one of bringing down the poor-rates. It was a much wider system than that, a system of finance and political economy, having as its aim the draining of increased amounts of wealth out of the countryside, and into the hands of the competitive classes, both landed and monied. The purpose of the scheme was to put even greater pressure upon the working people; to confront them even more immediately with the fact of starvation; to engender a greater competition between them; and in these ways to make them ever more malleable and more submissive.

It worked. The act triggered a long-term decline in the wages-bill – or, in other words, of produce consumed upon the spot, intercepted before it could reach the market. All labourers giving evidence before the Select Committee of 1837 had already suffered wage reductions. The earnings of Edward Pullen of Kidford had declined from 15s. to 11s. 6d.; Richard Ford's from 15s. 9d. to 9s.; and all others in proportion. The following year, the committee noted, presumably with approval, reductions in relief allowances, wages and task-work payments. Alexander Somerville, travelling around the country

---

3 Alexander Somerville. Whistler at the Plough. Pp. 257-259.

4 Ibid. P. 46.

5 K. D. M. Snell. Annals of the Labouring Poor. P. 133.

6 Alexander Somerville. Whistler at the Plough. P. 258.

during the 1840s, was constantly recording wage reductions. On Salisbury Plain, wages were being reduced on the pretext of a good harvest. The wages had been 9s.; they had come down to 8s. In parts of Dorset and Wiltshire, wages had been reduced to 7s., which was expected to be the prevailing figure before long. From Shaftesbury into Devon, wages were 7s.; in some places 6s.[7]

These were not wages that could support life; but downward pressure on them continued. A farmer told the Select Committee in 1838;-

"I could have as many men as I wanted, to do all my work at 1s. a day, or 6s. a week....if my conscience would let me."

But 6s. was now being suggested as the standard. A farmer from Clavering told a reporter from the Morning Chronicle;-

"A man with a family of five children will be nearly able with 6s. a week to buy bread enough, if he buys the coarsest flour; his rent he generally gets out of his harvest money; his clothes he gets by some means or other – people sometimes give them to him – and then, when he is unemployed.... we keep him in the workhouse."[8]

If 6s. was the standard, plenty fell below it. Around Preston and Lancaster, Somerville found wages at 9d. a day, or 4s. 6d. a week; and this figure was the norm amongst the framework-knitters of Leicestershire, Nottinghamshire and Derbyshire. By 1850 in the south of England, wages were generally between 65 per cent and 85 per cent of their 1833 levels, without taking into account the withdrawal of relief payments.[9]

Yet even with such wages as these, unemployment and underemployment were endemic. Work was "very scarce – uncertain, difficult to obtain and retain, in fact most casual". Less than half the labouring families were fully employed. The subsistence pressure placed upon the labourers compelled them to submit to the most horrendous hours of work.[10]

"At the time of the repeal of the Corn Laws, and soon after, we had to work from 4a.m. until 6 and 8p.m., lads for 4d. per day, and men, with eight or nine children, for 9s. per week".[11]

This was not unusual. Children barely beyond infancy were forced out to work. Joseph Boddington of Northampton started work with his father, aged six, "weather hot or cold"; this was common enough, though others might wait until seven, eight or nine. Wages for a child of six were 1s. a week; by the time he reached ten, maybe the same. As wages were forced down, and hours lengthened, the rents of cottages were on the rise. 1s.6d. was now a typical sum to be deducted from a man's wages weekly before he could even think about feeding himself and his family. The labourers of Dorset Somerville thought the poorest in England; yet there the "meanest hovels" with not a yard of garden ground, would rent for between three and four pounds a year.[12]

Those who had the management of the estates congratulated themselves on what they had achieved. Thomas Bennett was the Duke of Bedford's agent at Woburn; he wrote to His grace;-

"We may justly consider the market for labour in a sound and healthy state – I know of no farmer, who employed a man more than is absolutely necessary, and I have had no few applications from men wanting work during the period I have been here."[13]

7   K. D. M. Snell. Annals of the Labouring Poor. P. 126. Alexander Somerville. Whistler at the Plough. P. 29.
8   K. D. M. Snell. Annals of the Labouring Poor. P. 126.
9   Alexander Somerville. Whistler at the Plough. P. 91. J. G. Chambers. Nottinghamshire in the Eighteenth Century. P. 99. K. D. M. Snell. Annals of the Labouring Poor. P. 129.
10 See, e.g. The Hungry Forties. Pp. 135 and 260.
11 The Hungry Forties. P. 229.
12 The Hungry Forties. Pp. 83-84, 188-189, 58, 74, and 168. Alexander Somerville. Whistler at the Plough. Pp. 32 and 380.
13 A. Brundage. The Making of the New Poor Law. P. 109.

A decline in employment opportunities and an intensification of the competition between labourers were among what landowners and their agents saw as the beneficial effects of the New Poor Law; the symptoms of a sound and healthy labour market.

So what was to be done with all the wealth saved by reducing the subsistence of the working people? As Cobbett had foreseen, the passing of the New Poor Law ushered in a period of a much more intense financial exploitation of the agricultural estates, of which the farmer was almost as much a victim as the labourer. Rents began to rise almost immediately consequent upon the passing of the Act. The Duke of Rutland related to one of the officials that "his steward in Cambridgeshire had written that he had readily relet a farm at an advanced rent, solely from the effect of the Poor Law Amendment Act."[14] Landowners and their agents began routinely to keep a much tighter control over their tenants. Most were yearly tenants-at-will, removable at the pleasure of their landlords, and bound by elaborate contracts drawn up by lawyers. These might contain a variety of stipulations and restrictions, many of them virtually feudal in their nature; as well as a set of harsh penalties for infringement, with a wide discretion over the imposition and collection of these being given to the agents of the estate. Since votes at elections were part of the landowners' route to lucrative state office, tenants also had to be prepared to support the prescribed candidates.

The lifestyle of the landed aristocrat involved a competitive and ostentatious luxury, so many landlords lived beyond their income. This would leave the estates at the mercy of mortgagees – they were on tick to the Paper-Money Men, as Cobbett put it – and thus lawyers would be given an even freer rein to extract money, who were possessed of little or no agricultural expertise. Somerville quoted the eminent Scottish agriculturalist, James Hogg.

"The first thing required in England to make a successful farmer was *not* a practical knowledge of breeding and rearing and feeding sheep and cattle, of manuring and cropping land. Every qualification, he said, of an agricultural kind, was entirely subordinate to a knowledge of *law*. And he said the laws affecting the cultivator of the soil were so numerous, so completely interwoven into everything which a farmer could do; and the lawyers were so keen-scented and so plentiful – the estates being almost entirely committed to the management of lawyers…."[15]

The resulting sad plight of the tenant farmer was described by Alexander Somerville.

Farmers "might very well point to the ruinous prices they pay the landlords….bound….hand and foot, led by the nose by one agent, pinched behind their backs by another; obliged to pay high poor-rates to maintain a pauper population whom they cannot employ; compelled to endure game and pay for the crimes and punishments arising from game, because they dare not complain; compelled to be put to all manner of mean uses in political prostitution."[16]

A large proportion of the tenantry were now poor men. Here is the recollection of Samuel Nuttall, of Holywell in Wales.

"I was the son of a small farmer, and fared better than many a one, as we had plenty of food, as it was; but we were very hard up many a time, although we fared well….the only white or wheaten bread we had was a small loaf, the price of which was 2d., for tea on Sunday, and that was cut very thin and placed between two slices of black bread, and we thought we had luxuries."[17]

The white wheaten loaf, the exclusive dependence on which was once the symptom of the degradation of labouring families, was now completely unavailable to those families, and constituted a luxury even for a farmer.

---

14 K. D. M. Snell. Annals of the Labouring Poor. P. 124. A. Brundage. The Making of the New Poor Law. P. 126.
15 Alexander Somerville. Whistler at the Plough. Pp. 328-329.
16 Alexander Somerville. Whistler at the plough. P.333.
17 The Hungry Forties. Pp. 247-248.

The son of a farmer from Sussex lived on "cabbage and bacon all the year round, and sometimes very little of that", with a taste of roast beef about once a month on a Sunday.[18]

Impoverished farmers could not farm properly. Somerville noted countless instances of bad cultivation; around Shaftesbury, in Dorset, for example, the land was poorly drained, and covered in couch grass and thistles. And this meant also that they could not employ labour. Even if they could afford to do so, they were disabled by their tenancy agreements; landlords and their agents constantly endeavouring to reduce the labour costs on their estates. The tenant-at-will was "liable to be told what men they shall employ and what not". The terms of the lease would prohibit or severely restrict the more labour-intensive modes of cultivation. On the estate of Sir Alexander Hood, one of the tenants "made an attempt to drain and cultivate a portion of his farm, only a few acres out of several hundreds, so that he might grow some more winter feeding for his cattle, employ two or three men, and thus lessen the parish rates. But he was proceeded against for penalties, was forced into litigation, was sold up, expelled the farm, beggared, and made an example of". The labour-saving threshing-machine made its re-appearance, the labourers being now forced into such a position of submissiveness that there was nothing they could do to oppose it. At Sutton Scotney in Hampshire, Somerville met up with Joseph Carter, who had been a machine-breaker in the riots of 1830.

"They ha' got three sheens now in this place, now at this very time; and one farmer borrows one; and them four sheens does the work of eight men. They be a doin' of that at Sutton in this moment; and men be again doin' nothin'." The Earl of Abingdon did all he could physically to remove the poor from his estate; and yet, on his farms, "half the work is not done that should be done". Most of the work that was done was performed by young men and boys brought in from a distance, and paid between 2s. and 5s. per week. They "provide themselves with food and clothing out of their wages; sleep in a stable-loft or barn, having no fireside to go to; no hot dinners, but everlasting bread and lard, bread and lard, bread and lard!"

"We may very properly inquire if his Lordship is justified in making his tenants such slaves of uncertainty that they cannot employ labourers to the requisite extent of their farms."[19]

On the Duke of Richmond's estate in Sussex, Somerville noted the great reduction in the amount of labour employed on the farms.

"There used to be seven or eight men employed on each 100 acres, that was when farms were smaller. Now the highest number was five to the hundred acres; and that only on a very few farms."

On one farm of 300 acres there were but five men and two boys. Around Glastonbury, on the estate of Sir Alexander Hood, in spite of the "wretched farm workers....existing on half diet", the wages paid were "at the rate of one man at 7s.6d., and one boy at 3s., to each hundred acres of land. A great deal of the land lies in grass; it all wants draining."[20]

The vast amounts of wealth thus liberated from the farms were sucked up in rent, just as Cobbett had predicted. The son of a farmer from Sussex recalled his father paying 50s. per acre in rent, and 10s. in addition in tithe. Such rates as these were kept up by increasing competition between farmers. Somerville found himself in Surrey, on the estate near Farnham from which Cobbett had rented his last farm.

"I have been assured by several farmers, who are now offering for farms, that there is no chance of getting a new holding but at an advance on present rentals. This may not be so with the very large farms, for which there is not so great a competition; but for small ones, or those of moderate size, for which competition is great, an increase of rent is asked everywhere."[21]

18 Ibid. P. 155.
19 Alexander Somerville. Whistler at the Plough. Pp. 398, 249-250, 261-263 and 141-142.
20 Ibid. Pp, 407-408 and 249.
21 Ibid. P. 309.

The competition for farms, of course, was entirely unrelated to their potential profitability. Because of continual consolidating and engrossing, the number of available farms was constantly decreasing. On the other hand, farmers' families were "annually increasing". In earlier years, there had been plentiful employment opportunities for their offspring outside agriculture. More than half the shopkeepers in Stockport, for example, were the sons and daughters of farmers. But because of continual economic dislocation, these alternative outlets no longer existed.[22]

The Duke of Richmond maintained that if farmers were prepared to offer high rents, he was perfectly justified in taking them.

"It is not the worth of the farm that makes them compete for it", retorted Somerville, "it is their own numbers; they must get farms or be without the means of living."[23]

Many landlords sought actively to maximise rents, by putting farms out to competitive tender.

Out in the countryside, out of sight and out of mind, the system of high rents and minimal cultivation was completely ruinous. It was disastrous for labourers....

"I have known as many as sixteen men running about the village playing marbles simply because they had got nothing to do, and the farmers did not want them. What was the reason why they would not employ the men, do you ask? Why, because the rent of land was so high. The price of fairly good soil in the old days was £2 an acre to the farmer, and then he had to pay tithe and rates and taxes."[24]

....and it was disastrous for farmers. J. Besley was a farmer in the parish of Milverton in Somerset, who, according to his nephew, paid his workforce at the very lowest level.

"You will suppose my uncle made his fortune owing to paying such low wages. Nothing of the kind. My uncle failed, as nearly half the farmers in the county at that time, owing to the high rent and bad harvests. His wife and only daughter died early and left him dependent upon relatives. If he had not taken that farm he had capital sufficient to keep himself and his family in comfort."[25]

Alexander Somerville's former employer paid away all his farming capital, as well as a private inheritance, in rent, and the whole was transferred to the pocket of the landlord. He had a large family to support, and no alternative employment was on offer if he left the farm.[26]

Even for the landlords themselves, Somerville maintained that this system was short-sighted and counterproductive. In Oxfordshire, the Duke of Marlborough was a notoriously bad landlord.

"His princely domain of Blenheim is, palace and Park, the most noble, regal-like, that I have seen in any part of the kingdom; but worse farming, and poorer labourers are not to be found within the British shores than on the Duke's property. The estate is one vast wreck."[27]

Somerville accused landlords fairly uniformly of neglecting their estates. But was he missing the point somewhat? The years following the passing of the Poor Law Amendment Act were a time of the most magnificent prosperity and splendour for all the landed and monied classes. Henry Colman was a well-known American agriculturalist who toured England in the early 1840s. His company was eagerly sought by many of the great English landlords, by whom he was lavishly entertained. He recorded his experiences in a series of letters, which subsequently was published.

"The incomes of many noblemen and gentlemen here are indeed enormous. Earl __ is stated to have an annual income of upwards of £100,000 sterling. The Duke of __ has actually spent more than £40,000 sterling in draining and irrigating his property, so you may infer from that what possibly

22 Ibid. p. 91.
23 Ibid. P. 406.
24 Recollection of William Smith of Holme Hale in East Anglia in The Hungry Forties. Pp. 126-127.
25 Ibid. p. 181.
26 Alexander Somerville. Whistler at the Plough. P. 311.
27 Ibid. P. 140.

may be his possessions. That expenditure is not even felt by him. And Earl __ is estimated at least at £150,000 sterling per year. The accumulation of property here is in some cases amazing, and entirely beyond my arithmetic...."[28]

Colman stayed as the guest of Earl Spencer, at Althorp, in Northamptonshire.

"His home-place consists of ten thousand acres, all lying together, in wood, meadow, pasture, gardens, parks, and every thing in a style of superior beauty and order. There is, first, a very large house, forming three sides of a quadrangle, and furnishing sleeping-rooms for seventy guests, with extensive halls for servants; the entries and rooms are filled with pictures and statues; a gallery of pictures one hundred feet in length, containing many of the works of the first masters, and a library of most valuable books in elegant binding, covering the high walls of eight large rooms and halls, and making together more than fifty thousand volumes; said to be the finest private library in the world. Then, besides that, there are extensive ranges of stables as elegant as private dwellings, and equally neat; and greenhouses and conservatories, and the gamekeeper's house, and the dairy-house, and the dog-kennels, and the porter's lodge at the entrance of the park, and how many farm-houses I cannot say."[29]

While at Althorp, Colman received an invitation to visit the Duke of Richmond, at Goodwood House, in Sussex. At Goodwood, there were 23,000 acres; but Richmond also owned between two and three thousand acres in Scotland.

"Now, it is impossible to convey to you on paper a just idea of the magnificence and beauty of this palace and residence, filled with books, pictures, statues, curiosities, conveniences and elegancies. One of the large halls is covered with yellow silk, and with pictures in tapestry of the most exquisite workmanship, and splendid furniture. Then, the extensive parks, through which you literally ride for miles and miles, and, what was singularly beautiful, the herds of deer, of sheep, of cattle, and twenty-five race horses in the stable, with a groom for each of them; together with an aviary, an enclosure of six acres, with a high wall, a pond, a grove, a grotto, which the ladies of the house were seven years in adorning with varied shells, a keeper's house, and places for the parrots, canary birds, gold and silver fish, peacocks, and above all, the beautiful golden and silver pheasants, making one of the most romantic and delightful spots that can be imagined."[30]

Colman's letters overflowed with detailed information about the luxurious lifestyle enjoyed at such establishments as these. At Woburn Abbey, he observed;-

"The dress of the ladies was more splendid than I can describe, and the jewels and diamonds on the head, and neck, and wrists, and fingers, as brilliant as their own bright eyes."[31]

At Lambton Castle, County Durham;-

"The ladies, it is reported, never wear a pair of white satin shoes, or white gloves more than once; and some of them, if they find, on going into society, another person of inferior rank wearing the same dress as themselves, the dress upon being taken off, is at once thrown aside, and the lady's maid perfectly understands her perquisite."[32]

All of these palaces teemed with servants, whose number could range from around thirty, to over a hundred. At Lambton Castle, the total was between forty and fifty.[33]

"The servants' establishment is quite an affair by itself. The steward is at the head; he provides everything, and purchases all the supplies; he oversees all the other servants, and puts on, and where

---

28 Henry Colman. European Life and Manners. Vol. I. Pp. 114-115.
29 Ibid. Pp. 28-29.
30 Ibid. Pp. 30-32.
31 Ibid. P. 329.
32 Ibid. P. 91.
33 Ibid. Vol. II. P. 36.

the party is not large, takes everything off from the table, the other servants standing by and waiting upon him. He has a room to himself, well fitted up, and has a large salary. Next to him comes the butler, who takes care of all the wines, fruit, glasses, candlesticks, lamps and plate, and has an under butler for his adjunct. Next in equal authority with the steward, and having also an elegant parlour, is the housekeeper; she has all the care of the chambers, the linen, and the female servants. Then comes next in authority, and perfectly despotic in his own domain, the cook, who is generally French or Italian, and his subalterns. Then come the coachman, the footman, and the hostlers, who, the last, I believe, seldom come into the house. Then there is the porter, who in London houses always sits in the entry, and either has an office by the door, or else a table, with pen, ink, paper, &c., who receives and delivers messages, but does not leave his place, having always servants at hand to wait upon him. Then each gentleman in the house has his own private valet, and each lady her own maid...."[34]

Colman stayed at very many establishments such as these.

"In truth, in comfort and splendour, the living at all these houses is upon a common type."

But, for Colman, the pinnacle was Welbeck Abbey, home of the Duke of Portland, whose forbear had been Home Secretary during the 1790s.

"I had supposed I had seen, several times before, the summit of luxurious living, but this I confess went beyond what I had met with, and the beauty of the whole was, that though there were so many parts, wheel within wheel, and one spring depending for its tension and its movements upon another, yet there was not the slightest jarring or creaking."[35]

In the metropolis of London, things were wearing a much more prosperous aspect since the passing of the New Poor Law. The depression and stagnation of trade which afflicted the traders in luxury goods in the wake of the riots of 1830 was over. Trade was now booming.

"The merchants here are many of them men of great wealth; and the shops in London, Edinburgh, Manchester, and Glasgow, are extraordinarily elegant, and the windows are indescribably brilliant with the productions of the most exquisite and improved art. One is never tired of looking at them, and of admiring the wonderful skill displayed in the manufacture, the brilliancy of their colors, and the magnificence which a mixed collection, tastefully arranged, displays by gas light. Indeed, I think one of the most beautiful sights I have seen in London, has been on a ride down Regent Street, on the box-seat of an omnibus, in the evening, when the streets are crowded with people elegantly dressed, and the shops in long ranges, with their illuminated windows of immense wealth, and their interior, exhibiting an almost indefinite perspective, are all in their glory. It appears absolutely like fairy land, and the whole of this most magnificent street seems converted into the hall of an oriental palace on a Court Gala."[36]

In London were to be found "the most fashionable millinery and fancy store, and the largest jewellery store in the world. The capital in one of the stores is £200,000 sterling...; in the other, £300,000 sterling....I saw a mere envelope case, price sixty-five guineas; a blotting book for a lady's table, ninety guineas; and one single set of jewels, necklace, broach and earrings, £37,000 sterling.... We sober people in America can have no idea of such extravagance, and yet here, they say they will soon find a purchaser for these things."[37]

Colman was clearly mesmerised.

"I was curious enough one day, standing in Hyde Park, a pleasant afternoon, to count the carriages of the nobility and gentry, which passed me in a given time. In eighteen minutes there passed me two

---

34 Ibid. Vol. I. Pp. 90-91.
35 Ibid. Pp. 110, 146 and 122.
36 Ibid. Pp. 127-128.
37 Ibid. Pp. 36-37.

hundred of superb four-wheeled carriages and equipages, and these were all different, and taking the circuit of the Park."[38]

In the financial districts of the City, things had also moved on from the depressed trading conditions, the tightness of credit, and the talk of the suspension of payments, reported by William Cobbett in his final years. In Threadneedle Street, the Old Lady was no longer sick. Already by 1835, just a year after the passing of the Poor Law Amendment Act, money was plentiful, and the Bank's coffers were full; filled in part, no doubt, by the wealth sucked up by the mortgages with which the aristocratic families funded their ostentatious lifestyle. The prices of the funds were on the rise again, and the West Indian Slave Emancipation loan was floated in 1835, and the Bank boosted its price by lending to subscribers. By irresponsible lending, the Bank fuelled a speculative boom such as had not been seen since 1823-5. Quite apart from numerous transactions with provincial banks, bill-broking firms, and the House of Rothschild, the Bank financed paving and lighting in Birmingham, the Ellesmere and Birmingham canals, industrial ventures, and, most significantly, stoked up the mania for investment in railways. A craze for investing in America brought the inevitable crash already by 1836-7, with the usual spate of bankruptcies, causing the usual round of ruin and degradation for many. In April 1837, the distress in the cotton districts of Lancashire was said to be "intense and beyond example".

"In the manufacturing district things were bad. Batches of men, women and children wandered south in hopeless destitution, and, to use the words of an Oldham manufacturer, 'utter starvation prevailed'."

Nothing daunted, the bankers cranked up another boom; prices rose eleven per cent between 1835 and 1839, in which year the next crash came, followed, in 1840, by the next round of bankruptcies and distress. During the 1840s, the Bank of England continued its policy of low interest rates and easy credit. These years were the heyday of railway mania, and investment in railways was said to be sucking up £60 millions a year. 9,000 miles of railway were authorised between 1843 and 1848, and 1,900 miles became operational. There was further heavy investment in railways abroad; £40 millions being ventured on railways in France alone during the 1840s. Of course, it ended in tears, with the crash of 1847. Bankruptcies became prevalent first among major corn-dealers, then other big firms, then banks, then manufacturers.[39]

The problem is not that bankers never learn from experience; the problem is that they profit from the constant fluctuation. Alexander Baring was the man who first proposed in Parliament that outdoor relief should no longer be offered to the poor, in order to put pressure on them to emigrate. Baring's Bank did very well in the post-Poor Law era, as Joshua Bates, one of the partners, noted in 1846.

"Our business is too good and too extensive for us to keep it many years....As we now stand the permanent means of the House would enable us to buy all our competitors out and have half a million to spare."[40]

Of course, the sufferings caused to ordinary people by these operations of high finance are incalculable. But for all the members of the landed and monied elite it was party time. Henry Colman found himself invited along, and observed them at their feasting.

Colman was amazed, as well as impressed, by the amount of gold, silver and valuable porcelain that adorned the dinner tables of the wealthy. In November 1843, he was staying at Goodwood House, in Sussex.[41]

---

38 Ibid. P. 339.
39 Sir John Clapham. The Bank of England. Pp. 151-157, 162, 176 and 100-206. P. Ziegler. The Sixth Great Power. Pp. 138 and 141. The Hungry Forties. Pp. 143-144.
40 P. Ziegler. The Sixth Great Power. P. 137.
41 H. Colman. European Life and Manners. Pp.33-34.

"The service at dinner was always silver or gold throughout, plates and dishes, excepting for the jellies and puddings, and those of the most beautiful china. At breakfast, every article, cups and saucers, plates, &c., &c., were all of the most splendid china, and every one differed in its pattern from another, that is, one cup and saucer was different from another cup and saucer; one plate differed from another....There was an immense amount, not only of porcelain, but of Sevre's china; and to give you some idea of the value of the latter, which is of the finest description, the price of a single cup and saucer, now on sale in Oxford street, is thirty-five dollars."[42]

In February 1845, Colman dined with the Duke of Bedford, at Woburn Abbey.

"I have never seen anything so splendid. The service was all of gold and silver, except the dessert plates, which were of Sevres porcelain....I observed many large massive pieces of gold plate in the centre of the table, and a silver waiter or tray, to support them, more than eight feet long and nearly two wide. There were two large gold tureens, one at each end of the table. Besides the gold service on the table, there were, among other plate, two large gold waiters, on the side-board....The arms of the family are a deer; and there were four salts in my sight, being a deer, about five inches high, of silver, with antlers, and two panniers slung over his back, one containing coarse, and the other fine salt."[43]

Servants were an integral part of the dining experience.

"I never dined out yet, even in a private untitled family, with less than three or four, and at several places eight or nine even, for a party hardly as numerous; but each knows his place; all are in full dress, the liveried servants in livery, and the upper servants in plain gentlemanly dress, but all with white cravats."[44]

In October 1843, Colman was at Welbeck Abbey, home of the Duke of Portland.

"At breakfast, the side-table would have on it, cold ham, cold chicken, cold pheasant or partridge, which you ask for, or to which, as is most common, you get up and help yourself. On the breakfast table were several kinds of the best bread possible, butter always fresh, made that morning, as I have found at all these houses; and if you asked for coffee, or chocolate, it would be brought to you in a silver coffee-pot, and you helped yourself; if for tea, you would have a silver urn to each guest, heated by alcohol, placed by you, a small teapot, and a small caddie of black and green tea to make for yourself, or the servant for you. The papers of the morning....were then brought to you, and your letters if any."

Henry Colman rarely took lunch; however;-

"A lunch at such houses, is in fact a dinner; the table is set at half-past one, not quite so large as for dinner. Commonly, there is roast meat warm, birds, warm or cold, cold chicken, cold beef, cold ham, bread, butter, cheese, fruit, beer, ale and wines, and every one takes it as he pleases, standing, sitting, waiting for the rest, or not, and going away when he pleases."[45]

The event of the day at a great house was dinner. This took place around 7 o' clock, and diners were required to be in full dress.

"Sometimes no dishes are put upon the table until the soup is done with, but at other times there are two covers besides the soup....After soup, the fish cover is removed, and this is commonly served round without any vegetables, but certainly not more than one kind. After fish come the plain joints, roast or boiled, with potatoes, peas or beans, and cauliflowers. Then sherry wine is handed by the servants to every one. German wine is offered to those who prefer it; this is always drank in green glasses; then come the entrees, which are a variety of French dishes, and hashes; then

42 Ibid. P. 147.
43 Ibid. P. 329.
44 Ibid. P. 34.
45 Ibid. Pp. 122-123.

champagne is offered; after this remove, come ducks, or partridges, or other game; after this the bons bons, puddings, tarts, sweetmeats, blanc mange; then cheese and bread, and a glass of strong ale is handed round; then the removal of the upper cloth, and oftentimes the most delicious fruits and confectionary follow, such as grapes, peaches, melons, apples, dried fruits, &c., &c. After this is put upon the table a small bottle of Constantia wine, which is deemed very precious, and handed round in small wine glasses, or noyeau, or some other cordial. Finger glasses are always furnished, though in some cases I have seen a deep silver plate filled with rose water presented to each guest, in which he dips the corner of his napkin, to wipe his lips or his fingers."[46]

Closely surrounding the great country houses and the city mansions were millions of people whose bill of fare was in contrast to that which Colman described.

Meat was relatively cheap by the 1840s, owing to the general lack of purchasing power; most types were a distant memory in working families. Wheaten bread was a more recent, but fading memory. And the history of diet during these years is the history of the resourcefulness of the English people, in finding substitutes for these two staples, and expedients of many sorts, in the desperate struggle just to stay alive.

In the wake of the passing of the New Poor Law, the subsistence, if that is what it can be called, of the English people, consisted in potatoes, and various concoctions of the inferior grains. Oatmeal, in areas where it was produced, could be used in a variety of ways; ryebread was widely eaten; but barley bread was the most common, and the most complained about. Barley is essentially indigestible. The better-off might mix it with a little wheat flour in order to offset the worst of its effects; but most had no resort but complaint.

"You do not know what heartburn means till you have eaten barley bread."[47]

The adulteration of the food of the poor was common practice during the 1840s; but the quality of the bread was further impaired by the run of wet harvests. In these years, the corn used to make bread was often already sprouting. The rye bread was said to be very doughy.

"If you cut the crust off and threw the remainder at the wall it would stick there."

Bread made from sprouted corn turned out nearly black. Barley bread became very sour. The outside would be very hard; the inside the consistency of clay and foul-smelling. Such bread would not rise in the oven, and had to be turned into unleavened griddle cakes or "bannicks". These were dark brown in colour, and often had to be cut out of the oven, "or its top scooped out with the ladle." When even barley meal could not be afforded, the poor resorted to the various types of offal produced by the milling process.

"Many a mother, to appease the hunger and stop the crying of her children, made bran dumplings."

Toppings were used, or sharps, "which seemed to burn inside after we had eaten it."[48]

It was a crust of bread of this type that the labourer took to work with him for his lunch; which he washed down with a drink of water from the ditch.[49]

"Ah boy! hot dinner today", proclaimed a labourer from East Anglia. This labourer had an onion to accompany his crust. The better-off had onions. The worse-off, who had not even crusts, were wont to buckle their belts a hole tighter.[50]

The main evening meal of the day consisted generally of potatoes. It might be 'taters and shake-over – that is, with a little salt. Or it could be small potatoes cooked in a little bit of fat, to prevent

46 Ibid. Pp. 92-94.
47 The Hungry Forties. Pp. 67, 120, 58 and 261.
48 Ibid. Pp. 69, 123, 69-70, 247-248, 92, 146, 160, 230 and 95.
49 Alexander Somerville. Whistler at the Plough. P. 119.
50 The Hungry Forties. Pp.95 and 90.

them from burning. Or it might be potatoes boiled and mashed, with a penny-worth of suet melted and poured over.[51]

Occasionally, on a Sunday, working families could afford themselves a treat. Between a half a pound and a pound of pork, or salt pork, or fat bacon, would have to go round the entire family. Failing that, a red herring could be purchased cheaply, and divided between the family members; "the smell of which pervaded the air as you passed the workmen's cottages."[52]

Labouring families generally bought between half an ounce and an ounce of tea per week. When this ran out, they made tea out of dried herbs; or they coloured their tea with burnt crusts, or burnt barley cake, or old tea leaves, all of which were generally begged from the houses of the more opulent.[53]

In 1845, the potato blight arrived in England and decimated the crop. Alexander Somerville posed the question which is still puzzling today.

"It has appeared to me very extraordinary that so much should be written of the potato disease in Ireland, and so little said of it by the newspapers, or apparently known by them, or cared to be known, in England."

The working population of England suffered the acknowledged and inevitable fate of those who are reduced to dependence on the lowest possible article of subsistence. That article failed, and did so in a year of high prices.

"With bread high in price, and likely to rise, even a large supply of potatoes would not be enough this year. How much greater must the suffering be when to dearness of bread there is the companionship of scarcity of potatoes."[54]

What depth and what intensity of suffering for thousands of people is contained in this simple, dry statement of Somerville's, about the people of Somerset!

"For years past their daily diet is potatoes only. This year they have none."[55]

Potato blight, in varying degrees, was here to stay, and the place of the potato in the dietary of the poor was taken over by the swede and the turnip, "the last refuge of desperate poverty." Years later, the Rev. A. Barnard recalled;-

"A poor labourer said to me one Monday, 'I had fine fare yesterday. I had roast, baked and boiled.' 'Indeed', said I, 'you were in luck. What did you have? Explain.' 'Well', said he, 'I and my family had swede turnips, and nothing but swede turnips; but we thought we would have as much variety as we could, so we had roasted turnips, and baked turnips, and boiled turnips'."

These swedes were generally stolen from the fields by night, or else begged from the farmers.

"Sometimes we found a swede in the road, having fell off the farm cart. That was a treat indeed!"[56]

Needless to say, it all fell hardest on the children. Potatoes and salt might be all the nourishment they received; or else two slices of bread and lard would be a full day's ration. Children would "run like pigs after an apple-core in the street". The complaint of Mrs. Wilkins of Northwold in Suffolk that "my children I have had to put supperless to bed many and many a time" was a common one, and was echoed from around the whole country. Edward Cook, from Suffolk, left home aged eighteen, "although only a small ladie not more than 7 stone in weight....I can safely say during the first 18

51 Ibid. Pp. 151, 59 and 147.
52 Ibid. Pp. 61, 93, 122, 133, 147, 229, 67, 89 and 120.
53 Ibid. Pp. 84, 89, 118, 124, 161 and 257.
54 Alexander Somerville. The Whistler at the Plough. Pp. 413-414.
55 Ibid. P. 249.
56 The Hungry Forties. Pp. 61-62, 121, 151, 228, 263, 92 and 88-89.

years of my life my belly had not been properly filled 18 times since I was weaned from my mother's breast."[57]

Many and pathetic were the expedients resorted to by the poor in the attempt to avoid starvation. They robbed the pigs of their peas and their horse-beans, their barley-meal and their cooked small potatoes. Edward Cook relates;-

"My sister, who had evidently done the same thing before, took me to the cabbage bed and puled up some of the cabbage stalks, from which the cabbages had been cut, and peeled of the outer rine, and the centre we eate for our dinner, and many times after we did the same thing."[58]

Field weeds were collected up by the children; "these were boiled in the 'crock' and eaten to savour the barley-cake." "Nettles, when in season, be good vegetable eating", as a labourer from Strathfieldsaye told Alexander Somerville.[59]

"Joseph Pugh's wife and daughters used to go early into the meadows and eat snails."[60]

The desperate measures used by the poor to avert starvation during the famines of the 1790s had now become standard fare. But despite every desperate effort, this was not a diet that could support life. Many were dependent on charity. William Perry was a labourer from Charlton in Wiltshire, who kept five children on 7s. a week. He declared at a public meeting that "if there were not some good and charitable people in the country he should be starved"; and the reaction at the meeting showed that many were in just the same predicament.[61] But private charity was not equal to the scale of the problem.

"How to exist and keep honist was the mistrey that confronted my parents; final result, it could not be done. My father, therefore, like otheres in the same predicament, brought home from the farm potatoes, turnips, carrots &c., in fact anything that was eatiable."[62]

Subsistence crime was the ubiquitous consequence of endemic starvation.

"It makes one think on doing what one would never do, but for hunger", a Wiltshire labourer told Somerville.[63]

Sheep-stealing and poaching were necessary everyday occurrences.

"I was the oldest of 7 children; and when I was old enough I crept into the wood by the light of the moon, and brought out 5 pheasants to help keep my father, mother, brothers, and sister from starving."[64]

Here is S. L. Jacob, writing of his uncle's farm at Milverton in Somerset.

"What our labourers had for supper was a conglomeration of vegetables stued. You may well suppose they stole whatever they could lay their hands on, and no wonder!

"I don't think there was a month whilst I was on the farm but one or more of our men was in Taunton lock-up; and can you wonder at it? They were like hungry wolves. Continually we had sheep stolen. One December we had 21 fat turkeys stolen that we had been feeding for Tiverton Xmas market."[65]

Things were no better in Northamptonshire.

---

57 Ibid. Pp. 146, 148, 124 and 122.
58 Ibid. Pp. 92, 151, 162, 228 and 104.
59 The Hungry Forties. P. 161. Alexander Somerville. The Whistler at the Plough. P. 120.
60 The Hungry Forties. P. 84.
61 Alexander Somerville. The Whistler at the Plough. P. 384.
62 The Hungry Forties. P. 106.
63 Alexander Somerville. The Whistler at the Plough. P. 38.
64 Alexander Somerville. The Whistler at the Plough. P. 139. The Hungry Forties. P.81.
65 The Hungry Forties. Pp. 178-179.

"In 1844 it was not safe to go out after dark if you had any money on you. Burgaly, highway robbery, fowl stealing because men were starving."

The authorities by no means considered starvation a mitigating circumstance in the commission of subsistence crime. Punishment was savage.

"In 1844 men was brought to justice for sheep-stealing, sent to Van Demon's Land for 14 years. If you took a pheasant by night, 14 years. Two men in this village had 14, Jack Burrell and Bill Devenport....rioting was in every large town, and shops were guted. Rows of men chained together. I see as late as '53 men marched through Northampton streets to the gaol from Nottingham – there prison was full."[66]

G. Chambers made a similar observation.

"No wonder that men were riotous and clamorous; no wonder that they were shot down in my own native county town in the West of England because they clamoured for bread for their wives and little ones, who were starving."[67]

The word starvation was upon everybody's lips.

"I go with an empty belly so often that my grub ha'n't no name."

So a labourer told Somerville.[68]

The stark contrast between the magnificent splendour of the lifestyle enjoyed by the respectable, and the extreme and absolute destitution of the lower orders, was not lost upon Henry Colman. Here, he wrote of life in the capital.

"The extremes of human condition here are most affecting; and the cases of beggary, and wretchedness, and destitution, especially at this season (December 1843), make one's heart bleed with anguish. In the midst of the most extraordinary abundance, here are men, women and children dying of starvation; and running along side of the splendid chariot, with its gilded equipages, its silken linings, and its liveried footmen, are poor, forlorn, friendless, almost naked wretches, looking like mere fragments of humanity."[69]

Elsewhere, the situation was worse. Here are the recollections of John Bruce.

"In the cold winter, when the prevalence of frost and snow added to the terrors of the situation, I have seen them in groups and gangs, parading the streets of London, with hunger written on their faces, objects of pity, appealing for charity. Bad as they were, in the provincial towns they suffered more. The clamorous and silent victims of a criminal fiscal policy were everywhere. Riots were of daily occurrence, the military called out, and desperate encounters took place, always ending in bloodshed....

"But heartrending as the sights were in London and the towns, away in the rural districts the miseries were more pathetic and impressive. Subjugated by the landlords, whose tyranny was awfull, they bore with depressing patience, the hard lot to which they were assigned....Their diet was the meanest, and scanty, and barely sufficient to hold together body and soul, consisting of vegetables, bad brown bread, and inferior fat bacon, in small quantities; and their dwellings were rotten structures in which whole generations lived and died in squalid misery."[70]

The full extent of what the people of England suffered during these years we will never know. Most of the historical sources upon which we rely were written by those who saw the contrast between extreme opulence and absolute starvation as the just and rightful victory of the respectable and virtuous over the barbarous and dishonest; or by those who were dependent upon them. They

---

66 Ibid. Pp.79-80.
67 Ibid. Pp. 151-152.
68 Alexander Somerville. The Whistler at the Plough. P. 42.
69 Henry Colman. European Life and Manners. Vol. I .Pp. 164-165.
70 The Hungry Forties. Pp. 244-245.

were inclined either to deny to extreme distress any access to their consciousness, as was the case with Alexander Baring in 1830.

"BARING is reported to have said, some weeks back, that there was no *particular distress at this time*, and that the country must, '*from its* POSITION *and its population, always have some distress*', and that the labourers were *as well off* as ever they were. – This is a *great point*, at which all those aim who wish to uphold the present system."[71]

Or else to rationalise it in one of the ways detailed by the Adorno team.

"Most persons here are Malthusians, and presume to say that the human race is propagated too fast."[72]

Those who were genuinely concerned for the plight of humanity, as Cobbett frequently pointed out, could not bring themselves to describe its utmost degradations. Henry Colman went walking through Manchester, and was introduced "to exhibitions of the most disgusting and loathsome forms of destitution, and utter vice and profligacy. We went into thirty or more different houses, from the most squalid to those which would not be inaptly termed elegant; and marched directly into parlours, chambers, garrets and cellars, crowded….rather like a putrid carcass filled with vermin. But I cannot describe my visits here; the paper would, I fear, be absolutely offensive to the touch if I should send the details. It made me very sad; it shocked me with horror, and it will make my life hereafter an incessant thanksgiving that my children have not, in the inscrutable dispensation of Heaven been cast destitute, helpless, and orphans in such a country as this."[73]

In general, the authorities were reluctant to attribute mortalities to a "Want of the necessaries of life". Nevertheless, it seems clear that death by actual starvation was an accepted everyday occurrence in the England of the 1840s; and, indeed, likely that many thousands of people perished in this way. Here is Colman, back in London.

"Now I dare say there are thousands and tens of thousands of such cases, within a circuit of two miles from me, of persons actually dying by piecemeal, from starvation; and all this in the midst of a splendour, perfectly dazzling, and a wealth surpassing the dreams of Oriental magnificence."[74]

The 1840s were little more than a century and a half ago. Was this the lowest point for the people of England? The summariser of the series of letters entitled The Hungry Forties, Brougham Villiers, certainly thought so.

"Upon the whole, we are convinced, our country has never passed through so terrible a time before or since. Right through the Middle Ages sporadic famines occurred, and there were years of terrible dearth, due to defective harvests; but so continuous a period of systematic underfeeding of the whole nation never before occurred."[75]

Note the expression which he uses; "systematic underfeeding".

The idea that "underfeeding" was "systematic" lies at the heart of the great debate about poverty that took place during these years, a small proportion of which has been presented in this book. Malthus denied it. In the first (1798) edition of his Essay on the Principle of Population, he maintained that the disproportion between the rates of increase of population and subsistence made poverty ever-present, inevitable, irremediable.

71 William Cobbett. Political Register. 27/11/30.
72 Henry Colman. European Life and Manners. Vol. I. P.44.
73 Ibid. P. 103.
74 Ibid. Vol. II. Pp. 24-25.
75 The Hungry Forties. Pp. 253-254.

"Nature has scattered the seeds of life abroad with the most profuse and liberal hand. She has been comparatively sparing in the room and the nourishment necessary to rear them....This natural inequality of the two powers of population and of production in the earth....appears, therefore, to be decisive against the possible existence of a society, all the members of which should live in ease, happiness, and comparative leisure; and feel no anxiety about providing the means of subsistence for themselves and their families."

Poverty was not created by man; and therefore could not be removed by man.

"The truth is, that though human institutions appear to be the obvious and obtrusive causes of much mischief to mankind, yet in reality they are light and superficial, they are mere feathers that float on the surface, in comparison with those deeper seated causes of impurity that corrupt the springs and render turbid the whole stream of human life....To prevent the recurrence of misery, is, alas! beyond the power of man".[76]

William Cobbett took an opposite view. Poverty was not ever-present; for the great sufferings of the people which so exercised establishment writers as well as others during these years were a relatively recent phenomenon. Nor was it natural, nor inevitable, for it had a cause.

"The very *name* of England was pronounced throughout the world with respect. That very *name* was thought to mean high-spirit, impartial justice, freedom and happiness. What does it mean *now*? It means that which I have not the power to describe, nor the heart to describe, if I had the power. England now contains the most miserable people that ever trod the earth. It is the seat of greater human suffering; of more pain of body and of mind, than was ever before heard of in the world. In countries, which have been deemed the most wretched; there never has existed wretchedness equal to that, which is now exhibited in this once flourishing, free and happy country....

"This change never can have taken place without *a cause*. There must have been something, and something done *by man* too, to produce this change, this disgraceful, this distressing, this horrible change. God has not afflicted the country with pestilence or with famine; nor has the land been invaded and ravaged by an enemy. Providence has of late, been more than ordinarily benevolent to us. Three successive *harvests* of uncommon abundance have blessed, or would have blessed, these Islands. *Peace* has been undisturbed. War appears not to have been even thought possible....And yet, in the midst of profound peace and abundant harvests the nation seems to be convulsed with the last struggles of gnawing hunger.

"It is *man*, therefore, and not a *benevolent Creator*, who has been the cause of our sufferings, present and past, and of the more horrid sufferings, which we now but reasonably anticipate. To *man*, therefore, must we look for *an account* for these evils, into the cause of which let us, without any want of charity, but, at the same time, without fear and without self-deception, freely inquire."[77]

Malthus, however, altered his line of reasoning quite radically. By the time of the second edition of his Essay, he was characterising the poor as lacking in skill and industry, and therefore as undeserving. They brought their hardships on themselves by their want of frugality, and by their unwillingness to save up against contingencies. In all these vices, they were encouraged by the plentiful subsistence guaranteed to them by the Poor Laws.[78]

Most importantly, the poor reproduced themselves too quickly. In indulging their innate improvidence, irresponsibility and uncontrolled passion, they persistently brought beings into the world whom they had no hope of supporting. The fact that wages were in no way equal to the support of a family was, to them, of little consequence, because there existed the safety net of the Poor

---

76 T. R. Malthus. Essay on the Principle of Population. Penguin ed. Pp. 71-72 and 133.

77 William Cobbett. Political Register. 19/2/1820.

78 T. R. Malthus. An Essay on the Principle of Population. Second ed. P. James ed. Vol. I. Pp. 351-352 and 359.

Laws, through which the poor could throw the burden on to their more virtuous and hardworking neighbours. The Poor Laws, therefore, acted as an encouragement to early marriage, and thus as a stimulant to population, and to poverty.[79]

To Malthus, by this time, the poor were themselves the cause of their own poverty.[80]

Between them, Malthus and Cobbett drew up for us the main lines of debate about poverty, not only for their own times, but for all times. It is hard to think of any argument that does not broadly fit into one of the categories of reasoning used by these two writers – that a continual state of hunger is the natural state of a large part of mankind; that such a state is caused by exploitation by a class of accumulators; that it is brought about by the poor themselves.

Malthus always based his observations upon what he saw as a pre-existent class of proletarian poor; a polarisation between proprietors and labourers being, for him, an inevitable feature of every society that has advanced from the savage state. Malthus never tells us his reasons for this assumption, which conveniently removes from the equation the traditional agricultural community, or, at best, classifies it as part of savage life.

However, we have seen that the poor, as a class, were artificially created from the traditional cultivators of the soil. At Wigston Magna, the historian W. G. Hoskins observed this process taking place in some detail. Basing his remarks on the census report, Hoskins surveyed the state of his village in 1851.

"The peasant system had completely vanished by 1851 and in its place we have the large farm, the absentee landlord, and the capitalist tenant-farmer; and the native peasantry are small occupiers, if they are anything at all."[81]

The displaced farmers of the traditional village now made up a pauper population which it was virtually impossible to maintain. They lived in tiny brick cottages, newly-built by speculative builders; or else old, divided tumble-down farmhouses. The rents were exorbitant. The conditions of life in them were the worst, at least, since the 16th century. Diseases ran rampant and death-rates were high. Many of the dispossessed peasantry were now framework-knitters, whose earnings might be little more than 5s. per week.

"At Wigston we find among them the Dands, the Herricks, and descendants of several other old peasant families whose names have recurred as freeholders and copyholders of inheritance through several centuries. But where was his inheritance now?...The starved peasant looked at his ancestors' lands on his Sunday walk, but he looked in vain for even a single furrow of his own."[82]

In terms of the total amount of time that man has existed upon this earth as a species, it is a relatively short period during which he has produced his subsistence through agriculture. But, throughout the history of agriculture, there have been recurring episodes of exploitation. It has not always been the case. There is no necessary and inevitable connection between agriculture and exploitation, and plenty of examples can be found throughout history of autonomous agricultural communities left free to consume the fruits of their own farming operations , and possibly to trade their own surpluses. Indeed, there is reason to believe that agriculture started in this way. The first communities of farmers seem to have arisen in the near east and in south-eastern Europe. Here, they lived in villages or small towns, in houses made out of mud, and it seems likely that their social system was based on annually elected headmen, councils of elders, and communities of free citizens.[83] The village of Wigston Magna, up until around the middle of the 18th century, might be classed as a semi-

---

79   Ibid. Vol. II. Pp. 120, 88, 106. Vol. I. P. 364.

80   Ibid. Vol. II. P. 107.

81   W. G. Hoskins. The Midland Peasant. P. 267.

82   Ibid. P. 275-276.

83   Stuart Piggott. Ancient Europe. Pp. 40-44.

autonomous agricultural community, along with thousands of other English villages in the 16th and 17th centuries. From these, a certain amount of surplus produce might be drained off in the form of rent, taxes and tithes; but not only were these impositions not so heavy as to cause mass hardship, but certain advantages accrued to the villagers as a result of them. They procured the services of a parish priest. A sympathetic landlord with local affiliations could be a great blessing to a farming community; he might provide protection, both in a physical and a political sense, and be a source also of various economic advantages; charity, hospitality, consumption and employment. The English governments of the 16th and 17th centuries were quite paternalistic in their nature, and provided legal protection for the property rights of small farmers, and showed concern for the poor in the form of the Poor Laws, and the enforcement of the laws against monopolistic trading practices. Villagers elected their own officials, and took their own decisions about village and agricultural affairs.

Nevertheless, the connection between agriculture and exploitation is too recurrent to be merely coincidental; and there are various aspects of the agricultural way of life that render its practitioners peculiarly vulnerable to the depredations of the violent, the competitive and the parasitic. To begin with, unlike communities of hunters and gatherers, who only take from their environment what is necessary to keep themselves alive and comfortable, farmers can produce far more subsistence than they actually need, and this surplus produce, being capable of being drawn off whilst leaving the community intact, constitutes an obvious attraction to the exploitative mindset. In contrast again to the subsistence of hunters and gatherers, the principal article produced by farming communities, grain, has a long shelf-life; it can be transported over great distances; it can be traded, so that the exploiter can gain the benefit of far more of it than he can actually consume himself. In many ways, the agricultural lifestyle is an extremely vulnerable one. For much of the year, the entire subsistence of the village community lies exposed in the open air, in fields and pastures, clearly liable to destruction by any enemy or potential tyrant, with starvation the likely result. The production of this subsistence is labour-intensive, and time-consuming; working farmers do not have huge amounts of time to devote to warlike activities; and although, in 18th century England, conventional political wisdom had it that sturdy husbandmen made the best soldiers, the seasons wait for no man. Once again, it is worthwhile speculating on the comparative psychology of the community-based agriculturalist and his would-be oppressor. The mechanism of projectivity is important here. The members of farming communities might have been physically powerful and inured to hardship by their way of life; but they were not, on a psychological level, warlike, and were therefore, perhaps, trusting and slow to apprehend danger. The exploiter, on the other hand, has an aggressive mindset himself, and for that reason assumes aggression in the environment around him. The competitive mindset has constantly the advantage over the cooperative one. How far back in history Adorno's authoritarian, anti-democratic personality can be found can only, of course, be guessed at.

The system of exploitation which has been the subject of this book finds many parallels throughout history, all displaying features with which we have become familiar.

Superior physical force, of course, is the most basic and the most ubiquitous instrument of oppression. Its use for purposes of accumulating agricultural wealth can first be seen with the emergence, in the second millennium B.C., of the bronze age warrior aristocracy. Here, technological progress played the crucial part, as the advance of bronze-working enabled increasingly efficient methods of killing to be developed. The control over the trade upon which the working of bronze depended monopolised those methods of killing within an elite. In the later bronze age long slashing swords were in use across Europe, upon which came to be based the power and the wealth of a cosmopolitan aristocracy. From the period of their predominance we can date an early re-organisation of the agricultural system, which may have involved the breaking up of agricultural communities, but certainly resulted in the establishment of individual farms worked by extended families. This systematically organised landscape centred on the series of hillforts which were beginning to spring up, which seemed to combine the defensive functions of the Norman castle with the storage capacity of the mediaeval tithe-barn; and into these, perhaps, the ancient farmers were compelled to deposit their surpluses, particularly of grain and of spun woollen yarn.[84]

Exploitation by military conquest is discernible in the historical record at many points. The Roman occupation of Britain resulted in land and personal taxes being imposed both in money and in kind. Detailed assessment documents were drawn up containing numbers of the inhabitants, and valuations of their property and agricultural produce. Where a Romanised British aristocracy remained in charge, the tax-take seems to have represented around ten per cent of the produce. But the areas where the native aristocracy had resisted the Roman advance, and had consequently been eliminated, fell directly under the sway of the Roman army. Such areas included the fenlands, Cranborne Chase, Derbyshire and the north, and here around sixty per cent of the produce appears to have been drained out of the localities. One might speculate that the difference, around fifty per cent, constituted roughly the rent which the Roman overlords allowed the estate-owners to take in order to support their luxurious lifestyle. Taxes paid in coin were deposited in the Treasury of the Roman government. Taxes in kind, and particularly the corn-tax, were delivered over to the military authorities. Upon the agriculturalists fell the burden of the army by whom they were occupied. The ubiquitous fortifications were made at their expence. The roads upon which the army marched were kept in repair by native labour working under Roman military engineers. The Roman intelligence service was run using horses supplied by native farmers, or else requisitioned from them; large and luxurious posting stations were built along the way at their expence, And natives were themselves liable to be conscripted into the Roman army.[85]

The connection between agricultural exploitation and warfare is varying and complex; but almost invariably present. In the metamorphosis of the leaders of English society into its exploiters, which took place during the 18th century, warfare played a crucial role in concentrating political and financial power into the hands of those for whom war was the harvest. The kings of Celtic Britain, it has been suggested, may have promoted a state of constant warfare in order to consolidate their position as the protectors of communities. Over time, protection can easily develop into racket; and perhaps the biggest racket of all was the *pax Romana*.[86]

In England in the 9th century, as the annual incursions of Scandinavian raiders were causing devastation in the countryside, the Wessex dynasty of King Alfred placed the whole of society on a war footing. Under the pressure of this external violence, the landscape was yet again artificially re-organised on a large scale. Fortified burhs were set up along frontiers and in strategic places, and the people forced or encouraged to settle in and around them. The abandonment of archaeological sites testifies to mass movements of population, at the time of King Athelstan, for example, in the 920s and 930s; and the result was a system of nucleated villages, open fields and communal agriculture. The ever-present need for security placed a growing control over resources in the hands of the king and the military part of the nation. Progressively, the peasantry were forced to sacrifice personal liberty in return for protection, and to become the bondmen of great lords. The thegns drew the resources out of the countryside and used them in support of the king. The burdens on the land grew heavier, in terms of military and other services, taxation in money and supplies in kind. Ultimately, most of the burden fell on the cultivators of the soil. In the face of the Viking threat, the English monarchy, the powerful landed families, and the class of thegns all grew immensely rich and powerful at the

---

84 Ian Armit, Celtic Scotland. Pp. 19, 24, 46-48 and 69. Barry Cunliffe. Danebury. Pp. 43-46, 119-120, 123-126, 145-146 and 152.
85 Ian Richmond. Roman Britain. Pp. 130, 90-91 and 97.
86 Ian Armit. Celtic Scotland. P. 48.

expence of the rest of society, and there opened up a huge gulf between the agricultural and military sections of the population in terms of wealth, power and status.[87]

A productive agricultural country such as England was, with the strong and efficient system of administration and taxation which the Anglo-Saxon rulers put in place, was an obvious attraction for aggressive predators. In the 11th century, the Danish kings drained huge amounts of wealth out of the country. In 1018, Canute took £82,500, the equivalent of thirty tons of silver and two-thirds of all the coinage minted in the land.[88]

In 1066, William of Normandy took over, ready-made, the exploitative institutions of the Anglo-Saxon monarchy, and used them to his own advantage with a degree of savagery and ruthlessness which suggests sadism. Tax followed arbitrary tax. William's constant and foremost need was for fighting forces. In the winter of 1085, he raised an army so large that "people wondered how this country could maintain that army", and it was dispersed and quartered upon the countryside. In those areas that dared to resist, the land was laid waste, and the people massacred.

"Certainly in his time people had much oppression and very many injuries." The king "oppressed the poor"; he was "so very stark and deprived his subjects of many a mark of gold and more hundreds of pounds of silver, that he took with great injustice….for greediness he loved above all."

Like his Roman and Anglo-Saxon predecessors, William ordered to be made a catalogue of the taxable wealth of the kingdom.

"He ruled over England, and by his cunning it was so examined that there was not one hide in England that he did not know who owned it, and what it was worth, and then set it down in his record."

The making of the famous Domesday Book accompanied various renewed pieces of fiscal outrage perpetrated by William towards the end of his life.

The consequences of Norman rule to the English countryside, even those parts spared the wrath of the king, included hunger, diseases of man and beast, harvest deficiency, and the Great Famine of 1082. The progressive concentration of landownership into fewer and fewer hands, which was already taking place in Anglo-Saxon times as a result of constant warfare, reached a peak during the reign of William I. By the time of Domesday, eighty per cent of the heads of households were recorded as being in bondage of some sort to great men. Here is the polarisation that we have often observed between agricultural producers and militaristic consumers.

Robert Losinga, Bishop of Hereford, seems to have been a sort of 11th century William Cobbett.

"And the land was vexed with many calamities arising from the collection of the royal money."[89]

The exploitation of rural communities is generally carried out the more ruthlessly by oppressors who are of a different race, nationality or religion from their victims. In that situation, the aggressor is the more easily able to convince himself of the utter worthlessness or wickedness of his victim. The system of fiscal extortion which Cobbett named "the Thing" came into being as the result of the introduction of a Dutch king to the English throne in 1688, and of the wars which he saw it as in his interest to wage. Many of his counsellors arrived with him from Holland. The financial men who operated "the Thing" were also, many of them, outsiders with little or no feeling of English nationality. It was almost as if a new set of conquerors had arrived from overseas, and the English aristocrats, rather like their Romano-British predecessors, had cooperated with them, and acquiesced in their financial demands, and were allowed, in return, a growing opulence and an excessively luxurious lifestyle. Many, interestingly and significantly, claimed to be descended from the Norman

---

87 Michael Wood. Domesday. Pp. 94-107.
88 Ibid. Pp.146-147.
89 Michael Wood. Domesday. Pp. 18-21, 159 and 149.

conquerors; and in time their English language came to be spoken in a way intended to set them above the ordinary Englishman.

However, the oppression of the agricultural communities of Catholic Ireland, by landlords who were English or Protestant, was still more ruthless and intense even than that of their English counterparts.

The harshest exploiters, then, often tend to be invaders, outsiders or newcomers of some sort. The sword-wielding aristocrats of the bronze age were probably Celts – possibly the first Indo-European speakers to arrive on these islands – and whilst they lived off the productions of the indigenous Neolithic cultivators, it was perhaps the Celtic language that formed a principal line of demarcation between the producer and the consumer; between the out-group and the in-group.[90]

In Roman times, the distinction between the producer and the consumer was defined, in the minds of the dominant group, in cultural terms. The Romanised way of life, and Romanised manners, religion, literature and art all came increasingly to be what distinguished the new elite, whether of Roman or of native origin, from the rest of society. The Roman historian, Tacitus, thought that dining-rooms and bath-houses were foremost among the hallmarks of civility. Apart from the obvious ostentatious consumption involved in dining-rooms and bath-houses, an obsession with cleanliness can be found among the characteristics of the anti-democratic personality, which accompanies the stereotyping of the out-group as dirty, or "the great unwashed". In all these ways, the Roman elite distinguished the urban "civilisation" of the luxurious consumers from the rustic "barbarity" of the cultivators of the soil.[91]

Similar observations might be made of the Norman aristocracy imposed upon England by William I. These latest new overlords put their contempt for the English people on display in many ways. Most of the Anglo-Saxon cathedrals and churches were quickly demolished, and replaced with unnecessarily large and ostentatious buildings, with wealth sucked out of the countryside, and by labourers whose relationship with their Norman masters was such as may be guessed at. In propaganda, the necessary tool of every exploitative elite, the English culture was condemned as insular and backward; their literature as unworthy of note; and their language as the hallmark of barbarity.[92]

A luxury which is deliberately excessive, and has display as its purpose, seems to be a distinguishing feature of every exploitative elite, not excluding the sword-wielding aristocracy of the bronze age. Archaeologists find their substantial houses, not just in Britain, but throughout Europe. Their opulent single graves are clearly intended to magnify the status of individual warriors, and are easily differentiated from the humbler communal burials of their agricultural predecessors. At bronze age sites such as these evidence is found of luxurious and exotic artefacts both of weaponry, and of domestic use and display.[93]

We previously noted Henry Colman's observations on the dining habits of the English elite of the 1840s. Uncannily, in the luxurious homes of the Romano-British landlord class of the first few centuries A.D., things were little different. As in Victorian England, wine was the article of conspicuous consumption on which all the others centred, and vast amounts of it were imported, to grace the tables of the well-to-do on every occasion of lavish and elegant entertaining. The silver plate on which the food was served was the pride of the family, and was matched by the dishes, the jugs and the drinking vessels, all of the same metal, and imported from the Mediterranean or from Gaul. Other table furnishings were made from bronze, such as lamps and candelabra, heated dishes,

90 Ian Armit. Celtic Scotland. Pp. 22-26.
91 Ian Richmond. Roman Britain. P. 113.
92 Michael Wood. Domesday. P. 160.
93 Ian Armit. Celtic Scotland. Pp. 27 and 18.

containers and wine-strainers. Bronze work could be made more elaborate, with wine-ladles, cups and jars being enamelled and decorated. From the 4th century, archaeologists can identify Rhenish glass and glazed pottery, in the form of jugs, and bowls, and plates, and even Cobbett's despised decanters. It was almost as if a pattern had been set on which the 19th century wealthy elitist could model is own habits of conspicuous consumption – right down to the very finger-bowls![94]

In all systems of exploitation, there seems to be a tendency, over time, for the burden placed upon the productive classes to be gradually made heavier. The exploitative mindset is an essentially competitive one; and the competitive strains that arise within elites, and between their individual members, seem to dictate that an ever greater amount of wealth needs to be withdrawn from the productive economy. This leads to the polarisation which we have observed at so many points, as the personality needs of the in-group for a more and more elevated lifestyle lead to poverty and degradation in society at large.

Such a trend is clearly visible in later Roman times. From many of the provinces of the Roman Empire during the 4th and 5th centuries come complaints about rising and extortionate levels of taxation, which often carried off more than a quarter of the agricultural output. The economic effects of this were such as any reader of William Cobbett might be able to predict. Businesses were destroyed, and poorer soils went out of production. In Asia Minor this amounted to ten per cent of the land; in parts of north Africa, to between a third and a half. At the same time, landlords in Gaul, for example, many of whom were deserting the countryside for what they saw as the more civilised culture of the Romanised towns, were adding to the burdens of their tenants. Land was becoming concentrated more and more in the hands of the great landlord, the splendour of whose lifestyle was becoming ever more striking. In southern England, the effect of all this was the building of large numbers of villas, of increasing size and opulence. The growing prosperity of this class can be traced in the conversion of the modest villas of early Roman times into the corridor houses of the 3rd century, most of which were by now equipped with bath-houses and dining-rooms. The 4th century saw the further development of these houses into large courtyard villas, some truly massive, as at Bignor and Fishbourne in Sussex. The layout of these villas testifies to the priority given to leisure, entertaining and elegance. Households were divided, in order to keep the presiding family separate from the servants and the workpeople. At Hambledon, in Buckinghamshire, the main front of the house was reversed, so that the labourers and the farm buildings could no longer offend the genteel eyes of the occupants.[95] The parallel with the English aristocracy of the 18th and 19th centuries hardly needs a mention.

The reverse side of the coin was also as might be expected. In later Roman times, peasant farming became less and less viable; profit became impossible; subsistence difficult. With his capital gone, many a small farmer was forced into dependency upon great lords, and often it was in a servile capacity. There are suggestions of famines, and epidemics, and plagues….[96]

With the growth of opulence and luxury comes eventually also an element of decadence. The more outrageous the levels of wealth and display among the members of the elite, the greater their professed contempt for the producers of that wealth. We have seen how, in the England of William Cobbett some members of the ruling classes set out deliberately to humiliate their humbler neighbours; some took a kind of sordid pleasure in separating man from wife and parent from child; and personal abuse of this sort did more than anything to produce indignation among ordinary people.

The universal counterpart of decadence of this sort, involving humiliation and cruelty that is, at best unthinking and at worst deliberately sadistic, is unrest among the victims often leading to

---

94 Ian Richmond. Roman Britain. Pp. 171-177.
95 Ibid. Pp. 113-118.
96 Michael Wood. Domesday. P. 48.

physical violence. Towards the end of the iron age, the members of the aristocratic societies of Britain and Gaul seem to have acquired a passion for Italian wines; and a trade grew up based largely on the import of these wines in return for slaves taken from the indigenous communities, and exported to the consumer markets of Rome. A Roman writer observed that Gauls loved wine so much that they would give a slave for a single amphora![97]

Comeuppance came. At Danebury Ring in Hampshire, around 100 B.C., archaeologists have found that the main gateway giving access to the interior of the fort was burnt down, and that numbers of bodies had been thrown into pits. This was followed by the virtual abandonment of the fort. Other hillforts in the area seem to have suffered the same fate at about the same time. One prehistorian has ventured to speculate on "vitrified" hillforts, fired with such intense heat that could not have been obtained by accident or in battle, but fired in a deliberate and sustained manner; that their destruction was "a premeditated act of intense symbolic power as the seats of a warrior aristocracy were permanently and spectacularly razed."[98]

In later Roman times, the increasing exactions of the Romano-Gallic landlords led to disturbances and rebellion among their tenants. And the Roman Empire itself was finally sunk under the attacks of those whom it had labelled barbarian.

Previous to this destruction, the amount of the produce gathered up in taxes by the Roman government is estimated at around twenty-five per cent. But when William Cobbett rode his horse through the Valley of the Wiltshire Avon in 1826, he calculated that almost nineteen-twentieths of the produce of the cultivators were being carried away in one way or another. In the post-Poor Law era of the hungry forties, the proportion must have been greater still. In England, too, the populace was roused to violence by the treatment they received. The agricultural revolt of 1830 threatened to destroy the system of exploitation; it enjoyed short-term success. But in England the ruthless use of the army and the law subdued it; and the people's anger was left to simmer on, manifesting itself rather ineffectually from time to time in the anonymous firing of farmers' property....

A kind of progress is discernible in the history of exploitation. The more "primitive" systems of oppression involved the collection of tithes and taxes, of tributes and rent, in the form of actual produce; or else in personal services, either military or agricultural. These were the economies of the hillfort and the tithe-barn; of the lord's demesne and of his personal military retinue. During the last century or two before the Roman conquest, the use of money became more usual. In many systems wealth was accumulated in services, in kind and in money, in varying proportions; but over time there was a clear trend towards converting the produce of the cultivation of the soil into money before accumulating it into the hands of the elite. Elites themselves eventually became money-based, as well as land-based, as we have seen; and ultimately predominantly money-based.

This distinction, between the produce-based economy and the money-based one, is of crucial importance in determining the fate of agricultural communities. In societies where an exploitative elite gathers up the produce of those under its sway in the form of grain, woollen yarn, livestock etc., that elite has a powerful interest in some sort of minimum state of well-being for the agricultural system; where it is the manpower that is harvested, similar considerations apply. But the conversion of the produce into money, previously to its being gathered up by the wealthy in-group, puts an entirely different complexion upon the whole situation. We have seen how, in Cobbett's England, the theorists about the national wealth strenuously advocated the minimisation of consumption in the

97   Barry Cunliffe. Danebury. Pp.174-175.
98   Barry Cunliffe. Danebury. Pp. 73 and 172. Ian Armit. Celtic Scotland. P. 59.

countryside, in order to turn the greatest possible proportion of produce into money, which could then be collected up in rent and taxes. To this end, they recommended the re-organisation of agriculture; the amalgamation of farms; the conversion of tillage into labour-saving systems of capitalist farming, and livestock production in particular; a greater proportion of work came to be performed by horse and by machine; seasonal and specialist labour was employed wherever possible. And the object of it all was the breaking-up of the agricultural communities, and the clearing away from the countryside of the supposedly useless and unproductive mouths, that consumed the produce before it could be turned into money.

Those who controlled that money, the quantity of it, its value and its distribution, therefore exercised ultimate control over the distribution of all the wealth that was actually generated in the productive economy.

The idea was not new. The last century of Roman rule in Britain saw the development of an economy much more heavily orientated towards the use of money; and in the transactions of everyday life, particularly the collection of taxes, payment in coin came to replace payments in kind. Many of the tricks of which Cobbett accused the Paper-Money Men were foreshadowed by the artifices of this period. At one time, attempts were made to contract the circulating medium; at another the country was awash with coins of gold and silver. At one time the coinage would be debased, and official efforts were directed towards controlling the price rises inevitably consequent upon this; at another the intrinsic value of the coins was made equal to their face value, and prices remained stable. The effects upon the countryside of this fluctuating system of monetary exploitation will not seem unfamiliar to anyone conversant with the processes of agricultural change in the England of the 18th and 19th centuries.

The concentration, during this period, of landownership into the hands of a restricted group of wealthy landlords has already been mentioned. In some areas of southern England, this was accompanied by yet another re-organisation of the landscape, involving the conversion of tillage to pasture. The older field-systems were done away with, and in their place was laid out a system of large enclosures for livestock. Livestock production took the place of tillage, and became a renowned feature of the British economy in the 4th century. Wool seems to have been particularly important. From around Winchester to the north Cotswolds, wealthy villas sprang up everywhere, in connection with the fleeces produced in the British countryside. Woollen cloth and cattle hides came to figure largely among the exports from these islands.[99]

Of course, a rural economy geared up to livestock production suggests a relative sparseness of population. There is evidence from this period of the abandonment of agricultural villages; whether forced or not we can only surmise. But that some sort of man-made attempt was being made to keep population to a minimum is suggested by the practice of infanticide, which seems to have been associated with nearly all the villas.[100]

"What happened", one historian is prompted to ask, "to the mass of the workforce of Roman Britain, the dependent peasantry whose economic and social status sank to the level of tied labourers?"

What happened, in similar circumstances, to the dependent peasantry of 19th century England; when the great and all-pervading complexity of the money economy had advanced far beyond anything known even in Roman times; when paper currency and fictitious credit were important new factors in the equation?

Many thousands were starved, or killed by the diseases associated with malnutrition; many thousands more were forced to emigrate; many more moved into cities or into areas of intensive

---

99 Ian Richmond. Roman Britain. Pp, 182-185 and 131. Michael Wood. Domesday. Pp. 41, 46-48 and 55.

100 Ian Richmond. Roman Britain. Pp. 131 and 117.

industrial production, so that their children could earn a pittance in the factories; those who remained in the countryside were unemployed, or under-employed, and as paupers many alternated between seasonal work on the farms and the regime of the workhouse. The clearances in Scotland; the driving away of the peasantry from the estates of the Irish landlords; these are all symptoms of the desire to maximise, in money, the returns of the land to the governing classes. We may mark them down as the consequences that tend to follow from the intensive financial and monetary exploitation of a productive rural economy by a small but determined, aggressive and competitive elite.

More recent history abounds in examples of this process taking place all over the world; it takes many guises; there are an infinite number of variations on the theme; but all are modelled on what happened in England during the 18th and 19th centuries.

Colonial conquest has often been the trigger for the concentration of landownership into a few hands and the ejection of the traditional communities of cultivators. Brazil, under the Portuguese conquerors, came to have one of the most restricted systems of landownership in the world, with less than one per cent of proprietors in control of nearly half of total production. The indigenous agriculturalists of Brazil, now predominantly landless, were subjected to discriminatory policies and denied basic political rights; and this process of clearance is responsible for many of the social problems of Brazil today, with 32 million people said to be suffering from hunger in 1993.[101]

In South Africa, the story was similar. Under the policy of apartheid introduced in 1913, many thousands of black farming families were forced off the land, excluded from proper citizenship, and banned from owning land. It is not difficult to trace the many social problems of South Africa today back to this process.[102]

But the process can take place without any previous conquest by those with ambitions of empire. When the investment-hungry capitalists of the western world turn their attention to distant parts of the globe, similar consequences can ensue. In the later 19th century, American investment in the Philippines brought about the clearance of land for the production of crops wanted for export to the United States and to Europe – cotton, hemp, tobacco, and, most significantly, sugar. The peasants forced off the land had little choice but to become labourers in the clearing of land, and subsequently on the new farms. When the United States took the Philippines under direct control, there was an even more aggressive drive towards the clearing away of forest, and the conversion of farms producing rice for subsistence, to sugar production for export. Pools of displaced and dependent labour were constantly being created in this way, and the consequences of this policy could still be seen in the Philippines in recent times. On Negros Island, for example, where the descendants of the original cultivators now worked on the sugar plantations, unscrupulous gangmasters plied an illegal but lucrative trade in the supply of labour. This was enabled to happen by the constant surplus of labour and the comparatively low labour requirements of the sugar crop. Unemployment was chronic and growing. The work was seasonal, and only provided employment for half the year. Labourers were paid less than half the minimum wage. They lived in decrepit bunkhouses provided by the landlords, or else they built their own shacks around the plantations. Their diet consisted of unripe bananas, wild roots, frogs, mice and shellfish, with consequences in terms of nutritional status, disease and life expectancy that may be guessed at.[103]

---

101   Francisco Menezes and Candido Gzybowski in Farmers' World Network. Landmark Magazine. July 1998. Pp. 6-7.

102   Alastair Bradstock in Farmers' World Network. Landmark Magazine. August/September 1999. Pp. 10-11.

103   Dan Pollard and Jayson Cainglet in Farmers; World Network. Landmark Magazine. September/October 1998. Pp.3-5.

As in England, the wealth sucked out of the countryside by the displacement of the peasantry can lead to financial power, political power, and even military predominance. It can even alter the whole balance of power on a worldwide scale. After the Russian Revolution of 1917, the Soviet authorities determined on a policy of industrialisation and military aggrandizement. Already by 1921, there was famine, and Lenin was said to have echoed the sentiments of the English elite of the 18th and 19th centuries.

"Let the peasants starve."

And he ordered starving farmers to be hanged and their bodies displayed at the roadside.

A policy of forced appropriation of grain for export was already being pursued in the 1920s. Josef Stalin intensified the pressure. Land was seized, and its occupants forced into collective farms in order to create a greater surplus to be turned into money by exportation. When the system of collectivisation did not increase the surplus to the desired extent, Stalin decided on forcible land clearance to achieve his aims. Rather in the manner of a latter-day Duke of Portland, but with even greater savagery, he ordered war to be waged against virtually the whole of the rural population.

"We must break the back of the peasantry."

In the Ukraine, particularly, it being one of the most fertile areas, Stalin ordered grain to be forcibly taken from the farms and sold abroad. By December 1931, an artificial famine had been created, and the farming people were reduced to eating dogs, horses, rotten potatoes and the bark of trees; and eventually each other. As in England, political motives were ascribed to the hungry and discontented. Those guilty of subsistence crime were ordered to be shot under the "Misappropriation of Socialist Property Law". Stalin branded the farmers as "saboteurs" and declared "a fight to the death. These people deliberately tried to sabotage the Soviet stage".

As in England, the army was ordered into the affected areas, but, also as in England, not to bring food aid. The farming people were shot on sight, or herded into camps, or else transported to the vast empty spaces of Siberia. In total, between ten and fifteen million people are said to have been shot, starved or deported, and among the benefits that accrued to the human race as a result can be cited the cold war and the proliferation of nuclear weapons.[104]

With the passing acquaintance that we have acquired with the arguments of the English propagandists on the subject of poverty, it will come as no surprise that the perpetrators of acts of mass depredation such as this often present them as, in some way or other, contributing to the improvement of the human race. The doctrine of "development" was introduced to the world by President Harry Truman in his inaugural address in 1949.

"We must embark on a bold new programme for making the benefits of our scientific advances and industrial progress available for the improvement and growth of underdeveloped areas."

It was on this pretext that the many international institutions were set up, whose actual function over the years has turned out to be to confine the financial benefits of global production to a narrow in-group of governments and transnational companies. These included the World Bank, the International Monetary Fund, the G7 and G8, and the World Trade Organisation. The "developmental" explanation of poverty we can loosely place in the early Malthusian category of the Essay of 1798; that people are destitute in their natural and pre-existent state because there is simply not enough food to go around. According to this explanation, the solution to the problem of poverty is "growth". Here is Truman again.

"Greater production is the key to prosperity and peace. And the key to greater production is a wider and more vigorous application of modern scientific and technical knowledge."[105]

---

104 Simon Sebag Montefiore in Daily Mail. 26/7/2008.
105 Farooq Khan. Islam can make Poverty History. Pp.8-9.

By the time of the World Food Summit of 1974, the preoccupation was the same. Participants affected a concern with producing enough food on a worldwide scale to feed an increasing population. At the time, the United Nations defined food security as follows;-

"The availability at all times of adequate world supplies of basic food-stuffs….to sustain a steady expansion of food consumption….and to offset fluctuations in production and prices."

To this end, modern technologies were introduced in many countries where they had previously been unknown; and farmers were brought to a dependence on imported inputs such as machinery, pesticides, fertilizers and new varieties of seed. This was known as the Green Revolution, and in many areas it had the desired effect in raising yields. But the Green Revolution, like the Agricultural one before it, had the effect of confining the means of production to a wealthy few; of displacing the traditional cultivators from the land; and of concentrating on capitalist cash crops, rather than subsistence ones, often for export, where the end-product was not produce, but money; this was then drawn off in the form of rent, taxes, and through the costs of the new technology.

This process of "modernisation" accentuated even more the concentration of landownership in, for example, Brazil; where, during the 1970s and 1980s, 30 million people were displaced from the land by a combination of big landowners and agribusiness companies; and under the auspices of the military regime there. This was carried out with such force that much violence and many deaths resulted.[106]

In keeping with the aims of the Green Revolution was the plan known as "Vision 2020". This was a strategy drawn up by a team of American consultants for the modernising and mechanising of the agriculture of the Indian province of Andhra Pradesh. It involved the use of genetically modified crops, and aimed at a monocultural, intensive system of agriculture producing cash crops mainly for export. The most significant feature of the plan was the increase of farm size and the use of mechanisation which was to lead to the enforced displacement from the land of twenty million farming families. The strategy contained no provision as to what was to happen to these people; it was a mere trifling side-effect; and the vague references to employment in the service industries merely bring to mind once again that haunting phrase of Stephen Addington's from 1772.

"Some indeed say, 'Let the farmers starve'."[107]

Thus, under the doctrine of development, a plan which will clearly have the effect of concentrating wealth into the hands of an in-group, and impoverishing millions, can be presented as contributing to the elimination of poverty by promoting "growth".

The systems of agriculture promoted by the Green Revolution had a further undesirable effect – they contributed towards bringing the poorer nations into debt. Over a period of fifty years, 500 billion dollars were invested in Africa, but at the end of it Africans on average were poorer than they had been. Collectively, the nations of Africa were in debt to the tune of 293 billion dollars; and whilst 27 million dollars a day were being paid to financiers and investors, 70 per cent of people in sub-Saharan Africa were living on two dollars a day, and two hundred million people were going hungry every day.[108]

National debts, as we have seen, have certain political consequences. They seem invariably to lead to political corruption, and, because of the arbitrary nature of the taxation needed to service them, they tend necessarily towards anti-democratic government, and the by-passing, suspension or

---

106   Francisco Menezes and Candido Gzybowski in Farmers' World Network. Landmark Magazine. July 1998. Pp. 6-7.

107   Michael Hart in Farmers' World Network Landmark Magazine. September/October 2001. Pp. 13-14. Stephen Addington. An Inquiry into the Reasons for and against Inclosing Open-Fields. P. 32.

108   Farooq Khan. Islam can make Poverty History. P. 11.

abolition of the representative elements of national constitutions. The Rothschild family recognised long ago the power which indebtedness gave to the creditor over the debtor; to the great financiers over the governments of indebted nations.

Bangladesh is a case in point. In 1973-4, the per capita national debt there amounted to 6.59 dollars. By 1998-9, this had risen to 115.9 dollars. As a result, an alliance grew up between the corrupt ruling elite of Bangladesh and the international financial institutions of the western world. In 2003, it was estimated that 1.3 billion dollars were disappearing every year through endemic corruption; and the loss of such sums was clearly contributing to increase the debt still further. Massive amounts of money were being sucked into the inefficient workings of government departments; the oiling of the proceedings of parliament; grants and pensions to members of the political elite and their families; and unnecessary missions to foreign countries. Further squanderings went on in the building of monuments and bridges, and cultural and sporting functions which were little more than propaganda. William Cobbett might have recognised the symptoms. The upshot was that the influence of public opinion was excluded from the decision-making process. Electoral corruption determined the outcome of elections; the resulting government was accountable to no one; and taxes could be levied at will at any time.[109]

The political elite of Bangladesh joined forces with the financial institutions, and in return for the betrayal of their own people, were allowed to build their palaces, and to enjoy a luxurious lifestyle within.[110] Does nothing change?

The power which national indebtedness and budgetary deficit hand to the international financial institutions is exercised in negotiations over loans, debt restructuring and financial aid. Packages come with conditions attached; and in this way, in Bangladesh, for example, the World Bank has gained a control over the whole economy.[111]

The demands of the monied man are extremely inimical to the well-being of the populations of the countries where they operate. Conditions are laid down that multinational companies should be allowed free access the ownership of the natural resources of the countries in question. In Bangladesh, energy production is all in the hands of large foreign companies, and the ports, the canals and the railways have all fallen under foreign control. In South Africa, the lever of financial aid was used to deliver water resources into the hands of wealthy European companies, whilst IMF loans to, among others, Angola and Tanzania ensured that their water services went the same way. Africans no longer own their own water. Similarly in Bolivia, negotiations with the IMF compelled the government there to allow foreign companies to take control of the country's natural resources; the export of those resources cannot be taxed.[112] Thus, the financiers ensure that an indebted nation has no way to escape the trammels of debt; and is forced to throw the produce of its land on to the world market merely to keep its head above water.

Another condition often imposed is the creation of what is euphemistically termed an investment friendly environment. Instances of the consequences of this environment are to be seen in many countries of the world. From prawn farms to golf courses, "investment" projects frequently involve the ejection from the landscape of those who make their living there. In Malaysia in 1998, there was such a pressing need to become self-sufficient in food that even urban consumers with small gardens or window-boxes were being urged to produce some food of their own. And yet, in the fertile food-

109   Mujibul Islam. Bangladesh's Economic Crisis. Pp. 7-8, 21, 11 and 15.
110   Ibid. P. 25.
111   Ibid. P. 9.
112   Ibid. P. 8. Farooq Khan. Islam can make Poverty History. P. 12. Chris Emerson in Farmers' World Network Landmark Magazine. December 2004. Pp. 10-11.

producing region of north-west Penang, organic farmers were being driven from their farms to make way for projects of industrial development and urban growth.[113]

The government of the Philippines seems to have caved in to the international financial interest more completely than most. A combination of Philippino big business and foreign multinationals has been allowed free rein over the clearing of land and its conversion to cash crop production. Vast areas of forest have been felled by them for timber. They are the beneficiaries of generous mining concessions, covering six million hectares. And they engage in large-scale fishing operations, as well as intensive prawn production, much to the injury of the pre-existing population of farming and fisher folk. Most glaringly grotesque of all are the operations of the giant real estate companies. Hacienda Looc was a productive agricultural estate of 8650 hectares situated fifty-five miles south of Manila, that was home to 10,000 agricultural and fishing families. With the active cooperation of corrupt local and government officials, this region was illegally taken over by multinational developers for a tourist project which involved the building of four golf courses, two marinas, beach resorts and hotels. The amount of force needed to remove the inhabitants of this area resulted in the deaths of farmers; and was accompanied, predictably enough, by a campaign of anti-farmer propaganda. As a result, between 75 and 90 per cent of the farmers are now landless, with consequences for them and their families with which we have by now become familiar.[114]

The next concession demanded by the international financial institutions in return for maintaining the flow of aid and credit goes by the rather curious name of trade liberalisation. By this is meant the artificial exclusion, by monopolistic trade practices, of all small-scale native farmers from markets. The principle underlying this is simple enough, and can be seen in operation in any supermarket – sell a given category of produce at impossibly low prices until the small-scale competition has been forced out of business, and then, when a near monopoly has been attained, raise the prices to more profitable levels. In the modern world, this process can be seen in action across the globe. In Mexico, for example, the conditions imposed by the rescheduling of the debt led to the opening of its markets to imports of subsidised foodstuffs. In 1991, Mexico imported a quarter of a million tons of corn. By 1996, this had risen to five million tons, and over the same period imports of wheat quadrupled. Previously, Mexico had been an exporter of soya beans, green beans and sorghum, but by 1996 had become dependent on the multinational companies for its supply of these. Nicaragua had been self-sufficient in food, but by 2005 was importing food to the value of 200 million dollars a year. In Bolivia, the story was the same, with the value of food imports having risen by 2004 from one million dollars to ten million.[115]

Many of those countries which are insulted with the appellations of poor, third world or underdeveloped are also favoured with packages of what is called food aid, whereby corn is dumped on them completely free.

Indigenous communities of cultivators are completely unable to compete in this environment of market distortion, and families are forced out of business in their millions. In this way, countries that are perfectly capable of producing their own food are forced on to a dependence for their subsistence upon the multinational trading companies. When we have the benefit of hindsight, it will possibly

---

113   Jennifer Mourin in Farmers' World Network Landmark Magazine. November/December 1998. P. 4.

114   Jayson Cainglet in Farmers' World Network Landmark Magazine. November/December 1997. Pp. 11-12.

115   Victor Suarez Carrera in Farmers' World Network Landmark Magazine. October/November 1996. P. 9. Nicaragua Solidarity Campaign in Farmers' World Network Landmark Magazine. May 2005. Pp. 10-11. Chris Emerson in Farmers' World Network Landmark Magazine. December 2004. Pp. 10-11.

appear that this process of "trade liberalisation" has been the most efficient means yet devised of clearing the land of traditional farming families. In very many countries, it has had the effect of emptying the countryside of people and causing a mass migration to the cities or to other countries. In their place come the monocultural, capital-intensive, labour-saving systems of agriculture of international agribusiness, subsidised by governments, and producing cash crops for export.

When these objectives have been achieved, and dependency enforced, food aid can be withdrawn, as in the case of Bolivia, and the consumers of these countries forced on to world markets, where prices are routinely manipulated by international commodity speculators and the small number of big companies that trade in grain. In Mexico, for example, the result of this process has been a rapid advance in the price of food, to the extent that by 1996 nearly half of the population was in receipt of an income too low to purchase an adequate diet.[116]

The final part of this modern system of exploitation is perhaps the least noticed; but far from the least important. Agricultural countries are compelled to allow their currencies to float on the international markets. This permits international financiers and speculators to manipulate their economies; and for the probable consequences of this, in terms of the movements of prices and wages, and the increasingly unfavourable relationship between the two, it is only necessary to refer to William Cobbett.[117]

These are not, for the most part, poor countries. Bangladesh is a country of predominantly fertile agricultural land; it is favoured with great reserves of coal, gas and uranium; and it has a large workforce. The continent of Africa has plentiful reserves of oil, gas, uranium, copper diamonds and gold. The poverty that is to be found in all the countries that are denominated "third world" conforms much more closely to the Cobbettian model of starvation amidst plenty, than the early Malthusian one of the inability to produce enough subsistence to feed all those who are born into the world. In 1998, India was the world's third largest exporter of wheat, whilst malnutrition ran ever more rampant among its population. Brazil was the third largest exporter of soya, whilst half the people there went hungry. In Bangladesh, 45 million tons of rice a year are produced for a population that could subsist quite happily on 25 millions; and enough seafood plentifully to supply everyone. But in Bangladesh, the wages of a hard week's work are insufficient to maintain a family; millions are hungry or undernourished; clothing and shelter are at a premium; diseases are rife; and the economy as a whole finds, in many respects, an uncanny parallel in William Cobbett's description of the Valley of the Wiltshire Avon from 1826.[118]

"National wealth" has become "global wealth". The international financial and political elite operates through debt and taxation; through currency manipulation; through monopolistic and manipulative trading practices; through investment projects; through the direct ownership of natural resources; and through taking advantage of the vast pools of surplus labour which they themselves have created. The consequences of these latter-day agricultural and industrial revolutions are visible across the globe. Millions of hard-working and multi-skilled families are disconnected from the means of production; these are forced from the farms; birth-rates soar; they migrate across the world; or they settle in slums and shanty-towns on the edge of uncontrollably sprawling cities such as Lagos, Mexico

---

116 Chris Emerson in Farmers' World Network Landmark Magazine. December 2004. Pp. 10-11. Victor Suarez Carrera in Farmers' World Network Landmark Magazine October/November 1996. P. 9.

117 Mujibul Islam. Bangladesh's Economic Crisis. P. 9. Jennifer Mourin in Farmers' World Network Landmark Magazine. January/February 1998. P. 4.

118 Mujibul Islam. Bangladesh's Economic Crisis. Pp. 12-13, 18 and 25. Farooq Khan. Islam can make Poverty History. P. 11. Susan Atkinson in Farmers' World Network Landmark Magazine. May/June 2001. P. 11.

City and Rio de Janeiro; or they remain in the countryside to face unemployment and degradation. The 21,000 unemployed coffee workers said to be camped out along the roadsides in Nicaragua epitomise the inability or unwillingness of capitalist agriculture to soak up the manpower forced from the land. The resulting poverty and indebtedness bring with them child labour, child trafficking, and the actual enslavement of an estimated 27 million men women and children worldwide.[119]

The "developmental" explanation of poverty can be loosely categorised as belonging to the early Malthusian school; but with a happy ending. It posits a natural and pre-existing, chronic and endemic state of hunger and deprivation in the "pre-industrial economy". It ascribes this state to what it sees as "the weaknesses" of this economy – to the lack of technological progress; to the absence of market organisation, infrastructure or credit; and to the inadequacy of yield and produce. It characterises those who practise such economies, at best, as lacking in skill and application; at worst as backward and barbaric. In 18th century England, Arthur Young was perhaps the foremost promoter of this opinion. He contended that the increase of produce and employment generated by the new agriculture would cure the conditions of poverty endemic among the "Goths and Vandals" of the traditional open-field villages. In more modern times President Truman told the world that the solution to the pre-existing problem of hunger among the world's impoverished nations was the spreading of the multinational corporate system of finance and the introduction of technologies designed to increase production.

This view of poverty and history permeates, in a very fundamental way, our thinking and our perceptions about the world we live in. Basically, it is the view of a "progress" taking place, from a natural situation of poverty and misery, to a man-made one of comfort and opulence. It is a matter for never-ceasing astonishment that even those, who write sympathetically on the subject of the world's poor, persist in insulting them with the epithets of "developing" and "underdeveloped". Among these writers, it is widely acknowledged that it is the policies and systems of "development" that cause the deteriorating condition of the world's poor; yet still the remedy is seen as more development, or different development, or better development. In the time of Arthur Young, it was the capitalist agriculture of the enclosed and enlarged farm, which he advocated, which caused the poverty of the members of the traditional communities. The cause is represented as the cure.

At the many points in our history where we can recognise an intensive exploitation and monopolisation of resources by an aggressive elite, historians are to be found who will represent this as in some way progressive, and contributing to the improvement of mankind. Of the conquests of the Normans, it has been suggested that they brought with them a "new conception of the State", and that, in consequence, "it was the Normans who reshaped the life of Europe both politically and intellectually, and who set the development of European civilisation on a new course". This was quoted in a book called The Norman Achievement; and though, in a literal sense, the invasion and exploitation of England was the successful outcome of strenuous efforts directed towards a desired end; nevertheless one can surely be forgiven for wondering whether "achievement" is not too positive a word for the savage and unconscionable plundering of the English nation.[120] Of a similar mindset is the historian who sees the great poverty of the English people during the 18th and 19th centuries and rationalises it into an improving situation brought about by the "agricultural" and "industrial" "revolutions".

---

119   Nicaragua Solidarity Campaign in Farmers' World Network Landmark Magazine. May 2005. Pp. 10-11. Beth Herzfeld in Farmers' World Network Landmark Magazine. May/June 2001. Pp. 4-7.
120   D. C. Douglas. The Norman Achievement. P. 169.

The dichotomy appears almost inescapable and everlasting; Cobbett's dichotomy between the man who works and the man who lives without working; between the producer and the accumulator; which in the hands of the propagandist became the dichotomy between the lower orders and the respectable. An eminent prehistorian of more recent times has seen this dichotomy between the poor and the rich as prevalent in prehistoric times, as enduring throughout history, and as still being with us in the modern world. He characterises it as the distinction between the barbarous and the civilised. Barbarous means rural; civilised means living in a city. And although these words, in fact, convey a neutral and objective meaning, they have acquired negative and positive connotations respectively, according to the prejudices of those who use them. The eminent prehistorian contrasts a "simple peasantry" with a "complex urbanism"; and the crucial difference between the two he sees as the willingness to innovate – to progress technologically – and thus to acquire wealth and pre-eminence in the world.[121] Here is what he has to say about the barbarian agriculturalist. Observe the tone of slightly hostile contempt.

"We have not got to look far, even in the British Isles, for communities of conservators, where differentiation of behaviour, if it is associated with ideas not sanctioned by long tradition within the group, is difficult and dangerous. Nothing can recompense the alienation of the individual from his group; if his new ideas prosper he will be envied; if they fail he will be ridiculed….The tradition of a conserving society is to abide by tradition, even at the risk of prolonging an archaic and ineffective economy, or allowing itself to be superseded by an alien culture, at whose door at least all the blame can them be laid."[122]

This distinction, between the conservator and the innovator, Piggott implies, is, in part at least, genetic. He quotes Julian Huxley.

"Man is the most variable of all organisms – anatomically and physiologically, intellectually and temperamentally."[123]

Thus, he follows Joseph Townsend in asserting that the rich are inherently superior to the poor, and are rich for that reason.

The barbarian attitudes of "violence and hatred, cruelty and the enjoyment of killing, aggression and brutality" are with difficulty channelled and restrained by the advance of civilisation.

"Warfare, the brutal suppression of man by man, of class by class, of age group by age group, of one tribe by another, are as inseparable from the life of prehistoric village civilisation as they are implied by the organisation of even very humanistic town civilisations up to the present day."[124]

And this dichotomy, between the violent and aggressive conservators of the agricultural economy, and the technological innovators of civilised society, Piggott sees as having persisted into the modern world, and as having become the dichotomy between the underdeveloped and the developed. The underdeveloped – the genetically inferior – have resisted the technologies that have become available since the industrial revolution, whilst the more open-minded and innovative developed have embraced them and prospered.

Progress, therefore, consists in the gradual supersession of the negative attributes of rural man by the more positive ones of urban man. Piggott quotes Herbert Spencer from 1850.

---

121 Stuart Piggott. Ancient Europe. Chapter I.
122 Ibid. P. 18. I would very much like to know what the Adorno team would have made of this passage!
123 Ibid. P. 15.
124 Ibid. Pp. 14-15.

"Progress is not an accident but a necessity. It is a part of nature….Evil tends perpetually to disappear….Civilisation, instead of being artificial, is a part of nature; all of a piece with the development of the embryo, or the unfolding of a flower."[125]

Here, Piggott has set out for us what might be termed an orthodox view of progress and the world; embracing a developmental view of poverty; a Malthusian view, in fact, both in the sense that it sees poverty as a natural pre-existing state, and also in the sense that it sees the poor, as barbarian conservators, as themselves the reason why they have not moved on to better things.

In the chapters which follow, Piggott presents a meticulous, painstaking and detailed account of the sites and the finds that have contributed towards our archaeological knowledge of prehistoric times. He treats his data scientifically; he draws his conclusions with caution and propriety; he points out the limitations of the evidence at one point; the plurality of possible interpretations at another. And yet, when he comes to summarise his findings; to place them in a wider context; to abridge them in order that his readers might retain a clearer understanding of the whole; he draws a whole series of conclusions about the comparative mindsets of barbarian and civilised man that the evidence, by its very nature, does not even come close to justifying; and constructs thereupon a world view of poverty and progress.

In summarising his findings, Piggott has abandoned his role as a scientific investigator; and instead is showing an anxiety to make a statement about himself and about the present; and about the relationship between the two. He is wishing to place himself firmly in the progressive camp. As he himself says;-

"The point of view of Western historiography from its beginnings has been that of the innovating societies….The assumptions and beliefs of the innovating societies are familiar to us, for however much of their doctrines we may from time to time reject, we are their product….Much of our thinking on these matters has *inevitably* been coloured by the wish to see a pattern of progress in man's history….An implicit thesis has been that a development from barbarism to civilisation is, or rather should have been, the norm."[126]

Why inevitably?

The tendency to see the past in accordance with our assumptions about the world we live in was the subject of a brilliant little essay, published in 1931, by Herbert Butterfield, entitled The Whig Interpretation of History.

"It is part and parcel of the whig interpretation of history that it studies the past with reference to the present; and though there may be a sense in which this is unobjectionable if its implications are carefully considered, and there may be a sense in which it is inescapable, it has often been an obstruction to historical understanding because it has been taken to mean the study of the past with direct and perpetual reference to the present. Through this system of immediate reference to the present-day, historical personages can easily and irresistibly be classed into the men who furthered progress and the men who tried to hinder it; so that a handy rule of thumb exists by which the historian can select and reject, and can make his points of emphasis….The total result of this method is to impose a certain form upon the whole historical story, and to produce a scheme of general history which is bound to converge beautifully upon the present – all demonstrating throughout the ages the workings of an obvious principle of progress."[127]

The intellectual and psychological tendency which Butterfield describes here is the failing of the general historian; the summariser and the abridger; whose views of the past and of the world find their way into newspapers and school text-books, and into the mindsets and the assumptions of the

---

125 Ibid. Pp. 18-19.
126 Ibid. Pp. 18-20.
127 Herbert Butterfield. The Whig Interpretation of History. Pp. 11-12.

population at large. But when the research historian comes to carry out his detailed and scientific investigations into the minutiae of life in historic and prehistoric times – to perform, in other words, the true and proper task of the historian – he often comes across a mass of material which is completely at odds with the summary and the abridgment. And these two *personae* of the historian, as Stuart Piggott so neatly demonstrates for us, are often, perhaps generally, united in the same person. Here is Butterfield again.

"This attitude to history is not by any means the one which the historical specialist adopts at the precise moment when he is engaged upon his particular research; and indeed as we come closer to the past we find it impossible to follow these principles consistently even though we may have accepted them verbally. In spite of ourselves and in spite of our theories we forget that we had set out to study the past for the sake of the present, we cannot save ourselves from tumbling headlong into it and being immersed in it for its own sake; and very soon we may be concentrated upon the most useless things in the world – Marie Antoinette's earrings or the adventures of the Jacobites. But the attitude is one which we tend to adopt when we are visualising the general course of history or commenting on it, and it is one into which the specialist often slides when he comes to the point of relating his special piece of work to the larger historical story. In other words it represents a fallacy and an unexamined habit of mind into which we fall when we treat of history on the broad scale. It is something which intervenes between the work of the historical specialist and that work, partly of organisation and partly of abridgment, which the general historian carries out; it inserts itself at the change of focus that we make when we pass from the microscopic view of a particular period to our bird's-eye view of the whole; and when it comes it brings with it that whig interpretation of history which is so different from the story which the research student has to tell."[128]

In our capacity as the respected progressives of the modern world, we may be profoundly convinced, with Piggott, that the story which history has to tell is of a development from the barbarous communities of agricultural conservators to the more complex and sophisticated society of urban innovators; from rustic violence and aggression to a settled and civilised state of peace and good order; from a natural state of poverty and misery to an artificial one of opulence and comfort. But when we come to do our detailed historical investigations into technological advance, we find the agricultural communities of "conservators" constantly adapting and improving, as circumstance and environments change. When we turn our attention to warfare and aggression and conquest, we frequently find the weapons in the wrong hands and pointing in the wrong direction; the Celtic farmers did not conquer Rome; the Anglo-Saxon villagers did not invade Normandy; and innovations in warfare and weaponry were, indeed, associated with those whom we like to think of as civilisers. Adam Smith himself made an attempt to explain away this apparent paradox.

"In modern war the great expense of firearms gives an evident advantage to the nation which can best afford that expense, and consequently to an opulent and civilised over a poor and barbarous nation....The invention of firearms, an invention which at first sight appears to be so pernicious, is certainly favourable both to the permanency and to the extension of civilisation."[129]

Finally, when we study social conditions, we invariably find the greatest heights of civilisation and wealth accompanied by the deepest gulfs of poverty, degradation and slavery.

But, in spite of our detailed observations, we seldom allow our findings to make a great or significant impact upon our broad and overall view of progress and development. Here is Herbert Butterfield.

"The study of the past with one eye, so to speak, upon the present is the source of all sins and sophistries in history....And though it might be said that in any event all errors are corrected by

---

128   Ibid. Pp. 14-16.
129   Adam Smith. The Wealth of Nations. Penguin ed. Vol. II. Pp. 296-297.

more detailed study, it must be remembered that the thesis itself is one that has the effect of stopping enquiry; as against the view that we study the past for the sake of the past, it is itself an argument for the limitation of our aims and researches; it is the theory that history is very useful provided that we take it in moderation; and it can be turned into an apology for anything that does not tally with historical research. A more intensive study can only be pursued, as has been seen, in proportion as we abandon this thesis. And even so, even in the last resort, though a further enquiry has corrected so many of the more glaring errors that result from this fallacy, there is a sense in which, if we hold to the whig thesis, historical research can never catch up, for it can never break into the circle in which we are arguing. The specialist himself is cheated and he cries out to us to no purpose, if we re-cast his work from what we call the point of view of the present – still selecting what conforms to our principle, still patching the new research into the old story."[130]

Even aside from such patching, there is another way in which our preconceptions prevent research and enquiry. It is pointed out to us by Stuart Piggott.

"There then arises....the view that features which a nominally civilised community has in common with nominally barbarous societies have to be regarded as regrettable, and not in themselves an essential part of that civilisation, or indeed of civilisation as an abstract concept. We select the qualities we regard as desirable in terms of our own moral and ethical presuppositions of the moment, and constitute civilisation out of them alone."

And he quotes a historian of ancient Greece.

"We condemn slavery, and we are embarrassed for the Greeks, whom we admire so much; therefore we tend either to underestimate its role in their life, or we ignore it altogether, hoping that somehow it will quietly go away."[131]

Slavery, in fact, has been closely associated with most of the great civilised elites in history; probably with the warlike aristocracies of the bronze age and iron age; certainly with the Romans and the Normans; the landed and monied elites of 18th and 19th century England were great slave-owners, either in name, as in the West Indies, or in fact, at home; and slavery is a persistent feature of the global financial and commercial system of the modern world. On the other hand, it is difficult to see what role slavery might have in an autonomous or semi-autonomous agricultural community. Our connection of slavery with "barbarous" societies is merely part of our view of progress and development; a preconception based upon our view of ourselves, which comes to alter our perceptions of the past, and to form a part of that circular argument which, Butterfield complains, is so difficult for the conscientious researcher to break into.

The hope of the general, summarising historian, of the broader views, that certain things will go quietly away, is a prominent and glaring feature of the historiography of the period which forms the subject of this book. A great part of the early chapters of this book is based upon a brilliant study of the life of a Leicestershire village over a period of many centuries, written by W. G. Hoskins. It had to be based on this, because there is nothing else of the kind. The Midland Peasant was written over half a century ago, and should have been a pioneering study. There must be hundreds of villages scattered across England which would lend themselves to studies of this sort; these would yield huge amounts of information about our past in many critical areas of knowledge. But nobody has followed. Not only that, but my impression is that the Midland Peasant is very much under-used and under-valued both by students and by historians. If one were to try to account for this, one might speculate that it presents quite a positive picture of the life of a traditional agricultural community; and tells the story of the rapid deterioration of the conditions of life in the village brought about by the processes of

---

130   Herbert Butterfield. The Whig Interpretation of History. Pp. 31-33.
131   Stuart Piggott. Ancient Europe. Pp. 19-20.

development and modernisation. The solemn classification, in the census of 1851, of a ten year old boy of Wigston Magna as an agricultural labourer, provoked the following conclusion from Hoskins.

"A *labourer* of ten was necessary to the new system. To this pass the peasant village had come in the end. There had been more respect and rest for old age, more care-free happiness for small children, more leisure in the open air for all, in the so-called Dark Ages than in the early years of Queen Victoria's reign."[132]

Of course, Hoskins has it completely the wrong way around; no amount of patching will fit this conclusion into any of our conceptions of progress and poverty. It is said that this work is depressing; but is it depressing because of the sympathy we feel for the oppressed and unhappy villagers, or because of the challenge it poses to our most cherished and fundamental assumptions? Have the generality of historians and research students decided that it might be better never to visit Wigston Magna, or anywhere else like it, ever again?

If so, it is in good company. With the wealth of detailed studies available covering the time of Malthus and Cobbett, there remain some amazing gaps in our knowledge. Many of the despotic features of the British government have been, if not quite air-brushed from history, then at least badly under-researched. The financial system operated by Cobbett's "Paper-Money men" we know very little of. In spite of a few comprehensive biographies of its leading figures, the generality of the men who worked in the City of London are still a mystery to us. The all-pervading corruption of the institutions of government and representation is lightly treated of by many historians; or else rationalised by moral relativity – by some reference to "the standards of the time", when the fact was that most Englishmen of the time were profoundly shocked and appalled by the corruption of their government. The internal military system set up by Pitt and Castlereagh and Perceval and Palmerston has a shadowy existence which barely disturbs the pages of conventional histories; the division of the country into military districts and the building of barracks in town and country. The system of state espionage intrudes upon our consciousness at certain points, like the Derbyshire rising of 1817, but how little we know of its role in the everyday workings of the government, and in the life of its citizens! The corn trade, an important part of every system of despotism, is hardly researched; we know very little of the workings of the Mark Lane market, and of the dealings and speculations of the great capitalist traders. There is a story waiting to be told of the connections and influence of these great men with landowners, government and the financial system. The role of propaganda has not been properly appreciated or investigated. The glaring fact that neither Hannah More nor Arthur Young, to name but two, nor possibly even Malthus himself, believed what they wrote, desperately needs explaining. Once again, there is a host of shadowy figures about whom we know very little – John Bowles, William Jones, Sir Francis D'Ivernois. And the likes of Adam Smith, Malthus and the absurd David Ricardo are treated as serious economists instead of the establishment propagandists that they clearly were. Finally - because he impinges upon everything – there is the neglect of the bulk of the writings of William Cobbett; although widely recognised as a colourful character and a biographically interesting subject, in terms of what he actually said and believed he is too often treated as some sort of raging eccentric, shouting abuse from the sidelines, trying to obstruct humankind's continually advancing march of progress. Here is Butterfield again.

"If we see in each generation the conflict of the future against the past, the fight of what might be called progressive versus reactionary, we shall find ourselves organising the historical story upon what is really an unfolding principle of progress, and our eyes will be fixed upon certain people who appear as the special agencies of that progress."[133]

---

132 W. G. Hoskins. The Midland Peasant. P. 276.
133 Herbert Butterfield. The Whig Interpretation of History. Pp. 45-46.

And this is what happens in the broader summaries of the past which ignore the painstaking work of detailed investigation; which attempt to portray the world in terms of a preconceived view of life which the author wishes to promote or to be associated with; which attempt to mould the mind of the reader in a certain way, or to reinforce, or to tune in with, assumptions that are already present; which seek the approbation of the "right-minded"; which say to the reader, "I am a certain sort of person and so, of course, are you."

"It is perhaps a tragedy that the important work of abridging history is so often left to writers of text-books and professional manufacturers of commercial literature. It is unfortunate that so many abridgments of history are in reality not abridgments at all – not the condensation of a full mind but mere compilations from other abridgments. It would seem that abridgments are often falsified by the assumption that the essentials of the story can be told, leaving out the complications; an assumption which overlooks the fact that history is the whole network produced by countless complications perpetually involving one another. There is a danger that abridgment may be based more or less consciously upon some selective principle, as is the case with the whig interpretation which organises the whole course of centuries upon what is really a directing principle of progress. There is a danger in all abridgments that acquire certainty by reason of what they omit, and so answer all questions more clearly than historical research is ever able to do. Finally, there is the undoubted danger that we may pile too heavy a weight of inference upon the general statements of historians – statements from which all that complicates and qualifies has been abbreviated out of existence. These are the abuses of abridged history, but when all has been said they are only its abuses; they show how history-books may teach the reverse of what history teaches, and they show why history can so often be turned into propaganda...."[134]

Propaganda is an inescapable part of every despotic and exploitative regime; and as, in most cases, the despotism is only a means to an end; a way of facilitating the exploitation, and of enabling the few to benefit at the expence of the many; since the despotism nearly always means a deterioration in the conditions of life for the majority of the people; the associated propaganda will inevitably attempt to persuade people that conditions are better than they actually are; and that, in any case, though they may be far from perfect, they represent a decided improvement on what had gone before. A part of the propaganda of a despotic regime will nearly always concern the conditions under which people live; and the superiority of those conditions over those that used to prevail in the bad old days. In 1792, William Pitt stood up in the House of Commons and declared his belief that there was not "any existing grievance in this country that was felt at this hour. On the contrary, he believed that at this moment we actually did enjoy as much happiness as we should, or that a rational man ought to hope for. He believed that we were in a state of prosperity and progressive improvement rarely equalled, never excelled, by any nation at any period in the history of the world."[135]

The issues that form the raw material of much propaganda, therefore, are poverty and the causes of poverty, history and progress. And this we have seen time and again. This is how Cobbett saw it.

"Englishmen, until within the last fifty years, when long parliaments and banking and funding and borrowing and taxing began to produce poverty and misery and crimes were *always well off*, in the oldest of times....Those who, like me, are now fifty years of age, can well remember when it was thought a *sorrowful sight* to see a labouring man apply for parish relief....Well do I remember when old men, common labourers, used to wear to church good broad-cloth coats which they had worn at their weddings. They were frugal and careful, but they had encouragement to practise those virtues. The household goods of a labouring man, his clock, his trenchers and his pewter plates, his utensils of brass and copper, his chairs, his joint-stools, his substantial oaken tables, his bedding and

---

134   Ibid. Pp. 100-101.
135   Parliamentary History. Vol. 29. P. 1310.

all that belonged to him, form a contrast with his present miserable and worthless stuff that make one's heart ache to think of. His beer and his bread and meat are now exchanged for the cat-lap of the tea-kettle, taxed to more than three-fourths of its prime cost, and for the cold and heartless diet of the potato-plat....

"We complain that the people of this kingdom are *worse off* than they used to be. We talk of the *good old times* of our forefathers. We conclude, that we might, under a good system, be *as happy* as our forefathers were; and, this good system we (I do for one) most firmly believe, would be brought about speedily by a reform of the parliament, and this belief we have *proved* to be rational. The sons of Corruption meet us at the threshold of the argument, and assert, in the most unqualified manner, that we are much *better off* than our forefathers were, whom they represent as a set of despicable ragamuffins and vassals. To read the essays on this subject in the COURIER and the TIMES, one would suppose, that, until the days of Pitt, or thereabouts, Englishmen were a species of barbarians, clad in skins of wild animals, sleeping amongst ferns under hedges, and living upon hips and haws....

"The insolent sons of Corruption would fain have us believe....that we ought to be very *grateful* that we are not compelled to live, like blackbirds, upon wild berries and worms."

Thus it was argued in Cobbett's time; thus it has been argued by every regime that has abandoned the paternalistic role of the "natural magistracy" and sought aggressively to drain off the wealth of its citizens, from motives connected with wealth or power. Here is George Orwell, on an announcement emanating from the Ministry of Plenty, of the revolutionary government of Nineteen Eighty-Four.

"'Comrades!' cried an eager youthful voice. 'Attention, comrades! We have glorious news for you. We have won the battle for production! Returns now completed of the output of all classes of consumption goods show that the standard of living has risen by no less than 20 per cent over the past year. All over Oceania this morning there were irrepressible spontaneous demonstrations when workers marched out of factories and offices and paraded through the streets with banners voicing their gratitude to Big Brother for the new, happy life which his wise leadership has bestowed upon us....'

"The fabulous statistics continued to pour out of the telescreen. As compared with last year there was more food, more clothes, more houses, more furniture, more cooking-pots, more fuel, more ships, more helicopters, more books, more babies – more of everything except disease, crime and insanity....People today....lived longer, worked shorter hours, were bigger, healthier, stronger, happier, more intelligent, better educated, than the people of fifty years ago. Not a word of it could ever be proved or disproved. The party claimed, for example, that today 40 per cent of adult proles were literate; before the Revolution, it was said, the number had only been 15 per cent. The party claimed that the infant mortality rate was now only 160 per thousand, whereas before the Revolution it had been 300 – and so it went on....Year by year and minute by minute, everybody and everything was whizzing rapidly upwards."[136]

Big Brother reduced the chocolate ration from thirty grammes a week to twenty; and news came through that demonstrators had appeared on the streets thanking him for raising the chocolate ration to twenty grammes. Winston, Orwell's hero, observed the reactions of his companions.

"Was it possible that they could swallow that, after only twenty-four hours? Yes, they swallowed it. Parsons swallowed it easily, with the stupidity of an animal (sic). The eyeless creature at the other table swallowed it fanatically, passionately, with a furious desire to track down, denounce and vaporize anyone who should suggest that last week the ration had been thirty grammes. Syme, too – in some more complex way....swallowed it. Was he, then, *alone* in the possession of a memory?"[137]

---

136 George Orwell. Nineteen Eighty-Four. Pp. 50-51 and 63.
137 Ibid. P. 50.

An eminent historian once asserted that "the belief in a hard core of historical facts existing objectively and independently of the historian, is a preposterous fallacy."[138] On the basis of this obvious cop-out, history becomes whatever you want it to be. It becomes the circular argument of the propagandist. It becomes the indubitable proof of the correctness of every assumption and preconception underpinning the current order of things. It becomes the operation of orthodoxy on credulity. On the contrary, though historical truth may never be revealed to us in its entirety, it nevertheless exists, and we catch glimpses of it in our detailed researches. These show that the progressive, Malthusian, developmental model of poverty and history by no means constitutes a valid explanation either of our past or of our present. Still, for our own reasons, we cling to it. It is not historically correct; but it remains politically so.

In George Orwell's Nineteen Eighty-Four, Winston Smith reflects upon the nature of historical truth.

"At one time it had been a sign of madness to believe that the earth goes round the sun; today, to believe that the past is unalterable. He might be *alone* in holding that belief, and if alone, then a lunatic. But the thought of being a lunatic did not greatly trouble him; the horror was that he might be wrong.

"In the end the Party would announce that two and two made five, and you would have to believe it. It was inevitable that they would make that claim sooner or later; the logic of their position demanded it. Not merely the validity of experience, but the very existence of external reality, was tacitly denied by their philosophy. The heresy of heresies was common sense. And what was terrifying was not that they would kill you for thinking otherwise, but that they might be right. For, after all, how do we know that two and two make four? Or that the force of gravity works? Or that the past is unchangeable? If both the past and the external world exist only in the mind, and if the mind is controllable – what then?

"Everything faded into mist. The past was erased, the erasure was forgotten, the lie became the truth….The past not only changed, but changed continuously. What most afflicted him with the sense of nightmare was that he had never clearly understood *why* the huge imposture was undertaken. The immediate advantages of falsifying the past were obvious, but the ultimate motive was mysterious. He took up his pen again and wrote;

I understand HOW; *I do not understand* WHY."[139]

Material progress occupied only a part of the concerns of establishment writers. The happy and improving conditions of life enjoyed by the poor were harped upon by such writers as William Paley, Edmund Burke and Hannah More; and in the earlier 19th century this argument became transmogrified in the hands of, for example, Harriet Martineau and the writers of the Society for the Diffusion of Useful Knowledge, into the great benefits bestowed upon society by the accumulation of resources into the hands of the great capitalists. But all the while these lines of argument were accompanied by the expression of sentiments which we may categorise as anti-poor and anti-rural. Arthur Young and his fellow advocates of the modern agriculture attempted to stereotype the traditional countryman as idle, obstinately backward and prone to criminality. After the famines of the 1790s, in which the machinations of wealthy traders and financiers had played such an important part, Malthus wrote to dispel any sympathy for the victims, by labelling them as idle, improvident, and the guilty authors of their own misfortunes. During the troublous times of 1817, caused by the constant changes in the value of the currency, reprints were put into circulation recycling the anti-

138   E. H. Carr quoted in Stuart Piggott. Ancient Europe. P. 5.
139   George Orwell. Nineteen Eighty-Four. Pp. 63 and 67.

poor and anti-rural sentiments of Malthus, Joseph Townsend and Hannah More. The whole genre reached its apogee in the hands of Harriet Martineau, whose rabid rantings against the rural classes were to justify and facilitate the great suction of resources out of the countryside and into the financial system which the Poor Law Amendment Act was intended to bring about.

The insults thus offered to his countrymen aroused the ire of William Cobbett. In 1829, he took a Rural Ride amongst my ancestors and their neighbours at the eastern extremity of Sussex. He had heard that the parishes around Rye and Winchelsea were busy clearing away their inhabitants by means of emigration to the United States; and this caused him to reflect upon the abuse of those who were being compelled to make way for the purpose of increasing the national wealth.

"I cannot quit this subject, even for the present, without observing upon the conduct of those who ought to be the friends and protectors of the labouring people. They seem to look on them not as *men* and *women*, but merely as animals made for their service or their sport. Our ears are everlastingly dinned with the charges of *immoralities* committed by the poor. I have known *twenty* different projects for correcting the 'evil of pauperism', but never of one project for making the lot of the labourer better than it is. Look at the *letters* of these English labourers; go and look at the people themselves; and then remember the project of that insolent Irishman[140] who said that, rather than *indulge them in idleness*, he would make them '*dig holes one day and fill them up the next!*' There must be a day of *justice*; this ill-treatment of millions of good people never can pass off without producing some signal event. Every coxcomb Scotchman, and, indeed, almost every Irish political prattler, has his impudent jaws full of talk about the management of the English *peasantry*. 'Peasantry' back down the throats of the brazen blackguards! Let them go back home, and see if they can find there people to equal these 'paupers' shipped off from Sussex to America; people so neat in their houses and gardens, labourers so skilful and constant at their work, people so moral, and, in all respects, so good. And these are the people that the base and degenerate and cowardly English land-owners abandon to be scourged by hired overseers! They seem to regard the working classes as their *natural enemies*, though without them their estates are of no value; and their whole time seems to be spent in devising schemes for taking from the labouring man as much as possible of his means of existence. God is just, and *God will punish this.*"[141]

That the leaders of society, who were also the advocates of progress and modernisation, held such prejudiced views of the traditional rural class – that class which became transformed into "the poor" – and that they found it necessary, through stereotypy and vilification, to instil a hostility against them in the other classes of the community, is highly revealing. It provides the beginnings of a clue to solving that problem by which George Orwell found himself confronted.

"*I do not understand* WHY".

To the ordinary mortal, the idea of progress implies improvement. One envisages the whole of the human race marching forward together, both in a material sense and in less tangible ways, as a result of technological innovation and the growth of productivity. But in the world of Malthus and Cobbett, the process of development principally entailed, not the creation of wealth, but a transfer of it from one group to another. One large group was disconnected from the means of production, and another group, much smaller and more select, substituted in its place. Almost invariably, civilisation comes about at somebody else's expence.

The elitist mindset was a competitive one, and the doctrine of progress which it entertained was not, and was not even claimed to be, a doctrine of universal benevolence. Only the most outlandish eccentric would think of suggesting that the barbarian was to share in the blessings of civilisation. It was a doctrine of supersession; of elimination; of liquidation, either in a cultural or an actual sense.

---

140 Castlereagh.
141 William Cobbett. Political Register. 27/6/1820.

It aimed at the victory of the innovator over the conservator; of town man over village man; of the modern over the "forces of conservatism"; of the respectable over the lower orders.

At bottom, and in the last resort, we are brought to suspect that the dichotomy was the psychological one expounded by T. W. Adorno and his team in The Authoritarian Personality; for what was being aimed at was the victory of an in-group over a perceived out-group; and the victors wrote the history.

❋

We began this investigation from a premise, and that premise was that poverty has a cause. It is easily observable, in the environment of our countryside, that the deer and the foxes and the rabbits do not, under normal circumstances, live in a state of chronic starvation, *en masse*. The state of nature is not a state of poverty.

In England, on the other hand, by the earlier 19th century, a very large proportion of the people did live in a state of chronic starvation. And the reasons for that, therefore, have to be sought in the artificial state of society and economy in which they lived.

Like everything else in history, poverty was the effect of a number of interwoven causes acting upon a pre-existing situation.

That pre-existing situation was the agricultural way of life and of producing subsistence. This system, on the one hand, is capable of producing far more subsistence than can be consumed by those who work in it; on the other hand, it is a very vulnerable system, wide open to exploitation by the warlike and the parasitic. As mankind changed from hunters and gatherers, to roaming pastoralists, to agriculturalists, poverty was an accident waiting to happen.

Mankind has won his subsistence from cultivating the soil for a relatively short space of time, when considered in relation to the period of his existence as a species. It might be suggested, therefore, that, in relative terms, poverty is a feature mainly characteristic of the modern world.

The fields of the farmer lie exposed to the depredations of those with the will to exploit; whether those depredations take place through naked physical force; through the much more sophisticated means of fiscal and financial manipulation; or through actual dispossession. And we have speculated that the will to exploit may have its origin in social isolation, upbringing, psychology and personality formation.

The methods of exploitation fall into four categories – physical force, the corruption of government and the elimination of the popular will, the manipulation of the mind, and control over the mechanisms of exchange. These methods are used in differing proportions, and with differing degrees of sophistication, at different periods. The more modern systems of exploitation have involved a great development of the last method. The introduction and ever-increasing complexity of the money economy in recent times; the constantly fluctuating circulating medium; the lever of indebtedness; and the control over economy and society which these things put into the hands of the operators of the system; have had a profound and fundamental influence over the nature and effects of exploitation.

The exploiters of the agricultural way of life have, at many points in history, sought to reorganise the farming landscape to their own advantage. But the logic and implications of exploitation in a money economy – the doctrine of the national wealth – require the actual removal from the countryside of a great proportion of the cultivators of it, and it is this feature that distinguishes more modern systems of exploitation from more ancient ones. The corollary of displacement is proletarianisation – the disconnection of the productive classes of the community from the means of production. Globally, the proletarian tends often to be under-employed or unemployed, or under-paid, or dependent upon the charitable inclinations of governments. He is often forced physically from the land into the slums and shanty-towns of the great cities. He is often a migrant. He has no margin of safety to shield him from the effects of climatic vagaries or the misfortunes of everyday life. And he is immediately vulnerable to every shock and fluctuation brought about by those who operate the financial system. It is through proletarianisation that the rural classes become "the poor". A state of proletarianisation is one never very far removed from slavery.

Proletarianisation is surely one of the most important issues of the modern world, and it is really extraordinary how our mindsets are moulded over such issues. Proletarianisation is economically necessary to the capitalist system; and it is politically necessary to the socialist one. Throughout what is called the political spectrum, which in reality is nothing more than a straight line from left to right, there is no room for the man who says that proletarianisation is an evil; that mankind exists in a better condition where the ownership and control of the means of production are left more diffuse and widely distributed. As a political commentator put it on television recently, the only alternative to the avarice and irresponsibility of bankers is North Korea. But the truth is that not every shade of opinion can be represented along a straight line, and the absurd and persisting belief that it can leads us unthinkingly into the Malthusian assumption that the division of society into proprietors and proletarians is the natural state of any people that has progressed beyond the savage state.

A degree of control over the means of production is crucial to the well-being of every people on earth. This is surely so obvious as to be a platitude. Small and family farms, indeed small and family businesses of every description, are what shield mankind from hunger and poverty; but small and family farms most of all. The traditional cultivators of the soil are the people that have the skill, the hardiness, the ability to work, and the hereditary knowledge to bring forth the most, the best and the most varied produce; it is their methods of mixed farming that provide employment; and they are the people best able to decide which technologies are of use and which not. Humankind in general, if left to its own resources, is perfectly capable of forging for itself a more than adequate subsistence. It is not what you give to the poor that makes all the difference; it is what you have taken from them, and continue to take from them.

But, inevitably, the financial system draws everything towards itself. It is rapidly becoming a system of global monopoly; and if we thought about it deeply enough that is precisely what we should expect. Financial institutions have usurped to themselves the governmental prerogative of issuing currency. Just as water must always find its own level; just as nature abhors a vacuum; so money must always command an interest. Usury used to be illegal in this country, and is proscribed by some of the world's major religions. But in the modern world, with interest the driving force, huge amounts of currency are put into circulation that appear to have no basis in reality. Endless credit seems to be available; does nobody stop to ask where it all comes from? Can it be conjured without limit out of cyber-space? With a seemingly infinite money supply needing profitable investment opportunities, can we be surprised if that investment monopolises the earth's resources? Can we wonder if the payment of the interest eats up the subsistence of the world; indeed, threatens to destroy the very planet?

The exploitative financial system William Cobbett thought to be constantly on the brink of collapse. He frequently prophesied its imminent demise, and that all would soon be well for his suffering countrymen. But his hopes were disappointed.

"They will find base wretches enough to say; 'the thing *does* last'. This month of July lasts, but it will *surely end*. Man's life *lasts*, but it must come to an end."[142]

True; but the passing of two centuries has still failed to bring about the fulfilment of his prophecies. The Age of the Sentimental Mercenary goes on….

---

142 William Cobbett. Political Register. 18/12/1813.